PHILIP'S

ROAD ATLAS

2025 BIG ROAD ATLAS EUROPE

T0299430

www.philips-maps.co.uk

First published in 1998 as Philip's Multiscale Europe by Philip's, a division of Octopus Publishing Group Ltd
www.octopusbooks.co.uk
Carmelite House,
50 Victoria Embankment
London EC4Y 0DZ
An Hachette UK Company
www.hachette.co.uk

Twenty-fourth edition 2024
Second impression 2024

ISBN 978-1-84907-658-6 spiral-bound
ISBN 978-1-84907-657-9 paperback

This product includes mapping data licensed from Ordnance Survey®, with the permission of the Controller of His Majesty's Stationery Office
© Crown copyright 2024. All rights reserved.
Licence number AC0000851689

* is a registered Trade Mark of the Northern Ireland Department of Finance and Personnel. This product includes mapping data licensed from Ordnance Survey of Northern Ireland®, reproduced with the permission of Land and Property Services under delegated authority from the Controller of His Majesty's Stationery Office, © Crown Copyright 2024.

The maps of Ireland on pages 18 to 21 and the urban area map and town plan of Dublin are based upon the Crown Copyright and are reproduced with the permission of Land & Property Services under delegated authority from the Controller of His Majesty's Stationery Office,

© Crown Copyright and database right 2024, PMLPA No 100503, and on Ordnance Survey Ireland by permission of the Government

Ordnance Survey Ireland/Tailte Éireann Permit No. 9296
© Tailte Éireann/Government of Ireland

Cartography by Philip's
Copyright © Philip's 2024

Printed in Dubai

The UK's best-selling Europe atlases
Data from Nielsen Total Consumer Market 2023

CONTENTS

II **Key to map symbols**

III **Driving regulations**

1 **Key to route planning map pages** · Distance table

2 **Route planning maps** at 1: 3 200 000

17 **Key to road map pages**

18 **Road maps of Europe**

121 **Town plans and urban area maps**

121 Alicante **C**	**130** Göteborg Gothenburg **C**	**140** Oslo **C**
Antwerpen Antwerp **C**	Granada **C**	Paris **C**
122 Amsterdam **C U**	Hamburg **C U**	**141** Paris **U**
Athina Athens **U**	**131** Helsinki **C U**	**142** Praha Prague **C U**
123 Athina Athens **C**	İstanbul **U**	Rotterdam **C**
Barcelona **C U**	**132** København Copenhagen **C U**	Sankt Peterburg St Petersburg **U**
Basel **C**	Köln Cologne **C**	**143** Roma Rome **C U**
124 Berlin **C U**	**133** Lisboa Lisbon **C U**	**144** Sevilla Seville **C**
125 Beograd Belgrade **C**	**134** London **C**	Strasbourg **C U**
Bordeaux **C U**	London **U**	Stuttgart **C**
Bruxelles Brussels **U**	**135** Luxembourg **C**	**145** Stockholm **C U**
126 Bruxelles Brussels **C**	Lyon **C U**	**146** Torino Turin **U**
Budapest **C U**	Madrid **U**	Venézia Venice **C**
127 Dublin **C U**	**136** Madrid **C**	**147** Torino Turin **U**
Edinburgh **C**	Málaga **C**	Warszawa Warsaw **C U**
Düsseldorf **C**	Marseille Marseilles **C**	Wien Vienna **U**
128 Düsseldorf (Ruhrgebiet) **U**	**137** Milano Milan **C U**	**148** Wien Vienna **C**
129 Firenze Florence **C**	**138** Moskva Moscow **C U**	Zagreb **C**
Frankfurt **C**	München Munich **C U**	Zürich **C**
Genève Geneva **C**	**139** Nápoli Naples **C U**	
Génova Genoa **C**	Oslo **U**	

C = City street plan   **U** = Urban area map

149 **Index to road maps of Europe**

Inside back cover **Map of high-speed rail network**

Felus Robert Leverne / iStock

Legend to road maps pages 18–120

⑦ ⑧	**Motorway with junctions** – full, restricted access
◇ ◇	services, rest or parking area
	tunnel
	under construction
	Toll Motorway – with toll barrier
	Pre-pay motorway – 'vignette' must be purchased before travel
	Principal trunk highway – single / dual carriageway
	tunnel
	under construction
	Other main highway – single / dual carriageway
	Other important road
	Other road
E25	**European road number**
A49	**Motorway number**
135	**National road number**
Col Bayard 1248	**Mountain pass**
	Scenic route, gradient – arrow points uphill
143	**Distances** – in kilometres
	major
28	minor
	Principal railway
	tunnel
Nápoli	**Ferry route**
	Short ferry route
	International boundary
	National boundary
HEATHROW	**Airport**
KNOSSOS	**Ancient monument**
	Beach
SCHLOSS LAHNECK	**Castle or house**
GROTTE DE HAN-SUR-LESSE	**Cave**
GIVERNY	**Park or garden**
	National park
	Natural park
SANTA CRUZ	**Religious building**
	Ski resort
DISNEYLAND PARIS	**Theme park**
POMPEI	**World Heritage site**
PARQUE JURASSICO	**Other place of interest**
1754 ▲	**Spot height**
Sevilla	**World Heritage town**
Verona	**Town of tourist interest**
▣ ◉	**Town with Low Emission Zone**

Scales

Pages 18–110 and 120
1:753 800 • 1cm = 7.5km • 1 inch = 12 miles
0 4 8 12 16 20 24 28 32 36 40km
0 2 4 6 8 10 12 14 16 18 20 22 24 26 miles

Pages 111–119
1:1 507 600 • 1cm = 15km • 1 inch = 24 miles
0 8 16 24 32 40 48 56 64 72 80km
0 4 8 12 16 20 24 28 32 36 40 44 48 52 miles

HELP ME, PLEASE!

If you're in a difficult situation and need local help, then the following words and phrases might prove useful if language is a problem:

🇬🇧	🇫🇷	🇪🇸	🇮🇹	🇩🇪
Do you speak English?	Parlez-vous anglais?	¿Habla usted inglés?	Parla inglese?	Sprechen Sie Englisch?
Thank you (very much)	Merci (beaucoup)	(Muchas) Gracias	Grazie (mille)	Danke (sehr)
Is there a police station near here?	Est-ce qu'il y a un commissariat de police près d'ici?	¿Hay una comisaría cerca?	C'e' un commissariato qui vicino?	Gibt es ein Polizeirevier hier in der Nähe?
I have lost my passport	J'ai perdu mon passeport.	He perdido mi pasaporte	Ho perso il mio passaporto.	Ich have meinen Reisepass verloren
I have broken down	Je suis tombé en panne	Mi coche se ha averiado	Ho un guasto	Ich habe eine Panne
I have run out of fuel	Je suis tombé en panne d'essence.	Me he quedado sin gasolina.	Ho terminato la benzina.	Ich habe kein Benzin mehr.
I feel ill	Je me sens malade.	Me siento mal.	Mi sento male.	Mir ist schlecht.

Legend to route planning maps pages 2–16

	Motorway with selected junctions
	tunnel, under construction
	Toll motorway
	Pre-pay motorway
	Main through route
	Other major road
	Other road
25	**European road number**
56	**Motorway number**
55	**National road number**
56	**Distances** – in kilometres
	International boundary
	National boundary
LE HAVRE	**Car ferry and destination**
⥲ ✈ 1089 ▲	**Mountain pass, international airport, height in metres**

Town – population
MOSKVA ▣	5 million +
BERLIN ▣	2–5 million
MINSK ▣	1–2 million
Oslo ◉	500000–1million
Aarhus ⊙	200000–500000
Turku ◎	100000–200000
Gävle ⊙	50000–100000
Nybro ○	20000–50000
Ikast ○	10000–20000
Skjern ○	5000–10000
Lillesand ○	0–5000

Town – with Low Emission Zone
▣	5 million +
▣	2–5 million
▣	1–2 million
◉	500000–1million
●	200000–500000
●	100000–200000
●	50000–100000
●	20000–50000
●	10000–20000
○	5000–10000
○	0–5000

Scale
1:3 200 000 • 1cm = 32km • 1 inch = 50.51 miles
0 20 40 60 80 100 120 140 160 180 km
0 10 20 30 40 50 60 70 80 90 100 110 miles

Legend to city plans pages 121–148

	Motorway		**Car ferry**
	Major through route		**Railway**
	Through route		**Rail / bus station**
	Secondary road	⊖ Ⓤ Ⓜ Ⓣ	**Underground, metro station**
	Dual carriageway		**Cable car**
	Other road	†	**Abbey, cathedral**
	Tunnel	†	**Church of interest**
	Limited access / pedestrian road	✡	**Synagogue**
→	**One-way street**	✛	**Hospital**
Ⓟ	**Parking**	POL	**Police station**
A7	**Motorway number**	✉	**Post office**
447	**National road number**	i	**Tourist information**
E45	**European road number**	*Theatre*	**Place of interest**
GENT	**Destination**		

Legend to city approach maps pages 121–148

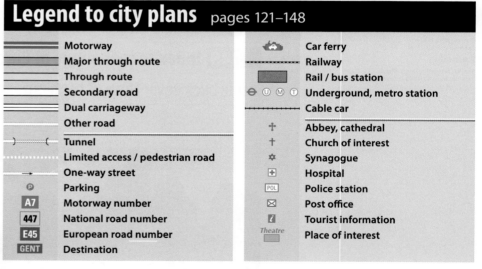

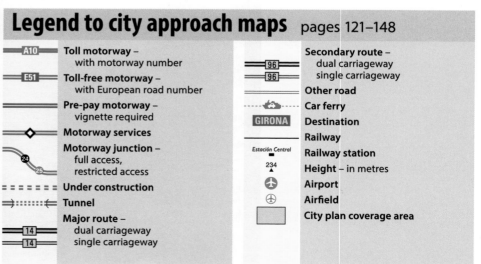

Driving regulations

The information below is for drivers visiting for fewer than 12 months, as different rules will apply for residents.

Vehicle
A national vehicle plate is always required when taking a vehicle abroad. Fitting headlamp converters or beam deflectors when taking a right-hand-drive car to a country where driving on the right (every country in Europe except the UK and Ireland) is compulsory.

A national vehicle plate is required when taking a vehicle abroad. The GB identifier was replaced by UK in September 2021 and is no longer valid. If you are driving a UK registered vehicle within the EU and its number plate does not include a UK identifier and the Union flag, you will need to attach a UK sticker. Outside the EU and in Cyprus, Malta and Spain, a UK sticker is required even if your number plate includes a UK identifier. A UK sticker is not required in Ireland.

Vehicle documentation
All countries require that you carry a vehicle registration document (V5C), hire certificate (VE103) or letter of authority for the use of someone else's vehicle, full driving licence/International Driving Permit and insurance documentation (and/or Green Card outside the EU – see also "Insurance" below). Minimum driving ages are often higher for people holding foreign licences. Drivers of vehicles over three years old should ensure that the MOT is up to date and take the certificate with them.

Travel documentation
All UK visitors' passports should be valid for at least six months. Some non-EU countries also require a visa. UK nationals may visit the EU Schengen area countries for up to 90 days in a 180-day period without a visa. A UK EHIC (UK European Health Insurance Card) or a UK GHIC (UK Global Health Insurance Card) will allow you to access state provided healthcare when visiting an EU country. They are available from the NHS website https://services.nhsbsa.nhs.uk/cra/start. Not all healthcare in the EU is free so you should also ensure you also have suitable travel insurance. In future, the GHIC card may cover additional countries outside the EU but it is not currently valid in Norway, Iceland, Liechtenstein or Switzerland.

Insurance
Third-party cover is compulsory across Europe. Most insurance policies give only basic cover when driving abroad, so you should check that your policy provides at least third-party cover for the countries in which you will be driving and upgrade it to the level that you require. You might be forced to take out extra cover at the frontier if you cannot produce acceptable proof that you have adequate insurance.

Licence
A photo licence is preferred. If you have an old-style paper driving licence or are visiting countries outside the EU, you may need to carry an IDP (International Driving Permit). Some non-EU countries may only recognise one of the three available types of IDP (1926, 1949 or 1968) so the correct one should be obtained, see www.gov.uk/driving-abroad/international-driving-permit.

If planning to hire a car abroad, you should check in advance if the hire company wish to check your licence for endorsements and permitted vehicles categories. If so, visit www.gov.uk/view-driving-licence to create a digital code (valid for 72 hours) that allows your licence details to be shared. For more information, contact the DVLA (0300 790 6802), www.dft.gov.uk/dvla.

Motorcycles
It is compulsory for all motorcyclists and passengers to wear crash helmets.
In France it is compulsory for them to carry reflective jackets.

Other
In countries in which reflective jackets are compulsory, one for each person should be carried in the passenger compartment (or motorcycle panniers). Warning triangles should also be carried here. The penalties for infringements of regulations vary considerable between countries. In many, the police have the right to impose on-the-spot fines (ask for a receipt). Serious infringements, such as exceeding the blood-alcohol limit, can result in immediate imprisonment.

Please note that driving regulations often change and it has not been possible to include the information for all types of vehicle.

The figures given for capitals' populations are for the entire metropolitan area.

The symbols used are:
- Speed limit in kilometres per hour (kph). These are the maximum speeds for the types of roads listed. In some places, and under certain conditions, they may be considerably lower. Always obey local signs.
- Motorway
- Dual carriageway / expressway
- Single carriageway
- Urban area
- Surfaced road
- Unsurfaced or gravel road
- Seat belts
- Children
- Blood alcohol level
- Warning triangle
- First aid kit
- Spare bulb kit
- Fire extinguisher
- Minimum driving age
- Additional documents required
- Mobile phones
- **LEZ** Low Emission Zone
- Dipped headlights
- Winter driving
- ★ Other information

The publishers have made every effort to ensure that the information given here was correct at the time of going to press. No responsibility can be accepted for any errors or their consequences.

Please note that driving regulations may change, and that it has not been possible to cover all the information for every type of vehicle.

Andorra Principat d'Andorra AND
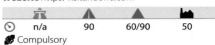

Area 468 sq km (181 sq miles)
Population 85,000 **Capital** Andorra la Vella (22,000)
Languages Catalan (official), French, Castilian and Portuguese **Currency** Euro = 100 cents
Website http://visitandorra.com

⊙	🏍	▲	▲	🏙
n/a	90	60/90		50

- Compulsory
- Under 10 and below 150 cm must travel in an EU-approved restraint system adapted to their size in the rear. Airbag must be deactivated if a child is in the front passenger seat.
- 0.05% △ 2 compulsory Recommended
- Compulsory Recommended 18
- Only allowed with hands-free kit
- Compulsory for motorcycles during day and for other vehicles during poor daytime visibility
- Snow chains must be carried or winter tyres fitted 1 Nov–15 May
- ★ On-the-spot fines imposed
- ★ Visibility vests compulsory
- ★ Wearers of contact lenses or spectacles should carry a spare pair

Austria Österreich A

Area 83,859 sq km (32,377 sq miles)
Population 8,941,000 **Capital** Vienna / Wien (1,960,000)
Languages German (official) **Currency** Euro = 100 cents
Website www.austria.info/en

⊙	🏍	▲	▲	🏙
130	100	100		30–50

If towing trailer under 750kg / over 750 kg

100/80	100/80	100/70		50

Minimum speed on motorways 60 kph

- Compulsory
- Under 14 and under 135cm cannot travel as a front or rear passenger unless they use a suitable child restraint; under 14 over 150cm must wear adult seat belt. Airbags must be deactivated if a rear-facing child seat is used in the front.
- 0.049% • 0.01% for professional drivers or if licence held less than 2 years
- △ Compulsory First aid kit Compulsory
- Recommended Recommended
- 18 (16 for motorbikes up to 125cc)
- Paper driving licences must be accompanied by photographic proof of identity.
- Only allowed with hands-free kit
- **LEZ** Several cities and regions have LEZs affecting HGVs that ban non-compliant vehicles, impose speed restrictions and night-time bans. Trucks in categories N1 to N3 must display an environmental badge (Umwelt-Pickerl) in these areas.
- Compulsory for motorcycles and in poor visibility for other vehicles. Headlamp converters compulsory for right-hand drive vehicles
- Winter tyres compulsory 1 Nov–15 Apr. Snow chains only permitted if road is fully covered by snow or ice.
- ★ On-the-spot fines imposed
- ★ Radar detectors and dashcams prohibited
- ★ To drive on motorways or expressways, a motorway sticker must be purchased at the border or main petrol station. These are available for 10 days, 2 months or 1 year. Vehicles 3.5 tonnes or over must purchase an on-board unit in order to pay a mileage-based toll.
- ★ Visibility vests compulsory
- ★ When traffic flow ceases on a motorway or dual carriageway, vehicles are required to form a corridor between lanes for use by emergency services.

Belarus BY

Area 207,600 sq km (80,154 sq miles)
Population 9,384,000 **Capital** Minsk (2,049,000)
Languages Belarusian, Russian (both official)
Currency Belarusian ruble = 100 kopek
Website www.belarus.by/en/government

⊙	🏍	▲	▲	🏙
110	90	90		60[1]

If towing trailer under 750kg

90	70	70		50

[1] In residential areas limit is 20 kph • Vehicle towing another vehicle 50 kph limit • If full driving licence held for less than 2 years, must not exceed 70 kph

- Compulsory in front seats, and rear seats if fitted
- Under 12 not allowed in front seat and must use appropriate child restraint
- 0.00% △ Compulsory
- Recommended Recommended
- Recommended 18
- Visa, 1968 International Driving Permit, green card recommended, local health insurance. Even with a green card, local third-party insurance may be imposed at the border.
- Only allowed with a hands-free kit
- Compulsory during the day in poor visibility or if towing or being towed. Headlamp converters compulsory for right-hand drive vehicles
- Winter tyres compulsory 1 Dec–1 Mar; snow chains recommended
- ★ A temporary vehicle import certificate must be purchased on entry and driver must be registered
- ★ It is illegal for vehicles to be dirty
- ★ Many road signs use only the Cyrillic alphabet
- ★ On-the-spot fines imposed
- ★ Radar-detectors prohibited
- ★ To drive on main motorways an on-board unit must be acquired at the border or a petrol station in order to pay tolls. See www.beltoll.by/index.php/en

Belgium Belgique (B)

Area 30,528 sq km (11,786 sq miles)
Population 11,914,000
Capital Brussels/Bruxelles (2,110,000)
Languages Dutch, French, German (all official)
Currency Euro = 100 cents
Website www.belgium.be/en

	🛣	▲	▲	🏘
⊙	120[1]	120[1]	90[2]	50[3]
Over 3.5 tonnes				
⊙	90	90	70[2]–90	50[3]

[1]Minimum speed of 70 kph may be applied in certain conditions on motorways and some dual carriageways. [2]70 kph in Flanders. [3]20 kph in residential areas, 30 kph near some schools, hospitals and churches, and in designated cycle zones.

- 💺 Compulsory
- 👶 All under 18s under 135 cm must wear an appropriate child restraint. Airbags must be deactivated if a rear-facing child seat is used in the front.
- 🍷 0.05% • 0.02% professional drivers △ Compulsory
- ⊞ Recommended (compulsory for vehicles registered in Belgium)
- 💡 Recommended 🧯 Recommended (compulsory for vehicles registered in Belgium) ⊖ 18
- 📱 Only allowed with a hands-free kit
- LEZ LEZs in operation in Antwerp, Brussels and Ghent. Preregistration necessary and fees payable for most vehicles.
- ◐ Mandatory at all times for motorcycles and during the day in poor conditions for other vehicles
- ❄ Winter tyres permitted 1 Oct to 31 Apr. Snow chains only permitted if road is fully covered by snow or ice. Vehicles with studded tyres restricted to 90 kph on motorways/dual carriageways and 60 kph on other roads.
- ★ If a tram or bus stops to allow passengers on or off, you must not overtake
- ★ Motorcyclists must wear fully protective clothing
- ★ On-the-spot fines imposed
- ★ Radar detectors prohibited
- ★ Sticker indicating maximum recommended speed for winter tyres must be displayed on dashboard if using them
- ★ Visibility vest compulsory
- ★ When a traffic jam occurs on a road with two or more lanes in the direction of travel, motorists should move aside to create a path for emergency vehicles between the lanes.

Bosnia and Herzegovina Bosna i Hercegovina (BIH)

Area 51,197 km² (19,767 mi²)
Population 3,808,000
Capital Sarajevo (555,000)
Languages Bosnian/Croatian/Serbian
Currency Convertible Marka = 100 convertible pfenniga
Website www.fbihvlada.gov.ba/english/index.php

	🛣	▲	▲	🏘
⊙	130	100	80	50

- 💺 Compulsory
- 👶 Under 12s must sit in rear using an appropriate child restraint. Under-2s may travel in a rear-facing child seat in the front only if the airbags have been deactivated.
- 🍷 0.03% • no person under the influence of alcohol may travel in front seats.
- △ 2 compulsory ⊞ Recommended
- 💡 Recommended 🧯 Compulsory for LPG vehicles
- ⊖ 18
- 📄 Original vehicle registration and ownership papers.
- 📱 Only allowed with hands-free kit
- ◐ Compulsory for all vehicles at all times
- ❄ Winter tyres compulsory 15 Nov–15 Apr; the use of snow chains is compulsory in thick snow or if indicated by road signs.
- ★ GPS must have fixed speed camera function deactivated; radar detectors prohibited.
- ★ On-the-spot fines imposed
- ★ Visibility vest, tow rope or tow bar recommended

Bulgaria Bulgariya (BG)

Area 110,912 sq km (42,822 sq miles)
Population 6,828,000
Capital Sofia (1,287,000)
Languages Bulgarian (official), Turkish
Currency Lev = 100 stotinki
Website www.government.bg/en

	🛣	▲	▲	🏘
⊙	140	120	90	50
If towing trailer				
⊙	100	90	70	50
Over 3.5 tonnes				
⊙	100	90	80	50

- 💺 Compulsory
- 👶 Under 3s not permitted in vehicles with no child restraints; 3–10 year olds must sit in rear in an appropriate restraint. Rear-facing child seats may be used in the front only if the airbag has been deactivated.
- 🍷 0.05% △ Compulsory ⊞ Compulsory
- 💡 Recommended 🧯 Compulsory ⊖ 18
- 📄 Photo driving licence preferred; a paper licence must be accompanied by an International Driving Permit.
- 📱 Only allowed with a hands-free kit
- ◐ Compulsory
- ❄ Winter tyres compulsory. Snow chains should be carried from 1 Nov–1 Mar. Max speed with chains 50 kph
- ★ GPS must have fixed speed camera function deactivated
- ★ On-the-spot fines imposed
- ★ A vignette is required to drive on motorways and main roads. These can be purchased at the border. Digital e-vignettes can be obtained from terminals at border checkpoints or online in advance: https://tollpass.bg/en
- ★ Visibility vest compulsory

Croatia Hrvatska (HR)

Area 56,538 km² (21,829 mi²)
Population 4,169,000 **Capital** Zagreb (1,107,000)
Languages Croatian
Currency Euro = 100 cents
Website https://vlada.gov.hr/en

	🛣	▲	▲	🏘
⊙	130	110	90	50
If towing				
⊙	90	90	80	50

Lower speed limits for newly qualified drivers; please check before travelling

- 💺 Compulsory if fitted
- 👶 Children under 12 not permitted in front seat and must use appropriate child seat or restraint in rear. Children under 2 may use a rear-facing seat in the front only if the airbag is deactivated.
- 🍷 0.05% • 0.00 % for drivers under 24 and professional drivers
- △ Compulsory (2 if towing)
- ⊞ Compulsory
- 💡 Compulsory except for xenon or LED lights
- 🧯 Recommended
- ⊖ 18
- 📱 Only allowed with hands-free kit
- ◐ Compulsory in reduced visibilty and at all times from the last weekend in October until the last weekend in March
- ❄ From 15 Nov to 15 Apr, winter tyres must be fitted, snow chains and shovel must be carried in vehicle. Winter tyres must have minimum tread of 4mm
- ★ Motorway tolls can be paid in cash or by credit or debit card. An electronic toll collection system is also available, for details see www.hac.hr/en
- ★ On-the-spot fines imposed
- ★ Radar detectors prohibited
- ★ Visibility vest compulsory

Czechia Česko (CZ)

Area 78,864 sq km (30,449 sq miles)
Population 10,706,000
Capital Prague/Praha (1,318,000)
Languages Czech (official), Moravian
Currency Czech Koruna = 100 haler
Website https://vlada.cz/en

	🛣	▲	▲	🏘
⊙	130	110/80[1]	90	50
If towing				
⊙	80	80	80	50

[1]80 kph on urban expressways.

- 💺 Compulsory
- 👶 Children under 36 kg and 150 cm must use appropriate child restraint. Only front-facing child retraints are permitted in the front in vehicles with airbags fitted. Airbags must be deactivated if a rear-facing child seat is used in the front.
- 🍷 0.00% △ Compulsory ⊞ Compulsory
- 💡 Compulsory 🧯 Recommended
- ⊖ 18 (17 for motorcycles under 125 cc)
- 📄 Licences with a photo preferred. Paper licences should be accompanied by an International Driving Permit.
- 📱 Only allowed with a hands-free kit
- LEZ Two-stage LEZ in Prague for vehicles over 3.5 and 6 tonnes. Permit system.
- ◐ Compulsory at all times
- ❄ Winter tyres compulsory 1 Nov–31 Mar if roads are icy/snow-covered or snow is expected. Also if winter equipment sign (circular blue sign with white car and snowflake) is displayed. Minimum tread depth 4mm.
- ★ GPS must have fixed speed camera function deactivated; radar detectors prohibited
- ★ On-the-spot fines imposed
- ★ Replacement fuses must be carried
- ★ Spectacles or contact lens wearers must carry a spare pair in their vehicle at all times
- ★ Vehicles up to 3.5 tonnes require e-vignette for motorway driving, available for 1 year, 30 days, 10 days. https://edalnice.cz/en. Vehicles over 3.5 tonnes are subject to tolls and must carry an electronic tag https://mytocz.eu/en
- ★ Visibility vest compulsory

Denmark Danmark (DK)

Area 43,094 sq km (16,638 sq miles)
Population 5,947,000
Capital Copenhagen / København (1,370,000)
Languages Danish (official)
Currency Krone = 100 øre
Website www.visitdenmark.com

	🛣	▲	▲	🏘
⊙	110-130[1]	80	80	50[2]
If towing				
⊙	100	80	80	50[2]

[1]Over 3.5 tonnes 80 kph [2]Central Copenhagen 40 kph

- 💺 Compulsory
- 👶 Under 135cm must use appropriate child restraint; in front permitted only in an appropriate rear-facing seat with any airbags disabled.
- 🍷 0.05% △ Compulsory
- ⊞ Recommended 💡 Recommended
- 🧯 Recommended ⊖ 18
- 📱 Only allowed with a hands-free kit
- LEZ Aalborg, Aarhus, Copenhagen/Frederiksberg and Odense. Older diesel-powered trucks, buses, vans and cars may not enter unless they have been retrofitted with a compliant particulate filter. Pre-registration required. Non-compliant vehicles banned. https://miljoezoner.dk/en
- ◐ Must be used at all times
- ❄ Studded tyres may be fitted 1 Nov–15 April, if used on all wheels
- ★ On-the-spot fines imposed
- ★ Radar detectors prohibited
- ★ Tolls apply on the on the Storebælt and Øresund bridges
- ★ Visibility vest recommended

Estonia Eesti (EST)

Area 45,100 sq km (17,413 sq miles)
Population 1,203,000 **Capital** Tallinn (427,000)
Languages Estonian (official), Russian
Currency Euro = 100 cents **Website** www.valitsus.ee/en

	🛣	▲	▲	🏘
⊙	n/a	90[1]	90	50

[1]In summer, the speed limit on some dual carriageways may be raised to 100/120 kph. The limit on ice roads varies between 10kph and 70 kph according to ice thickness.

- 💺 Compulsory if fitted
- 👶 Children too small for adult seatbelts must wear a seat restraint appropriate to their size. Rear-facing safety seats must not be used in the front if an air bag is fitted, unless this has been deactivated.
- 🍷 0.02% △ 2 compulsory
- ⊞ Recommended (compulsory for company cars)
- 💡 Recommended 🧯 Compulsory
- ⊖ 18
- 📱 Only allowed with a hands-free kit
- ◐ Compulsory at all times
- ❄ Winter tyres are compulsory from Dec–Mar; dates may be extended in severe weather. Studded winter tyres are allowed from 15 Oct–31 Mar, but this can be extended to start 1 October and/or end 30 April
- ★ A toll system is in operation in Tallinn
- ★ On-the-spot fines imposed
- ★ Radar detectors prohibited
- ★ 2 wheel chocks compulsory
- ★ Visibility vest compulsory

Finland Suomi (FIN)

Area 338,145 sq km (130,557 sq miles)
Population 5,615,000 **Capital** Helsinki (1,328,000)
Languages Finnish, Swedish (both official)
Currency Euro = 100 cents
Website https://valtioneuvosto.fi/en/frontpage

	🛣	▲	▲	🏘
⊙	100-120	80-100	80-100[1]	20/50
Vans, lorries and if towing				
⊙	80	80	60	20/50

[1]100 in summer • If towing a vehicle by rope, cable or rod, max speed limit 60 kph • Maximum of 80 kph for vans and lorries • Speed limits are often lowered in winter

- 💺 Compulsory
- 👶 Below 135 cm must use a child restraint or seat
- 🍷 0.05% △ Compulsory
- ⊞ Recommended 💡 Recommended
- 🧯 Recommended
- ⊖ 18
- 📱 Only allowed with hands-free kit
- ◐ Must be used at all times
- ❄ Winter tyres compulsory Dec–Feb
- ★ On-the-spot fines imposed
- ★ Radar-detectors are prohibited
- ★ Visibility vest compulsory

France (F)

Area 551,500 sq km (212,934 sq miles)
Population 68,522,000
Capital Paris (11,142,000)
Languages French (official), Breton, Occitan
Currency Euro = 100 cents
Website www.gouvernement.fr/en

	🛣	▲	▲	🏘
⊙	130	110	80	50
On wet roads or if full driving licence held for less than 3 years				
⊙	110	100	70	50
above 3.5 tonnes gross				
⊙	90	80	80	50

50kph on all roads if fog reduces visibility to less than 50m

- 💺 Compulsory in front seats and, if fitted, in rear
- 👶 Children up to age 10 must use suitable child seat or restraint and may only travel in the front if: • the vehicle has no rear seats • no rear seatbelts • the rear seats are already occupied by children up to age 10 • the child is a baby in a rear facing child seat and the airbag is deactivated.
- 🍷 0.05% • 0.02% if full driving licence held for less than 3 years • All drivers/motorcyclists are required to carry an unused breathalyser though this rule is not currently enforced.
- △ Compulsory
- ⊞ Recommended
- 💡 Recommended
- ⊖ 18 (16 for motorbikes up to 125cc)
- 📱 Use permitted only with hands-free kit. Must not be used with headphones or earpieces
- LEZ An LEZ operates in the Mont Blanc tunnel and such zones are being progressively introduced across French cities. Non-compliant vehicles are banned during operating hours. Crit'Air stickers must be displayed by compliant vehicles. See http://certificat-air.gouv.fr/en
- ◐ Compulsory in poor daytime visibility and at all times for motorcycles
- ❄ In mountainous areas (marked by signs), winter tyres must be fitted or snow chains available 1 Nov to 31 March
- ★ GPS must have fixed speed camera function deactivated; radar-detection equipment is prohibited
- ★ Headphones or earpieces must not be used for listening to music or making phone calls while driving.
- ★ Motorcyclists and passengers must have four reflective stickers on their helmets (front, back and both sides) and wear CE-certified gloves.
- ★ On-the-spot fines imposed
- ★ Tolls on motorways. Electronic tag needed if using automatic tolls.
- ★ Visibility vests, to be worn on the roadside in case of emergency or breakdown, must be carried for all vehicle occupants and riders.
- ★ Wearers of contact lenses or spectacles should carry a spare pair

Germany Deutschland (D)

Area 357,022 sq km (137,846 sq miles)
Population 84,220,000
Capital Berlin (3,571,000)
Languages German (official)
Currency Euro = 100 cents
Website www.bundesregierung.de/breg-en

	🛣	▲	▲	🏘
⊙	130[1]	130[1]	100	50
If towing				
⊙	80	80	80	50

[1]recommended maximum. • 50kph if visibility below 50m

- 💺 Compulsory
- 👶 Aged 3-12 and under 150cm must use an appropriate child seat or restraint and sit in the rear. Children under 3 must be in a suitable child restraint and may travel in a rear-facing seat in the front if airbags are deactivated.
- 🍷 0.05% • 0.00% for professional drivers, under 21s and those with less than 2 years full licence
- △ Compulsory ⊞ Compulsory
- 💡 Recommended 🧯 Recommended ⊖ 18
- 📱 Use permitted only with hands-free kit – also applies to drivers of motorbikes and bicycles
- LEZ Many cities have or are planning LEZs (Umweltzone). Vehicles must display a 'Plakette' sticker, indicating emissions category. Proof of compliance needed to acquire sticker. Non-compliant vehicles banned. www.umwelt-plakette.de/en
- ◐ Compulsory during poor daytime visibility and tunnels; recommended at other times. Compulsory at all times for motorcyclists.
- ❄ Winter tyres compulsory in all winter weather conditions; snow chains recommended
- ★ GPS must have fixed speed camera function deactivated; radar detectors prohibited
- ★ On-the-spot fines imposed
- ★ Tolls on autobahns for lorries
- ★ Visibility vest compulsory

Greece Ellas (GR)

Area 131,957 sq km (50,948 sq miles)
Population 10,498,000
Capital Athens / Athina (3,154,000)
Languages Greek (official) **Currency** Euro = 100 cents
Website www.visitgreece.gr

	🛣	▲	▲	🏘
⊙	130	110	90	50
If towing				
⊙	90–100	80–90	80	50

- 💺 Compulsory in front seats and, if fitted, in rear
- 👶 Under 12 or below 135cm must use appropriate child restraint. In front if child is in rear-facing child seat, any airbags must be deactivated.
- 🍷 0.05% • 0.02% for professional drivers or drivers with less than 2 years full licence
- △ Compulsory ⊞ Compulsory
- 💡 Recommended 🧯 Compulsory
- ⊖ 18
- 📱 Only allowed with a hands-free kit
- ◐ Compulsory during poor daytime visibility and at all times for motorcycles
- ❄ Snow chains permitted on ice- or snow-covered roads. Max speed 50 kph.
- ★ On-the-spot fines can be imposed but not collected by the police
- ★ Radar-detection equipment is prohibited
- ★ Tolls on several newer motorways.

Hungary Magyarország (H)

Area 93,032 sq km (35,919 sq miles)
Population 9,670,000
Capital Budapest (1,775,000)
Languages Hungarian (official)
Currency Forint = 100 filler
Website https://abouthungary.hu

	🛣	▲	▲	🏘
⊙	130	110	90	50[1]
If towing or if over 3.5 tonnes				
⊙	80	70	70	50[1]

[1]30 kph zones have been introduced in many cities

- 💺 Compulsory
- 👶 Under 150cm and over 3 must be seated in rear and use appropriate child restraint. Under 3 allowed in front only in rear-facing child seat with any airbags deactivated.
- 🍷 0.00% △ Compulsory
- ⊞ Recommended 💡 Recommended
- 🧯 Recommended ⊖ 17
- 📱 Only allowed with a hands-free kit

LEZ Budapest is divided into zones with varying restrictions on HGVs

◐ Compulsory during the day outside built-up areas; compulsory at all times for motorcycles

❄ Snow chains compulsory where conditions dictate. Max speed 50 kph.

★ Tolls apply to many motorways and are administered through an electronic vignette system with automatic number plate recognition https://nemzetiutdij.hu/en/

★ On-the-spot fines issued

★ Radar detectors prohibited

★ Tow rope recommended

★ Visibility vest recommended

Iceland Ísland (IS)

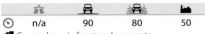

Area 103,000 sq km (39,768 sq miles)
Population 361,000
Capital Reykjavík (140,000)
Languages Icelandic
Currency Krona = 100 aurar
Website www.government.is

	🛣	🚗	🚗≈	🏙
⊙	n/a	90	80	50

⛓ Compulsory in front and rear seats

👶 Children up to 135 cm must use suitable child seat or restraint. Up to 150cm must not sit in front seat unless airbag is deactivated.

🍷 0.05%

△ Compulsory

✚ Recommended

💡 Recommended

🧯 Recommended

⊖ 17

📱 Only allowed with a hands-free kit

◐ Compulsory at all times

❄ Winter tyres compulsory c.1 Nov–14 Apr (variable). Snow chains may be used when necessary.

★ Driving off marked roads is forbidden

★ Highland roads are not suitable for ordinary cars and many are unusable in winter

★ On-the-spot fines imposed

Ireland Eire (IRL)

Area 70,273 sq km (27,132 sq miles)
Population 5,324,000
Capital Dublin (1,458,000)
Languages Irish, English (both official)
Currency Euro = 100 cents
Website www.gov.ie/en

	🛣	▲	▲	🏙
⊙	120	100	80	50[1]
If towing				
⊙	80	80	80	50[1]

[1]Dublin and some other areas have introduced 30 kph zones

⛓ Compulsory where fitted. Driver responsible for ensuring passengers under 17 comply

👶 Children under 150cm and 36 kg must use appropriate child restraint. Airbags must be deactivated if a rear-facing child seat is used in the front.

🍷 0.05% • 0.02% for novice and professional drivers

△ Recommended (compulsory for HGVs and buses)

✚ Recommended

💡 Recommended

🧯 Recommended

⊖ 17 (16 for motorbikes up to 125cc; 18–24 for over 125cc according to power).

📱 Only allowed with a hands-free kit

◐ Compulsory in poor visibility

★ Driving is on the left

★ GPS must have fixed speed camera function deactivated; radar detectors prohibited

★ On-the-spot fines imposed

★ Tolls are being introduced on some motorways; the M50 Dublin has barrier-free tolling with number-plate recognition. Tolls can be paid in cash or with an electronic toll tag; not all toll stations accept cards. www.etoll.ie/driving-on-toll-roads/information-for-visitors

Italy Italia (I)

Area 301,318 sq km (116,338 sq miles)
Population 61,022,000
Capital Rome / Roma (4,298,000)
Languages Italian (official)
Currency Euro = 100 cents
Website www.italia.it

	🛣	▲	▲	🏙
⊙	130	110	90	50
If towing				
⊙	80	70	70	50
When wet				
⊙	110	90	80	50

Some motorways with emergency lanes have speed limit of 150 kph

⛓ Compulsory in front seats and, if fitted, in rear

👶 Children under 150cm must use appropriate child restraint. In front, if child is in rear-facing child seat, any airbags must be deactivated. For foreign-registered cars, the country of origin's legislation applies.

🍷 0.05% • 0.00% for professional drivers or with less than 3 years full licence

△ Compulsory

✚ Recommended

💡 Recommended

🧯 Recommended

⊖ 18 (14 for mopeds, 16 up to 125cc)

📱 Only allowed with hands-free kit

LEZ Italy has many LEZs with varying standards and hours of operation. Milan and Palermo operate combined LEZ and urban road toll schemes.

◐ Compulsory outside built-up areas, in tunnels, on motorways and dual carriageways and in poor visibility; compulsory at all times for motorcycles

❄ Winter tyres or snow chains compulsory 15 Oct–15 Apr in certain areas where signs indicate. Max speed with snow chains 50 kph

★ On-the-spot fines imposed

★ Radar-detection equipment is prohibited

★ Tolls on motorways. Blue lanes accept credit cards; yellow lanes restricted to holders of Telepass pay-toll device.

★ Visibility vest compulsory

Kosovo Republika e Kosoves / Republika Kosovo (RKS)

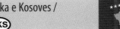

Area 10,887 sq km (4203 sq miles)
Population 1,964,000
Capital Pristina (162,000)
Languages Albanian, Serbian (both official), Bosnian, Turkish, Roma
Currency Euro (Serbian dinar in Serb enclaves)
Website http://kryeministri-ks.net/en

	🛣	▲	▲	🏙
⊙	110–130	100	80	50

⛓ Compulsory

👶 Under 12 must sit in rear seats in an appropriate restraint

🍷 0.01%

△ Compulsory

✚ Compulsory

💡 Compulsory

🧯 Compulsory

⊖ 18

📄 International Driving Permit recommended, locally purchased third-party insurance (green card is not recognised). Visitors from many non-EU countries also require documents with proof of ability to cover costs and valid reason for visiting.

📱 Only allowed with a hands-free kit

◐ Compulsory at all times

❄ Winter tyres or snow chains compulsory in poor winter weather conditions

Latvia Latvija (LV)

Area 64,589 sq km (24,942 sq miles)
Population 1,822,000
Capital Riga (870,000)
Languages Latvian (official), Russian
Currency Euro = 100 cents
Website www.mk.gov.lv/en

	🛣	▲	▲	🏙
⊙	n/a	90–100[1]	90[2]	50
If towing				
⊙	n/a	80	80	50

[1]100 on designated roads only during 1 Mar–1 Nov. • [2]80 on gravel roads. In residential areas limit is 20kph

⛓ Compulsory in front seats and if fitted in rear

👶 Children under 150cm must use suitable child restraint

🍷 0.05% • 0.02% with less than 2 years experience

△ Compulsory

✚ Recommended

💡 Recommended

🧯 Recommended

⊖ 18

📱 Only allowed with hands-free kit

◐ Must be used at all times all year round

❄ Winter tyres:compulsory 1 Dec–1 Mar on all vehicles up to 3.5 tonnes. Studded tyres allowed 1 Oct–30 Apr.

★ On-the-spot fines can be imposed but not collected by the police

★ Radar-detection equipment prohibited

★ Visibility vests recommended

Lithuania Lietuva (LT)

Area 65,200 sq km (25,173 sq miles)
Population 2,656,000
Capital Vilnius (854,000)
Languages Lithuanian (official), Russian, Polish
Currency Euro = 100 cents
Website https://lrv.lt/en

	🛣	▲	▲	🏙
⊙	130/110[1]	120/110[1]	70–90	50[2]
If towing				
⊙	90	90	70–90	50
If licence held for less than two years				
⊙	100	90	70–80	50

[1]Apr–Oct / Nov–Mar [2]20kph in some residential areas

⛓ Compulsory

👶 Under 12 or below 135 cm not allowed in front seats unless in suitable restraint; under 3 must use appropriate child seat. A rear-facing child seat may be used in front only if airbags are deactivated.

🍷 0.04% • 0.00% if full licence held less than 2 years

△ Compulsory

✚ Recommended

💡 Recommended

🧯 Recommended

⊖ 18

📄 Licences without a photograph must be accompanied by photographic proof of identity, e.g. a passport

📱 Only allowed with a hands-free kit

◐ Must be used at all times

❄ Winter tyres compulsory 10 Nov–10 Apr

★ On-the-spot fines imposed

★ Visibility vest recommended

Luxembourg (L)

Area 2,586 sq km (998 sq miles)
Population 661,000
Capital Luxembourg (133,000)
Languages Luxembourgian / Letzeburgish (official), French, German
Currency Euro = 100 cents
Website http://luxembourg.public.lu/en

	🛣	▲	▲	🏙
⊙	130/110[1]	90	90	50[2]
If towing				
⊙	90	75	75	50[2]

If full driving licence held for less than 2 years, must not exceed 75 kph • [1]110 in wet weather • [2]30 kph zones are progressively being introduced. 20 kph in zones where pedestrians have priority.

⛓ Compulsory

👶 Children under 3 must use an appropriate restraint system. Airbags must be disabled if a rear-facing child seat is used in the front. Children 3–18 and/or under 150 cm must use a restraint system appropriate to their size. If over 36kg a seatbelt may be used in the back only.

🍷 0.05%, 0.02% for young drivers, drivers with less than 2 years experience and drivers of taxis and commercial vehicles

△ Compulsory

✚ Recommended

💡 Recommended

🧯 Recommended

⊖ 18

📱 Use permitted only with hands-free kit

◐ Compulsory for motorcyclists and for other vehicles in poor visibility and in tunnels. Outside urban areas, full-beam headlights are compulsory at night and in poor visibility.

❄ Winter tyres compulsory in winter weather

★ On-the-spot fines imposed

★ Visibility vest recommended

North Macedonia Severna Makedonija (NMK)

Area 25,713 sq km (9,927 sq miles)
Population 2,131,000
Capital Skopje (607,000)
Languages Macedonian (official), Albanian
Currency Denar = 100 deni
Website

	🛣	▲	▲	🏙
⊙	130	110[1]	80	50

[1]if road reserved for motor vehicles, otherwise 80. Lower limits apply to newly qualified drivers

⛓ Compulsory

👶 Between 2 and 12 not allowed in front seats; under 5 must use an appropriate child restraint. Under 2 allowed in front seat in a rear-facing child seat if airbags are deactivated.

🍷 0.05% • 0.00% for business, commercial and professional drivers and with less than 2 years experience

△ Compulsory

✚ Recommended

💡 Recommended

🧯 Recommended; compulsory for LPG vehicles

⊖ 18 (16 with parental supervision, 16 for mopeds)

📄 International Driving Permit and green card recommended

📱 Use not permitted whilst driving

◐ Compulsory at all times

❄ Winter tyres or snow chains compulsory 15 Nov–15 Mar. Max speed 50 kph for vehicles using snow chains

★ GPS must have fixed speed camera function deactivated; radar detectors prohibited

★ Novice drivers are subject to restricted driving hours

★ On-the-spot fines imposed but paid later

★ Tolls apply on many roads

★ Tow rope recommended

★ Visibility vest recommended and should be kept in the passenger compartment and worn to leave the vehicle in the dark outside built-up areas

Moldova (MD)

Area 33,851 sq km (13,069 sq miles)
Population 3,251,000 **Capital** Chisinau (779,000)
Languages Moldovan / Romanian (official)
Currency Leu = 100 bani
Website www.moldova.md

	🛣	▲	▲	🏙
⊙	n/a	110	80	50[1]

[1]20kph in some residential areas

⛓ Compulsory in front seats and, if fitted, in rear seats

👶 Under 12 not allowed in front seats and must use an appropriate child restraint in the back

🍷 0.00%

△ Compulsory

✚ Recommended

💡 Recommended

🧯 Recommended

⊖ 18

📄 If not the vehicle owner, bring written permission from the owner, translated into Romanian and legalised; valid insurance (green card).

📱 Only allowed with a hands-free kit

◐ Must use dipped headlights at all times 1 Nov–31 Mar

❄ Winter tyres compulsory 1 Nov–31 Mar

★ On-the-spot-fines imposed

★ Vehicles not registered in Moldova require a vignette. These may be purchased from MAIB (Moldova-Agroindbank) branches or online https://evinieta.gov.md

Montenegro Crna Gora (MNE)

Area 14,026 sq km, (5,415 sq miles)
Population 602,000
Capital Podgorica (186,000)
Languages Serbian (of the ljekavian dialect)
Currency Euro = 100 cents
Website www.gov.me/en

	🛣	▲	▲	🏙
⊙	100	100	80	50

80kph speed limit if towing a caravan

⛓ Compulsory in front and rear seats

👶 Under 12 not allowed in front seats. Under-5s must use an appropriate child seat.

🍷 0.03% • 0.01% if aged up to 24 or licence held for less than 1 year.

△ Compulsory ✚ Recommended

💡 Recommended 🧯 Recommended

⊖ 18

📄 1968 International Driving Permit (1949 IDP may not be recognised); original vehicle registration document; vehicle insurance valid in Montenegro (green card recommended)

📱 Prohibited

◐ Must be used at all times

❄ Winter tyres compulsory 15 Nov–31 Mar.

★ On-the-spot fines imposed

★ Tolls in the Sozina tunnel between Lake Skadar and the sea. Toll charged on the open section of new A1 motorway (not yet completed)

★ Visibility vest recommended

Netherlands Nederland (NL)

Area 41,526 sq km (16,033 sq miles)
Population 17,464,000
Capital Amsterdam 1,166,000 • administrative capital 's-Gravenhage (The Hague) 2,390,000
Languages Dutch (official), Frisian
Currency Euro = 100 cents
Website www.government.nl

	🛣	▲	▲	🏙
⊙	100–130	80/100	80/100	50

⛓ Compulsory

👶 Under 3 must travel in the back, using an appropriate child restraint; 3–18 and under 135cm must use an appropriate child restraint. A rear-facing child seat may only be used in front if airbags are deactivated.

🍷 0.05% • 0.02% if full licence held less than 5 years and for moped riders under 24.

△ Compulsory ✚ Recommended

💡 Recommended

🧯 Recommended

⊖ 18

📱 Only allowed with a hands-free kit

LEZ LEZs for diesel vehicles operate in many Dutch cities. Restrictions depend on vehicle's Euro emissions standard. For information see https://www.milieuzones.nl/english

◐ Recommended in poor visibility and on open roads. Compulsory for motorcycles.

★ On-the-spot fines imposed

★ Radar-detection equipment is prohibited

★ Trams have priority over other traffic. You must wait if a bus or tram stops in the middle of the road to allow passengers on or off.

Norway Norge (N)

Area 323,877 sq km (125,049 sq miles)
Population 5,598,000
Capital Oslo (1,071,000)
Languages Norwegian (official), Lappish, Finnish
Currency Krone = 100 øre
Website www.norway.no/en/uk

	🛣	▲	▲	🏙
⊙	80–100	80	80	30/50
If towing trailer with brakes				
⊙	80	80	80	50
If towing trailer without brakes				
⊙	60	60	60	50

⛓ Compulsory in front seats and, if fitted, in rear

👶 Children shorter than 135cm or lighter than 36kg must use appropriate child restraint. Children under 4 must use child safety seat or safety restraint (cot). A rear-facing child seat may be used in front only if airbags are deactivated.

🍷 0.02%

△ Compulsory

✚ Recommended

💡 Recommended

🧯 Recommended

⊖ 18 (heavy vehicles 18/21)

📱 Only allowed with a hands-free kit

◐ Must be used at all times

❄ Winter tyres with at least 3mm tread compulsory during winter. Studded tyres may be used 1 Nov until first Sunday after Easter (15 Oct–1 May in Nordland, Troms, and Finnmark). There is a fee for using studded tyres within city boundaries of Oslo, Bergen and Trondheim. Vehicles under 3.5 tonnes must carry snow chains if snow or ice is expected.

★ On-the-spot fines imposed

★ Radar-detectors are prohibited

★ Tolls apply on some bridges, tunnels and access roads into Bergen, Haugesund, Kristiensand, Oslo, Stavangar, Tonsberg, Trondheim and others. Most use electronic fee payment collection only www.autopass.no/en/user/foreign-vehicles/

★ Some of the higher mountain passes can experience snowfall and ice even if conditions are warm at lower altitudes, particularly in spring and autumn.

★ Visibility vest compulsory

Poland Polska (PL)

Area 323,250 sq km (124,807 sq miles)
Population 37,992,000
Capital Warsaw / Warszawa (1,795,000)
Languages Polish (official)
Currency Zloty = 100 groszy
Website www.poland.travel/en

	🛣	▲	▲	🏘
⊙	140	120[1]/100	100[1]/90	20/50/60[2]
if towing				
⊙	80	80	70	20/50/60[2]

[1]Expressway, indicated by signs with white car on blue background • [2]residential / built-up area / built-up area 2300-0500

- 🔗 Compulsory in front seats and, if fitted, in rear
- 👶 Under 12 and below 150 cm must use an appropriate child restraint. A rear-facing child seat may be used in front only if airbags are deactivated.
- 🍸 0.02%
- △ Compulsory
- ✚ Recommended
- 💡 Recommended
- 🧯 Compulsory
- ⊖ 18 (mopeds and motorbikes under 125cc – 16)
- 📱 Only allowed with a hands-free kit
- 🔆 Compulsory for all vehicles
- ❄ Snow chains permitted only on roads completely covered in snow
- ★ On-the-spot fines imposed
- ★ Radar-detection equipment is prohibited
- ★ Vehicles under 3.5 tonnes pay tolls on some motorways https://etoll.gov.pl/en/light-vehicles • www.tolls.eu/poland
- ★ Visibility vests compulsory

Portugal (P)

Area 88,797 sq km (34,284 sq miles)
Population 10,223,000
Capital Lisbon / Lisboa (2,986,000)
Languages Portuguese (official)
Currency Euro = 100 cents
Website www.visitportugal.com/en

	🛣	▲	▲	🏘
⊙	120[1]	90/100	90	50/20
If towing				
⊙	100[1]	80	70	50/20

[1]50kph minimum; 90kph max if licence less than 1 year

- 🔗 Compulsory in front seats and, if fitted, in rear
- 👶 Under 12 and below 135cm must travel in the rear in an appropriate child restraint; rear-facing child seats permitted in front for under 3s only if airbags deactivated
- 🍸 0.05% • 0.02% for professional drivers or if full licence held less than 3 years
- △ Compulsory ✚ Recommended
- 💡 Recommended 🧯 Recommended
- ⊖ 18
- 🪪 IDP required if you have old-style paper licence, photographic proof of identity must be carried at all times
- 📱 Only allowed with hands-free kit
- LEZ Lisbon's LEZ has a minimum entry requirement of emission standard Euro 3 for the central zone and Euro 2 for the outer zone between 0700 and 2100.
- 🔆 Compulsory for motorcycles, compulsory for other vehicles in poor visibility and tunnels
- ★ On-the-spot fines imposed
- ★ Radar detectors and dash-cams prohibited
- ★ Some motorways use traditional toll booths (green lanes are reserved for auto-payment users) but others may only be used by vehicles registered with an automated billing system. www.portugaltolls.com/en
- ★ Visibility vest compulsory
- ★ Wearers of spectacles or contact lenses should carry a spare pair

Romania (RO)

Area 238,391 sq km (92,042 sq miles)
Population 18,326,000
Capital Bucharest / Bucuresti (1,785,000)
Languages Romanian (official), Hungarian
Currency Romanian leu = 100 bani
Website https://romaniatourism.com

	🛣	▲	▲	🏘
Cars and motorcycles				
⊙	130	100	90	50
If towing				
⊙	120	90	80	50

If full driving licence has been held for less than one year, speed limits are 20kph lower than those listed above.

- 🔗 Compulsory
- 👶 Under 12s not allowed in front and must use an appropriate restraint in the rear
- 🍸 0.00% △ Compulsory
- ✚ Compulsory 💡 Compulsory
- 🧯 Compulsory
- ⊖ 18
- 🪪 Green card recommended
- 📱 Only allowed with hands-free kit
- 🔆 Compulsory outside built-up areas, compulsory everywhere for motorcycles
- ❄ Winter tyres compulsory Nov–Mar if roads are snow- or ice-covered, especially in mountainous areas
- ★ Compulsory electronic road tax can be paid for at the border, post offices and some petrol stations and on-line www.roviniete.ro/en
- ★ On-the-spot fines imposed
- ★ Visibility vest compulsory

Russia Rossiya (RUS)

Area 17,075,000 sq km (6,592,800 sq miles)
Population 141,699,000 **Capital** Moscow / Moskva (12,641,000) **Languages** Russian (official), and many others
Currency Russian ruble = 100 kopeks
Website www.visitrussia.org.uk

	🛣	▲	▲	🏘
⊙	110	90	90	60/20
If licence held for under 2 years				
⊙	70	70	70	60/20

- 🔗 Compulsory if fitted
- 👶 Under 8 must use suitable child restraint in front and rear seats; under 12 must use suitable child restraint in front seat
- 🍸 0.03 % △ Compulsory
- ✚ Compulsory 💡 Compulsory
- 🧯 Compulsory ⊖ 18
- 🪪 1968 International Driving Permit with Russian translation, visa, green card may not be accepted – check with insurance company before travel, International Certificate for Motor Vehicles
- 📱 Only allowed with a hands-free kit
- 🔆 Compulsory during the day outside built-up areas
- ❄ Winter tyres compulsory 1 Dec–1 Mar
- ★ On-the-spot fines imposed but must be paid later
- ★ Picking up hitchhikers is prohibited
- ★ Radar detectors/blockers prohibited
- ★ Road tax payable at the border
- ★ Some toll roads, mainly payable in cash

Serbia Srbija (SRB)

Area 77,474 sq km, 29,913 sq miles
Population 6,693,000 **Capital** Belgrade / Beograd (1,405,000) **Languages** Serbian
Currency Dinar = 100 paras **Website** www.srbija.gov.rs

	🛣	▲	▲	🏘
⊙	130	100	80	50
If towing				
⊙	80	80	80	50

Speed limits vary so check local signage

- 🔗 Compulsory in front and rear seats
- 👶 Age 3–12 must be in rear seats and use an appropriate child restraint; under 3 in rear-facing child seat permitted in front only if airbag deactivated
- 🍸 0.029% • 0.00% for commercial drivers, motorcyclists, or if full licence held less than 1 year
- △ Compulsory ✚ Recommended
- 💡 Recommended 🧯 Recommended
- ⊖ 18
- 🪪 International Driving Permit recommended, insurance that is valid for Serbia or locally bought third-party insurance
- 📱 Only allowed with a hands-free kit
- 🔆 Compulsory
- ❄ Winter tyres compulsory 1 Nov–1 Apr for vehicles up to 3.5 tonnes. Carrying snow chains compulsory in winter as these must be fitted if driving on snow-covered roads when signs indicate.
- ★ 3-metre tow rope or bar and spare wheel compulsory
- ★ On-the-spot fines imposed
- ★ Radar detectors prohibited
- ★ Tolls on motorways ★ Visibility vest compulsory

Slovakia Slovenska Republika (SK)

Area 49,012 sq km (18,923 sq miles)
Population 5,425,000 **Capital** Bratislava (720,000)
Languages Slovak (official), Hungarian
Currency Euro = 100 cents
Website https://slovakia.travel/en

	🛣	▲	▲	🏘
⊙	130/90[1]	90	90	50

[1]rural roads / urban roads

- 🔗 Compulsory
- 👶 Under 12 or below 150cm must be in rear in appropriate child restraint
- 🍸 0.00% △ Compulsory
- ✚ Recommended 💡 Recommended
- 🧯 Recommended
- ⊖ 18
- 📱 Only allowed with a hands-free kit
- 🔆 Compulsory at all times
- ❄ Winter tyres compulsory when snow or ice on the road
- ★ On-the-spot fines imposed
- ★ Radar-detection equipment is prohibited
- ★ Tow rope recommended
- ★ Electronic vignette required for motorways, validity: 1 year, 30 days, 10 days https://eznamka.sk/en
- ★ Visibility vests recommended

Slovenia Slovenija (SLO)

Area 20,256 sq km (7,820 sq miles)
Population 2,100,000 **Capital** Ljubljana (538,000)
Languages Slovene **Currency** Euro = 100 cents
Website www.slovenia.info/en

	🛣	▲	▲	🏘
⊙	130	110	90	50[1]
If towing				
⊙	80	80	80	50[1]

[1] 30 kph and 20 kph zones are increasingly common in cities. 50 kph in poor visibility or with snow chains

- 🔗 Compulsory
- 👶 Below 150cm must use appropriate child restraint. A rear-facing baby seat may be used in front only if airbags are deactivated.
- 🍸 0.05% • 0.00% for commercial drivers, under 21s or with less than one year with a full licence
- △ Compulsory ✚ Recommended
- 💡 Recommended 🧯 Recommended
- ⊖ 18 (motorbikes up to 125cc – 16, up to 350cc – 18)
- 🪪 Licences without photographs must be accompanied by an International Driving Permit
- 📱 Only allowed with hands-free kit
- 🔆 Must be used at all times
- ❄ From 15 Nov to 15 Mar winter tyres must be fitted or snow chains must be carried ready for use in icy conditions. Winter tyres also compulsory in wintry conditions beyond those dates.
- ★ On-the-spot fines imposed
- ★ Radar detectors prohibited
- ★ An e-vignette must be purchased before a vehicle can enter a toll road, https://evinjeta.dars.si/en
- ★ Visibility vest recommended

Spain España (E)

Area 497,548 sq km (192,103 sq miles)
Population 47,223,000 **Capital** Madrid (6,714,000)
Languages Castilian Spanish (official), Catalan, Galician, Basque **Currency** Euro = 100 cents
Website www.spain.info/en

	🛣	▲	▲	🏘
⊙	120[1]	100[1]	90	50[1]
Passenger cars & vans with trailers, vehicles below 3.5 t				
⊙	90	80	80	50[1]

[1]Urban motorways and dual carriageways 80 kph. 20 kph zones are being introduced in many cities

- 🔗 Compulsory
- 👶 Up to 12 years or below 135cm must use an appropriate child restraint and sit in the rear, unless all rear seats being used by other children. Rear-facing baby seat permitted in front only if airbag deactivated.
- 🍸 0.05% • 0.03% if less than 2 years full licence or if vehicle is over 3.5 tonnes or carries more than 9 passengers
- △ 2 compulsory (one for in front, one for behind)
- ✚ Recommended 💡 Compulsory
- 🧯 Recommended. Compulsory for buses and LGVs
- ⊖ 18 (16 for motorbikes up to 125cc)
- 📱 Only allowed with a hands-free kit. Headphones and earpieces not permitted
- LEZ Many Spanish cities have LEZs, restricting access to vehicles which meet specific emission requirements. Advance registration is required. See https://urbanaccessregulations.eu/countries-mainmenu-147/spain
- 🔆 Compulsory for motorcycles and for other vehicles in poor daytime visibility and in tunnels
- ❄ Snow chains compulsory in areas indicated by signs
- ★ On-the-spot fines imposed
- ★ Radar-detection equipment is prohibited
- ★ Spare wheel compulsory
- ★ Tolls on motorways
- ★ Visibility vest compulsory

Sweden Sverige (S)

Area 449,964 sq km (173,731 sq miles)
Population 10,536,000 **Capital** Stockholm (1,679,000)
Languages Swedish (official), Finnish
Currency Swedish krona = 100 ore
Website https://sweden.se

	🛣	▲	▲	🏘
⊙	70–120	70	70	30–50
If towing trailer with brakes				
⊙	80	80	70	50

- 🔗 Compulsory in front and rear seats
- 👶 Under 135cm must use an appropriate child restraint and may sit in the front only if airbag is deactivated; rear-facing baby seat permitted in front only if airbag deactivated.
- 🍸 0.02% △ Compulsory ✚ Recommended
- 💡 Recommended 🧯 Recommended ⊖ 18
- 🪪 Licences without a photograph must be accompanied by photographic proof of identity, e.g. a passport
- 📱 Only allowed with hands-free kit
- LEZ Many Swedish cities have LEZs restricting access for lorries and buses; a small area of central Stockholm also restricts cars https://urbanaccessregulations.eu/countries-mainmenu-147/sweden-mainmenu-248
- 🔆 Must be used at all times
- ❄ 1 Dec–31 Mar and in wintry conditions outside these dates, winter tyres, anti-freeze screenwash additive and shovel compulsory
- ★ On-the-spot fines imposed
- ★ Radar-detection equipment is prohibited
- ★ Tolls on some roads and charges to use some bridges.
- ★ Tow rope recommended
- ★ Visibility vest recommended

Switzerland Schweiz (CH)

Area 41,284 sq km (15,939 sq miles)
Population 8,564,000 **Capital** Bern (134,000)
Languages French, German, Italian, Romansch (all official)
Currency Swiss Franc = 100 centimes / rappen
Website www.myswitzerland.com/en-gb

	🛣	▲	▲	🏘
⊙	120	80–100	80	50
If towing				
⊙	80	80	80	50

- 🔗 Compulsory
- 👶 Up to 12 years or below 150 cm must use an appropriate child restraint. A rear-facing child seat may only be used in the front if the airbag is deactivated.
- 🍸 0.05%, but 0.01% for commercial drivers or with less than 3 years with a full licence
- △ Compulsory ✚ Recommended 💡 Recommended
- 🧯 Recommended ⊖ 18 (mopeds up to 50cc – 16)
- 📱 Only allowed with a hands-free kit
- 🔆 Compulsory
- ❄ Winter tyres recommended Nov–Mar; snow chains compulsory in designated areas in poor winter weather
- ★ All vehicles under 3.5 tonnes must display a vignette on the windscreen. These are valid for one year and can be purchased at border crossings, petrol stations, post offices and online https://switzerlandtravelcentre.com/en/gbr/offer/vignette. Vehicles over 3.5 tonnes are subject to a heavy vehicle charge https://via.admin.ch/shop/dashboard.
- ★ GPS must have fixed speed camera function deactivated; radar detectors prohibited ★ On-the-spot fines imposed ★ Picking up hitchhikers is prohibited on motorways ★ Spectacles or contact lens wearers must carry a spare pair in their vehicle at all times ★ Visibility vests recommended

Turkey Türkiye (TR)

Area 774,815 sq km (299,156 sq miles)
Population 83,593,000 **Capital** Ankara (5,636,000)
Languages Turkish (official), Kurdish
Currency New Turkish lira = 100 kurus
Website www.mfa.gov.tr/default.en.mfa

	🛣	▲	▲	🏘
⊙	120	90	90	50
Motorbikes				
⊙	80	70	70	50

- 🔗 Compulsory if fitted
- 👶 Under 150 cm and below 36kg must use suitable child restraint. Under 3s can only travel in the front in a rear facing seat if the airbag is deactivated. Children 3–12 may not travel in the front seat.
- 🍸 0.05% immediate confiscation of licence if over limit • 0.00% for professional drivers and if towing trailer or caravan
- △ 2 compulsory (one in front, one behind)
- ✚ Compulsory 💡 Recommended
- 🧯 Compulsory ⊖ 18
- 🪪 1968 International Driving Permit advised, and required for use with licences without photographs, or UK licence with notarised copy in Turkish; note that Turkey is in both Europe and Asia, green card/UK insurance that covers whole of Turkey or locally bought insurance.
- 📱 Only allowed with hands-free kit
- 🔆 Compulsory in poor daytime visibility
- ★ On-the-spot fines imposed ★ GPS must have fixed speed camera function deactivated; radar detectors prohibited ★ Tolls on several motorways and the Bosphorus bridges; electronic payment required by purchasing HGS vignette or pre-payment card from Post Offices or service stations. ★ Winter tyres recommended

Ukraine Ukraina (UA)

Area 603,700 sq km (233,088 sq miles)
Population 43,306,000 **Capital** Kiev / Kyviv (3,010,000)
Languages Ukrainian (official), Russian
Currency Hryvnia = 100 kopiykas
Website www.kmu.gov.ua/en

	🛣	▲	▲	🏘
⊙	130	110	90	20/50

If driving licence held less than 2 years, must not exceed 70 kph. 50 kph if towing another vehicle.

- 🔗 Compulsory in front and rear seats
- 👶 Under 12 and below 145cm must use an appropriate child restraint and sit in rear
- 🍸 0.02% – if use of medication can be proved. Otherwise 0.00%.
- △ Compulsory ✚ Compulsory
- 💡 Compulsory 🧯 Compulsory ⊖ 18
- 🪪 1968 International Driving Permit, green card (check that insurance is recognised in Ukraine).
- 📱 Only allowed with a hands-free kit
- 🔆 Compulsory in poor daytime visibility and from 1 Oct–30 Apr
- ❄ Winter tyres compulsory Nov–Apr in snowy conditions
- ★ On-the-spot fines imposed
- ★ Visibility vest compulsory

United Kingdom (GB)

Area 241,857 sq km (93,381 sq miles)
Population 68,138,000 **Capital** London (9,541,000)
Languages English (official), Welsh (also official in Wales), Gaelic **Currency** Sterling (pound) = 100 pence
Website www.gov.uk

	🛣	▲	▲	🏘
⊙	112	112	96	48
If towing				
⊙	96	96	80	48

Several cities have introduced 32 kph (20 mph) zones away from main roads

- 🔗 Compulsory in front seats and if fitted in rear seats
- 👶 Under 3 must use appropriate child restraint in front and rear; 3-12 or under 135cm must use appropriate child restraint in front, in rear must use appropriate child restraint or seat belt if no child restraint is available (e.g. because two occupied restraints prevent fitting of a third).
- 🍸 0.08% (England, Northern Ireland, Wales) • 0.05% (Scotland)
- △ Recommended ✚ Recommended
- 💡 Recommended 🧯 Recommended
- ⊖ 17 (16 for mopeds)
- 📱 Only allowed with hands-free kit
- LEZ London's LEZ and ULEZ (ultra-low emission zone) operate by number-plate recognition; non-compliant vehicles face hefty daily charges. Foreign-registered vehicles must register.
- ★ Driving is on the left ★ On-the-spot fines imposed
- ★ Smoking is banned in all commercial vehicles
- ★ Tolls on some toll motorways, bridges and tunnels

1 : 3 200 000 map pages

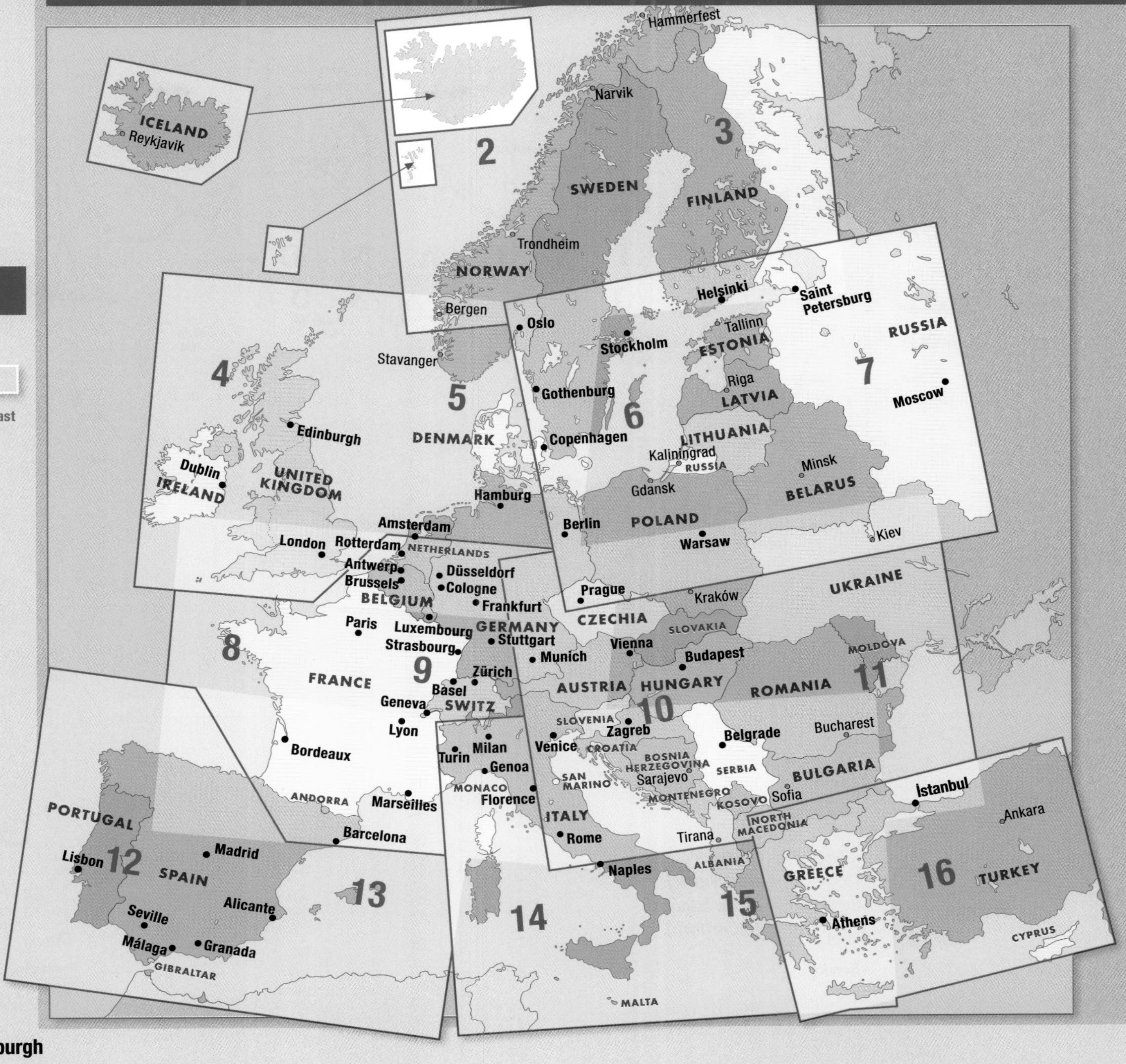

Map index with page grid numbers **2**–**16** and location labels:

ICELAND · Reykjavik · Hammerfest · Narvik · SWEDEN · FINLAND · NORWAY · Trondheim · Bergen · Stavanger · Oslo · Stockholm · Gothenburg · Helsinki · Tallinn · ESTONIA · Saint Petersburg · RUSSIA · Moscow · Riga · LATVIA · LITHUANIA · Kaliningrad RUSSIA · Minsk · BELARUS · Copenhagen · DENMARK · Hamburg · Berlin · POLAND · Warsaw · Gdansk · Kiev · UKRAINE · Amsterdam · NETHERLANDS · London · Rotterdam · Antwerp · Brussels · BELGIUM · Düsseldorf · Cologne · Frankfurt · Prague · Kraków · CZECHIA · SLOVAKIA · Dublin · IRELAND · UNITED KINGDOM · Edinburgh · Paris · Luxembourg · GERMANY · Strasbourg · Stuttgart · Munich · Vienna · Budapest · AUSTRIA · HUNGARY · Zürich · Basel · SWITZ · MOLDOVA · ROMANIA · FRANCE · Geneva · Lyon · Bordeaux · Turin · Milan · Genoa · Venice · Zagreb · SLOVENIA · CROATIA · Belgrade · Bucharest · Marseilles · ANDORRA · SAN MARINO · BOSNIA HERZEGOVINA · SERBIA · MONTENEGRO · KOSOVO · BULGARIA · Istanbul · Ankara · PORTUGAL · Lisbon · Madrid · SPAIN · Barcelona · Alicante · Seville · Granada · Málaga · GIBRALTAR · ITALY · Florence · Rome · MONACO · Naples · Tirana · ALBANIA · NORTH MACEDONIA · Sofia · GREECE · Athens · TURKEY · CYPRUS · MALTA

km

Distances

Dublin → Goteborg = 477 km

Distances shown in blue involve at least one ferry journey

	Calais	Dublin	Edinburgh	Frankfurt	Göteborg
Dublin	548				
Edinburgh	726	346			
Frankfurt	575	1123	1301		
Göteborg	1342	477	176	1067	
Hamburg	1189	760	477	1486	485	582

	Amsterdam	Athina	Barcelona	Bergen	Berlin	Bruxelles	Bucuresti	Budapest	Calais	Dublin	Edinburgh	Frankfurt	Göteborg	Hamburg	Helsinki	Istanbul	København	Köln	Lisboa	London	Luxembourg	Madrid	Marseille	Milano	Moskva	München	Oslo	Paris	Praha	Roma	Sevilla	Sofia	Stockholm	Warszawa	Wien
Athina	2945																																		
Barcelona	1505	3192																																	
Bergen	1484	3742	2803																																
Berlin	650	2412	1863	1309																															
Bruxelles	197	2895	1308	1586	764																														
Bucuresti	2245	1219	2644	3037	1707	2181																													
Budapest	1420	1530	1999	2212	882	1358	852																												
Calais	367	3100	1269	1783	956	215	2398	1573																											
Dublin	533	3630	1817	270	1504	763	3021	2196	548																										
Edinburgh	1093	3826	1995	176	1696	941	3124	2299	726	346																									
Frankfurt	441	2499	1313	1508	550	383	1804	979	575	1123	1301																								
Göteborg	1029	3080	2362	819	668	1145	1734	1550	1342	477	176	1067																							
Hamburg	447	2719	1780	1023	286	563	2014	1189	760	477	1486	485	582																						
Helsinki	1560	2539	2338	1063	475	1239	1834	1009	1431	1318	1236	1598	505	1113																					
Istanbul	2756	1145	2990	3653	2223	2706	690	1341	2911	3537	3657	2314	2891	2530	2350																				
København	965	2782	2090	1103	370	1081	2077	1252	1278	752	479	795	284	518	803	2593																			
Köln	256	2684	1376	1427	566	198	1983	1158	390	938	1116	180	986	404	1517	2499	714																		
Lisboa	2331	4460	1268	3723	2869	3141	3917	3222	2069	2617	2795	2400	3282	2700	3817	4342	3014	2339																	
London	480	3200	1387	458	1074	333	2591	1766	118	430	608	693	122	878	1991	3107	1188	508	2187																
Luxembourg	406	2661	1190	1613	749	209	2052	1227	424	972	1150	240	1172	590	1703	2472	900	186	2160	542															
Madrid	1790	3809	617	3183	2364	1600	3262	2622	1528	1634	2254	1930	2742	2160	3276	3589	2473	1798	651	1646	1628														
Marseille	1210	2683	509	2435	1541	1030	2154	1505	1063	1588	1789	1023	1994	1412	2525	2479	1722	1006	1777	1182	822	1126													
Milano	1085	2182	1038	2141	1060	890	1668	992	1072	1620	1798	683	1700	1118	1535	1993	1428	868	2315	1190	679	1655	538												
Moskva	2457	2930	3655	2223	1821	2585	1761	2099	2800	3348	3526	2312	1665	2115	1160	2605	2325	2387	4875	2918	2852	4224	3270	3027											
München	839	2106	1340	1788	594	789	1497	672	994	1524	1720	398	1347	765	1069	1907	969	580	2545	1094	555	2010	1011	473	2305										
Oslo	1347	3372	2680	503	960	1463	2667	1842	1660	773	729	1385	316	900	697	3089	590	1304	3604	1778	1490	3063	2312	2018	1823	1559									
Paris	510	2917	988	1922	1051	320	2307	1482	281	829	1007	591	1481	899	2012	2727	1209	495	1821	399	351	1280	782	857	2903	810	1799								
Praha	950	2067	1750	1675	345	888	1362	537	1097	1635	1816	512	1013	652	770	1878	715	690	2870	1205	753	2329	1399	853	1853	388	1305	1061							
Roma	1691	1140	1385	2706	1502	1520	1904	1263	1678	2226	2404	1289	2265	1683	1977	2237	1993	1474	2653	1796	1285	2002	876	606	3362	918	2583	1389	1309						
Sevilla	2347	4223	1031	3736	2894	2150	3709	3010	2078	2626	2804	2344	3295	2713	3826	4034	3023	2318	401	2196	2178	550	1540	2078	4774	2371	3613	1830	2781	2446					
Sofia	2206	828	2453	3103	1673	2156	391	790	2361	2891	3087	1764	2341	1980	1800	550	2043	1949	3706	2461	1922	3037	1929	1443	2252	1367	2632	2177	1328	1687	3484				
Stockholm	1393	3418	2726	1063	1006	1509	2713	1888	1673	2254	1069	1431	505	946	167	3185	590	1350	3650	1824	1536	3109	2358	2064	1228	1600	530	1845	1351	2629	3659	2679			
Warszawa	1256	2128	2366	1909	606	1350	1473	648	1542	2110	2268	1136	1274	886	361	1989	956	1152	3480	1680	1345	2960	2015	1469	1245	996	1506	1677	616	1853	3397	1439	1612		
Wien	1168	1772	1856	1970	640	1114	1067	242	1308	1954	2034	731	1308	947	1088	1583	1010	916	3100	1524	993	2473	1353	818	2137	430	1600	1240	295	1126	2876	1033	1646	727	
Zurich	816	2426	1030	1938	863	619	1810	985	804	1352	1530	464	1497	915	2164	2323	1433	589	2296	922	410	1647	699	292	2552	303	1815	592	691	898	2061	1173	1861	1307	743

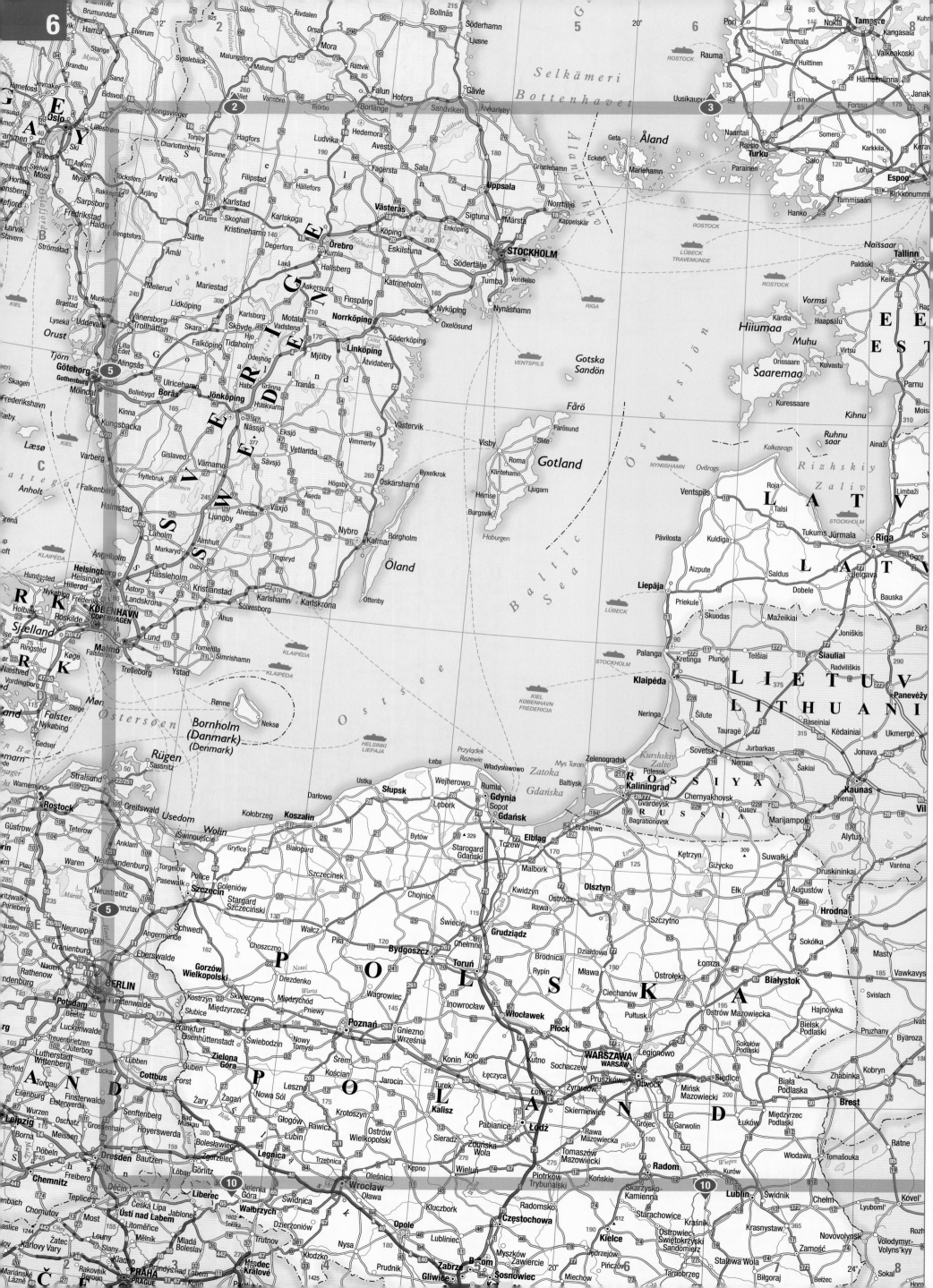

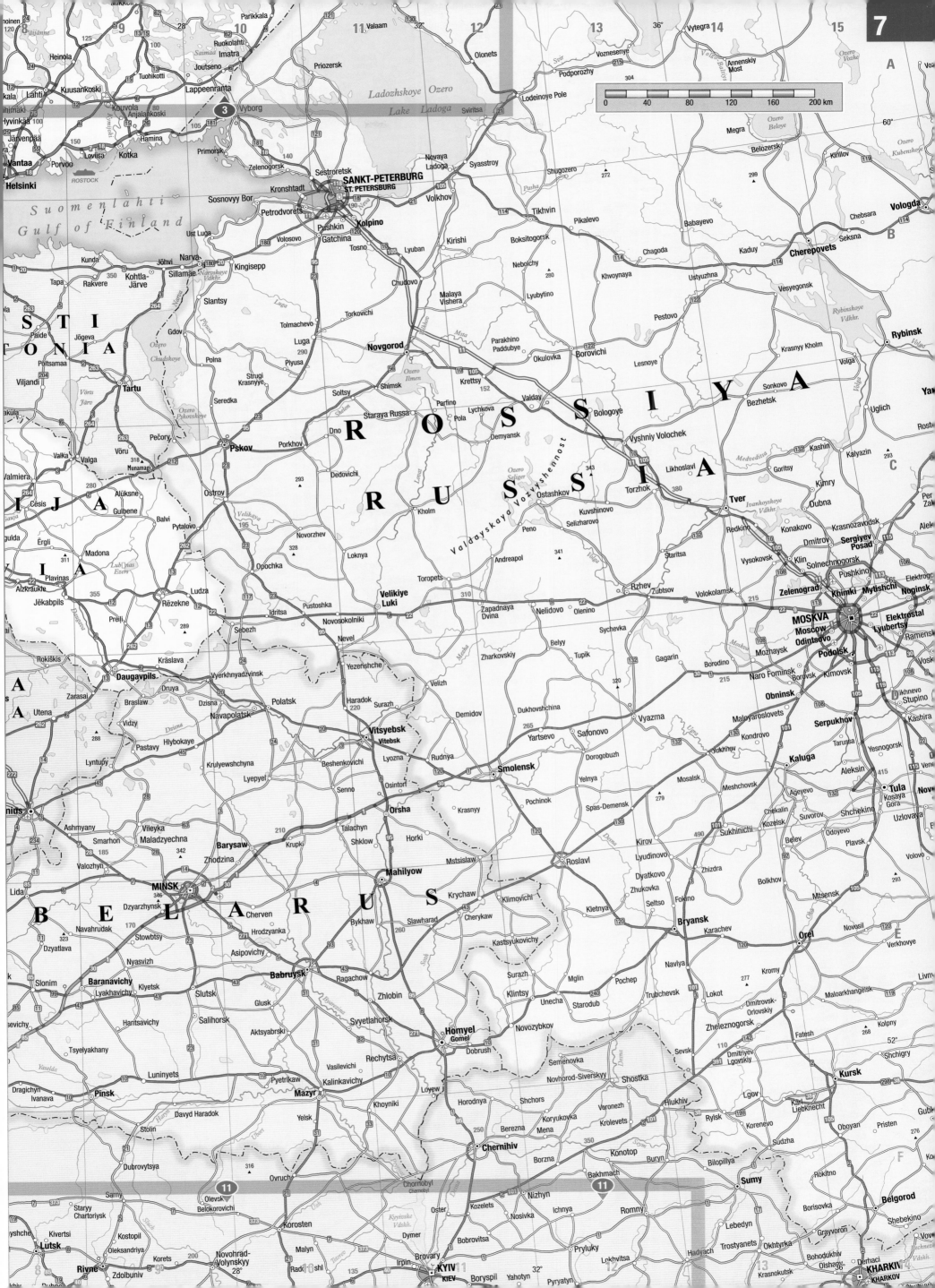

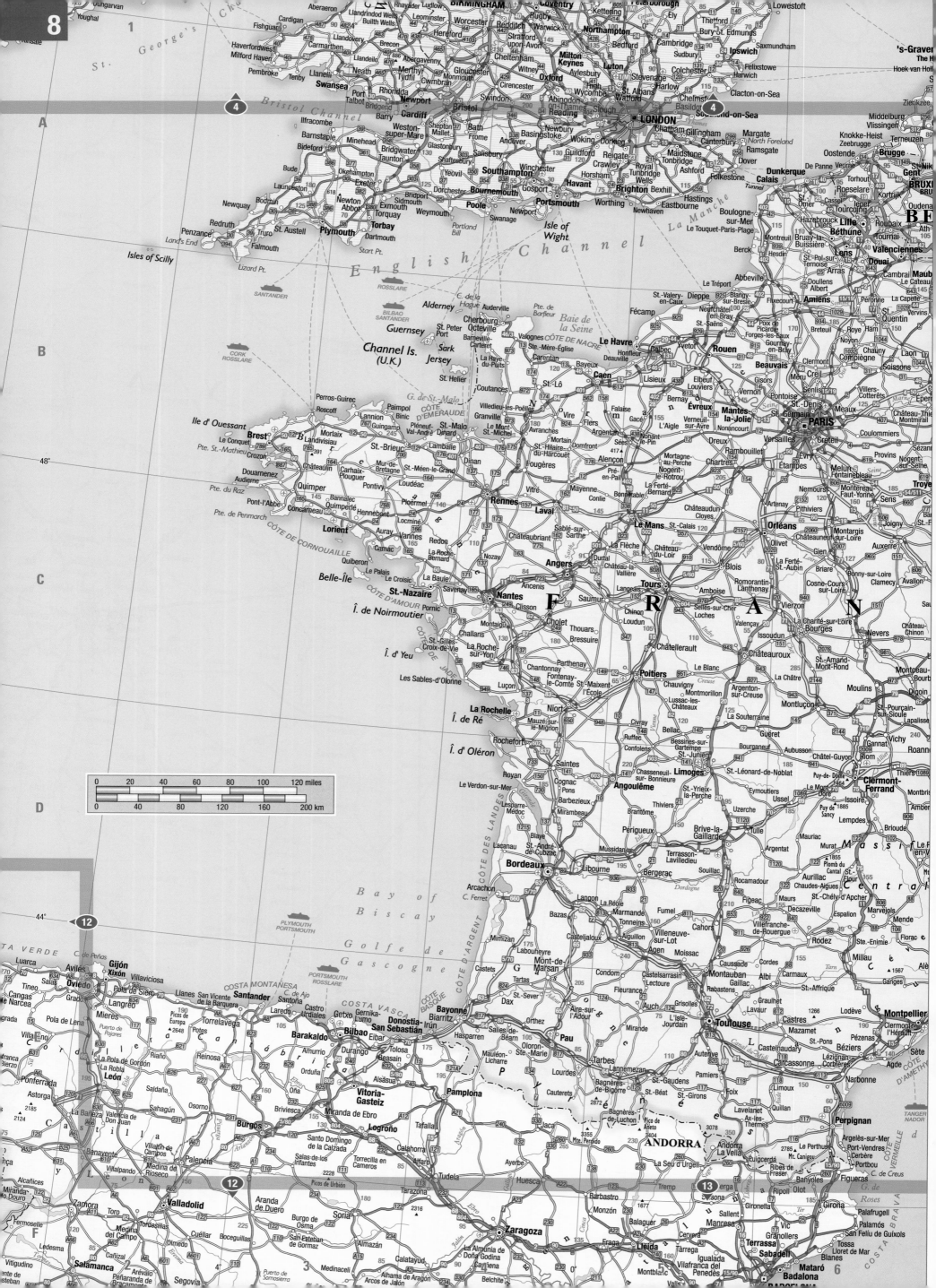

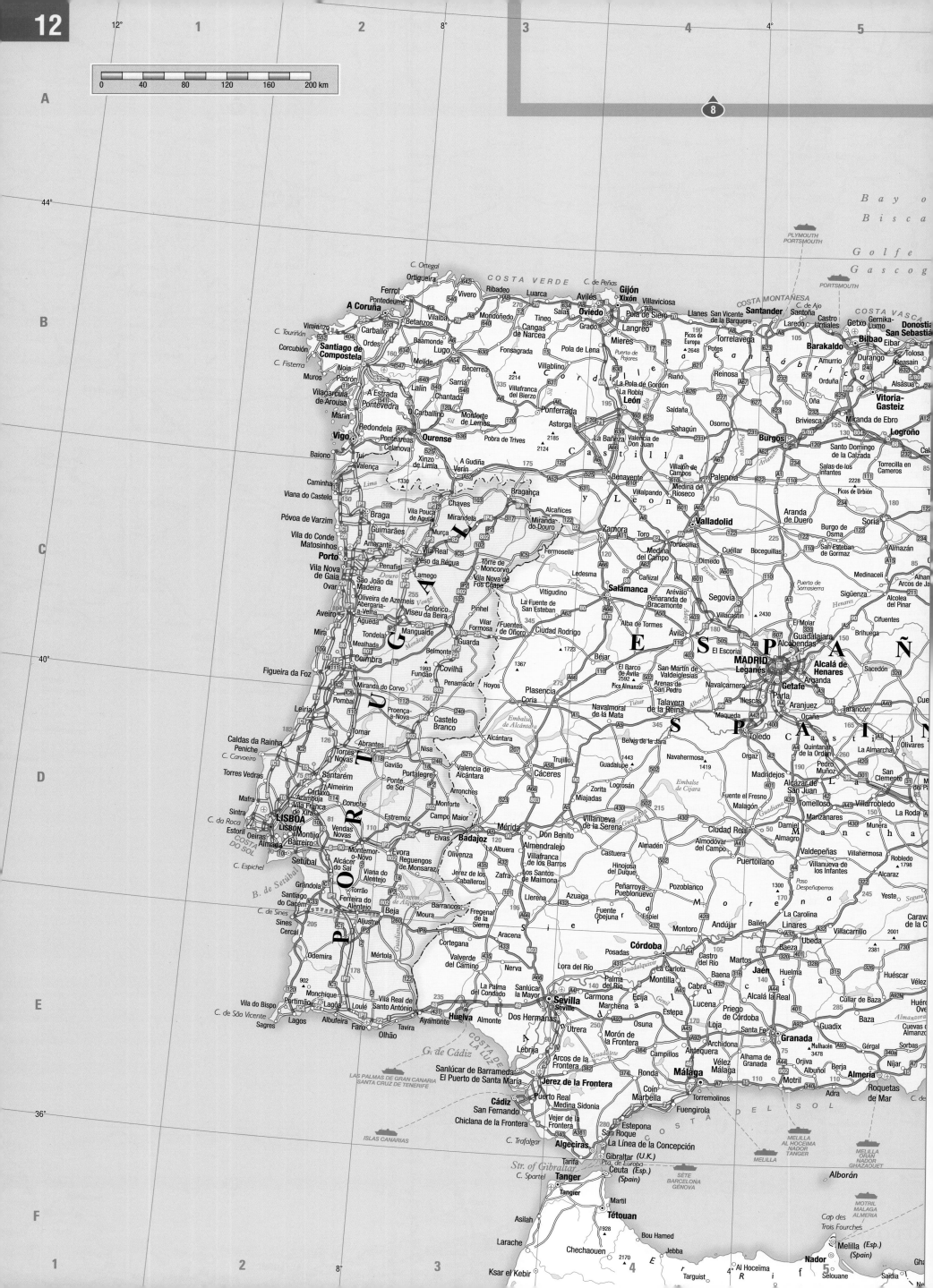

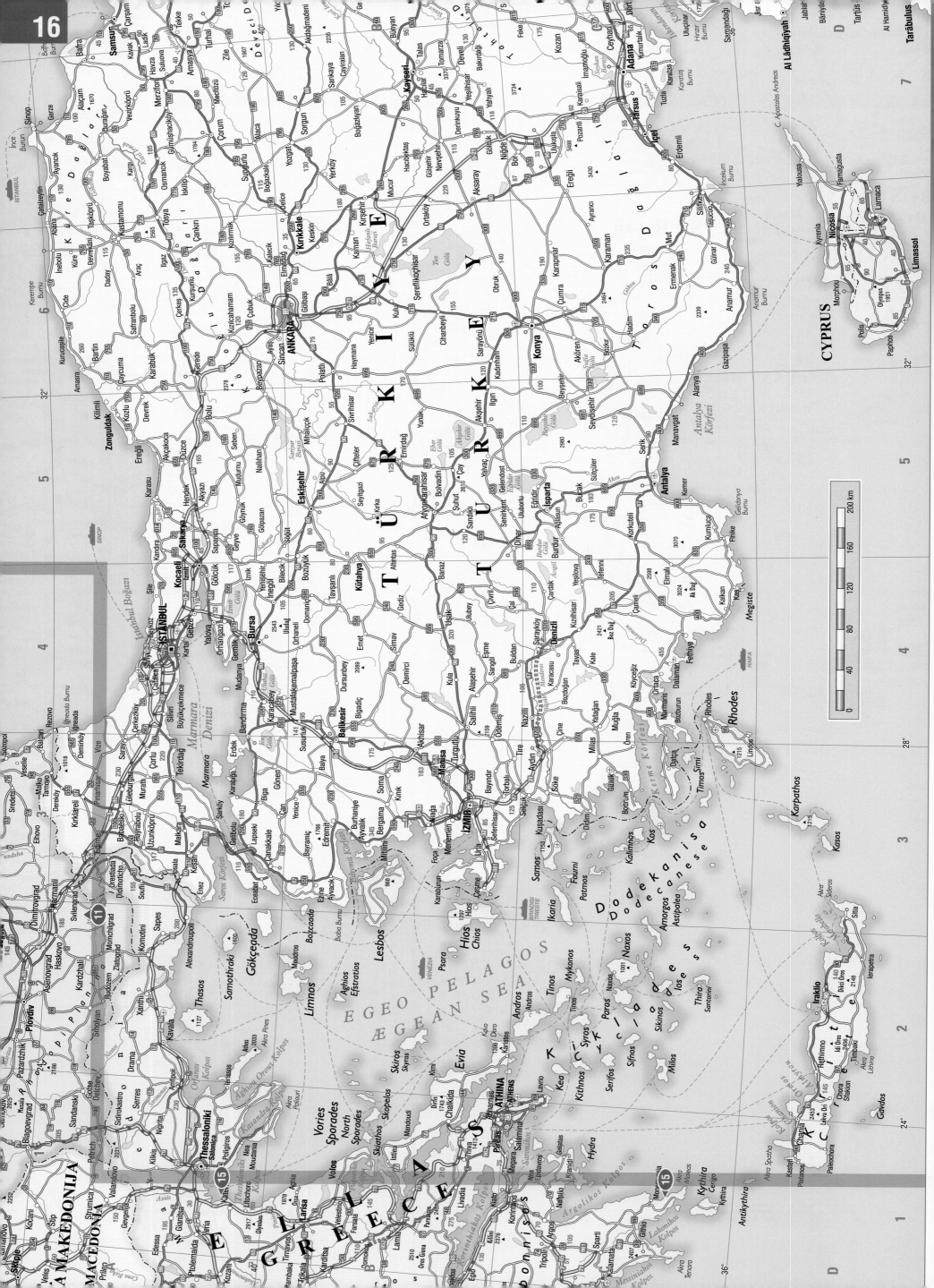

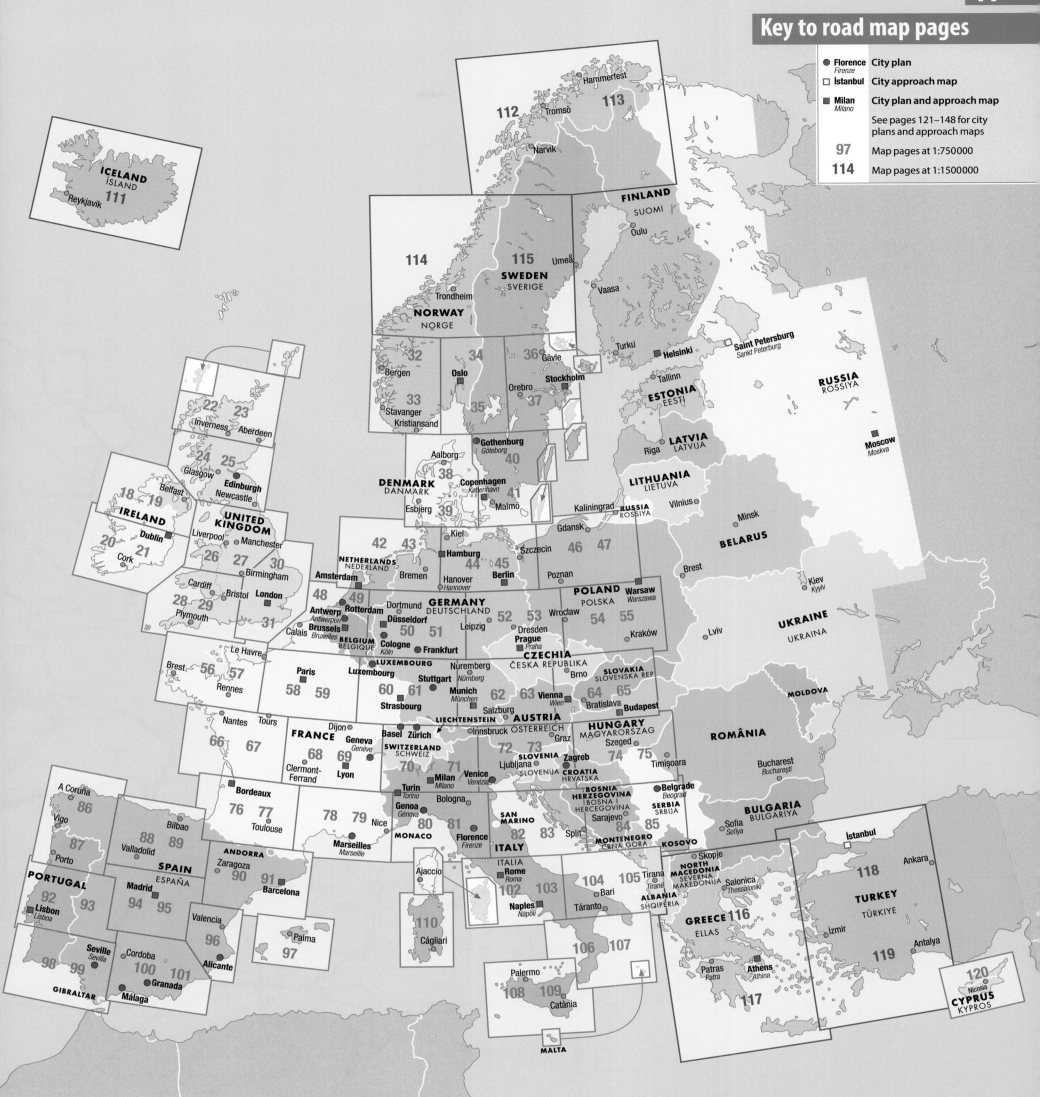

● Florence *Firenze*	City plan
□ İstanbul	City approach map
■ Milan *Milano*	City plan and approach map
	See pages 121–148 for city plans and approach maps
97	Map pages at 1:750000
114	Map pages at 1:1500000

Motorway vignettes

Some countries require you to purchase (and in some cases display) a vignette before using certain classes of road

In Austria you will need to purchase and display a vignette on the inside of your windscreen. These may be purchased at border crossings and petrol stations. Digital vignettes are also available. More details from www.asfinag.at/en/toll/vignette/

In Belarus all vehicles over 3.5 tonnes and cars and vans under 3.5 tonnes registered outside the Eurasion Economic Union are required to have a *BelToll* unit installed. This device enables motorway tolls to be automatically deducted from the driver's account. http://beltoll.by/index.php/en/

In Bulgaria a vignette is required to drive on motorways and main roads. These can be purchased at the border. Digital e-vignettes can be obtained from terminals at border checkpoints or online in advance: www.bgtoll.bg/en

In Czechia vehicles up to 3.5 tonnes require an e-vignette for motorway driving, these are available for periods of 1 year, 30 days or 10 days https://edalnice.cz/en. Vehicles over 3.5 tonnes are subject to tolls and must carry an electronic tag https://mytocz.eu/en

In Hungary tolls apply to many motorways and are administered through an electronic vignette system with automatic number plate recognition https://nemzetiutdij.hu/en

In Moldova vehicles not registered in Moldova require a vignette. These may be purchased from MAIB (Moldova-Agroindbank) branches or online https://evinieta.gov.md

In Slovakia an electronic vignette is required for motorways, validity: 1 year, 30 days, 10 days. https://eznamka.sk/en

In Slovenia an e-vignette must be purchased before a vehicle can enter a toll road https://evinjeta.dars.si/en

In Switzerland, all vehicles under 3.5 tonnes must display a vignette on the windscreen. These are valid for one year and can be purchased at border crossings, petrol stations, post offices and online https:// switzerlandtravelcentre.com/en/gbr/offer/ vignette. Vehicles over 3.5 tonnes are subject to a heavy vehicle charge https://via.admin.ch/shop/dashboard.

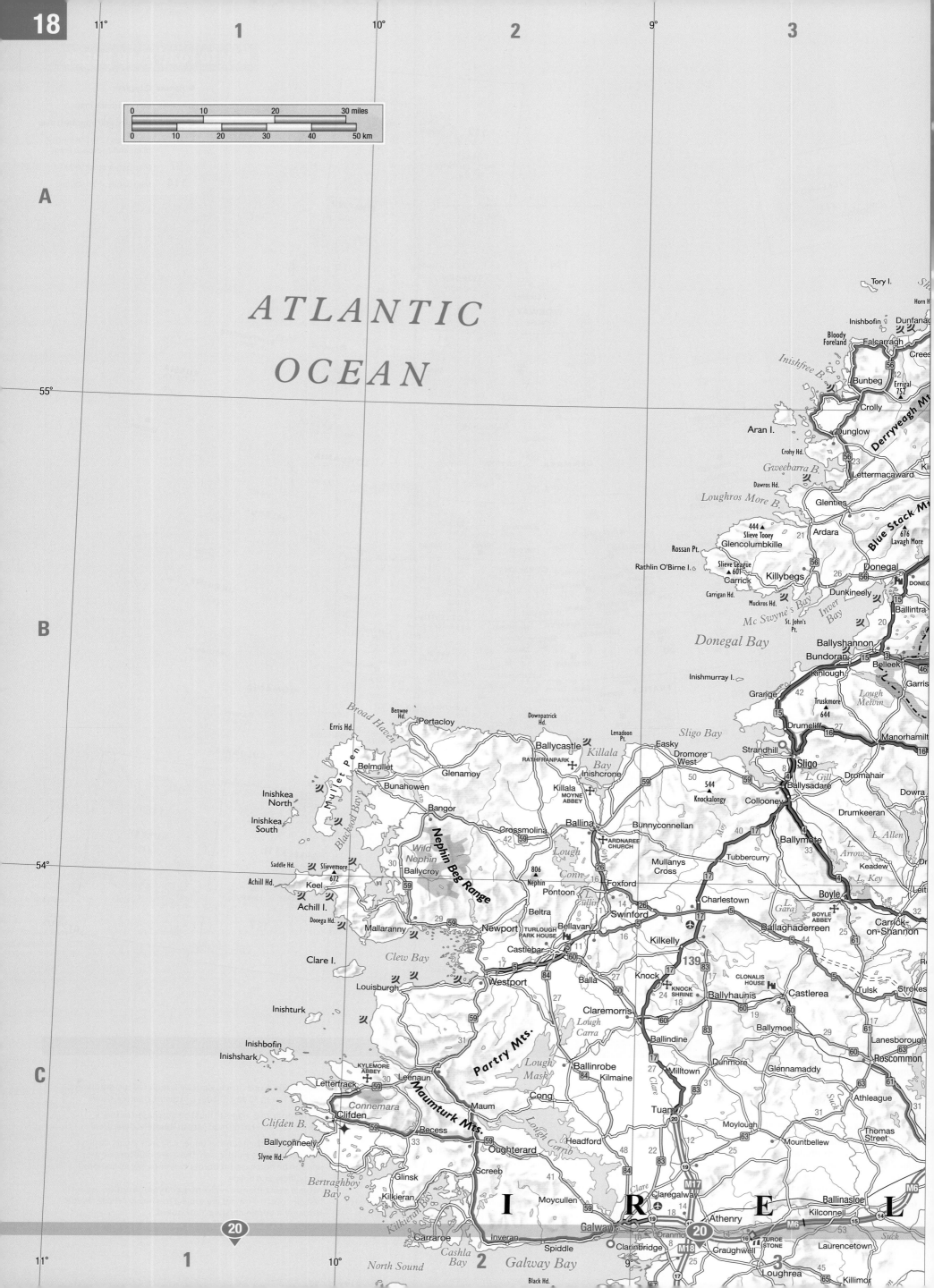

ATLANTIC

OCEAN

A

B

C

IRELAND

11°   1   10°   2   9°   3

0   10   20   30 miles
0   10   20   30   40   50 km

55°

54°

Tory I.

Inishbofin   Dunfanag
Bloody   Falcarragh   Crees
Foreland
Inishfree B.   Bunbeg   Errigal   752
Crolly
Aran I.   Dunglow   Derryveagh Mt.
Crohy Hd.   Lettermacaward   Ki
Gweebarra B.
Dawros Hd.   Glenties
Loughros More B.
444   Slieve Tooey   Ardara   676
Glencolumbkille   21   Lavagh More
Rossan Pt.   Slieve League   26   Donegal
Rathlin O'Birne I.   60   Carrick   Killybegs   Donec
Carrigan Hd.   Dunkineely   15
Muckros Hd.   Ballintra
Mc Swyne's Bay   St. John's   20
Pt.   Donegal   Ballyshannon
Donegal Bay   Bundoran   15   Belleek
Inishmurray I.   Kinlough   Lough
Grange   42   Truskmore   Melvin   Garris
644
Drumcliff   15   16   Manorhamilt
Broad   Benwee   Downpatrick   Sligo Bay   Strandhill   Sligo
Hd.   Hd.   Easky   Dromore   L. Gill   Dromahair   16
Erris Hd.   Portacloy   Ballycastle   Killala   Lenadoon   West   Ballysadare   Dowra
RATHFRANPARK   Bay   Pt.   Inishcrone   50   544   Colloney   L.
Belmullet   Glenamoy   Killala   59   Knockalongy   Ballymote   Allen
Bunahowen   MOYNE   33   Keadew
Inishkea   ABBEY   Mullanys   40   L. Key
North   Bangor   Crossmolina   Ballina   Bunnyconnellan   Cross   Tubbercurry   17   Boyle
Inishkea   42   59   ARDNAREE   May   Charlestown   Gara   BOYLE
South   Wild   CHURCH   26   17   ABBEY
Nephin   806   Lough   Foxford   9   5   Ballaghaderreen   25   Carrick-
Saddle Hd.   30   Nephin   Conn   14   Swinford   17   on-Shannon
Slievemore   Ballycroy   Pontoon   1   7   5   44   61
Achill Hd.   672   59   Beltra   16   Kilkelly   CLONALIS   Castlerea   Tulsk   Stroke
Keel   Newport   Bellavary   Knock   139   83   HOUSE   Tuam   33
Achill I.   29   59   TURLOUGH   60   24   KNOCK   18   Ballyhaunis   60   60
Dooega Hd.   PARK HOUSE   11   SHRINE   Ballymoe   19   Castlerea
Mallaranny   Castlebar   60   Balla   27   60   29   61   Lanesborough
Clare I.   Clew Bay   17   5   84   Claremorris   83   Ballindine   Dunmore   63   Roscommon
Louisburgh   Westport   27   Ballinrobe   60   Milltown   Glennamaddy   63
Inishturk   31   Lough   84   Kilmaine   27   Duhmore   31   Athleague   31
Cara   Cong   Clare   83   31   63   Thomas
Inishbofin   KYLEMORE   Partry Mts.   Lough   Ballinrobe   Moylough   Street
Inishshark   ABBEY   30   Leenaun   Mask   Tuam   63   Mountbellew
Letterfrack   59   Maum   Cong   20   12   83   19
Connemara   Maumturk Mts.   Lough   Headford   48   17   Ballinasloe   M6
Clifden B.   Clifden   Corrib   22   83   M17   Athenry   Kilconnell   15   M6
Ballyconneely   Recess   59   Oughterard   59   84   Clare   18   14   Galway   Craughwell
Slyne Hd.   33   Screeb   41   M17   Claregalway   19   TUROE
Glinsk   IRE   20   Moycullen   STONE
Bertraghboy   Kilkieran   Moyullen   M18   Oranmo   M8
Bay   Carraroe   Inveran   Spiddle   Galway   16   Laurencetown
20   Clarinbridge   M8   Loughrea   53   Suck
North Sound   Galway Bay   17   25   45   Killimor
Black Hd.

11°   1   10°   2   9°

Shetland Islands

Hermaness
Muckle Flugga
Baltasound
Norwick
Haroldswick
Unst
968
Balta
Cullivoe
16
Gutcher
Belmont
Pt. of Fethaland
26
Mid
Fetlar
Isbister
968
Yell
Funzie
The Faither
970
Rónas Hill
450
Yell
Esha Ness
6
15
Burravoe
Hillswick
20
Ulsta
St. Magnus Bay
Papa Stour
Brae
968
Vidlin
Muckle Roe
Whalsay
Voe
Symbister
Sandness
9
23
Neap
Dale
971
Aith
Lunna Ness
Out Skerries
Walls
29
970
Easter Skeld
Shetland
Bressay
Scalloway
Lerwick
Hamnavoe
I. of Noss
West Burra
42
Bard Hd.
Helli Ness
Aberdeen
Kirkwall
Northpunds
Scousburgh
970
Boddam
Tolob
Sumburgh
JARLSHOF PREHISTORIC SITE
Sumburgh Hd.

Foula

Fair Isle

Shetland Islands

Butt of Lewis
Dail bho Dheas
Port Nis
857
24
Barabhas
Tolastadh bho Thuath
Tolsta Hd.
Siabost
857
16
Bac
858
Broad Bay
Carlabhagh
292
Ben Mholach
Tiumpan Hd.
Great Bernera
Calanais
51
Newmarket
Port Nan Giuran
Timsgearraidh
Stornoway
866
Gallan Hd.
858
Mealabost
574
Lewis
Chicken Hd.
Mealisval
Giosla
859
Crosbost
48
Scarp
Kintarvie
Leumrabhagh
Grabhair
Husinish
572
Kebock Hd.
799
Beinn Mhor
Clisham
West L. Tarbert
Ardhasig
Taransay
Aird Asaig
Tairbeart
Scalpay
Toe Hd.
Shiant Is.
859
East L. Tarbert
Sgarasta Mhor
38
Pabbay
An t-Ob
Sd. of Pabbay
Roghadal
Berneray
Renish Pt.
Solas
48
865
North Uist
867
Loch nam Madadh
865
Clachan na Luib
Monach Is.
Baleshare
Ronay
Benbecula
Creag Ghoraidh
Wiay
865
Tobha Mor
53
South Uist
Machair
South Uist
865
Dalabrog
Loch Baghasdail
Pol a Charra
Sound of Barra
Eriskay
Barra
888
18
Bagh a Chaisteil
Vatersay
Sandray
Mingulay

Oban
Tiree

Rona

C. Wrath
Kyle of Durness
Durness
29
838
L. Inchard
Kinlochbervie
Rhiconich
North-West Sutherland
Foinaven
908
Scourie
Laxford Bridge
894
34
838
Eddrachillis Bay
L. More
Kylestrome
Kinloch
894
Pt. of Stoer
Drumbeg
Unapool
ARDVRECK CASTLE
Stoer
18
837
Inchnadamph
58
Rubha Coigeach
Lochinver
111
Assynt-Coigach
998
Ben More Assynt
Enard B.
Elphin
Achiltibuie
Ledmore
HYDROPONICUM GARDENS
835
837
L. Lurgainn
Strathkanaird
Oykel Bridge
Rosehall
25
Gruinard
Ullapool
L. Broom
26
837
Greenstone Pt.
LECKMELM ARBORETUM
Ardcharnich
CROICH CHURCH
Gruinard B.
Aultbea
62
Ardessie
835
Cove
832
Ardessie
Ben Dearg
1081
Melvaig
INVEREWE GARDEN
1062
An Teallach
17
Longa I.
Poolewe
Fionn Loch
Wester
Braemore
832
L. Gairloch
Gairloch
Ross
Port Henderson
Kerrysdale
1110
Sgurr Mor
Red Point
Talladale
29
832
L. Fannich
33
Kinlochewe
Garve
L. Torridon
24
832
15
Achnasheen
Rona
Torridon
890
25
Shieldaig
896
Scardoy
Achnashellach
Applecross
Coulags
27
Carron
L. Monar
Monar Lodge
Glen Strathfarrar
28
ATTADALE GARDEN
BEAULY
Ardarroch
Lochcarron
890
Liatrie
831
L. Carron
27
Stromeferry
Cannich
20
Drum
L. Carron
Kyle of Lochalsh
WOODLAND GARDEN
Auchtertyre
Glen Affric
CASTLE MOIL
L. Alsh
Dornie
Affric Lodge
19
URQ
Kyleakin
EILEAN CASTLE
87
18
Glen Affric
L. Mullardoch
12
Kintail
North
Glenelg
Shiel Bridge
30
Kylerhea
851
Glen Affric
Invermoriston
KNOCK CASTLE
21
L. Hourn
Fort Augustus
Teangue
L. Quoich
Tomdoun
87
Armadale
ARMADALE GARDENS
Knoydart
L. Garry
Invergarry
Pt. of Sleat
L. Nevis
Laggan
Mallaig
Murlaggan
L. Lochy
Clunes
LOCH NAN UAMH CAIRN
830
Lochailort
Glenfinnan
830
18
Spean Bridge
Arisaig
26
882
87
2
Gairlochy
Morar, Moidart
861
Roybridge
Corpach
Rhois-Bheinn
Loch

Inner Hebrides / Skye

Rubha Hunish
DUNTULM CASTLE
Staffin
855
51
Trotternish
Geary
Uig
Vaternish Pt.
L. Snizort
87
Rona
Dunvegan Hd.
Stein
23
The Storr
719
Sound of Raasay
DUNVEGAN CASTLE
Lephin
850
32
Carbost
Dunvegan
855
Inner Sound
Roskhill
863
Portree
34
Bracadale
Raasay
Skye
Clachan
Carbost
Drynoch
Scalpay
15
Sconser
L. Bracadale
Kyle of Lochalsh
Cuillin Hills
The Cuillin Hills
87
28
Broadford
Glenbrittle
L. Eishort
Soay
Elgol
Canna
Sanday
Rùm
Kinloch
Eigg
Galmisdale
The Small Isles
Sound of Rum
Muck

Scale:
0   10   20   30 miles
0 10 20 30 40 50 km

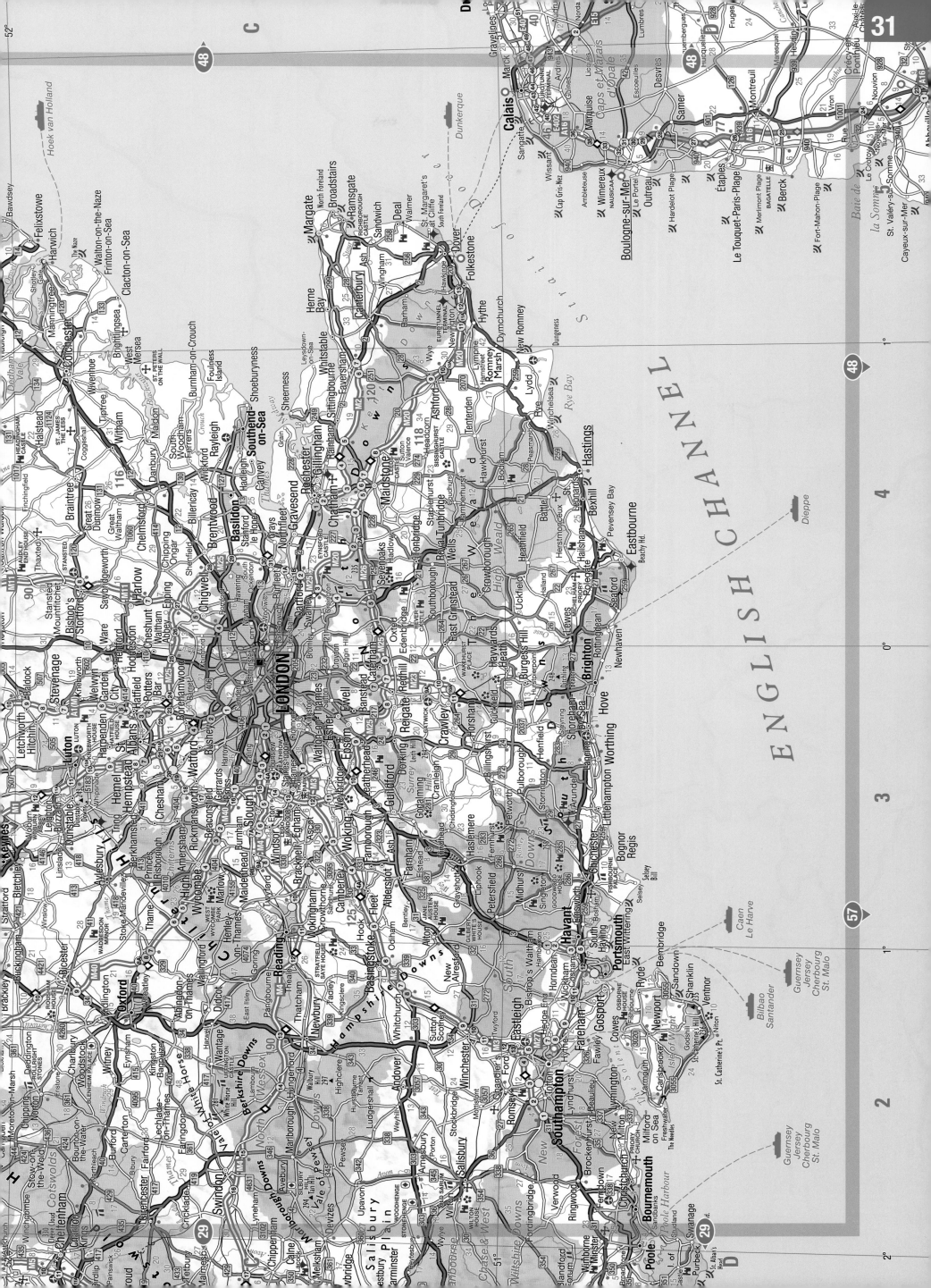

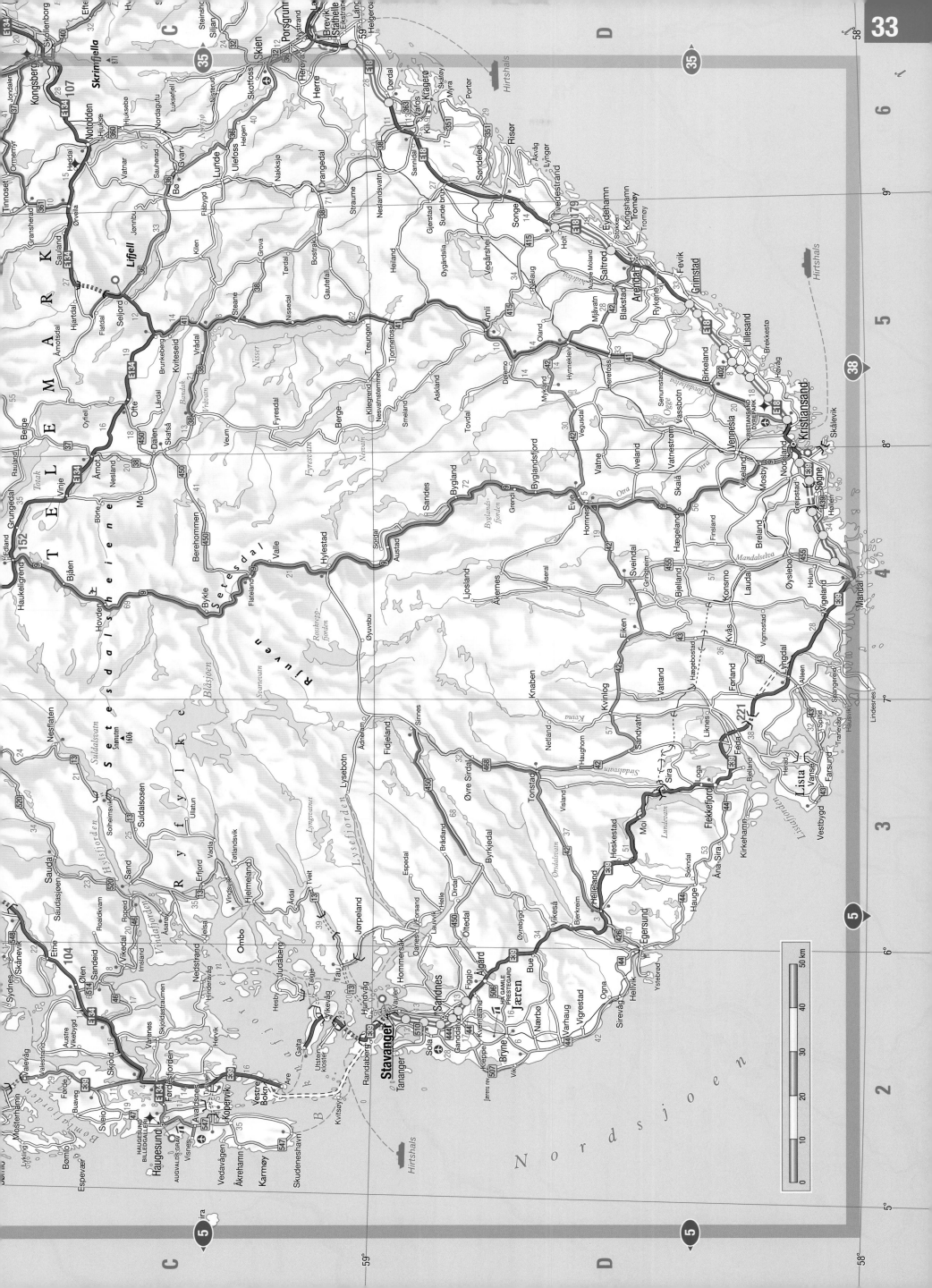

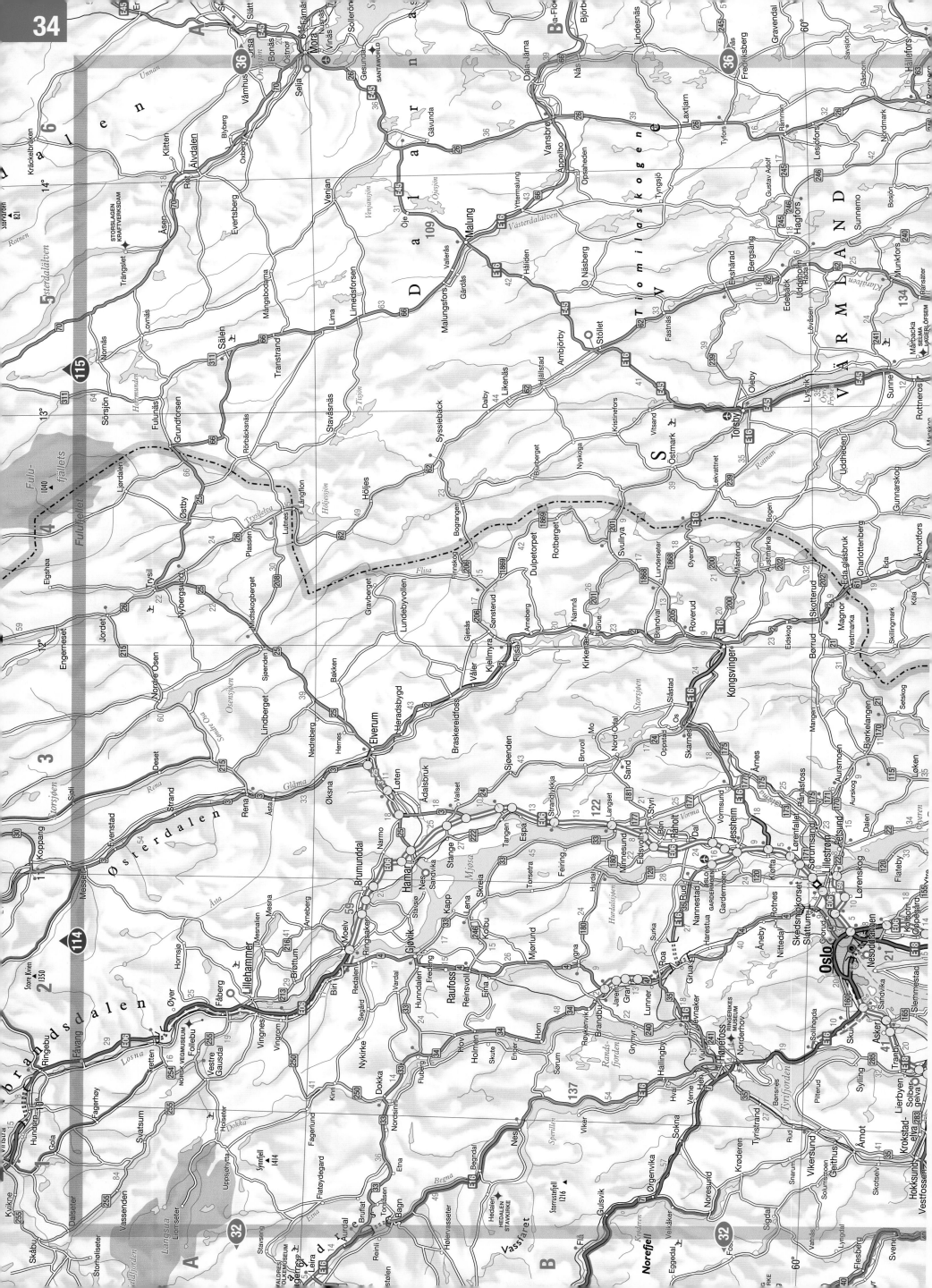

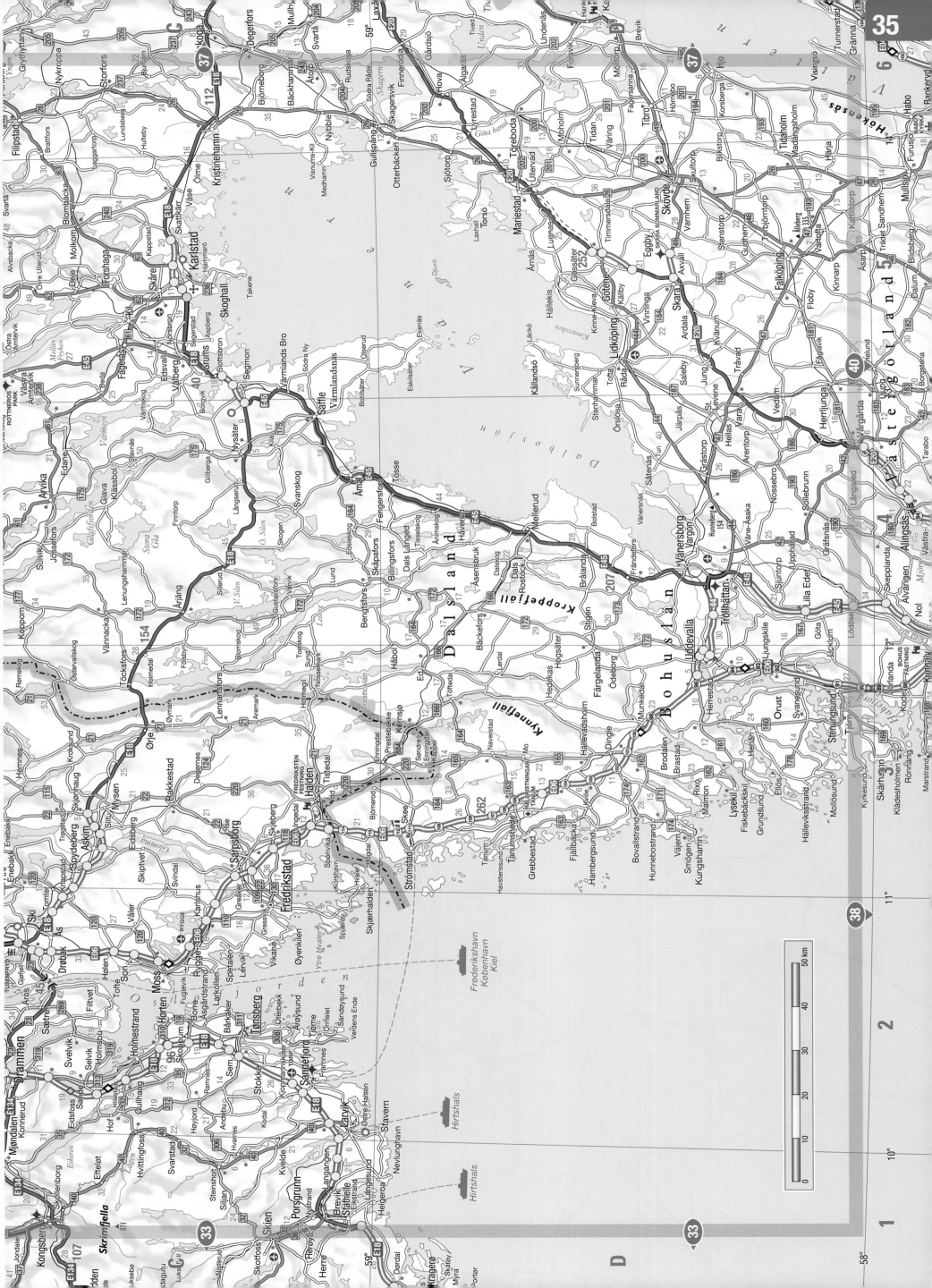

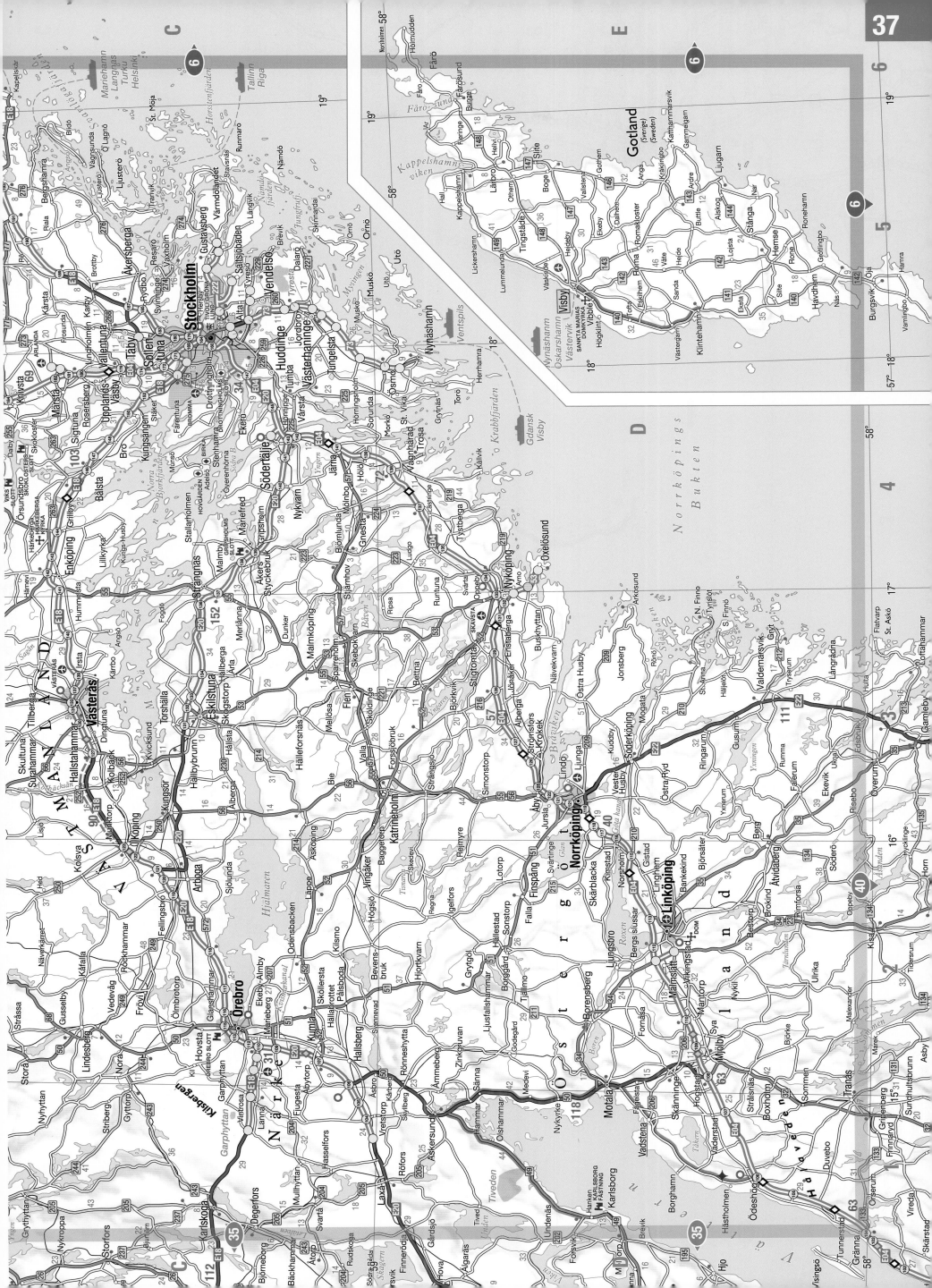

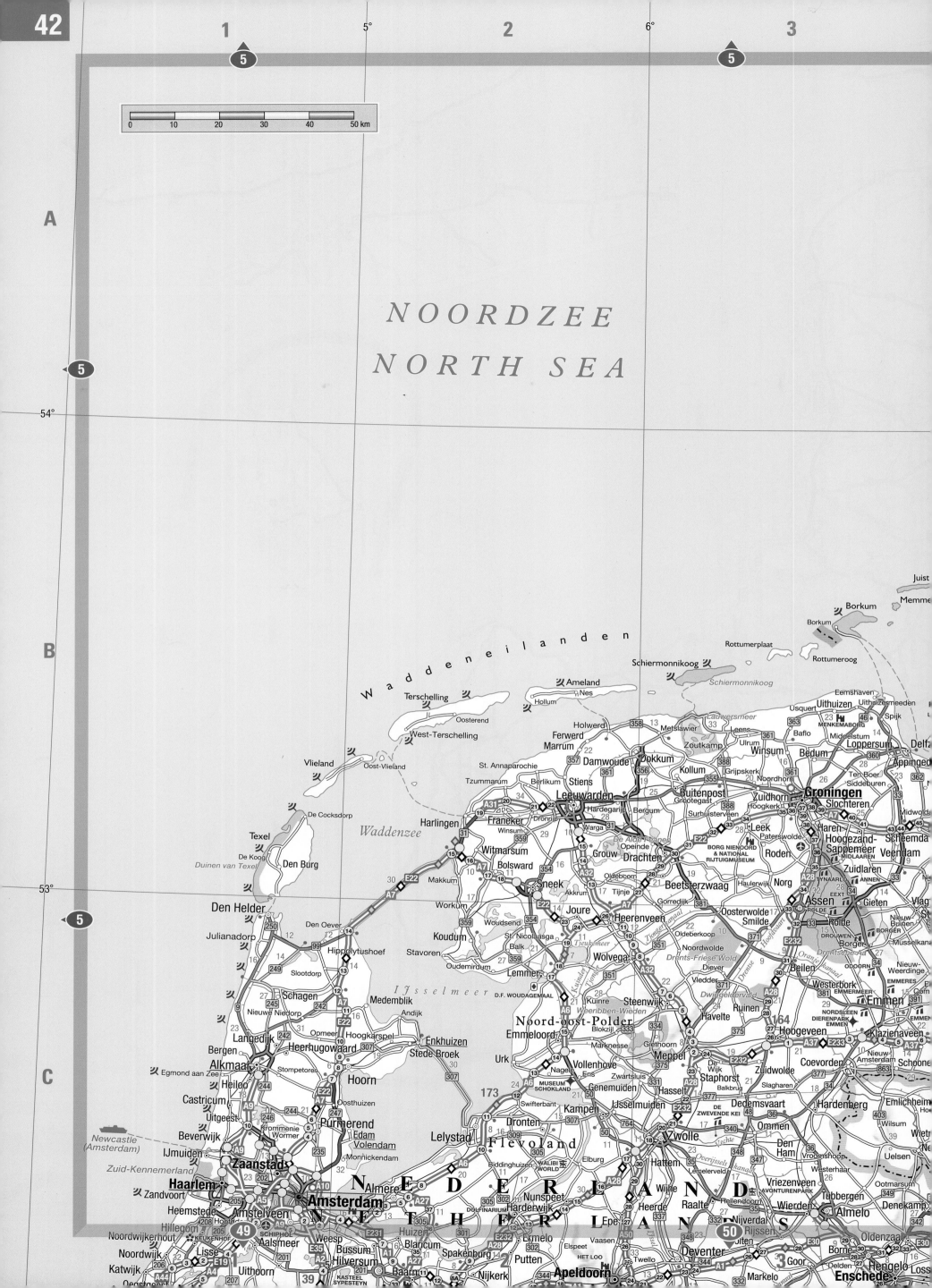

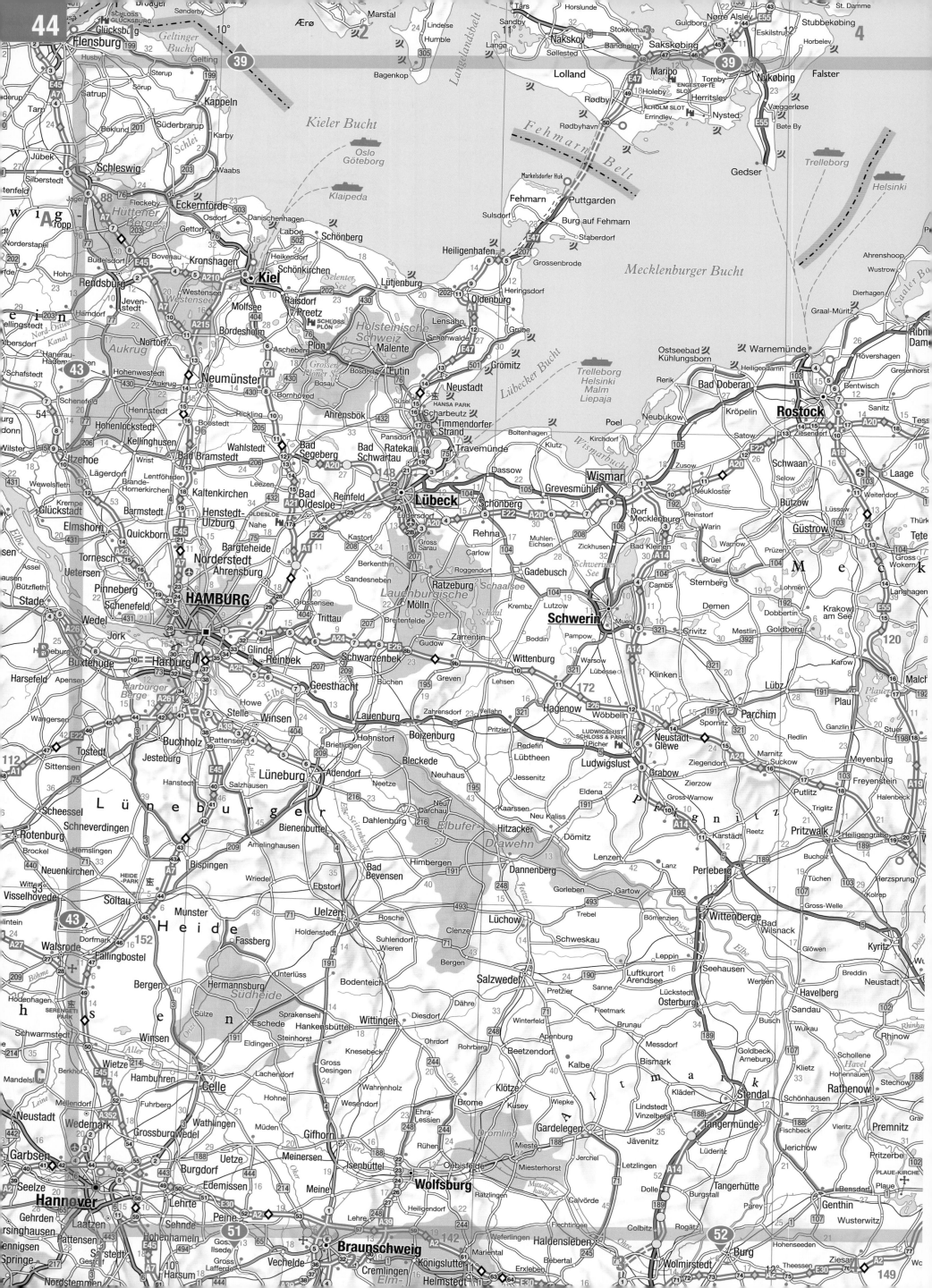

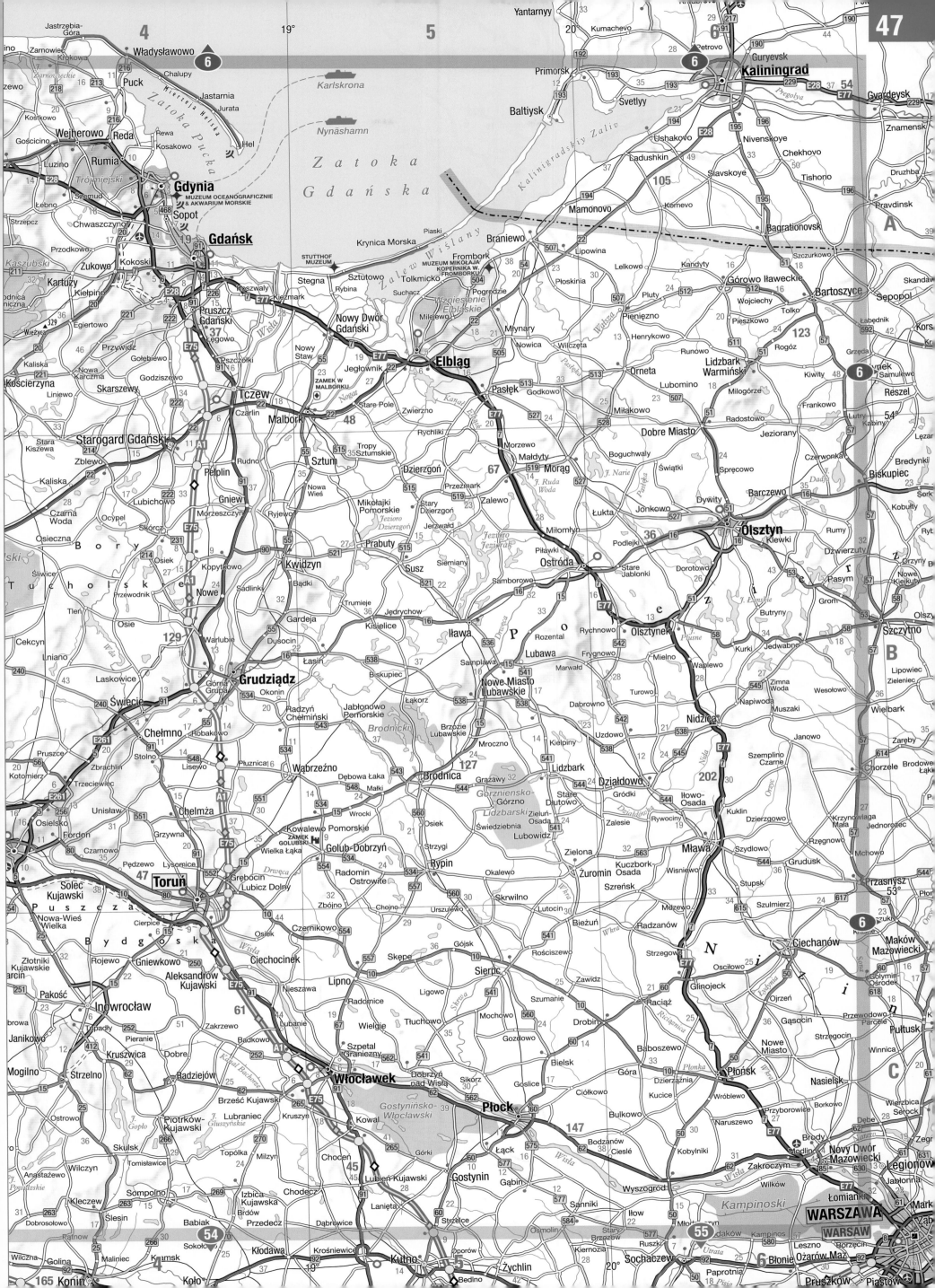

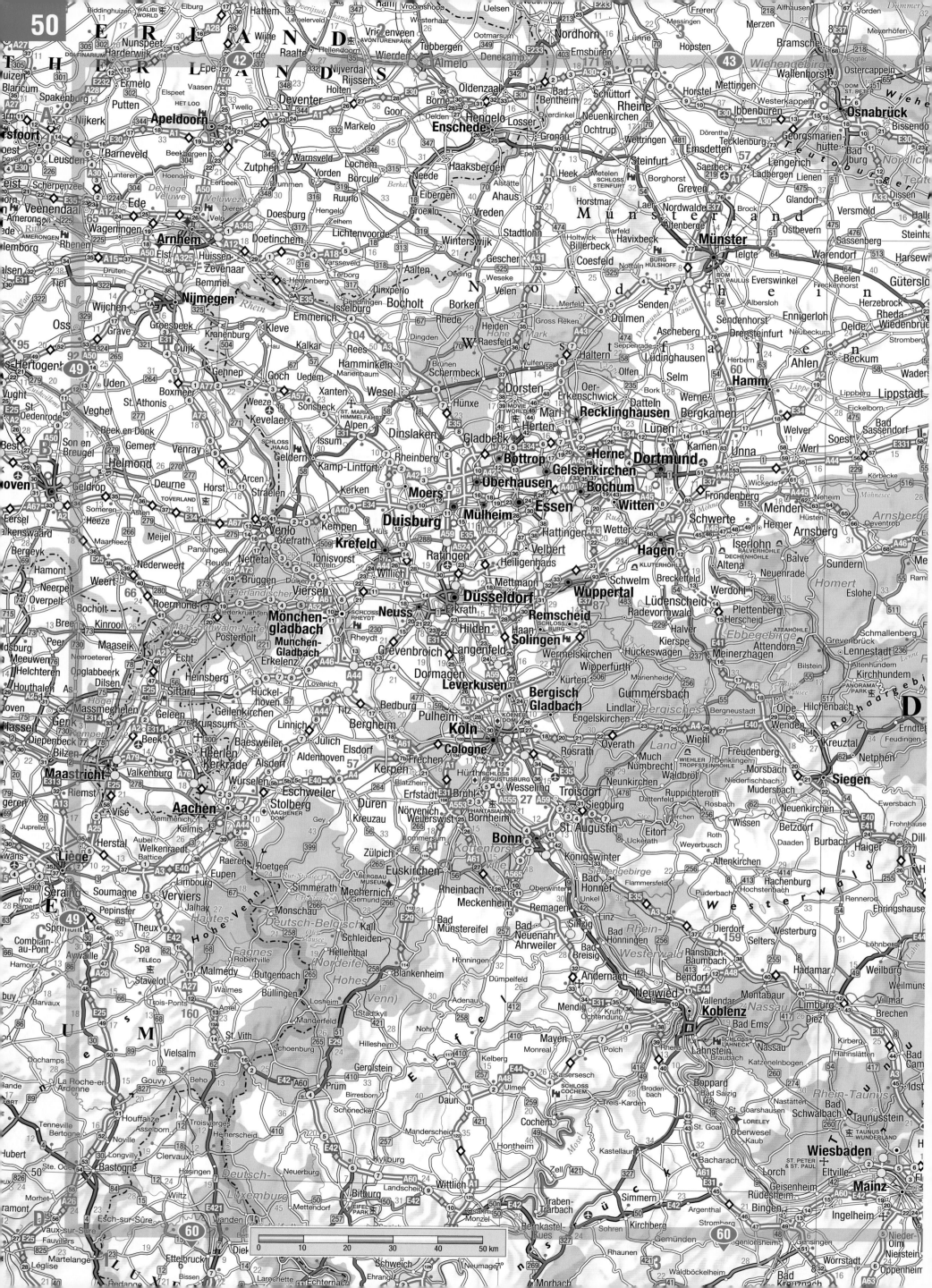

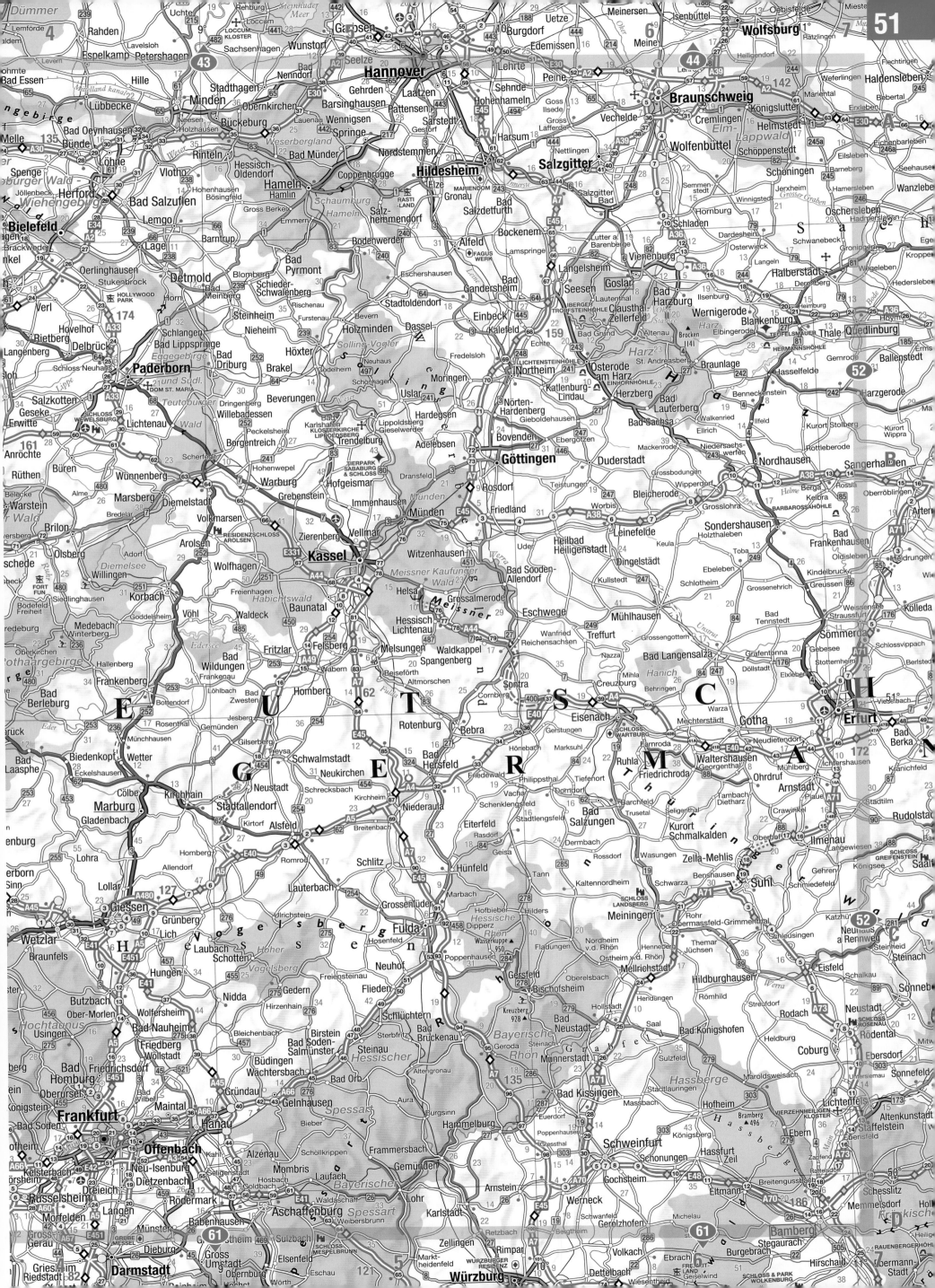

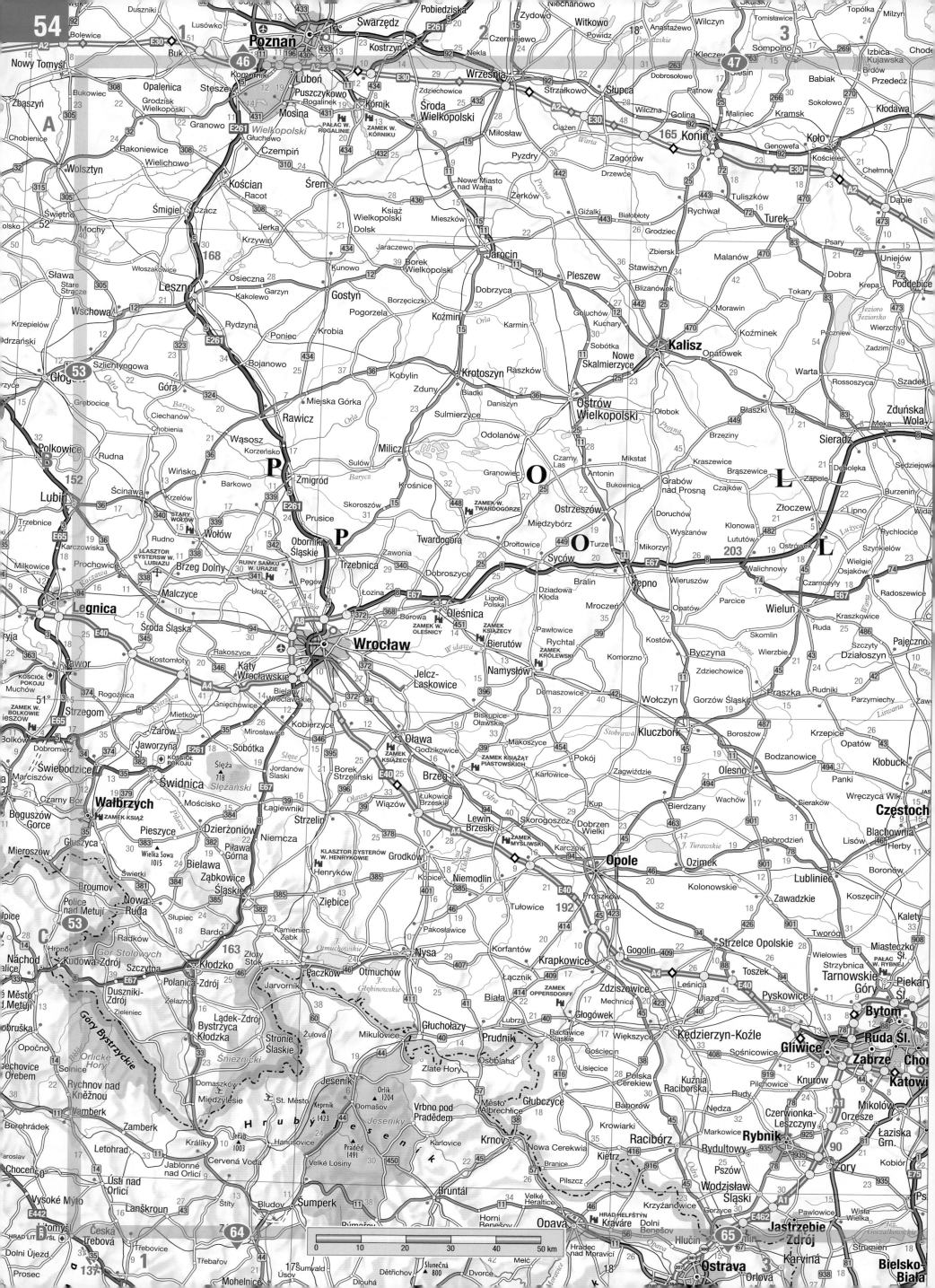

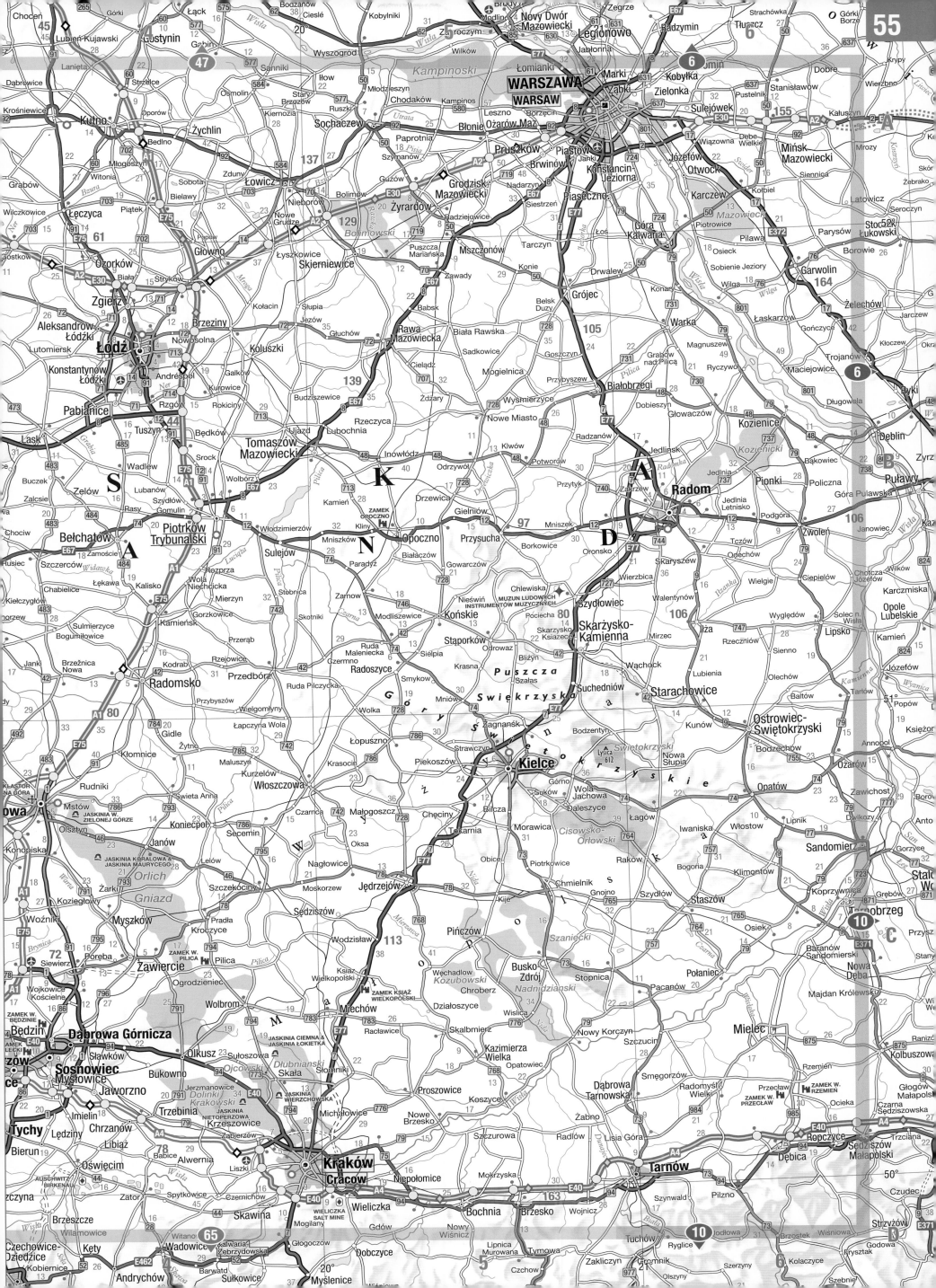

0 10 20 30 40 50 km

Le Havre Rouen Dieppe Amiens Beauvais Creil Senlis Chantilly

Lisieux Évreux Vernon Mantes-la-Jolie Pontoise Cergy Argenteuil St-Denis

PARIS Versailles Créteil Montreuil Évry Corbeil-Essonnes

Dreux Chartres Rambouillet Étampes Pithiviers

Le Mans Nogent-le-Rotrou Châteaudun Orléans

Vendôme Blois Beaugency Meung-sur-Loire

Tours Château-du-Loir

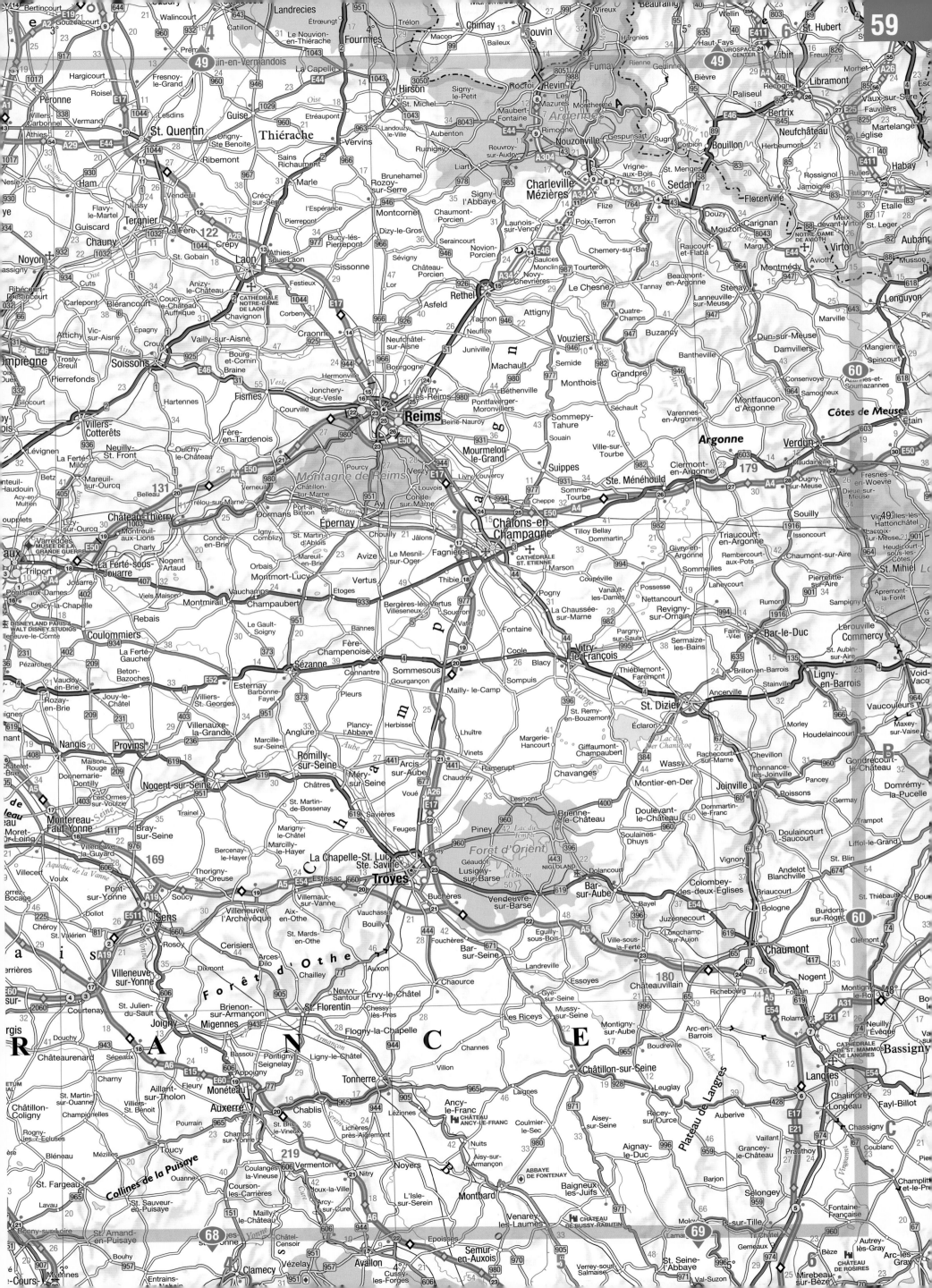

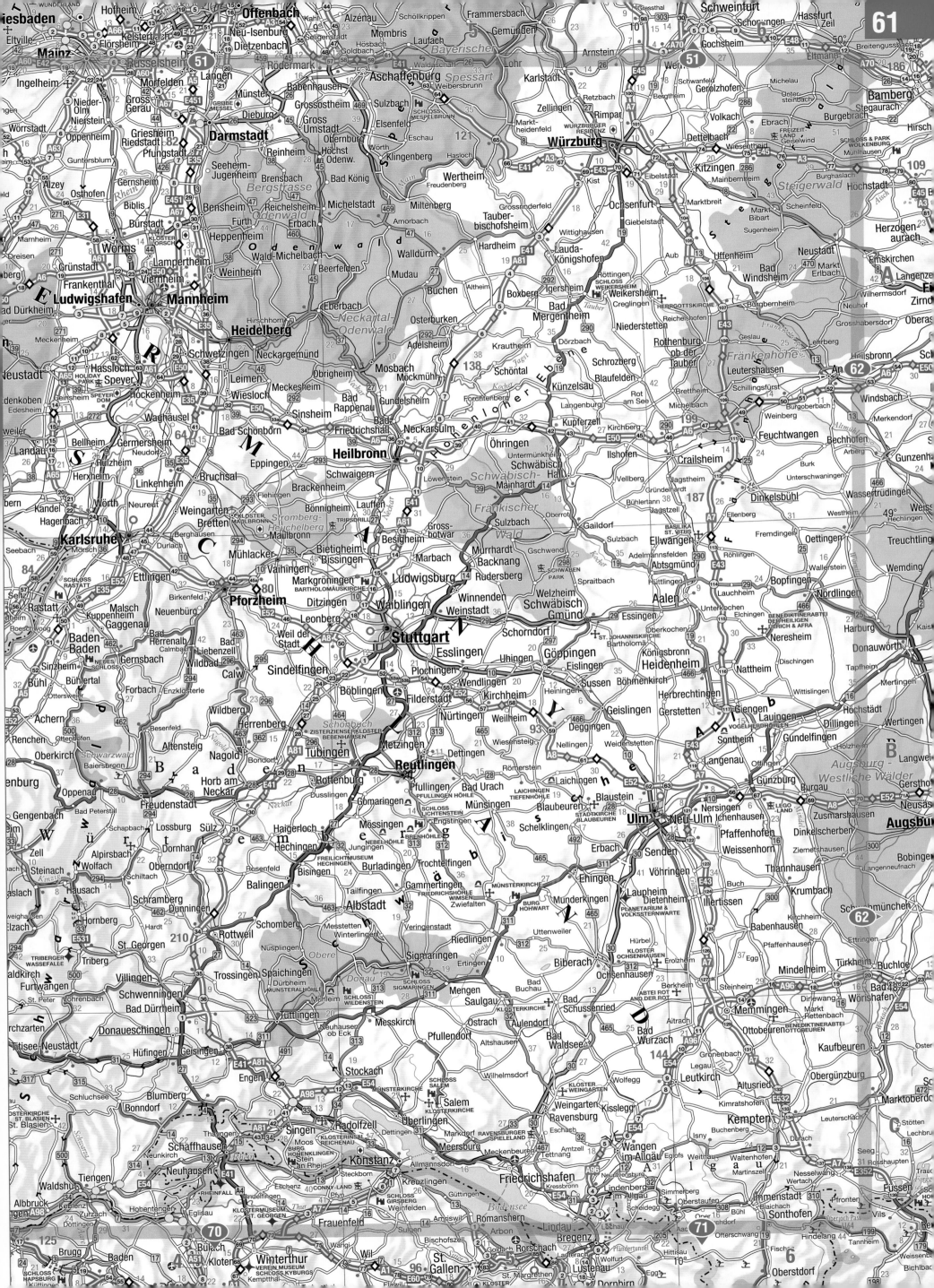

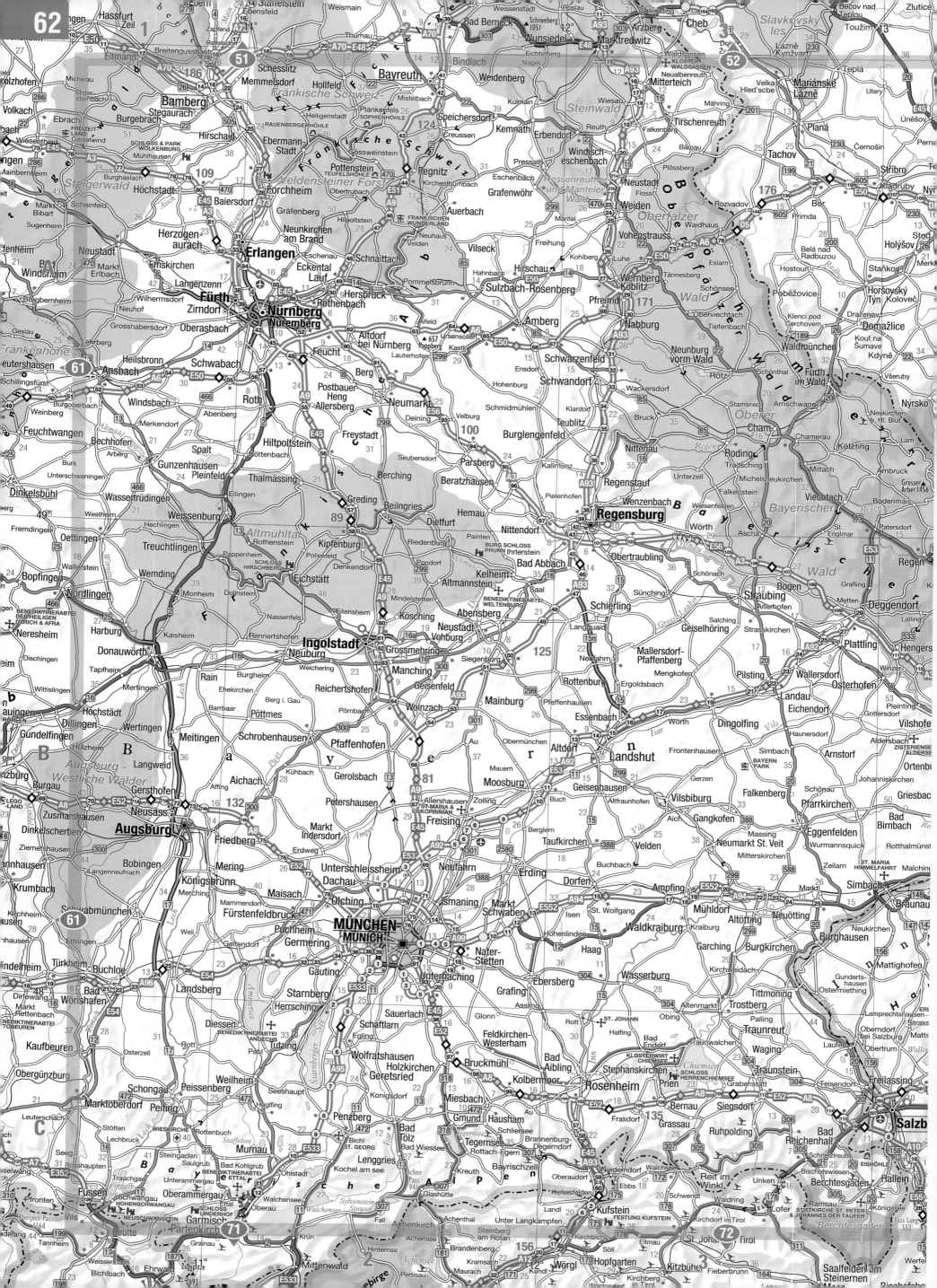

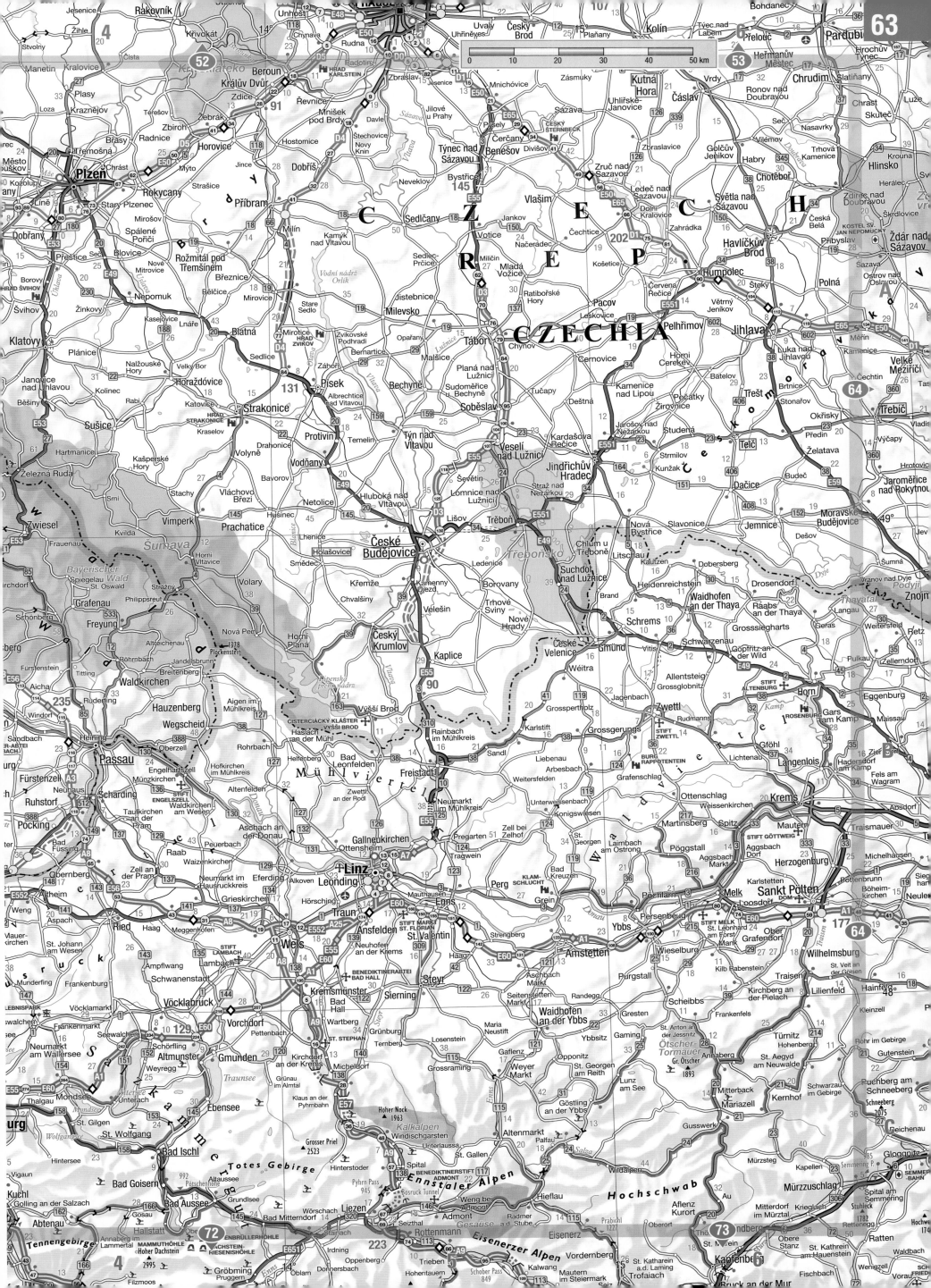

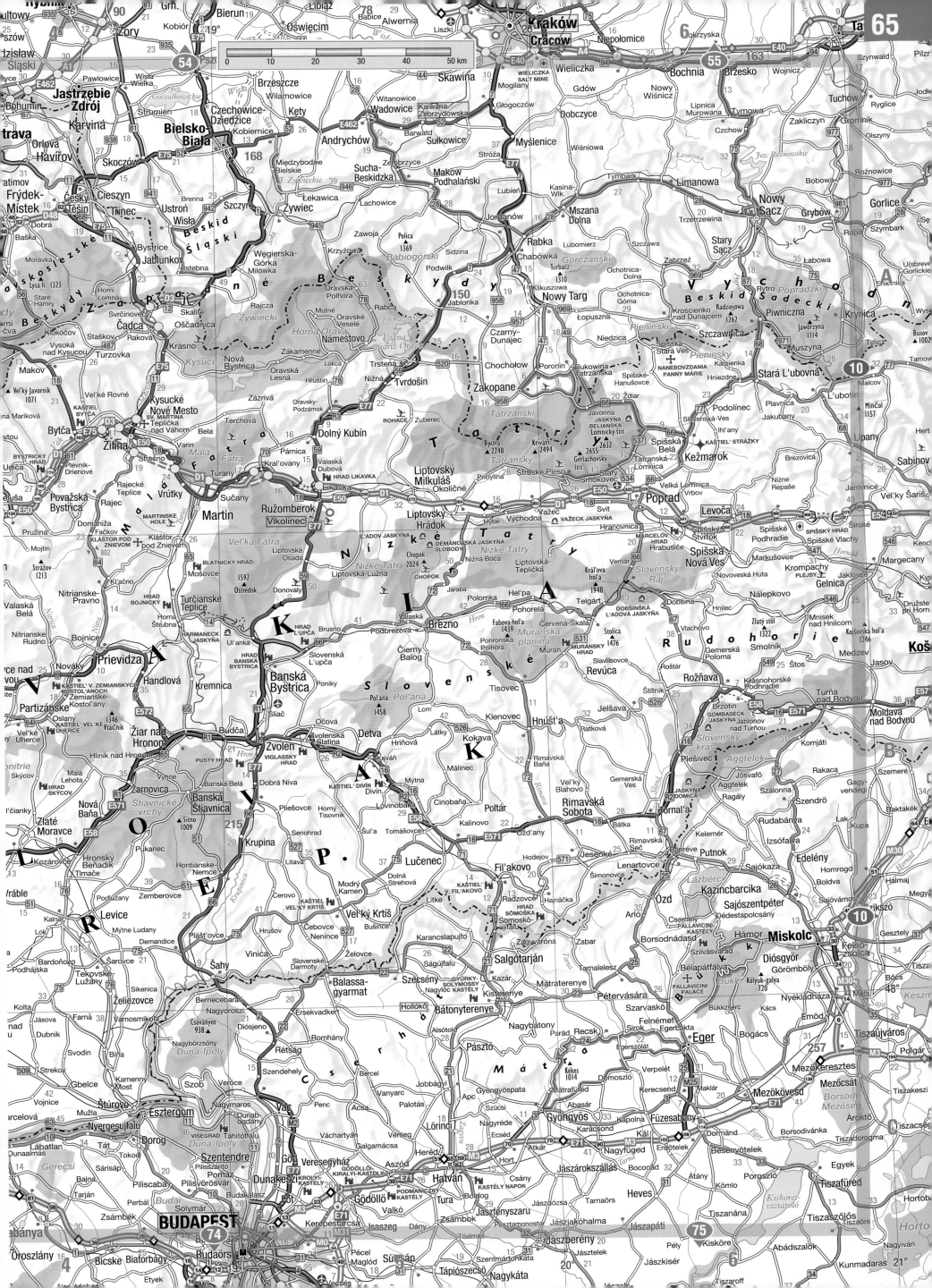

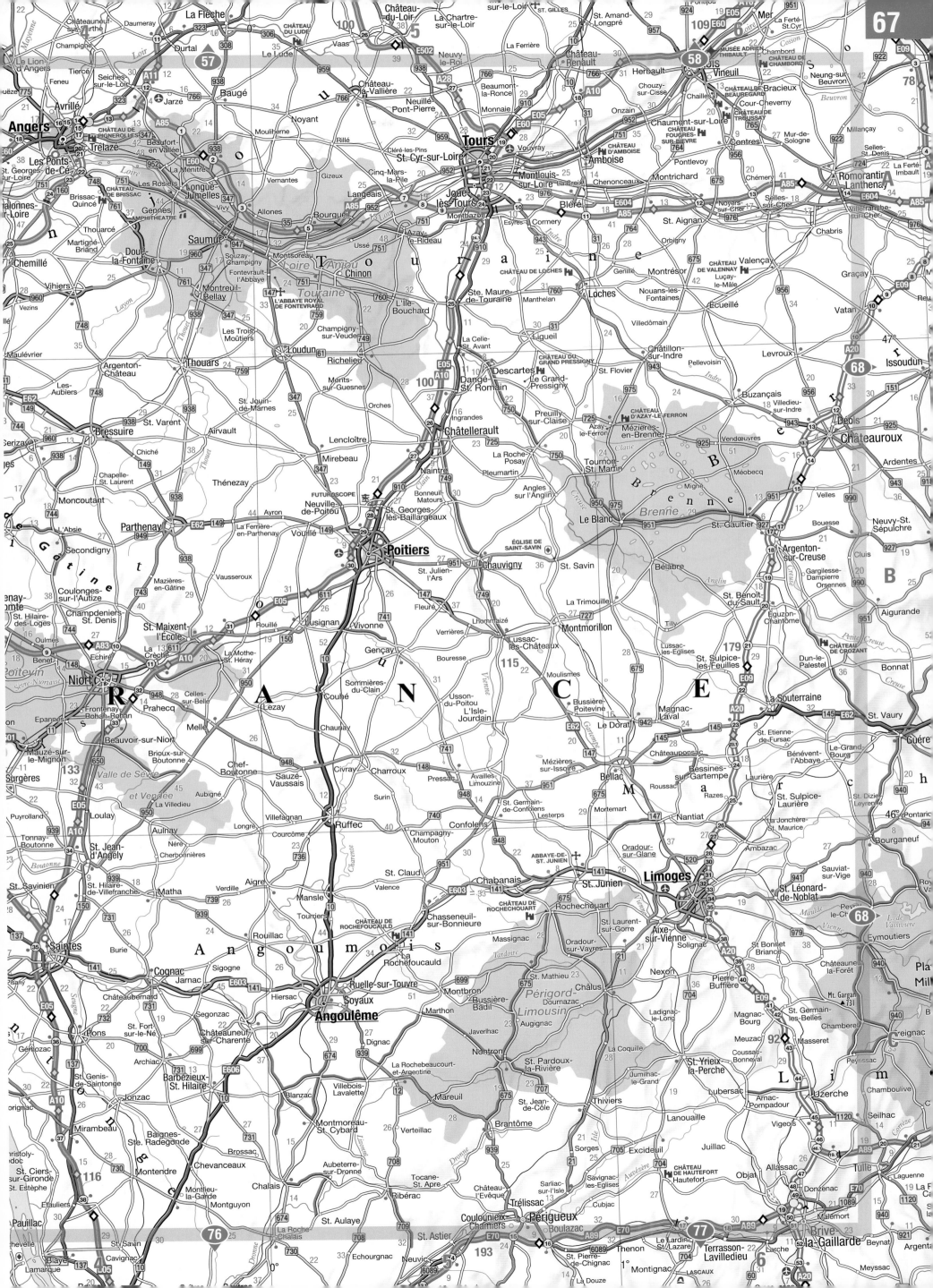

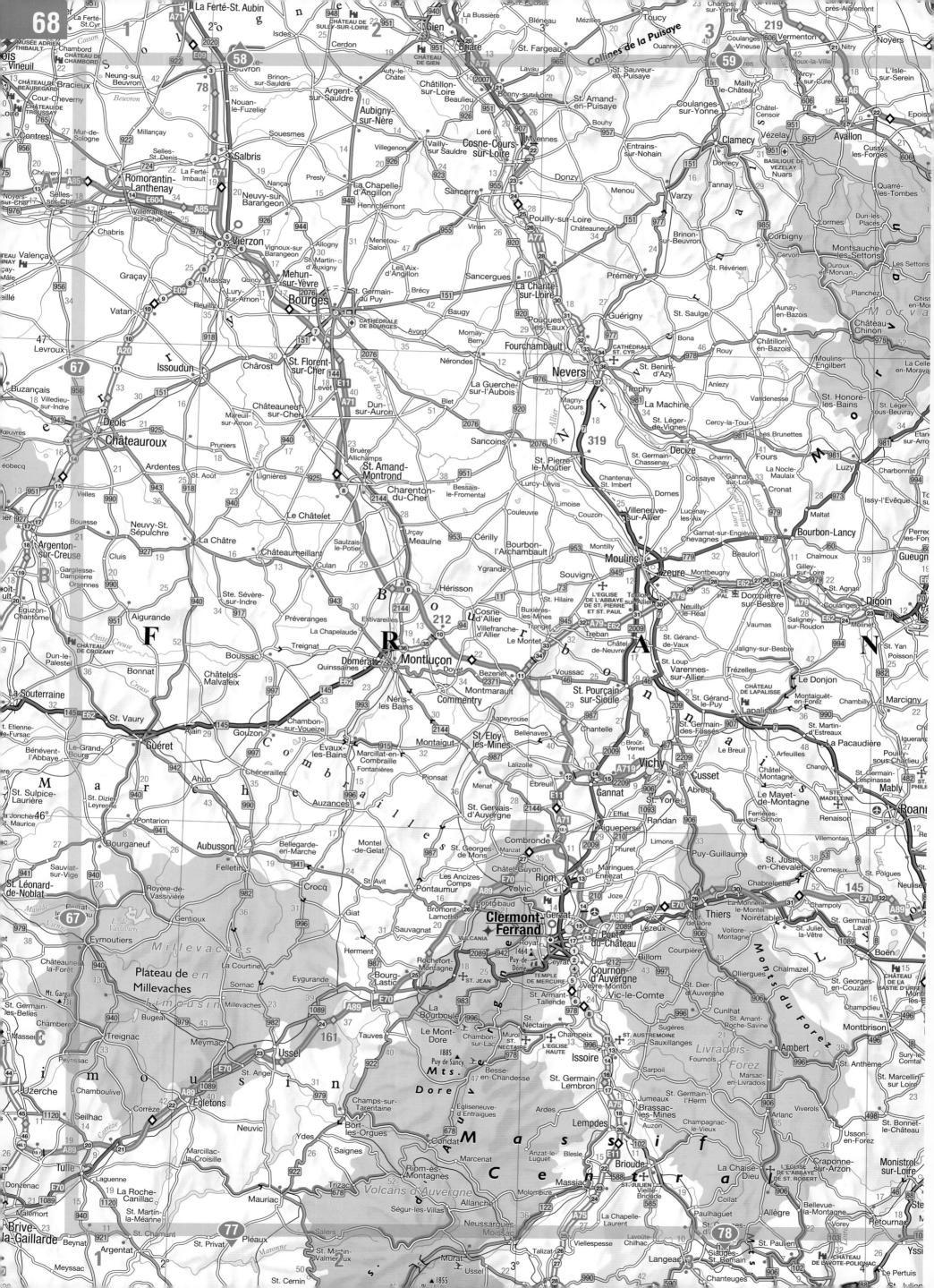

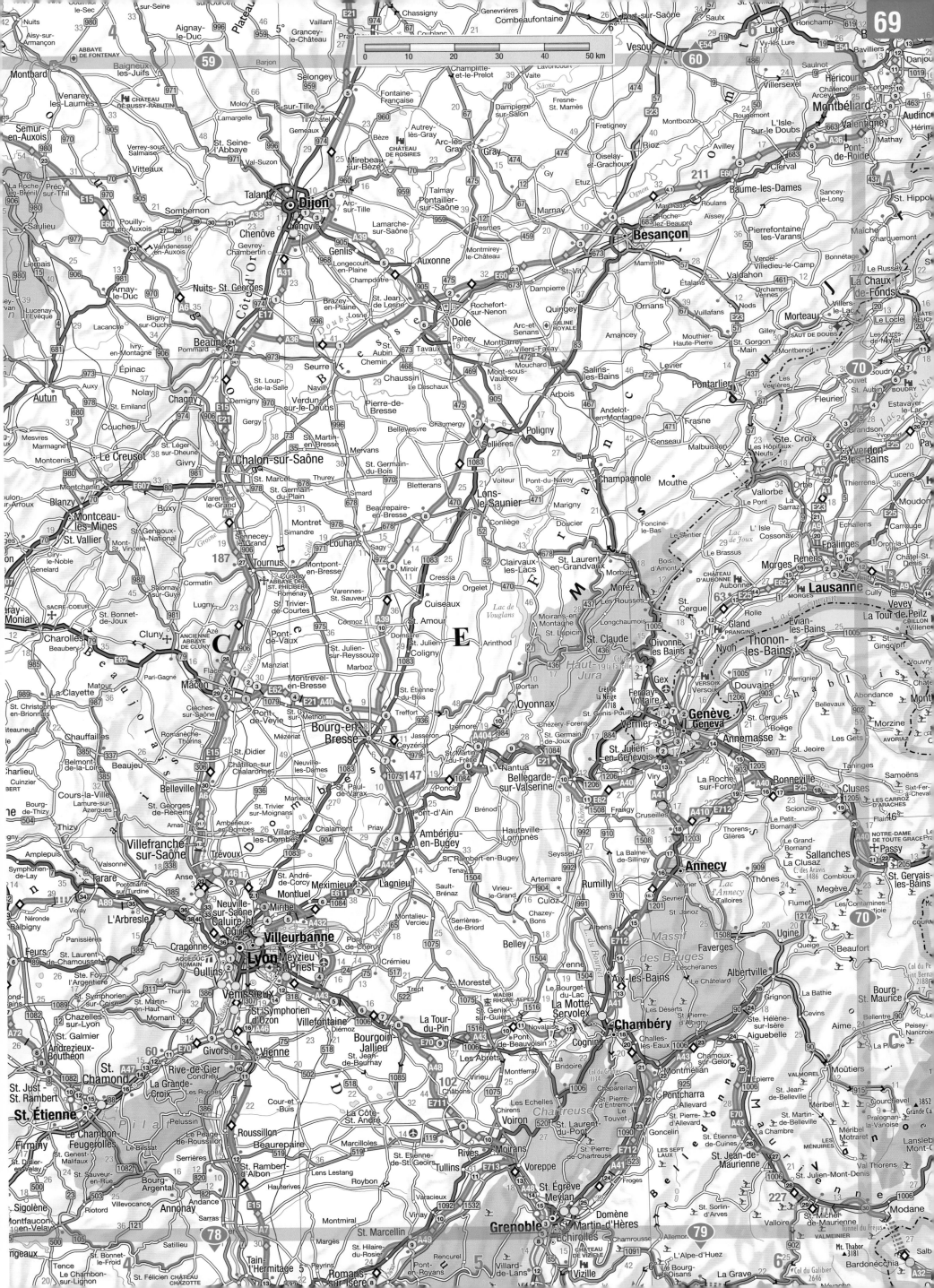

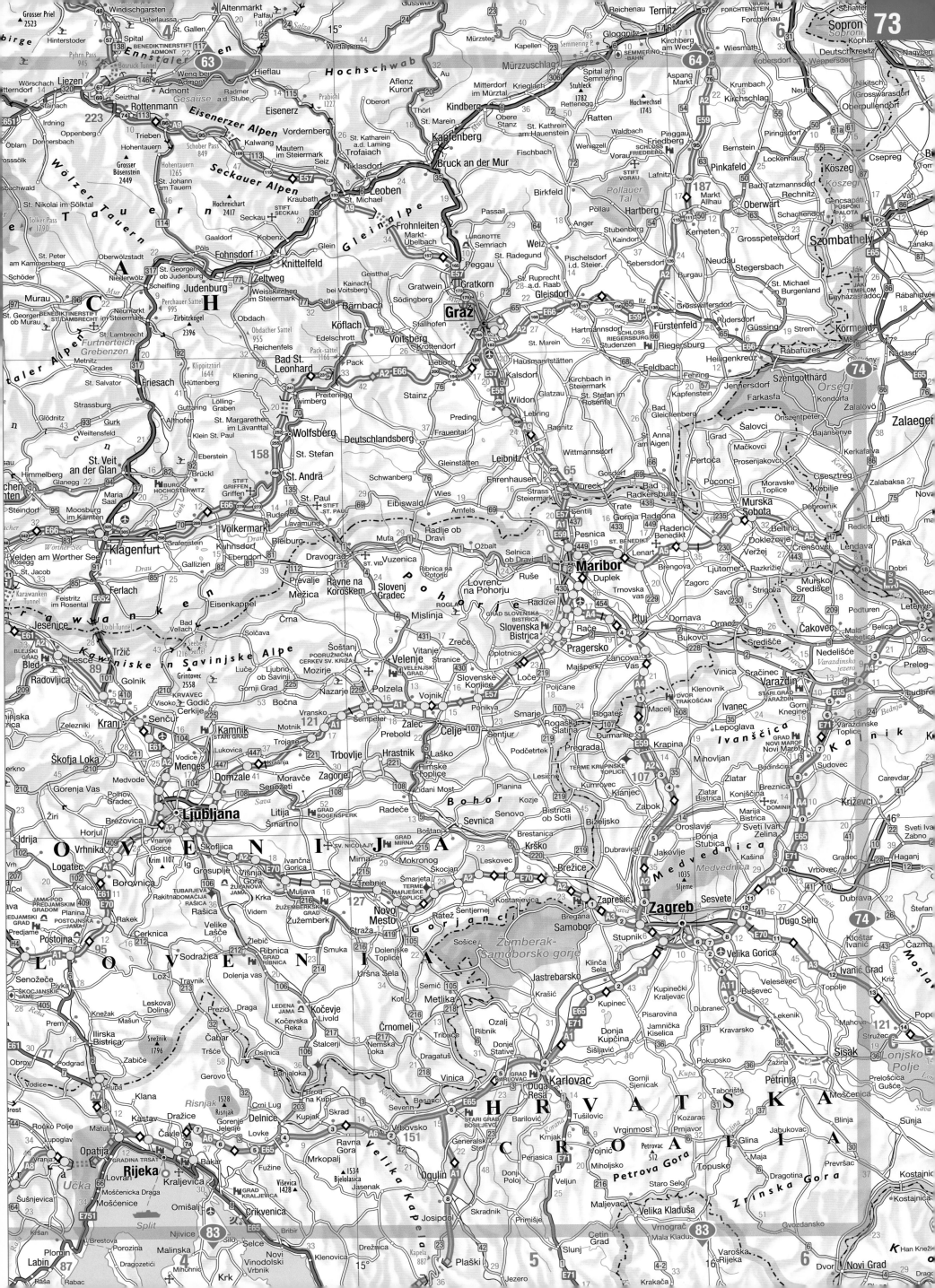

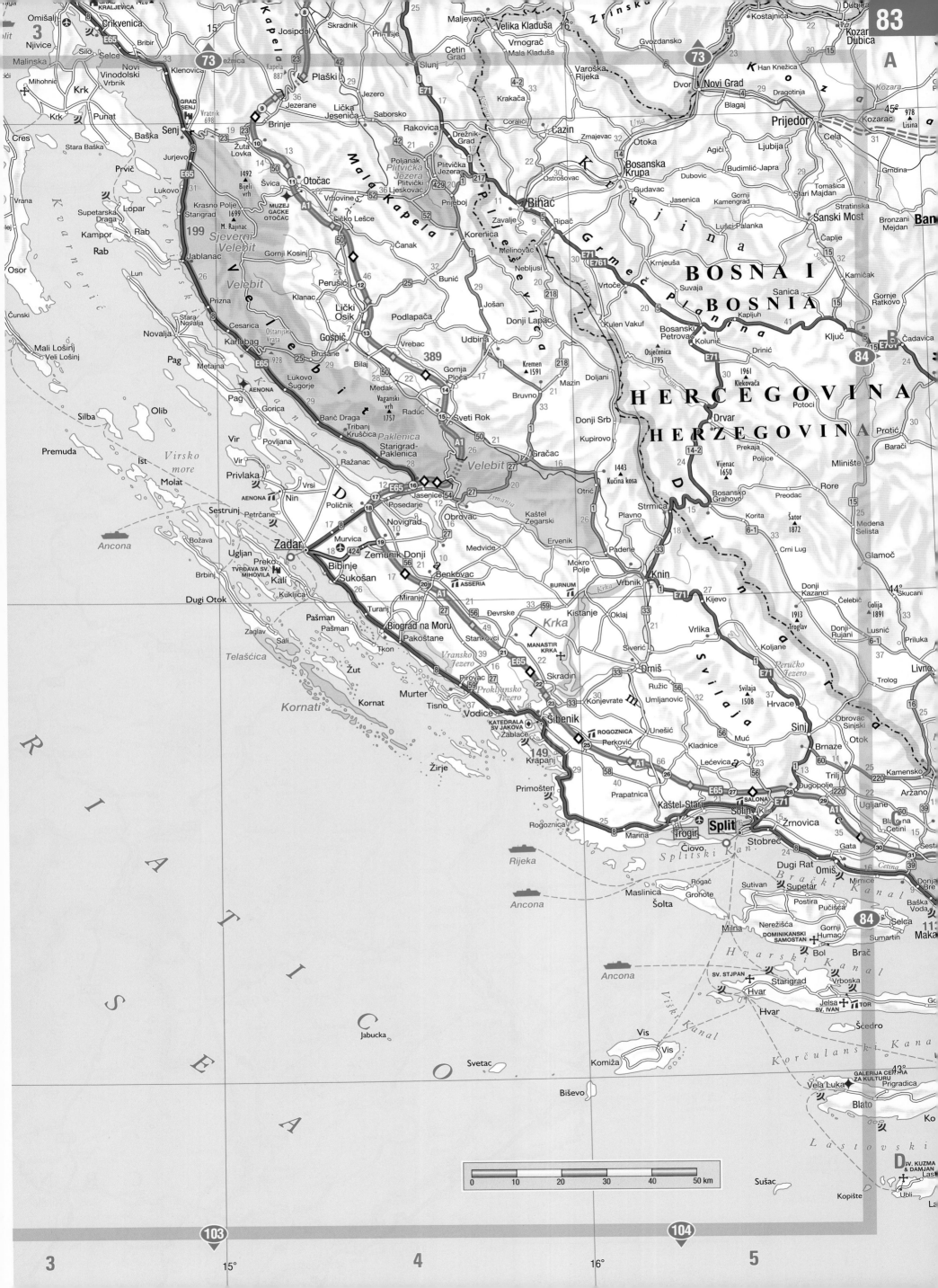

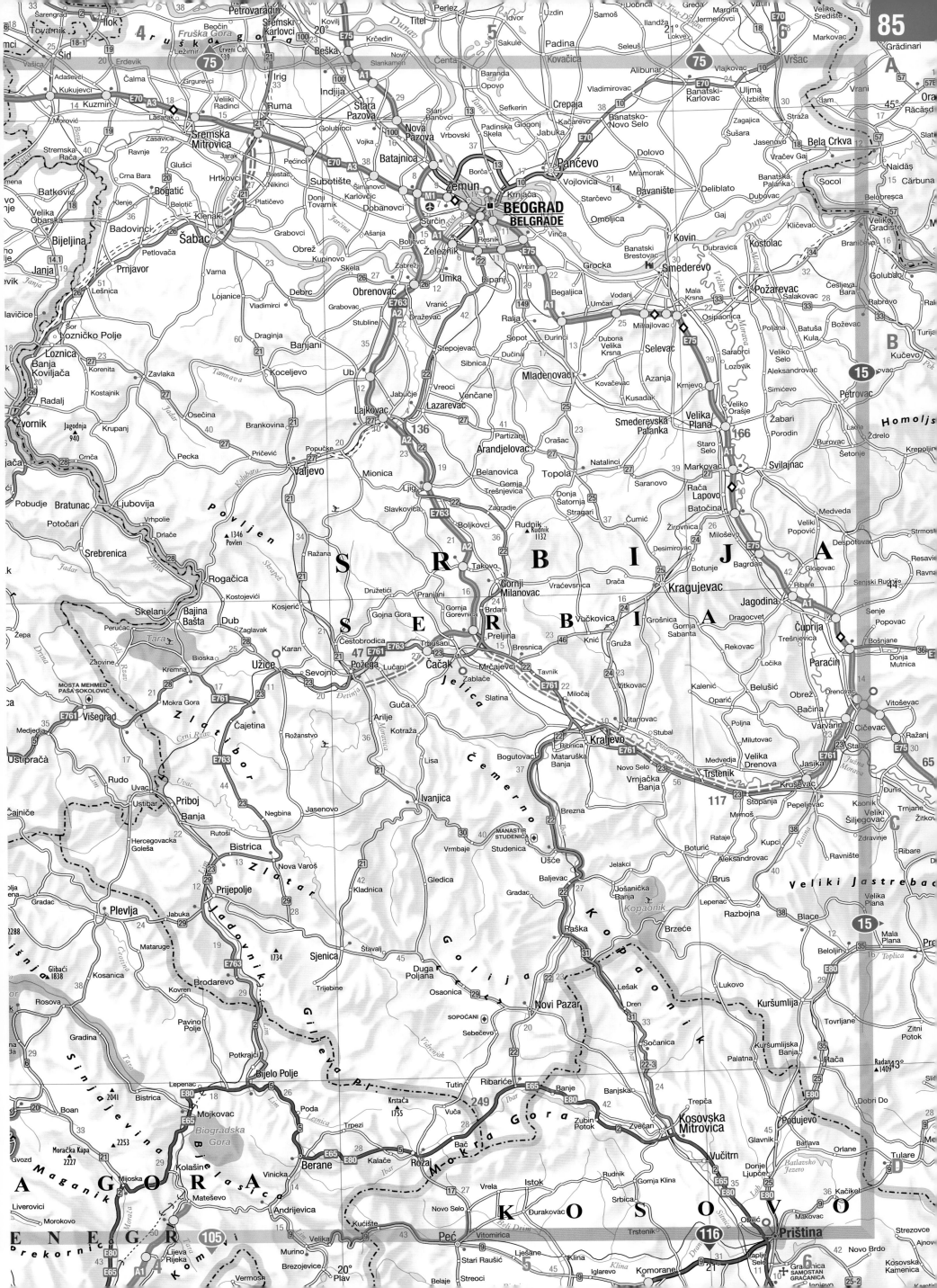

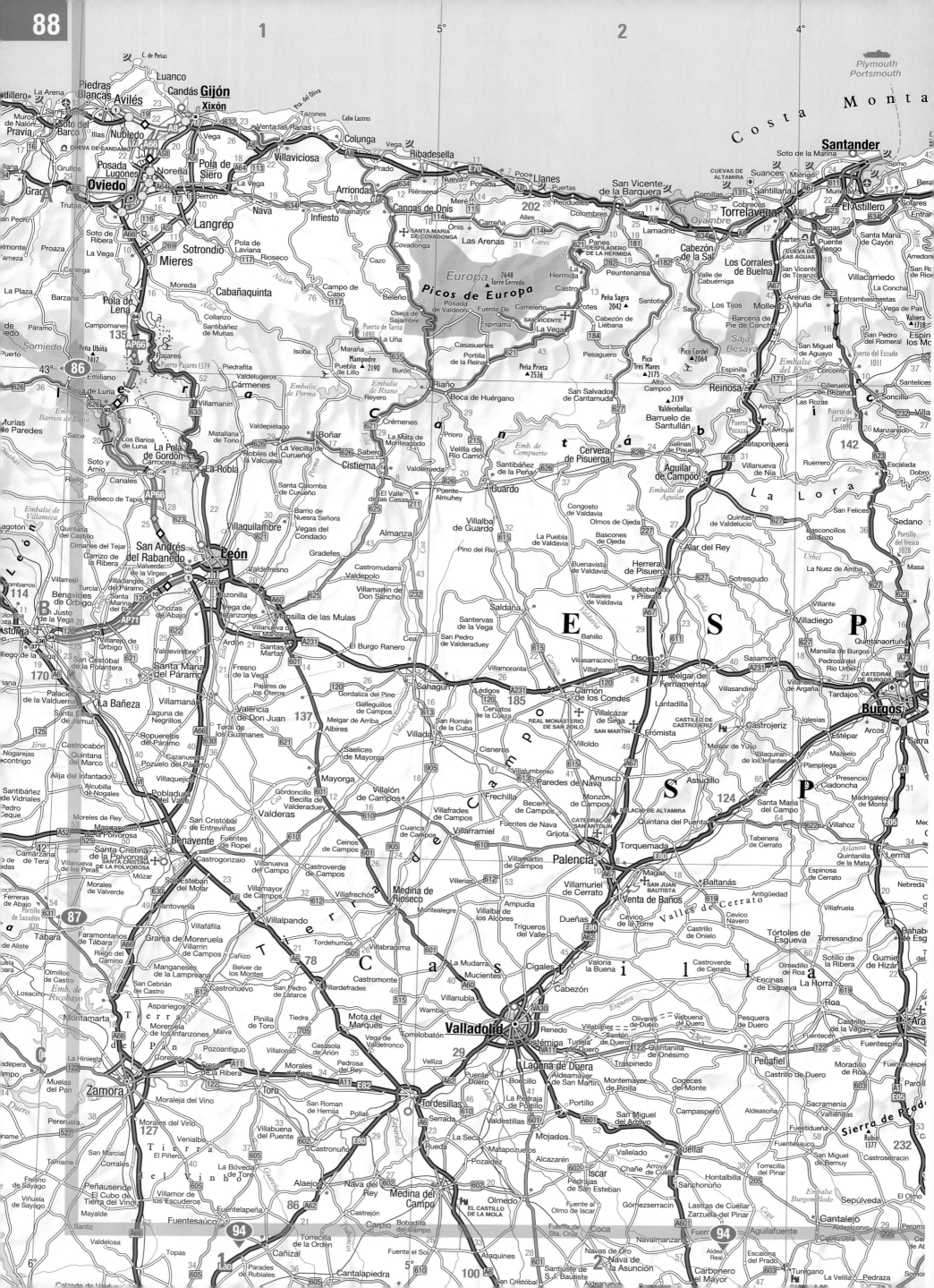

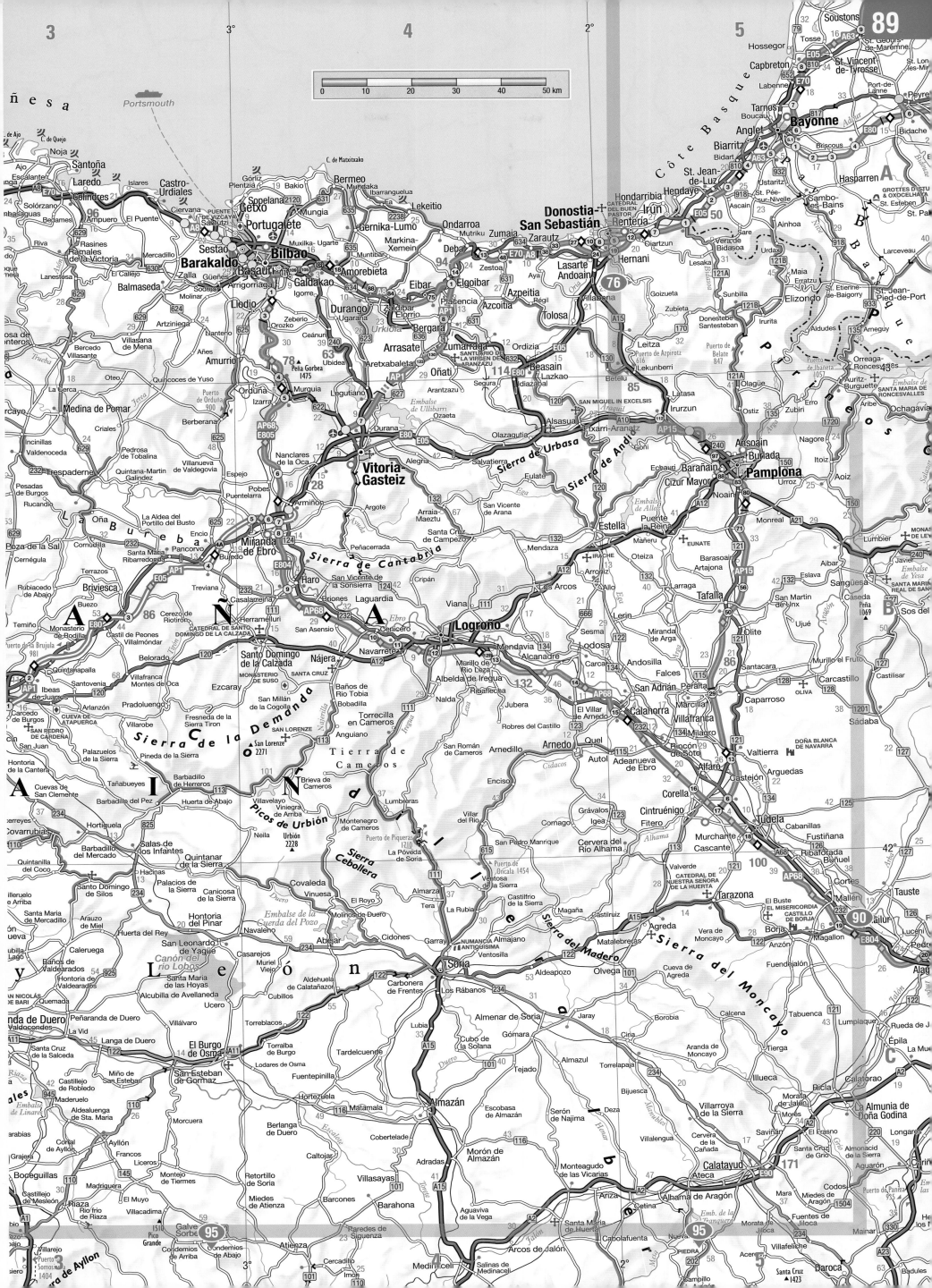

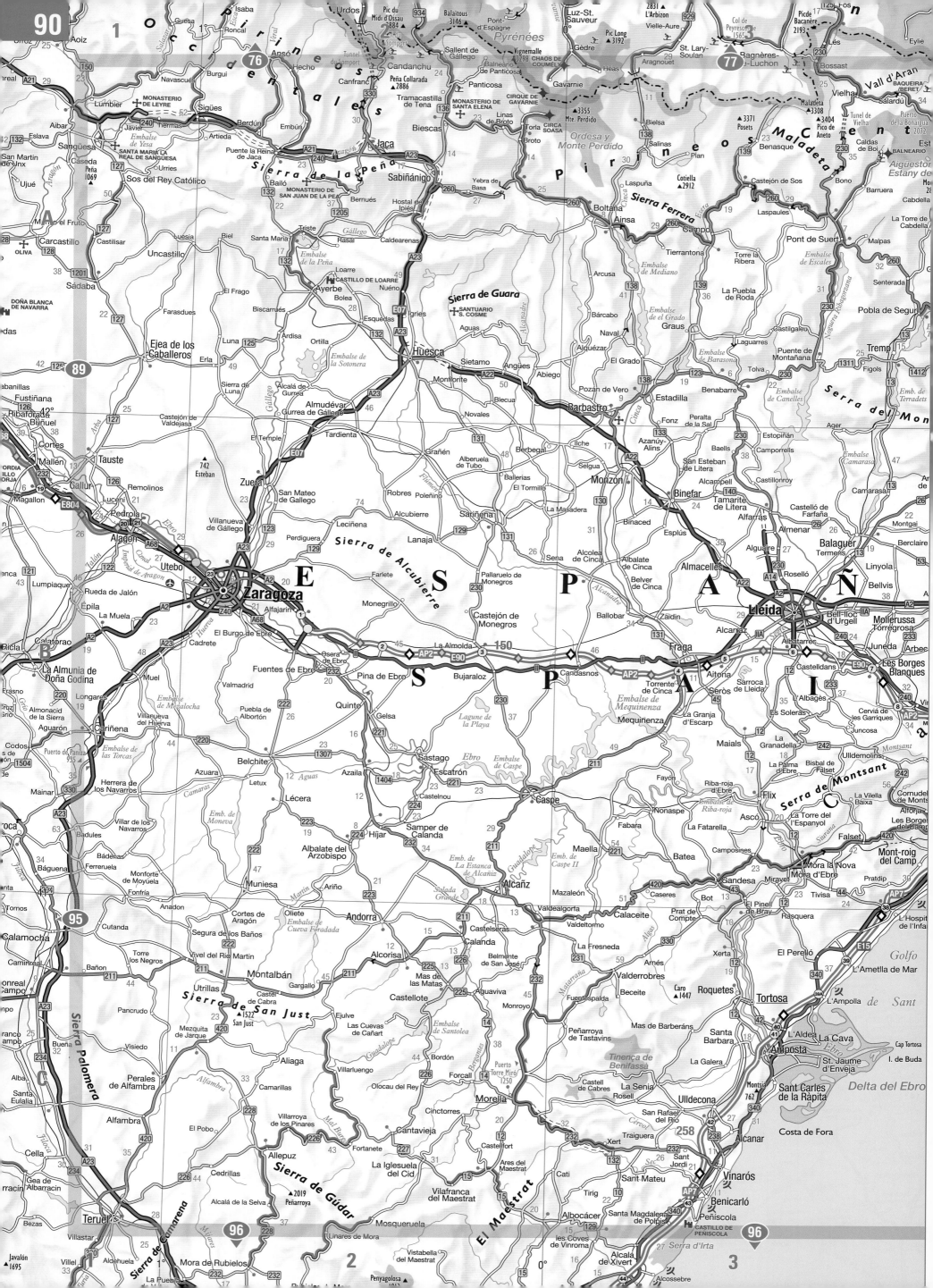

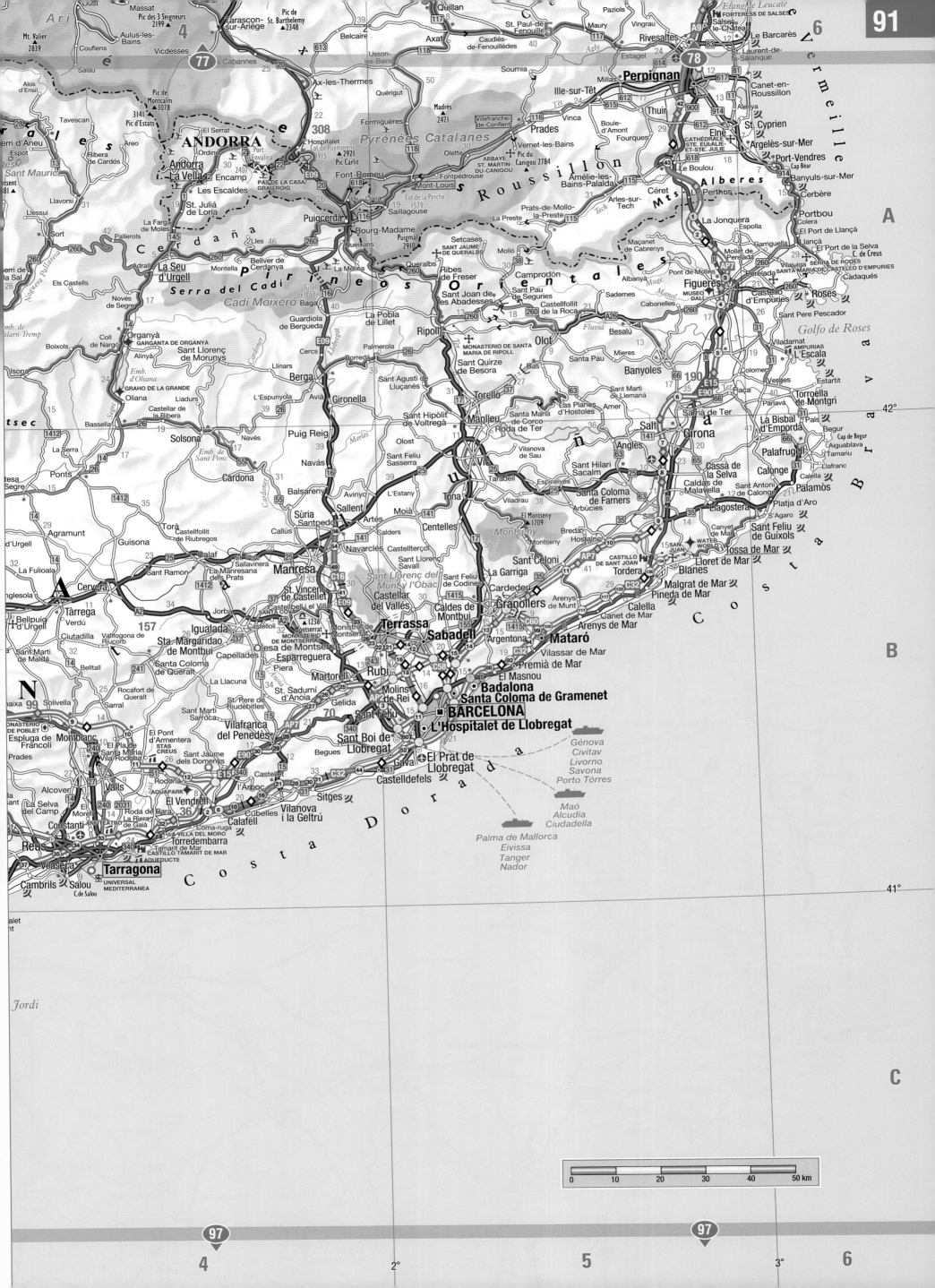

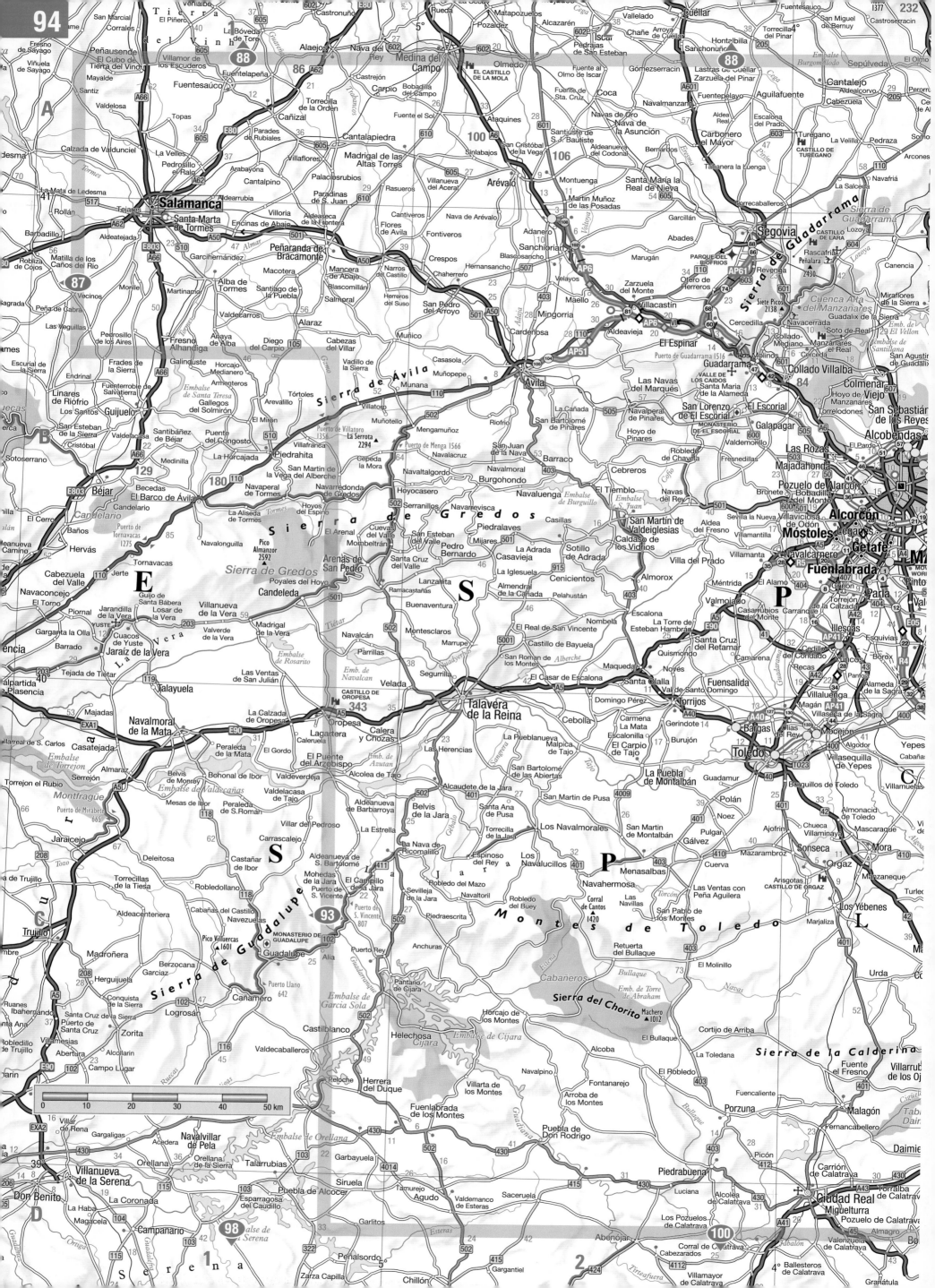

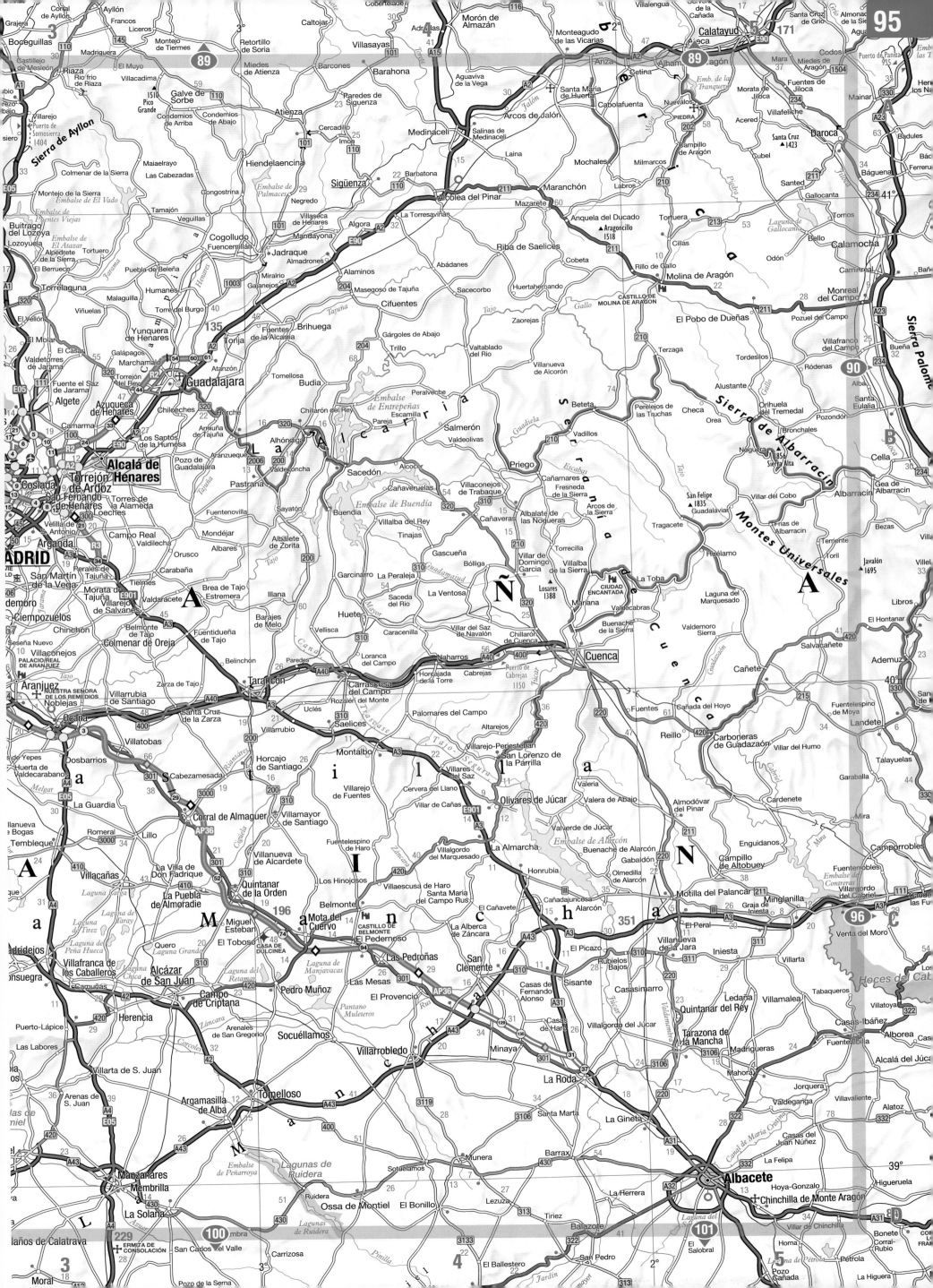

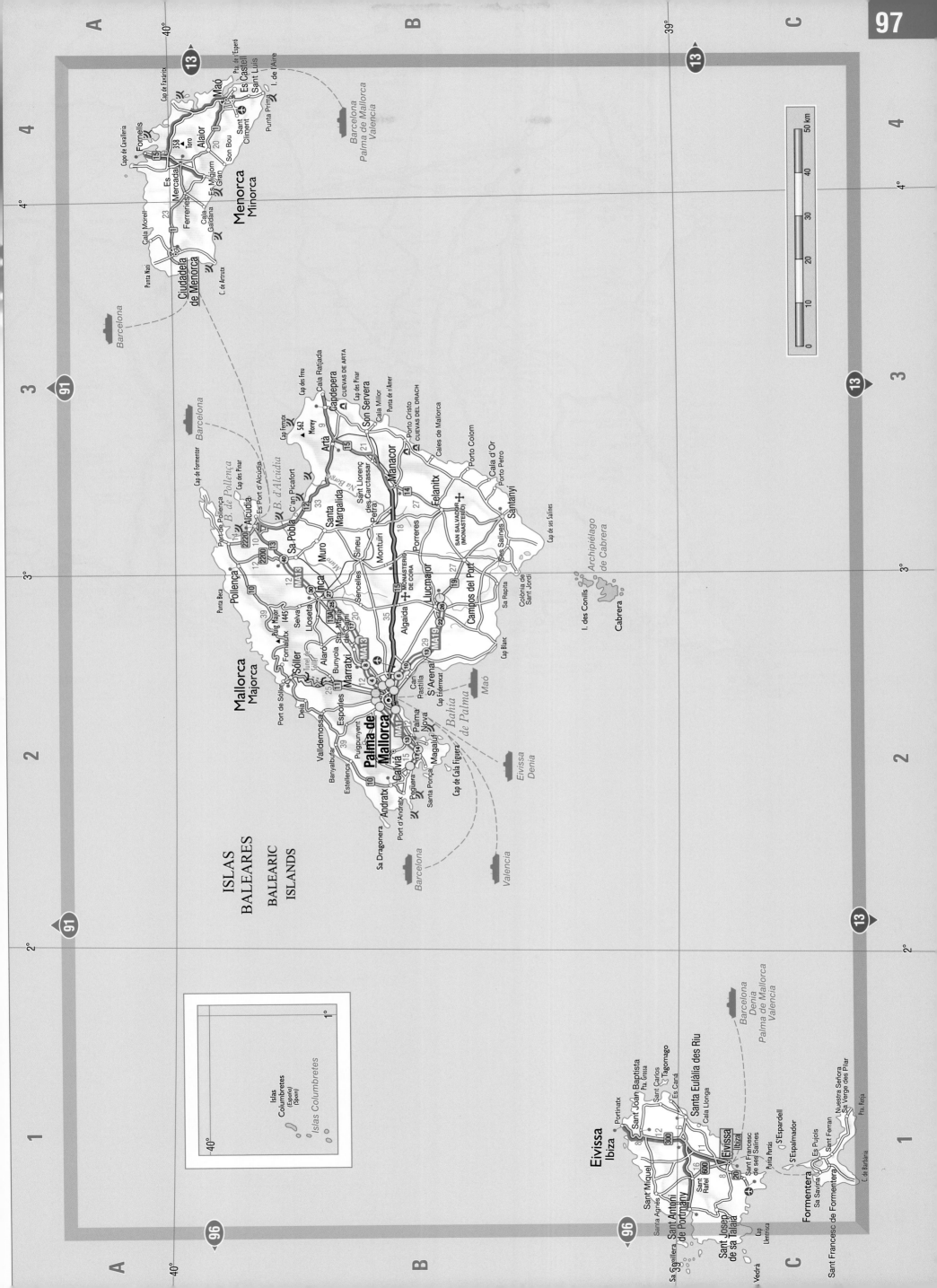

Menorca
Minorca

Cap de Cavalleria
Fornells
Cap de Favàritx
Pta. de l'Esperó
Maó
Es Castell
Sant Lluís
I. de l'Aire
Punta Prima
Son Bou
Sant Climent
Alaior
358 Toro
Es Mercadal
Es Migjorn Gran
Ferreries
Cala Galdana
Cala Morell
Punta Nati
C. de Artrutx
Ciudadela de Menorca

Barcelona
Palma de Mallorca
Valencia

Barcelona

Mallorca
Majorca

Cap de Formentor
Cap des Pinar
B. de Pollença
Pollença
Port de Pollença
Cap d'Alcúdia
B. d'Alcúdia
Alcúdia
Es Port d'Alcúdia
Can Picafort
Punta Beca
Puig Major 1445
Port de Sóller
Sóller
Fornalutx
Túnel de Sóller
Deià
Valldemossa
Banyalbufar
Estellencs
Esporles
Puigpunyent
Andratx
Port d'Andratx
Sa Dragonera
Cap de Cala Figuera
Santa Ponça
Peguera
Magaluf
Palma Nova
Calvià
Palma de Mallorca
Marratxí
Bunyola
Alaró
Sta. Maria del Camí
Lloseta
Selva
Inca
Sencelles
Sineu
Muro
Sa Pobla
Santa Margalida
Santa Margalida
Cala Ratjada
Capdepera
CUEVAS DE ARTA
Artà
Son Servera
Cap des Freu
Cap Ferrutx
562 Morey
Cala Millor
Cap del Pinar
Punta de l'Amer
Porto Cristo
CUEVAS DEL DRACH
Cales de Mallorca
Sant Llorenç des Cardassar
Petra
Manacor
Felanitx
Porto Colom
Cala d'Or
Porto Petro
Santanyí
SAN SALVADOR (MONASTERIO)
MONASTERIO DE CORA
Montuïri
Porreres
Llucmajor
Algaida
Campos del Port
S'Arenal
Can Pastilla
Cap Enderrocat
Cap Blanc
Sa Ràpita
Colònia de Sant Jordi
Ses Salines
Cap de ses Salines

Bahía de Palma
Maó
Eivissa
Denia
Barcelona
Valencia

Archipiélago de Cabrera
I. des Conills
Cabrera

ISLAS BALEARES
BALEARIC ISLANDS

Barcelona

Eivissa
Ibiza

Santa Eulàlia des Riu
Sant Joan Baptista
Sant Carles
Pta. Grossa
I. Tagomago
Es Canà
Cala Llonga
Portinatx
Sant Miquel
Santa Agnès
Sant Rafel
Sant Antoni de Portmany
Sant Josep de sa Talaia
Cap Llentrisca
Vedrà
Sa Sargellera
S'Espardell
EIVISSA / Ibiza
Sant Francesc de ses Salines
Punta Pedàs
S'Espalmador
Es Pujols
Sant Ferran
Nuestra Señora Sa Verge des Pilar
Formentera
Sa Savina
Sant Francesc de Formentera
Pta. Roja
C. de Barbaria

Barcelona
Denia
Palma de Mallorca
Valencia

Islas Columbretes
Islas Columbretes
Islas (España) (Spain)

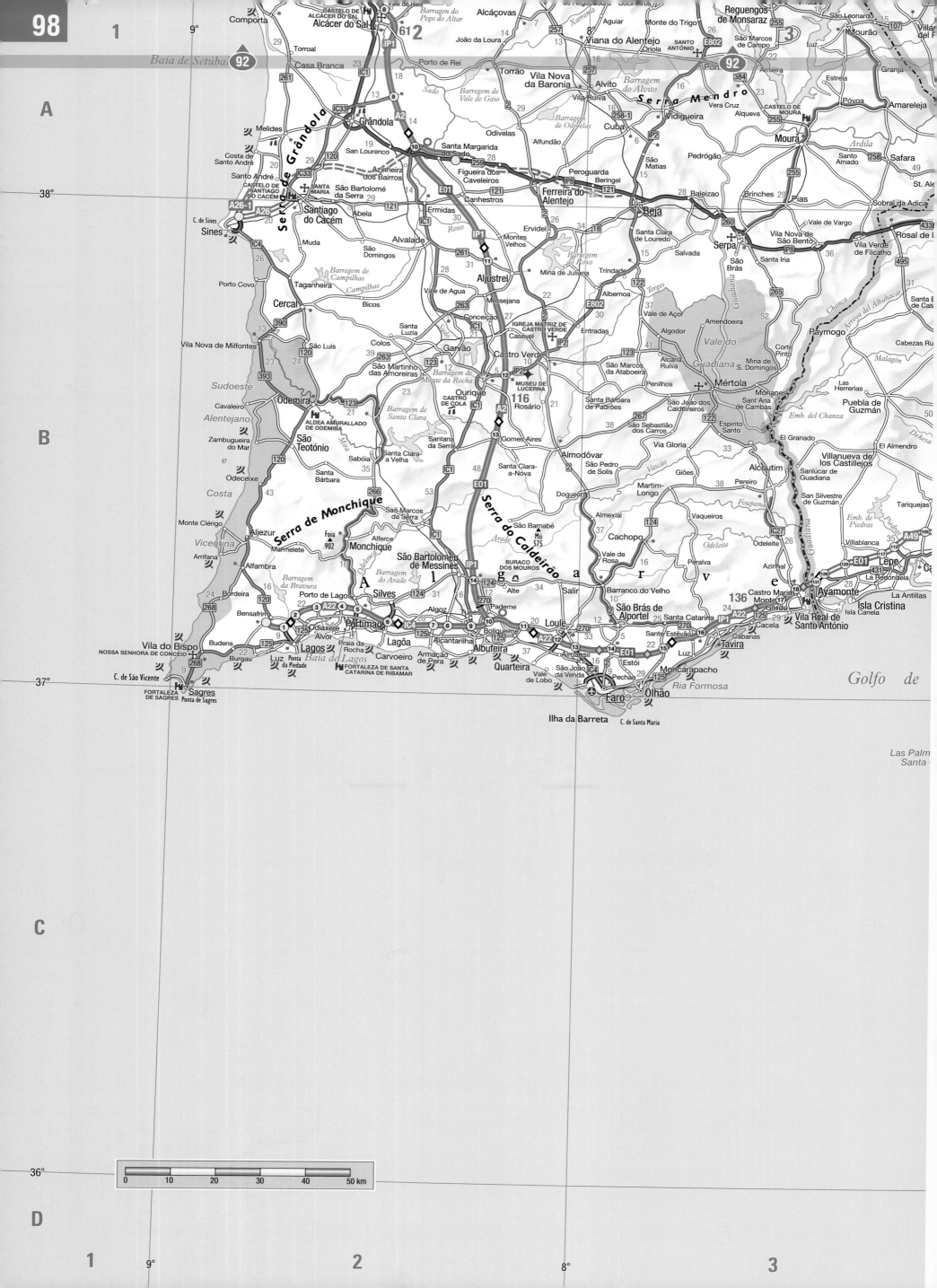

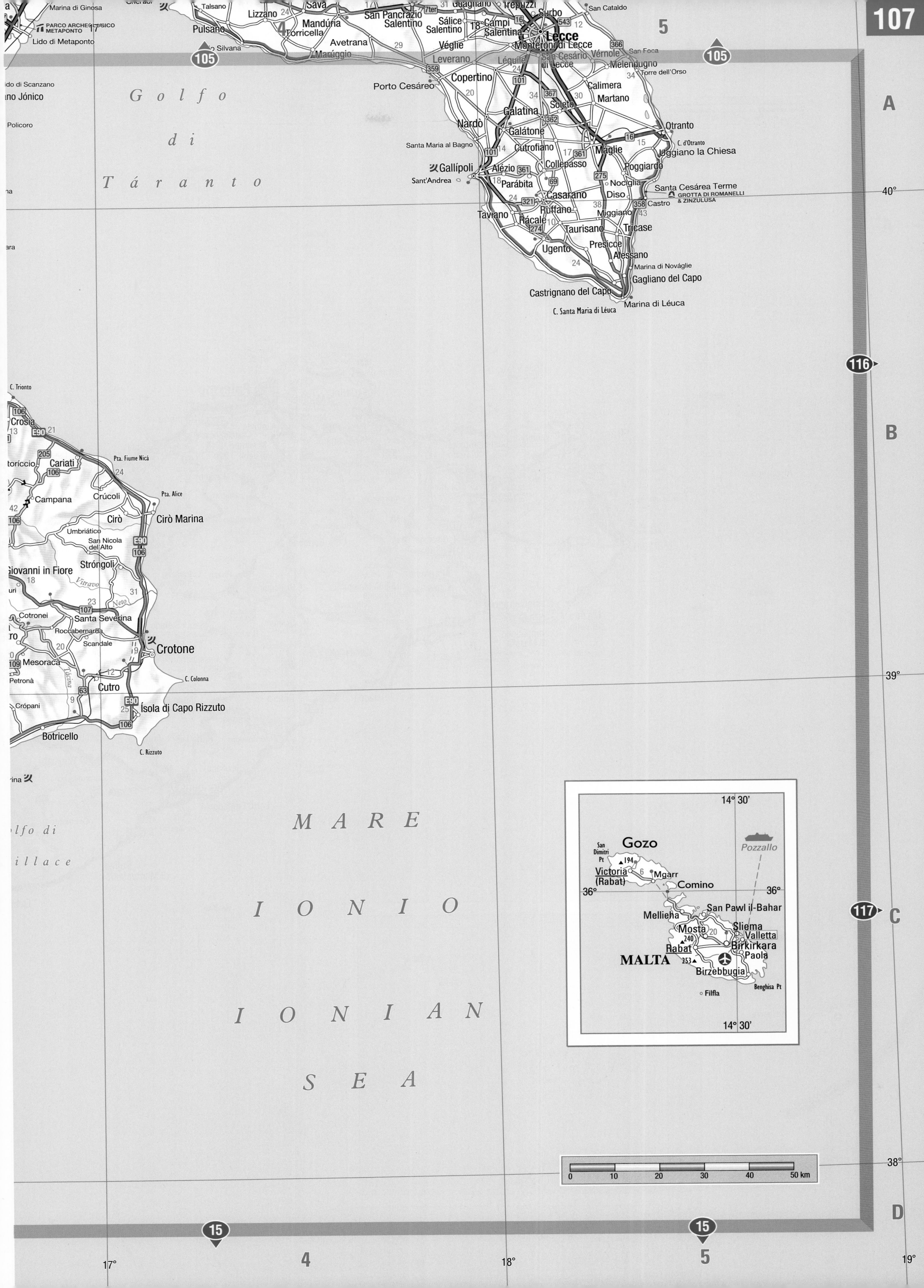

A

B

C

D

4

5

40°

39°

38°

17°

18°

19°

116

117

105

105

15

15

Marina di Ginosa

PARCO ARCHEOLOGICO
METAPONTO

Lido di Metaponto

Pulsano

Torricella

Mandúria

Avetrana

Manúggio

Silvana

Lizzano

Sava

Talsano

San Pancrazio
Salentino

Salice
Salentino

Véglie

Leverano

Copertino

Guagnano

Campi
Salentina

Trepuzzi

Surbo

Lecce

Monteroni di Lecce

San Césario
di Lecce

Léquile

San Cataldo

Vérnole

Melendugno

Torre dell'Orso

San Foca

Calimera

Martano

Soleto

Galatina

Nardò

Galátone

Cútrofiano

Maglie

Otranto

C. d'Otranto

Uggiano la Chiesa

Santa Maria al Bagno

Gallípoli

Alézio

Parábita

Collepásso

Poggiardo

Nociglia

Santa Cesárea Terme

GROTTA DI ROMANELLI
& ZINZULUSA

Sant'Andrea

Casarano

Diso

Castro

Taviano

Rácale

Ruffano

Taurisano

Tricase

Miggiano

Ugento

Presicce

Alessano

Marina di Nováglie

Gagliano del Capo

Castrignano del Capo

C. Santa Maria di Léuca

Marina di Léuca

Golfo
di
Táranto

Golfo di
Squillace

C. Trionto

Crosia

Cariati

Campana

Crúcoli

Cirò

Cirò Marina

Umbriático

San Nicola
dell'Alto

Stróngoli

Giovanni in Fiore

Santa Severina

Cotronei

Roccabernarda

Scandale

Mesoraca

Petronà

Crótone

Cutro

Crópani

Ísola di Capo Rizzuto

Botricello

C. Colonna

C. Rizzuto

Pta. Fiume Nicá

Pta. Alice

Vitravo

Neto

MARE

IONIO

IONIAN

SEA

Porto Cesáreo

Lido di Scanzano

Policoro

Golfo
Jónico

Gozo

San
Dimitri
Pt

Victoria
(Rabat)

Mgàrr

Comino

Pozzallo

San Pawl il-Bahar

Mellieha

Mosta

Rabat

MALTA

Sliema

Valletta

Birkirkara

Paola

Birzebbugia

Filfla

Benghisa Pt

14° 30'

36°

36°

14° 30'

0   10   20   30   40   50 km

A map of western Sicily (Sicilia), showing the provinces of Trapani, Palermo, and Agrigento, with inset maps of Pantelleria and the Ísole Pelágie (Isole Pelagie).

Scale: 0 10 20 30 40 50 km

Golfo di Castellammare

Golfo di Términi Imerese

Ústica

Livorne
Nápoli
Génova
Salerno
Civitavécchia

Cágliari
Tunis

Cágliari

Palermo

Isola delle Fémmine
Mondello
C. Gallo

Terrasini
Capaci
Carini
Monreale
Ficarazzi
Bagheria
Trabia
Términi Imerese
Campofelice di Roccella

C. San Vito
San Vito lo Capo
M. Spáragio
Scopello
Balestrate
Altofonte
Casteldáccia
Misilmeri
Marineo
Bolognetta
Cáccamo
Cerda

Pizzolungo
Érice
Valdérice
Castellammare del Golfo
Pártinico
San Cipirello
Piana degli Albanesi
Villafrati
Ciminna
Montemaggiore Belsito
Caltavuturo

Trápani
Paceco
Fulgatore
Álcamo
Camporeale
Mezzojuso
Vicari
Roccapalumba
Valledolmo

Lévanzo
Ísole Égadi
Calatafimi
TEMPIO GRECO DI SEGESTA
Roccamena
Rca. Busambra 1613
Prizzi
Lercara Friddi

Maréttimo
Favignana
Rillievo
Salemi
Gibellina Nuova
Corleone
Bisacquino
Santo Stéfano Quisquina
Vallelunga Pratameno
Villalba

Stagnone
CASE ROMANA
Santa Ninfa
Partanna
Salaparuta
Campofiorito
Chiusa Scláfani
Palazzo Adriano
Bivona
Cammarata
Mussomeli
Marianópoli

Marsala
Mataroco
Santa Margherita di Belice
Sambuca di Sicília
San Carlo
Búrgio
Alessándria della Rocca
Casteltérmini
Campofránco

Strasatti
L. della Trinità Délia
Menfi
Caltabellotta
Cianciana
Ribera
San Biágio Plátani
Montedoro
Serradifalco

Mazara del Vallo
Campobello di Mazara
CITTÀ GRECA DI SELINUNTE
Marinella
Sciacca
Cattólica Eraclea
Raffadali
Aragona
Racalmuto
Canicatti

Granitola-Torretta
C. Granitola
C. S. Marco
HERACLEA MINOA
Montallegro
Siculiana
Agrigento
Favara
Castrofilippo
Délia

Porto Empédocle
Naro
Camastra
Palma di Montechiaro
Licata

Linosa
Lampedusa

Canale di Sicilia / Strait of Sicily

Trápani
Pantelleria
Pantelleria
Pantelleria (Italia) (Italy) ▲ 836

Porto Empédocle
Linosa

Ísole Pelágie (Italia) (Italy)

Lampione
Lampedusa

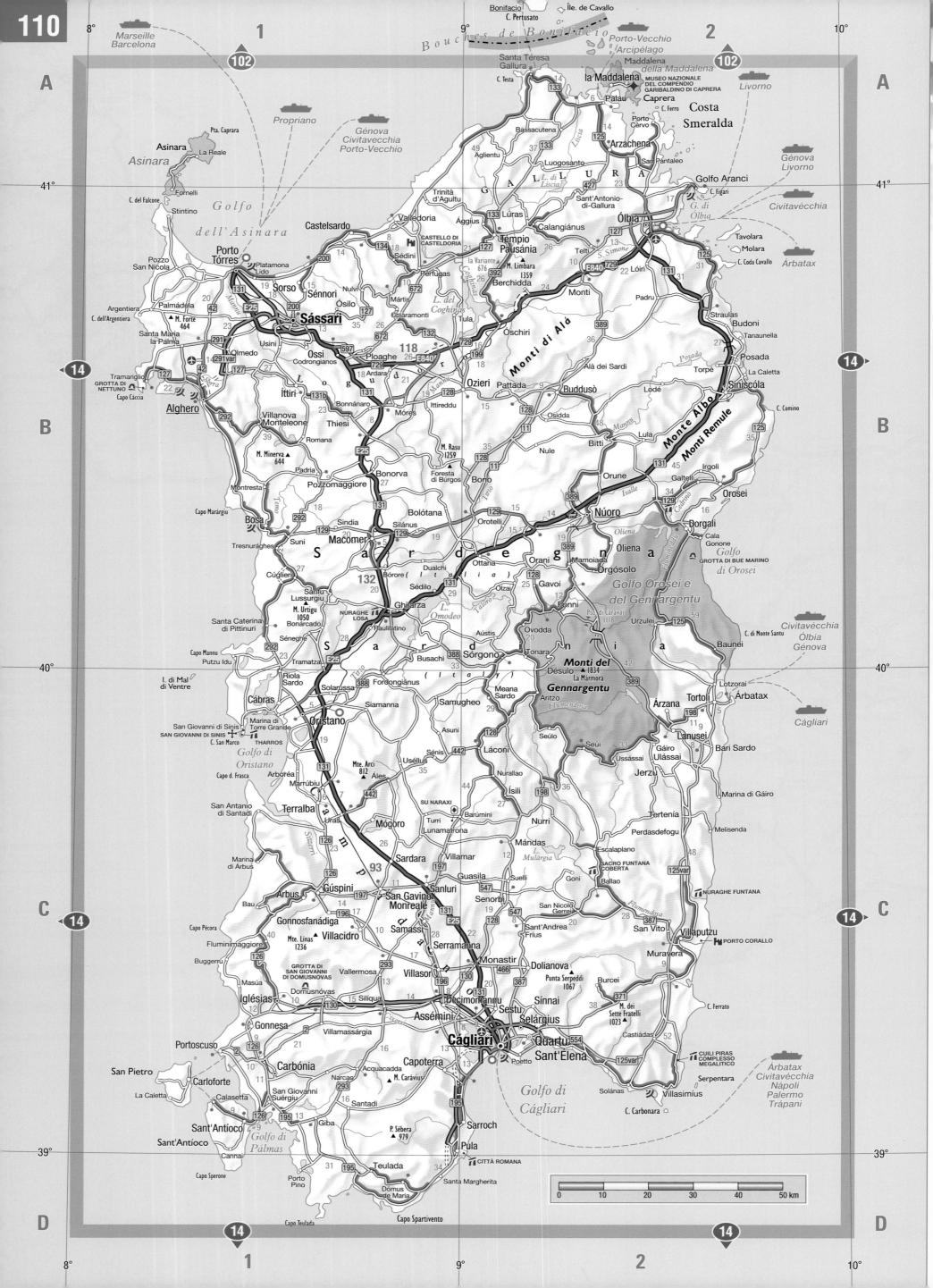

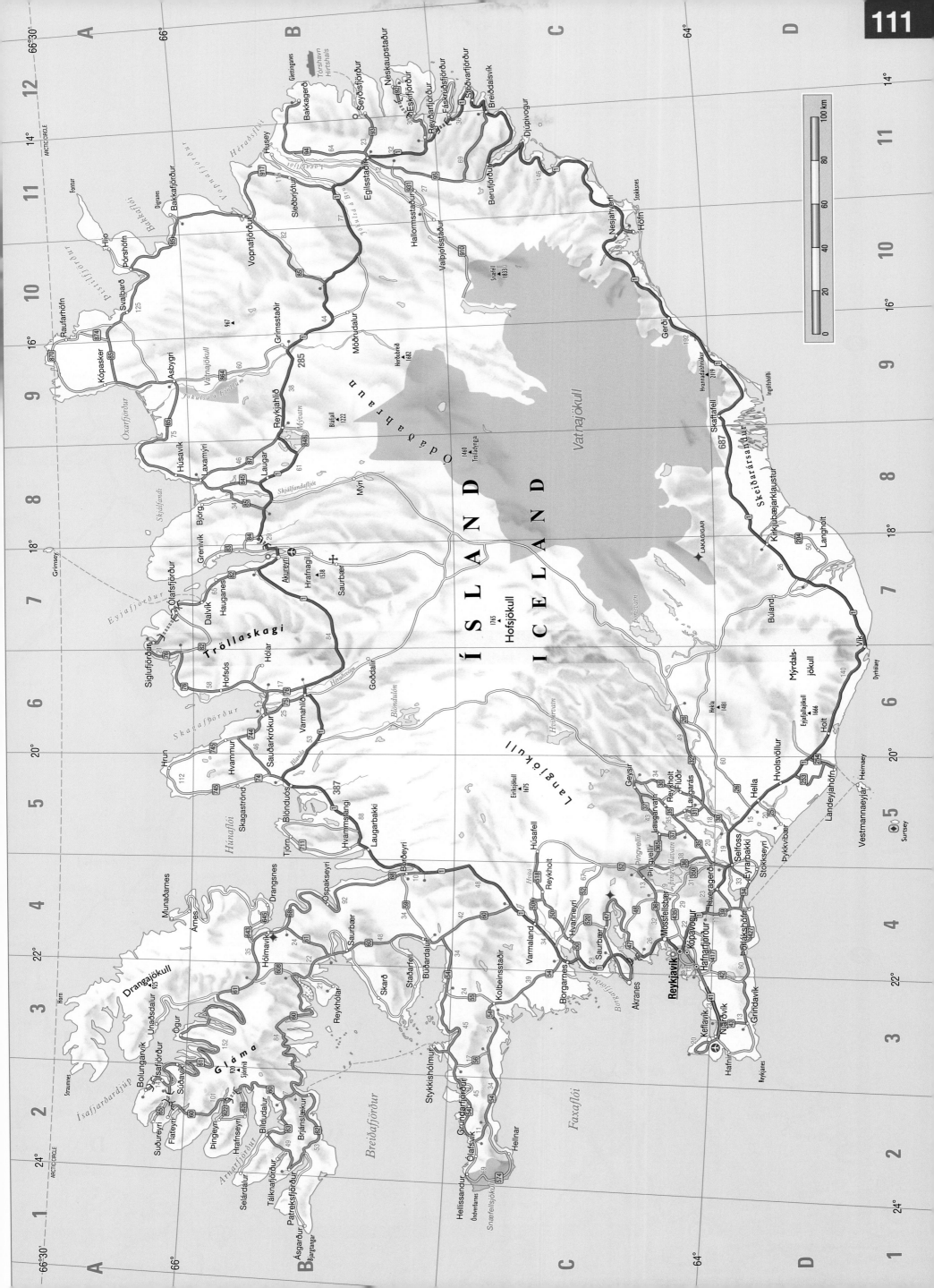

Í S L A N D   I C E L A N D

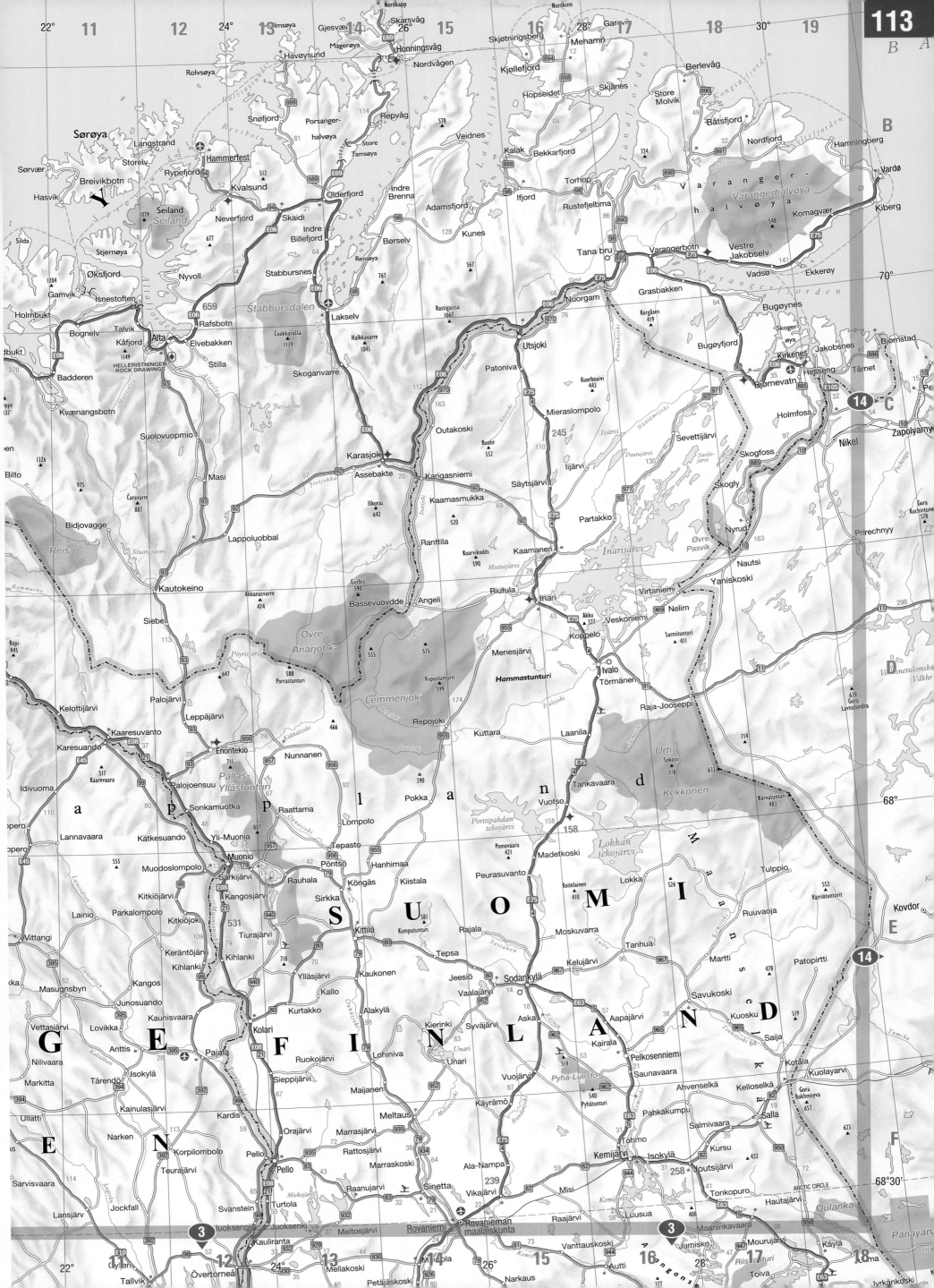

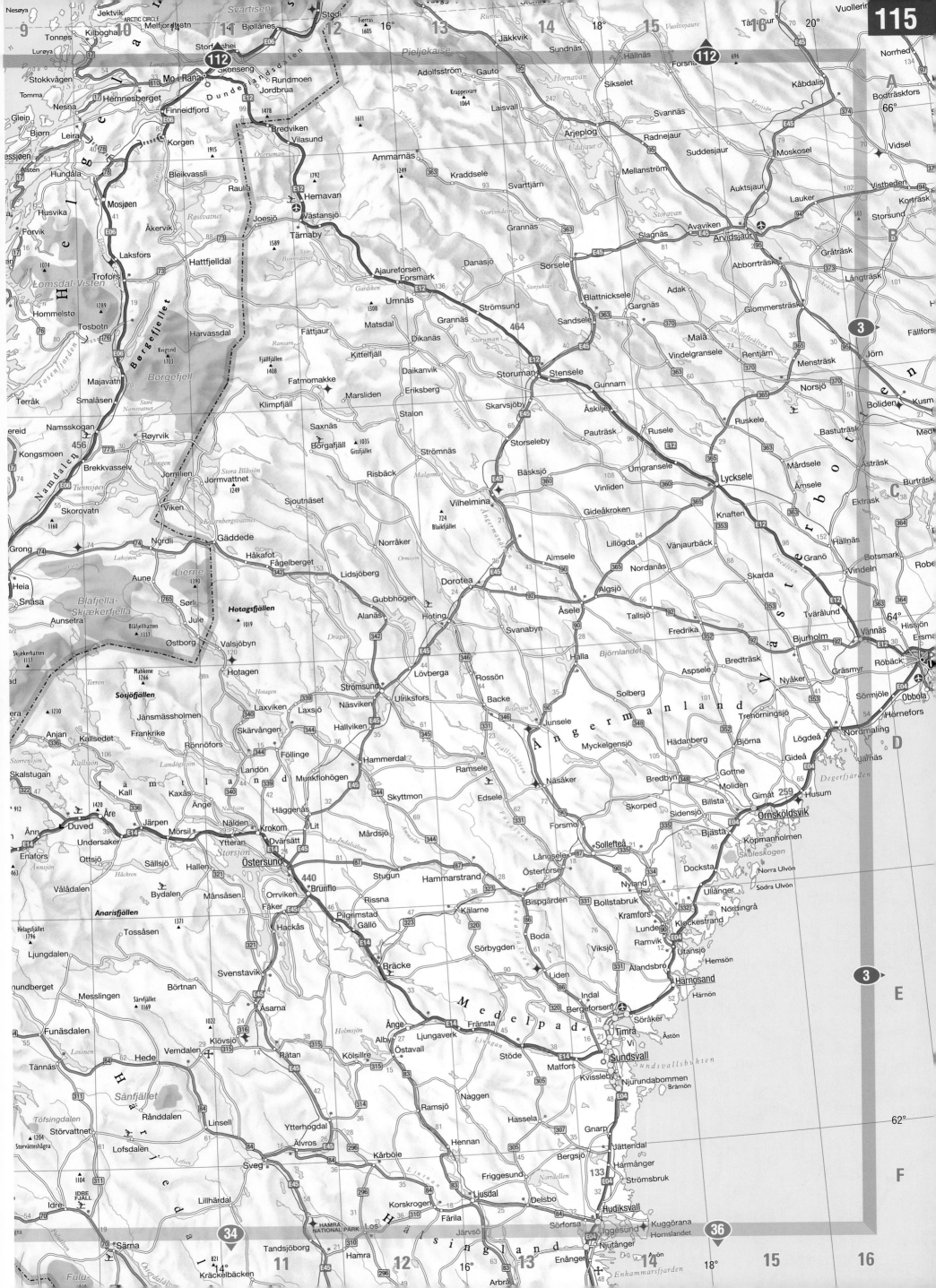

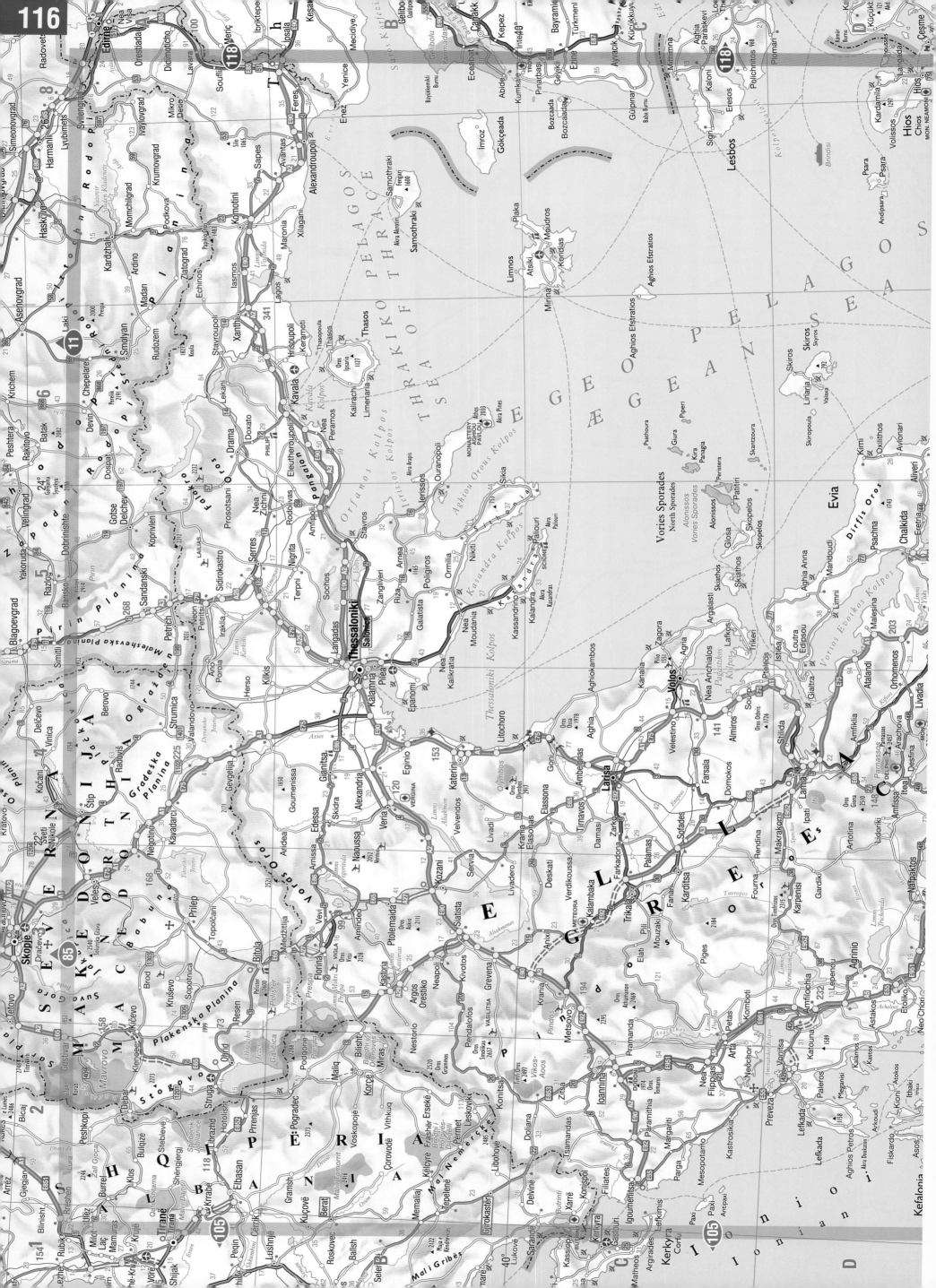

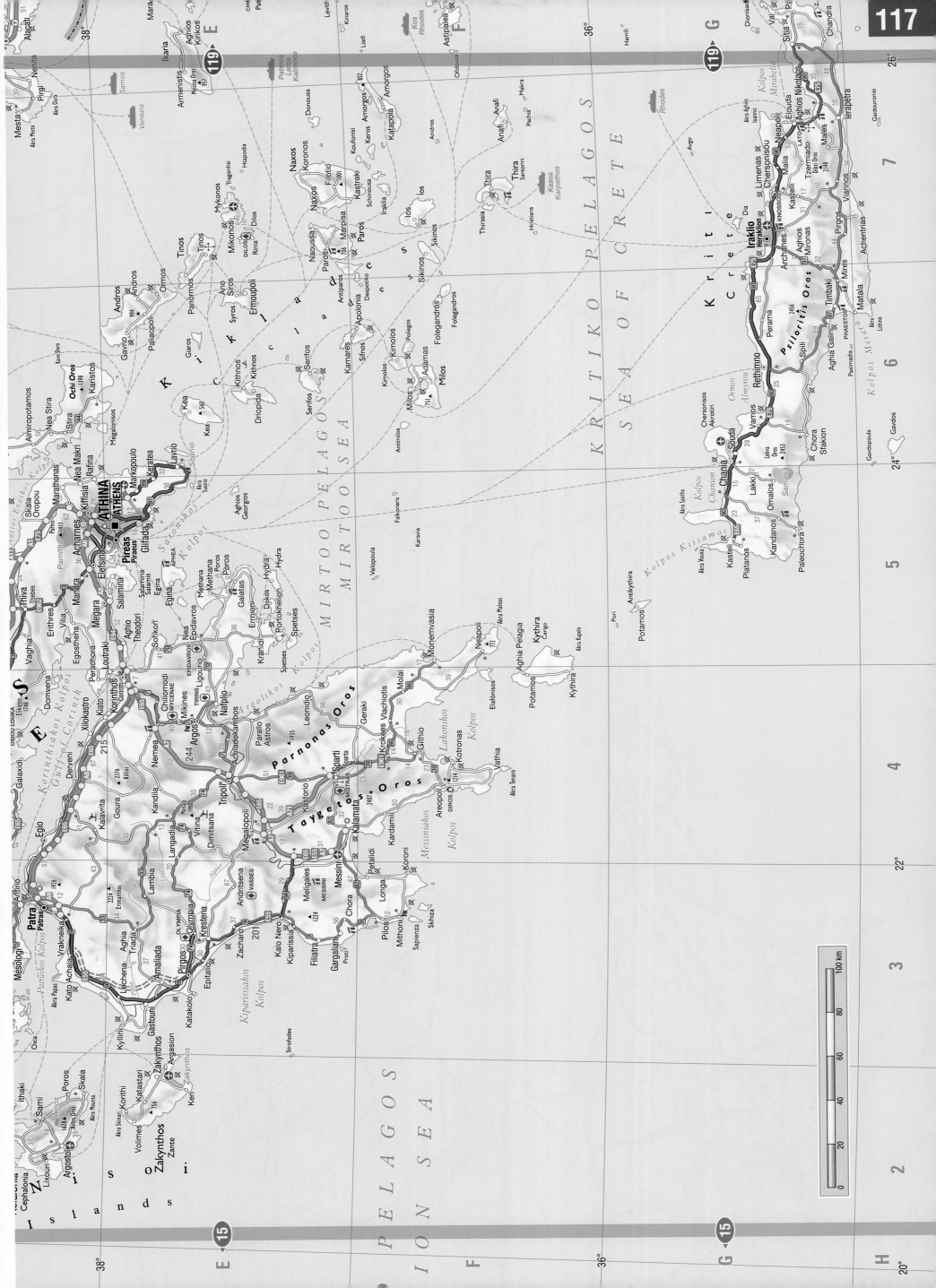

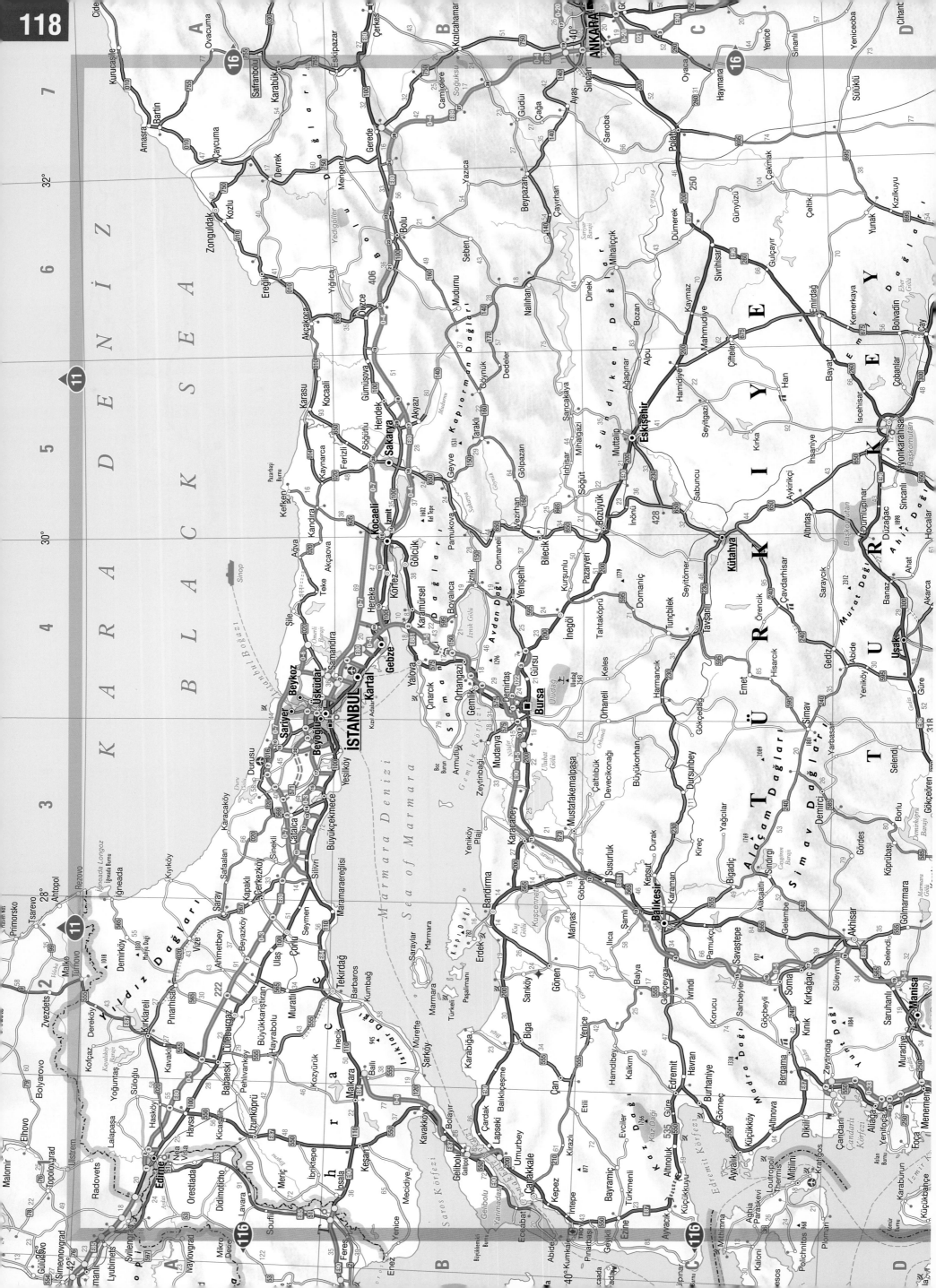

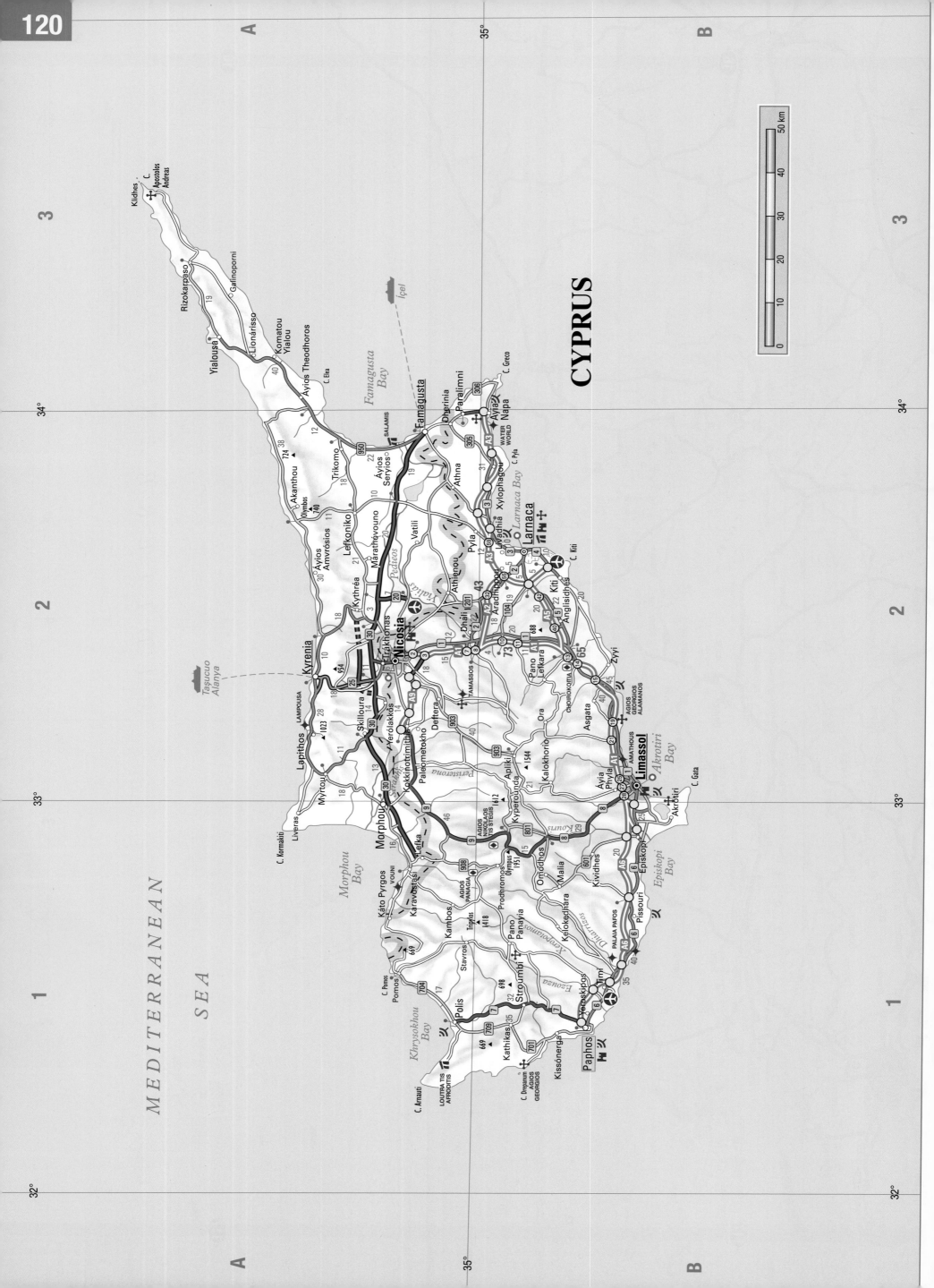

CYPRUS

MEDITERRANEAN SEA

Khrysokhou Bay

Morphou Bay

Famagusta Bay

Larnaca Bay

Akrotiri Bay

Episkopi Bay

C. Apostolos Andreas

Klidhes

Rizokarpaso

Yialousa

Lionárisso

Komatou Yialou

Ayios Theodhoros

C. Elea

Akanthou

Olymbos

Trikomo

Ayios Servios

SALAMIS

Famagusta

Dherinia

Paralimni

Ayia Napa

C. Greco

WATER WORLD

C. Pyla

Xylophagou

Livachia

Larnaca

C. Kiti

Kiti

Anglisidhes

Athna

Athienou

Pyla

Marathóvouno

Lefkoniko

Kythréa

Ayios Amvrósios

Nicosia

Trákhonas

Kyrenia

Lapithos

Lampousa

Myrtou

Skilloura

Yerólakkos

Kokkinotrimithi

Paleometokho

Deftera

Dháli

TAMASSOS

Pano Lekara

Zyyi

Ora

Asgata

CHOIROKOITIA

AGIOS GEORGIOS ALAMANOS

AMATHOUS

Limassol

Akrotiri

C. Gata

Ayia Phyla

Kalokhorio

Malia

Onnódhos

Kyperounda

Apliki

PERISTERONA

AGIOS NIKOLAOS TIS STEGIS

Prodhromos

Olympus

Pano Panayia

AGIOS PANAGIA

Tinjptos

Kambos

Stavros

Kelokedhara

Kividhes

Episkopi

Pissouri

Kato Pyrgos

Karavostasi

VOUNI

Lefka

Morphou

Kokkina

Liveras

Lapithos

C. Kormakiti

C. Pomos

Pomos

C. Arnauti

LOUTRA TIS ARODITIS

Polis

Kathikas

Stroumbi

Kissónerga

C. Drepaum AGIOS GEORGIOS

Paphos

Yeroskipos

Timi

PALAIA PAFOS

Kouklia

MEDITERRANEAN SEA

Pedieos

Yialias

Kouris

Dhiarizos

Xeropotamos

Ezousa

Kryos

Tașucu Alanya

İçel

City plans • Plans de villes
Stadtpläne • Piante di città

Motorway	Autoroute	Autobahn	Autostrada
Major through route	Route principale majeur	Hauptstrecke	Strada di grande communicazione
Through route	Route principale	Schnellstrasse	Strada d'importanza regionale
Secondary road	Route secondaire		
Dual carriageway	Chaussées séparées	Nebenstrasse	Strada d'interesse locale
Other road	Autre route	Zweispurig Schnellstrasse	Strada a carreggiate doppie
Tunnel	Tunnel	Nebenstrecke	Altra strada
Limited access / pedestrian road	Rue réglementée / rue piétonne	Tunnel	Galleria stradale
One-way street	Sens unique	Beschränkter Zugang/ Fussgängerzone	Strada pedonale / a accesso limitato
Parking	Parc de stationnement	Einbahnstrasse	Senso unico
Motorway number A7	Numéro d'autoroute	Parkplatz	Parcheggio
National road number 447	Numéro de route nationale	Autobahnnummer A7	Numero di autostrada
European road number E45	Numéro de route européenne	Nationalstrassen- nummer 447	Numero di strada nazionale
Destination GENT	Destination	Europäische Strassennummer E45	Numero di strada europea
Car ferry	Bac passant les autos	Ziel GENT	Destinazione
Railway	Chemin de fer	Autofähre	Traghetto automobili
Rail / bus station	Gare / gare routière	Eisenbahn	Ferrovia
Underground, metro station	Station de métro	Bahnhof / Busstation	Stazione ferrovia / pullman
Cable car	Téléférique	U-Bahnstation	Metropolitano
Abbey, cathedral	Abbaye, cathédrale	Drahtseilbahn	Funivia
Church of interest	Église intéressante	Abtei, Kloster, Kathedrale	Abbazia, duomo
Synagogue	Synagogue	Interessante Kirche	Chiesa da vedere
Hospital	Hôpital	Synagoge	Sinagoga
Police station	Police	Krankenhaus	Ospedale
Post office	Bureau de poste	Polizeiwache	Polizia
Tourist information	Office de tourisme	Postamt	Ufficio postale
Place of interest Theatre	Autre curiosité	Informationsbüro	Ufficio informazioni turistiche
		Sonstige Sehenswürdigkeit Theatre	Luogo da vedere

Approach maps • Agglomérations
Carte régionale • Regionalkarte

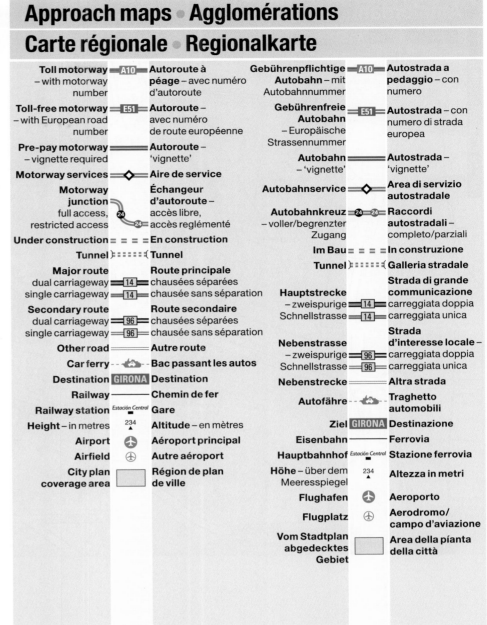

Toll motorway – with motorway number A10	Autoroute à péage – avec numéro d'autoroute	Gebührenpflichtige Autobahn – mit Autobahnnummer A10	Autostrada a pedaggio – con numero
Toll-free motorway – with European road number E51	Autoroute – avec numéro de route européenne	Gebührenfreie Autobahn – Europäische Strassennummer E51	Autostrada – con numero di strada europea
Pre-pay motorway – vignette required	Autoroute – 'vignette'	Autobahn – 'vignette'	Autostrada – 'vignette'
Motorway services	Aire de service	Autobahnservice	Area di servizio autostradale
Motorway junction full access, restricted access 24	Échangeur d'autoroute – accès libre, accès réglementé 24	Autobahnkreuz – voller/begrenzter Zugang 24	Raccordi autostradali – completo/parziali
Under construction	En construction	Im Bau	In construzione
Tunnel	Tunnel	Tunnel	Galleria stradale
Major route dual carriageway 14 single carriageway 14	Route principale chausées séparées chausée sans séparation	Hauptstrecke – zweispurige 14 Schnellstrasse 14	Strada di grande communicazione carreggiata doppia carreggiata unica
Secondary route dual carriageway 96 single carriageway 96	Route secondaire chausées séparées chausée sans séparation	Nebenstrasse – zweispurige 96 Schnellstrasse 96	Strada d'interesse locale carreggiata doppia carreggiata unica
Other road	Autre route	Nebenstrecke	Altra strada
Car ferry	Bac passant les autos	Autofähre	Traghetto automobili
Destination GIRONA	Destination	Ziel GIRONA	Destinazione
Railway	Chemin de fer	Eisenbahn	Ferrovia
Railway station Estación Central	Gare	Hauptbahnhof Estación Central	Stazione ferrovia
Height – in metres 234	Altitude – en mètres 234	Höhe – über dem Meeresspiegel 234	Altezza in metri 234
Airport	Aéroport principal	Flughafen	Aeroporto
Airfield	Autre aéroport	Flugplatz	Aerodromo/ campo d'aviazione
City plan coverage area	Région de plan de ville	Vom Stadtplan abgedecktes Gebiet	Area della pianta della città

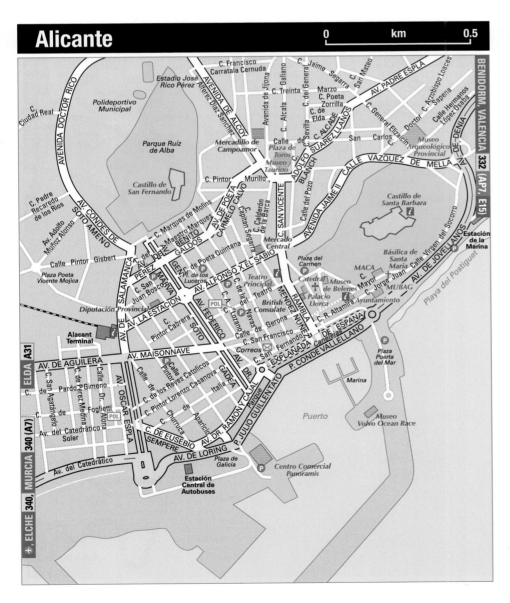

Alicante   0 km 0,5

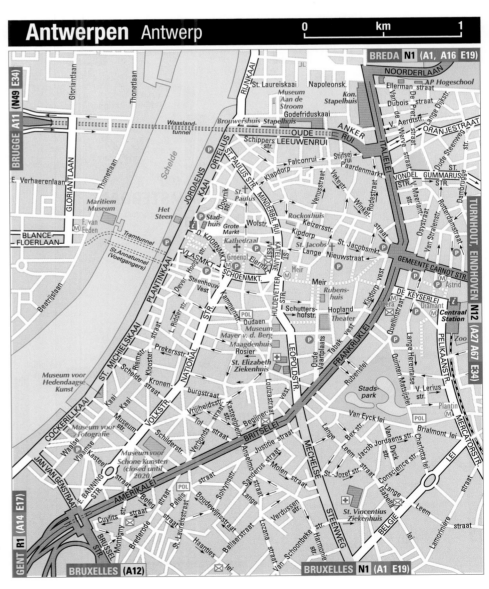

Antwerpen Antwerp   0 km 1

Amsterdam

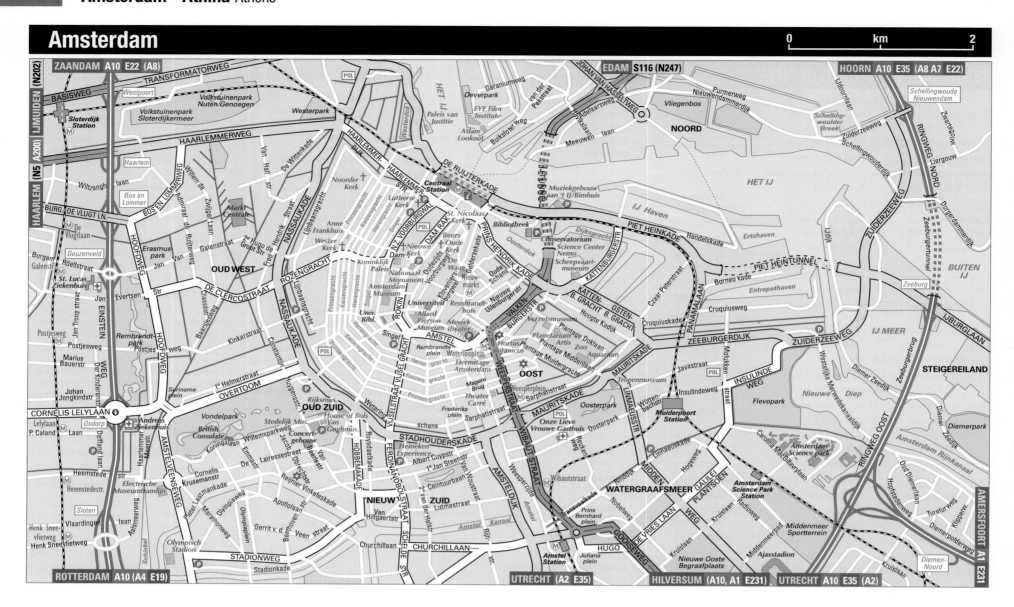

Amsterdam

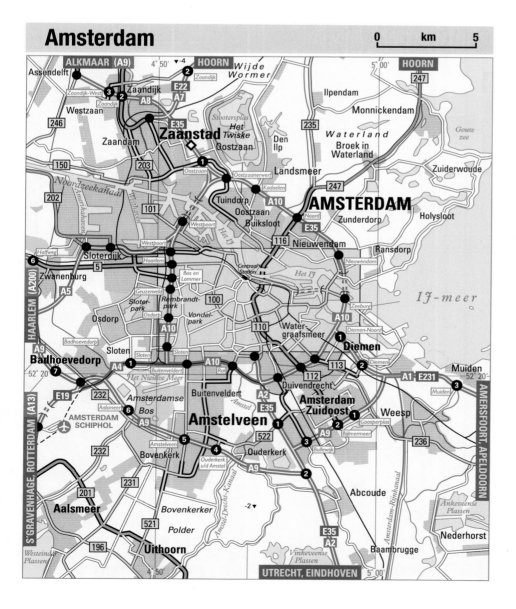

Athina Athens

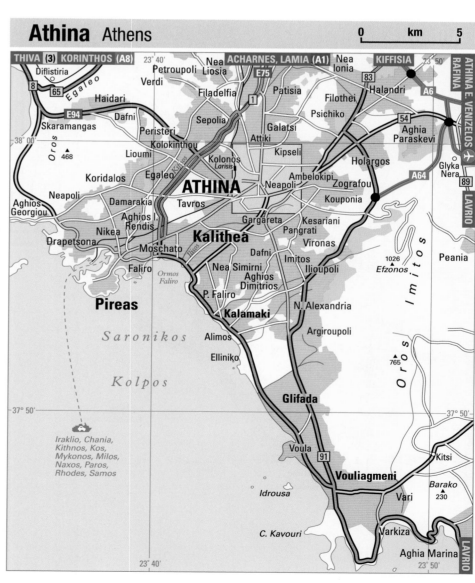

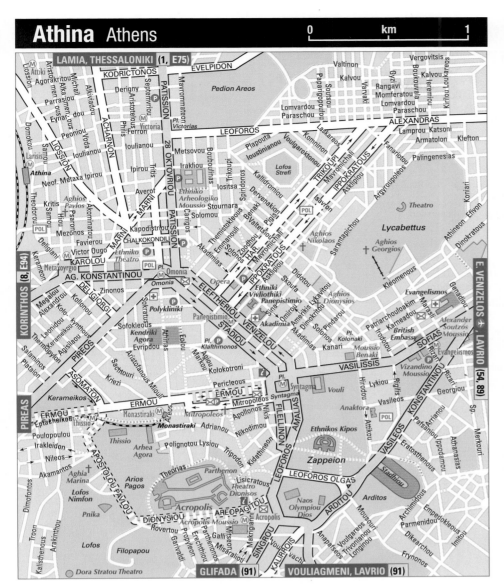

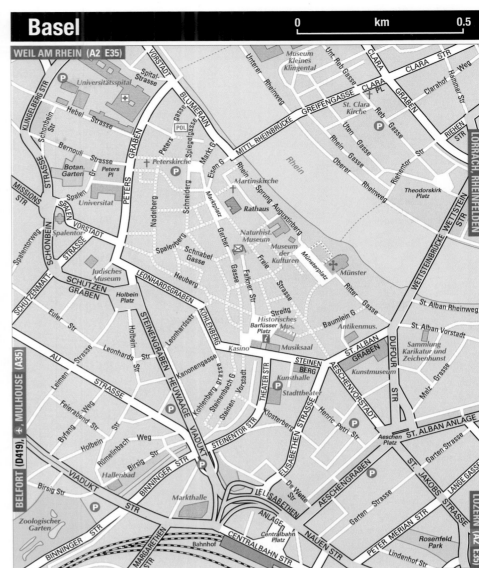

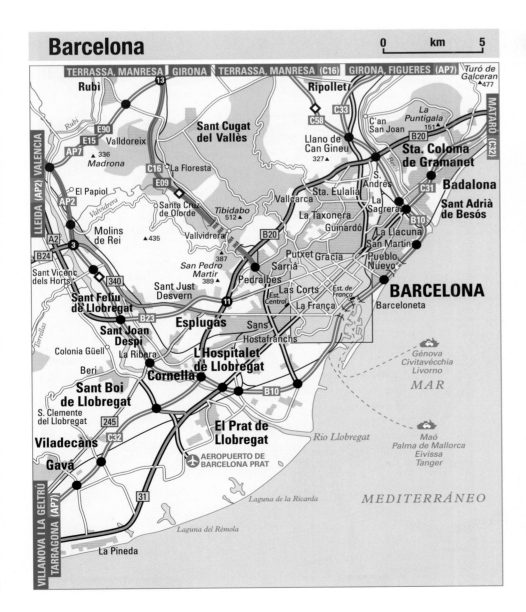

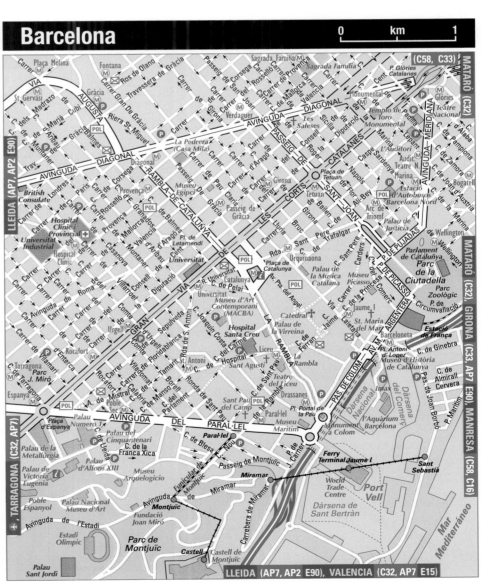

Berlin

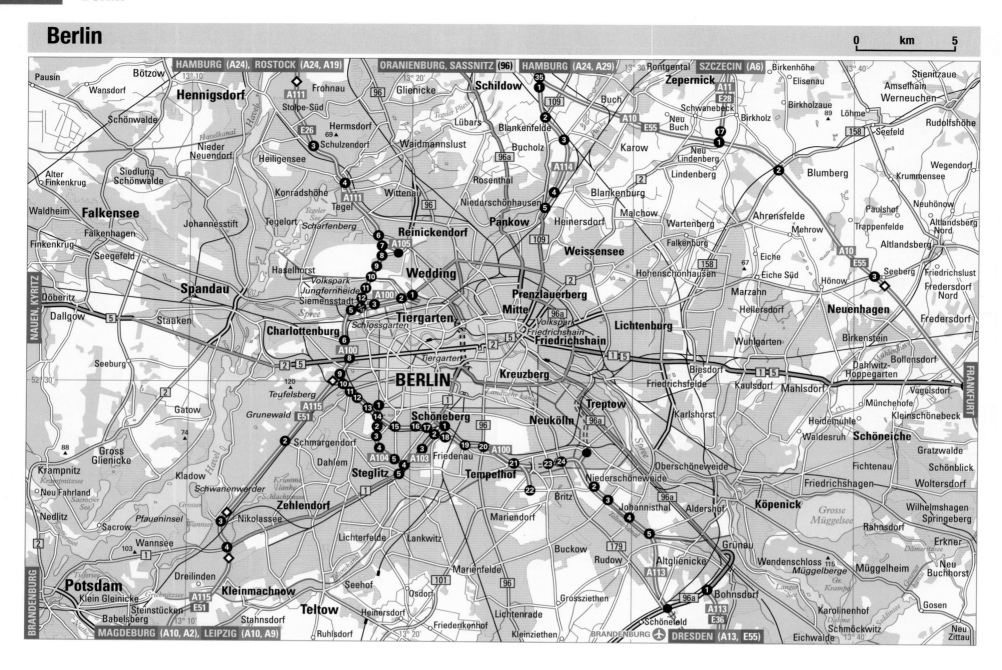

Berlin

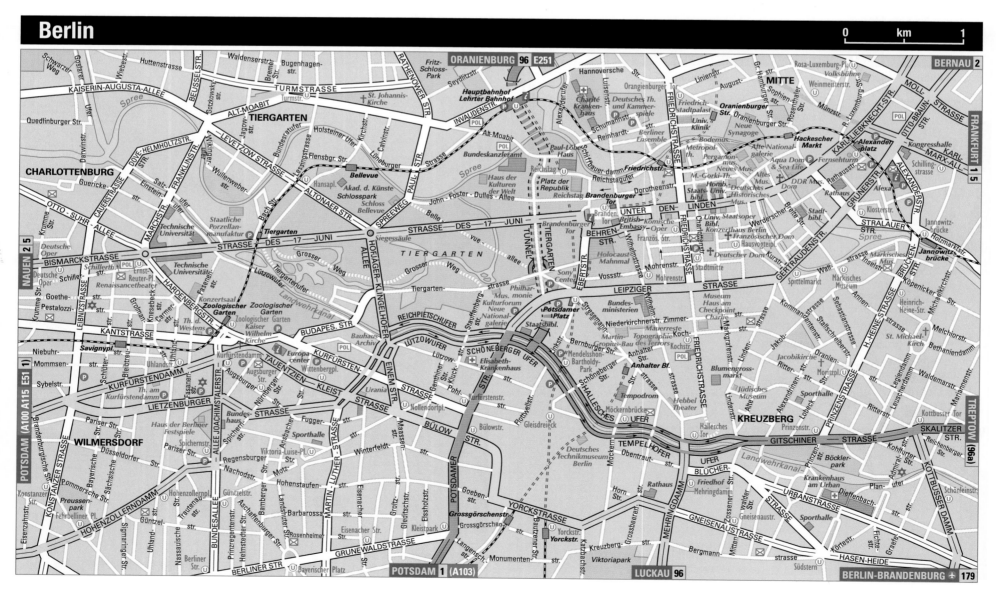

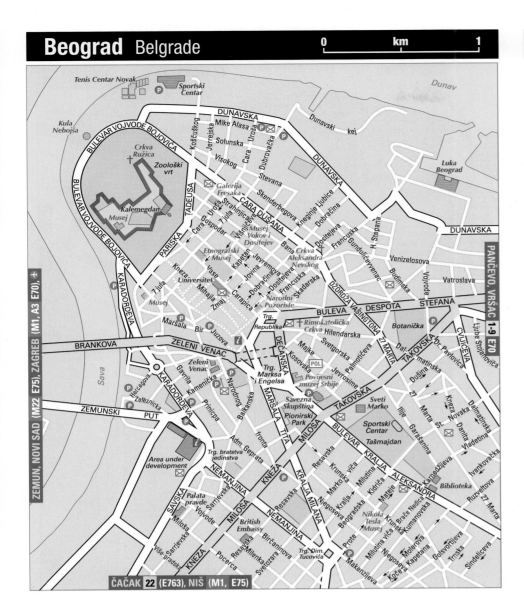

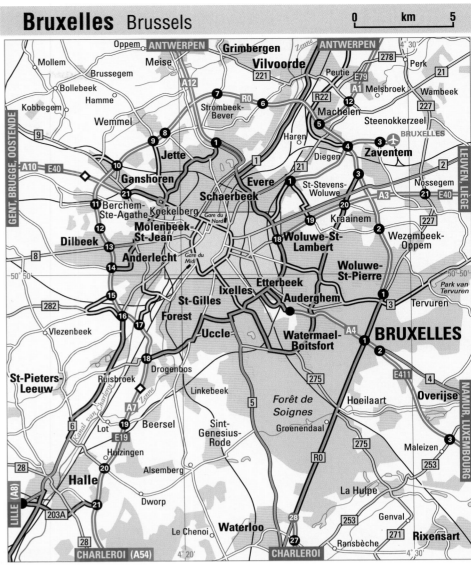

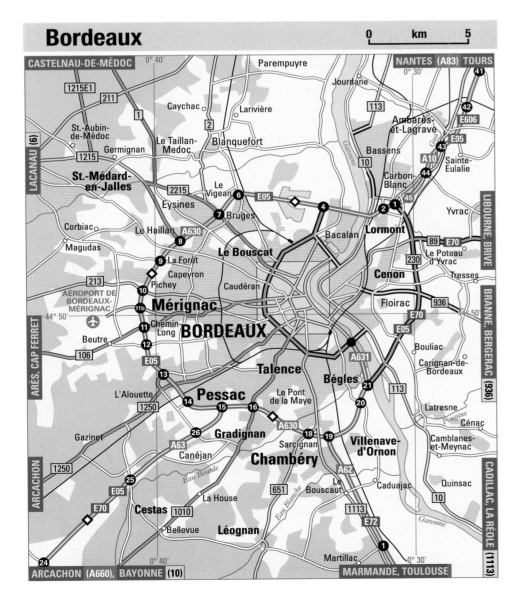

Bruxelles Brussels

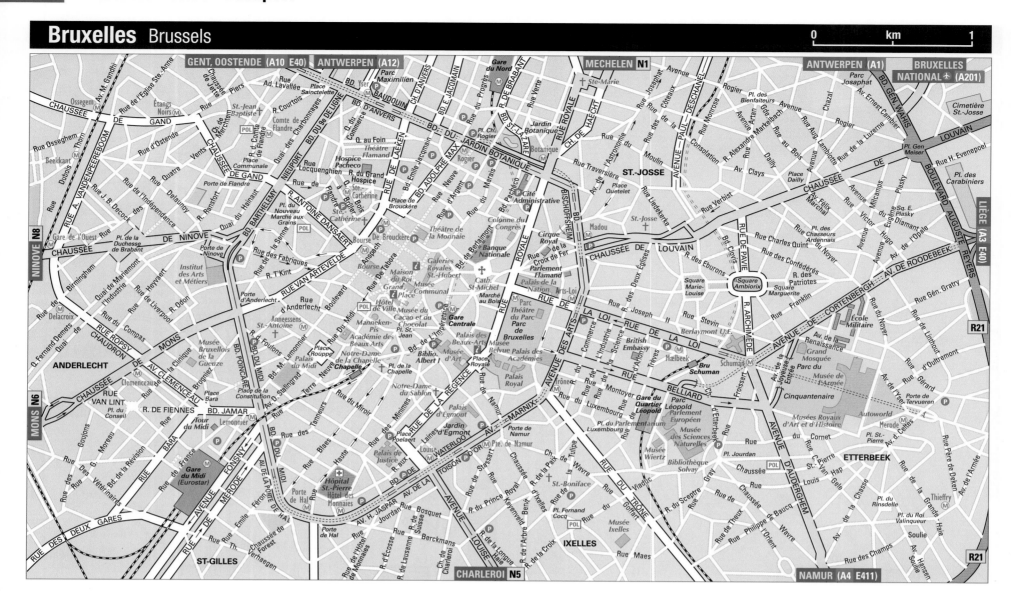

Budapest

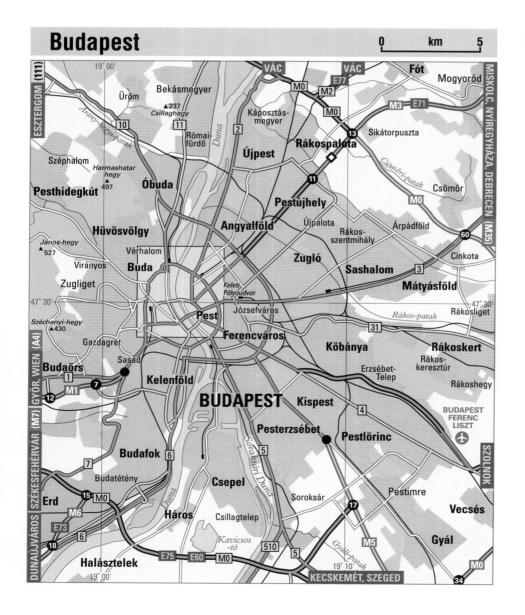

Budapest

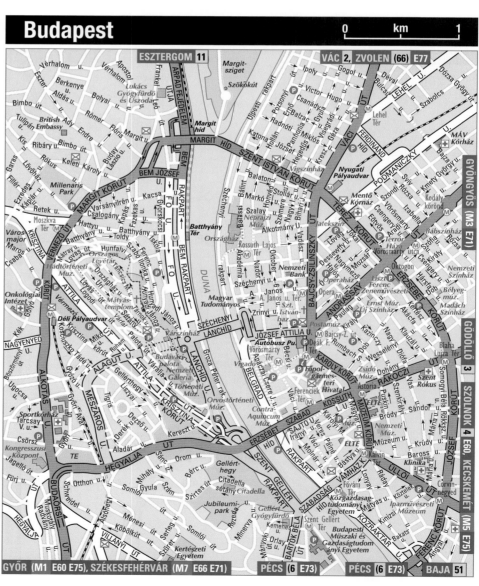

Dublin

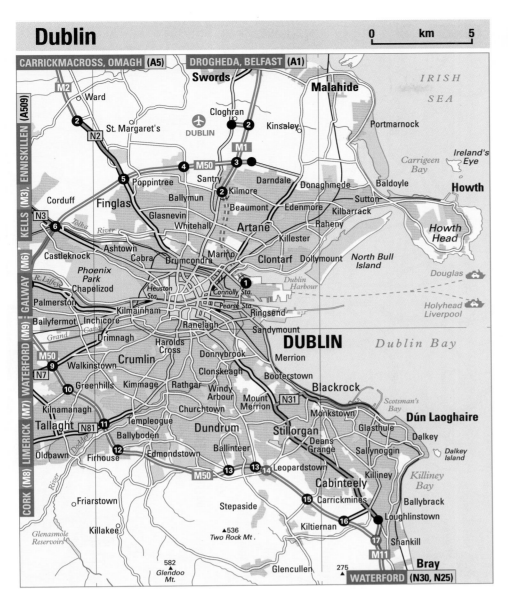

Dublin

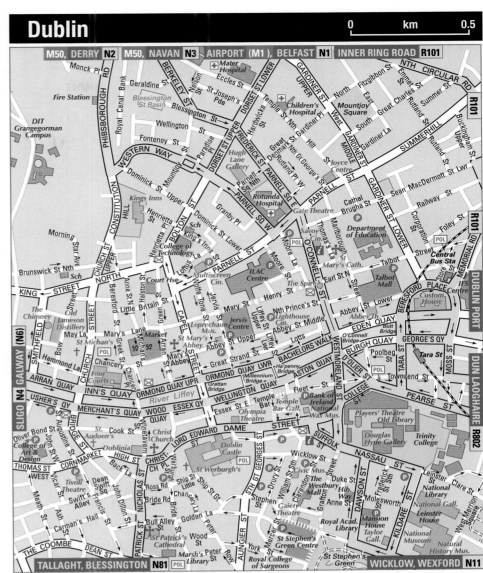

Düsseldorf

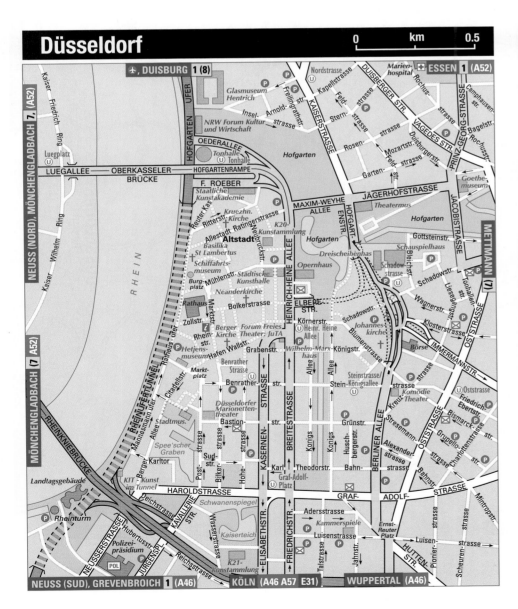

Edinburgh

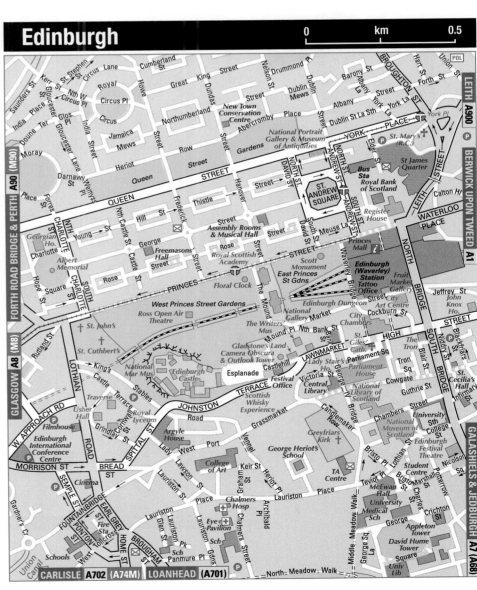

For **Cologne** see page 132
For **Copenhagen** see page 132

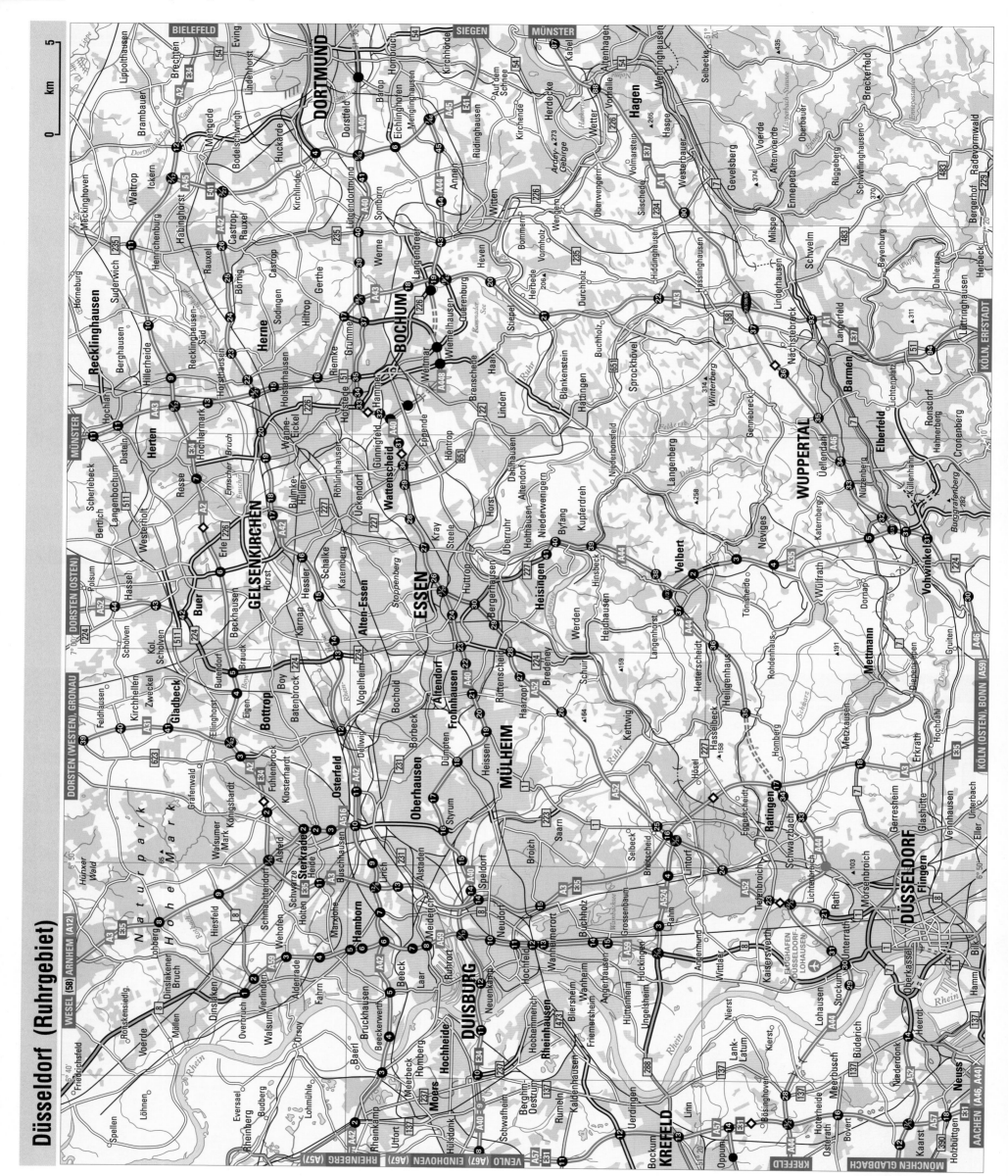

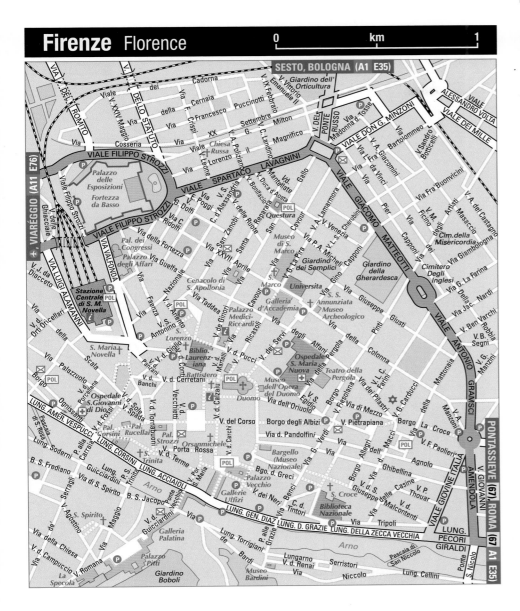

Firenze Florence

Frankfurt

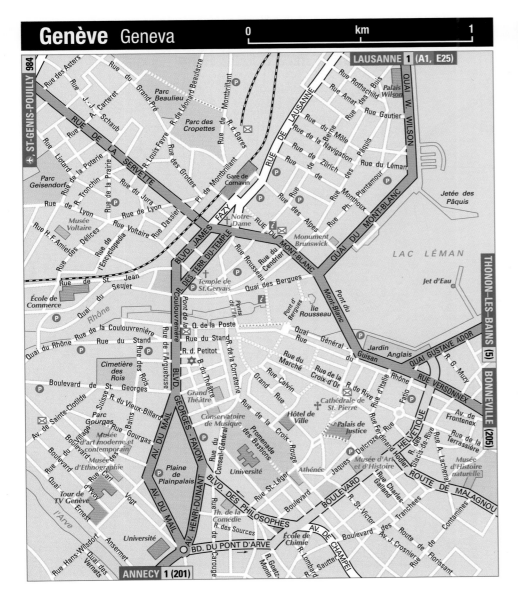

Genève Geneva

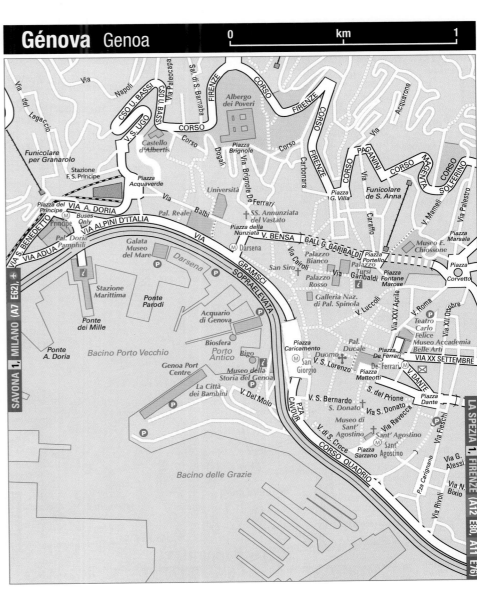

Génova Genoa

Granada

0 km 0.5

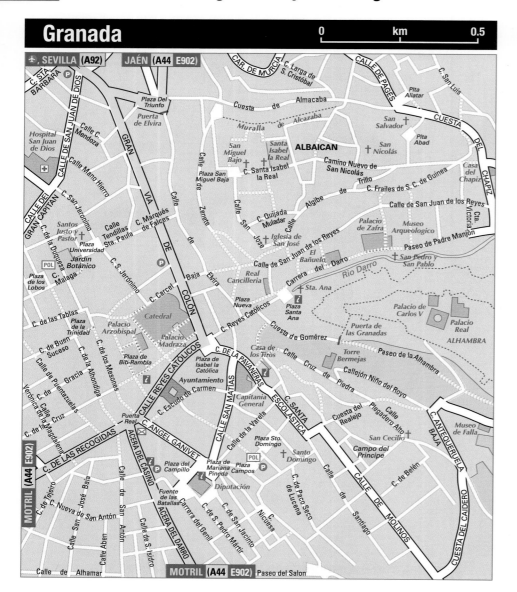

Göteborg Gothenburg

0 km 1

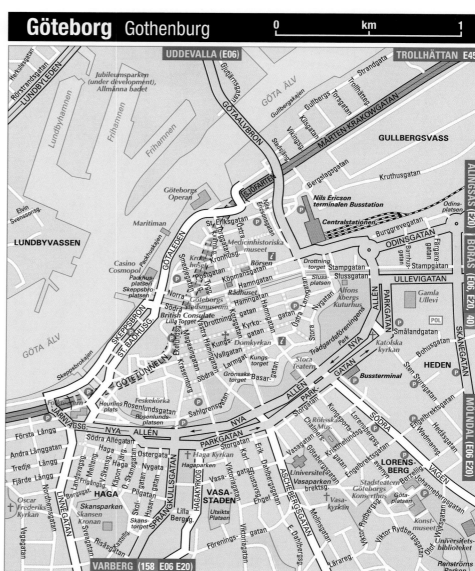

Hamburg

0 km 5

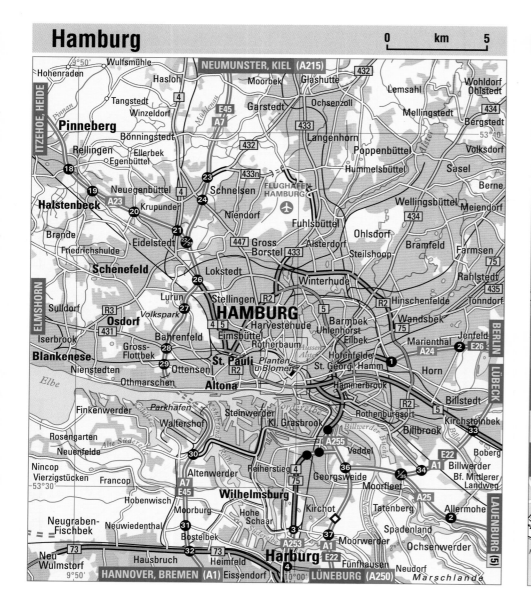

Hamburg

0 km 1

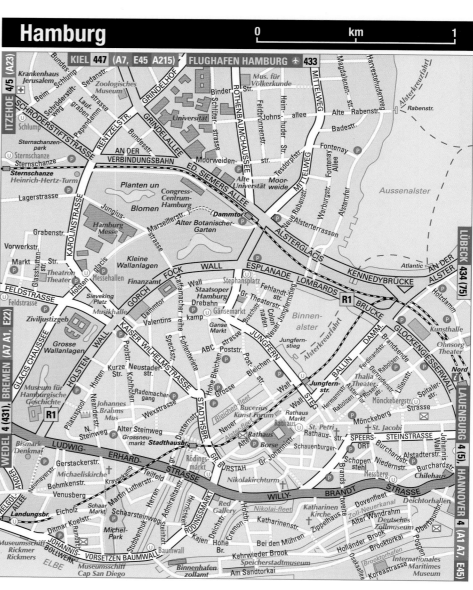

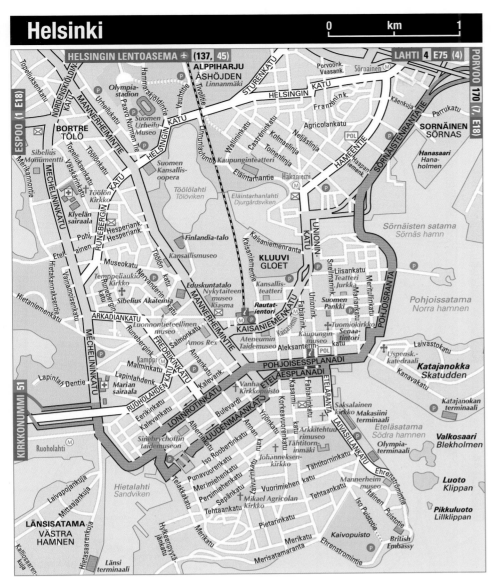

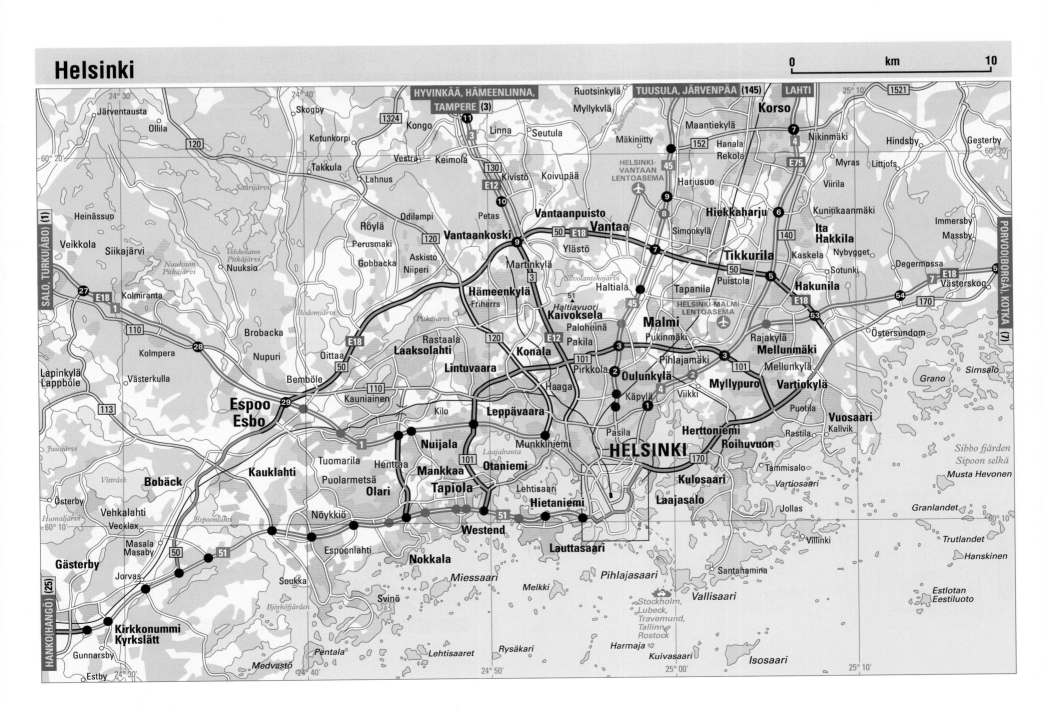

København Copenhagen

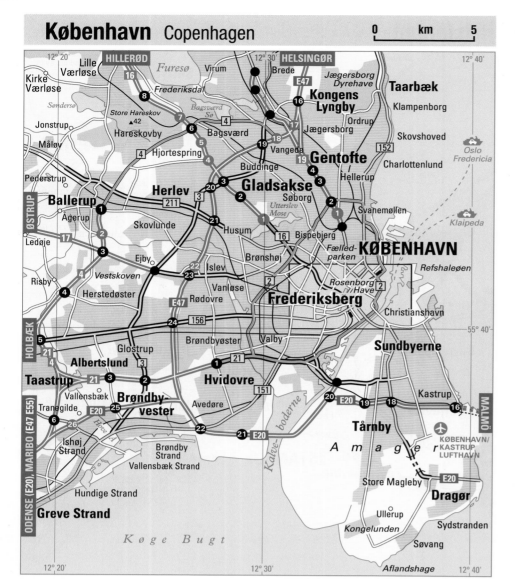

Köln Cologne

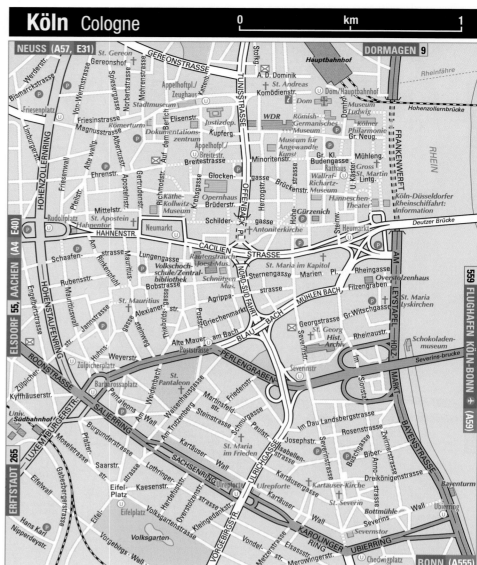

København Copenhagen

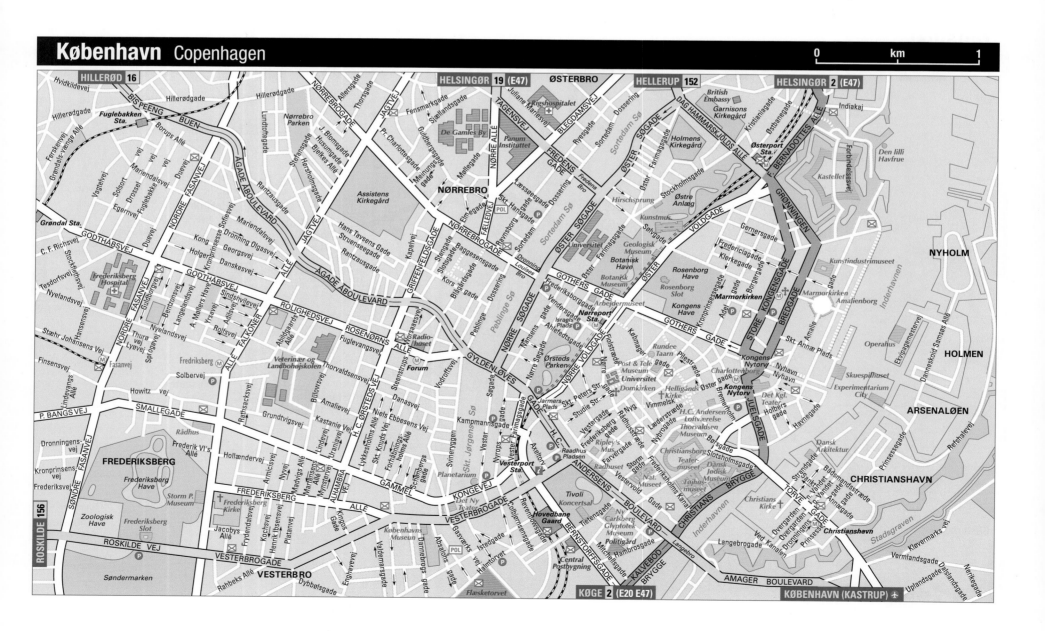

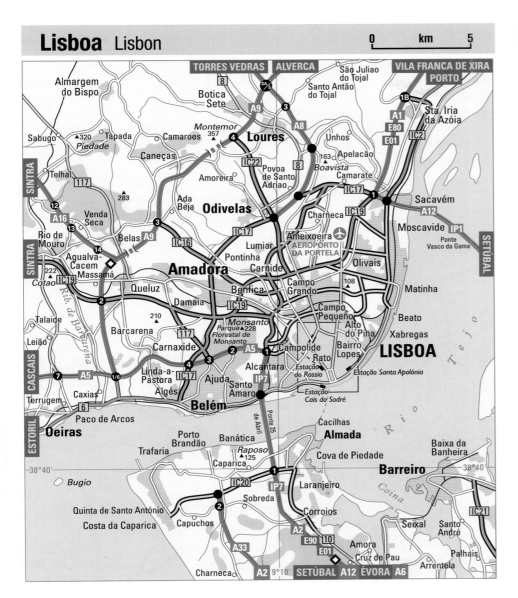

Lisboa Lisbon

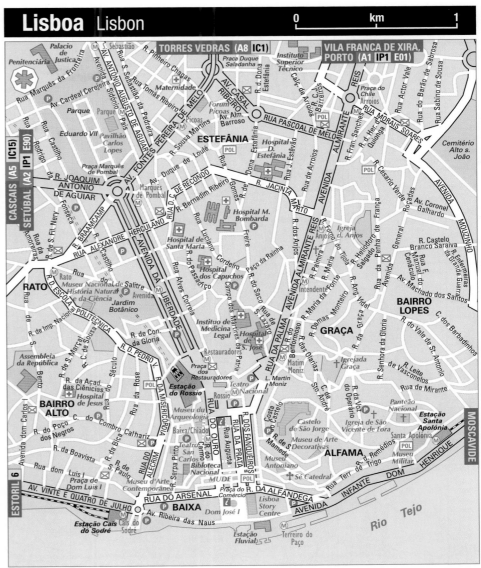

Lisboa Lisbon

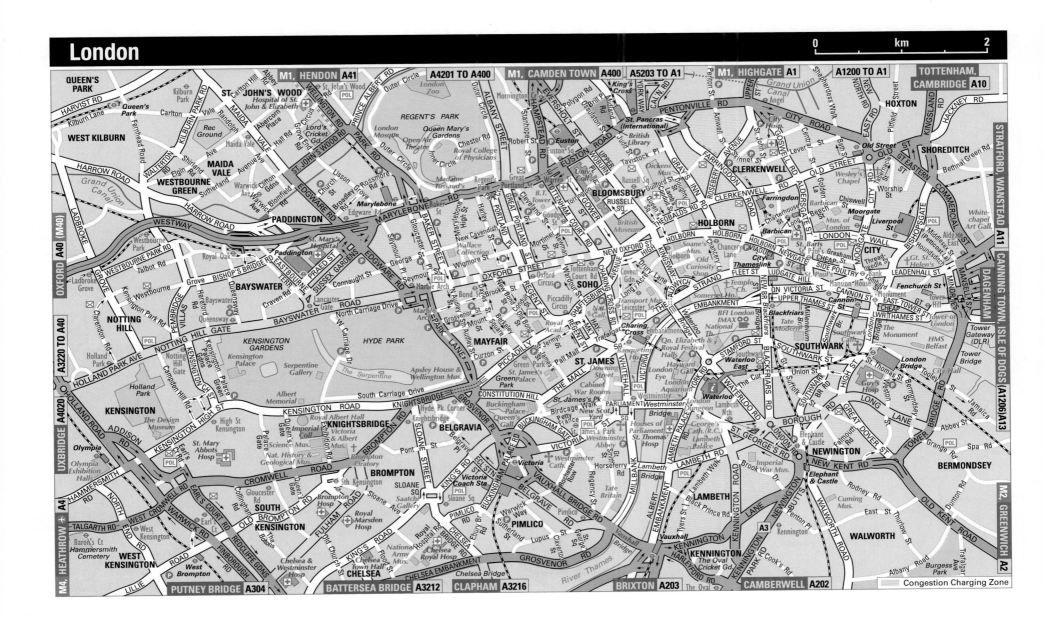

London

London

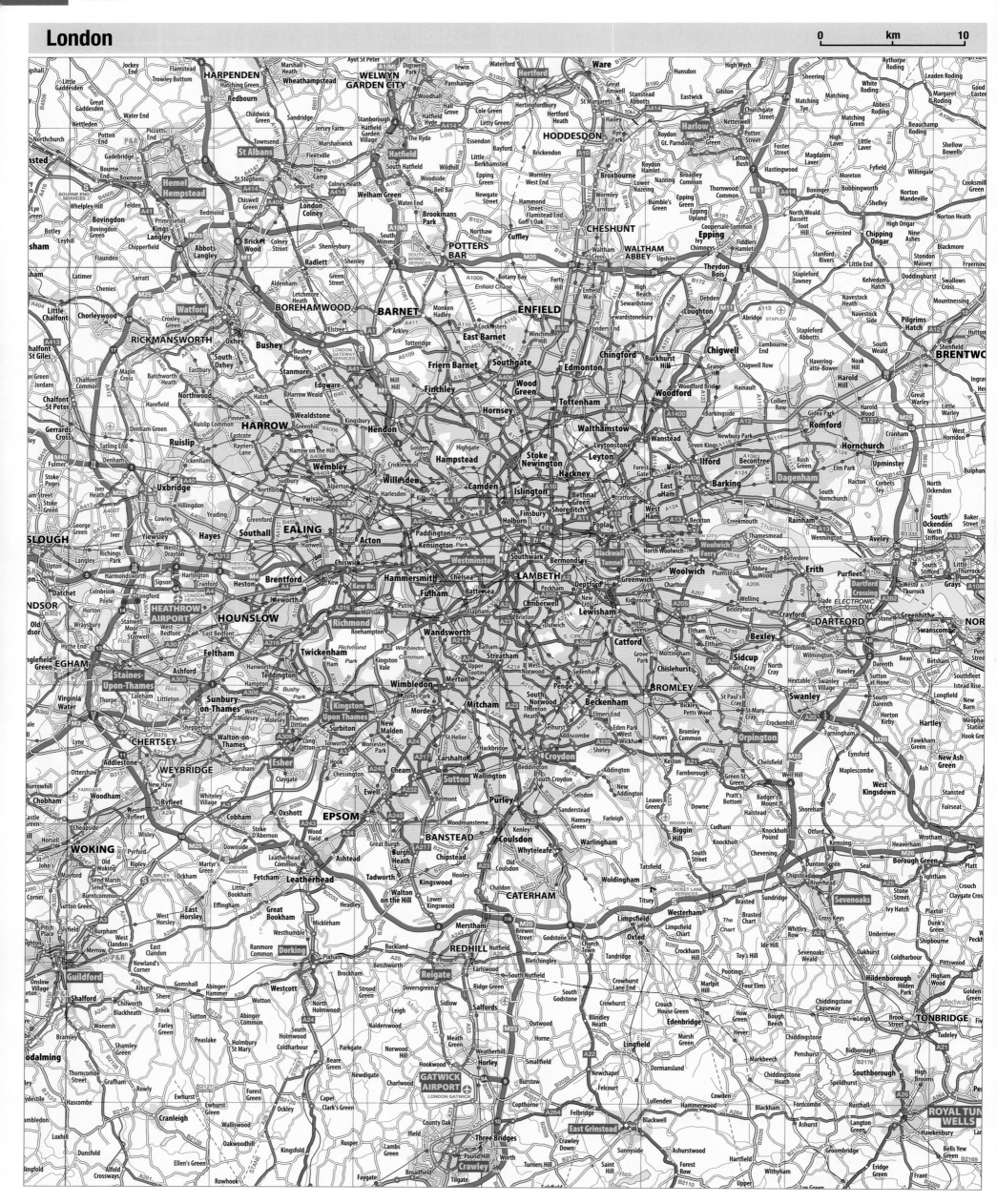

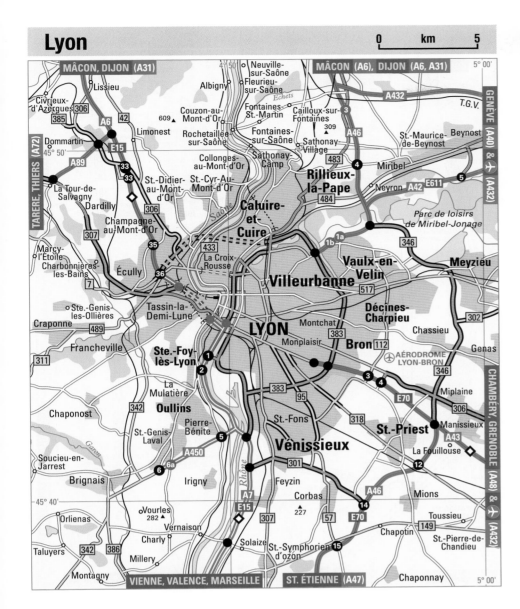

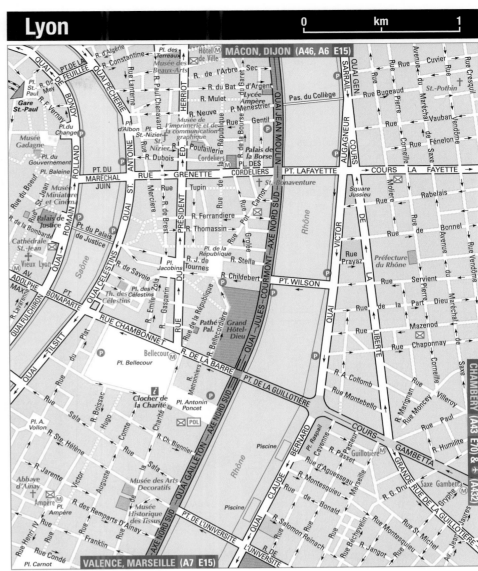

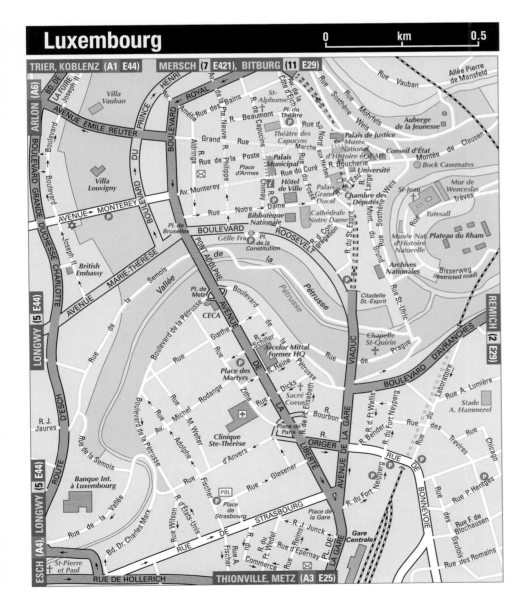

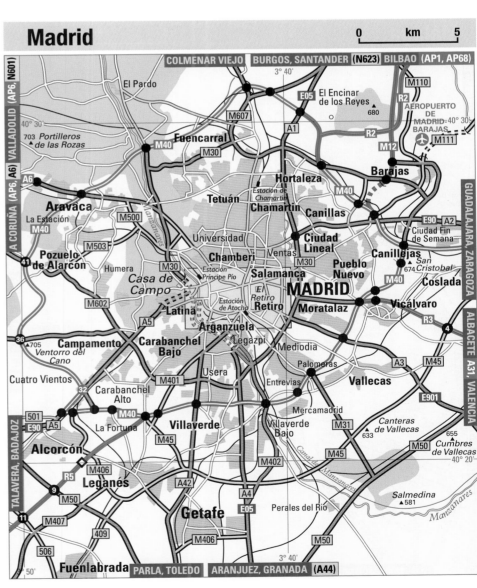

Madrid

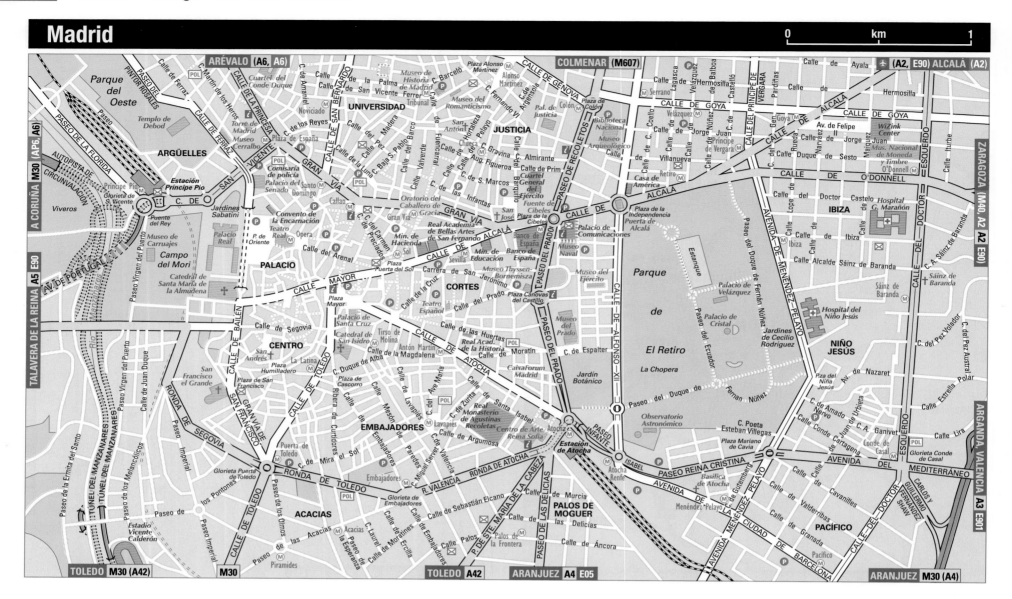

Málaga

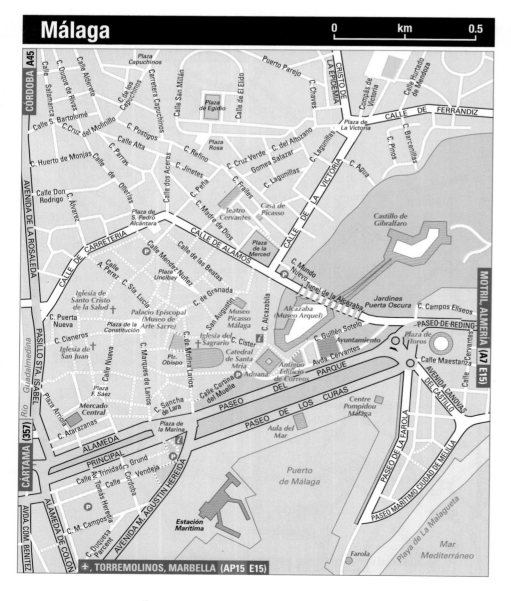

Marseille / Marseilles

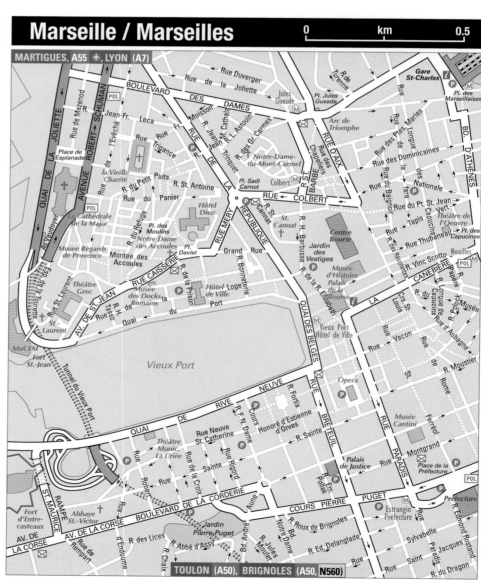

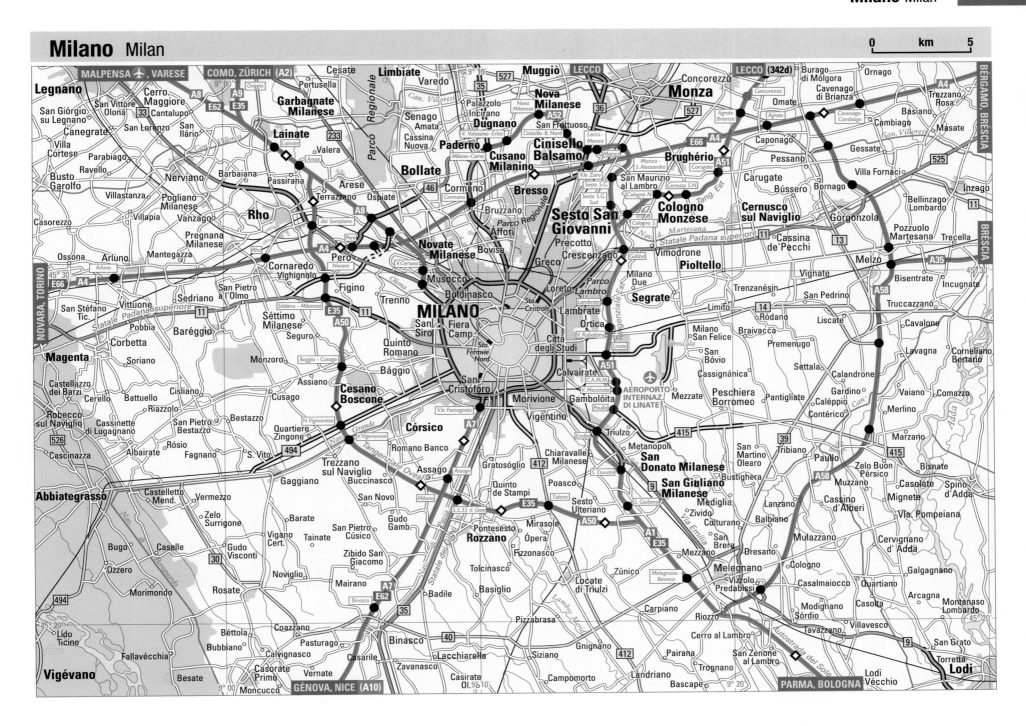

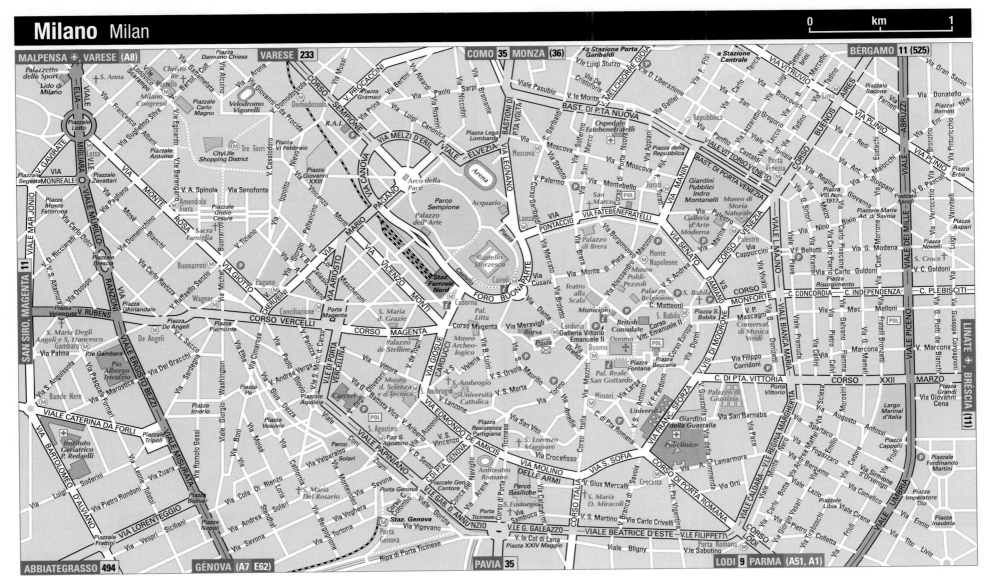

Moskva Moscow

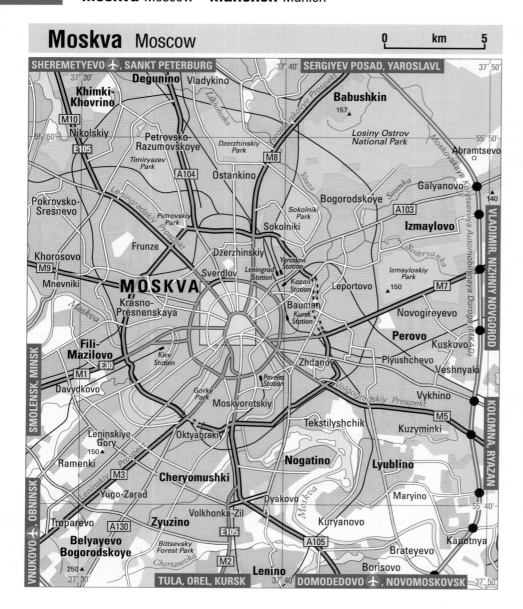

Moskva Moscow

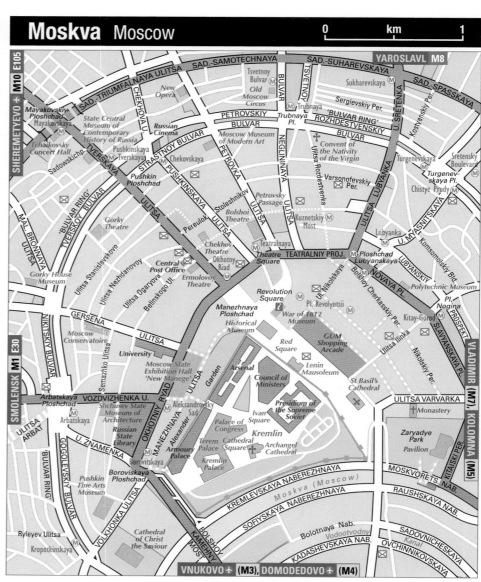

München Munich

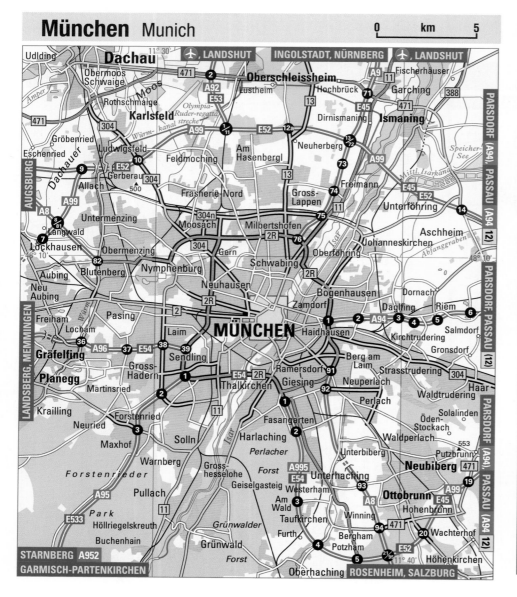

München Munich

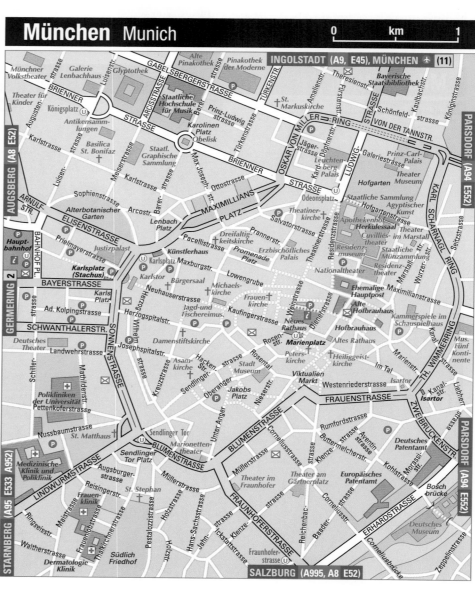

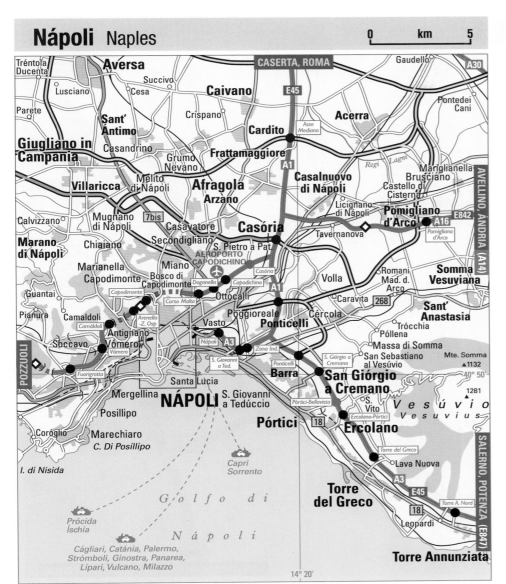

Nápoli Naples

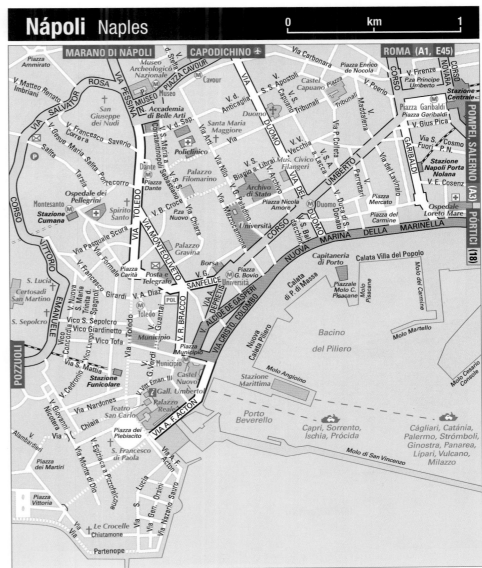

Nápoli Naples

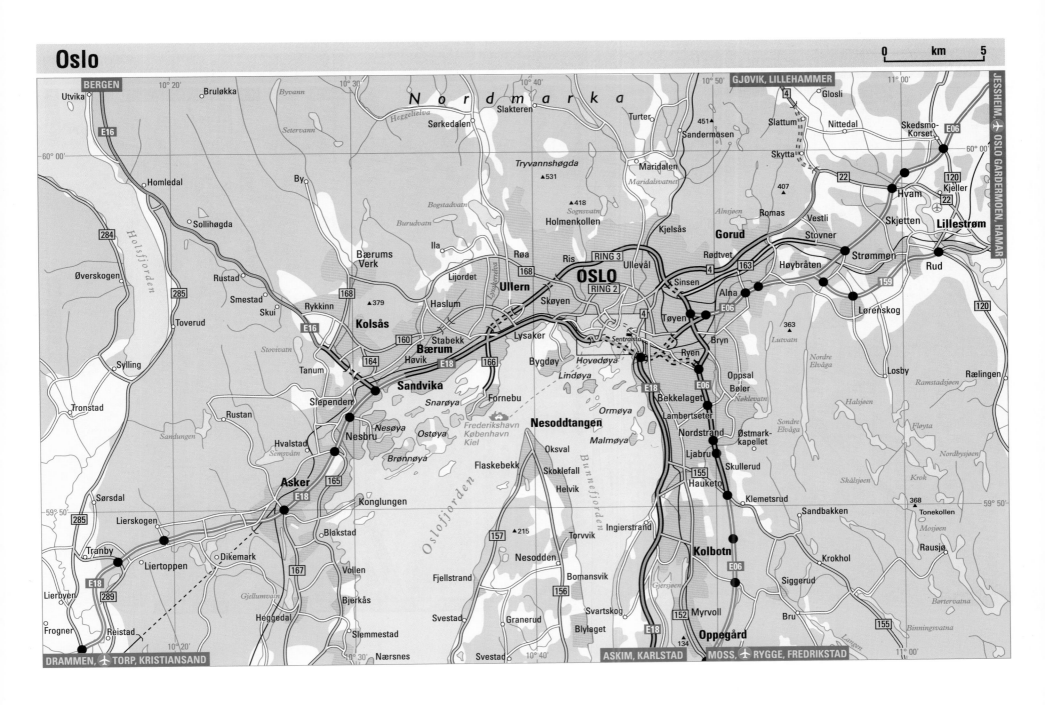

Oslo

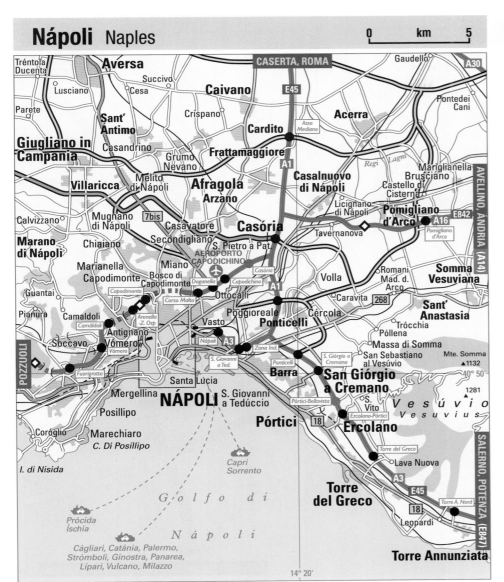

Nápoli Naples

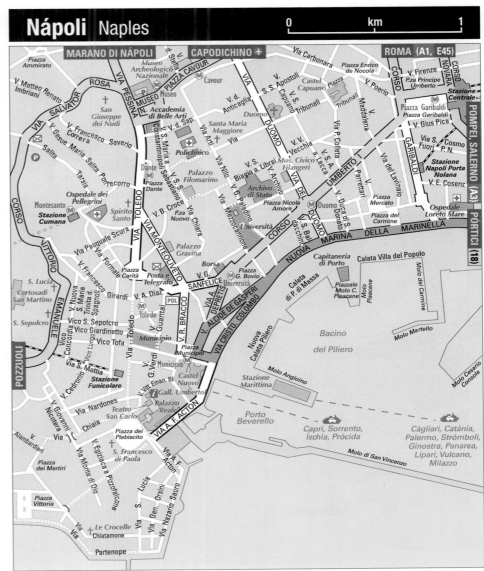

Nápoli Naples

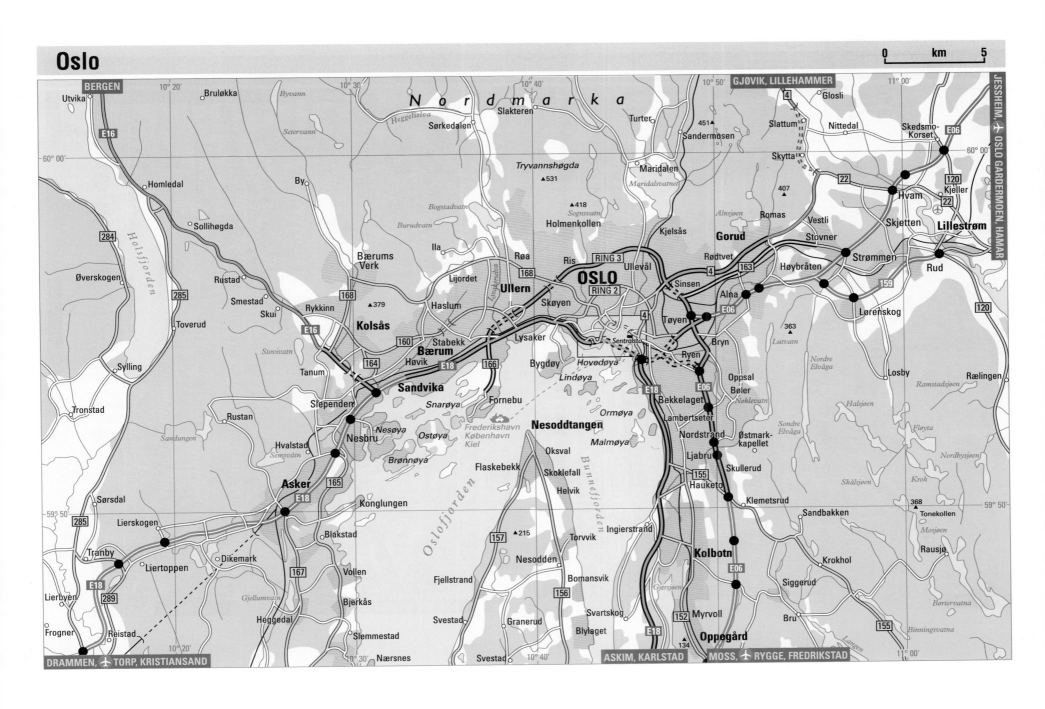

Oslo

Oslo

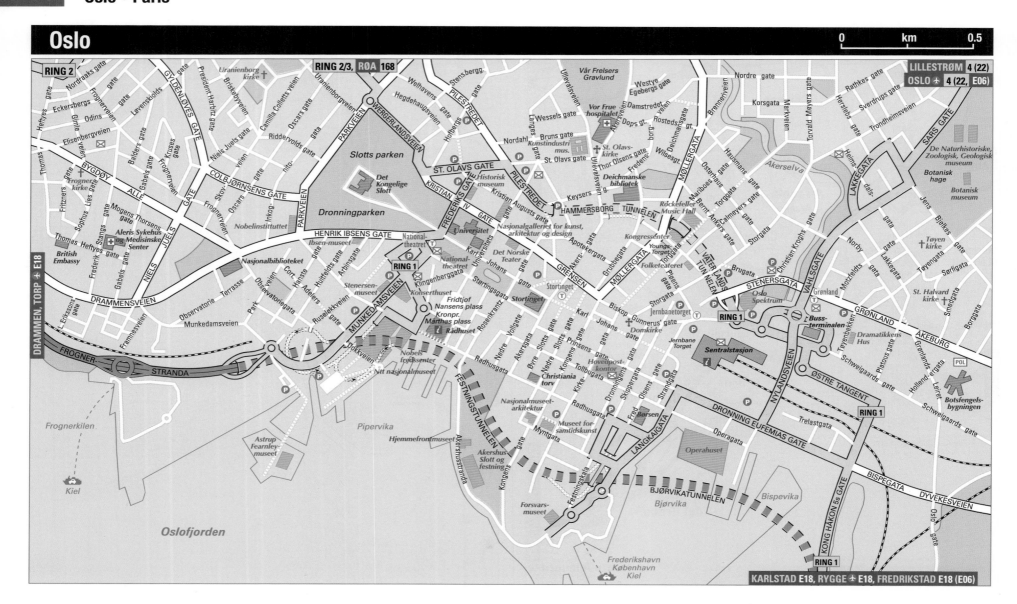

Paris

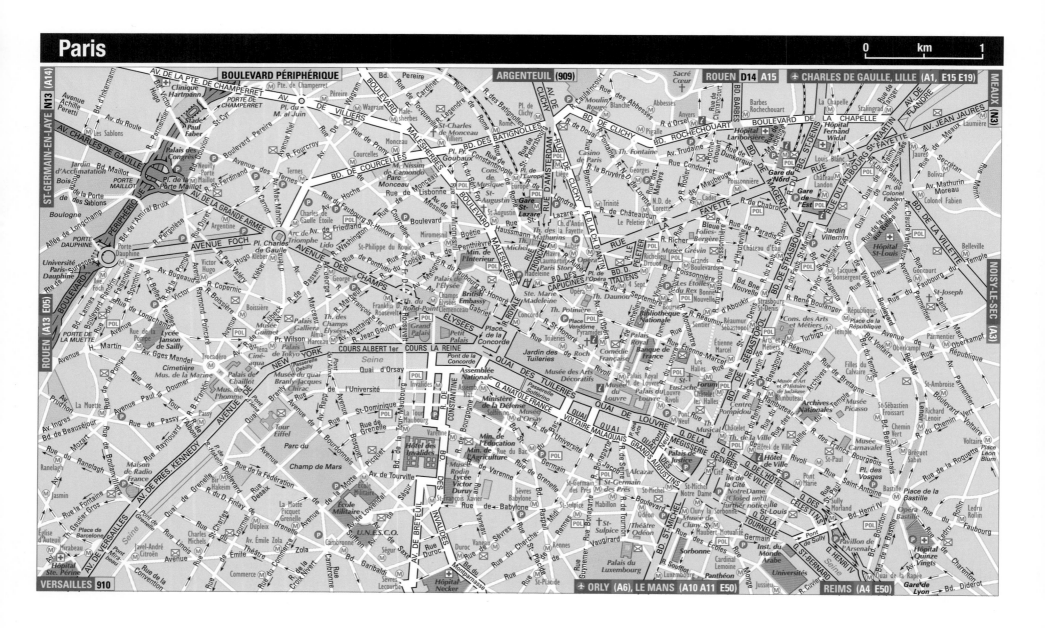

Paris

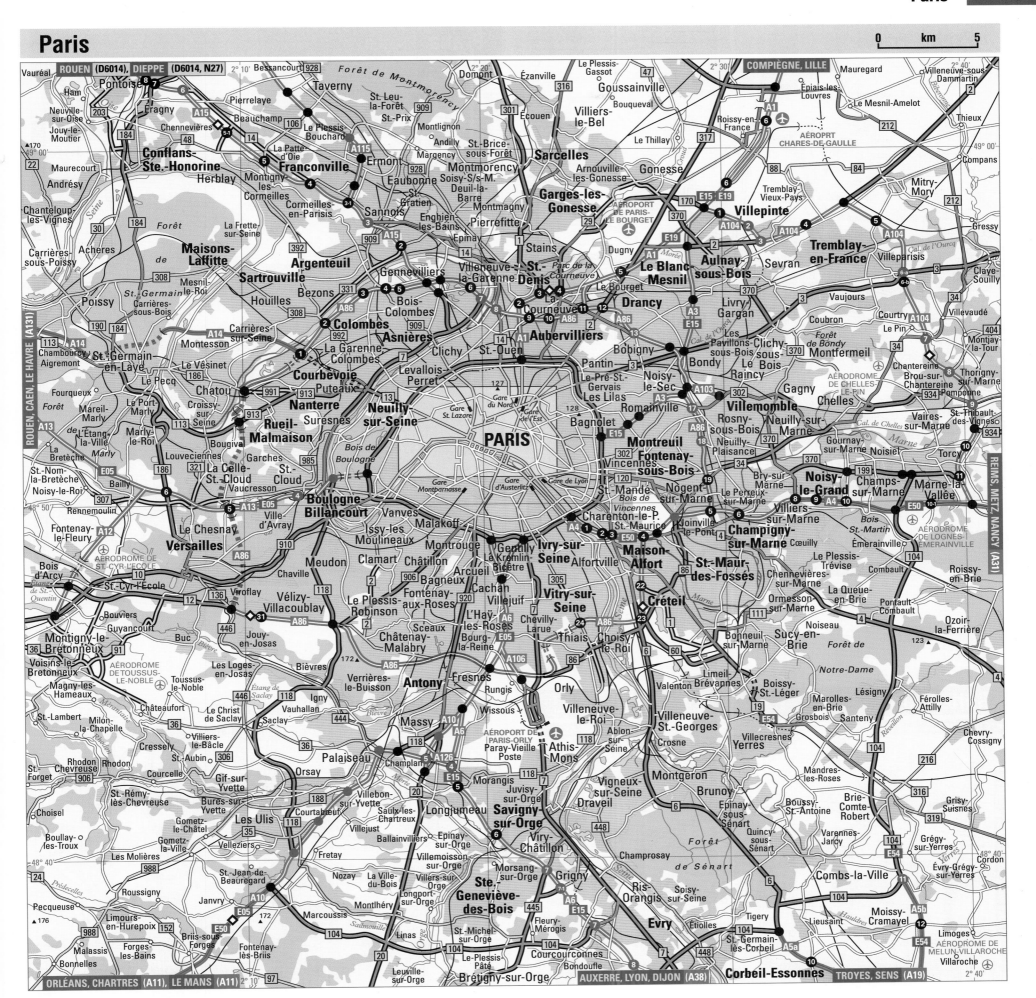

Praha Prague

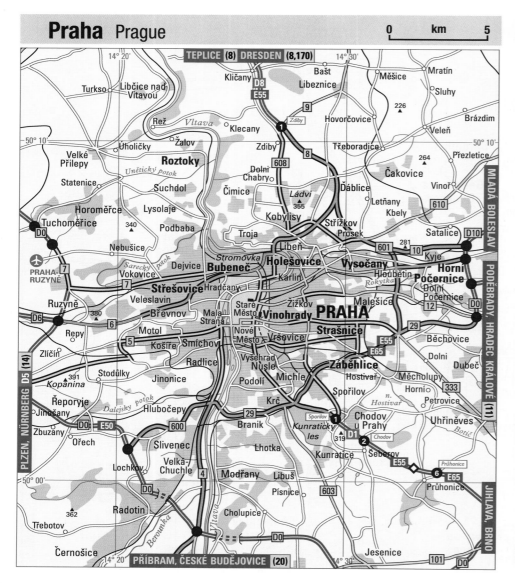

Praha Prague

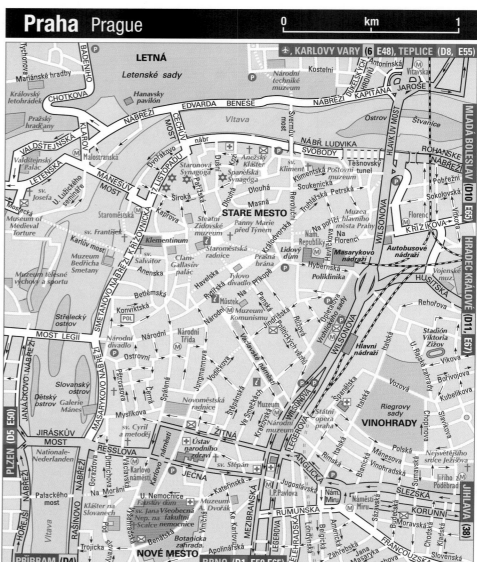

Rotterdam

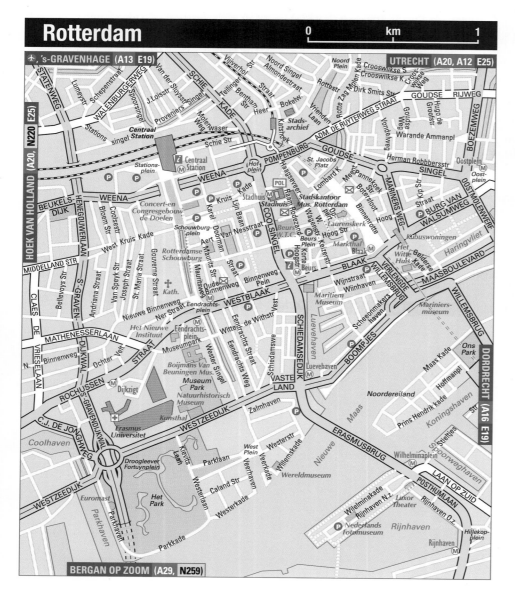

Sankt-Peterburg St. Petersburg

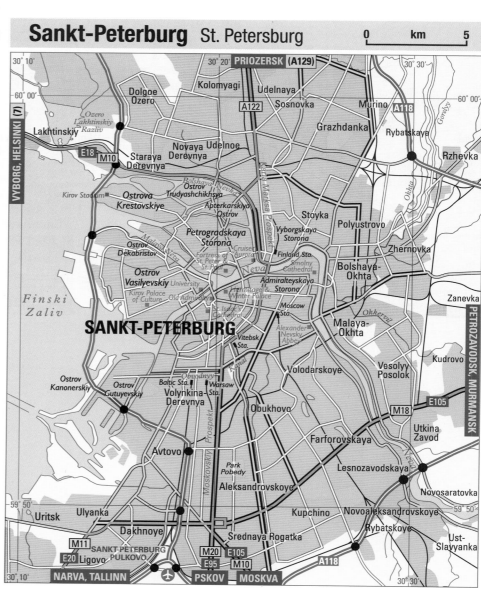

For **Rome** see page 143

Roma Rome

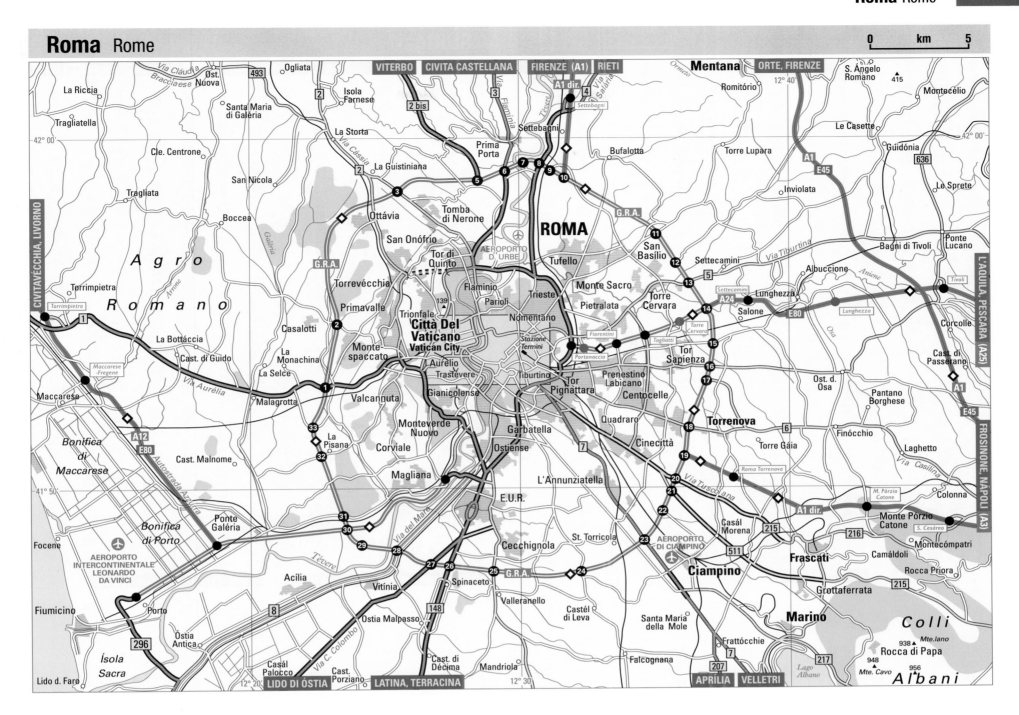

Roma Rome

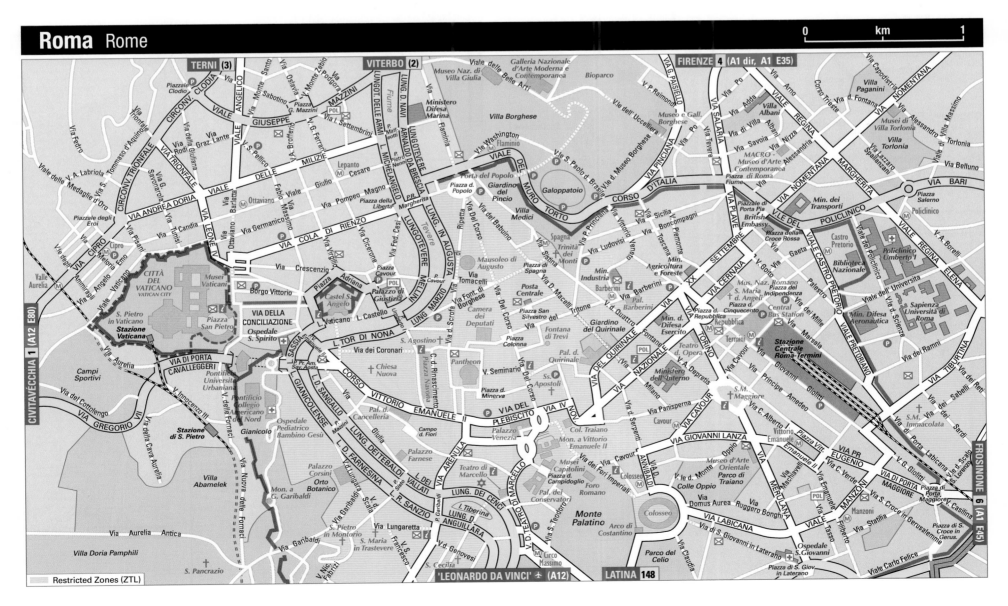

Restricted Zones (ZTL)

Sevilla Seville

0 km 0.5

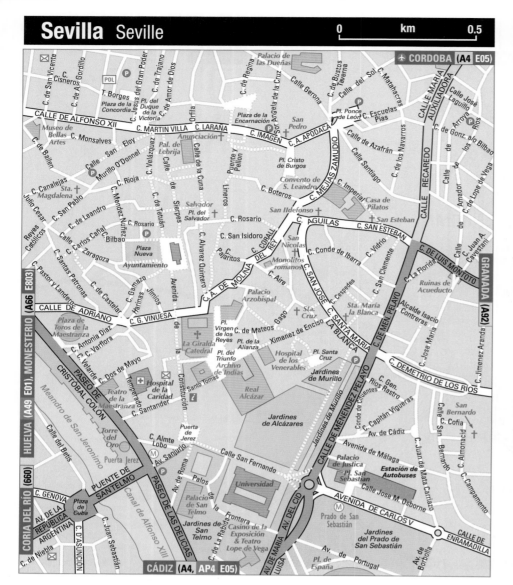

Stuttgart

0 km 0.5

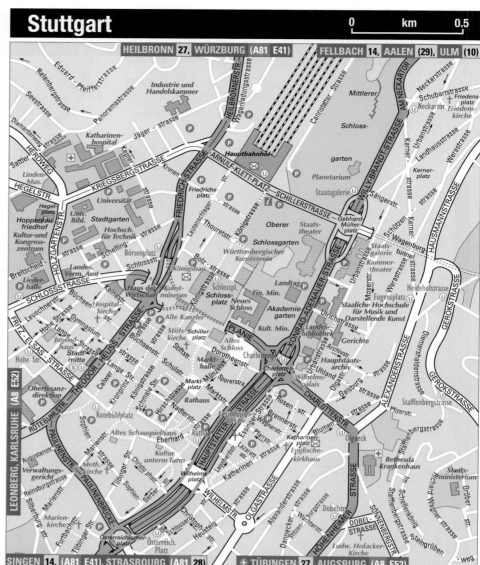

Strasbourg

0 km 5

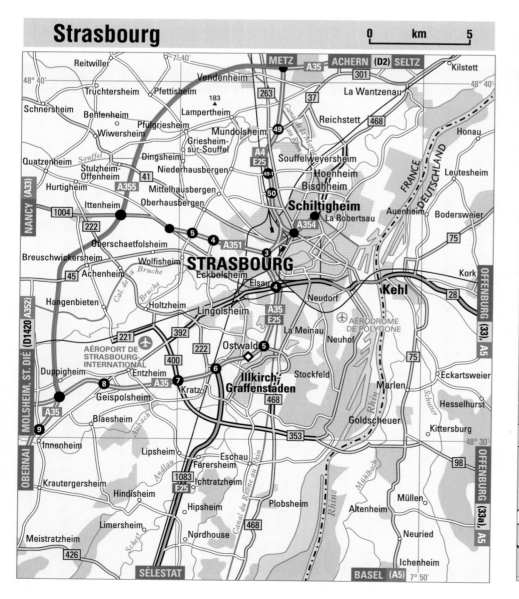

Strasbourg

0 km 0.5

Stockholm

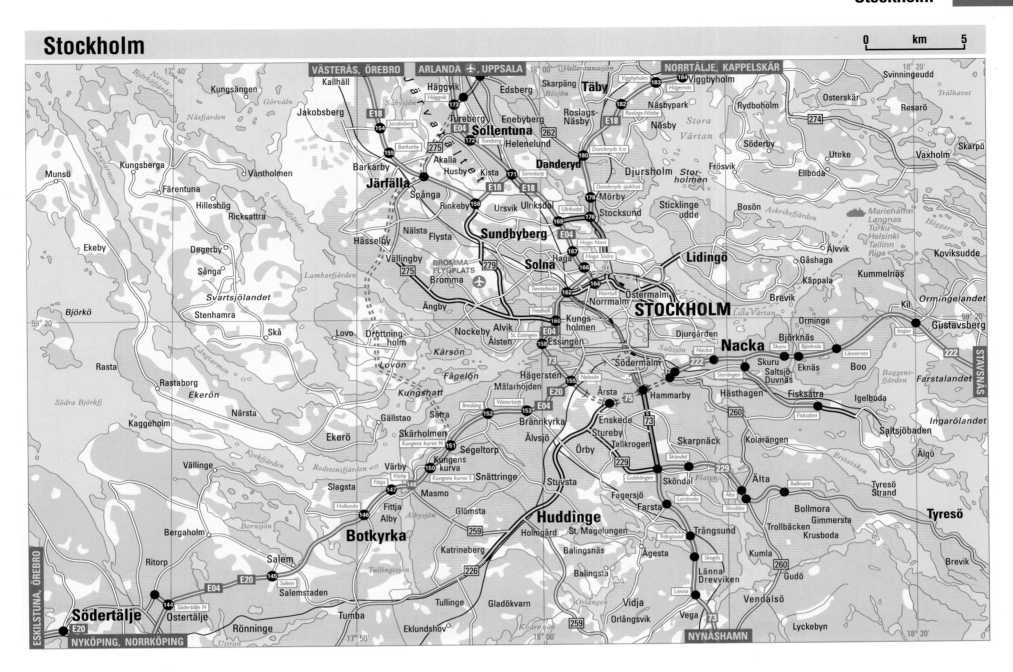

Stockholm

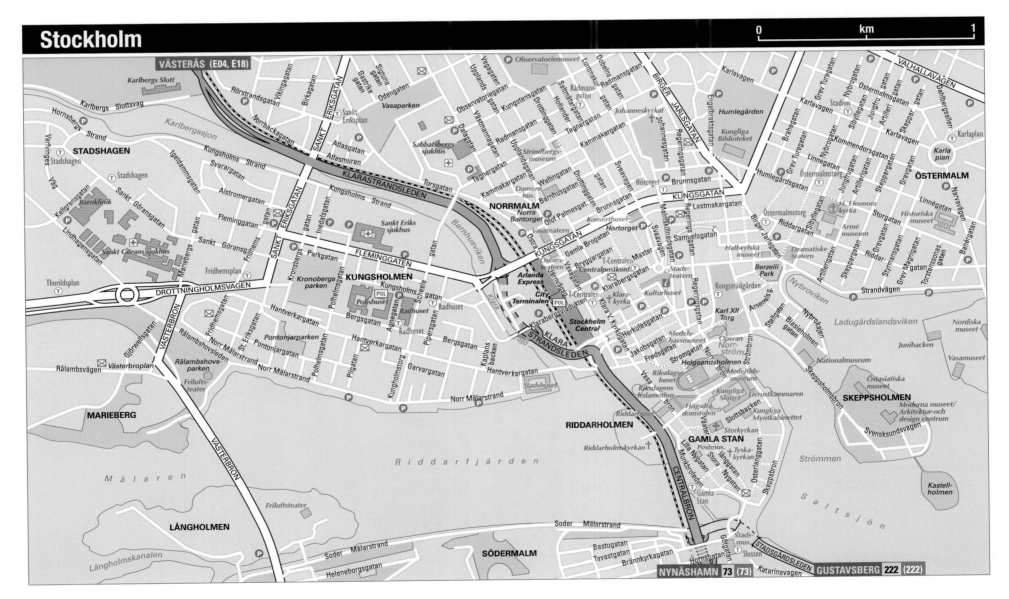

Torino Turin

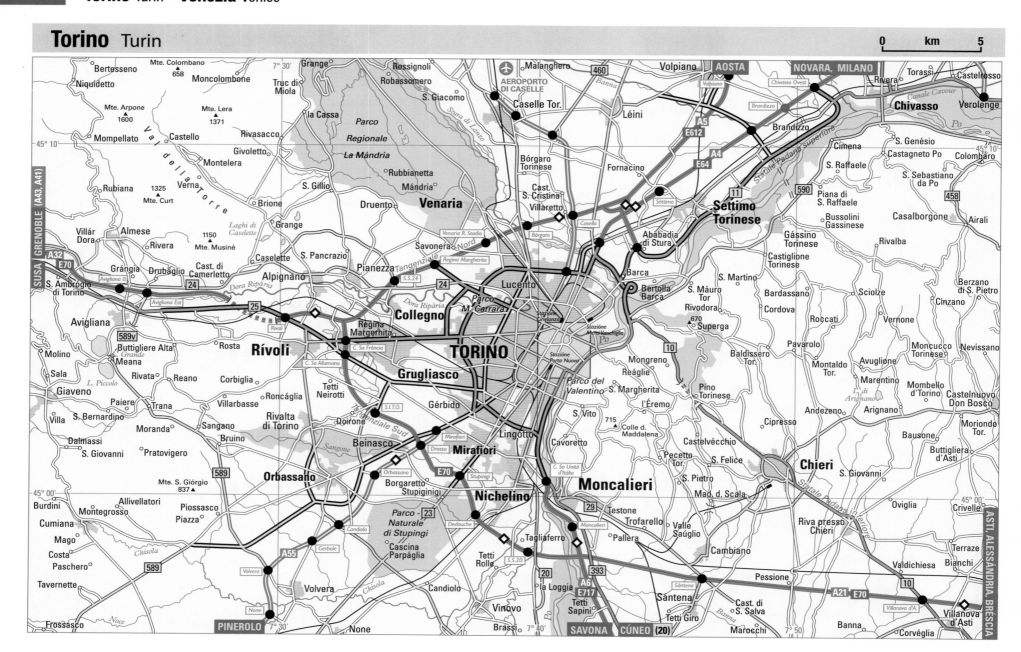

Venézia Venice

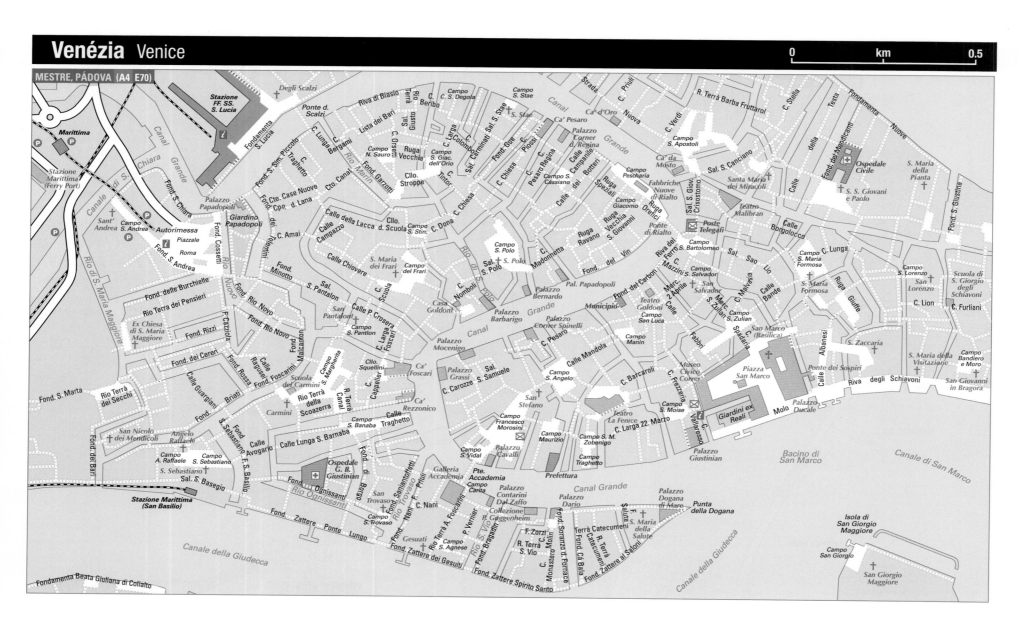

Torino Turin

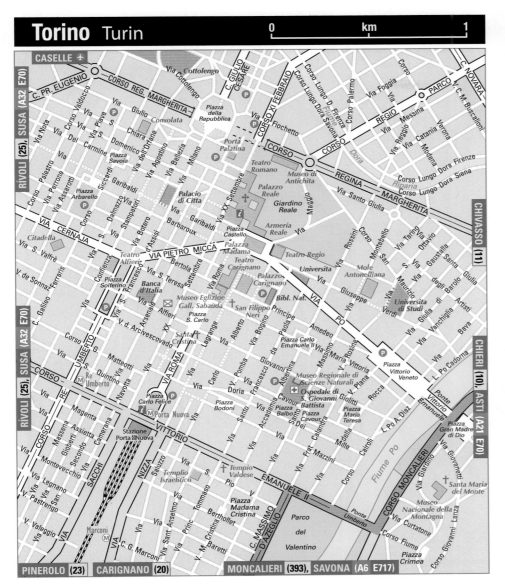

Wien Vienna

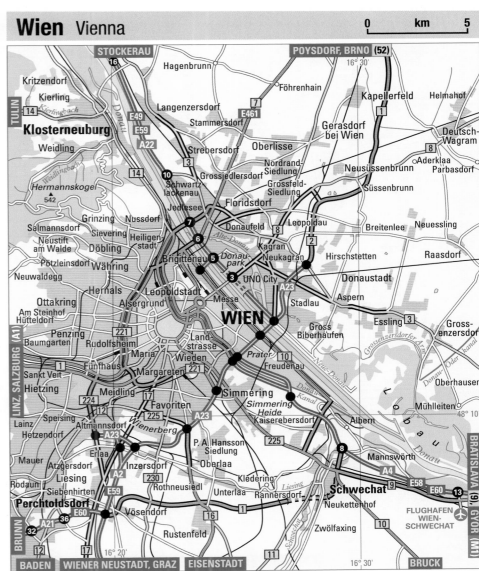

Warszawa Warsaw

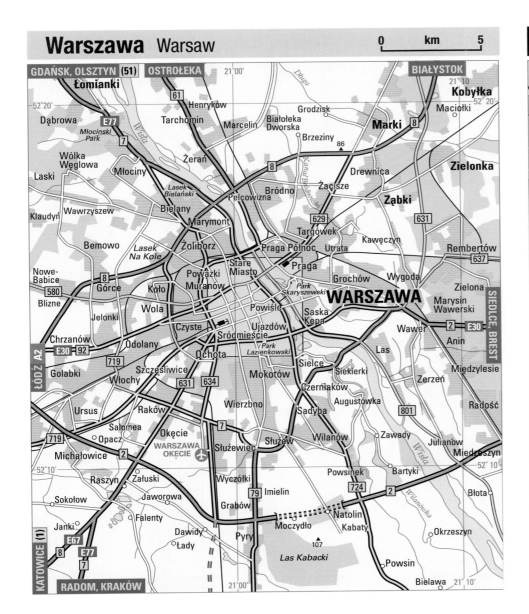

Warszawa Warsaw

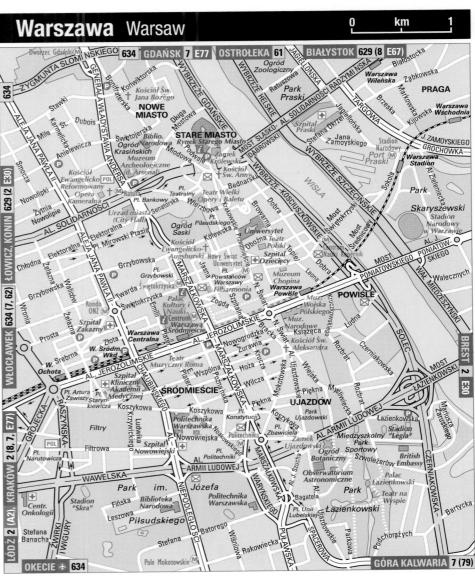

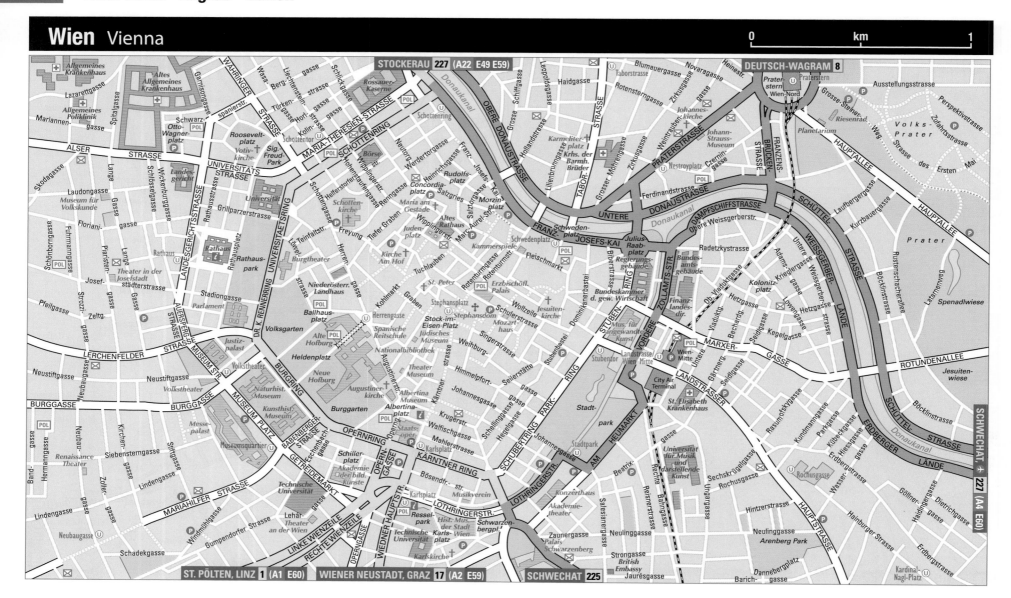

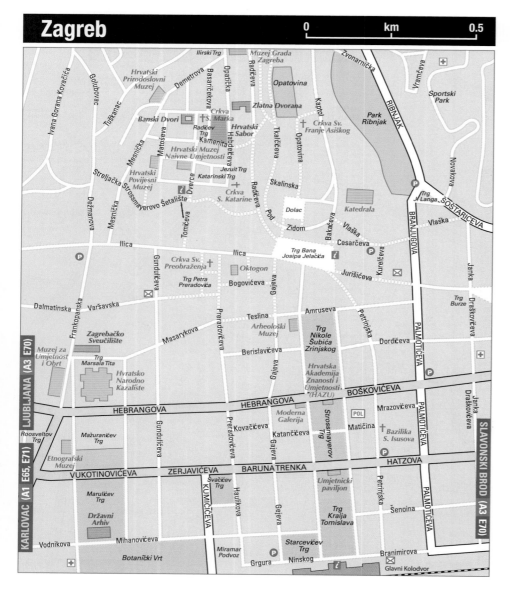

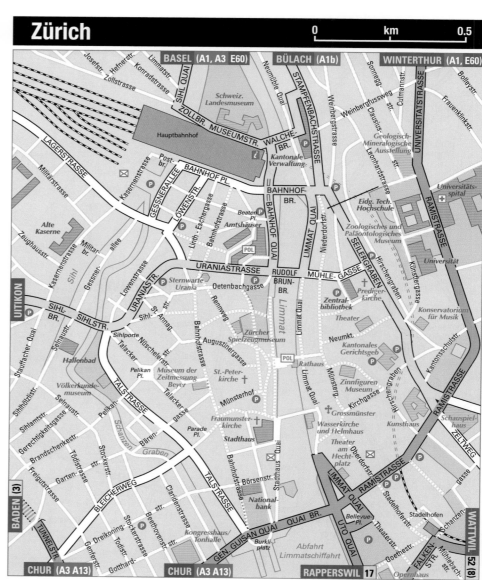

	English	French	German	Italian
(A)	Austria	Autriche	Österreich	Austria
(AL)	Albania	Albanie	Albanien	Albania
(AND)	Andorra	Andorre	Andorra	Andorra
(B)	Belgium	Belgique	Belgien	Belgio
(BG)	Bulgaria	Bulgarie	Bulgarien	Bulgaria
(BIH)	Bosnia-Herzegovin	Bosnia-Herzegovine	Bosnien-Herzegowina	Bosnia-Herzogovina
(BY)	Belarus	Belarus	Weissrussland	Bielorussia
(CH)	Switzerland	Suisse	Schweiz	Svizzera
(CY)	Cyprus	Chypre	Zypern	Cipro
(CZ)	Czechia	République Tchèque	Tschechische Republik	Repubblica Ceca
(D)	Germany	Allemagne	Deutschland	Germania
(DK)	Denmark	Danemark	Dänemark	Danimarca
(E)	Spain	Espagne	Spanien	Spagna
(EST)	Estonia	Estonie	Estland	Estonia
(F)	France	France	Frankreich	Francia
(FIN)	Finland	Finlande	Finnland	Finlandia
(FL)	Liechtenstein	Liechtenstein	Liechtenstein	Liechtenstein
(FO)	Faeroe Islands	Îles Féroé	Färöer-Inseln	Isole Faroe
(GBZ)	Gibraltar	Gibraltar	Gibraltar	Gibilterra
(GR)	Greece	Grèce	Griechenland	Grecia
(H)	Hungary	Hongrie	Ungarn	Ungheria
(HR)	Croatia	Croatie	Kroatien	Croazia
(I)	Italy	Italie	Italien	Italia
(IRL)	Ireland	Irlande	Irland	Irlanda
(IS)	Iceland	Islande	Island	Islanda
(KOS)	Kosovo	Kosovo	Kosovo	Kosovo
(L)	Luxembourg	Luxembourg	Luxemburg	Lussemburgo
(LT)	Lithuania	Lituanie	Litauen	Lituania
(LV)	Latvia	Lettonie	Lettland	Lettonia
(M)	Malta	Malte	Malta	Malta
(MC)	Monaco	Monaco	Monaco	Monaco
(MD)	Moldova	Moldavie	Moldawien	Moldavia
(MNE)	Montenegro	Monténégro	Montenegro	Montenegro
(N)	Norway	Norvège	Norwegen	Norvegia
(NL)	Netherlands	Pays-Bas	Niederlande	Paesi Bassi
(NMK)	North Macedonia	Macédoine du Nord	Nordmakedonien	Macedonia del Nord
(P)	Portugal	Portugal	Portugal	Portogallo
(PL)	Poland	Pologne	Polen	Polonia
(RO)	Romania	Roumanie	Rumanien	Romania
(RSM)	San Marino	Saint-Marin	San Marino	San Marino
(RUS)	Russia	Russie	Russland	Russia
(S)	Sweden	Suède	Schweden	Svezia
(SK)	Slovakia	République Slovaque	Slowak Republik	Repubblica Slovacca
(SLO)	Slovenia	Slovénie	Slowenien	Slovenia
(SRB)	Serbia	Serbie	Serbien	Serbia
(TR)	Turkey	Turquie	Türkei	Turchia
(UA)	Ukraine	Ukraine	Ukraine	Ucraina
(UK)	United Kingdom	Royaume Uni	Grossbritannien und Nordirland	Regno Unito

A

Aab – And

Aabenraa DK 39 D2
Aabybro DK 38 B2
Aach D 71 A4
Aachen D 50 C2
Aalborg DK 38 B2
Aalen D 61 B6
Aalestrup DK 38 C2
Aalsmeer NL 49 A5
Aalst B 49 C6
Aalter B 49 B4
Äänekoski FIN 3 E26
Aapajärvi FIN 113 E16
Agapınar TR 118 C5
Aarau CH 70 A3
Aarberg CH 70 A2
Aarburg CH 70 A2
Aardenburg NL 49 B4
Aarhus DK 39 C3
Aars DK 38 C2
Aarschot B 49 C5
Aarup DK 39 D3
Aba H 74 A3
Abádanes E 95 B4
Abades E 94 B2
Abadín E 86 A3
Abádszalók H 75 A5
Abaliget H 74 B3
Abana TR 16 A7
A Baña E 86 B2
Abanilla E 101 A4
Abano Terme I 72 C1
Abarán E 101 A4
Abasár H 65 C6
Abbadia San Salvatore I 81 D5
Abbasanta I 110 B1
Abbehausen D 43 B5
Abbekäs S 41 D3
Abbeville F 48 C2
Abbey IRL 20 A3
Abbeydorney IRL 20 B2
Abbeyfeale IRL 20 B2
Abbeyleix IRL 21 B4
Abbey Town UK 25 D4
Abbiategrasso I 70 C3
Abborrträsk S 115 B16
Abbots Bromley UK 27 C4
Abbotsbury UK 29 C5
Abda H 64 C3
Abejar E 89 C4
Abela P 98 B2
Abelvær N 114 C8
Abenberg D 62 A1
Abenójar E 100 A1
Abensberg D 62 B2
Aberaeron UK 28 A3
Abercarn UK 29 B4
Aberchirder UK 23 D6
Aberdare UK 29 B4
Aberdaron UK 26 C1
Aberdeen UK 23 D6
Aberdulais UK 28 B4
Aberdyfi UK 26 C1
Aberfeldy UK 25 B4
Aberffraw UK 26 B1
Aberfoyle UK 24 B3
Abergavenny UK 29 B4
Abergele UK 26 B2
Abergynolwyn UK 26 C2
Aberporth UK 28 A3
Abersoch UK 26 C1
Abertillery UK 29 B4
Abertura E 93 B5
Aberystwyth UK 28 A3
Abetone I 81 B4
Abfaltersbach A 72 B2
Abide
  Çanakkale TR 118 B1
  Kütahya TR 118 D4
Abiego E 90 A2
Abild DK 39 E1
Abingdon-on-Thames UK 31 C2
Abington UK 25 C4
Abisko S 112 D7
Abiul P 92 B2
Abla E 101 B3
Ablis F 58 B2
Abondance F 70 B1
Abony H 75 A5
Aboyne UK 23 D6
Abrantes P 92 B2
Abreiro P 87 C3
Abreschviller F 60 B3
Abrest F 68 B3
Abriès F 79 B5
Abrud RO 11 C7
Absdorf A 64 B1
Abtenau A 72 A3
Abtsgmünd D 61 B5
Abusejo E 93 A4
Åby
  Kronoberg S 40 B4
  Östergötland S 37 D3
Åbyggeby S 36 B4
Åbytorp S 37 C2
A Cañiza E 87 B2
A Capela E 86 A2
Acate I 109 B3
Accadía I 103 B8
Accéglio I 79 B5
Accettura I 104 C2
Acciaroli I 106 A2
Accous F 76 D2
Accrington UK 26 B3
Accúmoli I 82 D2
Acedera E 93 B5
Acehúche E 93 B4
Acered E 95 A5
Acerenza I 104 C1
Acerno I 103 C8
Acerra I 103 C7
Aceuchal E 93 C4
Acharacle UK 24 B2
Acharnes GR 117 D5
Achavanich UK 23 C5
Achene B 49 C6
Achenkirch A 72 A1
Achensee A 72 A1
Achenthal A 72 A1
Achentrias GR 117 H7
Achern D 61 B4
Acheux-en-Amienois F 48 C3
Achiltibuie UK 22 C3
Achim D 43 B6
Achladokambos GR 117 E4
Achnasheen UK 22 D3
Achnashellach UK 22 D3
Achosnich UK 24 B1
Aci Castello I 109 B4
Aci Catena I 109 B4
Acilia I 102 B5
Acıpayam TR 119 E4
Acireale I 109 B4
Acle UK 30 B5
A Coruña E 86 A2
Acqua Doria I 102 B1
Acquacadda I 110 C1
Acquanegra sul Chiese I 71 C5
Acquapendente I 81 D5
Acquasanta Terme I 82 D2
Acquasparta I 102 A5
Acquaviva I 81 C5
Acquaviva delle Fonti I 104 C2
Acquaviva Picena I 82 D2
Acquigny F 58 A2
Acqui Terme I 80 B2
Acri I 106 B3
Acsa H 65 C5
Ácsteszér H 74 A2
Acy-en-Multien F 59 A3
Adak S 115 B15
Ådalsbruk N 34 B3
Adamas GR 117 F6
Adamsfjord N 113 B15
Adamuz E 100 A1
Adana TR 16 C7
Ádánd H 74 B3
Adanero E 94 B2
Adare IRL 20 B3
Adaševci SRB 85 A4
Adeanueva de Ebro E 89 B5
Adelboden CH 70 B2
Adelebsen D 51 B5
Adélfia I 104 B2
Adelmannsfelden D 61 B6
Adelsheim D 61 A5
Adelsö S 37 C4
Ademuz E 96 A1
Adenau D 50 C2
Adendorf D 44 B2
Adenkerke B 48 B3
Adjud RO 11 C9
Adliswil CH 70 A3
Admont A 63 C5
Adneram N 33 C3
Adolfsström S 115 A13
Adony H 74 A3
Adorf
  Hessen D 51 B4
  Sachsen D 52 C2
Adra E 100 C2
Adradas E 89 C4
Adrall E 91 A4
Adrano I 109 B3
Adria I 72 C2
Adrigole IRL 20 C2
Adwick le Street UK 27 B4
Adzaneta E 96 A2
Aesch CH 70 A2
A Estrada E 86 B2
Afandou GR 119 F3
Åfarnes N 114 E4
Affing D 62 B1
Affoltern CH 70 A3
Affric Lodge UK 22 D3
Åfjord N 114 D7
Aflenz Kurort A 73 A5
A Fonsagrada E 86 A3
Afragóla I 103 C7
Afritz A 72 B3
Agazzano I 80 B3
Agde F 78 C2
Agdenes N 114 D6
Ager E 90 B3
Agerbæk DK 39 D1
Agerskov DK 39 D2
Ageyevo RUS 7 D14
Agger DK 38 C1
Aggersund DK 38 B2
Aggius I 110 B2
Aggsbach Dorf A 63 B6
Aggsbach Markt A 63 B6
Aghalee UK 19 B5
Aghia GR 116 C4
Aghia Anna GR 116 D5
Aghia Galini GR 117 G6
Aghia Marina GR 119 G1
Aghia Paraskevi GR 118 C1
Aghia Pelagia GR 117 F4
Aghia Triada GR 117 E3
Aghiokambos GR 116 C4
Aghios Efstratios GR 116 C6
Aghios Kirikos GR 119 E1
Aghios Mathaios GR 116 C1
Aghios Mironas GR 117 G7
Aghios Nikolaos GR 117 G7
Aghios Petros GR 116 D2
Aghio Theodori GR 117 E5
Agići BIH 83 B5
Agira I 109 B3
Aglientu I 110 A2
Agnières F 79 B4
Agno CH 70 C3
Agnone I 103 B7
Agolada E 86 B2
Agon Coutainville F 57 A4
Agordo I 72 B2
Agost E 96 C2
Agramón E 101 A4
Agramunt E 91 B4
Agreda E 89 C5
Agria GR 116 C4
Agrigento I 108 B2
Agrinio GR 116 D3
Agrón E 100 B2
Agrópoli I 103 C7
Aguadulce
  Almería E 101 C3
  Sevilla E 100 B1
Agualada E 86 A2
Agua Longa P 87 C2
A Guarda E 87 C2
Aguarón E 89 C5
Aguas E 90 A2
Aguas Belas P 92 B2
Aguas de Busot E 96 C2
Aguas de Moura P 92 C2
Aguas Frias P 87 C3
Aguas Santas P 87 C2
Aguaviva E 90 C2
Aguaviva de la Vega E 89 C4
Agudo E 100 A1
Águeda P 92 A2
Aguessac F 78 B2
Agugliano I 82 C2
Aguiar P 92 C3
Aguiar da Beira P 87 D3
Aguilafuente E 94 A2
Aguilar de Campóo E 88 B2
Aguilar de la Frontera E 100 B1
Aguilas E 101 B4
Agunnaryd S 40 C4
Ahat TR 118 D4
Ahaus D 50 A2
Åheim N 114 E2
Ahigal E 93 A4
Ahigal de Villarino E 87 C4
Ahillones E 99 A5
Ahlbeck D 45 B6
Ahlen D 50 B3
Ahlhorn D 43 C5
Ahmetbey TR 118 A2
Ahmetler TR 119 D4
Ahmetli TR 119 D2
Ahoghill UK 19 B5
Ahrensbök D 44 A2
Ahrensburg D 44 B2
Ahrenshoop D 44 A4
Ahun F 68 B2
Åhus S 41 D4
Ahvenselkä FIN 113 F17
Aibar E 89 B5
Aich D 62 B3
Aicha D 63 B4
Aichach D 62 B2
Aidone I 109 B3
Aiello Cálabro I 106 B3
Aigen im Mühlkreis A 63 B4
Aigle CH 70 B1
Aignan F 76 C3
Aignay-le-Duc F 59 C5
Aigre F 67 C5
Aigrefeuille-d'Aunis F 66 B4
Aigrefeuille-sur-Maine F 66 A3
Aiguablava E 91 B6
Aiguebelle F 69 C6
Aigueperse F 68 B3
Aigues-Mortes F 78 C3
Aigues-Vives F 78 C1
Aiguilhe F 78 A2
Aiguillon F 77 B3
Aigurande F 68 B1
Ailefroide F 79 B5
Aillant-sur-Tholon F 59 C4
Ailly-sur-Noye F 58 A3
Ailly-sur-Somme F 58 A3
Aimargues F 78 C3
Aime F 69 C6
Ainaži LV 6 C8
Ainet A 72 B2
Ainhoa F 76 C1
Ainsa E 90 A3
Airaines F 48 D2
Aird Asaig Tairbeart UK 22 D2
Airdrie UK 25 C4
Aire-sur-l'Adour F 76 C2
Aire-sur-la-Lys F 48 C3
Airole I 80 C1
Airolo CH 70 B3
Airvault F 67 B4
Aisey-sur-Seine F 59 C5
Aïssey F 69 A6
Aisy-sur-Armançon F 59 C5
Aiterhofen D 62 B3
Aith
  Orkney UK 23 B6
  Shetland UK 22 A7
Aitona E 90 B3
Aitrach D 61 C6
Aiud RO 11 C7
Aix-en-Othe F 59 B4
Aix-en-Provence F 79 C4
Aix-les-Bains F 69 C5
Aizenay F 66 B3
Aizkraukle LV 7 C8
Aizpute LV 6 C6
Ajac F 77 C5
Ajaccio F 102 B1
Ajain F 68 B1
Ajaureforsen S 115 B12
Ajdovščina SLO 72 C3
Ajka H 74 A2
Ajo E 89 A3
Ajofrin E 94 C3
Ajuda P 93 C3
Akanthou CY 120 A2
Akarca TR 118 D4
Akasztó H 75 B4
Akçakoca TR 118 A6
Akçay TR 119 F4
Aken D 52 B2
Åkerby S 36 B4
Åkernes N 33 C4
Åkersberga S 37 C5
Åkers Styckebruk S 37 C4
Åkervik N 115 B10
Akhisar TR 118 D2
Åkirkeby DK 41 D4
Akköy TR 119 E2
Akkrum NL 42 B2
Akören TR 119 F7
Akra N 33 C3
Akranes IS 111 C3
Akrehamn N 33 C2
Akrotiri CY 120 B1
Aksaray TR 16 B7
Akşehir TR 119 D6
Akseki TR 119 E6
Aksla N 33 D3
Aksu TR 119 F5
Aktsyabrski BY 7 E10
Akureyri IS 111 B7
Åkvåg N 33 D6
Akyazı TR 118 B5
Al I 32 B5
Ala I 71 C6
Alaca TR 16 A7
Alacant = Alicante E 96 C2
Alaçam TR 16 A7
Alaçatı TR 119 D1
Aladağ TR 16 C7
Alaejos E 88 C1
Alaior E 97 B4
Alájar E 99 B4
Alakurtti RUS 3 C29
Alakylä FIN 113 E13
Alameda E 100 B1
Alameda de la Sagra E 94 B3
Alamedilla E 100 B2
Alamillo E 100 A1
Alaminos E 95 B4
Ala-Nampa FIN 113 F15
Alanäs S 115 C12
Alandroal P 92 C3
Älandsbro S 115 E14
Alange E 93 C4
Alaniemi FIN 3 D26
Alanís E 99 A5
Alanno I 103 A6
Alanya TR 16 C6
Alap H 74 B3
Alaquàs E 96 B2
Alar del Rey E 88 B2
Alaraz E 94 B1
Alarcón E 95 C4
Alaró E 97 B2
Alatoz E 96 B1
Alatri I 103 B6
Alavus FIN 3 E25
Alba
  E 95 B5
  I 80 B2
Alba Adriática I 82 D2
Albacete E 95 D5
Albaching D 62 B3
Alba de Tormes E 94 B1
Alba de Yeltes E 93 A4
Alba-Iulia RO 11 C7
Albal E 96 B2
Albaladejo E 101 A3
Albala del Caudillo E 93 B4
Albalat E 96 B2
Albalate de Cinca E 90 B3
Albalate del Arzobispo E 90 C2
Albalate de las Nogueras E 95 B4
Albalate de Zorita E 95 B4
Albánchez E 101 B3
Albanchez de Ubeda E 100 B2
Albano Laziale I 102 B5
Albanyà E 91 A5
Albaredo d'Adige I 71 C6
Albares E 95 B3
Albarracín E 95 B5
Albatana E 101 A4
Albatarrec E 90 B3
Albatera E 101 A5
Albbruck D 61 C4
Albedin E 100 B1
Albelda de Iregua E 89 B4
Albenga I 80 B2
Albens F 69 C5
Alberga
  Södermanland S 37 C3
  Södermanland S 37 D3
Albergaria-a-Nova P 87 D2
Albergaria-a-Velha P 92 A2
Albergaria dos Doze P 92 B2
Alberge P 92 C2
Alberic E 96 B2
Albernoa P 98 B3
Alberobello I 104 C3
Alberoni I 72 C2
Albersdorf D 43 A6
Albersloh D 50 B3
Albert F 48 D3
Albertirsa H 75 A4
Albertville F 69 C6
Alberuela de Tubo E 90 B2
Albi F 77 B5
Albidona I 106 B3
Albínia I 81 D5
Albino I 71 C4
Albinshof D 45 B5
Albires E 88 B1
Albisola Marina I 80 B2
Albocácer E 90 C3
Albolote E 100 B2
Albondón E 100 C2
Alborea E 96 B1
Alborge E 90 B2
Albox E 101 B3
Albrechtice nad Vltavou CZ 63 A5
Albstadt D 61 B5
Albufeira P 98 B2
Albuñol E 100 C2
Albuñuelas E 100 C2
Alburquerque E 92 B3
Alby
  Öland S 41 C6
  Västernorrland S 115 E12
Alcácer do Sal P 92 C2
Alcáçovas P 92 C2
Alcadozo E 101 A4
Alcafoces P 92 B3
Alcains P 92 B3
Alcalá de Guadaira E 99 B5
Alcalá de Gurrea E 90 A2
Alcalá de Henares E 95 B3
Alcalá de la Selva E 90 C2
Alcalá del Júcar E 96 B1
Alcaládei Sardi I 70 C2
Alcalá del Río E 99 B5
Alcalá del Valle E 99 C5
Alcalá de Xivert E 90 C3
Alcalá la Real E 100 B2
Alcamo I 108 B1
Alcampell E 90 B3
Alcanadre E 89 B4
Alcanar E 90 C3
Alcanede P 92 B2
Alcanena P 92 B2
Alcañices E 87 C4
Alcántara E 93 B4
Alcantarilha P 98 B2
Alcantarilla E 101 A4
Alcañiz E 90 C2
Alcaracejos E 100 A1
Alcara il Fusi I 109 A3
Alcaraz E 101 A3
Alcaria Ruiva P 98 B3
Alcarraz E 90 B3
Alcaudete E 100 B1
Alcaudete de la Jara E 94 C2
Alcázar de San Juan E 95 C3
Alcazarén E 88 C2
Alceda E 88 A2
Alcester UK 29 A6
Alcoba E 94 C2
Alcobaça P 92 B1
Alcobendas E 94 B3
Alcocer E 95 B4
Alcoceber E 90 C3
Alcochete P 92 C1
Alcoentre P 92 B1
Alcoholel UK 24 B2
Alcolea
  Almería E 100 C3
  Córdoba E 100 B1
Alcolea de Calatrava E 94 D2
Alcolea de Cinca E 90 B3
Alcolea del Pinar E 95 B4
Alcolea del Rio E 99 B5
Alconchel E 93 C3
Alconera E 93 C4
Alcontar E 101 B3
Alcora E 96 A2
Alcorcón E 94 B3
Alcorisa E 90 C2
Alcossebre E 90 C3
Alcoutim P 98 B3
Alcover E 91 B4
Alcoy E 96 C2
Alcsútdoboz H 74 A3
Alcubierre E 90 B2
Alcubilla de Avellaneda E 89 C3
Alcubilla de Nogales E 88 B1
Alcublas E 96 B2
Alcúdia E 97 B3
Alcudia de Guadix E 100 B2
Alcuéscar E 93 B4
Aldbrough UK 27 B5
Aldeacentenera E 93 B5
Aldeadávila de la Ribera E 87 C4
Aldea del Cano E 93 B4
Aldea del Obispo E 87 D4
Aldea del Rey E 100 A2
Aldea de Trujillo E 93 B5
Aldealcorvo E 94 A3
Aldealuenga de Santa María E 89 C3
Aldeamayor de San Martín E 88 C2
Aldeanueva de Barbarroya E 94 C1
Aldeanueva del Camino E 93 A5
Aldeanueva del Codonal E 94 A2
Aldeanueva de San Bartolomé E 94 C1
Aldeapozo E 89 C4
Aldeaquemada E 100 A2
Aldea Real E 94 A2
Aldeavieja E 94 B2
Aldekerk D 50 B2
Aldeburgh UK 30 B5
Aldeia da Serra P 92 C3
Aldeia do Bispo P 93 A4
Aldeia do Mato P 92 B2
Aldeia Gavinha P 92 B1
Aldeonte E 89 C3
Aldersbach D 62 B4
Aldershot UK 31 C3
Aldudes F 76 C1
Aled S 40 C3
Aledo E 101 B4
Alegria E 89 B4
Aleksa Šantić SRB 75 C4
Aleksandrovac SRB 85 C6
Aleksandrów Kujawski PL 47 C4
Aleksandrów Łódzki PL 55 B4
Ålem S 40 C6
Alençon F 57 B6
Alenquer P 92 B1
Alenya F 91 A5
Aléria F 102 A2
Alès F 78 B3
Alessándria I 80 B2
Alessándria della Rocca I 108 B2
Alessano I 105 C4
Ålesund N 114 E3
Aletshausen D 61 B6
Alet-les-Bains F 77 D5
Alexandria
  GR 116 B4
  RO 11 E8
  UK 24 C3
Alexandroupoli GR 116 B7
Aleyrac F 78 B3
Alézio I 105 C4
Alfacar E 100 B2
Alfaiates P 93 A4
Alfajarín E 90 B2
Alfambra
  E 95 A5
  P 98 B2
Alfândega da Fé P 87 C4
Alfarim P 92 C1
Alfarnate E 100 C1
Alfaro E 89 B5
Alfarrás E 90 B3
Alfaz del Pi E 96 C2
Alfedena I 103 B7
Alfeizarão P 92 B1
Alfeld
  Bayern D 62 A2
  Niedersachsen D 51 B5
Alfena P 87 C2
Alferce P 98 B2
Alfhausen D 43 C4
Alfonsine I 81 B6
Alford
  Aberdeenshire UK 23 D6
  Lincolnshire UK 27 B6
Alforja E 90 B3
Alfoz E 86 A3
Algaida E 97 B2
Algar E 99 C5
Älgarås S 35 D6
Ålgård N 33 D2
Algarinejo E 100 B1
Algarrobo E 100 C1
Algatocin E 99 C5
Algeciras E 99 C5
Algemesí E 96 B2
Algés P 92 C1
Algete E 95 B3
Alghero I 110 B1
Alghult S 40 B5
Alginet E 96 B2
Algodonales E 99 C5
Algodor E 94 C3
Algora E 95 B4
Algoso P 87 C4
Algoz P 98 B2
Algutsrum S 41 C6
Algyő H 75 B5
Alhama de Almería E 101 C3
Alhama de Aragón E 89 C5
Alhama de Granada E 100 C2
Alhama de Murcia E 101 B4
Alhambra E 100 A2
Alhandra P 92 C1
Alhaurin de la Torre E 100 C1
Alhaurín el Grande E 100 C1
Alhóndiga E 95 B4
Ali I 109 B4
Ália I 108 B2
Aliaga E 90 C2
Aliağa TR 118 D1
Aliano I 106 A3
Alíartos GR 116 D4
Alibunar SRB 85 A5
Alicante = Alacant E 96 C2
Alicún de Ortega E 100 B2
Alife I 103 B7
Alija del Infantado E 88 B1
Alijó P 87 C3
Alimena I 109 B3
Alingsås S 40 B2
Aliseda E 93 B4
Aliveri GR 116 D6
Alixan F 79 B4
Aljaraque E 99 B3
Aljezur P 98 B2
Aljorra E 101 B4
Aljubarrota P 92 B2
Aljucén E 93 B4
Aljustrel P 98 B2
Alken B 49 C6
Alkmaar NL 42 C1
Allaines F 58 B2
Allaire F 57 C3
Allanche F 68 C2
Alland A 64 B2
Allariz E 87 B3
Allassac F 67 C6
Alleen N 33 D4
Alleghe I 72 B2
Allemont F 69 C6
Allendale Town UK 25 D5
Allendorf D 51 C4
Allentsteig A 63 B6
Allepuz E 90 C2
Aller E 88 A1
Allersberg D 62 A2
Allershausen D 62 B2
Alles E 88 A2
Allevard F 69 C6
Allex F 79 B4
Allgunnen S 40 B5
Allinge DK 41 C5
Alloa UK 25 B4
Allogny F 68 A2
Alloluokta S 112 E8
Allones
  Eure-et-Loire F 58 B2
  Maine-et-Loire F 67 A5
Allonnes F 57 C6
Allons F 76 B2
Allos F 79 B5
Alloza E 90 C2
Allstedt D 52 B1
Alltwalis UK 28 B3
Allumiere I 102 A4
Almaceda P 92 B3
Almacelles E 90 B3
Almáchar E 100 C1
Almada P 92 C1
Almadén E 100 A1
Almadén de la Plata E 99 B4
Almadenejos E 100 A1
Almadrones E 95 B4
Almagro E 100 A2
Almajano E 89 C4
Almansa E 96 C1
Almansil P 98 B2
Almanza E 88 B1
Almaraz E 93 B5
Almargen E 99 C5
Almarza E 89 C4
Almásfüzitő H 65 C4
Almassora E 96 B2
Almazán E 89 C4
Almazul E 89 C4
Almeida
  E 87 C4
  P 93 A4
Almeirim P 92 B2
Almelo NL 42 C3
Almenar E 90 B3
Almenar de Soria E 89 C4
Almendra P 87 D3
Almendral E 93 C4
Almendral de la Cañada E 94 B2
Almendralejo E 93 C4
Almendros E 95 C4
Almenno San Bartolomeo I 71 C4
Almere NL 42 C2
Almería E 101 C3
Almese I 70 C2
Almexial P 98 B3
Almhult S 40 C4
Almiropotamos GR 116 D6
Almiros GR 116 C4
Almodóvar P 98 B2
Almodóvar del Campo E 100 A1
Almodóvar del Pinar E 95 C5
Almodóvar del Río E 99 B5
Almofala P 87 D3
Almogía E 100 C1
Almoharín E 93 B4
Almonacid de la Sierra E 90 B1
Almonacid de Toledo E 94 C3
Almonaster la Real E 99 B4
Almonte E 99 B4
Almoradí E 96 C2
Almoraima E 99 C5
Almoster P 92 B2
Almsele S 115 C14
Almudena E 101 A4
Almudévar E 90 A2
Almuñécar E 100 C2
Almunge S 36 C5
Almuradiel E 100 A2
Almussafes E 96 B2
Almvik S 40 B6
Alnwick UK 25 C6
Åloppe S 36 C4
Álora E 100 C1
Alosno E 99 B3
Alozaina E 100 C1
Alpbach A 72 A1
Alpedrete de la Sierra E 95 B3
Alpedrinha P 92 A3
Alpen D 50 B2
Alpera E 96 C1
Alphen aan de Rijn NL 49 A5
Alpiarça P 92 B2
Alpignano I 70 C2
Alpirsbach D 61 B4
Alpu TR 118 C5
Alpuente E 96 B1
Alpullu TR 118 A2
Alqueva P 98 A3
Alquézar E 90 A3
Als DK 38 C3
Alsasua E 89 B4
Alsdorf D 50 C2
Alselv DK 39 D1
Alsfeld D 51 C5
Alsike S 36 C4
Alskog S 37 E5
Alsleben D 52 B1
Alsónémedi H 75 A4
Alsótold H 65 C5
Alsóújlak H 74 A1
Alstad N 112 E4
Alstätte D 50 A2
Alsterbro S 40 C5
Alstermo S 40 C5
Alston UK 25 D5
Alsvåg N 112 D4
Alsvik N 112 E3
Alta N 113 C12
Altamura I 104 C2
Altarejos E 95 C4
Altaussee A 63 C4
Altavilla Irpina I 103 B7
Altavilla Silentina I 103 C8
Altdöbern D 53 B4
Altdorf
  CH 70 B3
  D 62 B3
Altdorf bei Nürnberg D 62 A2
Alt Duvenstedt D 43 A6
Alte P 98 B2
Altea E 96 C2
Altedo I 81 B5
Alteidet N 113 B11
Altena D 50 B3
Altenau D 51 B6
Altenberg D 53 C3
Altenberge D 50 A3
Altenburg D 52 C2
Altenfelden A 63 B4
Altengronau D 51 C5
Altenheim D 60 B3
Altenhundem D 50 B4
Altenkirchen
  Mecklenburg-Vorpommern D 45 A5
  Radom D 50 C3
Altenkunstadt D 52 C1
Altenmarkt
  A 63 C5
  D 62 B3
Altenmarkt im Pongau A 72 A3
Altensteig D 61 B4
Altentreptow D 45 B5
Altenwalde D 43 B5
Alten-weddingen D 52 A1
Alter do Chão P 92 B3
Altfraunhofen D 62 B3
Altheim
  A 63 B4
  D 61 B5
Althofen A 73 B4
Altınoluk TR 118 C1
Altınova TR 118 C1
Altıntaş TR 118 C5
Altkirch F 60 C3
Altlandsberg D 45 C5
Altlengbach A 64 B1
Altmannstein D 62 B2
Altmorschen D 51 B5
Altmünster A 63 C4
Altnaharra UK 23 C4
Alto Campóo E 88 A2
Altofonte I 108 A2
Altomonte I 106 B3
Alton
  Hampshire UK 31 C3
  Staffordshire UK 27 C4
Altopáscio I 81 C4
Altötting D 62 B3
Altreichenau D 63 B4
Alt Ruppin D 45 C4
Altshausen D 61 C5
Altstätten CH 71 A4
Altura E 96 B2
Altusried D 61 C6
Alūksne LV 7 C9
Alunda S 36 B5
Alustante E 95 B5
Alvaiázere P 92 B2
Alvalade P 98 B2
Älvängen S 38 B5
Alvarenga P 87 D2
Alvares P 92 A2
Alvdal N 114 E7
Alverca P 92 C1
Alversund N 32 B2
Alvesta S 40 C4
Alvignac F 77 B4
Alvignano I 103 B7
Alvik N 32 B3
Alvik S 36 B1
Alvimare F 58 A1
Alviobeira P 92 B2
Alvito P 98 A3
Älvkarleby S 36 B4
Älvkarleö bruk S 36 B4
Alvor P 98 B2
Alvorge P 92 B2
Alvros S 115 F10
Alvsbacka S 35 C5
Älvsbyn S 3 D24
Älvsered S 40 B2
Amélia I 102 A5
Amélie-les-Bains-Palalda F 91 A5
Amelinghausen D 44 B2
Amendoa P 92 B2
Amendoeira P 98 B3
Améndola I 104 B1
Amendolara I 106 B3
Amer E 91 A5
A Merca E 87 B3
Amerongen NL 49 A6
Amersfoort NL 49 A6
Amersham UK 31 C3
Amesbury UK 29 B6
Amfiklia GR 116 D4
Amfilochia GR 116 D3
Amfipoli GR 116 B5
Amfissa GR 116 D4
Amièira P 98 A3
Amieiro P 92 A2
Amiens F 58 A3
Amindeo GR 116 B3
Åminne FIN 3 E25
Åmli N 33 D5
Amlwch UK 26 B1
Ammanford UK 28 B4
Ammarnäs S 115 B13
Ämmeberg S 37 D1
Amorbach D 61 A5
Amorebieta E 89 A4
Amorgos GR 117 F7
Amorosi I 103 B7
Åmot
  Buskerud N 34 C1
  Telemark N 33 C4
  S 36 B3
Åmotfors S 35 C4
Åmotsdal N 33 C5
Amou F 76 C2
Ampezzo I 72 B2
Ampfing D 62 B3
Amplepuis F 69 C4
Ampilly F 30 B3
Amposta E 90 C3
Ampudia E 88 C2
Ampuero E 89 A3
Amriswil CH 71 A4
Amsele S 115 C16
Amsterdam NL 42 C1
Amstetten A 63 B5
Amulree UK 25 B4
Amurrio E 89 A4
Anacapri I 103 C7
Anadia P 92 A2
Anadon E 90 C1
Anafi GR 117 F7
Anagni I 102 B6
Anamur TR 16 C6
Ananyiv UA 11 C10
Anascaul IRL 20 B1
Ånäset S 3 D24
Ana-Sira N 33 D3
Anaya de Alba E 94 B1
Anca P 92 A2
Ancaster UK 27 C5
Ancede P 87 C2
Ancenis F 66 A3
Ancerville F 59 B6
Ancona I 82 C2
Ancrum UK 25 C5
Ancy-le-Franc F 59 C5
Åndalsnes N 114 E4
Andau A 64 C3
Andebu N 35 C2
Andelfingen CH 70 A3
Andelot-Blancheville F 59 B6
Andelot-en-Montagne F 69 B5
Andenes N 112 C5
Andenne B 49 C6
Anderlues B 49 C5
Andermatt CH 70 B3
Andernach D 50 C3
Andernos-les-Bains F 76 B1
Anderslöv S 41 D3
Anderstorp S 40 B3
Andijk NL 42 C2
Andoain E 89 A4
Andocs H 74 B2
Andorra E 90 C2
Andorra La Vella AND 91 A4
Andosilla E 89 B5
Andover UK 31 C2
Andratx E 97 B2
Andreapol RUS 7 C11
Andreas UK 26 A1
Andréspol PL 55 B4
Andretta I 103 C8
Andrijevica MNE 85 D4
Andritsena GR 117 E3

Andros GR 117 E6
Andrychów PL 65 A5
Andselv N 112 C7
Andújar E 100 A1
Anduze F 78 B2
Åneby N 34 B2
Aneby S 40 B4
Añes E 89 A3
Anet F 58 B2
Anfo I 71 C5
Ang S 40 B4
Anga S 37 E5
Angaïs F 76 C2
Ånge S 115 D11
Ånge S 115 E12
Angeja P 92 A2
Ängelholm S 41 C2
Angeli FIN 113 D14
Ängelsberg S 36 C3
Anger A 73 A5
Angera I 70 C3
Angermünde D 45 B6
Angern A 64 B2
Angers F 67 A4
Angerville F 58 B3
Anghiari I 82 C1
Angle UK 28 B2
Anglès E 91 B5
Anglés F 77 C5
Angles F 66 B3
Anglesola E 91 B4
Angles sur l'Anglin F 67 B5
Anglet F 76 C1
Anglisidhes CY 120 B2
Anglure F 59 B4
Angoulême F 67 C5
Angoulins F 66 B3
Angsö S 37 C3
Angueira P 87 C4
Angües E 90 A2
Anguiano E 89 B4
Anguillara Sabazia I 102 A5
Anguillara Véneta I 72 C1
Anhée B 49 C5
Anholt DK 38 C4
Aniane F 78 C2
Aniche F 49 C4
Ånimskog S 35 D4
Anina RO 10 D6
Anixi GR 116 C3
Anizy-le-Château F 59 A4
Anjalankoski FIN 3 F27
Anjan S 115 D9
Ankara TR 118 C7
Ankaran SLO 72 C3
Ankarsrum S 40 B6
Ankerlia N 112 C9
Anklam D 45 B5
Ankum D 43 C4
Anlauftal A 72 A3
Anlezy F 68 B3
Ånn S 115 D9
Annaberg A 63 C6
Annaberg-Buchholz
D 52 C3
Annaberg im
Lammertal A 72 A3
Annaburg D 52 B3
Annahütte D 53 B3
Annalong UK 19 B6
Annan UK 25 D4
Anndalsvågen N 115 B9
Anneberg
Halland S 38 B5
Jönköping S 40 B4
Annecy F 69 C6
Annelund S 40 B3
Annemasse F 69 B6
Annenskiy Most RUS 7 A14
Annerstad S 40 C3
Annestown IRL 21 B4
Annevoie-Rouillon B 49 C5
Annonay F 69 C4
Annot F 79 C5
Annweiler D 60 A3
Ano Poroia GR 116 A5
Añora E 100 A1
Ano Siros GR 117 E6
Anould F 60 B2
Anquela del Ducado
E 95 B4
Anröchte D 51 B4
Ans DK 39 C2
Ansager DK 39 D1
Ansbach D 62 A1
Anse F 69 C4
Anseroeul B 49 C4
Ansfelden A 63 B5
Ansião P 92 B2
Ansó E 76 D2
Ansoain E 76 D1
Anstruther UK 25 B5
Antalya TR 119 F5
Antas E 101 B4
Antegnate I 71 C4
Antequera E 100 B1
Anterselva di Mezzo I 72 B2
Antibes F 79 C6
Antigüedad E 88 C2
Antillo I 109 B4
Antirio GR 117 D3
An t-Ob UK 22 D1
Antoing B 49 C4
Antonin PL 54 B2
Antrain F 57 B4
Antrim UK 19 B5
Antrodoco I 102 A6
Antronapiana I 70 B3
Anttis S 113 E11
Antuzede P 92 A2
Antwerp = Antwerpen
B 49 B5
Antwerpen = Antwerp
B 49 B5
Anversa d'Abruzzi I 103 B6
Anvin F 48 C3
Anzat-le-Luguet F 68 C3
Anzi I 104 C1
Ánzio I 102 B5
Anzola d'Emilia I 81 B5
Anzón E 89 C5
Aoiz E 76 D1
Aosta I 70 C2
Apalhão P 92 B3
Apátfalva H 75 B5
Apatin SRB 75 C4
Apatity RUS 3 C30
Apc H 65 C5
Apécchio I 82 C1
Apeldoorn NL 50 A1
Apen D 43 B4
Apenburg D 44 C3
Apensen D 43 B6
A Peroxa E 86 B3
Apiro I 82 C2
Apliki CY 120 B2
Apolda D 52 B1
Apolonia GR 117 F6
A Pontenova E 86 A3
Apostag H 75 B3
Äppelbo S 34 B6
Appennino I 82 D2
Appenzell CH 71 A4
Appiano I 71 B6
Appingedam NL 42 B3
Appleby-in-
Westmorland UK 26 A3
Applecross UK 22 D3
Appledore UK 28 B3
Appoigny F 59 C4
Apremont-la-Forêt F 60 B1
Aprica I 71 B5
Apricena I 103 B8
Aprigliano I 106 B3
Aprília I 102 B5
Apt F 79 C4
Apúlia P 87 C2
Aquiléia I 72 C3
Aquilónia I 103 C8
Aquino I 103 B6
Ar S 37 E5
Arabayona E 94 A1
Arabba I 72 B1
Araç TR 16 A6
Aracena E 99 B4
Arachova GR 116 D4
Arad RO 75 B6
Aradac SRB 75 C5
Aradhippou CY 120 B2
Aragnouet F 76 D3
Aragona I 108 B2
Arahal E 99 B5
Aramits F 76 C2
Aramon F 78 C3
Aranda de Duero E 88 C3
Aranda de Moncayo E 89 C5
Arandjelovac SRB 85 B5
Aranjuez E 95 B3
Arantzazu E 89 B4
Aranzueque E 95 B3
Aras de Alpuente E 96 B1
Arauzo de Miel E 89 C3
Arazede P 92 A2
Arbas F 77 D3
Árbatax I 110 C2
Arbeca E 90 B3
Arberg D 62 A1
Arbesbach A 63 B5
Arboga S 37 C2
Arbois F 69 B5
Arbon CH 71 A4
Arboréa I 110 C1
Arbório I 70 C3
Årbostad N 112 D6
Arbrå S 36 A3
Arbroath UK 25 B5
Arbùcies E 91 B5
Arbuniel E 100 B2
Arbus I 110 C1
Arcachon F 76 B1
Arce I 103 B6
Arcen NL 50 B2
Arc-en-Barrois F 59 C5
Arces-Dilo F 59 B4
Arc-et-Senans F 69 A5
Arcévia I 82 C1
Arcey F 70 A1
Archanes GR 117 G7
Archangelos GR 119 F3
Archena E 101 A4
Archez E 100 C2
Archiac F 67 C4
Archidona E 100 B1
Archiestown UK 23 D5
Archivel E 101 A4
Arcidosso I 81 D5
Arcille I 81 D5
Arcis-sur-Aube F 59 B5
Arc-lès-Gray F 69 A5
Arco I 71 C5
Arcones E 94 A3
Arcos E 88 B3
Arcos de Jalón E 95 A4
Arcos de la Frontera E 99 C5
Arcos de la Sierra E 95 B4
Arcos de las Salinas E 96 B1
Arcos de Valdevez P 87 C2
Arcozelo P 92 A3
Arc-sur-Tille F 69 A5
Arcusa E 90 A3
Arcy-sur-Cure F 59 C4
Ardagh IRL 20 B2
Årdal N 33 C3
Ardala S 35 D5
Ardales E 100 C1
Årdalstangen N 32 A4
Ardara
I 110 B1
IRL 18 B3
Ardarroch UK 22 D3
Ardbeg UK 24 C1
Ardcharnich UK 22 D3
Ardchyle UK 24 B3
Ardee IRL 19 C5
Arden DK 38 C2
Ardentes F 68 B1
Ardenza I 81 C4
Ardersier UK 23 D4
Ardes F 68 C3
Ardessie UK 22 D3
Ardez CH 71 B5
Ardfert IRL 20 B2
Ardgay UK 23 D4
Ardglass UK 19 B6
Ardgroom IRL 20 C2
Ardhasig UK 22 D2
Ardino BG 116 A7
Ardisa E 90 A2
Ardkearagh IRL 20 C1
Ardlui UK 24 B3
Ardlussa UK 24 B2
Ardón E 88 B1
Ardooie B 49 C4
Ardore I 106 C3
Ardrahan IRL 20 A3
Ardre S 37 E5
Ardres F 48 C2
Ardrishaig UK 24 B2
Ardrossan UK 24 C3
Are N 33 C2
Åre S 115 D10
Areia Branca P 92 B1
Aremark N 35 C3
Arenales de San
Gregorio E 95 C3
Arenas E 100 C1
Arenas de Iguña E 88 A2
Arenas del Rey E 100 C2
Arenas de San Juan E 95 C3
Arenas de San Pedro
E 94 B1
Arendal N 33 D5
Arendonk B 49 B6
Arengosse F 76 B2
Arentorp S 35 D4
Arenys de Mar E 91 B5
Arenys de Munt E 91 B5
Arenzano I 80 B2
Areo E 91 A4
Areopoli GR 117 F4
Ares E 86 A2
Arès F 76 B1
Ares del Maestrat E 90 C2
Aresvika N 114 D5
Arette F 76 C2
Aretxabaleta E 89 A4
Arevalillo E 93 A5
Arévalo E 94 A2
Arez P 92 B3
Arezzo I 81 C5
Arfeuilles F 68 B3
Argalasti GR 116 C5
Argallón E 99 A5
Argamasilla de Alba
E 95 C3
Argamasilla de
Calatrava E 100 A1
Arganda E 95 B3
Arganil P 92 A2
Argasion GR 117 E2
Argegno I 71 C4
Argelès-Gazost F 76 C2
Argelès-sur-Mer F 91 A6
Argenta I 81 B5
Argentan F 57 B5
Argentat F 77 A4
Argentera I 79 B5
Argenteuil F 58 B3
Argenthal D 50 D3
Argentiera I 110 B1
Argentona E 91 B5
Argenton-Château F 67 B4
Argenton-
sur-Creuse F 67 B6
Argentré F 57 B5
Argentré-du-Plessis F 57 B4
Argent-sur-Sauldre F 68 A2
Argirades GR 116 C1
Argıthanı TR 119 D6
Argos GR 117 E4
Argos Orestiko GR 116 B3
Argostoli GR 117 D2
Argote E 89 B4
Arguedas E 89 B5
Argueil F 58 A2
Arholma S 36 C6
Ariano Irpino I 103 B8
Ariano nel Polésine I 82 B1
Aribe E 76 D1
Aridea GR 116 B4
Arienzo I 103 B7
Arild S 41 C2
Arileod UK 24 B1
Arilje SRB 85 C5
Arinagour UK 24 B1
Ariño E 90 B2
Arinthod F 69 B5
Arisaig UK 24 B2
Arisgotas E 94 C3
Aritzo I 110 C2
Ariza E 89 C4
Årjäng S 35 C4
Arjeplog S 115 A14
Arjona E 100 B1
Arjonilla E 100 B1
Arkasa GR 119 G2
Arkelstorp S 41 C4
Arklow IRL 21 B5
Arkösund S 37 D3
Ärla S 37 C3
Arlanc F 68 C3
Arlanzón E 89 B3
Arlebosc F 78 A3
Arlena di Castro I 102 A4
Arles F 78 C3
Arles-sur-Tech F 91 A5
Arló H 65 B6
Arlon B 60 A1
Armação de Pera P 98 B2
Armadale
Highland UK 22 D3
West Lothian UK 25 C4
Armagh UK 19 B5
Armamar P 87 C3
Armenistis GR 117 E8
Armeno I 70 C3
Armenteros E 93 A5
Armentières F 48 C3
Armilla E 100 B2
Armiñón E 89 B4
Armoy UK 19 A5
Armuña de Tajuña E 95 B3
Armutlu
Bursa TR 118 B3
İzmir TR 119 D2
Arnac-Pompadour F 67 C6
Arnafjord N 32 A3
Arnage F 57 C6
Arnas F 69 B4
Årnäs S 35 D5
Arnay-le-Duc F 69 A4
Arnborg DK 39 C2
Arnbruck D 62 A3
Arnea GR 116 B5
Arneberg
Hedmark N 34 A2
Hedmark N 34 B4
Arneburg D 44 C4
Arnedillo E 89 B4
Arnedo E 89 B4
Arneguy F 76 C1
Arnés E 90 C3
Árnes IS 111 A4
Årnes
Akershus N 34 B3
Troms N 112 C7
Arnfels A 73 B5
Arnhem NL 50 B1
Arnissa GR 116 B3
Arno S 37 D4
Arnold UK 27 B4
Arnoldstein A 72 B3
Arnsberg D 50 B4
Arnschwang D 62 A3
Arnsdorf D 53 B3
Årnset N 114 D6
Arnside UK 26 A3
Arnstadt D 51 C6
Arnstein D 51 D5
Arnstorf D 62 B3
Arnum DK 39 D1
Aroche E 99 B4
Arolla CH 70 B2
Arolsen D 51 B5
Arona I 70 C3
Äros N 35 C2
Arosa
CH 71 B4
P 87 C2
Ærøskøbing DK 39 E3
Arøsund DK 39 D2
Arouca P 87 D2
Årøysund N 35 C2
Arpajon F 58 B3
Arpajon-sur-Cère F 77 B5
Arpino I 103 B6
Arquata del Tronto I 82 D2
Arques F 48 C3
Arques-la-Bataille F 58 A2
Arquillos E 100 A2
Arraia-Maeztu E 89 B4
Arraiolos P 92 C2
Arrancourt F 60 B2
Arras F 48 C3
Arrasate E 89 A4
Årre DK 39 D1
Arreau F 77 D3
Arredondo E 89 A3
Arrens-Marsous F 76 D2
Arriate E 99 C5
Arrifana P 98 B2
Arrigorriaga E 89 A4
Arriondas E 88 A1
Arroba de
los Montes E 94 C2
Arrochar UK 24 B3
Arromanches-
les-Bains F 57 A5
Arronches P 92 B3
Arroniz E 89 B4
Arrou F 58 B2
Arroya E 88 B2
Arroya de Cuéllar E 88 C2
Arroyal E 88 B2
Arroyo de la Luz E 93 B4
Arroyo del Ojanco E 100 A3
Arroyo de San Servan
E 93 C4
Arroyomolinos
de León E 99 A4
Arroyomolinos de
Montánchez E 93 B4
Arruda dos Vinhos P 92 C1
Arsac F 76 B2
Ars-en-Ré F 66 B3
Arsiè I 72 C1
Arsiero I 71 C6
Årslev DK 39 D3
Ársoli I 102 A6
Ars-sur-Moselle F 60 A2
Årsunda S 36 B3
Artà E 97 B3
Arta GR 116 C3
Artajona E 89 B5
Artegna I 72 B3
Arteixo E 86 A2
Artemare F 69 C5
Arten I 72 B1
Artena I 102 B5
Artenay F 58 B2
Artern D 52 B1
Artés E 91 B4
Artesa de Segre E 91 B4
Arth CH 70 A3
Arthez-de-Béarn F 76 C2
Arthon-en-Retz F 66 A3
Arthurstown IRL 21 B5
Artieda E 90 A2
Artix F 76 C2
Artotina GR 116 D4
Artsyz UA 11 C10
Artziniega E 89 A3
A Rúa E 87 B3
Arudy F 76 C2
Arundel UK 31 D3
Arveyres F 76 B2
Arvidsjaur S 115 B16
Arvieux F 79 B5
Arvika S 35 C4
Åryd
Blekinge S 41 C5
Kronoberg S 40 C4
Arzachena I 110 A2
Arzacq-Arraziguet F 76 C2
Árzana I 110 C2
Arzano F 56 C2
Aržano HR 84 C1
Arzberg D 52 C2
Arzignano I 71 C6
Arzila P 92 A2
Arzl im Pitztal A 71 A5
Arzúa E 86 B2
As B 49 B6
Aš CZ 52 C2
Ås N 35 C2
Åsa S 40 B2
Asaa DK 38 B3
Aşağıçiğil TR 119 D6
Ašanja SRB 85 B5
Åsarna S 115 E11
Åsarøy N 33 C3
Åsarp S 40 A3
Asasp F 76 C2
Åsbro S 37 C2
Åsby S 40 B2
Asby S 40 B5
Asbygri IS 111 A9
Ascain F 76 C1
Ascea I 106 A2
Ascha D 62 A3
Aschach an
der Donau A 63 B5
Aschaffenburg D 51 D5
Aschbach Markt A 63 B5
Ascheberg
Nordrhein-Westfalen
D 50 B3
Schleswig-Holstein D 44 A2
Aschendorf D 43 B4
Aschersleben D 52 B1
Asciano I 81 C5
Ascó E 90 B3
Asco F 102 A2
Áscoli Piceno I 82 D2
Áscoli Satriano I 104 B1
Ascona CH 70 B3
Ascot UK 31 C3
Ascoux F 58 B3
Åse N 112 C4
Åseda S 40 B5
Åsele S 115 C14
Åsen
N 114 D8
S 34 A5
Asendorf D 43 C6
Asenovgrad BG 11 E8
Åsensbruk S 35 D4
Åseral N 33 D4
Asfeld F 59 A5
Åsgårdstrand N 35 C2
Ásgarður IS 111 B1
Asgate CY 120 B2
Ash
Kent UK 31 C5
Surrey UK 31 C3
Åshammar S 36 B3
Ashbourne
IRL 21 A5
UK 27 B4
Ashburton UK 28 C4
Ashby-de-la-Zouch
UK 27 C4
Ashchurch UK 29 B5
Åsheim N 114 F8
Ashford UK 31 C4
Ashington UK 25 C6
Ashley UK 26 C3
Ashmyany BY 7 D8
Ashton-under-Lyne
UK 26 B3
Ashwell UK 30 B3
Asiago I 71 C6
Asipovichy BY 7 E10
Aska FIN 113 E15
Askam-in-Furness UK 26 A2
Askeaton IRL 20 B3
Asker N 34 C2
Askersund S 37 D1
Åskilje S 115 C14
Askim N 35 C3
Askland N 33 D5
Äsköping S 37 C3
Askvoll N 32 A2
Åsljunga S 41 C3
Asnæs DK 39 D4
As Neves E 87 B2
As Nogaís E 86 B3
Ásola I 71 C5
Asolo I 72 C1
Asos GR 116 D2
Asotthalom H 75 B4
Aspach A 63 B4
Aspang Markt A 64 C2
Aspariegos E 88 C1
Asparn an der Zaya A 64 B2
Aspatria UK 26 A2
Aspberg S 35 C5
Aspe E 101 A5
Aspet F 77 C3
Äspö S 41 C5
As Pontes de García
Rodríguez E 86 A3
Aspres-sur-Buëch F 79 B4
Aspsele S 115 D15
Assafora P 92 C1
Asse B 49 C5
Assebakte N 113 C14
Assel D 43 B6
Asselborn L 50 C1
Asséminì I 110 C1
Assen NL 42 C3
Assenede B 49 B4
Assens
Aarhus Amt. DK 38 C3
Fyns Amt. DK 39 D2
Assesse B 49 C6
Assisi I 82 C1
Åsskard N 114 D5
Assling D 62 C3
Asso I 71 C4
Asson F 76 C2
Ássoro I 109 B3
Assumar P 92 B3
Åsta N 34 A3
Astaffort F 77 B3
Astakos GR 116 D3
Asten NL 50 B1
Asti I 80 B2
Astipalea GR 119 F1
Astorga E 86 B4
Åstorp S 41 C2
Åsträsk S 115 C16
Astudillo E 88 B2
Asuni I 110 C1
Asványráró H 64 C3
Aszód H 65 C5
Aszófö H 74 B2
Atabey TR 119 E5
Atalaia P 92 B3
Atalandi GR 116 D4
Atalho P 92 C2
Átány H 65 C6
Atanzón E 95 B3
Ataquines E 94 A2
Atarfe E 100 B2
Atça TR 119 E3
Ateca E 89 C5
A Teixeira E 87 B3
Atella I 104 C1
Atessa I 103 A7
Ath B 49 C4
Athboy IRL 19 C5
Athea IRL 20 B2
Athenry IRL 20 A3
Athens = Athina GR 117 E5
Atherstone UK 27 C4
Athienou CY 120 A2
Athies F 59 A3
Athies-sous-Laon F 59 A4
Athina = Athens GR 117 E5
Athleague IRL 20 A3
Athlone IRL 21 A4
Athna CY 120 A2
Athy IRL 21 B5
Atienza E 95 A4
Atina I 103 B6
Atkár H 65 C5
Atlantı TR 119 D7
Atna N 114 F7
Åtorp S 35 C6
Atrå N 32 C5
Ätran S 40 B2
Atri I 103 A6
Atripalda I 103 C7
Atsiki GR 116 C7
Attendorn D 50 B3
Attichy F 59 A4
Attigliano I 102 A5
Attigny F 59 A5
Attleborough UK 30 B5
Åtvidaberg S 37 D2
Atzendorf D 52 B1
Au
Steiermark A 63 C6
Vorarlberg A 71 A4
Bayern D 62 B2
Bayern D 62 C2
Aub D 61 A6
Aubagne F 79 C4
Aubange B 60 A1
Aubel B 50 C1
Aubenas F 78 B3
Aubenton F 59 A5
Auberive F 59 C6
Aubeterre-
sur-Dronne F 67 C5
Aubiet F 77 C3
Aubigné F 67 B4
Aubigny F 66 B3
Aubigny-au-Bac F 49 C4
Aubigny-en-Artois F 48 C3
Aubigny-sur-Nère F 68 A2
Aubin F 77 B5
Aubonne CH 69 B6
Aubrac F 78 B1
Aubusson F 68 C2
Auch F 77 C3
Auchencairn UK 25 D4
Auchinleck UK 24 C3
Auchterarder UK 25 B4
Auchtermuchty UK 25 B4
Auchtertyre UK 22 D3
Auchy-au-Bois F 48 C3
Audenge F 76 B1
Auderville F 57 A4
Audierne F 56 B1
Audincourt F 70 A1
Audlem UK 26 C3
Audruicq F 48 C3
Audun-le-Roman F 60 A1
Audun-le-Tiche F 60 A1
Aue
Nordrhein-Westfalen
D 50 B4
Sachsen D 52 C2
Auerbach
Bayern D 62 A2
Sachsen D 52 C2
Auffach A 72 A2
Augher UK 19 B4
Aughnacloy UK 19 B5
Aughrim IRL 21 B5
Augignac F 67 C5
Augsburg D 62 B1
Augusta I 109 B4
Augusten-borg DK 39 E2
Augustfehn D 43 B4
Augustów PL 6 E7
Aukrug D 44 A1
Auktsjaur S 115 B16
Auldearn UK 23 D5
Aulendorf D 61 C5
Auletta I 103 C8
Aulla I 81 B3
Aullène F 102 B2
Aulnay F 67 B4
Aulnoye-Aymeries F 49 C4
Ault F 48 C2
Aultbea UK 22 D3
Aulum DK 39 C1
Aulus-les-Bains F 77 D4
Auma D 52 C1
Aumale F 58 A2
Aumetz F 60 A1
Aumont-Aubrac F 78 B2
Aunay-en-Bazois F 68 A3
Aunay-sur-Odon F 57 A5
Aune N 115 C10
Auneau F 58 B2
Auneuil F 58 A2
Auning DK 39 C3
Aunsetra N 115 C9
Aups F 79 C5
Aura D 51 C5
Auray F 56 C3
Aurdal N 32 B6
Aure N 114 D5
Aurich D 43 B4
Aurignac F 77 C3
Aurillac F 77 B5
Auriol F 79 C4
Auritz-Burguette E 76 D1
Aurlandsvangen N 32 B4
Auronzo di Cadore I 72 B2
Auros F 76 B2
Auroux F 78 B2
Aurskog N 34 C3
Aursmoen N 34 C3
Ausónia I 103 B6
Ausservillgraton A 72 B2
Austad N 33 D4
Austbygda N 32 B5
Aústis I 110 B2
Austmarka N 34 B4
Austre Moland N 33 D5
Austre Vikebygd N 33 C2
Austrheim N 32 B1
Auterive F 77 C4
Autheuil-Authouillet
F 58 A2
Authon F 79 B5
Authon-du-Perche F 58 B1
Autol E 89 B5
Autreville F 60 B1
Autrey-lès-Gray F 69 A5
Autun F 69 B4
Auty-le-Châtel F 58 C3
Auvelais B 49 C5
Auvillar F 77 B3
Auxerre F 59 C4
Auxi-le-Château F 48 C3
Auxon F 59 B4
Auxonne F 69 A5
Auxy F 69 B4
Auzances F 68 B2
Auzon F 68 C3
Ağva TR 118 A4
Availles-Limouzine F 67 B5
Avaldsnes N 33 C2
Avallon F 68 A3
Avantas GR 116 B7
Avaviken S 115 B15
Avebury UK 29 B6
A Veiga E 87 B3
Aveiras de Cima P 92 B2
Aveiro P 92 A2
Avelgem B 49 C4
Avellino I 103 C7
Avenches CH 70 B2
A-Ver-o-Mar P 87 C2
Aversa I 103 C7
Avesnes-le-Comte F 48 C3
Avesnes-sur-Helpe F 49 C4
Avesta S 36 B3
Avetrana I 105 C3
Avezzano I 103 A6
Avià E 91 A4
Aviano I 72 B2
Aviemore UK 23 D5
Avigliana I 80 A1
Avigliano I 104 C1
Avignon F 78 C3
Ávila E 94 B2
Avilés E 88 A1
Avilley F 69 A6
Avintes P 87 C2
Avinyo E 91 B4
Àvio I 71 C5
Avioth F 59 A6
Avis P 92 B3
Avize F 59 B5
Avlonari GR 116 D6
Ávola I 109 C4
Avon F 58 B3
Avonmouth UK 29 B5
Avord F 68 A2
Avranches F 57 B4
Avril F 60 A1
Avrillé F 67 A4
Avtovac BIH 84 C3
Awans B 49 C6
Axams A 71 A6
Axat F 77 D5
Axbridge UK 29 B5
Axel NL 49 B4
Ax-les-Thermes F 77 D4
Axmarby S 36 B4
Axmarsbruk S 36 A4
Axminster UK 29 C4
Axvall S 35 D5
Ay F 59 A5
Aya E 89 A4
Ayamonte E 98 B3
Ayancık TR 16 A7
Ayaş TR 118 B7
Aydın TR 119 E2
Ayelo de Malferit E 96 C2
Ayer CH 70 B2
Ayerbe E 90 A2
Ayette F 48 C3
Ayia Napa CY 120 B2
Áyia Phyla CY 120 B2
Áyios Amvrósios CY 120 A2
Áyios Seryios CY 120 A2
Áyios Theodhoros
CY 120 A3
Aykirikçi TR 118 C5
Aylesbury UK 31 C3
Ayllón E 89 C3
Aylsham UK 30 B5
Ayna E 101 A3
Ayódar E 96 B2
Ayora E 96 B1
Ayr UK 24 C3
Ayrancı TR 16 C6
Ayrancılar TR 119 D2
Ayron F 67 B5
Aysgarth UK 27 A4
Ayton UK 25 C5
Aytos BG 11 E9
Ayvacık TR 118 C1
Ayvalık TR 118 C1
Aywaille B 49 C6
Azaila E 90 B2
Azambuja P 92 B2
Azambujeira P 92 B2
Azanja SRB 85 B5
Azannes-et-
Soumazannes F 60 A1
Azanúy-Alins E 90 B3
Azaruja P 92 C3
Azay-le-Ferron F 67 B6
Azay-le-Rideau F 67 A5
Azcoitia E 89 A4
Azé F 69 B4
Azeiteiros P 92 B3
Azenhas do Mar P 92 C1
Azinhaga P 92 B2
Azinhal P 98 B3
Azinheira dos Bairros
P 98 A2
Aznalcázar E 99 B4
Aznalcóllar E 99 B4
Azóia P 92 B2
Azpeitia E 89 A4
Azuaga E 99 A5
Azuara E 90 B2
Azuqueca de Henares
E 95 B3
Azur F 76 C1
Azzano Décimo I 72 C2

B

Baad A 71 A5
Baamonde E 86 A3
Baar CH 70 A3
Bağarasi TR 119 E2
Baarle-Nassau B 49 B5
Baarn NL 49 A6
Babadağ TR 119 E3
Babadag RO 11 D10
Babaeski TR 118 A2
Babayevo RUS 7 B13
Babenhausen
Bayern D 61 B6
Hessen D 51 D4
Babiak PL 54 A3
Babice PL 55 C4
Babigoszcz PL 45 B6
Babimost PL 53 A5
Babina Greda HR 84 A3
Babócsa H 74 B2
Bábolma H 64 C3
Baborów PL 54 C2
Baboszewo PL 47 C6
Babót H 64 C3
Babruysk BY 7 E10
Babsk PL 55 B5
Bač
MNE 85 D5
SRB 75 C4
Bac UK 22 C2
Bacares E 101 B3
Bacău RO 11 C9
Baccarat F 60 B2
Bacharach D 50 C3
Bačina SRB 85 C6
Backa S 36 B2
Bačka Palanka SRB 75 C4
Backaryd S 41 C5
Bačka Topola SRB 75 C4
Backe S 115 D13
Bäckebo S 40 C6
Bäckefors S 35 D4
Bäckhammar S 35 C6
Bački Breg SRB 75 C3
Bački-Brestovac SRB 75 C4
Bački Monoštor SRB 75 C3
Bački Petrovac SRB 75 C4
Bački Sokolac SRB 75 C4
Backnang D 61 B5
Bačko Gradište SRB 75 C5
Bačko Novo Selo SRB 75 C4
Bačko Petrovo Selo
SRB 75 C5
Bácoli I 103 C7
Bacqueville-
en-Caux F 58 A2
Bácsalmás H 75 B4
Bácsbokod H 75 B4
Bad Abbach D 62 B3
Badacsonytomaj H 74 B2
Bad Aibling D 62 C3
Badajoz E 93 C4
Badalona E 91 B5
Badalucco I 80 C1
Bad Aussee A 63 C4
Bad Bederkesa D 43 B5
Bad Bentheim D 50 A3
Bad Bergzabern D 60 A3
Bad Berka D 52 C1
Bad Berleburg D 51 B4
Bad Berneck D 52 C1
Bad Bevensen D 44 B2
Bad Bibra D 52 B1
Bad Birnbach D 62 B4
Bad Blankenburg D 52 C1
Bad Bleiberg A 72 B3
Bad Brambach D 52 C2
Bad Bramstedt D 44 B1
Bad Breisig D 50 C3
Bad Brückenau D 51 C5
Bad Buchau D 61 B5
Bad Camberg D 50 C4
Badderen N 113 C11
Bad Doberan D 44 A3
Bad Driburg D 51 B5
Bad Düben D 52 B2
Bad Dürkheim D 61 A4
Bad Dürrenberg D 52 B2
Bad Dürrheim D 61 B4
Bad Elster D 52 C2
Bad Ems D 50 C3
Baden
A 64 B2
CH 70 A3
Bádenas E 90 B1
Baden-Baden D 61 B4
Bad Endorf D 62 C3
Badenweiler D 60 C3
Baderna HR 72 C3
Bad Essen D 50 A4
Bad Fischau A 64 C2
Bad Frankenhausen
D 52 B1
Bad Freienwalde D 45 C6
Bad Friedrichshall D 61 A5
Bad Füssing D 63 B4
Bad Gandersheim D 51 B6
Bad Gastein A 72 A3
Bad Gleichenberg A 73 B5
Bad Goisern A 63 C4
Bad Gottleuba D 53 C3
Bad Grund D 51 B6
Bad Hall A 63 B5
Bad Harzburg D 51 B6
Bad Herrenalb D 61 B4
Bad Hersfeld D 51 C5
Bad Hofgastein A 72 A3
Bad Homburg D 51 C4
Bad Honnef D 50 C3
Bad Hönningen D 50 C3
Badia Calavena I 71 C6
Badia Polésine I 81 A5
Badia Pratáglia I 81 C5
Badia Tedalda I 82 C1
Bad Iburg D 50 A4
Bad Innerlaterns A 71 A4
Bad Ischl A 63 C4
Bad Karlshafen D 51 B5
Bad Kemmeriboden
CH 70 B2
Bądki PL 47 B4
Bad Kissingen D 51 C6
Bad Kleinen D 44 B3
Bad Kohlgrub D 62 C2
Bad König D 61 A5
Bad Königshofen D 51 C6
Bad Köstritz D 52 C2
Badkowo PL 47 C4
Bad Kreuzen A 63 B5
Bad Kreuznach D 60 A3
Bad Krozingen D 60 C3
Bad Laasphe D 51 C4
Bad Langensalza D 51 B6
Bad Lauchstädt D 52 B1
Bad Lausick D 52 B2
Bad Lauterberg D 51 B6
Bad Leonfelden A 63 B5
Bad Liebenwerda D 52 B3
Bad Liebenzell D 61 B4
Bad Lippspringe D 51 B4
Badljevina HR 74 C2
Bad Meinberg D 51 B4
Bad Mergentheim D 61 A5
Bad Mitterndorf A 72 A3
Bad Münder D 51 A5
Bad Münstereifel D 50 C2
Bad Muskau D 53 B4
Bad Nauheim D 51 C4
Bad Nenndorf D 43 C6
Bad Neuenahr-
Ahrweiler D 50 C3
Bad Neustadt D 51 C6
Bad Oeynhausen D 51 A4
Badolato I 106 C3
Badolatosa E 100 B1
Bad Oldesloe D 44 B2
Badonviller F 60 B2
Bad Orb D 51 C5
Badovinci SRB 85 B4
Bad Peterstal D 61 B4
Bad Pyrmont D 51 B5
Bad Radkersburg A 73 B5
Bad Ragaz CH 71 B4
Bad Rappenau D 61 A5
Bad Reichenhall D 62 C3
Bad Saarow-
Pieskow D 53 A4
Bad Sachsa D 51 B6
Bad Säckingen D 70 A2
Bad Salzdetfurth D 51 A6
Bad Salzig D 50 C3
Bad Salzuflen D 51 A4
Bad Salzungen D 51 C6
Bad Sankt
Leonhard A 73 B4
Bad Sassendorf D 50 B4
Bad Schandau D 53 C4
Bad Schmiedeberg D 52 B2
Bad Schönborn D 61 A4
Bad Schussenried D 61 B5
Bad Schwalbach D 50 C4
Bad Schwartau D 44 B2
Bad Segeberg D 44 B2
Bad Soden D 51 C4
Bad Soden-
Salmünster D 51 C5
Bad Sooden-
Allendorf D 51 B5
Bad Sulza D 52 B1
Bad Sülze D 45 A4
Bad Tatzmannsdorf A 73 A6
Bad Tennstedt D 51 B6
Bad Tölz D 62 C2
Badules E 90 B1
Bad Urach D 61 B5
Bad Vellach A 73 B4
Bad Vilbel D 51 C4
Bad Vöslau A 64 C2
Bad Waldsee D 61 C5
Bad Wiessee D 62 C2
Bad Wildungen D 51 B5
Bad Wilsnack D 44 C3
Bad Windsheim D 61 A6
Bad Wörishafen D 62 B1
Bad Wurzach D 61 C5
Bad Zwesten D 51 B5
Bad Zwischenahn D 43 B5
Baells E 90 B3
Baena E 100 B1
Baesweiler D 50 C2
Baeza E 100 B2
Baflo NL 42 B3
Bafra TR 16 A7
Baga E 91 A4
Bagaladi I 106 C2
Bagenkop DK 39 E3
Baggetorp S 37 C3
Bagh a Chaisteil UK 22 E1
Bagheria I 108 A2
Bagn N 32 B6
Bagnacavallo I 81 B5
Bagnáia I 102 A5
Bagnara Cálabra I 106 C2
Bagnasco I 80 B2
Bagnères-
de-Bigorre F 76 C3
Bagnères-
de-Luchon F 77 D3
Bagni del Másino I 71 B4
Bagni di Lucca I 81 B4
Bagni di Rabbi I 71 B5
Bagni di Tivoli I 102 B5
Bagno di Romagna I 81 C5
Bagnoles-de-l'Orne F 57 B5
Bagnoli dei Trigno I 103 B7
Bagnoli di Sopra I 72 C1
Bagnoli Irpino I 103 C8
Bagnolo Mella I 71 C5
Bagnols-en-Forêt F 79 C5
Bagnols-sur-Cèze F 78 B3
Bagnorégio I 102 A5
Bagolino I 71 C5
Bagrationovsk RUS 47 A6
Bagrdan SRB 85 B6
Báguena E 95 A5
Bahabón
de Esgueva E 88 C3
Bahillo E 88 B2
Báia delle Zágare I 104 B2
Báia Domizia I 103 B6
Baia Mare RO 11 C7
Baiano I 103 C7
Baião P 87 C2
Baiersbronn D 61 B4
Baiersdorf D 62 A2
Baignes-
Ste Radegonde F 67 C4
Baigneux-les-Juifs F 59 C5
Baildon UK 27 B4
Bailén E 100 A2
Băileşti RO 11 D7
Baileux B 49 C5
Bailieborough IRL 19 C5
Bailleul F 48 C3
Baillonville B 49 C6
Bailó E 90 A2
Bain-de-Bretagne F 57 C4
Bains F 78 A2
Bains-les-Bains F 60 B2
Bainton UK 27 B5
Baio E 86 A2
Baiona E 87 B2
Bais F 57 B5
Baiso I 81 B4
Baiuca P 92 A3
Baja H 75 B3
Bajánsenye H 73 B6
Bajina Bašta SRB 85 C4
Bajmok SRB 75 C4
Bajna H 65 C4
Bajovo Polje MNE 84 C3
Bajram Curri AL 105 A6
Bajša SRB 75 C4
Bajzë AL 105 A5
Bak H 74 B1
Bakar HR 73 C4
Bakewell UK 27 B4
Bakhmach UA 7 F12
Bakio E 89 A4
Bakırdağı TR 16 B7
Bakka N 32 C6
Bakkafjörður IS 111 A11
Bakkagerði IS 111 B12
Bække DK 39 D2
Bakken N 34 B3
Baklan TR 119 E4
Bækmarksbro DK 39 C1
Bakonybél H 74 A2
Bakonycsernye H 74 A3
Bakonyjákó H 74 A2
Bakonyszentkirály H 74 A2
Bakonyszombathely
H 74 A2
Bakov nad Jizerou CZ 53 C4
Bąkowiec PL 55 B6
Baks H 75 B5
Baksa H 74 C3
Bakum D 43 C5
Bâlâ TR 16 B6
Bala UK 26 C2
Balaguer E 90 B3
Balassagyarmat H 65 B5
Balástya H 75 B5
Balatonakali H 74 B2
Balatonalmádi H 74 A3
Balatonboglár H 74 B2
Balatonbozsok H 74 B3
Balatonederics H 74 B2
Balatonfenyves H 74 B2
Balatonföldvár H 74 B2
Balatonfüred H 74 B2
Balatonfüzfö H 74 A3
Balatonkenese H 74 A3
Balatonkiliti H 74 B3
Balatonlelle H 74 B2
Balatonszabadi H 74 B3
Balatonszemes H 74 B2
Balatonszentgyörgy
H 74 B2
Balazote E 101 A3
Balbeggie UK 25 B4
Balbigny F 69 C4
Balboa E 86 B4
Balbriggan IRL 19 C5
Balchik BG 11 E10
Balçova TR 119 D2
Baldock UK 31 C3
Bale HR 82 A2
Baleira E 86 A3
Baleizao P 98 A3
Balen B 49 B6
Balerma E 100 C3
Balestrand N 32 A3
Balestrate I 108 A2
Balfour UK 23 B6
Bälganet S 41 C5
Balgari BG 11 E9
Balıkesir TR 118 C2
Balıklıçeşme TR 118 B2
Bälinge S 36 C4
Balingen D 61 B4
Balingsta S 36 C4
Balintore UK 23 D5
Balizac F 76 B2
Baljevac SRB 85 C5
Balk NL 42 C2
Balkbrug NL 42 C3
Balla IRL 18 C2
Ballachulish UK 24 B2
Ballaghaderreen IRL 18 C3
Ballancourt-
sur-Essonne F 58 B3
Ballantrae UK 24 C3
Ballao I 110 C2
Ballasalla UK 26 A1
Ballater UK 23 D5
Ballen DK 39 D3
Ballenstedt D 52 B1
Ballerias E 90 B2
Balleroy F 57 A5
Ballerup DK 41 D2
Ballesteros
de Calatrava E 100 A2
Ballı TR 118 B2
Ballina IRL 18 B2
Ballinalack IRL 19 C4
Ballinamore IRL 19 B4
Ballinascarty IRL 20 C3
Ballinasloe IRL 20 A3
Ballindine IRL 18 C3
Balling DK 38 C1
Ballingarry
Limerick IRL 20 B3
Tipperary IRL 21 B4
Ballingeary IRL 20 C2
Ballinhassig IRL 20 C3
Ballinluig UK 25 B4
Ballino I 71 C5
Ballinrobe IRL 18 C2
Ballinskelligs IRL 20 C1
Ballinspittle IRL 20 C3
Ballintra IRL 18 B3
Ballivor IRL 21 A5
Ballobar E 90 B3
Ballon
F 58 B1
IRL 21 B5
Ballószög H 75 B4
Ballsh AL 105 C5
Ballstad N 112 D2
Ballum DK 39 D1
Ballybay IRL 19 B5
Ballybofey IRL 19 B4
Ballybunion IRL 20 B2
Ballycanew IRL 21 B5
Ballycarry UK 19 B6
Ballycastle
IRL 18 B2
UK 19 A5
Ballyclare UK 19 B6
Ballyconneely IRL 18 C1
Ballycotton IRL 20 C3
Ballycroy IRL 18 B2
Ballydehob IRL 20 C2
Ballyferriter IRL 20 B1
Ballygawley UK 19 B4
Ballygowan UK 19 B6
Ballyhaunis IRL 18 C3
Ballyheige IRL 20 B2
Ballyjamesduff IRL 19 C4
Ballylanders IRL 20 B3
Ballylynan IRL 21 B4
Ballymahon IRL 21 A4
Ballymena UK 19 B5
Ballymoe IRL 18 C3
Ballymoney UK 19 A5
Ballymore IRL 21 A4
Ballymote IRL 18 B3
Ballynacorra IRL 20 C3
Ballynagore IRL 21 A4
Ballynahinch UK 19 B6
Ballynure UK 19 B6
Ballyragget IRL 21 B4
Ballysadare IRL 18 B3
Ballyshannon IRL 18 B3
Ballyvaughan IRL 20 A2
Ballyvourney IRL 20 C2
Ballywalter UK 19 B6
Balmaclellan UK 24 C3
Balmaseda E 89 A3
Balme I 70 C2
Balmedie UK 23 D6
Balmuccia I 70 C3
Balna-paling UK 23 D4
Balneario
de Panticosa E 76 D2
Balotaszállás H 75 B4
Balsa P 87 C3
Balsareny E 91 B4
Balsorano-Nuovo I 103 B6
Bålsta S 37 C4
Balsthal CH 70 A2
Balta UA 11 B10
Baltanás E 88 C2
Baltar E 87 C3
Baltasound UK 22 A8
Bălţi MD 11 C9
Baltimore IRL 20 C2
Baltinglass IRL 21 B5
Baltiysk RUS 47 A5
Baltów PL 55 B6
Balugães P 87 C2
Bælum DK 38 C3
Balve D 50 B3
Balvi LV 7 C9
Balvicar UK 24 B2
Balya TR 118 C2
Balzo I 82 D2
Bamberg D 62 A1
Bamburgh UK 25 C6
Banatska Palanka SRB 85 B6
Banatski Brestovac
SRB 85 B5
Banatski Despotovac
SRB 75 C5
Banatski Dvor SRB 75 C5
Banatski-Karlovac
SRB 85 A6
Banatsko Arandjelovo
SRB 75 B5
Banatsko-Novo Selo
SRB 85 B5
Banaz TR 118 D4
Banbridge UK 19 B5
Banbury UK 30 B2
Banchory UK 23 D6
Bande
B 49 C6
E 87 B3
Bandholm DK 39 E4
Bandırma TR 118 B2
Bandol F 79 C4
Bandon IRL 20 C3
Bañeres E 96 C2
Banff UK 23 D6
Bangor
F 66 A1
IRL 18 B2
Down UK 19 B6
Gwynedd UK 26 B1
Bangsund N 114 C8
Banie PL 45 B6
Banja SRB 85 C4
Banja Koviljača SRB 85 B4
Banjaloka SLO 73 C4
Banja Luka BIH 84 B2
Banjani SRB 85 B4
Banja Vručica BIH 84 B2
Banje KOS 85 D5
Banjska KOS 85 D5
Banka SK 64 B3
Bankekind S 37 D2
Bankend UK 25 C4
Bankeryd S 40 B4
Bankfoot UK 25 B4
Bankso BG 116 A5
Banloc RO 75 C6
Bannalec F 56 C2
Bannes F 59 B4
Bannockburn UK 25 B4
Bañobárez E 87 D4
Bañon E 90 C1
Banon F 79 B4
Baños E 93 A5
Baños de Gigonza E 99 C5
Baños de la Encina E 100 A2
Baños de Molgas E 87 B3
Baños de Rio Tobia E 89 B4
Baños
de Valdearados E 89 C3
Bánov CZ 64 B3
Banova Jaruga HR 74 C1
Bánovce
nad Bebravou SK 64 B4
Banovići BIH 84 B3
Banoviči Selo BIH 84 B3
Bánréve H 65 B6
Bansin D 45 B6
Banská Belá SK 65 B4
Banská Bystrica SK 65 B5
Banská Štiavnica SK 65 B4
Banstead UK 31 C3
Banteer IRL 20 B3
Bantheville F 59 A6
Bantry IRL 20 C2
Bantzenheim F 60 C3
Banyalbufar E 97 B2
Banyoles E 91 A5
Banyuls-sur-Mer F 91 A6
Bapaume F 48 C3
Bar
MNE 105 A5
UA 11 B9
Barabhas UK 22 C2
Barači BIH 84 B1
Baracs H 74 B3
Baracska H 74 A3
Barahona E 89 C4
Barajes de Melo E 95 B4
Barakaldo E 89 A4
Baralla E 86 B3
Barañain E 76 D1
Baranavichy BY 7 E9
Báránd H 75 A6
Baranda SRB 85 A5
Baranello I 103 B7
Baranów
Sandomierski PL 55 C6
Baraqueville F 77 B5
Barasoain E 89 B5
Barbacena P 92 C3
Barbadás E 87 B3
Barbadillo E 94 B1
Barbadillo
de Herreros E 89 B3
Barbadillo
del Mercado E 89 B3
Barbadillo del Pez E 89 B3
Barban HR 82 A3
Barbarano Vicento I 71 C6
Barbariga HR 82 B2
Barbaros TR 118 B2
Barbastro E 90 A3
Barbate E 99 C5
Barbatona E 95 A4
Barbâtre F 66 B2
Barbazan F 77 C3
Barbeitos E 86 A3
Barbentane F 78 C3
Barberino
di Mugello I 81 B5
Barbezieux-
St Hilaire F 67 C4
Barbonne-Fayel F 59 B4
Barbotan-
les-Thermes F 76 C2
Barby D 52 B1
Bárcabo E 90 A3
Barca de Alva P 87 C4
Barcarrota E 93 C4
Barcellona-Pozzo di
Gotto I 109 A4
Barcelona E 91 B5
Barcelonette F 79 B5
Barcelos P 87 C2
Bárcena del
Monasterio E 86 A4
Barcena de
Pie de Concha E 88 A2
Barchfeld D 51 C6
Barcin PL 46 C3
Barcino PL 46 A2
Bárcis I 72 B2
Barco P 92 A3
Barcones E 89 C4
Barcs H 74 C2
Barcus F 76 C2
Barczewo PL 47 B6
Bardejov SK 10 B6
Bårdesø DK 39 D3
Bardi I 81 B3
Bardney UK 27 B5
Bardo PL 54 C1
Bardolino I 71 C5
Bardonécchia I 79 A5
Bardoňovo SK 65 B4
Barèges F 76 D3
Barenstein D 52 C3
Barentin F 58 A1
Barenton F 57 B5
Barevo BIH 84 B2
Barfleur F 57 A4
Barga I 81 B4
Bargas E 94 C2
Barge I 79 B6
Bargemon F 79 C5
Barghe I 71 C5
Bargoed UK 29 B4
Bargrennan UK 24 C3
Bargteheide D 44 B2
Barham UK 31 C5
Bari I 104 B2
Barič Draga HR 83 B4
Barilović HR 73 C5
Bari Sardo I 110 C2
Barisciano I 103 A6
Barjac F 78 B3
Barjols F 79 C4
Barjon F 59 C5
Bårkåker N 35 C2
Barkald N 114 F7
Barkowo
Dolnośląskie PL 54 B1
Pomorskie PL 46 B3
Bârlad RO 11 C9
Bar-le-Duc F 59 B6
Barles F 79 B5
Barletta I 104 B2
Barlinek PL 45 C7
Barmouth UK 26 C1
Barmstedt D 43 B6
Barnard Castle UK 27 A4
Barnarp S 40 B4
Bärnau D 62 A3
Bärnbach A 73 A5
Barneberg D 52 A1
Barnenitz D 45 C4
Barnet UK 31 C3
Barnetby le Wold UK 27 B5
Barneveld NL 49 A6
Barneville-Carteret F 57 A4
Barnoldswick UK 26 B3
Barnowko PL 45 C6
Barnsley UK 27 B4
Barnstädt D 52 B1
Barnstaple UK 28 B3
Barnstorf D 43 C5
Barntrup D 51 B5
Baron F 58 A3
Baronissi I 103 C7
Barqueiro P 92 B2
Barquinha P 92 B2
Barr
F 60 B3
UK 24 C3
Barra P 92 A2
Barracas E 96 A2
Barraco E 94 B2
Barrado E 93 A5
Barrafranca I 109 B3
Barranco do Velho P 98 B3
Barrancos P 99 A4
Barrax E 95 C4
Barrbaar D 62 B1
Barre-des-Cevennes
F 78 B2
Barreiro P 92 C1
Barreiros E 86 A3
Barrême F 79 C5
Barret-le-Bas F 79 B4
Barrhead UK 24 C3
Barrhill UK 24 C3
Barrio de
Nuesra Señora E 88 B1
Barrowford UK 26 B3
Barrow-in-Furness UK 26 A2
Barrow upon
Humber UK 27 B5
Barruecopardo E 87 C4
Barruelo
de Santullán E 88 B2
Barruera E 90 A3
Barry UK 29 B4
Bårse DK 39 D4
Barsinghausen D 51 A5
Barssel D 43 B4
Bar-sur-Aube F 59 B5
Bar-sur-Seine F 59 B5
Barth D 45 A4
Bartholomä D 61 B5
Bartin TR 118 A7
Barton-
upon-Humber UK 27 B5
Bartoszyce PL 47 A6
Barúmini I 110 C1
Baruth D 52 A3
Barvaux B 49 C6
Barver D 43 C5
Barwatd PL 65 A5
Barwice PL 46 B2
Barysaw BY 7 D10
Barzana E 88 A1
Bârzava RO 10 C6
Bárzio I 71 C4
Bas E 91 A5
Bašaid SRB 75 C5
Basaluzzo I 80 B2
Basarabeasca MD 11 C10
Basauri E 89 A4
Baschi I 82 D1
Baschurch UK 26 C3
Basconcillos
del Tozo E 88 B3
Bascones de Ojeda E 88 B2
Basécles B 49 C4
Basel CH 70 A2
Basélice I 103 B7
Basildon UK 31 C4
Basingstoke UK 31 C2
Baška
CZ 65 A4
HR 83 B3
Baška Voda HR 84 C1
Bäsksjö S 115 C14
Baslow UK 27 B4
Başmakçı TR 119 E5
Basovizza I 72 C3
Bassacutena I 110 A2
Bassano del Grappa I 72 C1
Bassano Romano I 102 A5
Bassecourt CH 70 A2
Bassella E 91 A4
Bassevuovdde N 113 D14
Bassou F 59 C4
Bassoues F 76 C3
Bassum D 43 C5
Båstad S 40 C2
Bastardo I 82 D1
Bastelica F 102 A2
Bastelicaccia F 102 B1
Bastia
F 102 A2
I 82 C1

Bastogne B 50 C1
Baston UK 30 B3
Bastuträsk S 115 C17
Bata H 74 B3
Batajnica SRB 85 B5
Batalha P 92 B2
Bátaszék H 74 B3
Batea E 90 B3
Batelov CZ 63 A6
Bath UK 29 B5
Bathgate UK 25 C4
Batida H 75 B5
Batignano I 81 D5
Batina HR 74 C3
Bátka SK 65 B6
Batković BIH 85 B4
Batlava KOS 85 D6
Batley UK 27 B4
Batnfjordsøra N 114 E4
Batočina SRB 85 B6
Bátonyterenye H 65 C5
Batrina HR 74 C2
Båtsfjord N 113 B18
Battaglia Terme I 72 C1
Bätterkinden CH 70 A2
Battice B 50 C1
Battipáglia I 103 C7
Battle UK 31 D4
Battonya H 75 B6
Batuša SRB 85 B6
Bátya H 75 B3
Bau I 110 C1
Baud F 56 C2
Baudour B 49 C4
Baugé F 67 A4
Baugy F 68 A2
Bauma CH 70 A3
Baume-les-Dames F 69 A6
Baumholder D 60 A3
Baunatal D 51 B5
Baunei I 110 B2
Bauska LV 6 C8
Bautzen D 53 B4
Bavanište SRB 85 B5
Bavay F 49 C4
Bavilliers F 60 C2
Bavorov CZ 63 A5
Bawdsey UK 31 B5
Bawinkel D 43 C4
Bawtry UK 27 B4
Bayat TR 118 D5
Bayel F 59 B5
Bayeux F 57 A5
Bayındır TR 119 D2
Bayon F 60 B2
Bayonne F 76 C1
Bayons F 79 B5
Bayramiç TR 118 C1
Bayreuth D 52 D1
Bayrischzell D 62 C3
Baza E 101 B3
Bazas F 76 B2
Baziege F 77 C4
Bazoches-les-Gallerandes F 58 B3
Bazoches-sur-Hoëne F 58 B1
Bazzano I 81 B5
Beaconsfield UK 31 C3
Beade E 87 B2
Beadnell UK 25 C6
Beaminster UK 29 C5
Bearsden UK 24 C3
Beas E 99 B4
Beasain E 89 A4
Beas de Segura E 100 A3
Beattock UK 25 C4
Beaubery F 69 B4
Beaucaire F 78 C3
Beaufort
F 69 C6
IRL 20 B2
Beaufort-en Vallée F 67 A4
Beaugency F 58 C2
Beaujeu
Alpes-de-Haute-Provence F 79 B5
Rhône F 69 B4
Beaulac F 76 B2
Beaulieu
F 68 A2
UK 31 D2
Beaulieu-sous-la-Roche F 66 B3
Beaulieu-sur-Dordogne F 77 B4
Beaulieu-sur-Mer F 80 C1
Beaulon F 68 B3
Beauly UK 23 D4
Beaumaris UK 26 B1
Beaumesnil F 58 A1
Beaumetz-lès-Loges F 48 C3
Beaumont
B 49 C5
F 77 B3
Beaumont-de-Lomagne F 77 C3
Beaumont-du-Gâtinais F 58 B3
Beaumont-en-Argonne F 59 A6
Beaumont-Hague F 57 A4
Beaumont-la-Ronce F 58 C1
Beaumont-le-Roger F 58 A1
Beaumont-sur-Oise F 58 A3
Beaumont-sur-Sarthe F 57 B6
Beaune F 69 A4
Beaune-la-Rolande F 58 B3
Beaupréau F 66 A4
Beauraing B 49 C5
Beaurepaire F 69 C5
Beaurepaire-en-Bresse F 69 B5
Beaurières F 79 B4
Beauvais F 58 A3
Beauval F 48 C3
Beauville F 77 B3
Beauvoir-sur-Mer F 66 B2
Beauvoir-sur-Niort F 67 B4
Beba Veche RO 75 B5
Bebertal D 52 A1
Bebington UK 26 B2
Bebra D 51 C5
Bebrina HR 84 A2
Beccles UK 30 B5
Becedas E 93 A5
Beceite E 90 C3
Bečej SRB 75 C5
Becerreá E 86 B3
Becerril de Campos E 88 B2
Bécherel F 57 B4
Bechhofen D 61 A6
Bechyně CZ 63 A5
Bečići MNE 105 A4
Becilla de Valderaduey E 88 B1
Beckfoot UK 25 D4
Beckingham UK 27 B5
Beckum D 50 B4
Beco P 92 B2
Bécon-les-Granits F 66 A4
Bečov nad Teplou CZ 52 C2
Becsehely H 74 B1
Bedale UK 27 A4
Bedames E 89 A3
Bédar E 101 B4
Bédarieux F 78 C2
Bédarrides F 78 B3
Bedburg D 50 C2
Beddgelert UK 26 B1
Beddingestrand S 41 D3
Bédée F 57 B4
Bedegkér H 74 B3
Beden TR 119 F7
Bedford UK 30 B3
Będków PL 55 B4
Bedlington UK 25 C6
Bedlno PL 55 A4
Bedmar E 100 B2
Bédoin F 79 B4
Bedónia I 80 B3
Bedretto CH 70 B3
Bedsted DK 38 C1
Bedum NL 42 B3
Bedwas UK 29 B4
Bedworth UK 30 B2
Będzin PL 55 C4
Beekbergen NL 50 A1
Beek en Donk NL 49 B6
Beelen D 50 B4
Beelitz D 52 A2
Beer UK 29 C4
Beerfelde D 45 C6
Beerfelden D 61 A4
Beernem B 49 B4
Beeskow D 53 A4
Beetsterzwaag NL 42 B3
Beetzendorf D 44 C3
Beflelay CH 70 A2
Begaljica SRB 85 B5
Bégard F 56 B2
Begejci SRB 75 C5
Begijar E 100 B2
Begijnendijk B 49 B5
Begndal N 34 B1
Begues E 91 B4
Beguildy UK 26 C2
Begur E 91 B6
Beho B 50 C1
Behringen D 51 B6
Beilen NL 42 C3
Beilngries D 62 A2
Beine-Nauroy F 59 A5
Beinwil CH 70 A3
Beiseförth D 51 B5
Beith UK 24 C3
Beitostølen N 32 A5
Beiuş RO 11 C7
Beja P 98 A3
Béjar E 93 A5
Bekçiler TR 119 F4
Békés H 75 B6
Békéscsaba H 75 B6
Bekilli TR 119 D4
Bekkarfjord N 113 B16
Bela SK 65 A4
Bélâbre F 67 B6
Bela Crkva SRB 85 B6
Belalcázar E 93 C5
Belánad Radbuzou CZ 62 A3
Belanovica SRB 85 B5
Bélapátfalva H 65 B6
Bělápod Bezdězem CZ 53 C4
Belcaire F 77 D4
Bełchatów PL 55 B4
Belchite E 90 B2
Bělčice CZ 63 A4
Belcoo UK 19 B4
Belecke D 51 B4
Beled H 74 A2
Belej HR 83 B3
Beleño E 88 A1
Bélesta F 77 D4
Belev RUS 7 E14
Belevi TR 119 D2
Belfast UK 19 B6
Belford UK 25 C6
Belfort F 60 C2
Belgentier F 79 C4
Belgern D 52 B3
Belgioioso I 71 C4
Belgodère F 102 A2
Belgooly IRL 20 C3
Belgorod RUS 7 F14
Belgrade = Beograd SRB 85 B5
Belhade F 76 B2
Belica HR 74 B1
Beli Manastir HR 74 C3
Belin-Bèliet F 76 B2
Belinchón E 95 B3
Belišće HR 74 C3
Bělkovice-Lašt'any CZ 64 A3
Bella I 104 C1
Bellac F 67 B6
Bellágio I 71 C4
Bellananagh IRL 19 C4
Bellano I 71 B4
Bellária I 82 B1
Bellavary IRL 18 C2
Belleau F 59 A4
Belleek UK 18 B3
Bellegarde
Gard F 78 C3
Loiret F 58 C3
Bellegarde-en-Diois F 79 B4
Bellegarde-en-Marche F 68 C2
Bellegarde-sur-Valserine F 69 B5
Belle-Isle-en-Terre F 56 B2
Bellême F 58 B1
Bellenaves F 68 B3
Bellentre F 70 C1
Bellevaux F 69 B6
Bellevesvre F 69 B5
Belleville F 69 B4
Belleville-sur-Vie F 66 B3
Bellevue-la-Montagne F 68 C3
Belley F 69 C5
Bellheim D 61 A4
Bellinge DK 39 D3
Bellingham UK 25 C5
Bellinzago Novarese I 70 C3
Bellinzona CH 70 B4
Bell-lloc d'Urgell E 90 B3
Bello E 95 B5
Bellpuig d'Urgell E 91 B4
Bellreguart E 96 C2
Bellsbank UK 24 C3
Belltall E 91 B4
Belluno I 72 B2
Bellver de Cerdanya E 91 A4
Bellvis E 90 B3
Bélmez E 93 C5
Belmez de la Moraleda E 100 B2
Belmont UK 22 A8
Belmont-de-la-Loire F 69 B4
Belmonte
Asturias E 86 A4
Cuenca E 95 C4
P 92 A3
Belmonte de San José E 90 C2
Belmonte de Tajo E 95 B3
Belmont-sur-Rance F 78 C1
Belmullet IRL 18 B2
Belobresca RO 85 B6
Beloeil B 49 C4
Belogradchik BG 11 E7
Belokorovichi UA 11 A10
Beloljin SRB 85 C6
Belorado E 89 B3
Belotič SRB 85 B4
Bělotín CZ 64 A3
Belozersk RUS 7 B14
Belp CH 70 B2
Belpasso I 109 B3
Belpech F 77 C4
Belper UK 27 B4
Belsay UK 25 C6
Belsh AL 105 C5
Belsk Duzy PL 55 B5
Beltinci SLO 73 B6
Beltra IRL 18 C2
Belturbet IRL 19 B4
Beluša SK 64 A4
Belušić SRB 85 C6
Belvedere Marittimo I 106 B2
Belver de Cinca E 90 B3
Belver de los Montes E 88 C1
Belvès F 77 B3
Belvezet F 78 B2
Belvis de la Jara E 94 C2
Belvis de Monroy E 93 B5
Belyy RUS 7 D12
Belz F 56 C2
Bełżec PL 11 A7
Belzig D 52 A2
Bembibre E 86 B4
Bembridge UK 31 D2
Bemmel NL 50 B1
Bemposta
Bragança P 87 C4
Santarém P 92 B2
Benabarre E 90 A3
Benacazón E 99 B4
Benaguacil E 96 B2
Benahadux E 101 C3
Benalmádena E 100 C1
Benalúa de Guadix E 100 B2
Benalúa de las Villas E 100 B2
Benalup E 99 C5
Benamargosa E 100 C1
Benamaurel E 101 B3
Benameji E 100 B1
Benamocarra E 100 C1
Benaocaz E 99 C5
Benaoján E 99 C5
Benarrabá E 99 C5
Benasque E 90 A3
Benátky nad Jizerou CZ 53 C4
Benavente
E 88 B1
P 92 C2
Benavides de Órbigo E 88 B1
Benavila P 92 B3
Bendorf D 50 C3
Benedikt SLO 73 B5
Benejama E 101 A5
Benejúzar E 101 A5
Benešov CZ 63 A5
Bénestroff F 60 B2
Benet F 67 B4
Bene Vagienna I 80 B1
Bénévent-l'Abbaye F 67 B6
Benevento I 103 B7
Benfeld F 60 B3
Benfica P 92 B2
Bengtsfors S 35 C4
Bengtsheden S 36 B2
Beničanci HR 74 C3
Benicarló E 90 C3
Benicássim E 96 A3
Benidorm E 96 C2
Benifaió E 96 B2
Beniganim E 96 C2
Benington UK 27 B6
Benisa E 96 C3
Benkovac HR 83 B4
Benllech UK 26 B1
Benneckenstein D 51 B6
Bénodet F 56 C1
Benquerencia de la Serena E 93 C5
Bensafrim P 98 B2
Bensdorf D 44 C4
Benshausen D 51 C6
Bensheim D 61 A4
Bentley UK 31 C3
Bentwisch D 44 A4
Beočin SRB 75 C4
Beograd = Belgrade SRB 85 B5
Beragh UK 19 B4
Berane MNE 85 D4
Beranga E 89 A3
Berat AL 105 C5
Bérat F 77 C4
Beratzhausen D 62 A2
Bérbaltavár H 74 A1
Berbegal E 90 B2
Berbenno di Valtellina I 71 B4
Berberana E 89 B3
Bercedo E 89 A3
Bercel H 65 C5
Bercenay-le-Hayer F 59 B4
Berceto I 81 B3
Berchem B 49 C4
Berchidda I 110 B2
Berching D 62 A2
Berchtesgaden D 62 C4
Bérchules E 100 C2
Bercianos de Aliste E 87 C4
Berck F 48 C2
Berclaire d'Urgell E 90 B3
Berdoias E 86 A1
Berducedo E 86 A4
Berdún E 90 A2
Berdychiv UA 11 B10
Bere Alston UK 28 C3
Bereguardo I 70 C4
Berehommen N 33 C4
Berehove UA 11 B7
Berek BIH 84 A2
Beremend H 74 C3
Bere Regis UK 29 C5
Berestechko UA 11 A8
Berettyóújfalu H 10 C6
Berezhany UA 11 B8
Berezivka UA 11 C11
Berezna UA 7 F11
Berg
D 62 A2
N 114 B9
S 37 D3
Berga
Sachsen-Anhalt D 51 B7
Thüringen D 52 C2
E 91 A4
S 40 B6
Bergama TR 118 C2
Bérgamo I 71 C4
Bergara E 89 A4
Bergby S 36 B4
Berge
Brandenburg D 45 C4
Niedersachsen D 43 C4
Telemark N 33 C5
Bergeforsen S 115 E14
Bergen
Mecklenburg-Vorpommern D 45 A5
Niedersachsen D 44 C1
Niedersachsen D 44 C2
N 32 B2
NL 42 C1
Bergen op Zoom NL 49 B5
Bergerac F 77 B3
Bergères-lès-Vertus F 59 B5
Bergeyk NL 49 B6
Berghausen D 61 B4
Bergheim D 50 C2
Berghem S 40 B2
Berg im Gau D 62 B2
Bergisch Gladbach D 50 C3
Bergkamen D 50 B3
Bergkvara S 41 C6
Berglern D 62 B2
Bergneustadt D 50 B3
Bergsäng S 34 B5
Bergshamra S 37 C5
Bergsjö S 115 F14
Bergs slussar S 37 D2
Bergtheim D 61 A6
Bergues F 48 C3
Bergum NL 42 B2
Bergün Bravuogn CH 71 B4
Bergwitz D 52 B2
Berhida H 74 A3
Beringel P 98 A3
Beringen B 49 B6
Berja E 100 C3
Berkåk N 114 E7
Berkeley UK 29 B5
Berkenthin D 44 B2
Berkhamsted UK 31 C3
Berkheim D 61 B6
Berkhof D 43 C6
Berkovići BIH 84 C3
Berkovitsa BG 11 E7
Berlanga E 99 A5
Berlanga de Duero E 89 C4
Berlevåg N 113 B18
Berlikum NL 42 B2
Berlin D 45 C5
Berlstedt D 52 B1
Bermeo E 89 A4
Bermillo de Sayago E 87 C4
Bern CH 70 B2
Bernalda I 104 C2
Bernardos E 94 A2
Bernartice
Jihočeský CZ 63 A5
Vychodočeský CZ 53 C5
Bernau
Baden-Württemberg D 61 C4
Bayern D 62 C3
Brandenburg D 45 C5
Bernaville F 48 C3
Bernay F 58 A1
Bernburg D 52 B1
Berndorf A 64 C2
Berne D 43 B5
Bernecebarati H 65 B4
Bernhardsthal A 64 B2
Bernkastel-Kues D 60 A3
Bernolakovo SK 64 B3
Bernsdorf D 53 B4
Bernstadt D 53 B4
Bernstein A 73 A6
Bernués E 90 A2
Beromünster CH 70 A3
Beroun CZ 53 D4
Berovo NMK 116 A4
Berre-l'Etang F 79 C4
Berriedale UK 23 C5
Berriew UK 26 C2
Berrocal E 99 B4
Bersenbrück D 43 C4
Bershad' UA 11 B10
Bertamiráns E 86 B2
Berthåga S 36 C4
Berthelming F 60 B2
Bertincourt F 48 C3
Bertinoro I 82 B1
Bertogne B 49 C6
Bertrix B 59 A6
Berufjörður IS 111 C11
Berville-sur-Mer F 58 A1
Berwick-upon-Tweed UK 25 C5
Berzasca RO 10 D6
Berzence H 74 B2
Berzocana E 93 B5
Besalú E 91 A5
Besançon F 69 A6
Besenfeld D 61 B4
Besenyötelek H 65 C6
Besenyszög H 75 A5
Beshenkovichi BY 7 D10
Besigheim D 61 B5
Běšiny CZ 63 A4
Beška SRB 75 C5
Beşkonak TR 119 E6
Besle F 57 C4
Besnyő H 74 A3
Bessais-le-Fromental F 68 B2
Bessan F 78 C2
Besse-en-Chandesse F 68 C2
Bessèges F 78 B3
Bessé-sur-Braye F 58 C1
Bessines-sur-Gartempe F 67 B6
Best NL 49 B6
Bestorp S 37 D2
Betanzos E 86 A2
Betelu E 76 C1
Bétera E 96 B2
Beteta E 95 B4
Béthenville F 59 A5
Bethesda UK 26 B1
Béthune F 48 C3
Beton-Bazoches F 59 B4
Bettembourg L 60 A2
Betterdorf L 60 A2
Bettna S 37 D3
Béttola I 80 B3
Bettona I 82 C1
Bettyhill UK 23 C4
Betws-y-Coed UK 26 B2
Betxi E 96 B2
Betz F 59 A3
Betzdorf D 50 C3
Beuil F 79 B5
Beulah UK 29 A4
Beuzeville F 58 A1
Bevagna I 82 D1
Bevens-bruk S 37 C2
Beveren B 49 B5
Beverley UK 27 B5
Bevern D 51 B5
Beverstedt D 43 B5
Beverungen D 51 B5
Beverwijk NL 42 C1
Bex CH 70 B2
Bexhill UK 31 D4
Beyazköy TR 118 A2
Beychevelle F 76 A2
Beydağ TR 119 D3
Beyeğaç TR 119 E3
Beykoz TR 118 A4
Beynat F 68 C1
Beyoğlu TR 118 A4
Beypazarı TR 118 B6
Beyşehir TR 119 E6
Bezas E 95 B5
Bezau A 71 A4
Bezdan SRB 75 C3
Bèze F 69 A5
Bezenet F 68 B2
Bezhetsk RUS 7 C14
Béziers F 78 C2
Bezzecca I 71 C5
Biadki PL 54 B2
Biała
Łódzkie PL 55 B4
Opolskie PL 54 C2
Białaczów PL 55 B5
Biała Podlaska PL 6 E7
Biała Rawska PL 55 B5
Biale Błota PL 46 B3
Białobłoty PL 54 A2
Białobrzegi PL 55 B5
Białogard PL 46 B1
Białośliwie PL 46 B3
Białowąs PL 46 B2
Biały Bór PL 46 B2
Białystok PL 6 E7
Biancavilla I 109 B3
Bianco I 106 C3
Biandrate I 70 C3
Biar E 101 A5
Biarritz F 76 C1
Bias F 76 B1
Biasca CH 70 B3
Biatorbágy H 74 A3
Bibbiena I 81 C5
Bibbona I 81 C4
Biberach
Baden-Württemberg D 61 B4
Baden-Württemberg D 61 B5
Bibinje HR 83 B4
Bibione I 72 C3
Biblis D 61 A4
Bibury UK 29 B6
Biccari I 103 B8
Bicester UK 31 C2
Bichl D 62 C2
Bichlbach A 71 A5
Bicorp E 96 B2
Bicos P 98 B2
Bicske H 74 A3
Bidache F 76 C1
Bidart F 76 C1
Biddinghuizen NL 42 C2
Biddulph UK 26 B3
Bideford UK 28 B3
Bidford-on-Avon UK 29 A6
Bidjovagge N 113 C11
Bie S 37 C3
Bieber D 51 C5
Biebersdorf D 53 B3
Biedenkopf D 51 C4
Biel E 90 A2
Bielany Wroclawskie PL 54 B1
Bielawa PL 54 C1
Bielawy PL 55 A4
Biel/Bienne CH 70 A2
Bielefeld D 51 A4
Biella I 70 C3
Bielsa E 90 A3
Bielsk PL 47 C5
Bielsko-Biała PL 65 A5
Bielsk Podlaski PL 6 E7
Bienenbuttel D 44 B2
Bieniow PL 53 B5
Bienservida E 101 A3
Bienvenida E 93 C4
Bierdzany PL 54 C3
Bierné F 57 C5
Biersted DK 38 B2
Bierun PL 55 C4
Bierutów PL 54 B2
Bierwart B 49 C6
Bierzwina PL 46 B1
Bierzwnik PL 46 B1
Biescas E 90 A2
Biesenthal D 45 C5
Biesiekierz PL 46 A2
Bietigheim-Bissingen D 61 B5
Bièvre B 49 D6
Bieżuń PL 47 C5
Biga TR 118 B2
Bigadiç TR 118 C3
Biganos F 76 B2
Bigas P 87 D3
Bigastro E 101 A5
Bigbury UK 28 C4
Biggar UK 25 C4
Biggin Hill UK 31 C4
Biggleswade UK 30 B3
Bignasco CH 70 B3
Biguglia F 102 A2
Bihać BIH 83 B4
Biharnagybajom H 75 A6
Bijela MNE 105 A4
Bijeljani BIH 84 C3
Bijeljina BIH 85 B4
Bijelo Polje MNE 85 C4
Bijuesca E 89 C5
Bilaj HR 83 B4
Bila Tserkva UA 11 B11
Bilbao E 89 A4
Bilcza PL 55 C5
Bíldudalur IS 111 B2
Bileća BIH 84 D3
Bilecik TR 118 B4
Biled RO 75 C5
Biłgoraj PL 11 A7
Bilhorod-Dnistrovskyy UA 11 C11
Bílina CZ 53 C3
Bilisht AL 116 B2
Bilje HR 74 C3
Billdal S 38 B4
Billerbeck D 50 B3
Billericay UK 31 C4
Billesholm S 41 C2
Billingborough UK 30 B3
Billinge S 41 D3
Billingham UK 27 A4
Billinghay UK 27 B5
Billingsfors S 35 D4
Billingshurst UK 31 C3
Billom F 68 C3
Billsta S 115 D15
Billund DK 39 D2
Bilopillya UA 7 F13
Bílovec CZ 64 A4
Bilstein D 50 B4
Bilthoven NL 49 A6
Bilto N 112 C10
Bilzen B 49 C6
Bíňa SK 65 C4
Binaced E 90 B3
Binasco I 71 C4
Binbrook UK 27 B5
Binche B 49 C5
Bindlach D 52 D1
Bindslev DK 38 B3
Binefar E 90 B3
Bingen D 50 D3
Bingham UK 27 C5
Bingley UK 27 B4
Bingsjö S 36 A2
Binic F 56 B3
Binz D 45 A5
Bioče MNE 105 A5
Biograd na Moru HR 83 C4
Bionaz I 70 C2
Bioska SRB 85 C4
Birda RO 75 C6
Birdlip UK 29 B5
Biri N 34 B2
Birkeland N 33 D5
Birkenfeld
Baden-Württemberg D 61 B4
Rheinland-Pfalz D 60 A3
Birkenhead UK 26 B2
Birkerød DK 41 D2
Birkfeld A 73 A5
Birkirkara M 107 C5
Birmingham UK 27 C4
Birr IRL 21 A4
Birresborn D 50 C2
Birstein D 51 C5
Biržai LT 6 C8
Birzebbugia M 107 C5
Bisáccia I 103 B8
Bisacquino I 108 B2
Bisbal de Falset E 90 B3
Biscarosse F 76 B1
Biscarosse Plage F 76 B1
Biscarrués E 90 A2
Biscéglie I 104 B2
Bischheim F 60 B3
Bischofsheim D 51 C5
Bischofshofen A 72 A3
Bischofswerda D 53 B4
Bischofswiesen D 62 C3
Bischofszell CH 71 A4
Bischwiller F 60 B3
Bisenti I 103 A6
Bishop Auckland UK 27 A4
Bishop's Castle UK 26 C3
Bishops Lydeard UK 29 B4
Bishop's Stortford UK 31 C4
Bishop's Waltham UK 31 D2
Bisignano I 106 B3
Bisingen D 61 B4
Biskupice-Oławskie PL 54 B2
Biskupiec PL 47 B5
Bismark D 44 C3
Bismo N 114 F5
Bispgården S 115 D13
Bispingen D 44 B1
Bissen L 60 A2
Bissendorf D 50 A4
Bisserup DK 39 D4
Bistango I 80 B2
Bistarac Donje BIH 84 B3
Bistrica
BIH 84 B2
MNE 85 D4
SRB 85 C4
Bistrica ob Sotli SLO 73 B5
Bistriţa RO 11 C8
Bisztynek PL 47 A6
Bitburg D 50 D2
Bitche F 60 A3
Bitetto I 104 B2
Bitola NMK 116 A3
Bitonto I 104 B2
Bitschwiller F 60 C3
Bitterfeld D 52 B2
Bitti I 110 B2
Biville-sur-Mer F 48 D2
Bivona I 108 B2
Biwer L 60 A2
Bizeljsko SLO 73 B5
Bizovac HR 74 C3
Bjåen N 33 C4
Bjärnum S 41 C3
Bjärred S 41 D3
Bjästa S 115 D15
Bjelland
Vest-Agder N 33 D3
Vest-Agder N 33 D4
Bjelovar HR 74 C1
Bjerkreim N 33 D3
Bjerkvik N 112 D6
Bjerreby DK 39 E3
Bjerregrav DK 38 C2
Bjerringbro DK 39 C2
Bjøberg N 32 B5
Bjøllånes N 112 F3
Björbo S 36 B1
Bjordal N 32 A2
Björg IS 111 B8
Bjørkåsen N 112 D5
Björke
Gävleborg S 36 B4
Östergötland S 37 D2
Bjørkelangen N 34 C3
Björketorp S 40 B2
Björkholmen S 112 F8
Björkliden S 112 D7
Björklinge S 36 B4
Björko S 36 C6
Björkö S 38 B4
Björköby S 40 B4
Björkvik S 37 D3
Bjørn N 115 A9
Björna S 115 D15
Björneborg S 35 C6
Björnerod S 35 C3
Bjørnevatn N 113 C18
Björnlunda S 37 C4
Bjørnstad N 113 C19
Björsäter S 37 D3
Bjurberget S 34 B4
Bjurholm S 115 D16
Bjursås S 36 B2
Bjurtjärn S 35 C6
Bjuv S 41 C2
Blace SRB 85 C6
Blachownia PL 54 C3
Blackburn UK 26 B3
Blackpool UK 26 B2
Blackstad S 40 B6
Blackwater IRL 21 B5
Blackwaterfoot UK 24 C2
Blacy F 59 B5
Bladåker S 36 B5
Blaenau Ffestiniog UK 26 C2
Blaenavon UK 29 B4
Blaengarw UK 29 B4
Blagaj
BIH 83 A5
BIH 84 C2
Blagdon UK 29 B5
Blagnac F 77 C4
Blagoevgrad BG 11 E7
Blaichach D 61 C6
Blain F 66 A3
Blainville-sur-l'Eau F 60 B2
Blair Atholl UK 25 B4
Blairgowrie UK 25 B4
Blajan F 77 C3
Blakeney UK 29 B5
Blakstad N 33 D5
Blâmont F 60 B2
Blanca E 101 A4
Blancos E 87 C3
Blandford Forum UK 29 C5
Blanes E 91 B5
Blangy-sur-Bresle F 58 A2
Blankaholm S 40 B6
Blankenberge B 49 B4
Blankenburg D 51 B6
Blankenfelde D 45 C5
Blankenhain D 52 C1
Blankenheim D 50 C2
Blanquefort F 76 B2
Blansko CZ 64 A2
Blanzac F 67 C5
Blanzy F 69 B4
Blaricum NL 49 A6
Blarney IRL 20 C3
Blascomillán E 94 B1
Blascosancho E 94 B2
Błaszki PL 54 B3
Blatná CZ 63 A4
Blatné SK 64 B3
Blatnice CZ 64 B3
Blatnika BIH 84 B2
Blato HR 84 D1
Blato na Cetini HR 84 C1
Blatten CH 70 B2
Blattnicksele S 115 B14
Blatzheim D 50 C2
Blaubeuren D 61 B5
Blaufelden D 61 A5
Blaustein D 61 B5
Blaydon UK 25 D6
Blaye F 76 A2
Blaye-les-Mines F 77 B5
Blázquez E 93 C5
Bleckede D 44 B2
Blecua E 90 A2
Bled SLO 73 B4
Bleiburg A 73 B4
Bleichenbach D 51 C5
Bleicherode D 51 B6
Bleik N 112 C4
Bleikvassli N 115 B10
Bléneau F 59 C3
Blentarp S 41 D3
Blera I 102 A5
Blérancourt F 59 A4
Bléré F 67 A5
Blesle F 68 C3
Blessington IRL 21 A5
Blet F 68 B2
Bletchley UK 31 C3
Bletterans F 69 B5
Blidö S 37 C5
Blidsberg S 40 B3
Blieskastel D 60 A3
Bligny-sur-Ouche F 69 A4
Blikstorp S 35 D6
Blinisht AL 105 B6
Blinja HR 73 C6
Blizanówek PL 54 B3
Bliżyn PL 55 B5
Blois F 58 C2
Blokhus DK 38 B2
Blokzijl NL 42 C2
Blombacka S 35 C5
Blomberg D 51 B5
Blomskog S 35 C4
Blomstermåla S 40 C6
Blomvåg N 32 B1
Blönduós IS 111 B5
Błonie PL 55 A5
Blonville-sur-Mer F 57 A6
Blötberget S 36 B2
Blovice CZ 63 A4
Bloxham UK 31 B2
Blšany CZ 52 C3
Bludenz A 71 A4
Bludov CZ 64 A2
Blumberg D 61 C4
Blyberg S 34 A6
Blyth
Northumberland UK 25 C6
Nottinghamshire UK 27 B4
Blyth Bridge UK 25 C4
Blythburgh UK 30 B5
Blythe Bridge UK 26 C3
Bø
Nordland N 112 D3
Telemark N 33 C6
Boal E 86 A4
Boan MNE 85 D4
Boario Terme I 71 C5
Boat of Garten UK 23 D5
Boa Vista P 92 B2
Boğazkale TR 16 A7
Boğazlıyan TR 16 B7
Boba H 74 A2
Bobadilla
Logroño E 89 B4
Málaga E 100 B1
Bobadilla del Campo E 94 A1
Bobadilla del Monte E 94 B3
Bóbbio I 80 B3
Bóbbio Pellice I 79 B6
Bobigny F 58 B3
Bobingen D 62 B1
Böblingen D 61 B5
Bobolice PL 46 B2
Boboras E 87 B2
Bobowa PL 65 A6
Bobrinets UA 11 B12
Bobrová CZ 64 A2
Bobrovitsa UA 11 A11
Bobrowice PL 53 B5
Bobrówko PL 46 C1
Boca de Huérgano E 88 B2
Bocairent E 96 C2
Bočar SRB 75 C5
Bocchigliero I 106 B3
Boceguillas E 89 C3
Bochnia PL 55 D5
Bocholt
B 49 B6
D 50 B2
Bochov CZ 52 C3
Bochum D 50 B3
Bockara S 40 B6
Bockenem D 51 A6
Bockfliess A 64 B2
Bockhorn D 43 B5
Bočna SLO 73 B4
Bocognano F 102 A2
Boconád H 65 C6
Boczów PL 45 C6
Boda S 36 A2
Böda S 41 B7
Boda
Stockholm S 36 B5
Värmland S 35 C5
Västernorrland S 115 E13
Bodafors S 40 B4
Boda Glasbruk S 40 C5
Bodajk H 74 A3
Boddam
Aberdeenshire UK 23 D7
Shetland UK 22 B7
Boddin D 44 B3
Bödefeld-Freiheit D 51 B4
Boden S 3 D24
Bodenmais D 62 A4
Bodenteich D 44 C2
Bodenwerder D 51 B5
Bodiam UK 31 C4
Bodinnick UK 28 C3
Bodio CH 70 B3
Bodjani SRB 75 C4
Bodmin UK 28 C3
Bodø N 112 E3
Bodonal de la Sierra E 99 A4
Bodrum TR 119 E2
Bodstedt D 45 A4
Bodzanów PL 47 C6
Bodzanowice PL 54 C3
Bodzechów PL 55 C6
Bodzentyn PL 55 C5
Boecillo E 88 C2
Boëge F 69 B6
Boën F 68 C3
Bogács H 65 C6
Bogadmindszent H 74 C3
Bogajo E 87 D4
Bogarra E 101 A3
Bogarre E 100 B2
Bogatić SRB 85 B4
Bogatynia PL 53 C4
Bogdaniec PL 45 C7
Bogë AL 105 A5
Boge S 37 E5
Bogen
D 62 B3
Nordland N 112 D5
Nordland N 112 E4
S 34 B4
Bogense DK 39 D3
Bogetići MNE 84 D3
Bognanco Fonti I 70 B3
Bognelv N 113 B11
Bognes N 112 D5
Bogno CH 70 B4
Bognor Regis UK 31 D3
Bogoria PL 55 C6
Bograngen S 34 B4
Boguchwaly PL 47 B6
Bogumiłowice PL 55 B4
Boguslav UA 11 B11
Boguszów-Gorce PL 53 C6
Bogutovac SRB 85 C5
Bogyiszló H 74 B3
Bohain-en-Vermandois F 49 D4
Böheimkirchen A 64 B1
Bohinjska Bistrica SLO 72 B3
Böhlen D 52 B2
Böhmenkirch D 61 B5
Bohmte D 43 C5
Bohonal de Ibor E 93 B5
Böhönye H 74 B2
Bohumin CZ 65 A4
Boiro E 86 B2
Bois-d'Amont F 69 B6
Boisseron F 78 C3
Boitzenburg D 45 B5
Boixols E 91 A4
Boizenburg D 44 B2
Bojadła PL 53 B5
Bojano I 103 B7
Bojanowo PL 54 B1
Bøjden DK 39 D3
Bojkovice CZ 64 A3
Bojná SK 64 B4
Bojnice SK 65 B4
Boka SRB 75 C5
Böklund D 43 A6
Bokod H 74 A3
Böksholm S 40 B4
Boksitogorsk RUS 7 B12
Bol HR 83 C5
Bolaños de Calatrava E 100 A2
Bolayır TR 118 B1
Bolbec F 58 A1
Bölcske H 75 B3
Bolderslev DK 39 E2
Boldog H 65 C5
Boldva H 65 B6
Bolea E 90 A2
Bolekhiv UA 11 B7
Bolesławiec PL 53 B5
Boleszkowice PL 45 C6
Bolewice PL 46 C2
Bólgheri I 81 C4
Bolhrad UA 11 D10
Boliden S 3 D24
Bolimów PL 55 A5
Boliqueime P 98 B2
Boljevci SRB 85 B5
Boljkovci SRB 85 B5
Bolkhov RUS 7 E14
Bolków PL 53 C6
Bollebygd S 40 B2
Bollène F 78 B3
Bólliga E 95 B4
Bollnäs S 36 A3
Bollstabruk S 115 E14
Bollullos E 99 B4
Bollullos par del Condado E 99 B4
Bologna I 81 B5
Bologne F 59 B6
Bolognetta I 108 B2
Bolognola I 82 D2
Bologoye RUS 7 C13
Bolótana I 110 B1
Bolsena I 102 A4
Bolshaya Vradiyevka UA 11 C11
Bolsover UK 27 B4
Bolstad S 35 D4
Bolsward NL 42 B2
Boltaña E 90 A3
Boltenhagen D 44 B3
Boltigen CH 70 B2
Bolton UK 26 B3
Bolu TR 118 B6
Bolungarvík IS 111 A2
Bolvadin TR 118 D6
Bóly H 74 C3
Bolzaneto I 80 B2
Bolzano I 71 B6
Bomba I 103 A7
Bombarral P 92 B1
Bömenzien D 44 C3
Bomlitz D 43 C6
Bømlo N 33 C2
Bøn N 34 B3
Bona F 68 A3
Bonaduz CH 71 B4
Bonanza E 99 C4
Boñar E 88 B1
Bonarbridge UK 23 D4
Bonárcado I 110 B1
Bonares E 99 B4
Bonäs S 36 A1
Bonassola I 80 B3
Bonawe UK 24 B2
Bondal N 32 C5
Bondeno I 81 B5
Bondorf D 61 B4
Bondstorp S 40 B3
Bon-Encontre F 77 B3
Bo'ness UK 25 B4
Bonete E 101 A4
Bonifacio F 102 B2
Bonigen CH 70 B2
Bonin PL 46 A2
Bonn D 50 C3
Bonnánaro I 110 B1
Bonnåsjøen N 112 E4
Bonnat F 68 B1
Bonndorf D 61 C4
Bonnétable F 58 B1
Bonnétage F 70 A1
Bonneuil-les-Eaux F 58 A3
Bonneuil-Matours F 67 B5
Bonneval F 58 B2
Bonneval-sur-Arc F 70 C2
Bonneville F 69 B6
Bonnières-sur-Seine F 58 A2
Bonnieux F 79 C4
Bönnigheim D 61 A5
Bonnyrigg UK 25 C4
Bonny-sur-Loire F 68 A2
Bono
E 90 A3
I 110 B2
Bonorva I 110 B1
Bønsnes N 34 B2
Bonyhád H 74 B3
Boom B 49 B5
Boos F 58 A2
Boostedt D 44 A2
Bootle
Cumbria UK 26 A2
Merseyside UK 26 B2
Bopfingen D 61 B6
Boppard D 50 C3
Boqueixón E 86 B2
Bor
CZ 62 A3
S 40 B4
SRB 11 D7
TR 16 C7
Boran-sur-Oise F 58 A3
Borås S 40 B2
Borba P 92 C3
Borbona I 102 A6
Borča SRB 85 B5
Borci BIH 84 C3
Borculo NL 50 A2
Bordány H 75 B4
Bordeaux F 76 B2
Bordeira P 98 B2
Bordesholm D 44 A2
Borðeyri IS 111 B4
Bordighera I 80 C1
Bording DK 39 C2
Bordón E 90 C2
Bore I 81 B3
Borehamwood UK 31 C3
Borek Strzeliński PL 54 C2
Borek Wielkopolski PL 54 B2
Boreland UK 25 C4
Borello I 82 B1
Borensberg S 37 D2
Borgafjäll S 115 C12
Borgarnes IS 111 C4
Borgentreich D 51 B5
Börger D 43 C4
Borger NL 42 C3
Borggård S 37 D2
Borghamn S 37 D1
Borghetta di Vara I 81 B3
Borghetto d'Arróscia I 80 B1
Borghetto Santo Spirito I 80 B2
Borgholm S 41 C6
Borghorst D 50 A3
Bórgia I 106 C3
Borgloon B 49 C6
Børglum DK 38 B2
Borgo F 102 A2
Borgo alla Collina I 81 C5
Borgo a Mozzano I 81 C4
Borgoforte I 81 A4
Borgofranco d'Ivrea I 70 C2
Borgomanero I 70 C3
Borgomasino I 70 C2
Borgonovo Val Tidone I 80 A3
Borgo Pace I 82 C1
Borgorose I 102 A6
Borgo San Dalmazzo I 80 B1
Borgo San Lorenzo I 81 C5
Borgosésia I 70 C3
Borgo Val di Taro I 81 B3
Borgo Valsugana I 71 B6
Borgo Vercelli I 70 C3
Borgstena S 40 B3
Borgue UK 24 D3
Borgund N 32 A4
Borgvik S 35 C4
Borisovka RUS 7 F14
Borja E 89 C5
Bork D 50 B3
Borken D 50 B2
Borkenes N 112 D5
Børkop DK 39 D2
Borkowice PL 55 B5
Borkowo PL 47 C6
Borkum D 42 B3
Borlänge S 36 B2
Borlu TR 118 D3
Bormes-les-Mimosas F 79 C5
Bórmio I 71 B5
Bormujos E 99 B4
Borna D 52 B2
Borne NL 50 A2
Bornes P 87 C3
Borne Sulinowo PL 46 B2
Bornheim D 50 C2
Bornhöved D 44 A2
Börnicke D 45 C4
Bornos E 99 C5
Borobia E 89 C5
Borodino RUS 7 D13
Borohrádek CZ 53 C6
Boronów PL 54 C3
Bórore I 110 B1
Borosźow PL 54 C3
Borota H 75 B4
Boroughbridge UK 27 A4
Borovany CZ 63 B5
Borovichi RUS 7 B12
Borovnica SLO 73 C4
Borovo HR 75 C3
Borovsk RUS 7 D14
Borovy CZ 63 A4
Borowa PL 54 B2
Borowie PL 55 B6
Borox E 94 B3
Borrby S 41 D4
Borre
DK 41 E2
N 35 C2
Borredá E 91 A4
Borrenes E 86 B4
Borriol E 96 A2
Borris
DK 39 D1
IRL 21 B5
Borris-in-Ossory IRL 21 B4
Borrisokane IRL 20 B3
Borrisoleigh IRL 21 B4
Borrowdale UK 26 A2
Børrud N 34 C4
Borşa RO 11 C8
Borsdorf D 52 B2
Børselv N 113 B14
Borsfa H 74 B1
Borský Mikuláš SK 64 B3
Borsodivánka H 65 C6
Borsodnádasd H 65 B6
Börte N 33 C4
Borth UK 26 C1
Bort-les-Orgues F 68 C2
Börtnan S 115 E10
Børtnes N 32 B6
Borup DK 39 D4
Boryslav UA 11 B7
Boryspil UA 11 A11
Boryszyn PL 46 C1
Borzęciczki PL 54 B2
Borzęcin PL 55 A5
Borzna UA 7 F12
Borzonasca I 80 B3
Borzyszkowy PL 46 A3
Borzytuchom PL 46 A3
Bosa I 110 B1
Bošáca SK 64 B3
Bosanci HR 73 C5
Bosanska Krupa BIH 83 B5
Bosanski Petrovac BIH 83 B5
Bosansko Grahovo BIH 83 B5
Bošany SK 64 B4
Bösárkány H 64 C3
Bosau D 44 A2
Bósca H 75 B4
Boscastle UK 28 C3
Bosco I 80 B2
Bosco Chiesanuova I 71 C6
Bösdorf D 44 A2
Bösel D 43 B4
Bosham UK 31 D3
Bösingfeld D 51 A5
Bosjön S 34 C5
Boskoop NL 49 A5
Boskovice CZ 64 A2
Bošnjaci HR 84 A3
Bošnjane SRB 85 C6
Bossast E 77 D3
Bossolasco I 80 B2
Boštanj SLO 73 B5
Boston UK 27 C5
Bostrak N 33 C5
Böszénfa H 74 B2
Bot E 90 B3
Botajica BIH 84 B3
Bøte By DK 44 A3
Bothel UK 26 A2
Boticas P 87 C3
Botilsäter S 35 C5
Botngård N 114 D6
Botoš SRB 75 C5
Botoşani RO 11 C9
Botricello I 107 C3
Bottendorf D 51 B4
Bottesford UK 27 C5
Bottnaryd S 40 B3
Bottrop D 50 B2
Botunje SRB 85 B6
Boturić SRB 85 C5
Bötzingen D 60 B3
Bouaye F 66 A3
Bouça P 87 C3
Boucau F 76 C1
Bouchain F 49 C4
Bouchoir F 58 A3
Boudreville F 59 C5
Boudry CH 70 B1
Bouesse F 67 B6
Bouguenais F 66 A3
Bouhy F 68 A3
Bouillargues F 78 C3
Bouillon B 59 A6
Bouilly F 59 B4
Bouin F 66 B3
Boulay-Moselle F 60 A2
Boulazac F 67 C5
Boule-d'Amont F 91 A5
Bouligny F 60 A1
Boulogne-sur-Gesse F 77 C3
Boulogne-sur-Mer F 48 C2
Bouloire F 58 C1
Bouquemaison F 48 C3
Bourbon-Lancy F 68 B3
Bourbon l'Archambault F 68 B3
Bourbonne-les-Bains F 60 C1
Bourbourg F 48 C3
Bourbriac F 56 B2
Bourcefranc-le-Chapus F 66 C3
Bourdeaux F 79 B4
Bouresse F 67 B5
Bourg F 76 A2
Bourg-Achard F 58 A1
Bourganeuf F 68 C1
Bourg-Argental F 69 C4
Bourg-de-Péage F 79 A4
Bourg-de-Thizy F 69 B4
Bourg-de-Visa F 77 B3
Bourg-en-Bresse F 69 B5
Bourges F 68 A2
Bourg-et-Comin F 59 A4
Bourg-Lastic F 68 C2
Bourg-Madame F 91 A4
Bourgneuf-en-Retz F 66 A3
Bourgogne F 59 A5
Bourgoin-Jallieu F 69 C5
Bourg-St Andéol F 78 B3
Bourg-St Maurice F 70 C1
Bourgtheroulde F 58 A1
Bourgueil F 67 A5
Bourmont F 60 B1
Bourne UK 30 B3
Bournemouth UK 29 C6
Bourneville F 58 A1
Bournezeau F 66 B3
Bourran F 77 B3
Bourret F 77 C4
Bourron-Marlotte F 58 B3
Bourton-on-the-Water UK 29 B6
Boussac F 68 B2
Boussens F 77 C3
Boutersem B 49 C5
Bouttencourt F 48 D2
Bouvières F 79 B4
Bouvron F 66 A3
Bouxwiller F 60 B3
Bouzas E 87 B2
Bouzonville F 60 A2
Bova I 106 D2
Bovalino Marina I 106 C3
Bovallstrand S 35 D3
Bova Marina I 106 D2
Bovec SLO 72 B3
Bóveda E 86 B3
Bóvegno I 71 C5
Bovenau D 44 A1
Bovenden D 51 B5
Bøverdal N 114 F5
Boves F 58 A3
Bóves I 80 B1
Bovey Tracey UK 28 C4
Bovino I 103 B8
Bøvlingbjerg DK 38 C1
Bovolenta I 72 C1
Bovolone I 71 C6
Bowes UK 27 A4
Bowmore UK 24 C1
Bowness-on-Windermere UK 26 A3
Box UK 29 B5
Boxberg
Baden-Württemberg D 61 A5
Sachsen D 53 B4
Boxholm S 37 D2
Boxmeer NL 50 B1
Boxtel NL 49 B6
Boyabat TR 16 A7
Boyalıca TR 118 B4
Boyle IRL 18 C3
Bozan TR 118 C6
Božava HR 83 B3
Bozburun TR 119 F3
Bozcaada TR 116 C8
Bozdoğan TR 119 E3
Bożepole Wielkie PL 46 A3
Boževac SRB 85 B6
Božice CZ 64 B2
Boží Dar CZ 52 C2
Bozkır TR 119 E7
Bozouls F 78 B1
Bozova TR 119 E5
Bozüyük TR 118 C5
Bózzolo I 81 A4
Bra I 80 B1
Braås S 40 B5
Brabrand DK 39 C3
Bracadale UK 22 D2
Bracciano I 102 A5
Bracieux F 67 A6
Bräcke S 115 E12
Brackenheim D 61 A5
Brackley UK 30 B2
Bracklin IRL 19 C5
Bracknell UK 31 C3
Brackwede D 51 B4
Braco UK 25 B4
Brad RO 11 C7
Bradford UK 27 B4
Bradford on Avon UK 29 B5
Bradina BIH 84 C3
Brådland N 33 D3
Brædstrup DK 39 D2
Brae UK 22 A7
Braemar UK 23 D5
Braemore UK 22 D3
Braga P 87 C2
Bragança P 87 C4
Brăila RO 11 D9
Braine F 59 A4
Braine-le-Comte B 49 C5
Braintree UK 31 C4
Braives B 49 C6
Brake D 43 B5
Brakel
B 49 C4
D 51 B5
Bräkne-Hoby S 41 C5
Brålanda S 35 D4
Bralin PL 54 B2
Brallo di Pregola I 80 B3
Bram F 77 C5
Bramafan F 79 C5
Bramberg am Wildkogel A 72 A2
Bramdrupdam DK 39 D2
Bramming DK 39 D1
Brampton UK 25 D5
Bramsche D 43 C4
Branca I 82 C1
Brancaleone Marina I 106 D3
Brancaster UK 30 B4
Brand
Nieder Östereich A 63 B6
Vorarlberg A 71 A4
Brandbu N 34 B2
Brande DK 39 D2
Brande-Hornerkirchen D 43 B6
Brandenberg A 72 A1
Brandenburg D 45 C4
Brand-Erbisdorf D 52 C3
Brandis D 52 B2
Brando F 102 A2
Brandomil E 86 A2
Brandon UK 30 B4
Brandshagen D 45 A5
Brandval N 34 B4
Brandýs nad Labem CZ 53 C4
Branice PL 54 C2
Braničevo SRB 85 B6
Braniewo PL 47 A5
Branik SLO 72 C3
Brankovina SRB 85 B4
Branky CZ 64 A3
Branne F 76 B2
Brannenburg-Degerndorf D 62 C3
Brantôme F 67 C5
Branzi I 71 B4
Bras d'Asse F 79 C5
Braskereidfoss N 34 B3
Braslaw BY 7 D9
Braşov RO 11 D8
Brasparts F 56 B2
Brassac F 77 C5
Brassac-les-Mines F 68 C3
Brasschaat B 49 B5
Brastad S 35 D3
Břasy CZ 63 A4
Brąszewice PL 54 B3
Brataj AL 105 C5
Bratislava SK 64 B3
Brattfors S 35 C6
Brattvåg N 114 E3
Bratunac BIH 85 B4
Braubach D 50 C3
Braunau A 62 B4
Braunfels D 51 C4
Braunlage D 51 B6
Braunsbedra D 52 B1
Braunschweig D 51 A6
Bray IRL 21 A5
Bray Dunes F 48 B3
Bray-sur-Seine F 59 B4
Bray-sur-Somme F 48 D3
Brazatortas E 100 A1
Brazey-en-Plaine F 69 A5
Brbinj HR 83 B4
Brčko BIH 84 B3
Brdani SRB 85 C5
Brdów PL 47 C4
Brea de Tajo E 95 B3
Brécey F 57 B4
Brechen D 50 C4
Brechin UK 25 B5
Brecht B 49 B5
Brecketfeld D 50 B3
Břeclav CZ 64 B2
Brecon UK 29 B4
Brécy F 68 A2
Breda
E 91 B5
NL 49 B5
Bredaryd S 40 B3
Bredbyn S 115 D15
Breddin D 44 C4
Bredebro DK 39 D1
Bredelar D 51 B4
Bredenfelde D 45 B5
Bredsjö S 36 C1
Bredstedt D 43 A5
Bredsten DK 39 D2
Bredträsk S 115 D15
Bredviken S 115 A11
Bree B 49 B6
Bregana HR 73 C5
Breganze I 72 C1
Bregenz A 71 A4
Bréhal F 57 B4
Brehna D 52 B2
Breiðdalsvík IS 111 C11
Breidenbach F 60 A3
Breil-sur-Roya F 80 C1
Breisach D 60 B3

Breitenbach
CH 70 A2
D 51 C5
Breitenberg D 63 B4
Breitenfelde D 44 B2
Breitengussbach D 51 D6
Breivikbotn N 113 B11
Brejning DK 39 D2
Brekke N 32 A2
Brekken N 114 E8
Brekkestø N 33 D5
Brekkvasselv N 115 C10
Brekstad N 114 D6
Breland N 33 D4
Bremanger N 114 F1
Bremen D 43 B5
Bremerhaven D 43 B5
Bremervörde D 43 B6
Bremgarten CH 70 A3
Bremsnes N 114 D4
Brem-sur-Mer F 66 B3
Brenderup DK 39 D2
Brenes E 99 B5
Brengova SLO 73 B5
Brenna PL 65 A4
Breno I 71 C5
Brénod F 69 B5
Brensbach D 61 A4
Brentwood UK 31 C4
Brescello I 81 B4
Bréscia I 71 C5
Breskens NL 49 B4
Bresles F 58 A3
Bresnica SRB 85 C5
Bressana I 80 A3
Bressanone I 72 B1
Bressuire F 67 B4
Brest
BY 6 E7
F 56 B1
HR 72 C3
Brestač SRB 85 B4
Brestanica SLO 73 B5
Brestova HR 82 A3
Brestovac HR 74 C2
Bretenoux F 77 B4
Breteuil
Eure F 58 B1
Oise F 58 A3
Brétigny-sur-Orge F 58 B3
Bretten D 61 A4
Bretteville-sur-Laize
F 57 A5
Brettheim D 61 A6
Breuil-Cervínia I 70 C2
Breukelen NL 49 A6
Brevik
N 35 C1
Stockholm S 37 C5
Västra Götaland S 37 D1
Breza BIH 84 B3
Brežice SLO 73 C5
Bréziers F 79 B5
Brezna SRB 85 C5
Breznica HR 73 B6
Breznica Našička HR 74 C3
Březnice CZ 63 A4
Brezno SK 65 B5
Brezojevice MNE 85 D4
Brezolles F 58 B2
Brezovánad Svitavou
CZ 64 A2
Brezovápod Bradlom
SK 64 B3
Brezovica
SK 65 A6
SLO 73 B4
Brezovo Polje Selo
BIH 84 B3
Briançon F 79 B5
Brianconnet F 79 C5
Briare F 58 C3
Briatexte F 77 C4
Briático I 106 C3
Briaucourt F 59 B6
Bribir HR 73 C4
Bricquebec F 57 A4
Bridgend
Argyll & Bute UK 24 C1
Bridgend UK 29 B4
Bridge of Cally UK 25 B4
Bridge of Don UK 23 D6
Bridge of Earn UK 25 B4
Bridge of Orchy UK 24 B3
Bridgnorth UK 26 C3
Bridgwater UK 29 B5
Břidličná CZ 64 A3
Bridlington UK 27 A5
Bridport UK 29 C5
Briec F 56 B1
Brie-Comte-Robert F 58 B3
Brienne-le-Château F 59 B5
Brienon-sur-Armançon
F 59 C4
Brienz CH 70 B3
Brienza I 104 C1
Briesen D 45 C6
Brieskow Finkenheerd
D 53 A4
Brietlingen D 44 B2
Brieva de Cameros E 89 B4
Briey F 60 A1
Brig CH 70 B3
Brigg UK 27 B5
Brighouse UK 27 B4
Brightlingsea UK 31 C5
Brighton UK 31 D3
Brignogan-Plage F 56 B1
Brignoles F 79 C5
Brigstock UK 30 B3
Brihuega E 95 B4
Brijuni HR 82 B2
Brillon-en-Barrois F 59 B6
Brilon D 51 B4
Brimnes N 32 B3
Brinches P 98 A3
Bríndisi I 105 C3
Brinje HR 83 A4
Brinon-sur-Beuvron F 68 A3
Brinon-sur-Sauldre F 68 A2
Brinyan UK 23 B5
Brión E 86 B2
Briones E 89 B4
Brionne F 58 A1
Brioude F 68 C3
Brioux-sur-Boutonne
F 67 B4
Briouze F 57 B5
Briscous F 76 C1
Brisighella I 81 B5
Brissac-Quincé F 67 A4
Brissago CH 70 B3
Bristol UK 29 B5
Brive-la-Gaillarde F 67 C6
Briviesca E 89 B3
Brixham UK 29 C4
Brixlegg A 72 A1
Brjánslækur IS 111 B2
Brka BIH 84 B3
Brnaze HR 83 C5
Brněnec CZ 64 A2
Brno CZ 64 A2
Bro S 37 C4
Broadclyst UK 29 C4
Broadford
IRL 20 B3
UK 22 D3
Broad Haven UK 28 B2
Broadstairs UK 31 C5
Broadstone UK 29 C5
Broadway UK 29 A6
Broager DK 39 E2
Broaryd S 40 B3
Broby S 41 C4
Brobyværk DK 39 D3
Bročanac BIH 84 C2
Broćanac MNE 84 D3
Brocas F 76 B2
Brock D 50 A3
Brockel D 43 B6
Brockenhurst UK 31 D2
Broczyno PL 46 B2
Brod
BIH 84 A2
NMK 116 A3
Brodalen S 35 D3
Brodarevo SRB 85 C4
Broddbo S 36 C3
Brodek u Přerova CZ 64 A3
Broden-bach D 50 C3
Brodick UK 24 C2
Brod na Kupi HR 73 C4
Brodnica PL 47 B5
Brodnica Graniczna
PL 47 A4
Brody
Lubuskie PL 53 A5
Lubuskie PL 53 B4
Mazowieckie PL 47 C6
UA 11 A8
Broglie F 58 B1
Brójce PL 53 A5
Brokind S 37 D2
Brolo I 109 A3
Brome D 44 C2
Bromley UK 31 C4
Bromölla S 41 C4
Bromont-Lamothe F 68 C2
Brömsebro S 41 C5
Bromsgrove UK 29 A5
Bromyard UK 29 A5
Bronchales E 95 B5
Bronco E 93 A4
Brønderslev DK 38 B2
Broni I 80 A3
Brønnøysund N 114 B9
Brøns DK 39 D1
Bronte I 109 B3
Bronzani Mejdan BIH 84 B1
Bronzolo I 71 B6
Broons F 57 B3
Broquies F 78 B1
Brora UK 23 C5
Brørup DK 39 D2
Brösarp S 41 D4
Brossac F 67 C4
Brostrud N 32 B5
Brotas P 92 C2
Brötjärna S 36 B2
Broto E 90 A2
Brottby S 37 C5
Brøttum N 34 A2
Brou F 58 B2
Brouage F 66 C3
Brough UK 26 A3
Broughshane UK 19 B5
Broughton UK 25 C4
Broughton-
in-Furness UK 26 A2
Broumov CZ 53 C6
Broût-Vernet F 68 B3
Brouvelieures F 60 B2
Brouwershaven NL 49 B4
Brovary UA 11 A11
Brovst DK 38 B2
Brownhills UK 27 C4
Brozas E 93 B4
Brozzo I 71 C5
Brtnice CZ 63 A6
Brtonigla HR 72 C3
Bruay-la-Buissière F 48 C3
Bruchhausen-Vilsen
D 43 C6
Bruchsal D 61 A4
Bruck D 62 A3
Brück D 52 A2
Bruck an der
Grossglocknerstrasse
A 72 A2
Bruck an der Leitha A 64 B2
Bruck an der Mur A 73 A5
Brückl A 73 B4
Bruckmühl D 62 C2
Brue-Auriac F 79 C4
Brüel D 44 B3
Bruen CH 70 B3
Bruère-Allichamps F 68 B2
Bruff IRL 20 B3
Bruflat N 32 B6
Brugg CH 70 A3
Brugge B 49 B4
Brüggen D 50 B2
Brühl D 50 C2
Bruinisse NL 49 B5
Brûlon F 57 C5
Brumano I 71 C4
Brumath F 60 B3
Brummen NL 50 A2
Brumov-Bylnice CZ 64 A4
Brumunddal N 34 B2
Brunau D 44 C3
Brunehamel F 59 A5
Brünen D 50 B2
Brunete E 94 B2
Brunflo S 115 D11
Brunico I 72 B1
Brunkeberg N 33 C5
Brunn D 45 B5
Brunnen CH 70 B3
Brunsbüttel D 43 B6
Brunssum NL 50 C1
Bruntál CZ 54 D2
Brus SRB 85 C6
Brušane HR 83 B4
Brusasco I 70 C3
Brusio CH 71 B5
Brusno SK 65 B5
Brusque F 78 C1
Brussels = Bruxelles B 49 C5
Brusson I 70 C2
Brüssow D 45 B6
Brusy PL 46 B3
Bruton UK 29 B5
Bruvno HR 83 B4
Bruvoll N 34 B3
Bruxelles = Brussels B 49 C5
Bruyères F 60 B2
Bruz F 57 B4
Bruzaholm S 40 B5
Brwinów PL 55 A5
Bryansk RUS 7 E13
Brynamman UK 28 B4
Bryncrug UK 26 C1
Bryne N 33 D2
Brynmawr UK 29 B4
Bryrup DK 39 C2
Brzeće SRB 85 C5
Brzeg PL 54 C2
Brzeg Dolny PL 54 B1
Brześć Kujawski PL 47 C4
Brzesko PL 55 D5
Brzeszcze PL 55 D4
Brzezie PL 46 B2
Brzeziny
Łódzkie PL 55 B4
Wielkopolskie PL 54 B3
Brzeźnica PL 53 B5
Brzežnica Nowa PL 55 B4
Brzeżno PL 46 B1
Brzotin SK 65 B6
Brzozie Lubawskie PL 47 B5
Bua S 40 B2
Buarcos P 92 A2
Buaveg N 33 C2
Bubbio I 80 B2
Bubry F 56 C2
Buca TR 119 D2
Bucak TR 119 E5
Bučany SK 64 B3
Buccheri I 109 B3
Buccino I 103 C8
Bucelas P 92 C1
Buch
Bayern D 61 B6
Bayern D 62 B3
Buchach UA 11 B8
Bucharest = Bucureşti
RO 11 D9
Buchbach D 62 B3
Buchboden A 71 A4
Buchen D 61 A5
Büchen D 44 B2
Buchenberg D 61 C6
Buchères F 59 B5
Buchholz D 44 B1
Buchloe D 62 B1
Buchlovice CZ 64 A3
Buchlyvie UK 24 B3
Bucholz D 44 B4
Buchs CH 71 A4
Buchy F 58 A2
Bückeburg D 51 A5
Buckfastleigh UK 28 C4
Buckhaven UK 25 B4
Buckie UK 23 D6
Buckingham UK 31 B3
Buckley UK 26 B2
Bückwitz D 44 C4
Bučovice CZ 64 A3
Bucsa H 75 A6
Bucureşti = Bucharest
RO 11 D9
Bucy-lés-Pierrepont F 59 A4
Buczek PL 55 B4
Bud N 114 E3
Budakalasz H 65 C5
Budakeszi H 75 A3
Budal N 114 E7
Budaörs H 75 A3
Budapest H 75 A4
Búðardalur IS 111 B4
Budča SK 65 B5
Buddusò I 110 B2
Bude UK 28 C3
Budeč CZ 63 A6
Büdelsdorf D 43 A6
Budens P 98 B2
Budia E 95 B4
Budimlić-Japra BIH 83 B5
Büdingen D 51 C5
Budinšćina HR 73 B6
Budišov CZ 64 A3
Budleigh Salterton UK 29 C4
Budmerice SK 64 B3
Budoni I 110 B2
Búdrio I 81 B5
Budva MNE 105 A4
Budyněnad Ohří CZ 53 C4
Budziszewice PL 55 B4
Budzyń PL 46 C2
Bue N 33 D2
Bueña E 95 B5
Buenache de Alarcón
E 95 C4
Buenache de la Sierra
E 95 B5
Buenaventura E 94 B2
Buenavista
de Valdavia E 88 B2
Buendia E 95 B4
Bueu E 87 B2
Buezo E 89 B3
Bugac H 75 B4
Bugarra E 96 B2
Bugeat F 68 C1
Buggerru I 110 C1
Bugojno BIH 84 B2
Bugøyfjord N 113 C18
Bugøynes N 113 C18
Bugyi H 75 A4
Buharkent TR 119 E3
Bühl
Baden-Württemberg
D 61 B4
Bayern D 61 C6
Bühlertal D 61 B4
Bühlertann D 61 A5
Buia I 72 B3
Builth Wells UK 29 A4
Buin N 32 B6
Buis-les-Baronnies F 79 B4
Buitenpost NL 42 B3
Buitrago del Lozoya
E 94 B3
Bujalance E 100 B1
Bujaraloz E 90 B2
Buje HR 72 C3
Bujedo E 89 B3
Bük H 74 A1
Buk PL 46 C2
Bükkösd H 74 B2
Bükkzsérc H 65 C6
Bukovci SLO 73 B5
Bukowiec PL 53 A6
Bukowina Tatrzańska
PL 65 A6
Bukownica PL 54 B3
Bukowno PL 55 C4
Bülach CH 70 A3
Búland IS 111 D7
Buldan TR 119 D3
Bulgnéville F 60 B1
Bulgurca TR 119 D2
Bülkau D 43 B5
Bulken N 32 B3
Bulkowo PL 47 C6
Bullas E 101 A4
Bulle CH 70 B2
Büllingen B 50 C2
Bulqizë AL 116 A2
Buna BIH 84 C2
Bunahowen IRL 18 B2
Bunbeg IRL 18 A3
Bunclody IRL 21 B5
Buncrana IRL 19 A4
Bunde D 43 B4
Bünde D 51 A4
Bundoran IRL 18 B3
Bunessan UK 24 B1
Bungay UK 30 B5
Bunge S 37 E6
Bunić HR 83 B4
Bunmahon IRL 21 B4
Bunnyconnellan IRL 18 B2
Buño E 86 A2
Buñol E 96 B2
Bunratty IRL 20 B3
Bunsbeek B 49 C5
Buñuel E 89 C5
Bünyan TR 16 B7
Bunyola E 97 B2
Buonabitácolo I 104 C1
Buonalbergo I 103 B7
Buonconvento I 81 C5
Buonvicino I 106 B2
Burano I 72 C2
Burbach D 50 C4
Burcei I 110 C2
Burdons-sur-Rognon
F 59 B6
Burdur TR 119 E5
Bureå S 3 D24
Burela E 86 A3
Büren D 51 B4
Büren an der Aare CH 70 A2
Burford UK 29 B6
Burg
Cottbus D 53 B4
Magdeburg D 52 A1
Schleswig-Holstein D 43 B6
Burgas BG 11 E9
Burgau
A 73 A6
D 61 B6
P 98 B2
Burg auf Fehmarn D 44 A3
Burgbernheim D 61 A6
Burgdorf
CH 70 A2
D 44 C2
Burgebrach D 62 A1
Bürgel D 52 C1
Burgess Hill UK 31 D3
Burghaslach D 61 A6
Burghausen D 62 B3
Burghead UK 23 D5
Burgheim D 62 B2
Burgh le Marsh UK 27 B6
Búrgio I 108 B2
Burgkirchen D 62 B3
Burgkunstadt D 52 C1
Burglengenfeld D 62 A3
Burgo P 87 D2
Burgoberbach D 61 A6
Burgohondo E 94 B2
Burgos E 88 B3
Burgsinn D 51 C5
Burgstädt D 52 C2
Burgstall D 44 C3
Burg Stargard D 45 B5
Burgsvik S 37 E5
Burgui E 76 D2
Burguillos E 99 B5
Burguillos
del Cerro E 93 C4
Burguillos de Toledo
E 94 C3
Burhaniye TR 118 C1
Burhave D 43 B5
Burie F 67 C4
Burjassot E 96 B2
Burk D 61 A6
Burkhardtsdorf D 52 C2
Burlada E 76 D1
Burladingen D 61 B5
Burlage D 43 B4
Burness UK 23 B6
Burnham UK 31 C3
Burnham Market UK 30 B4
Burnham-
on-Crouch UK 31 C4
Burnham-on-Sea UK 29 B5
Burniston UK 27 A5
Burnley UK 26 B3
Burntisland UK 25 B4
Burón E 88 A1
Buronzo I 70 C3
Burovac SRB 85 B6
Burow D 45 B5
Burravoe UK 22 A7
Burrel AL 105 B6
Burret F 77 D4
Burriana E 96 B2
Burry Port UK 28 B3
Bürs A 71 A4
Bursa TR 118 B4
Burseryd S 40 B3
Bürstadt D 61 A4
Burton UK 26 A3
Burton Agnes UK 27 A5
Burton Bradstock UK 29 C5
Burton Latimer UK 30 B3
Burton upon Stather
UK 27 B5
Burton upon Trent UK 27 C4
Burujón E 94 C2
Burwell UK 30 B4
Burwick UK 23 C6
Bury UK 26 B3
Buryn UA 7 F12
Bury St Edmunds UK 30 B4
Burzenin PL 54 B3
Busachi I 110 B1
Busalla I 80 B2
Busana I 81 B4
Busano I 70 C2
Busca I 80 B1
Busch D 44 C3
Buševec HR 73 C6
Bushat AL 105 B5
Bushey UK 31 C3
Bushmills UK 19 A5
Bušince SK 65 B5
Buskhyttan S 37 D3
Busko-Zdrój PL 55 C5
Busot E 96 C2
Busovača BIH 84 B2
Busquistar E 100 C2
Bussang F 60 C2
Busseto I 81 B4
Bussière-Badil F 67 C5
Bussière-Poitevine F 67 B5
Bussolengo I 71 C5
Bussoleno I 70 C2
Bussum NL 49 A6
Busto Arsízio I 70 C3
Büsum D 43 A5
Butera I 109 B3
Butgenbach B 50 C2
Butler's Bridge IRL 19 B4
Butryny PL 47 B6
Bütschwil CH 70 A4
Buttermere UK 26 A2
Buttevant IRL 20 B3
Buttle S 37 E5
Buttstädt D 52 B1
Butzbach D 51 C4
Bützfleth D 43 B6
Bützow D 44 B3
Buxières-les-Mines F 68 B2
Buxtehude D 43 B6
Buxton UK 27 B4
Buxy F 69 B4
Büyükçekmece TR 118 A3
Büyükkariştiran TR 118 A2
Büyükorhan TR 118 C3
Buzançais F 67 B6
Buzancy F 59 A5
Buzău RO 11 D9
Buzet HR 72 C3
Buzsák H 74 B2
Buzy F 76 C2
By S 36 B3
Byala BG 11 E8
Byaroza BY 6 E8
Byczyna PL 54 B3
Bydalen S 115 D10
Bydgoszcz PL 47 B4
Bygdin N 32 A5
Bygland N 33 D4
Byglandsfjord N 33 D4
Bygstad N 32 A2
Bykhaw BY 7 E11
Bykle N 33 C4
Bylderup-Bov DK 39 E2
Byrkjedal N 33 D3
Byrkjelo N 114 F3
Byrum DK 38 B3
Byšice CZ 53 C4
Byske S 3 D24
Býškovice CZ 64 A3
Bysław PL 46 B3
Bystré CZ 64 A2
Bystřice CZ 63 A5
Bystrice CZ 65 A4
Bystřice nad
Pernštejnem CZ 64 A2
Bystřice pod
Hostýnem CZ 64 A3
Bystrzyca Kłodzka PL 54 C1
Bytča SK 65 A4
Bytnica PL 53 A5
Bytom PL 54 C3
Bytom Odrzański PL 53 B5
Bytów PL 46 A3
Byxelkrok S 41 B7
Bzenec CZ 64 B3
Bzince SK 64 B3

C

Çağa TR 118 B7
Cabacos P 92 B2
Cabaj-Čápor SK 64 B4
Cabana E 86 A2
Cabanac-et-
Villagrains F 76 B2
Cabañaquinta E 88 A1
Cabanas P 98 B3
Cabañas del Castillo
E 93 B5
Cabañas de Yepes E 95 C3
Cabanelles E 91 A5
Cabanes E 96 A3
Cabanillas E 89 B5
Čabar HR 73 C4
Cabasse F 79 C5
Cabdella E 91 A4
Cabeceiras de Basto
P 87 C2
Cabeço de Vide P 92 B3
Cabella Ligure I 80 B3
Cabeza del Buey E 93 C5
Cabeza la Vaca E 99 A4
Cabezamesada E 95 C3
Cabezarados E 100 A1
Cabezarrubias del
Puerto E 100 A1
Cabezas del Villar E 94 B1
Cabezas Rubias E 98 B3
Cabezón E 88 C2
Cabezón de la Sal E 88 A2
Cabezón de Liébana
E 88 A2
Cabezuela E 94 A3
Cabezuela del Valle E 93 A5
Cabo de Gata E 101 C3
Cabo de Palos E 101 B5
Cabolafuenta E 95 A4
Cabourg F 57 A5
Cabra
E 100 B1
P 92 A3
Cabrach UK 23 D5
Cabra del
Santo Cristo E 100 B2
Cábras I 110 C1
Cabreiro P 87 C2
Cabreiros E 86 A3
Cabrejas E 95 B4
Cabrela P 92 C2
Cabrillas E 87 D4
Cabuna HR 74 C2
Cacabelos E 86 B4
Čačak SRB 85 C5
Cáccamo I 108 B2
Caccuri I 107 B3
Cacela P 98 B3
Cacém P 92 C1
Cáceres E 93 B4
Cachafeiro E 86 B2
Cachopo P 98 B3
Čachtice SK 64 B3
Cacin E 100 B2
Čačinci HR 74 C2
Cadafais P 92 C1
Cadalen F 77 C5
Cadalso E 93 A4
Cadaqués E 91 A6
Cadaval P 92 B1
Cadavedo E 86 A4
Čadavica BIH 84 B1
Čadca SK 65 A4
Cadéac F 77 D3
Cadelbosco di Sopra
I 81 B4
Cadenazzo CH 70 B3
Cadenberge D 43 B6
Cadenet F 79 C4
Cadeuil F 66 C4
Cádiar E 100 C2
Cadillac F 76 B2
Cádiz E 99 C4
Čadjavica HR 74 C2
Cadouin F 77 B3
Cadours F 77 C4
Cadrete E 90 B2
Caen F 57 A5
Caerleon UK 29 B5
Caernarfon UK 26 B1
Caerphilly UK 29 B4
Caersws UK 26 C2
Cafede P 92 B3
Caggiano I 104 C1
Cagli I 82 C1
Cágliari I 110 C2
Čaglin HR 74 C2
Cagnano Varano I 104 B1
Cagnes-sur-Mer F 79 C6
Caher IRL 21 B4
Caherciveen IRL 20 C1
Caherdaniel IRL 20 C1
Cahors F 77 B4
Cahul MD 11 D10
Caiazzo I 103 B7
Caion E 86 A2
Cairndow UK 24 B3
Cairnryan UK 24 D2
Cairo Montenotte I 80 B2
Caister-on-Sea UK 30 B5
Caistor UK 27 B5
Caivano I 103 C7
Cajarc F 77 B4
Čajetina SRB 85 C4
Čajniče BIH 84 C4
Çakırlar TR 119 F5
Çakmak TR 118 C6
Čakovec HR 73 B6
Cakran AL 105 C5
Çal TR 119 D4
Cala E 99 B4
Calabritto I 103 C8
Calaceite E 90 C3
Calacuccia F 102 A2
Cala d'Or E 97 B3
Calaf E 91 B4
Calafat RO 11 D7
Calafell E 91 B4
Cala Galdana E 97 B3
Cala Gonone I 110 B2
Calahonda
Granada E 100 C2
Málaga E 100 C1
Calahorra E 89 B5
Calais F 48 C2
Cala Llonga E 97 C1
Calalzo di Cadore I 72 B2
Cala Millor E 97 B3
Calamocha E 95 B5
Calamonte E 93 C4
Cala Morell E 97 A3
Calanais UK 22 C2
Calañas E 99 B4
Calanda E 90 C2
Calangiánus I 110 B2
Călăraşi RO 11 D9
Cala Ratjada E 97 B3
Calascibetta I 109 B3
Calasetta I 110 C1
Calasparra E 101 A4
Calatafimi I 108 B1
Calatayud E 89 C5
Calatorao E 89 C5
Calau D 53 B3
Calbe D 52 B1
Calcena E 89 C5
Calcinelli I 82 C1
Calco I 71 C4
Caldarola I 82 C2
Caldaro sulla
strada del Vino I 71 B6
Caldas da Rainha P 92 B1
Caldas de Boì E 90 A3
Caldas de Malavella E 91 B5
Caldas de Reis E 86 B2
Caldas de San Jorge
P 87 D2
Caldas de Vizela P 87 C2
Caldaso de
los Vidrios E 94 B2
Caldbeck UK 26 A2
Caldearenas E 90 A2
Caldelas P 87 C2
Calders E 91 B4
Caldes de Montbui E 91 B5
Caldicot UK 29 B5
Caldirola I 80 B3
Caledon UK 19 B5
Calella
Barcelona E 91 B5
Girona E 91 B6
Calenzana F 102 A1
Calera de León E 99 A4
Calera y Chozas E 94 C2
Caleruega E 89 C3
Caleruela E 93 B5
Cales de Mallorca E 97 B3
Calestano I 81 B4
Calfsound UK 23 B6
Calgary UK 24 B1
Calimera I 105 C4
Calitri I 103 C8
Calizzano I 80 B2
Callac F 56 B2
Callan IRL 21 B4
Callander UK 24 B3
Callas F 79 C5
Calliano
Piemonte I 80 A2
Trentino Alto Adige I 71 C6
Callington UK 28 C3
Callosa de Ensarriá E 96 C2
Callosa de Segura E 101 A5
Callús E 91 B4
Čalma SRB 85 A4
Calmbach D 61 B4
Calne UK 29 B6
Calolziocorte I 71 C4
Calonge E 91 B6
Čalovec SK 64 C3
Calpe E 96 C3
Caltabellotta I 108 B2
Caltagirone I 109 B3
Caltanissetta I 109 B3
Caltavuturo I 108 B2
Çaltılıbük TR 118 C3
Caltojar E 89 C4
Caluire-et-Cuire F 69 C4
Caluso I 70 C2
Calvello I 104 C1
Calvi F 102 A1
Calviá E 97 B2
Calvinet F 77 B5
Calvisson F 78 C3
Calvörde D 44 C3
Calw D 61 B4
Calzada
de Calatrava E 100 A2
Calzada
de Valdunciel E 94 A1
Calzadilla
de los Barros E 93 C4
Cam UK 29 B5
Camaiore I 81 C4
Camarasa E 90 B3
Camarena E 94 B2
Camarès F 78 C1
Camaret-sur-Aigues
F 78 B3
Camaret-sur-Mer F 56 B1
Camarillas E 90 C2
Camariñas E 86 A1
Camarma E 95 B3
Camarzana de Tera E 87 B4
Camas E 99 B4
Camastra I 108 B2
Cambados E 86 B2
Cambarinho P 92 A2
Camberley UK 31 C3
Cambil E 100 B2
Cambligeu F 48 C3
Cambo-les-Bains F 76 C1
Camborne UK 28 C2
Cambourne UK 30 B3
Cambrai F 49 C4
Cambre E 86 A2
Cambridge UK 30 B4
Cambrils E 91 B4
Cambs D 44 B3
Camburg D 52 B1
Camden UK 31 C3
Cameleño E 88 A2
Camelford UK 28 C3
Çameli TR 119 E4
Camelle E 86 A1
Camerano I 82 C2
Camerino I 82 C2
Camerota I 106 A2
Camigliatello Silano
I 106 B3
Caminha P 87 C2
Caminomorisco E 93 A4
Caminreal E 95 B5
Camisano Vicentino I 72 C1
Camlıdere TR 118 B7
Cammarata I 108 B2
Camogli I 80 B3
Camors F 56 C3
Camp IRL 20 B2
Campagna I 103 C8
Campagnano di Roma
I 102 A5
Campagnático I 81 D5
Campan F 76 C3
Campana I 107 B3
Campanario E 93 C5
Campanillas E 100 C1
Campano E 99 C4
Campaspero E 88 C2
Campbeltown UK 24 C2
Campello E 96 C2
Campelos P 92 B1
Campi Bisénzio I 81 C5
Campico López E 101 B4
Campíglia Maríttima
I 81 C4
Campillo de Altobuey
E 95 C5
Campillo de Aragón
E 95 A5
Campillo de Arenas
E 100 B2
Campillo de Llerena E 93 C5
Campillos E 100 B1
Câmpina RO 11 D8
Campi Salentina I 105 C4
Campli I 82 D2
Campo E 90 A3
Campobasso I 103 B7
Campobello di Licata
I 108 B2
Campobello
di Mazara I 108 B1
Campo da Feira E 86 A3
Campodársego I 72 C1
Campo de Bacerros E 87 B3
Campo de Caso E 88 A1
Campo de Criptana E 95 C3
Campodolcino I 71 B4
Campofelice
di Roccella I 108 B2
Campofiorito I 108 B2
Campofórmido I 72 B3
Campofranco I 108 B2
Campofrio E 99 B4
Campogalliano I 81 B4
Campo Ligure I 80 B2
Campolongo I 72 B2
Campo Lugar E 93 B5
Campo Maior P 93 B3
Campomanes E 88 A1
Campomarino I 103 B8
Campo Molino I 79 B6
Campomono F 102 B1
Campo Real E 95 B3
Camporeale I 108 B2
Camporeggiano I 82 C1
Camporrells E 90 B3
Camporrobles E 96 B1
Campos P 87 C3
Camposa P 87 C2
Camposampiero I 72 C1
Camposanto I 81 B5
Campos del Port E 97 B3
Camposines E 90 B3
Campotéjar E 100 B2
Campotosto I 103 A6
Campo Túres I 72 B1
Camprodón E 91 A5
Campsegret F 77 B3
Camrose UK 28 B2
Camuñas E 95 C3
Çamyolu TR 119 F7
Çan TR 118 B2
Cana I 81 D5
Cañada del Hoyo E 95 C5
Cañadajuncosa E 95 C4
Cañada Rosal E 99 B5
Čanak HR 83 B4
Çanakkale TR 118 B1
Canale I 80 B1
Canales
Asturias E 88 B1
Castellón de la Plana
E 96 B2
Canals E 96 C2
Canal San Bovo I 72 B1
Cañamares E 95 B4
Cañamero E 93 B5
Cañar E 100 C2
Cañate la Real E 99 C5
Cañaveral E 93 B4
Cañaveral de León E 99 A4
Cañaveras E 95 B4
Cañaveruelas E 95 B4
Canazei I 72 B1
Cancale F 57 B4
Cancellara I 104 C1
Cancello ed Arnone
I 103 B7
Cancon F 77 B3
Canda E 87 B4
Candamil E 86 A3
Candanchu E 76 D2
Çandarlı TR 118 D1
Candas E 88 A1
Candasnos E 90 B3
Candé F 66 A3
Candela I 104 B1
Candelario E 93 A5
Candeleda E 93 A5
Cándia Lomellina I 70 C3
Candide
Casamazzagno I 72 B2
Candin E 86 B4
Candosa P 92 A3
Canecas P 92 C1
Canelli I 80 B2
Canena E 100 A2
Canencia E 94 B3
Canero E 86 A4
Canet F 78 C2
Canet de Mar E 91 B5
Canet d'en Berenguer
E 96 B2
Cañete E 95 B5
Cañete de las Torres
E 100 B1
Canet-en-Roussillon
F 91 A6
Canfranc E 76 D2
Cangas
Lugo E 86 A3
Pontevedra E 87 B2
Cangas de Narcea E 86 A4
Cangas de Onís E 88 A1
Canha P 92 C2
Canhestros P 98 A2
Canicattì I 108 B2
Canicattini Bagni I 109 B4
Canicosa de la Sierra
E 89 C3
Caniles E 101 B3
Canillas de
Aceituno E 100 C1
Canino I 102 A4
Canisy F 57 A4
Cañizal E 94 A1
Cañizo E 88 C1
Canjáyar E 101 C3
Çankırı TR 16 A6
Cannai I 110 C1
Cannara I 82 C1
Cánnero Riviera I 70 B3
Cannes F 79 C6
Canneto
Sicilia I 106 C1
Toscana I 81 C4
Canneto sull'Oglio I 71 C5
Cannich UK 22 D4
Cannóbio I 70 B3
Cannock UK 26 C3
Canonbie UK 25 C5
Canosa di Púglia I 104 B2
Can Pastilla E 97 B2
C'an Picafort E 97 B3
Cantalapiedra E 94 A1
Cantalejo E 94 A3
Cantalgallo E 99 A4
Cantalice I 102 A5
Cantalpino E 94 A1
Cantalupo in Sabina
I 102 A5
Cantanhede P 92 A2
Cantavieja E 90 C2
Čantavir SRB 75 C4
Canterbury UK 31 C5
Cantiano I 82 C1
Cantillana E 99 B5
Cantiveros E 94 B2
Cantoria E 101 B3
Cantù I 71 C4
Canvey UK 31 C4
Cany-Barville F 58 A1
Canyet de Mar E 91 B5
Caol UK 24 B2
Cáorle I 72 C2
Caorso I 81 A3
Capáccio I 103 C8
Capaci I 108 A2
Capálbio I 102 A4
Capánnori I 81 C4
Caparde BIH 84 B3
Caparroso E 89 B5
Capbreton F 76 C1
Capdenac-Gare F 77 B5
Capdepera E 97 B3
Cap-de-Pin F 76 B2
Capel Curig UK 26 B2
Capellades E 91 B4
Capena I 102 A5
Capendu F 77 C5
Capestang F 78 C2
Capestrano I 103 A6
Cap Ferret F 76 B1
Capileira E 100 C2
Capinha P 92 A3
Ca'Pisani I 82 B1
Capistrello I 103 B6
Capizzi I 109 B3
Čaplje BIH 83 B5
Čapljina BIH 84 C2
Capo di Ponte I 71 B5
Caposile I 72 C2
Capoterra I 110 C1
Cappamore IRL 20 B3
Cappeln D 43 C5
Cappoquin IRL 21 B4
Capracotta I 103 B7
Capránica I 102 A5
Caprarola I 102 A5
Capretta I 82 D1
Capri I 103 C7
Capriati a Volturno I 103 B7
Caprino Veronese I 71 C5
Captieux F 76 B2
Cápua I 103 B7
Capurso I 104 B2
Capvern F 77 C3
Carabaña E 95 B3
Carabias E 88 C3
Caracal RO 11 D8
Caracenilla E 95 B4
Caráglio I 80 B1
Caraman F 77 C4
Caramánico Terme I 103 A7
Caranga E 86 A4
Caranguejeira P 92 B2
Caransebeş RO 11 D7
Carantec F 56 B2
Carapelle I 104 B1
Carasco I 80 B3
Carate Brianza I 71 C4
Caravaca de la Cruz
E 101 A4
Caravággio I 71 C4
Carbajal E 100 C1
Carbajo E 93 B3
Carballeda E 86 B3
Carballeda de Avia E 87 B2
Carballo E 86 A2
Carbis Bay UK 28 C2
Carbon-Blanc F 76 B2
Carbonera
de Frentes E 89 C4
Carboneras E 101 C4
Carboneras de
Guadazaón E 95 C5
Carbonero el Mayor E 94 A2
Carboneros E 100 A2
Carbónia I 110 C1
Carbonin I 72 B2
Carbonne F 77 C4
Carbost UK 22 D2
Carcaboso E 93 A4
Carcabuey E 100 B1
Carcaixent E 96 B2
Carcans F 76 A1
Carcans-Plage F 76 A1
Carção P 87 C4
Carcar E 89 B5
Cárcare I 80 B2
Carcassonne F 77 C5
Carcastillo E 89 B5
Carcedo de Burgos E 89 B3
Carcelén E 96 B1
Carcès F 79 C5
Carchelejo E 100 B2
Çardak
Çanakkale TR 118 B1
Denizli TR 119 E4
Cardedeu E 91 B5
Cardeña E 100 A1
Cardenete E 95 C5
Cardeñosa E 94 B2
Cardeto I 109 A4
Cardiff UK 29 B4
Cardigan UK 28 A3
Cardona E 91 B4
Cardosos P 92 B2
Carei RO 11 C7
Carentan F 57 A4
Carentoir F 57 C3
Careri I 106 C3
Carevdar HR 74 B1
Cargèse F 102 A1
Carhaix-Plouguer F 56 B2
Caria P 92 A3
Cariati I 107 B3
Carignan F 59 A6
Carignano I 80 B1
Cariñena E 90 B1
Carini I 108 A2
Cariño E 86 A3
Carínola I 103 B6
Carisbrooke UK 31 D2
Carlabhagh UK 22 C2
Carlepont F 59 A4
Carlet E 96 B2
Carlingford IRL 19 B5
Carlisle UK 25 D5
Carloforte I 110 C1
Carlópoli I 106 B3
Carlow
D 44 B2
IRL 21 B5
Carlton UK 27 C4
Carluke UK 25 C4
Carmagnola I 80 B1
Carmarthen UK 28 B3
Carmaux F 77 B5
Carmena E 94 C2
Cármenes E 88 B1
Carmine I 80 B1
Carmona E 99 B5
Carmonita E 93 B4
Carmyllie UK 25 B5
Carnac F 56 C2
Carndonagh IRL 19 A4
Carnew IRL 21 B5
Carnforth UK 26 A3
Cárnia I 72 B3
Carnlough UK 19 B6
Carno UK 26 C2
Carnon Plage F 78 C2
Carnota E 86 B1
Carnoustie UK 25 B5
Carnwath UK 25 C4
Carolei I 106 B3
Carolinensiel D 43 B4
Carolles F 57 B4
Carona I 71 B4
Caronía I 109 A3
Carovigno I 104 C3
Carovilli I 103 B7
Carpaneto
Piacentino I 81 B3
Carpegna I 82 C1
Carpenédolo I 71 C5
Carpentras F 79 B4
Carpi I 81 B4
Carpignano Sésia I 70 C3
Carpineti I 81 B4
Carpineto Romano I 102 B6
Cărpinis RO 75 C5
Carpino I 104 B1
Carpinone I 103 B7
Carpio E 94 A1
Carquefou F 66 A3
Carqueiranne F 79 C5
Carral E 86 A2
Carranque E 94 B3
Carrapichana P 92 A3
Carrara I 81 B4
Carraroe IRL 20 A2
Carrascalejo E 93 B5
Carrascosa
del Campo E 95 B4
Carratraca E 100 C1
Carrazeda
de Ansiães P 87 C3
Carrazedo de
Montenegro P 87 C3
Carrbridge UK 23 D5
Carregal do Sal P 92 A2
Carreña E 88 A2
Carrick IRL 18 B3
Carrickart IRL 19 A4
Carrickfergus UK 19 B6
Carrickmacross IRL 19 C5
Carrick-on-Shannon
IRL 18 C3
Carrick-on-Suir IRL 21 B4
Carrigallen IRL 19 C4
Carrión E 99 B4
Carrión de
Calatrava E 94 C3
Carrión de
los Condes E 88 B2
Carrizo de la Ribera E 88 B1
Carrizosa E 100 A3
Carro F 79 C4
Carrocera E 88 B1
Carros F 79 C6
Carrouge CH 70 B1
Carrouges F 57 B5
Carrù I 80 B1
Carryduff UK 19 B6
Carry-le-Rouet F 79 C4
Carsóli I 102 A6
Carsphairn UK 24 C3
Cartagena E 101 B5
Cártama E 100 C1
Cartaxo P 92 B2
Cartaya E 98 B3
Carteret F 57 A4
Cartes E 88 A2
Carúnchio I 103 B7
Carviçães P 87 C4
Carvin F 48 C3
Carvoeira P 92 B1
Carvoeiro P 98 B2
Casabermeja E 100 C1
Casa Branca
Portalegre P 92 C3
Setúbal P 98 A2
Casacalenda I 103 B7
Casa Castalda I 82 C1
Casaio E 87 B4
Casa l'Abate I 105 C4
Casalarreina E 89 B4
Casalbordino I 103 A7
Casalborgone I 70 C2
Casalbuono I 104 C1
Casalbuttano
ed Uniti I 71 C4
Casàl di Principe I 103 B7
Casalécchio di Reno I 81 B5
Casale Monferrato I 70 C3
Casalina I 82 D1
Casalmaggiore I 81 B4
Casalnuovo
Monterotaro I 103 B8
Casaloldo I 71 C5
Casalpusterlengo I 71 C4
Casamássima I 104 C2
Casamicciola Terme
I 103 C6
Casamozza F 102 A2
Casarabonela E 100 C1
Casarano I 107 A5
Casar de Cáceres E 93 B4
Casar de Palomero E 93 A4
Casarejos E 89 C3
Casares E 99 C5
Casares de las Hurdes
E 93 A4
Casariche E 100 B1
Casarrubios
del Monte E 94 B2
Casas de Don Pedro E 93 B5
Casas de Fernando
Alonso E 95 C4
Casas de Haro E 95 C4
Casas de Juan Gil E 96 B1
Casas del Juan Núñez
E 95 C5
Casas del Puerto E 101 A4
Casas del Rio E 96 B1
Casas de Millán E 93 B4
Casas de Reina E 99 A5
Casas de Ves E 96 B1
Casas-Ibáñez E 96 B1
Casasimarro E 95 C4
Casas Nuevas E 101 B4
Casasola E 94 B2
Casasola de Arión E 88 C1
Casasuertes E 88 A2
Casatejada E 93 B5
Casavieja E 94 B2
Casazza I 71 C4
Cascais P 92 C1
Cascante E 89 C5
Cascante del Rio E 96 A1
Cáscia I 82 D2
Casciana Terme I 81 C4
Cáscina I 81 C4
Cáseda E 89 B5
Casekow D 45 B6
Casella I 80 B3
Caselle Torinese I 70 C2
Casemurate I 82 B1
Casenove I 82 D1
Caseres E 90 B3
Caserío Benali E 96 B2
Caserta I 103 B7
Casével P 98 B2
Cashel IRL 21 B4
Casillas E 94 B2
Casillas de Coria E 93 B4
Casina I 81 B4
Casinos E 96 B2
Čáslav CZ 63 A6
Cásola Valsénio I 81 B5
Cásole d'Elsa I 81 C5
Cásoli I 103 A7
Casória I 103 C7
Caspe E 90 B2
Cassàde la Selva E 91 B5
Cassagnas F 78 B2
Cassagnes-Bégonhès
F 77 B5
Cassano allo Iónio I 106 B3
Cassano d'Adda I 71 C4
Cassano delle Murge
I 104 C2
Cassano Magnago I 70 C3
Cassano Spinola I 80 B2
Cassel F 48 C3
Cassíbile I 109 C4
Cassine I 80 B2
Cassino I 103 B6
Cassis F 79 C4
Cassolnovo I 70 C3
Cassuéjouls F 78 B1
Častá SK 64 B3
Castagnaro I 71 C6
Castagneto Carducci
I 81 C4
Castagnola CH 70 B3
Castalla E 96 C2
Castañar de Ibor E 93 B5
Castanheira de Pêra
P 92 A2
Cástano Primo I 70 C3
Castasegna CH 71 B4
Castéggio I 80 A3
Casteição P 87 D3
Castejón E 89 B5
Castejón de Monegros
E 90 B2
Castejón de Sos E 90 A3
Castejón de Valdejasa
E 90 B2
Castèl Baronia I 103 B8
Castel Bolognese I 81 B5
Castelbuono I 109 B3
Casteldáccia I 108 A2
Castel d'Aiano I 81 B4
Castel d'Ario I 71 C5
Castel de Cabra E 90 C2
Casteldelfino I 79 B6
Castél del Monte I 103 A6
Castel del Piano I 81 D5
Castel di Iúdica I 109 B3
Castel di Rio I 81 B5
Castèl di Sangro I 103 B7
Castél di Tora I 102 A5
Castelfidardo I 82 C2
Castelfiorentino I 81 C4
Castelforte I 103 B6
Castelfranco Emília I 81 B5
Castelfranco
in Miscano I 103 B8
Castelfranco Véneto I 72 C1
Castèl Frentano I 103 A7
Casteljaloux F 76 B3
Castellabate I 103 C7
Castellammare del
Golfo I 108 A1
Castellammare di
Stábia I 103 C7
Castellamonte I 70 C2
Castellana Grotte I 104 C3
Castellane F 79 C5
Castellaneta I 104 C2
Castellaneta Marina
I 104 C2
Castellar E 100 A2
Castellarano I 81 B4
Castellar de la Frontera
E 99 C5
Castellar de la Ribera
E 91 A4
Castellar del Vallés E 91 B5
Castellar de Santiago
E 100 A2
Castell Arquato I 81 B3
Castell'Azzara I 81 D5
Castellbell i Villar E 91 B4
Castelldans E 90 B3
Castell de Cabres E 90 C3
Castell de Castells E 96 C2
Castelldefels E 91 B4
Castell de Ferro E 100 C2
Castelleone I 71 C4
Castellet E 91 B4
Castelletto di Brenzone
I 71 C5
Castellfollit de la Roca
E 91 A5
Castellfollit de
Riubregos E 91 B4
Castellfort E 90 C2
Castellina in Chianti I 81 C5
Castellina Marittima I 81 C4
Castellóde Farfaña E 90 B3
Castellóde la Plana E 96 B2
Castello d'Empùries
E 91 A6
Castello di Fiemme I 71 B6
Castelloli E 91 B4
Castellón de Rugat E 96 C2
Castellote E 90 C2
Castello Tesino I 72 B1
Castellterçol E 91 B5
Castellúcchio I 71 C5
Castellúccio de'Sáuri
I 103 B8
Castelluccio Inferiore
I 106 B2
Castelmassa I 81 A5
Castelmáuro I 103 B7
Castelmoron-sur-Lot
F 77 B3
Castelnaudary F 77 C4
Castelnau-de-Médoc
F 76 A2
Castelnau-de-
Montmirail F 77 C4
Castelnau-
Magnoac F 77 C3
Castelnau-Montratier
F 77 B4
Castelnou E 90 B2
Castelnovo ne'Monti
I 81 B4
Castelnuovo
Berardenga I 81 C5
Castelnuovo della
Dáunia I 103 B8
Castelnuovo di
Garfagnana I 81 B4
Castelnuovo di Val di
Cécina I 81 C4
Castelnuovo
Don Bosco I 80 A1
Castelnuovo Scrivia I 80 B2
Castelo Branco
Bragança P 87 C4
Castelo Branco P 92 B3
Castelo de Paiva P 87 C2
Castelo de Vide P 92 B3
Castelo do Neiva P 87 C2
Castelo Mendo P 93 A4
Castelraimondo I 82 C2
Castel San Gimignano
I 81 C5
Castèl San Giovanni I 80 A3
Castèl San Pietro Terme
I 81 B5
Castelsantángelo I 82 D2
Castél Sant'Elia I 102 A5
Castelsaraceno I 106 A2
Castelsardo I 110 B1
Castelsarrasin F 77 B4
Castelserás E 90 C2
Casteltérmini I 108 B2
Castelvecchio
Subéquo I 103 A6
Castelvetrano I 108 B1
Castél Volturno I 103 B6
Castenédolo I 71 C5
Castets F 76 C1
Castiádas I 110 C2
Castiglioncello I 81 C4
Castiglione I 102 A6
Castiglione
Chiavarese I 80 B3
Castiglione d'Adda I 71 C4
Castiglione dei Pepoli
I 81 B5
Castiglione del Lago I 81 C6
Castiglione della
Pescáia I 81 D4
Castiglione delle
Stiviere I 71 C5
Castiglione di Sicília
I 109 B4
Castiglione d'Órcia I 81 C5
Castiglione Messer
Marino I 103 B7
Castiglione Messer
Raimondo I 103 A6
Castiglion Fibocchi I 81 C5
Castiglion Fiorentino
I 81 C5
Castilblanco E 94 C1
Castilblanco de los
Arroyos E 99 B5
Castil de Peones E 89 B3
Castilfrio de la Sierra
E 89 C4
Castilgaleu E 90 A3
Castilisar E 90 A1
Castilleja E 99 B4
Castillejar E 101 B3
Castillejo de Martin
Viejo E 93 A4
Castillejo de Mesleón
E 89 C3
Castillejo de Robledo
E 89 C3
Castillo de Bayuela E 94 B2
Castillo de Locubín
E 100 B2
Castillonès F 77 B3
Castillon-la-Bataille F 76 B2
Castillon-
Len-Couserans F 77 D4
Castillonroy E 90 B3
Castilruiz E 89 C4
Castione CH 70 B4
Castions di Strada I 72 C3
Castirla F 102 A2
Castlebar IRL 18 C2
Castlebellingham IRL 19 C5
Castleblaney IRL 19 B5
Castlebridge IRL 21 B5
Castle Cary UK 29 B5
Castlecomer IRL 21 B4
Castlederg UK 19 B4
Castledermot IRL 21 B5
Castle Douglas UK 25 D4
Castleford UK 27 B4
Castleisland IRL 20 B2
Castlemaine IRL 20 B2
Castlemartyr IRL 20 C3
Castlepollard IRL 19 C4
Castlerea IRL 18 C3
Castleton UK 27 B4
Castletown
Highland UK 23 C5
Isle of Man UK 26 A1
Castletown
Bearhaven IRL 20 C2
Castletownroche IRL 20 B3
Castlewellan UK 19 B6
Casto I 71 C5
Castrejón E 88 C1
Castrelo del Valle E 87 C3
Castres F 77 C5
Castricum NL 42 C1
Castries F 78 C2
Castrignano
del Capo I 107 B5
Castril E 101 B3
Castrillo de Duero E 88 C3
Castrillo de la Vega E 88 C3
Castrillo de Onielo E 88 C2
Castro
E 88 A2
I 107 A5
Castrocabón E 88 B1
Castro-Caldelas E 87 B3
Castrocaro Terme I 81 B5
Castrocontrigo E 87 B4
Castro Daire P 87 D3
Castro dei Volsci I 103 B6
Castro del Río E 100 B1
Castro de Rey E 86 A3
Castrofilippo I 108 B2
Castrogonzaio E 88 B1
Castrojeriz E 88 B2
Castro Laboreiro P 87 B2
Castro Marim P 98 B3
Castromonte E 88 C1
Castromudarra E 88 B1
Castronuevo E 88 C1
Castronuño E 88 C1
Castropol E 86 A3
Castroreale I 109 A4
Castroserracin E 88 C3
Castro-Urdiales E 89 A3
Castroverde E 86 A3
Castro Verde P 98 B2
Castroverde
de Campos E 88 C1
Castroverde
de Cerrato E 88 C2
Castrovíllari I 106 B3
Castuera E 93 C5
Catadau E 96 B2
Cataéggio I 71 B4
Çatalca TR 118 A3
Çatallar TR 119 F5
Çatalzeytin TR 16 A7
Catánia I 109 B4
Catanzaro I 106 C3
Catanzaro Marina I 106 C3
Catarroja E 96 B2
Catarruchos P 92 A2
Catcleugh UK 25 C5
Catenanuova I 109 B3
Caterham UK 31 C3
Cati E 90 C3

Čatići BIH 84 B3
Catignano I 103 A6
Catillon F 49 C4
Catoira E 86 B2
Caton UK 26 A3
Catral E 101 A5
Catterick UK 27 A4
Cattólica I 82 C1
Cattólica Eraclea I 108 B2
Catton UK 25 D5
Caudebec-en-Caux F 58 A1
Caudete E 101 A5
Caudete de las Fuentes E 96 B1
Caudiel E 96 B2
Caudiès-de-Fenouillèdes F 77 D5
Caudry F 49 C4
Caulkerbush UK 25 D4
Caulnes F 57 B3
Caulónia I 106 C3
Caumont-l'Evente F 57 A5
Caunes-Minervois F 77 C5
Cauro F 102 B1
Caussade F 77 B4
Causse-de-la-Selle F 78 C2
Cauterets F 76 D2
Cava de Tirreni I 103 C7
Cavaglia I 70 C3
Cavaillon F 79 C4
Cavalaire-sur-Mer F 79 C5
Cavaleiro P 98 B2
Cavalese I 71 B6
Cavallermaggiore I 80 B1
Cavallino I 72 C2
Cavan IRL 19 C4
Cavárzere I 72 C2
Çavdarhisar TR 118 C4
Çavdır TR 119 E4
Cavernães P 87 D3
Cavezzo I 81 B5
Cavignac F 76 A2
Čavle HR 73 C4
Cavo I 81 D4
Cavour I 80 B1
Cavtat HR 84 D3
Cawdor UK 23 D5
Çay TR 118 D6
Çaycuma TR 118 A7
Cayeux-sur-Mer F 48 C2
Cayiralan TR 16 B7
Çayırhan TR 118 B6
Caylus F 77 B4
Cayres F 78 B2
Cazalilla E 100 B2
Cazalla de la Sierra E 99 B5
Cazals F 77 B4
Cazanuecos E 88 B1
Cazaubon F 76 C2
Cazaux F 76 B1
Cazavet F 77 C4
Cazères F 77 C4
Cazin BIH 83 B4
Cazis CH 71 B4
Čazma HR 74 C1
Cazo E 88 A1
Cazorla E 100 B3
Cazouls-lès-Béziers F 78 C2
Cea
León E 88 B1
Orense E 86 B3
Ceánuri E 89 A4
Ceauce F 57 B5
Cebolla E 94 C2
Čebovce SK 65 B5
Cebreros E 94 B2
Čečava BIH 84 B2
Ceccano I 103 B6
Cece H 74 B3
Cecenowo PL 46 A3
Čechtice CZ 63 A6
Čechtin CZ 64 A1
Cécina I 81 C4
Ceclavín E 93 B4
Cedégolo I 71 B5
Cedeira E 86 A2
Cedillo E 92 B3
Cedillo del Condado E 94 B3
Cedrillas E 90 C2
Cedynia PL 45 C6
Cée E 86 B1
Cefalù I 109 A3
Céggia I 72 C2
Cegléd H 75 A4
Ceglédbercel H 75 A4
Céglie Messápica I 104 C3
Cehegín E 101 A4
Ceilhes-et-Rocozels F 78 C2
Ceinos de Campos E 88 B1
Ceira P 92 A2
Čejč CZ 64 B2
Cekcyn PL 47 B4
Cela BIH 83 B5
Čelákovice CZ 53 C4
Celano I 103 A6
Celanova E 87 B3
Celbridge IRL 21 A5
Čelebič BIH 83 C5
Celenza Valfortore I 103 B7
Čelić BIH 84 B3
Čelinac BIH 84 B2
Celje SLO 73 B5
Cella E 95 B5
Celldömölk H 74 A2
Celle D 44 C2
Celle Ligure I 80 B2
Celles B 49 C5
Celles-sur-Belle F 67 B4
Cellino San Marco I 105 C3
Celorico da Beira P 92 A3
Celorico de Basto P 87 C2
Çeltik TR 118 C6
Çeltikçi TR 119 E5
Cemaes UK 26 B1
Cembra I 71 B6
Čemerno BIH 84 C3
Cenad RO 75 B5
Cencenighe Agordino I 72 B1
Cenei RO 75 C5
Ceneselli I 81 A5
Cenicero E 89 B4
Cenicientos E 94 B2
Censeau F 69 B6
Čenta SRB 85 A5
Centallo I 80 B1
Centelles E 91 B5
Cento I 81 B5
Centúripe I 109 B3
Cepeda la Mora E 94 B1
Cépet F 77 C4
Čepin HR 74 C3
Čepinski Martinci HR 74 C3
Cepovan SLO 72 B3
Ceprano I 103 B6
Čeralije HR 74 C2
Cerami I 109 B3
Cerano I 70 C3
Cérans Foulletourte F 57 C6
Ceraso I 106 A2
Cerbaia I 81 C5
Cerbère F 91 A6
Cercadillo E 95 A4
Cercal
Lisboa P 92 B1
Setúbal P 98 B2
Čerčany CZ 63 A5
Cerceda E 94 B3
Cercedilla E 94 B2
Cercemaggiore I 103 B7
Cercs E 91 A4
Cercy-la-Tour F 68 B3
Cerda I 108 B2
Cerdedo E 86 B2
Cerdeira P 93 A3
Cerdon F 58 C3
Cerea I 71 C6
Ceres
I 70 C2
UK 25 B5
Cerese I 81 A4
Ceresole-Reale I 70 C2
Cereste F 79 C4
Céret F 91 A5
Cerezo de Abajo E 95 A3
Cerezo de Riotirón E 89 B3
Cerfontaine B 49 C5
Cergy F 58 A3
Cerignola I 104 B1
Cérilly F 68 B2
Cerisiers F 59 B4
Cerizay F 67 B4
Çerkeş TR 16 A6
Çerkezköy TR 118 A3
Cerkije SLO 73 B4
Cerknica SLO 73 C4
Cerkno SLO 72 B3
Cerkwica PL 45 A7
Çermë-Proshkë AL 105 B5
Cerna HR 74 C3
Černá Hora CZ 64 A2
Cernavodă RO 11 D10
Cernay F 60 C3
Cerne Abbas UK 29 C5
Cernégula E 89 B3
Cernik HR 74 C2
Cernóbbio I 70 C4
Černošin CZ 62 A3
Cernovice CZ 63 A5
Cérons F 76 B2
Cerovlje HR 73 C4
Cerovo SK 65 B5
Cerqueto I 82 D1
Cerralbo E 87 D4
Cerreto d'Esi I 82 C1
Cerreto Sannita I 103 B7
Cerrigydrudion UK 26 B2
Cërrik AL 105 B5
Cerro Muriano E 100 A1
Certaldo I 81 C5
Certosa di Pésio I 80 B1
Cerva P 87 C3
Cervaro I 103 B6
Cervatos de la Cueza E 88 B2
Červena Řečice CZ 63 A6
Červená-Skala SK 65 B6
Cervená Voda CZ 54 C1
Cerveny Kostelec CZ 53 C6
Cervera E 91 B4
Cervera de la Cañada E 89 C5
Cervera del Llano E 95 C4
Cervera del Río Alhama E 89 B5
Cervera de Pisuerga E 88 B2
Cervéteri I 102 B5
Cérvia I 82 B1
Cerviá de les Garriques E 90 B3
Cervignano del Friuli I 72 C3
Cervinara I 103 B7
Cervione F 102 A2
Cervo E 86 A3
Cervon F 68 A3
Cesana Torinese I 79 B5
Cesarica HR 83 B4
Cesarò I 109 B3
Cesena I 82 B1
Cesenático I 82 B1
Cēsis LV 7 C8
Česká Belá CZ 63 A6
Česká Kamenice CZ 53 C4
Česká Lípa CZ 53 C4
Česká Třebová CZ 64 A2
České Budějovice CZ 63 B5
České Velenice CZ 63 B5
Český Brod CZ 53 C4
Český Dub CZ 53 C4
Český Krumlov CZ 63 B5
Český Těšin CZ 65 A4
Ćešljeva Bara SRB 85 B6
Çeşme TR 119 D1
Cessenon F 78 C2
Cesson-Sévigné F 57 B4
Cestas F 76 B2
Čestobrodica SRB 85 C5
Cesuras E 86 A2
Cetina E 89 C5
Cetin Grad HR 73 C5
Cetinje MNE 105 A4
Cetraro I 106 B2
Ceuta E 99 D5
Ceuti E 101 A4
Ceva I 80 B2
Cevico de la Torre E 88 C2
Cevico Navero E 88 C2
Cevins F 69 C6
Cévio CH 70 B3
Cevizli TR 119 E6
Čevo MNE 105 A4
Cewice PL 46 A3
Ceyhan TR 16 C7
Ceylan TR 119 F4
Ceyrat F 68 C3
Ceyzériat F 69 B5
Chaam NL 49 B5
Chabanais F 67 C5
Chabeuil F 79 B4
Chabielice PL 55 B4
Chablis F 59 C4
Châbons F 69 C5
Chabówka PL 65 A5
Chabreloche F 68 C3
Chabris F 67 A6
Chagford UK 28 C4
Chagny F 69 B4
Chagoda RUS 7 B13
Chaherrero E 94 B2
Chailland F 57 B5
Chaillé-les-Marais F 66 B3
Chailles F 67 A6
Chailley F 59 B4
Chalabre F 77 D5
Chalais F 67 C5
Chalamont F 69 C5
Châlette-sur-Loing F 58 B3
Chalindrey F 59 C6
Chalkida GR 116 D5
Challacombe UK 28 B4
Challans F 66 B3
Challes-les-Eaux F 69 C5
Chalmazel F 68 C3
Chalmoux F 68 B3
Chalonnes-sur-Loire F 66 A4
Châlons-en-Champagne F 59 B5
Chalon-sur-Saône F 69 B4
Chalupy PL 47 A4
Châlus F 67 C5
Cham
CH 70 A3
D 62 A3
Chamberet F 68 C1
Chambéry F 69 C5
Chambilly F 68 B4
Chambley F 60 A1
Chambly F 58 A3
Chambois F 57 B6
Chambon-sur-Lac F 68 C2
Chambon-sur-Voueize F 68 B2
Chambord F 58 C2
Chamborigaud F 78 B2
Chamboulive F 68 C1
Chamerau D 62 A3
Chamonix-Mont Blanc F 70 C1
Chamoux-sur-Gelon F 69 C6
Champagnac-le-Vieux F 68 C3
Champagney F 60 C2
Champagnole F 69 B5
Champagny-Mouton F 67 B5
Champaubert F 59 B4
Champdeniers-St Denis F 67 B4
Champdieu F 68 C4
Champdôtre F 69 A5
Champeix F 68 C3
Champéry CH 70 B1
Champigne F 57 C5
Champignelles F 59 C4
Champigny-sur-Veude F 67 A5
Champlitte-et-le-Prelot F 60 C1
Champoluc I 70 C2
Champoly F 68 C3
Champorcher I 70 C2
Champrond-en-Gâtine F 58 B2
Champs-sur-Tarentaine F 68 C2
Champs-sur-Yonne F 59 C4
Champtoceaux F 66 A3
Chamrousse F 69 C5
Chamusca P 92 B2
Chanac F 78 B2
Chanaleilles F 78 B2
Chandler's Ford UK 31 D2
Chandra GR 117 G8
Chandrexa de Queixa E 87 B3
Chañe E 88 C2
Changy F 68 B3
Chania GR 117 G6
Channes F 59 C5
Chantada E 86 B3
Chantelle F 68 B3
Chantenay-St Imbert F 68 B3
Chanteuges F 78 A2
Chantilly F 58 A3
Chantonnay F 66 B3
Chão de Codes P 92 B2
Chaource F 59 B5
Chapa E 86 B2
Chapareillan F 69 C5
Chapel en le Frith UK 27 B4
Chapelle Royale F 58 B2
Chapelle-St Laurent F 67 B4
Charbonnat F 68 B4
Chard UK 29 C5
Charenton-du-Cher F 68 B2
Charlbury UK 31 C2
Charleroi B 49 C5
Charlestown
IRL 18 C3
UK 28 C3
Charlestown of Aberlour UK 23 D5
Charleville IRL 20 B3
Charleville-Mézières F 59 A5
Charlieu F 68 B4
Charlottenberg S 34 C4
Charlton Kings UK 29 B5
Charly F 59 B4
Charmes F 60 B2
Charmes-sur-Rhône F 78 B3
Charmey CH 70 B2
Charminster UK 29 C5
Charmont-en-Beauce F 58 B3
Charny F 59 C4
Charolles F 69 B4
Chârost F 68 B2
Charquemont F 70 A1
Charrin F 68 B3
Charroux F 67 B5
Chartres F 58 B2
Charzykow PL 46 B3
Chasseneuil-sur-Bonnieure F 67 C5
Chassigny F 59 C6
Château-Arnoux F 79 B5
Châteaubernard F 67 C4
Châteaubourg F 57 B4
Châteaubriant F 57 C4
Château-Chinon F 68 A3
Château-d'Oex CH 70 B2
Château-d'Olonne F 66 B3
Château-du-Loir F 58 C1
Châteaudun F 58 B2
Châteaugiron F 57 B4
Château-Gontier F 57 C5
Château-Landon F 58 B3
Château-la-Vallière F 67 A5
Château-l'Evêque F 67 C5
Châteaulin F 56 B1
Châteaumeillant F 68 B2
Châteauneuf
Nièvre F 68 A3
Saône-et-Loire F 69 B4
Châteauneuf-de-Randon F 78 B2
Châteauneuf-d'Ille-et-Vilaine F 57 B4
Châteauneuf-du-Faou F 56 B2
Châteauneuf-du-Pape F 78 B3
Châteauneuf-en-Thymerais F 58 B2
Châteauneuf la-Forêt F 67 C6
Châteauneuf-le-Rouge F 79 C4
Châteauneuf-sur-Charente F 67 C4
Châteauneuf-sur-Cher F 68 B2
Châteauneuf-sur-Loire F 58 C3
Châteauneuf-sur-Sarthe F 57 C5
Châteauponsac F 67 B6
Château-Porcien F 59 A5
Châteauredon F 79 B5
Châteaurenard
Bouches du Rhône F 78 C3
Loiret F 59 C3
Château-Renault F 58 C1
Châteauroux F 68 B1
Châteauroux-les-Alpes F 79 B5
Château-Salins F 60 B2
Château-Thierry F 59 A4
Châteauvillain F 59 B5
Châtel F 70 B1
Châtelaillon-Plage F 66 B3
Châtelaudren F 56 B3
Châtel-Censoir F 68 A3
Châtel-de-Neuvre F 68 B3
Châtelet B 49 C5
Châtel-Guyon F 68 C3
Châtellerault F 67 B5
Châtel-Montagne F 68 B3
Châtel-St Denis CH 70 B1
Châtel-sur-Moselle F 60 B2
Châtelus-Malvaleix F 68 B2
Châtenois F 60 B1
Châtenois-les-Forges F 70 A1
Chatham UK 31 C4
Châtillon I 70 C2
Châtillon-Coligny F 59 C3
Châtillon-en-Bazois F 68 A3
Châtillon-en-Diois F 79 B4
Châtillon-sur Chalaronne F 69 B4
Châtillon-sur-Indre F 67 B6
Châtillon-sur-Loire F 58 C3
Châtillon-sur-Marne F 59 A4
Châtillon-sur-Seine F 59 C5
Châtres F 59 B4
Chatteris UK 30 B4
Chatton UK 25 C6
Chauchina E 100 B2
Chaudes-Aigues F 78 B2
Chaudrey F 59 B5
Chauffailles F 69 B4
Chaulnes F 58 A3
Chaument Gistoux B 49 C5
Chaumergy F 69 B5
Chaumont F 59 B6
Chaumont-en-Vexin F 58 A2
Chaumont-Porcien F 59 A5
Chaumont-sur-Aire F 59 B6
Chaumont-sur-Loire F 67 A6
Chaunay F 67 B5
Chauny F 59 A4
Chaussin F 69 B5
Chauvigny F 67 B5
Chavagnes-en-Paillers F 66 B3
Chavanges F 59 B5
Chaves P 87 C3
Chavignon F 59 A4
Chazelles-sur-Lyon F 69 C4
Chazey-Bons F 69 C5
Cheadle
Greater Manchester UK 26 B3
Staffordshire UK 27 C4
Cheb CZ 52 C2
Chebsara RUS 7 B15
Checa E 95 B5
Chęciny PL 55 C5
Cheddar UK 29 B5
Cheddleton UK 26 B3
Chef-Boutonne F 67 B4
Chekalin RUS 7 D14
Chekhovo RUS 47 A6
Cheles E 93 C3
Chella E 96 B2
Chelles F 58 B3
Chełm PL 11 A7
Chełmno
Kujawsko-Pomorskie PL 47 B4
Wielkopolskie PL 54 A3
Chelmsford UK 31 C4
Chełmża PL 47 B4
Cheltenham UK 29 B5
Chelva E 96 B1
Chémery F 67 A6
Chemery-sur-Bar F 59 A5
Chemillé F 67 A4
Chemin F 69 B5
Chemnitz D 52 C2
Chénérailles F 68 B2
Cheniménil F 60 B2
Chenonceaux F 67 A6
Chenôve F 69 A4
Chepelare BG 116 A6
Chepstow UK 29 B5
Chera E 96 B2
Cherasco I 80 B1
Cherbonnières F 67 C4
Cherbourg F 57 A4
Cherchiara di Calábria I 106 B3
Cherepovets RUS 7 B14
Cherkasy UA 11 B12
Chernihiv UA 7 F11
Chernivtsi UA 11 B8
Chernobyl = Chornobyl UA 7 F11
Chernyakhovsk RUS 6 D6
Chéroy F 59 B3
Cherven BY 7 E10
Chervonohrad UA 11 A8
Cherykaw BY 7 E11
Chesham UK 31 C3
Cheshunt UK 31 C3
Chessy-lès-Pres F 59 B4
Cheste E 96 B2
Chester UK 26 B3
Chesterfield UK 27 B4
Chester-le-Street UK 25 D6
Chevagnes F 68 B3
Chevanceaux F 67 C4
Chevillon F 59 B6
Chevilly F 58 B2
Chew Magna UK 29 B5
Chézery-Forens F 69 B5
Chialamberto I 70 C2
Chiampo I 71 C6
Chianale I 79 B6
Chianciano Terme I 81 C5
Chiaramonte Gulfi I 109 B3
Chiaramonti I 110 B1
Chiaravalle I 82 C2
Chiaravalle Centrale I 106 C3
Chiaréggio I 71 B4
Chiari I 71 C4
Chiaromonte I 106 A3
Chiasso CH 70 C4
Chiávari I 80 B3
Chiavenna I 71 B4
Chiché F 67 B4
Chichester UK 31 D3
Chiclana de la Frontera E 99 C4
Chiclana de Segura E 100 A2
Chiddingfold UK 31 C3
Chieri I 80 A1
Chiesa in Valmalenco I 71 B4
Chieti I 103 A7
Chieti Scalo I 103 A7
Chiéuti I 103 B8
Chigirin UA 11 B12
Chigwell UK 31 C4
Chiliomodi GR 117 E4
Chillarón de Cuenca E 95 B4
Chillarón del Rey E 95 B4
Chilleurs-aux-Bois F 58 B3
Chillón E 100 A1
Chilluevar E 100 B2
Chiloeches E 95 B3
Chimay B 49 C5
Chimeneas E 100 B2
Chinchilla de Monte Aragón E 96 C1
Chinchón E 95 B3
Chingford UK 31 C4
Chinon F 67 A5
Chióggia I 72 C2
Chiomonte I 79 A5
Chipiona E 99 C4
Chippenham UK 29 B5
Chipping Campden UK 29 A6
Chipping Norton UK 31 C2
Chipping Ongar UK 31 C4
Chipping Sodbury UK 29 B5
Chirac F 78 B2
Chirbury UK 26 C2
Chirens F 69 C5
Chirivel E 101 B3
Chirk UK 26 C2
Chirnside UK 25 C5
Chişinău = Khisinev MD 11 C10
Chişineu Criş RO 10 C6
Chissey-en-Morvan F 69 A4
Chiusa I 71 B6
Chiusa di Pésio I 80 B1
Chiusaforte I 72 B3
Chiusa Sclàfani I 108 B2
Chiusi I 81 C5
Chiva E 96 B2
Chivasso I 70 C2
Chlewiska PL 55 B5
Chludowo PL 46 C2
Chlumec nad Cidlinou CZ 53 C5
Chlum u Třeboně CZ 63 B5
Chmielnik PL 55 C5
Chobienia PL 54 B1
Chobienice PL 53 A5
Choceň CZ 53 D6
Choceń PL 47 C5
Chochołow PL 65 A5
Chocianów PL 53 B5
Chociw PL 55 B4
Chociwel PL 46 B1
Choczewo PL 46 A3
Chodaków PL 55 A5
Chodecz PL 47 C5
Chodov CZ 52 C2
Chodzież PL 46 C2
Chojna PL 45 C6
Chojnice PL 46 B3
Chojno
Kujawsko-Pomorskie PL 47 C5
Wielkopolskie PL 46 C2
Chojnów PL 53 B5
Cholet F 66 A4
Chomérac F 78 B3
Chomutov CZ 52 C3
Chop UA 11 B7
Chora GR 117 E3
Chora Sfakion GR 117 G6
Chorges F 79 B5
Chorley UK 26 B3
Chornobyl = Chernobyl UA 7 F11
Chortkiv UA 11 B8
Chorzew PL 54 B3
Chorzów PL 54 C3
Choszczno PL 46 B1
Chotcza-Józefów PL 55 B6
Chotěboř CZ 63 A6
Chouilly F 59 A5
Chouto P 92 B2
Chouzy-sur-Cisse F 67 A6
Chozas de Abajo E 88 B1
Chrast CZ 64 A1
Chrást CZ 63 A4
Chrastava CZ 53 C4
Chřibská CZ 53 C4
Christchurch UK 29 C6
Christiansfeld DK 39 D2
Chroberz PL 55 C5
Chropyně CZ 64 A3
Chrudim CZ 53 D5
Chrzanów PL 55 C4
Chtelnica SK 64 B3
Chudovo RUS 7 B11
Chueca E 94 C3
Chulmleigh UK 28 C4
Chur CH 71 B4
Church Stretton UK 26 C3
Churriana E 100 C1
Churwalden CH 71 B4
Chvalšiny CZ 63 B5
Chwaszczyno PL 47 A4
Chynava CZ 53 C4
Chýnov CZ 63 A5
Ciacova RO 75 C6
Ciadîr-Lunga MD 11 C10
Ciadoncha E 88 B3
Cianciana I 108 B2
Ciano d'Enza I 81 B4
Ciążen PL 54 A2
Cibakhaza H 75 B5
Ciborro P 92 C2
Cicagna I 80 B3
Cicciano I 103 C7
Cičevac SRB 85 C6
Ciciliano I 102 B5
Cicognolo I 71 C5
Cidadelhe P 87 D3
Cide TR 16 A6
Cidones E 89 C4
Ciechanów
Dolnośląskie PL 54 B1
Mazowieckie PL 47 C6
Ciechocinek PL 47 C4
Cielądz PL 55 B5
Ciemnik PL 46 B1
Ciempozuelos E 95 B3
Ciepielów PL 55 B6
Čierny Balog SK 65 B5
Cierp-Gaud F 77 D3
Cierpice PL 47 C4
Ciervana E 89 A3
Cierznie PL 46 B3
Cieslé PL 47 C6
Cieszyn PL 65 A4
Cieutat F 76 C3
Cieza E 101 A4
Cifer SK 64 B3
Çifteler TR 118 C6
Cifuentes E 95 B4
Cigales E 88 C2
Cigliano I 70 C3
Cihanbeyli TR 16 B6
Čilipi HR 105 A4
Cillas E 95 B5
Cilleros E 93 A4
Cilleruelo de Arriba E 88 C3
Cilleruelo de Bezana E 88 B3
Cimalmotto CH 70 B3
Cimanes del Tejar E 88 B1
Ciminna I 108 B2
Cimişlia MD 11 C10
Cimoláis I 72 B2
Cîmpulung RO 11 D8
Çınarcık TR 118 B4
Cinctorres E 90 C2
Cinderford UK 29 B5
Çine TR 119 E3
Činěves CZ 53 C5
Ciney B 49 C6
Cinfães P 87 C2
Cingia de Botti I 81 A4
Cíngoli I 82 C2
Cinigiano I 81 D5
Cinobaňa SK 65 B5
Cinq-Mars-la-Pile F 67 A5
Cinquefrondí I 106 C3
Cintegabelle F 77 C4
Cintruénigo E 89 B5
Ciółkowo PL 47 C5
Ciperez E 87 D4
Cirat E 96 A2
Cirella I 106 B2
Cirencester UK 29 B6
Cirey-sur-Vezouze F 60 B2
Ciria E 89 C5
Ciriè I 70 C2
Cirigliano I 104 C2
Cirò I 107 B4
Cirò Marina I 107 B4
Ciry-le-Noble F 69 B4
Cislău RO 11 D9
Cismon del Grappa I 72 C1
Cisneros E 88 B2
Cissac-Médoc F 66 C4
Čista CZ 52 C3
Cisterna di Latina I 102 B5
Cistérniga E 88 C2
Cisternino I 104 C3
Cistierna E 88 B1
Čitluk BIH 84 C2
Cítov CZ 53 C4
Cittadella I 72 C1
Città della Pieve I 81 D6
Città del Vaticano = Vatican City I 102 B5
Città di Castello I 82 C1
Cittaducale I 102 A5
Cittanova I 106 C3
Città Sant'Angelo I 103 A7
Ciudadela de Menorca E 97 B3
Ciudad Real E 94 D3
Ciudad Rodrigo E 93 A4
Ciutadilla E 91 B4
Cividale del Friuli I 72 B3
Cívita I 102 A6
Cívita Castellana I 102 A5
Civitanova Alta I 82 C2
Civitanova Marche I 82 C2
Civitavécchia I 102 A4
Civitella di Romagna I 81 B5
Civitella di Tronto I 82 D2
Civitella Roveto I 103 B6
Civray F 67 B5
Çivril TR 119 D4
Cizur Mayor E 76 D1
Clabhach UK 24 B1
Clachan UK 22 D2
Clachan na Luib UK 22 D1
Clacton-on-Sea UK 31 C5
Cladich UK 24 B2
Claggan UK 24 B2
Clairvaux-les-Lacs F 69 B5
Clamecy F 68 A3
Claonaig UK 24 C2
Clarecastle IRL 20 B3
Claregalway IRL 20 A3
Claremorris IRL 18 C2
Clarinbridge IRL 20 A3
Clashmore
IRL 21 B4
UK 23 D4
Claudy UK 19 B4
Clausthal-Zellerfeld D 51 B6
Cláut I 72 B2
Clay Cross UK 27 B4
Claye-Souilly F 58 B3
Cléder F 56 B1
Cleethorpes UK 27 B5
Clefmont F 60 B1
Cléguérec F 56 B2
Clelles F 79 B4
Clenze D 44 C2
Cleobury Mortimer UK 29 A5
Cléon-d'Andran F 78 B3
Cléré-les-Pins F 67 A5
Clères F 58 A2
Clermont F 58 A3
Clermont-en-Argonne F 59 A6
Clermont-Ferrand F 68 C3
Clermont-l'Hérault F 78 C2
Clerval F 69 A6
Clervaux L 50 C2
Clèry-St André F 58 C2
Cles I 71 B6
Clevedon UK 29 B5
Cleveleys UK 26 B2
Cley UK 30 B5
Clifden IRL 18 C1
Clifford UK 29 A4
Clisson F 66 A3
Clitheroe UK 26 B3
Clogh IRL 21 B4
Cloghan
Donegal IRL 19 B4
Offaly IRL 21 A4
Clogheen IRL 21 B4
Clogher UK 19 B4
Cloghjordan IRL 20 B3
Clohars-Carnoët F 56 C2
Clonakilty IRL 20 C3
Clonaslee IRL 21 A4
Clondalkin IRL 21 A5
Clones IRL 19 B4
Clonmany IRL 19 A4
Clonmel IRL 21 B4
Clonmellon IRL 19 C4
Clonord IRL 21 A4
Clonroche IRL 21 B5
Cloone IRL 19 C4
Cloppenburg D 43 C5
Closeburn UK 25 C4
Clough UK 19 B6
Clova UK 25 B4
Clovelly UK 28 C3
Clowne UK 27 B4
Cloyes-sur-le-Loir F 58 C2
Cloyne IRL 20 C3
Cluis F 68 B1
Cluj-Napoca RO 11 C7
Clun UK 26 C2
Clunes UK 24 B3
Cluny F 69 B4
Cluses F 69 B6
Clusone I 71 C4
Clydach UK 28 B4
Clydebank UK 24 C3
Coachford IRL 20 C3
Coagh UK 19 B5
Coalisland UK 19 B5
Coalville UK 27 C4
Coaña E 86 A4
Çobanlar TR 118 D5
Cobas E 86 A2
Cobertelade E 89 C4
Cobeta E 95 B4
Cóbh IRL 20 C3
Cobreces E 88 A2
Coburg D 51 C6
Coca E 94 A2
Cocentaina E 96 C2
Cochem D 50 C3
Cockburnspath UK 25 C5
Cockermouth UK 26 A2
Codigoro I 82 B1
Codogno I 71 C4
Codos E 89 C5
Codróipo I 72 C2
Codrongianos I 110 B1
Coelhoso P 87 C4
Coesfeld D 50 B3
Coevorden NL 42 C3
Cofrentes E 96 B1
Cogeces del Monte E 88 C2
Coggeshall UK 31 C4
Cognac F 67 C4
Cogne I 70 C2
Cognin F 69 C5
Cogolin F 79 C5
Cogollos de Guadix E 100 B2
Cogollos-Vega E 100 B2
Cogolludo E 95 B3
Coimbra P 92 A2
Coín E 100 C1
Coirós E 86 A2
Čoka SRB 75 C5
Col SLO 73 C4
Colares P 92 C1
Cölbe D 51 C4
Colbitz D 52 A1
Colchester UK 31 C4
Coldingham UK 25 C5
Colditz D 52 B2
Coldstream UK 25 C5
Colebrooke UK 28 C4
Colera E 91 A6
Coleraine UK 19 A5
Colfiorito I 82 C1
Cólico I 71 B4
Coligny F 69 B5
Colindres E 89 A3
Collado-Mediano E 94 B2
Collado Villalba E 94 B3
Collagna I 81 B4
Collanzo E 88 A1
Collat F 68 C3
Coll de Nargó E 91 A4
Collécchio I 81 B4
Colledimezzo I 103 B7
Colle di Val d'Elsa I 81 C5
Colleferro I 102 B6
Colle Isarco I 71 B6
Collelongo I 103 B6
Collepasso I 107 A5
Collepepe I 82 D1
Collesalvetti I 81 C4
Colle Sannita I 103 B7
Collesano I 108 B2
Colli a Volturno I 103 B7
Collin UK 25 C4
Collinée F 56 B3
Collingham
Nottinghamshire UK 27 B5
West Yorkshire UK 27 B4
Collinghorst D 43 B4
Cóllio I 71 C5
Collobrières F 79 C5
Collon IRL 19 C5
Collooney IRL 18 B3
Colmar F 60 B3
Colmars F 79 B5
Colmenar E 100 C1
Colmenar de la Sierra E 95 A3
Colmenar de Oreja E 95 B3
Colmenar Viejo E 94 B3
Colmonel UK 24 C3
Colne UK 26 B3
Colobraro I 106 A3
Cologna Véneta I 71 C6
Cologne F 77 C3
Cologne = Köln D 50 C2
Cologne al Serio I 71 C4
Colombey-les-Belles F 60 B1
Colombey-les-deux-Églises F 59 B5
Colombres E 88 A2
Colomera E 100 B2
Colomers E 91 A5
Colomiers F 77 C4
Colònia de Sant Jordi E 97 B3
Colorno I 81 B4
Colos P 98 B2
Cölpin D 45 B5
Colpy UK 23 D6
Colsterworth UK 30 B3
Coltishall UK 30 B5
Colunga E 88 A1
Colwell UK 25 C5
Colwyn Bay UK 26 B2
Colyford UK 29 C4
Comácchio I 82 B1
Coma-ruga E 91 B4
Combarros E 86 B4
Combeaufontaine F 60 C1
Comber UK 19 B6
Comblain-au-Pont B 49 C6
Combloux F 70 C1
Combourg F 57 B4
Combronde F 68 C3
Comeglians I 72 B2
Comillas E 88 A2
Comines F 49 C4
Cómiso I 109 C3
Comloşu Mare RO 75 C5
Commensacq F 76 B2
Commentry F 68 B2
Commerau D 53 B4
Commercy F 60 B1
Como I 71 C4
Cómpeta E 100 C2
Compiègne F 58 A3
Comporta P 92 C2
Comps-sur-Artuby F 79 C5
Comrat MD 11 C10
Comrie UK 25 B4
Comunanza I 82 D2
Cona
Emilia Romagna I 81 B5
Veneto I 72 C2
Concarneau F 56 C2
Conceição P 98 B2
Conches-en-Ouche F 58 B1
Concordia Sagittária I 72 C2
Concordia sulla Sécchia I 81 B4
Concots F 77 B4
Condat F 68 C2
Condé-en-Brie F 59 B4
Condeixa P 92 A2
Condemios de Abajo E 95 A3
Condemios de Arriba E 95 A3
Condé-sur-l'Escaut F 49 C4
Conde-sur-Marne F 59 A5
Condé-sur-Noireau F 57 B5
Condino I 71 C5
Condom F 77 C3
Condove I 70 C2
Condrieu F 69 C4
Conegliano I 72 C2
Conflans-sur-Lanterne F 60 C2
Confolens F 67 B5
Conforto E 86 A3
Cong IRL 18 C2
Congleton UK 26 B3
Congosto E 86 B4
Congosto de Valdavia E 88 B2
Congostrina E 95 A3
Conil de la Frontera E 99 C4
Coningsby UK 27 B5
Coniston UK 26 A2
Conlie F 57 B5
Conliège F 69 B5
Conna IRL 20 B3
Connah's Quay UK 26 B2
Connantre F 59 B4
Connaugh IRL 20 B3
Connaux F 78 B3
Connel UK 24 B2
Connerré F 58 B1
Cononbridge UK 23 D4
Čonoplja SRB 75 C4
Conques F 77 B5
Conques-sur-Orbiel F 77 C5
Conquista E 100 A1
Conquista de la Sierra E 93 B5
Consándolo I 81 B5
Consélice I 81 B5
Conselve I 72 C1
Consenvoye F 59 A6
Consett UK 25 D6
Consolacão P 92 B1
Constancia P 92 B2
Constanţa RO 11 D10
Constanti E 91 B4
Constantina E 99 B5
Consuegra E 95 C3
Consuma I 81 C5
Contarina I 82 A1
Contay F 48 D3
Conthey CH 70 B2
Contigliano I 102 A5
Contis-Plage F 76 B1
Contrada I 103 C7
Contres F 67 A6
Contrexéville F 60 B1
Controne I 103 C8
Contursi Termi I 103 C8
Conty F 58 A3
Conversano I 104 C3
Conwy UK 26 B2
Cookstown UK 19 B5
Coole F 59 B5
Coolgreany IRL 21 B5
Cooneen UK 19 B4
Cootehill IRL 19 B4
Cope E 101 B4
Copenhagen = København DK 41 D2
Copertino I 105 C4
Copparo I 81 B5
Coppenbrugge D 51 A5
Corabia RO 11 E8
Córaci I 106 B3
Coralići BIH 83 B4
Corato I 104 B2
Coray F 56 B2
Corbeil-Essonnes F 58 B3
Corbeny F 59 A4
Corbera E 96 B2
Corbie F 58 A3
Corbigny F 68 A3
Corbion B 59 A5
Corbridge UK 25 D5
Corby UK 30 B3
Corconte E 88 A3
Corcubión E 86 B1
Corcumello I 103 A6
Cordenòns I 72 C2
Cordes-sur-Ciel F 77 B4
Córdoba E 100 B1
Cordobilla de Lácara E 93 B4
Cordovado I 72 C2
Corella E 89 B5
Coreses E 88 C1
Corfe Castle UK 29 C5
Corga de Lobão P 87 D2
Cori I 102 B5
Coria E 93 B4
Coria del Río E 99 B4
Corigliano Cálabro I 106 B3
Corinaldo I 82 C1
Corinth = Korinthos GR 117 E4
Cório I 70 C2
Coripe E 99 C5
Coristanco E 86 A2
Cork IRL 20 C3
Corlay F 56 B2
Corleone I 108 B2
Corleto Monforte I 103 C8
Corleto Perticara I 104 C2
Çorlu TR 118 A2
Cormainville F 58 B2
Cormatin F 69 B4
Cormeilles F 58 A1
Cormery F 67 A5
Cormòns I 72 C3
Cormoz F 69 B5
Cornago E 89 B4
Cornberg D 51 B5
Cornellana E 86 A4
Corneşti MD 11 C10
Corníglio I 81 B4
Cornimont F 60 C2
Corniolo I 81 C5
Cornuda I 72 C2
Cornudella de Montsant E 90 B3
Cornudilla E 89 B3
Cornus F 78 C2
Çorovodë AL 116 B2
Corpach UK 24 B2
Corps F 79 B4
Corps Nuds F 57 C4
Corral de Almaguer E 95 C3
Corral de Ayllon E 89 C3
Corral de Calatrava E 100 A1
Corrales E 88 C1
Corral-Rubio E 101 A4
Corran UK 24 B2
Corredoiras E 86 A2
Corréggio I 81 B4
Corrèze F 68 C1
Corridónia I 82 C2
Corris UK 26 C2
Corrubedo E 86 B1
Córsico I 71 C4
Corsock UK 25 C4
Corte F 102 A2
Corteconcepción E 99 B4
Corte de Peleas E 93 C4
Cortegaca P 87 D2
Cortegada E 87 B2
Cortegana E 99 B4
Cortemaggiore I 81 B3
Cortemilia I 80 B2
Corte Pinto P 98 B3
Cortes E 89 C5
Cortes de Aragón E 90 C2
Cortes de Arenoso E 96 A2
Cortes de Baza E 101 B3
Cortes de la Frontera E 99 C5
Cortes de Pallás E 96 B2
Cortiçadas P 92 C2
Cortico P 87 C3
Cortijo de Arriba E 94 C2
Cortijos Nuevos E 101 A3
Cortina d'Ampezzo I 72 B2
Corton UK 30 B5
Cortona I 81 C5
Coruche P 92 C2
Corullón E 86 B4
Çorum TR 16 A7
Corvara in Badia I 72 B1
Corvera E 101 B4
Corwen UK 26 C2
Cosenza I 106 B3
Cosham UK 31 D2
Coslada E 95 B3
Cosne-Cours-sur-Loire F 68 A2
Cosne d'Allier F 68 B2
Cospeito E 86 A3
Cossato I 70 C3
Cossaye F 68 B3
Cossé-le-Vivien F 57 C5
Cossonay CH 69 B6
Costa da Caparica P 92 C1
Costa de Santo André P 98 A2
Costalpino I 81 C5
Costa Nova P 92 A2
Costaros F 78 B2
Costeşti RO 11 D8
Costigliole d'Asti I 80 B2
Costigliole Saluzzo I 80 B1
Coswig
Sachsen D 52 B3
Sachsen-Anhalt D 52 B2
Cotherstone UK 27 A4
Cotronei I 107 B3
Cottbus D 53 B4
Cottenham UK 30 B4
Cottingham UK 27 B5
Coublanc F 60 C1
Couches F 69 B4
Couço P 92 C2
Coucouron F 78 B2
Coucy-le-Château-Auffrique F 59 A4
Couëron F 66 A3
Couflens F 77 D4
Couhé F 67 B5
Couiza F 77 D5
Coulags UK 22 D3
Coulanges F 68 B3
Coulanges-la-Vineuse F 59 C4
Coulanges-sur-Yonne F 68 A3
Couleuvre F 68 B2
Coulmier-le-Sec F 59 C5
Coulommiers F 59 B4
Coulonges-sur-l'Autize F 67 B4
Coulounieix-Chamiers F 67 C5
Coulport UK 24 B3
Coupar Angus UK 25 B4
Coupéville F 59 B5
Couptrain F 57 B5
Coura P 87 C2
Courcelles B 49 C5
Courcelles-Chaussy F 60 A2
Courchevel F 70 C1
Cour-Cheverny F 67 A6
Courcôme F 67 C5
Courçon F 66 B4
Cour-et-Buis F 69 C4
Courgenay CH 70 A2
Courmayeur I 70 C1
Courniou F 78 C1
Cournon d'Auvergne F 68 C3
Cournonterral F 78 C2
Courpière F 68 C3
Coursan F 78 C2
Courseulles-sur-Mer F 57 A5
Cours-la-Ville F 69 B4
Courson-les-Carrières F 59 C4
Courtalain F 58 B2
Courtenay F 59 B4
Courtomer F 58 B1
Courville
Eure-et-Loire F 58 B2
Marne F 59 A4
Coussac-Bonneval F 67 C6
Coutances F 57 A4
Couterne F 57 B5
Coutras F 76 A2
Couvet CH 70 B1
Couvin B 49 C5
Couzon F 68 B3
Covadonga E 88 A1
Covaleda E 89 C4
Covarrubias E 89 B3
Covas P 87 C2
Cove UK 22 D3
Coventry UK 30 B2
Coverack UK 28 C2
Covigliáio I 81 B5
Covilhã P 92 A3
Cowbridge UK 29 B4
Cowdenbeath UK 25 B4
Cowes UK 31 D2
Cox F 77 C4
Cózar E 100 A2
Cozes F 66 C4
Cozzano F 102 B2
Craco I 104 C2
Cracow = Kraków PL 55 C4
Craibstone UK 23 D6
Craighouse UK 24 C2
Craignure UK 24 B2
Crail UK 25 B5
Crailsheim D 61 A6
Craiova RO 11 D7
Cramlington UK 25 C6
Cranleigh UK 31 C3
Craon F 57 C5
Craonne F 59 A4
Craponne F 69 C4
Craponne-sur-Arzon F 68 C3
Crathie UK 23 D5
Crato P 92 B3
Craughwell IRL 20 A3
Craven Arms UK 26 C3
Crawford UK 25 C4
Crawinkel D 51 C6
Crawley UK 31 C3
Creag Ghoraidh UK 22 D1
Crecente E 87 B2
Crèches-sur-Saône F 69 B4
Crécy-en-Ponthieu F 48 C2
Crécy-la-Chapelle F 59 B3
Crécy-sur-Serre F 59 A4
Crediton UK 29 C4
Creeslough IRL 19 A4
Creetown UK 24 D3
Creeve UK 19 B5
Creglingen D 61 A6
Creil F 58 A3
Creissels F 78 B2
Crema I 71 C4
Cremeaux F 68 C3
Crémenes E 88 B1
Crémieu F 69 C5
Cremlingen D 51 A6
Cremona I 81 A4
Creney F 59 B5
Črenšovci SLO 73 B6
Créon F 76 B2
Crepaja SRB 85 A5
Crépey F 60 B1
Crépy F 59 A4
Crépy-en-Valois F 59 A3
Cres HR 83 B3
Crescentino I 70 C3
Crespino I 81 B5
Crespos E 94 B2
Cressage UK 26 C3
Cressensac F 77 A4
Cressia F 69 B5
Crest F 79 B4
Cresta CH 71 B4
Créteil F 58 B3
Creully F 57 A5
Creussen D 62 A2
Creutzwald F 60 A2
Creuzburg D 51 B6
Crevalcore I 81 B5
Crèvecoeur-le-Grand F 58 A3
Crevillente E 101 A5
Crévola d'Ossola I 70 B3
Crewe UK 26 B3
Crewkerne UK 29 C5
Criales E 89 B3
Crianlarich UK 24 B3
Criccieth UK 26 C1
Crickhowell UK 29 B4
Cricklade UK 29 B6
Crieff UK 25 B4
Criel-sur-Mer F 48 C2
Crikvenica HR 73 C4
Crillon F 58 A2
Crimmitschau D 52 C2
Crimond UK 23 D7
Crinitz D 53 B3
Cripán E 89 B4
Criquetot-l'Esneval F 57 A6
Crispiano I 104 C3
Crissolo I 79 B6
Cristóbal E 93 A5
Crivitz D 44 B3
Črna SLO 73 B4
Crna Bara
Srbija SRB 85 B4
Vojvodina SRB 75 C5
Crnac HR 74 C2
Crnča SRB 85 B4
Crni Lug
BIH 83 B5
HR 73 C4
Črni Vrh SLO 73 C4
Crnjelovo Donje BIH 85 B4
Črnomelj SLO 73 C5
Crocketford UK 25 C4
Crocq F 68 C2
Crodo I 70 B3
Croglin UK 25 D5
Crolly IRL 18 A3
Cromarty UK 23 D4
Cromer UK 30 B5
Cronat F 68 B3
Crookhaven IRL 20 C2
Crookstown IRL 20 C3
Croom IRL 20 B3
Cropalati I 106 B3
Crópani I 107 C3
Crosbost UK 22 C2
Crosby UK 26 B2
Crosía I 106 B3
Crossakiel IRL 19 C4
Cross-Hands UK 28 B3
Crosshaven IRL 20 C3
Crosshill UK 24 C3
Crossmolina IRL 18 B2
Crotone I 107 B4
Crottendorf D 52 C2
Crouy F 59 A4
Crowborough UK 31 C4
Crowland UK 30 B3
Crowthorne UK 31 C3
Croyde UK 28 B3
Croydon UK 31 C3
Crozon F 56 B1
Cruas F 78 B3
Cruceni RO 75 B6
Crúcoli I 107 B4
Cruden Bay UK 23 D7
Crudgington UK 26 C3
Cruis F 79 B4
Crumlin UK 19 B5
Cruseilles F 69 B6
Crusheen IRL 20 B3
Cruz de Incio E 86 B3
Crvenka SRB 75 C4
Črveny Kamen SK 64 A4
Csabacsüd H 75 B5
Csabrendek H 74 A2
Csákánydoroszló H 74 B1
Csákvár H 74 A3
Csanádapáca H 75 B5
Csanádpalota H 75 B5
Csány H 65 C5
Csanytelek H 75 B5
Csapod H 74 A1
Császár H 74 A3
Császártöltés H 75 B4
Csávoly H 75 B4
Csemö H 75 A4
Csengöd H 75 B4
Csépa H 75 B5
Csepreg H 74 A1
Cserkeszölö H 75 B5
Csernely H 65 B6
Csesztreg H 74 B1
Csökmö H 75 A6
Csököly H 74 B2
Csokonyavisonta H 74 B2
Csólyospálos H 75 B4
Csongrád H 75 B5
Csopak H 74 B2
Csorna H 64 C3
Csorvás H 75 B5
Csurgo H 74 B2
Cuacos de Yuste E 93 A5
Cualedro E 87 C3
Cuanca de Campos E 88 B1
Cuba P 98 A3
Cubel E 95 A5
Cubelles E 91 B4
Cubillos E 89 C4
Cubillos del Sil E 86 B4
Cubjac F 67 C5
Cubo de la Solana E 89 C4
Çubuk TR 16 A6
Cuckfield UK 31 C3
Cucuron F 79 C4
Cudillero E 86 A4
Cuéllar E 88 C2
Cuenca E 95 B4
Cuers F 79 C5
Cuerva E 94 C2
Cueva de Agreda E 89 C5
Cuevas Bajas E 100 B1
Cuevas del Almanzora E 101 B4
Cuevas del Becerro E 99 C5
Cuevas del Campo E 100 B3
Cuevas del Valle E 94 B1
Cuevas de San Clemente E 89 B3
Cuevas de San Marcos E 100 B1
Cuges-les-Pins F 79 C4
Cúglieri I 110 B1
Cugnaux F 77 C4
Cuijk NL 50 B1
Cuinzier F 69 B4
Cuiseaux F 69 B5
Cuisery F 69 B5
Culan F 68 B2
Culemborg NL 49 B6
Cúllar E 101 B3
Cullaville UK 19 B5
Cullera E 96 B2
Cullivoe UK 22 A7
Cullompton UK 29 C4
Cully CH 70 B1
Culoz F 69 C5
Cults UK 23 D6
Cumbernauld UK 25 C4
Cumbres de San Bartolomé E 99 A4
Cumbres Mayores E 99 A4
Cumiana I 80 B1
Čumić SRB 85 B5
Cumnock UK 24 C3
Çumra TR 16 C6
Cúneo I 80 B1
Cunlhat F 68 C3
Čunski HR 83 B3
Cuntis E 86 B2
Cuorgnè I 70 C2
Cupar UK 25 B4
Cupello I 103 A7
Cupra Maríttima I 82 C2
Cupramontana I 82 C2
Ćuprija SRB 85 C6
Curinga I 106 C3
Currelos E 86 B3
Currie UK 25 C4
Curtea de Argeş RO 11 D8
Curtici RO 75 B6
Curtis E 86 A2
Curtis Santa Eulalia E 86 A2
Čurug SRB 75 C5
Cusano Mutri I 103 B7
Cushendall UK 19 A5
Cusset F 68 B3
Cussy-les-Forges F 68 A4
Custines F 60 B2
Cutanda E 90 C1
Cutro I 107 B3
Cutrofiano I 107 A5
Cuts F 59 A4
Cuvilly F 58 A3
Cuxhaven D 43 B5
Cvikov CZ 53 C4
Cwmbran UK 29 B4
Cybinka PL 53 A4
Czacz PL 54 A1
Czajków PL 54 B3
Czaplinek PL 46 B2
Czarlin PL 47 A4
Czarna-Dąbrówka PL 46 A3
Czarna Woda PL 47 B4
Czarnca PL 55 C4
Czarne PL 46 B2
Czarnków PL 46 C2
Czarnowo PL 47 B4
Czarnozyly PL 54 B3
Czarny Bór PL 53 C6
Czarny-Dunajec PL 65 A5
Czarny Las PL 54 B2
Czchow PL 65 A6
Czechowice-Dziedzice PL 65 A4
Czempiń PL 54 A1
Czermno PL 55 B5
Czernichow PL 55 D4
Czerniejewo PL 46 C3
Czernikowo PL 47 C4
Czersk PL 46 B3
Czerwieńsk PL 53 A5
Czerwionka-Leszczyny PL 54 C3
Czerwonka PL 47 B6
Częstochowa PL 55 C4
Czeszewo PL 46 C3
Człopa PL 46 B2
Człuchów PL 46 B3
Czołpino PL 46 A3

D

Dağ TR 119 E5
Daaden D 50 C3
Dabas H 75 A4
Dąbie PL 54 A3
Dąbki PL 46 A2
Dabo F 60 B3
Dabrowa PL 46 C3
Dąbrowa Górnicza PL 55 C4
Dąbrowa Tarnowska PL 55 C5
Dąbrowice PL 55 A4
Dabrowno PL 47 B6
Dachau D 62 B2
Dačice CZ 63 A6
Daday TR 16 A6
Dagali N 32 B5
Dägebüll D 39 E1
Dagmersellen CH 70 A2
Dahlen D 52 B2
Dahlenburg D 44 B2
Dahme D 52 B3
Dahn D 60 A3
Dähre D 44 C2
Daikanvik S 115 B13
Dail bho Dheas UK 22 C2
Dailly UK 24 C3
Daimiel E 95 C3
Daingean IRL 21 A4
Đakovica KOS 10 E6
Đakovo HR 74 C3
Dal
Akershus N 34 B3
Telemark N 32 C5
Dalaas A 71 A5
Dalabrog UK 22 D1
Dala-Floda S 36 B1
Dala-Husby S 36 B2
Dala-Järna S 36 B1
Dalaman TR 119 F3
Dalarö S 37 C5
Dalbeattie UK 25 D4
Dalby
DK 39 D3
Skåne S 41 D3
Uppsala S 37 C4
Värmland S 34 B4
Dale
Hordaland N 32 B2
Sogn og Fjordane N 32 A2
Pembrokeshire UK 28 B2
Shetland UK 22 A7
Dalen
Akershus N 34 C3
Telemark N 33 C5
Daleszyce PL 55 C5
Dalhalvaig UK 23 C5
Dalheim L 60 A2
Dalhem S 37 E5
Dalias E 100 C3
Dalj HR 75 C3
Dalkeith UK 25 C4
Dalkey IRL 21 A5

Dalmally UK 24 B3
Dalmellington UK 24 C3
Dalmose DK 39 D4
Daløy N 32 A1
Dalry
Dumfries & Galloway UK 24 C3
North Ayrshire UK 24 C3
Dalrymple UK 24 C3
Dalseter N 32 A6
Dalsjöfors S 40 B3
Dalskog S 35 D4
Dals Långed S 35 D4
Dals Rostock S 35 D4
Dalston UK 25 D5
Dalstorp S 40 B3
Dalton-in-Furness UK 26 A2
Daluis F 79 B5
Dalum
D 43 C4
S 40 B3
Dalvík IS 111 B7
Dalwhinnie UK 24 B3
Dalyan TR 119 F3
Damasi GR 116 C4
Damasławek PL 46 C3
Damazan F 76 B3
Damës AL 105 C5
Damgan F 56 C3
Dammarie-les-Lys F 58 B3
Dammartin-en-Goële F 58 A3
Damme D 43 C5
Damnica PL 46 A3
Dampierre F 69 A5
Dampierre-sur-Salon F 69 A5
Damüls A 71 A4
Damville F 58 B2
Damvillers F 59 A6
Damwoude NL 42 B2
Danasjö S 115 B13
Danbury UK 31 C4
Dångebo S 40 C5
Dangers F 58 B2
Dangé-St Romain F 67 B5
Dangeul F 58 B1
Danilovgrad MNE 105 A5
Danischenhagen D 44 A2
Daniszyn PL 54 B2
Danjoutin F 60 C2
Dannas S 40 B3
Dannemarie F 60 C3
Dannemora S 36 B4
Dannenberg D 44 B3
Dánszentmiklós H 75 A4
Dány H 75 A4
Daoulas F 56 B1
Darabani RO 11 B9
Darány H 74 C2
Darda HR 74 C3
Dardesheim D 51 B6
Darfeld D 50 A3
Darfo I 71 C5
Dargiń PL 46 A2
Dargun D 45 B4
Darlington UK 27 A4
Darłowo PL 46 A2
Darmstadt D 61 A4
Darney F 60 B2
Daroca E 95 A5
Darque P 87 C2
Darragh IRL 20 B2
Dartford UK 31 C4
Dartington UK 28 C4
Dartmouth UK 29 C4
Darton UK 27 B4
Daruvar HR 74 C2
Darvas H 75 A6
Darvel UK 24 C3
Darwen UK 26 B3
Dassel D 51 B5
Dassow D 44 B2
Datça TR 119 F2
Datteln D 50 B3
Dattenfeld D 50 C3
Daugard DK 39 D2
Daugavpils LV 7 D9
Daumeray F 57 C5
Daun D 50 C2
Daventry UK 30 B2
Davle CZ 63 A5
Davor HR 84 A2
Davos CH 71 B4
Davutlar TR 119 E2
Davyd Haradok BY 7 E9
Dawlish UK 29 C4
Dax F 76 C1
Dazkırı TR 119 E4
Deal UK 31 C5
Deauville F 57 A6
Deba E 89 A4
Debar NMK 116 A2
Debe Wielkie PL 55 A6
Dębica PL 55 C6
Dębnica Kaszubska PL 46 A3
Dębno PL 45 C6
Dębolęka PL 54 B3
Dębowa Łaka PL 47 B5
Debrc SRB 85 B4
Debrecen H 10 C6
Debrznica PL 53 A5
Debrzno PL 46 B3
Debstedt D 43 B5
Decazeville F 77 B5
Dechtice SK 64 B3
Decima I 102 B5
Decimomannu I 110 C1
Děčín CZ 53 C4
Decize F 68 B3
De Cocksdorp NL 42 B1
Decollatura I 106 B3
Decs H 74 B3
Dedaj AL 105 A5
Deddington UK 31 C2
Dedeler TR 118 B5
Dedelow D 45 B5
Dedemli TR 119 E7
Dedemsvaart NL 42 C3
Dédestapolcsány H 65 B6
Dedovichi RUS 7 C10
Deeping St Nicholas UK 30 B3
Deftera CY 120 A2
Dég H 74 B3
Degaña E 86 B4
Degeberga S 41 D4
Degerby FIN 36 B7
Degerfors S 37 C1
Degerhamn S 41 C6
Degernes N 35 C3
Deggendorf D 62 B3
Deggingen D 61 B5
Dego I 80 B2
Degolados P 93 B3
De Haan B 49 B4
Dehesas de Guadix E 100 B2
Dehesas Viejas E 100 B2
Deia E 97 B2
Deining D 62 A2
Deinze B 49 C4
Déiva Marina I 80 B3
Dej RO 11 C7
Deje S 35 C5
De Koog NL 42 B1
Delabole UK 28 C3
Delary S 40 C3
Delbrück D 51 B4
Delden NL 50 A2
Deleitosa E 93 B5
Delekovec HR 74 B1
Delémont CH 70 A2
Delft NL 49 A5
Delfzijl NL 42 B3
Délia I 108 B2
Delianuova I 106 C2
Deliblato SRB 85 B6
Delice TR 16 B6
Deliceto I 103 B8
Delitzsch D 52 B2
Dellach A 72 B3
Delle F 70 A2
Delme F 60 B2
Delmen-horst D 43 B5
Delnice HR 73 C4
Delsbo S 115 F13
Delvin IRL 19 C4
Delvinë AL 116 C2
Demandice SK 65 B4
Demen D 44 B3
Demidov RUS 7 D11
Demigny F 69 B4
Demirci TR 118 C3
Demirköy TR 118 A2
Demirtaş TR 118 B4
Demmin D 45 B5
Demonte I 79 B6
Demyansk RUS 7 C12
Denain F 49 C4
Denbigh UK 26 B2
Den Burg NL 42 B1
Dender-monde B 49 B5
Denekamp NL 42 C3
Den Ham NL 42 C3
Den Helder NL 42 C1
Denholm UK 25 C5
Denia E 96 C3
Denizli TR 119 E4
Denkendorf D 62 B2
Denklingen D 50 C3
Denny UK 25 B4
Den Oever NL 42 C2
Denta RO 75 C6
Déols F 68 B1
De Panne B 48 B3
Derbent TR 119 D3
Derby UK 27 C4
Derebucak TR 119 E6
Dereköy TR 118 A2
Derenberg D 51 B6
Derinkuyu TR 16 B7
Dermbach D 51 C6
Dermulo I 71 B6
Deronje SRB 75 C4
Derrygonnelly UK 19 B4
Derrylin UK 19 B4
Derry/Londonderry UK 19 B4
Dersingham UK 30 B4
Deruta I 82 D1
Dervaig UK 24 B1
Derval F 57 C4
Derveni GR 117 D4
Derventa BIH 84 B2
Dervock UK 19 A5
Desana I 70 C3
Descartes F 67 B5
Desenzano del Garda I 71 C5
Deset N 34 A3
Deševa BIH 84 C3
Desfina GR 116 D4
Desimirovac SRB 85 B5
Désio I 71 C4
Deskati GR 116 C3
Deskle SLO 72 B3
Desná CZ 53 C5
Dešov CZ 63 B6
Despotovac SRB 85 B6
Despotovo SRB 75 C4
Dessau D 52 B2
Deštná CZ 63 A5
Destriana E 87 B4
Désulo I 110 B2
Desvres F 48 C2
Deszk H 75 B5
Deta RO 75 C6
Detmold D 51 B4
Dětřichov CZ 64 A3
Dettelbach D 61 A6
Dettingen
Baden-Württemberg D 61 B5
Baden-Württemberg D 61 C5
Dettwiller F 60 B3
Detva SK 65 B5
Deurne NL 50 B1
Deutschkreutz A 64 C2
Deutschlandsberg A 73 B5
Deutsch Wagram A 64 B2
Deva RO 11 D7
Dévaványa H 75 A5
Devecikonağı TR 118 C3
Devecser H 74 A2
Develi TR 16 B7
Deventer NL 50 A2
Devil's Bridge UK 28 A4
Devin BG 116 A6
Devinska Nova Ves SK 64 B2
Devizes UK 29 B6
Devonport UK 28 C3
Devrek TR 118 A6
Devrekâni TR 16 A6
Ðevrske HR 83 C4
De Wijk NL 42 C3
Dewsbury UK 27 B4
Deza E 89 C4
Dežanovac HR 74 C2
Dezzo I 71 C5
Dhali CY 120 A2
Dherinia CY 120 A2
Dhërmi AL 105 C5
Diamante I 106 B2
Dianalund DK 39 D4
Diano d'Alba I 80 B2
Diano Marina I 80 C2
Dicomano I 81 C5
Didcot UK 31 C2
Didim TR 119 E2
Didimoticho GR 118 A1
Die F 79 B4
Diebling F 60 A2
Dieburg D 61 A4
Diego del Carpio E 93 A5
Diekirch L 60 A2
Diélette F 57 A4
Diemelstadt D 51 B5
Diémoz F 69 C5
Dienten am Hochkönig A 72 A2
Diepenbeck B 49 C6
Diepholz D 43 C5
Dieppe F 58 A2
Dierberg D 45 B4
Dierdorf D 50 C3
Dieren NL 50 A2
Dierhagen D 44 A4
Diesdorf D 44 C2
Diessen D 62 C2
Diest B 49 C6
Dietenheim D 61 B6
Dietfurt D 62 A2
Dietikon CH 70 A3
Dietzenbach D 51 C4
Dieue-sur-Meuse F 60 A1
Dieulefit F 79 B4
Dieulouard F 60 B2
Dieuze F 60 B2
Diever NL 42 C3
Diez D 50 C4
Diezma E 100 B2
Differdange L 60 A1
Digermulen N 112 D4
Dignac F 67 C5
Dignano I 72 B2
Digne-les-Bains F 79 B5
Digny F 58 B2
Digoin F 68 B3
Dijon F 69 A5
Dikanäs S 115 B13
Dikili TR 118 C1
Diksmuide B 48 B3
Dilar E 100 B2
Dillenburg D 50 C4
Dillingen
Bayern D 61 B6
Saarland D 60 A2
Dilsen B 50 B1
Dimaro I 71 B5
Dimitrovgrad BG 11 E8
Dimitsana GR 117 E4
Dinami I 106 C3
Dinan F 57 B3
Dinant B 49 C5
Dinar TR 119 D5
Dinard F 57 B3
Dinek TR 118 C6
Dingden D 50 B2
Dingelstädt D 51 B6
Dingle
IRL 20 B1
S 35 D3
Dingolfing D 62 B3
Dingtuna S 37 C3
Dingwall UK 23 D4
Dinkelsbühl D 61 A6
Dinkelscherben D 62 B1
Dinklage D 43 C5
Dinslaken D 50 B2
Dinxperlo NL 50 B2
Diö S 40 C4
Diósgyör H 65 B6
Diósjeno H 65 C5
Diou F 68 B3
Dippen UK 24 C2
Dipperz D 51 C5
Dippoldiswalde D 53 C3
Dirdal N 33 D3
Dirksland NL 49 B5
Dirlewang D 61 C6
Dischingen D 61 B6
Disentis CH 70 B3
Diso I 107 A5
Diss UK 30 B5
Dissen D 50 A4
Distington UK 26 A2
Ditzingen D 61 B5
Ditzum D 43 B4
Divača SLO 72 C3
Dives-sur-Mer F 57 A5
Divín SK 65 B5
Divion F 48 C3
Divišov CZ 63 A5
Divjakë AL 105 C5
Divonne les Bains F 69 B6
Dixmont F 59 B4
Dizy-le-Gros F 59 A5
Djúpivogur IS 111 C11
Djupvasshytta N 114 E4
Djura S 36 B1
Djurås S 36 B2
Djurmo S 36 B2
Djursdala S 40 B5
Dlouhá Loucka CZ 64 A3
Długowola PL 55 B6
Dmitriyev Lgovskiy RUS 7 E13
Dmitrov RUS 7 C14
Dmitrovsk-Orlovskiy RUS 7 E13
Dno RUS 7 C10
Doade E 86 B3
Doğanhisar TR 119 D6
Dobanovci SRB 85 B5
Dobbertin D 44 B4
Dobbiaco I 72 B2
Dobczyce PL 65 A6
Dobele LV 6 C7
Döbeln D 52 B3
Doberlug-Kirchhain D 52 B3
Dobern D 53 B4
Dobersberg A 63 B6
Dobiegniew PL 46 C1
Dobieszyn PL 55 B6
Doboj BIH 84 B3
Dobošnica BIH 84 B3
Doboz H 75 B6
Dobrá CZ 65 A4
Dobra
Wielkopolskie PL 54 B3
Zachodnio-Pomorskie PL 45 B6
Zachodnio-Pomorskie PL 45 B7
Dobrá Niva SK 65 B5
Dobřany CZ 63 A4
Dobre
Kujawsko-Pomorskie PL 47 C4
Mazowieckie PL 55 A6
Dobre Miasto PL 47 B6
Dobreta-Turnu-Severin RO 11 D7
Dobri H 74 B1
Dobrica SRB 75 C5
Dobrich BG 11 E9
Dobri Do SRB 85 D6
Dobrinishte BG 116 A5
Dobříš CZ 63 A5
Dobro E 89 B3
Dobrodzień PL 54 C3
Döbrököz H 74 B3
Dobromierz PL 53 C6
Dobrosołowo PL 47 C4
Dobroszyce PL 54 B2
Dobrota MNE 105 A4
Dobrovnik SLO 73 B6
Dobrush BY 7 E11
Dobruška CZ 53 C6
Dobrzany PL 46 B1
Dobrzen Wielki PL 54 C2
Dobrzyca
Wielkopolskie PL 46 B2
Wielkopolskie PL 54 B2
Zachodnio-Pomorskie PL 46 A1
Dobrzyńad Wisłą PL 47 C5
Dobšiná SK 65 B6
Dobwalls UK 28 C3
Dochamps B 49 C6
Docking UK 30 B4
Docksta S 115 D15
Doddington UK 25 C5
Döderhultt S 40 B6
Doesburg NL 50 A2
Doetinchem NL 50 B2
Dogliani I 80 B1
Dogueno P 98 B3
Doische B 49 C5
Dois Portos P 92 B1
Dojč SK 64 B3
Dokka N 34 B2
Dokkedal DK 38 C3
Dokkum NL 42 B2
Doklezovje SLO 73 B6
Doksy CZ 53 C4
Dokuz TR 119 D7
Dolancourt F 59 B5
Dolceácqua I 80 C1
Dol-de-Bretagne F 57 B4
Dole F 69 A5
Dølemo N 33 D5
Dolenja vas SLO 73 C4
Dolenjske Toplice SLO 73 C5
Dolfor UK 26 C2
Dolgarrog UK 26 B2
Dolgellau UK 26 B2
Doliana GR 116 C2
Dolianova I 110 C2
Dolice PL 45 B7
Doljani HR 83 B5
Döllach im Mölltal A 72 B2
Dolle D 44 C3
Dollnstein D 62 B2
Dollot F 59 B4
Döllstadt D 51 B6
Dolná Strehová SK 65 B5
Dolné Saliby SK 64 B3
Dolni Benešov CZ 64 A4
Dolni Bousov CZ 53 C5
Dolni Kounice CZ 64 A2
Dolni Kralovice CZ 63 A6
Dolni Ujezd CZ 64 A2
Dolni Žandov CZ 52 C2
Dolný Kubín SK 65 A5
Dolo I 72 C2
Dolores E 96 C2
Dolovo SRB 85 B5
Dölsach A 72 B2
Dolsk PL 54 B2
Dolwyddelan UK 26 B2
Dolynska UA 11 B12
Domaljevac BIH 84 A3
Domaniç TR 118 C4
Domaniža SK 65 A4
Domanovići BIH 84 C2
Domašov CZ 54 C2
Domaszék H 75 B4
Domaszków PL 54 C1
Domaszowice PL 54 B2
Domat-Ems CH 71 B4
Domažlice CZ 62 A3
Dombås N 114 E6
Dombasle-sur-Meurthe F 60 B2
Dombegyház H 75 B6
Dombóvár H 74 B3
Domène F 69 C5
Dómerat F 68 B2
Domfessel F 60 B3
Domfront F 57 B5
Domfront-en-Champagne F 57 B6
Domingão P 92 B2
Domingo Pérez
Granada E 100 B2
Toledo E 94 C2
Dömitz D 44 B3
Dommartin F 59 B5
Dommartin-le-Franc F 59 B5
Domme F 77 B4
Dommitzsch D 52 B2
Domodóssola I 70 B3
Domokos GR 116 C4
Domoszló H 65 C6
Dompaire F 60 B2
Dompierre-du-Chemin F 57 B4
Dompierre-sur-Besbre F 68 B3
Dompierre-sur-Mer F 66 B3
Domrémy-la-Pucelle F 60 B1
Dömsöd H 75 A4
Domsure F 69 B5
Dómus de Maria I 110 D1
Domusnóvas I 110 C1
Domvena GR 117 D4
Domžale SLO 73 B4
Donado E 87 B4
Donaghadee UK 19 B6
Don Alvaro E 93 C4
Doña Mencía E 100 B1
Donaueschingen D 61 C4
Donauwörth D 62 B1
Don Benito E 93 C5
Doncaster UK 27 B4
Donegal IRL 18 B3
Donestebe-Santesteban E 76 C1
Donges F 66 A2
Dongo I 71 B4
Donington UK 30 B3
Doniños E 86 A2
Donja Bebrina HR 84 A3
Donja Brela HR 84 C1
Donja Dubica BIH 84 A3
Donja Dubrava HR 74 B1
Donja Kupčina HR 73 C5
Donja Mutnica SRB 85 C6
Donja Šatornja SRB 85 B5
Donja Stubica HR 73 C5
Donje Brišnik BIH 84 C2
Donje Ljupče KOS 85 D6
Donje Stative HR 73 C5
Donji-Andrijevci HR 74 C3
Donji Kazanci BIH 83 C5
Donji Koričáni BIH 84 B2
Donji Lapac HR 83 B4
Donji Malovan BIH 84 C2
Donji Miholjac HR 74 C3
Donji Mosti HR 74 B1
Donji Poloj HR 73 C5
Donji-Rujani BIH 83 C5
Donji Srb HR 83 B5
Donji Svilaj BIH 84 A3
Donji Tovarnik SRB 85 B4
Donji Vakuf BIH 84 B2
Donnalucata I 109 C3
Donnemarie-Dontilly F 59 B4
Donnersbach A 73 A4
Donnersbachwald A 73 A4
Donnerskirchen A 64 C2
Donorático I 81 C4
Donostia-San Sebastián E 76 C1
Donovaly SK 65 B5
Donzenac F 67 C6
Donzère F 78 B3
Donzy F 68 A3
Doonbeg IRL 20 B2
Doorn NL 49 A6
Dor E 86 A1
Dorchester UK 29 C5
Dørdal N 33 D6
Dordrecht NL 49 B5
Dörenthe D 50 A3
Dores UK 23 D4
Dorfen D 62 B3
Dorfgastein A 72 A3
Dorfmark D 43 C6
Dorf Mecklenburg D 44 B3
Dorgali I 110 B2
Dorking UK 31 C3
Dormagen D 50 B2
Dormánd H 65 C6
Dormans F 59 A4
Dornava SLO 73 B5
Dornbirn A 71 A4
Dornburg D 52 B1
Dorndorf D 51 C6
Dornecy F 68 A3
Dornes F 68 B2
Dornhan D 61 B4
Dornie UK 22 D3
Dornoch UK 23 D4
Dornum D 43 B4
Dorog H 65 C4
Dorogobuzh RUS 7 D12
Dorohoi RO 11 C9
Dorotea S 115 C13
Dorotowo PL 47 B6
Dörpen D 43 C4
Dorsten D 50 B2
Dortan F 69 B5
Dortmund D 50 B3
Doruchów PL 54 B3
Dorum D 43 B5
Dörverden D 43 C6
Dörzbach D 61 A5
Dos Aguas E 96 B2
Dosbarrios E 95 C3
Döşemealtı TR 119 E5
Dos Hermanas E 99 B5
Dospat BG 116 A6
Dos-Torres E 100 A1
Dötlingen D 43 C5
Dottignies B 49 C4
Döttingen CH 70 A3
Douai F 49 C4
Douarnenez F 56 B1
Douchy F 59 C4
Douchy-les-Mines F 49 C4
Doucier F 69 B5
Doudeville F 58 A1
Doué-la-Fontaine F 67 A4
Douglas
Isle of Man UK 26 A1
South Lanarkshire UK 25 C4
Doulaincourt-Saucourt F 59 B6
Doulevant-le-Château F 59 B5
Doullens F 48 C3
Dounby UK 23 B5
Doune UK 24 B3
Dounreay UK 23 C5
Dour B 49 C4
Dourdan F 58 B3
Dourgne F 77 C5
Dournazac F 67 C5
Douro Calvo P 87 D3
Douvaine F 69 B6
Douvres-la-Délivrande F 57 A5
Douzy F 59 A6
Dover UK 31 C5
Dovje SLO 72 B3
Dovre N 114 F6
Downham Market UK 30 B4
Downhill UK 19 A5
Downpatrick UK 19 B6
Dowra IRL 18 B3
Doxato GR 116 A6
Doyet F 68 B2
Dozule F 57 A5
Drača SRB 85 B5
Dračevo BIH 84 D3
Drachten NL 42 B3
Draga SLO 73 C4
Drăgășani RO 11 D8
Dragatuš SLO 73 C5
Dragichyn BY 7 E8
Draginja SRB 85 B4
Dragobi AL 105 A5
Dragocvet SRB 85 C6
Dragolovci BIH 84 B2
Dragoni I 103 B7
Dragør DK 41 D2
Dragotina HR 73 C6
Dragotinja BIH 83 A5
Dragozetići HR 82 A3
Draguignan F 79 C5
Drahnsdorf D 52 B3
Drahonice CZ 63 A5
Drahovce SK 64 B3
Drama GR 116 A6
Drammen N 35 C2
Drangedal N 33 C6
Drangsnes IS 111 B4
Dransfeld D 51 B5
Dranske D 45 A5
Draperstown UK 19 B5
Drassburg A 64 C2
Drávaszabolcs H 74 C3
Dravograd SLO 73 B5
Drawno PL 46 B1
Drawsko Pomorskie PL 46 B1
Drayton UK 30 B5
Draženov CZ 62 A3
Draževac SRB 85 B5
Dražice HR 73 C4
Drebkau D 53 B4
Dreieich D 51 C4
Dreisen D 61 A4
Dren KOS 85 C5
Drenovac SRB 85 C6
Drenovci HR 84 B3
Drensteinfurt D 50 B3
Dresden D 53 B3
Dretyń PL 46 A2
Dreux F 58 B2
Dřevohostice CZ 64 A3
Drevsjø N 114 F9
Drewitz D 52 A2
Drezdenko PL 46 C1
Drežnica HR 83 A4
Drežnik-Grad HR 83 B4
Drietona SK 64 B3
Driffield UK 27 A5
Drimnin UK 24 B2
Drimoleague IRL 20 C2
Dringenberg D 51 B5
Drinić BIH 83 B5
Drinjača BIH 85 B4
Drinovci BIH 84 C2
Driopida GR 117 E6
Drivstua N 114 E6
Drlače SRB 85 B4
Drnholec CZ 64 B2
Drniš HR 83 C5
Drnje HR 74 B1
Drnovice CZ 64 A2
Dro I 71 C5
Drøbak N 35 C2
Drobin PL 47 C6
Drochia MD 11 B9
Drochtersen D 43 B6
Drogheda IRL 19 C5
Drohobych UA 11 B7
Droitwich Spa UK 29 A5
Drołtowice PL 54 B2
Dromahair IRL 18 B3
Dromcolliher IRL 20 B3
Dromore
Down UK 19 B5
Tyrone UK 19 B4
Dromore West IRL 18 B3
Dronero I 79 B6
Dronfield UK 27 B4
Drongan UK 24 C3
Dronninglund DK 38 B3
Dronrijp NL 42 B2
Dronten NL 42 C2
Drosendorf A 63 B6
Drösing A 64 B2
Drottningholm S 37 C4
Droué F 58 B2
Drulingen F 60 B3
Drumbeg UK 22 C3
Drumcliff IRL 18 B3
Drumgask UK 23 D4
Drumkeeran IRL 18 B3
Drummore UK 24 D3
Drumnadrochit UK 23 D4
Drumquin UK 19 B4
Drumshanbo IRL 19 B3
Drumsna IRL 19 C4
Drunen NL 49 B6
Druskininkai LT 6 D7
Druten NL 49 B6
Druya BY 7 D9
Družetići SRB 85 B5
Drvar BIH 83 B5
Drvenik HR 84 C2
Drwalew PL 55 B6
Drymen UK 24 B3
Drynoch UK 22 D2
Drzewce PL 54 A2
Drzewiany PL 46 B2
Drzewica PL 55 B5
Dualchi I 110 B1
Duas Igrejas P 87 C4
Dub SRB 85 C4
Dubá CZ 53 C4
Dubăsari MD 11 C10
Duben D 53 B3
Dübendorf CH 70 A3
Dubi CZ 53 C3
Dubica HR 74 C1
Dublin IRL 21 A5
Dubna RUS 7 C14
Dubňany CZ 64 B3
Dubnica nad Váhom SK 64 B4
Dubnik SK 65 C4
Dubno UA 11 A8
Dubodiel SK 64 B4
Dubona SRB 85 B5
Dubovac SRB 85 B6
Dubovic BIH 83 B5
Dubranec HR 73 C5
Dubrava HR 74 C1
Dubrave BIH 84 B3
Dubravica
HR 73 C5
SRB 85 B6
Dubrovnik HR 84 D3
Dubrovytsya UA 7 F9
Ducey F 57 B4
Duchcov CZ 53 C3
Ducherow D 45 B5
Dučina SRB 85 B5
Duclair F 58 A1
Dudar H 74 A2
Duddington UK 30 B3
Duderstadt D 51 B6
Dudeşti Vechi RO 75 B5
Dudley UK 26 C3
Dueñas E 88 C2
Duesund N 32 B2
Dueville I 72 C1
Duffel B 49 B5
Duffield UK 27 C4
Dufftown UK 23 D5
Duga Poljana SRB 85 C5
Duga Resa HR 73 C5
Dugi Rat HR 83 C5
Dugny-sur-Meuse F 59 A6
Dugopolje HR 83 C5
Dugo Selo HR 73 C6
Duino I 72 C3
Duisburg D 50 B2
Dukat AL 105 C5
Dukhovshchina RUS 7 D12
Dukovany CZ 64 A2
Duleek IRL 19 C5
Dülken D 50 B2
Dülmen D 50 B3
Dulovo BG 11 E9
Dulpetorpet N 34 B4
Dulverton UK 29 B4
Dumbarton UK 24 C3
Dümerek TR 118 C6
Dumfries UK 25 C4
Dumlupınar TR 118 D4
Dümpelfeld D 50 C2
Dunaalmás H 65 C4
Dunabogdány H 65 C5
Dunafalva H 74 B3
Dunaföldvár H 74 B3
Dunaharaszti H 75 A4
Dunajská Streda SK 64 C3
Dunakeszi H 65 C5
Dunakiliti H 64 C3
Dunakömlöd H 74 B3
Dunapataj H 75 B3
Dunaszekcső H 74 B3
Dunaszentgyorgy H 74 B3
Dunatetétlen H 75 B4
Dunaújváros H 74 B3
Dunavecse H 75 B3
Dunbar UK 25 B5
Dunbeath UK 23 C5
Dunblane UK 25 B4
Dunboyne IRL 21 A5
Dundalk IRL 19 B5
Dundee UK 25 B5
Dundrennan UK 25 D4
Dundrum UK 19 B6
Dunfanaghy IRL 19 A4
Dunfermline UK 25 B4
Dungannon UK 19 B5
Dungarvan IRL 21 B4
Dungiven UK 19 B5
Dunglow IRL 18 B3
Dungourney IRL 20 C3
Duninowo PL 46 A2
Đunis SRB 85 C6
Dunkeld UK 25 B4
Dunker S 37 C3
Dunkerque = Dunkirk F 48 B3
Dunkineely IRL 18 B3
Dunkirk = Dunkerque F 48 B3
Dun Laoghaire IRL 21 A5
Dunlavin IRL 21 A5
Dunleer IRL 19 C5
Dun-le-Palestel F 67 B6
Dun-les-Places F 68 A4
Dunlop UK 24 C3
Dunloy UK 19 A5
Dunmanway IRL 20 C2
Dunmore IRL 18 C3
Dunmore East IRL 21 B5
Dunmurry UK 19 B5
Dunnet UK 23 C5
Dunningen D 61 B4
Dunoon UK 24 C3
Duns UK 25 C5
Dunscore UK 25 C4
Dunsford UK 28 C4
Dunshaughlin IRL 21 A5
Dunstable UK 31 C3
Dunster UK 29 B4
Dun-sur-Auron F 68 B2
Dun-sur-Meuse F 59 A6
Dunvegan UK 22 D2
Duplek SLO 73 B5
Dupnitsa BG 11 E7
Durağan TR 16 A7
Durach D 61 C6
Durak TR 118 C3
Đurakovac KOS 85 D5
Durana E 89 B4
Durance F 76 B3
Durango E 89 A4
Durankulak BG 11 E10
Duras F 76 B3
Durban-Corbières F 78 D1
Dürbheim D 61 B4
Durbuy B 49 C6
Dúrcal E 100 C2
Ðurdjenovac HR 74 C3
Ðurdjevac HR 74 B2
Ðurdjevik BIH 84 B3
Düren D 50 C2
Durham UK 25 D6
Ðurinci SRB 85 B5
Durlach D 61 B4
Ðurmanec HR 73 B5
Durness UK 22 C4
Dürnkrut A 64 B2
Dürrboden CH 71 B4
Dürrenboden CH 70 B3
Durrës AL 105 B5
Durrow IRL 21 B4
Durrus IRL 20 C2
Dursunbey TR 118 C3
Durtal F 57 C5
Durup DK 38 C1
Durusu TR 118 A3
Dusina BIH 84 C2
Dusnok H 75 B3
Dusocin PL 47 B4
Düsseldorf D 50 B2
Dusslingen D 61 B5
Duszniki PL 46 C2
Duszniki-Zdrój PL 54 C1
Dutovlje SLO 72 C3
Duvebo S 40 A4
Duved S 115 D9
Düzağac TR 118 D5
Düzce TR 118 B6
Dvärsätt S 115 D11
Dvor HR 83 A5
Dvorce CZ 64 A3
Dvorníky SK 64 B3
Dvory nad Žitavou SK 64 C4
Dvůr Králové nad Labem CZ 53 C5
Dyatkovo RUS 7 E13
Dybvad DK 38 B3
Dyce UK 23 D6
Dygowo PL 46 A1
Dykehead UK 25 B4
Dymchurch UK 31 C5
Dymer UA 11 A11
Dyrnes N 114 D4
Dywity PL 47 B6
Džaniči BIH 84 C2
Dziadowa Kłoda PL 54 B2
Działdowo PL 47 B6
Działoszyce PL 55 C5
Działoszyn PL 54 B3
Dziemiany PL 46 A3
Dzierząźnia PL 47 C6
Dzierzgoń PL 47 B5
Dzierzgowo PL 47 B6
Dzierżoniów PL 54 C1
Dzisna BY 7 D10
Dziwnów PL 45 A6
Dzyarzhynsk BY 7 E9
Dzyatlava BY 7 E8

E

Ea E 89 A4
Eaglesfield UK 25 C4
Ealing UK 31 C3
Eardisley UK 29 A4
Earls Barton UK 30 B3
Earl Shilton UK 30 B2
Earlston UK 25 C5
Easington UK 27 B6
Easky IRL 18 B3
Eastbourne UK 31 D4
East Calder UK 25 C4
East Dereham UK 30 B4
Easter Skeld UK 22 A7
East Grinstead UK 31 C4
East Ilsley UK 31 C2
East Kilbride UK 24 C3
Eastleigh UK 31 D2
East Linton UK 25 C5
East Markham UK 27 B5
Easton UK 29 C5
East Wittering UK 31 D3
Eaton Socon UK 30 B3
Eaux-Bonnes F 76 D2
Eauze F 76 C3
Ebberup DK 39 D2
Ebbs A 62 C3
Ebbw Vale UK 29 B4
Ebeleben D 51 B6
Ebeltoft DK 39 C3
Ebene Reichenau A 72 B3
Eben im Pongau A 72 A3
Ebensee A 63 C4
Ebensfeld D 51 C6
Eberbach D 61 A4
Ebergötzen D 51 B6
Ebermann-Stadt D 62 A2
Ebern D 51 C6
Eberndorf A 73 B4
Ebersbach D 53 B4
Ebersberg D 62 B2
Ebersdorf
Bayern D 52 C1
Niedersachsen D 43 B6
Eberstein A 73 B4
Eberswalde D 45 C5
Ebnat-Kappel CH 71 A4
Éboli I 103 C8
Ebrach D 61 A6
Ebreichsdorf A 64 C2
Ebreuil F 68 B3
Ebstorf D 44 B2
Ecclefechan UK 25 C4
Eccleshall UK 26 C3
Eceabat TR 118 B1
Echallens CH 69 B6
Echauri E 76 D1
Echinos GR 116 A7
Echiré F 67 B4
Échirolles F 69 C5
Echourgnac F 76 A3
Echt NL 50 B1
Echte D 51 B6
Echternach L 60 A2
Ecija E 99 B5
Ečka SRB 75 C5
Eckartsberga D 52 B1
Eckelshausen D 51 C4
Eckental D 62 A2
Eckernförde D 44 A1
Eckerö FIN 36 B6
Eckington UK 27 B4
Éclaron F 59 B5
Écommoy F 58 C1
Écouché F 57 B5
Ecouis F 58 A2
Ecséd H 65 C5
Ecsegfalva H 75 A5
Écueillé F 67 A6
Ed S 35 D3
Eda S 34 C4
Eda glasbruk S 34 C4
Edam NL 42 C2
Edane S 35 C4
Edderton UK 23 D4
Ede NL 49 A6
Edebäck S 34 B5
Edebo S 36 B5
Edelény H 65 B6
Edelschrott A 73 A5
Edemissen D 44 C2
Edenbridge UK 31 C4
Edenderry IRL 21 A4
Edenkoben D 61 A4
Edesheim D 61 A4
Edessa GR 116 B4
Edewecht D 43 B4
Edgeworthstown IRL 19 C4
Edinburgh UK 25 C4
Edinet MD 11 B9
Edirne TR 118 A1
Edland N 33 C4
Edolo I 71 B5
Edøy N 114 D5
Edremit TR 118 C2
Edsbro S 36 C5
Edsbruk S 40 A6
Edsbyn S 36 A2
Edsele S 115 D13
Edsleskog S 35 C4
Edsvalla S 35 C5
Eekloo B 49 B4
Eemshaven NL 42 B3
Eerbeek NL 50 A2
Eersel NL 49 B6
Eferding A 63 B5
Effiat F 68 B3
Efteløt N 35 C1
Egeln D 52 B1
Eger H 65 C6
Egerbakta H 65 C6
Egernsund DK 39 E2
Egersund N 33 D3
Egerszólát H 65 C6
Egervár H 74 B1
Egg
A 71 A4
D 61 B6
Eggby S 35 D5
Eggedal N 32 B6
Eggenburg A 64 B1
Eggenfelden D 62 B3
Eggesin D 45 B6
Eggum N 112 D2
Egham UK 31 C3
Éghezée B 49 C5
Egiertowo PL 47 A4
Egilsstaðir IS 111 B11
Egina GR 117 E5
Egínio GR 116 B4
Egio GR 117 D4
Égletons F 68 C2
Egling D 62 C2
Eglinton UK 19 A4
Eglisau CH 61 C4
Égliseneuve-d'Entraigues F 68 C2
Eglofs D 61 C5
Egmond aan Zee NL 42 C1
Egna I 71 B6
Egosthena GR 117 D5
Egremont UK 26 A2
Egtved DK 39 D2
Eguilles F 79 C4
Eguilly-sous-Bois F 59 B5
Éguzon-Chantôme F 67 B6
Egyek H 65 C6
Egyházasrádóc H 74 A1
Ehekirchen D 62 B2
Ehingen D 61 B5
Ehra-Lessien D 44 C2
Ehrang D 60 A2
Ehrenfriedersdorf D 52 C2
Ehrenhain D 52 C2
Ehrenhausen A 73 B5
Ehringshausen D 51 C4
Ehrwald A 71 A5
Eibar E 89 A4
Eibelstadt D 61 A6
Eibenstock D 52 C2
Eibergen NL 50 A2
Eibiswald A 73 B5
Eichenbarleben D 52 A1
Eichendorf D 62 B3
Eichstätt D 62 B2
Eickelborn D 50 B4
Eide
Hordaland N 32 B3
Møre og Romsdal N 114 E4
Eidet N 112 C7
Eidfjord N 32 B4
Eidsberg N 35 C3
Eidsbugarden N 32 A5
Eidsdal N 114 E4
Eidsfoss N 35 C2
Eidskog N 34 B4
Eidsvåg
Hordaland N 32 B2
Møre og Romsdal N 114 E5
Eidsvoll N 34 B3
Eikefjord N 114 F2
Eikelandsosen N 32 B2
Eiken N 33 D4
Eikesdal N 114 E5
Eikstrand N 35 C1
Eilenburg D 52 B2
Eilsleben D 52 A1
Eina N 34 B2
Einbeck D 51 B5
Eindhoven NL 49 B6
Einsiedeln CH 70 A3
Einville-au-Jard F 60 B2
Eisenach D 51 C6
Eisenberg
Rheinland-Pfalz D 61 A4
Thüringen D 52 C1
Eisenerz A 73 A4
Eisenhüttenstadt D 53 A4
Eisenkappel A 73 B4
Eisenstadt A 64 C2
Eisentratten A 72 B3
Eisfeld D 51 C6
Eisleben D 52 B1
Eislingen D 61 B5
Eitensheim D 62 B2
Eiterfeld D 51 C5
Eitorf D 50 C3
Eivindvik N 32 B2
Eivissa = Ibiza E 97 C1
Eixo P 92 A2
Ejby DK 39 D2
Ejea de los Caballeros E 90 A1
Ejstrupholm DK 39 D2
Ejulve E 90 C2
Eke B 49 C4
Ekeby
Gotland S 37 E5
Skåne S 41 D2
Uppsala S 36 B5
Ekeby-Almby S 37 C2
Ekenäs S 35 D5
Ekenässjön S 40 B5
Ekerö S 37 C4
Eket S 41 C3
Eketorp S 41 C6
Ekevik S 40 A6
Ekkerøy N 113 B19
Ekshärad S 34 B5
Eksingedal N 32 B2
Eksjö S 40 B4
Eksta S 37 E5
Ekträsk S 115 C16
El Alamo
Madrid E 94 B3
Sevilla E 99 B4
El Algar E 101 B5
El Almendro E 98 B3
El Alquián E 101 C3
Élancourt F 58 B2
El Arenal E 94 B1
El Arguellite E 101 A3
Elassona GR 116 C4
El Astillero E 88 A3
Elati GR 116 C3
Żelazno PL 54 C1
El Ballestero E 101 A3
El Barco de Ávila E 93 A5
Elbasan AL 116 A2
El Berrón E 88 A1
El Berrueco E 95 B3
Elbeuf F 58 A1
Elbingerode D 51 B6
Elbląg PL 47 A5
El Bodón E 93 A4
El Bonillo E 95 D4
El Bosque E 99 C5
El Bullaque E 94 C2
Elburg NL 42 C2
El Burgo E 100 C1
El Burgo de Ebro E 90 B2
El Burgo de Osma E 89 C3
El Burgo Ranero E 88 B1
El Buste E 89 C5
El Cabaco E 93 A4
El Callejo E 89 A3
El Campillo E 99 B4
El Campillo de la Jara E 94 C1
El Cañavete E 95 C4
El Carpio E 100 B1
El Carpio de Tajo E 94 C2
El Casar E 95 B3
El Casar de Escalona E 94 B2
El Castillo de las Guardas E 99 B4
El Centenillo E 100 A2
El Cerro E 93 A5
El Cerro de Andévalo E 99 B4
Elche E 96 C2
Elche de la Sierra E 101 A3
Elchingen D 61 B6
El Comenar E 99 C5
El Coronil E 99 B5
El Crucero E 86 A4
El Cubo de Tierra del Vino E 88 C1
El Cuervo E 99 C4
Elda E 101 A5
Eldena D 44 B3
Eldingen D 44 C2
Elefsina GR 117 D5
El Ejido E 101 C3
Elek H 75 B6
Elemir SRB 75 C5
El Escorial E 94 B2
El Espinar E 94 B2
Eleutheroupoli GR 116 B6
El Frago E 90 A2
El Franco E 86 A4
El Frasno E 89 C5
Elgå N 114 E8
El Garrobo E 99 B4
El Gastor E 99 C5
Elgin UK 23 D5
Elgoibar E 89 A4
Elgol UK 22 D2
El Gordo E 93 B5
El Grado E 90 A3
El Granado E 98 B3
El Grao de Castelló E 96 B3
El Grau E 96 C2
Elgshøa N 34 A4
El Higuera E 100 B1
El Hijate E 101 B3
El Hontanar E 96 A1
Elhovo BG 11 E9
El Hoyo E 100 A2
Elie UK 25 B5
Elizondo E 76 C1
Ełk PL 6 E7
Ellenberg D 61 A6
Ellesmere UK 26 C3
Ellesmere Port UK 26 B3
Ellezelles B 49 C4
Ellingen D 62 A1
Ellmau A 72 A2
Ellon UK 23 D6
Ellös S 35 D3
Ellrich D 51 B6
Ellwangen D 61 B6
Elm
CH 71 B4
D 43 B6
Elmadağ TR 16 B6
El Madroño E 99 B4
El Maillo E 93 A4
Elmalı TR 119 F4
El Masnou E 91 B5
El Mirón E 93 A5
El Molar E 95 B3
El Molinillo E 94 C2
El Morell E 91 B4
Elmshorn D 43 B6
Elmstein D 60 A3
El Muyo E 89 C3
Elne F 91 A5
Elnesvågen N 114 E4
El Olmo E 88 C3
Előszállás H 74 B3
Elouda GR 117 G7
Éloyes F 60 B2
El Palo E 100 C1
El Pardo E 94 B3
El Payo E 93 A4
El Pedernoso E 95 C4
El Pedroso E 99 B5
El Peral E 95 C5
El Perelló
Tarragona E 90 C3
Valencia E 96 B2
Elphin UK 22 C3
El Picazo E 95 C4
El Pinell de Bray E 90 B3
El Piñero E 88 C1
El Pla de Santa Maria E 91 B4
El Pobo E 90 C2
El Pobo de Dueñas E 95 B5
El Pont d'Armentera E 91 B4
El Port de la Selva E 91 A6
El Port de Llançà E 91 A6
El Port de Sagunt E 96 B2
El Prat de Llobregat E 91 B5
El Provencio E 95 C4
El Puente E 89 A3
El Puente del Arzobispo E 93 B5
El Puerto E 86 A4
El Puerto de Santa María E 99 C4
El Real de la Jara E 99 B4
El Real de San Vincente E 94 B2
El Robledo E 94 C2
El Rocio E 99 B4
El Rompido E 99 B3
El Ronquillo E 99 B4
El Royo E 89 C4
El Rubio E 100 B1
El Sabinar E 101 A3
El Saler E 96 B2
El Salobral E 101 A4
El Saucejo E 99 B5
Els Castells E 91 A4
Elsdorf D 50 C2
Elsenfeld D 61 A5
El Serrat AND 91 A4
Elsfleth D 43 B5
Elspeet NL 50 A1
Elst NL 50 B1
Elstead UK 31 C3
Elster D 52 B2
Elsterberg D 52 C2
Elsterwerda D 52 B3
Elstra D 53 B4
El Temple E 90 B2
El Tiemblo E 94 B2
Eltmann D 51 D6
El Toboso E 95 C4
El Tormillo E 90 B2
El Torno E 93 A5
Eltville D 50 C4
El Valle de las Casas E 88 B1
Elvas P 93 C3
Elvebakken N 113 C12
El Vellón E 95 B3
Elven F 56 C3
El Vendrell E 91 B4
Elverum N 34 B3
El Villar de Arnedo E 89 B4
Elvington UK 27 B5
El Viso E 100 A1
El Viso del Alcor E 99 B5
Elxleben D 51 B6
Ely UK 30 B4
Elzach D 61 B4
Elze D 51 A5
Emådalen S 36 A1
Embleton UK 25 C6
Embonas GR 119 F2
Embrun F 79 B5
Embún E 90 A2
Emden D 43 B4
Emecik TR 119 F2
Emet TR 118 C4
Emirdağ TR 118 C6
Emlichheim D 42 C3
Emmaboda S 40 C5
Emmaljunga S 41 C3
Emmeloord NL 42 C2
Emmen
CH 70 A3
NL 42 C3
Emmendingen D 60 B3
Emmer-Compascuum NL 43 C4
Emmerich D 50 B2
Emmern D 51 A5
Emöd H 65 C6
Émpoli I 81 C4
Emsbüren D 43 C4
Emsdetten D 50 A3
Emsfors S 40 B6
Emskirchen D 62 A1
Emstek D 43 C5
Emsworth UK 31 D3
Emyvale IRL 19 B5
Enafors S 115 D9
Enånger S 115 F14
Encamp AND 91 A4
Encarnaçao P 92 C1
Encinas de Abajo E 94 B1
Encinas de Esgueva E 88 C2
Encinasola E 99 A4
Encinas Reales E 100 B1
Encio E 89 B3
Enciso E 89 B4
Enden N 114 F7
Endingen D 60 B3
Endrinal E 93 A5
Endröd H 75 B5
Enebakk N 34 C3
Eneryda S 40 C4
Enese H 64 C3
Enez TR 116 B8
Enfield IRL 21 A5
Eng A 72 A1
Engelberg CH 70 B3
Engelhartszell A 63 B4
Engelskirchen D 50 C3
Engen D 61 C4
Enger N 34 B2
Engerdal N 114 F8
Engerneset N 34 A4
Enge-sande D 39 E1
Engesvang DK 39 C2
Enghien B 49 C5
Engstingen D 61 B5
Engter D 43 C5
Enguera E 96 C2
Enguidanos E 95 C5
Enkenbach D 60 A3
Enkhuizen NL 42 C2
Enklinge FIN 36 B7
Enköping S 37 C4
Enna I 109 B3
Ennezat F 68 C3
Ennigerloh D 50 B4
Enningdal N 35 D3
Ennis IRL 20 B3
Enniscorthy IRL 21 B5
Enniskean IRL 20 C3
Enniskillen UK 19 B4
Ennistimon IRL 20 B2
Enns A 63 B5
Eno FIN 3 E29
Enontekiö FIN 113 D12
Ens NL 42 C2
Enschede NL 50 A2
Ensdorf D 62 A2
Ensisheim F 60 C3
Enstaberga S 37 D3
Enstone UK 31 C2
Entlebuch CH 70 A3
Entrácque I 80 B1
Entradas P 98 B2
Entrains-sur-Nohain F 68 A3
Entrambasaguas E 88 A3
Entrambasmestas E 88 A3
Entraygues-sur-Truyère F 77 B5
Entre-os-Rios P 87 C2
Entrevaux F 79 C5
Entrin Bajo E 93 C4
Entroncamento P 92 B2
Entzheim F 60 B3
Envermeu F 58 A2
Enviken S 36 B2
Enying H 74 B3
Enzingerboden A 72 A2
Enzklösterle D 61 B4
Épagny F 59 A4
Epalinges CH 70 B1
Epannes F 67 B4
Epanomi GR 116 B4
Epe
D 50 A3
NL 42 C2
Épernay F 59 A4
Épernon F 58 B2
Epfig F 60 B3
Epierre F 69 C6
Épila E 90 B1
Épinac F 69 B4
Épinal F 60 B2
Episcopia I 106 A3
Episkopi CY 120 B1
Epitalio GR 117 E3
Epoisses F 69 A4
Eppenbrunn D 60 A3
Eppendorf D 52 C3
Epping UK 31 C4
Eppingen D 61 A4
Epsom UK 31 C3
Epworth UK 27 B5
Eraclea I 72 C2
Eraclea Mare I 72 C2
Erba I 71 C4
Erbach
Baden-Württemberg D 61 B5
Hessen D 61 A4
Erbalunga F 102 A2
Erbendorf D 62 A3
Érchie I 105 C3
Ercolano I 103 C7
Ercsi H 74 A3
Érd H 74 A3
Erdek TR 118 B2
Erdemli TR 16 C7
Erdevik SRB 85 A4
Erding D 62 B2
Erdőtelek H 65 C6
Erdut HR 75 C4
Erdweg D 62 B2
Ereğli
Konya TR 16 C7
Zonguldak TR 118 A6
Erenkaya TR 119 E7
Eresfjord N 114 E5
Eresos GR 116 C7
Eretria GR 116 D5
Erfde D 43 A6
Erfjord N 33 C3
Erfstadt D 50 C2
Erfurt D 52 C1
Ergli LV 7 C8
Ergoldsbach D 62 B3
Eriboll UK 22 C4
Érice I 108 A1
Ericeira P 92 C1
Eğridir TR 119 E5
Eriksberg S 115 B12
Eriksmåla S 40 C5
Eringsboda S 41 C5
Eriswil CH 70 A2
Erithres GR 117 D5
Erkelenz D 50 B2
Erkner D 45 C5
Erkrath D 50 B2
Erla E 90 A2
Erlangen D 62 A2
Erli I 80 B2
Erlsbach A 72 B2
Ermelo NL 49 A6
Ermenak TR 16 C6
Ermenonville F 58 A3
Ermezinde P 87 C2
Ermidas P 98 A2
Ermioni GR 117 E5
Ermoupoli GR 117 E6
Ermsleben D 52 B1
Erndtebrück D 50 C4
Ernée F 57 B5
Ernestinovo HR 74 C3
Ernstbrunn A 64 B2
Erolzheim D 61 B6
Erquelinnes B 49 C5
Erquy F 56 B3
Erra P 92 C2
Erratzu E 76 C1
Errindlev DK 44 A3
Erro E 76 D1
Ersa F 102 A2
Érsekcsanád H 75 B3
Ersekë AL 116 B2
Érsekvadkert H 65 C5
Erstein F 60 B3
Erstfeld CH 70 B3
Ertebølle DK 38 C2
Ertingen D 61 B5
Ervedal
Coimbra P 92 A2
Portalegre P 92 B3
Ervenik HR 83 B4
Ervidel P 98 B2
Ervy-le-Châtel F 59 B4
Erwitte D 51 B4
Erxleben D 52 A1
Erzsébet H 74 B3
Esbjerg DK 39 D1
Esbly F 58 B3
Escacena del Campo E 99 B4
Escairón E 86 B3
Escalada E 88 B3
Escalante E 89 A3
Escalaplano I 110 C2
Escalona E 94 B2
Escalona del Prado E 94 A2
Escalonilla E 94 C2
Escalos de Baixo P 92 B3
Escalos de Cima P 92 B3
Escamilla E 95 B4
Es Caná E 97 B1
Escañuela E 100 B1
Es Castell E 97 B4
Escatrón E 90 B2
Eschach D 61 C5
Eschau D 61 A5
Eschede D 44 C2
Eschenau D 62 A2
Eschenbach D 62 A2
Eschenz CH 61 C4
Eschershausen D 51 B5
Esch-sur-Alzette L 60 A1
Esch-sur-Sûre L 60 A1
Eschwege D 51 B6
Eschweiler D 50 C2
Escobasa de Almazán E 89 C4
Escoeuilles F 48 C2
Escombreras E 101 B5
Escos F 76 C1
Escource F 76 B1
Escragnolles F 79 C5
Escrick UK 27 B4
Escurial E 93 B5
Escurial de la Sierra E 93 A5
Esens D 43 B4
Esgos E 87 B3
Esher UK 31 C3
Eskdalemuir UK 25 C4
Eskifjörður IS 111 B12
Eskilhem S 37 E5
Eskilsäter S 35 D5
Eskilstrup DK 39 E4
Eskilstuna S 37 C3
Eskipazar TR 118 B7
Eskişehir TR 118 C5
Eslarn D 62 A3
Eslava E 89 B5
Eslida E 96 B2
Eslohe D 50 B4
Eslöv S 41 D3
Eşme TR 119 D3

Es Mercadal E 97 B4
Es Migjorn Gran E 97 B4
Espa N 34 B3
Espalion F 78 B1
Esparragalejo E 93 C4
Esparragosa del Caudillo E 93 C5
Esparragossa de la Serena E 93 C5
Esparreguera E 91 B4
Esparron F 79 C4
Espe N 32 B3
Espedal N 33 D3
Espejo
Álava E 89 B3
Córdoba E 100 B1
Espeland N 32 B2
Espelkamp D 43 C5
Espeluche F 78 B3
Espeluy E 100 A2
Espera E 99 C5
Esperança P 93 B3
Espéraza F 77 D5
Espéria I 103 B6
Espevær N 33 C2
Espiel E 99 A5
Espinama E 88 A2
Espiñaredo E 86 A3
Espinasses F 79 B5
Espinelves E 91 B5
Espinhal P 92 A2
Espinho P 87 C2
Espinilla E 88 A2
Espinosa de Cerrato E 88 C3
Espinosa de los Monteros E 89 A3
Espinoso del Rey E 94 C2
Espirito Santo P 98 B3
Espluga de Francolí E 91 B4
Esplús E 90 B3
Espolla E 91 A5
Espoo FIN 6 A8
Esporles E 97 B3
Es Port d'Alcúdia E 97 B3
Esposende P 87 C2
Espot E 91 A4
Es Pujols E 97 C1
Esquedas E 90 A2
Esquivias E 94 B3
Essay F 57 B6
Essen
B 49 B5
Niedersachsen D 43 C4
Nordrhein-Westfalen D 50 B3
Essenbach D 62 B3
Essertaux F 58 A3
Essingen D 61 B6
Esslingen D 61 B5
Es Soleràs E 90 B3
Essoyes F 59 B5
Estacas E 87 B2
Estadilla E 90 A3
Estagel F 78 D1
Estaires F 48 C3
Estang F 76 C2
Estarreja P 87 D2
Estartit E 91 A6
Estavayer-le-Lac CH 70 B1
Este I 72 C1
Esteiro E 86 A2
Estela P 87 C2
Estella E 89 B4
Estellencs E 97 B2
Estepa E 100 B1
Estépar E 88 B3
Estepona E 99 C5
Esternay F 59 B4
Esterri d'Aneu E 91 A4
Esterwegen D 43 C4
Estissac F 59 B4
Estivadas E 87 B3
Estivareilles F 68 B2
Estivella E 96 B2
Estói P 98 B3
Estopiñán E 90 B3
Estoril P 92 C1
Estoublon F 79 C5
Estrée-Blanche F 48 C3
Estrées-St Denis F 58 A3
Estrela P 98 A3
Estremera E 95 B3
Estremoz P 92 C3
Estuna S 36 C5
Esyres F 67 A5
Esztergom H 65 C4
Etables-sur-Mer F 56 B3
Étain F 60 A1
Étalans F 69 A6
Etalle B 60 A1
Étampes F 58 B3
Etang-sur-Arroux F 69 B4
Étaples F 48 C2
Etauliers F 67 C4
Etili TR 118 C1
Etna N 34 B1
Etne N 33 C2
Etoges F 59 B4
Etoliko GR 116 D3
Eton UK 31 C3
Etréaupont F 59 A4
Étréchy F 58 B3
Étrépagny F 58 A2
Étretat F 57 A6
Étroeungt F 49 C4
Étroubles I 70 C2
Ettal D 62 C2
Ettelbruck L 60 A2
Etten NL 49 B5
Ettenheim D 60 B3
Ettington UK 29 A6
Ettlingen D 61 B4
Ettringen D 62 B1
Etuz F 69 A5
Etxarri-Aranatz E 89 B4
Etyek H 74 A3
Eu F 48 C2
Euerdorf D 51 C6
Eulate E 89 B4
Eupen B 50 C2
Europoort NL 49 B5
Euskirchen D 50 C2
Eutin D 44 A2
Evanger N 32 B3
Évaux-les-Bains F 68 B2
Evciler
Afyon TR 119 D4
Çanakkale TR 118 C1
Evenskjær N 112 D5
Evenstad N 34 A3
Evercreech UK 29 B5
Evergem B 49 B4
Everöd S 41 D4
Eversberg D 51 B4
Everswinkel D 50 B3
Evertsberg S 34 A5
Evesham UK 29 A6
Évian-les-Bains F 69 B6
Evisa F 102 A1
Evje N 33 D4
Evolène CH 70 B2
Évora P 92 C3
Evoramonte P 92 C3
Evran F 57 B4
Evrecy F 57 A5
Évreux F 58 A2
Évron F 57 B5
Évry F 58 B3
Ewell UK 31 C3
Ewersbach D 50 C4
Excideuil F 67 C6
Exeter UK 29 C4
Exmes F 57 B6
Exminster UK 29 C4
Exmouth UK 29 C4
Eydehamn N 33 D5
Eye
Peterborough UK 30 B3
Suffolk UK 30 B5
Eyemouth UK 25 C5
Eyguians F 79 B4
Eyguières F 79 C4
Eygurande F 68 C2
Eylie F 77 D3
Eymet F 77 B3
Eymoutiers F 68 C1
Eynsham UK 31 C2
Eyrarbakki IS 111 D4
Eystrup D 43 C6
Ezaro E 86 B1
Ezcaray E 89 B4
Ezcároz E 76 D1
Ezine TR 118 C1
Ezmoriz P 87 D2

F

Fabara E 90 B3
Fábbrico I 81 B4
Fåberg N 34 A2
Fabero E 86 B4
Fábiánsebestyén H 75 B5
Fåborg DK 39 D3
Fabrègues F 78 C2
Fabriano I 82 C1
Fabrizia I 106 C3
Facha P 87 C2
Facinas E 99 C5
Fačkov SK 65 A4
Fadagosa P 92 B3
Fadd H 74 B3
Faédis I 72 B3
Faenza I 81 B5
Fafe P 87 C2
Fagagna I 72 B3
Făgăras RO 11 D8
Fågelberget S 115 C11
Fågelfors S 40 B5
Fågelmara S 41 C5
Fågelsta S 37 D2
Fagerås S 35 C5
Fagerheim N 32 B4
Fagerhøy N 34 A1
Fagerhult S 40 B5
Fagerlund N 34 B2
Fagernes
Oppland N 32 B6
Troms N 112 C8
Fagersanna S 35 D6
Fagersta S 36 B2
Fåglavik S 35 D5
Fagnano Castello I 106 B3
Fagnières F 59 B5
Faido CH 70 B3
Fains-Véel F 59 B6
Fairford UK 29 B6
Fairlie UK 24 C3
Fajsz H 74 B3
Fakenham UK 30 B4
Fåker S 115 D11
Fakse DK 39 D5
Fakse Ladeplads DK 41 D2
Falaise F 57 B5
Falcade I 72 B1
Falcarragh IRL 18 A3
Falces E 89 B5
Fălciu RO 11 C10
Falconara I 109 B3
Falconara Maríttima I 82 C2
Falcone I 109 A4
Faldingworth UK 27 B5
Falerum S 37 D3
Fălești MD 11 C9
Falkenberg
Bayern D 62 A3
Bayern D 62 B3
Brandenburg D 52 B3
S 40 C2
Falkensee D 45 C5
Falkenstein
Bayern D 62 A3
Sachsen D 52 C2
Falkenthal D 45 C5
Falkirk UK 25 B4
Falkland UK 25 B4
Falköping S 35 D5
Fall D 62 C2
Falla S 37 D2
Fallingbostel D 43 C6
Falmouth UK 28 C2
Falset E 90 B3
Fălticeni RO 11 C9
Falun S 36 B2
Famagusta CY 120 A2
Fammestad N 32 B2
Fana N 32 B2
Fanano I 81 B4
Fanari GR 116 C3
Fanjeaux F 77 C5
Fano I 82 C2
Fântânele RO 75 B6
Fão P 87 C2
Fara in Sabina I 102 A5
Faramontanos de Tábara E 88 C1
Fara Novarese I 70 C3
Farasdues E 90 A1
Fårbo S 40 B6
Fareham UK 31 D2
Färentuna S 37 C4
Färgelanda S 35 D3
Färila S 115 F12
Faringdon UK 31 C2
Faringe S 36 B5
Farini I 80 B3
Fariza E 87 C4
Färjestaden S 41 C6
Farkadona GR 116 C4
Farkasfa H 73 B6
Farlete E 90 B2
Färlöv S 41 C4
Farmos H 75 A4
Farnå SK 65 C4
Färnäs S 36 B1
Farnborough UK 31 C3
Farnese I 102 A4
Farnham UK 31 C3
Farnroda D 51 C6
Faro P 98 B3
Fåro S 37 E6
Fårösund S 37 E6
Farra d'Alpago I 72 B2
Farranfore IRL 20 B2
Farre DK 39 C2
Farsala GR 116 C4
Farsø DK 38 C2
Farsund N 33 D3
Farum DK 41 D2
Fårup DK 38 C2
Fasana I 103 C8
Fasano I 104 C3
Fáskrúðsfjörður IS 111 C11
Fassberg D 44 C2
Fastiv UA 11 A10
Fastnäs S 34 B4
Fatesh RUS 7 E13
Fátima P 92 B2
Fatmomakke S 115 B12
Fättjaur S 115 B12
Faucogney-et-la-Mer F 60 C2
Fauguerolles F 76 B3
Faulenrost D 45 B4
Faulquemont F 60 A2
Fauquembergues F 48 C3
Fauske N 112 E4
Fauville-en-Caux F 58 A1
Fauvillers B 60 A1
Fåvang N 34 A2
Favara
E 96 B2
I 108 B2
Faverges F 69 C6
Faverney F 60 C2
Faversham UK 31 C4
Favignana I 108 B1
Fawley UK 31 D2
Fay-aux-Loges F 58 C3
Fayence F 79 C5
Fayet F 78 C1
Fayl-Billot F 60 C1
Fayón E 90 B3
Fearn UK 23 D5
Fécamp F 58 A1
Feda N 33 D3
Fedje N 32 B1
Feeny UK 19 B4
Fegen S 40 B3
Fegyvernek H 75 A5
Fehrbellin D 45 C4
Fehring A 73 B6
Feichten A 71 A5
Feiring N 34 B3
Feistritz im Rosental A 73 B4
Feke TR 16 C7
Feketić SRB 75 C4
Felanitx E 97 B3
Feld am See A 72 B3
Feldbach A 73 B5
Feldberg D 45 B5
Feldkirch A 71 A4
Feldkirchen in Kärnten A 73 B4
Feldkirchen-Westerham D 62 C2
Felgueiras P 87 C2
Felitto I 103 C8
Félix E 101 C3
Felixstowe UK 31 C5
Felizzano I 80 B2
Felletin F 68 C2
Fellingsbro S 37 C2
Felnac RO 75 B6
Felnémet H 65 C6
Felpéc H 74 A2
Fels am Wagram A 64 B1
Felsberg D 51 B5
Felsönyék H 74 B3
Felsöszentiván H 75 B4
Felsöszentmárton H 74 C2
Felsözsolca H 65 B6
Felsted DK 39 E2
Feltre I 72 B1
Femsjö S 40 C3
Fenagh IRL 19 B4
Fene E 86 A2
Fenestrelle I 79 A6
Fénétrange F 60 B3
Feneu F 57 C5
Fengersfors S 35 D4
Fenit IRL 20 B2
Fensmark DK 39 D4
Fenwick UK 24 C3
Feolin Ferry UK 24 C1
Ferbane IRL 21 A4
Ferdinandovac HR 74 B2
Ferdinandshof D 45 B5
Fère-Champenoise F 59 B4
Fère-en-Tardenois F 59 A4
Ferentillo I 102 A5
Ferentino I 103 B6
Feres GR 116 B8
Feria E 93 C4
Feričanci HR 74 C2
Ferizli TR 118 B5
Ferla I 109 B3
Ferlach A 73 B4
Ferleiten A 72 A2
Fermil P 87 C3
Fermo I 82 C2
Fermoselle E 87 C4
Fermoy IRL 20 B3
Fernancabellero E 94 C3
Fernán Nuñéz E 100 B1
Fernán Peréz E 101 C3
Fernão Ferro P 92 C1
Fernay-Voltaire F 69 B6
Ferndown UK 29 C6
Ferness UK 23 D5
Fernhurst UK 31 C3
Ferns IRL 21 B5
Ferpécle CH 70 B2
Ferrals-les-Corbières F 78 C1
Ferrandina I 104 C2
Ferrara I 81 B5
Ferrara di Monte Baldo I 71 C5
Ferreira E 86 A3
Ferreira do Alentejo P 98 A2
Ferreira do Zêzere P 92 B2
Ferreras de Abajo E 87 C4
Ferreras de Arriba E 87 C4
Ferreries E 97 B4
Ferreruela E 90 B1
Ferreruela de Tabara E 87 C4
Ferret CH 70 C2
Ferrette F 70 A2
Ferriere I 80 B3
Ferrière-la-Grande F 49 C4
Ferrières
Hautes-Pyrénées F 76 C2
Loiret F 58 B3
Oise F 58 A3
Ferrières-sur-Sichon F 68 B3
Ferrol E 86 A2
Ferryhill UK 27 A4
Fertörakos H 64 C2
Fertöszentmiklós H 64 C2
Ferwerd NL 42 B2
Festieux F 59 A4
Festøy N 114 E3
Festvåg N 112 E3
Fetești RO 11 D9
Fethard
Tipperary IRL 21 B4
Wexford IRL 21 B5
Fethiye TR 119 F4
Fetsund N 34 C3
Fettercairn UK 25 B5
Feucht D 62 A2
Feuchtwangen D 61 A6
Feudingen D 51 C4
Feuges F 59 B5
Feuquières F 58 A2
Feurs F 69 C4
Fevik N 33 D5
Ffestiniog UK 26 C2
Fiamignano I 102 A6
Fiano I 70 C2
Ficarazzi I 108 A2
Ficarolo I 81 B5
Fichtelberg D 52 C1
Ficulle I 82 D1
Fidenza I 81 B4
Fidjeland N 33 D3
Fieberbrunn A 72 A2
Fier AL 105 C5
Fiera di Primiero I 72 B1
Fiesch CH 70 B3
Fiesso Umbertiano I 81 B5
Figari F 102 B2
Figeac F 77 B5
Figeholm S 40 B6
Figgjo N 33 D2
Figline Valdarno I 81 C5
Figols E 90 A3
Figueira da Foz P 92 A2
Figueira de Castelo Rodrigo P 87 D4
Figueira dos Caveleiros P 98 A2
Figueiredo P 92 B3
Figueiredo de Alva P 87 D3
Figueiródos Vinhos P 92 B2
Figueres E 91 A5
Figueroles E 96 A2
Figueruela de Arriba E 87 C4
Filadélfia I 106 C3
Fil'akovo SK 65 B5
Filderstadt D 61 B5
Filey UK 27 A5
Filiași RO 11 D7
Filiates GR 116 C2
Filiatra GR 117 E3
Filipstad S 35 C6
Filisur CH 71 B4
Fillan N 114 D5
Filotio GR 117 E7
Filottrano I 82 C2
Filskov DK 39 D2
Filton UK 29 B5
Filtvet N 35 C2
Filzmoos A 72 A3
Finale Emilia I 81 B5
Finale Ligure I 80 B2
Fiñana E 101 B3
Finby FIN 36 B7
Fincham UK 30 B4
Finchingfield UK 31 C4
Findhorn UK 23 D5
Findochty UK 23 D6
Finike TR 119 F5
Finkenberg A 72 A1
Finnea IRL 19 C4
Finneidfjord N 115 A10
Finnerödja S 37 D1
Finnskog N 34 B4
Finnsnes N 112 C7
Finntorp S 35 C4
Finócchio I 102 B5
Finsjö S 40 B6
Finsland N 33 D4
Finspång S 37 D2
Finsterwalde D 53 B3
Finsterwolde NL 43 B4
Finstown UK 23 B5
Fintona UK 19 B4
Fionnphort UK 24 B1
Fiorenzuola d'Arda I 81 B3
Firenze = Florence I 81 C5
Firenzuola I 81 B5
Firmi F 77 B5
Firminy F 69 C4
Firmo I 106 B3
Fischamend Markt A 64 B2
Fischbach
A 73 A5
D 60 A3
Fischbeck D 44 C4
Fischen D 71 A5
Fishbourne UK 31 D2
Fishguard UK 28 B3
Fiskardo GR 116 D2
Fiskebäckskil S 35 D3
Fiskebøl N 112 D3
Fismes F 59 A4
Fisterra E 86 B1
Fitero E 89 B5
Fitjar N 32 C2
Fiuggi I 102 B6
Fiumata I 102 A6
Fiumefreddo Brúzio I 106 B3
Fiumefreddo di Sicília I 109 B4
Fiumicino I 102 B5
Fivemiletown UK 19 B4
Fivizzano I 81 B4
Fjälkinge S 41 C4
Fjällåsen S 112 E9
Fjällbacka S 35 D3
Fjæra N 32 C3
Fjärdhundra S 36 C3
Fjellerup DK 38 C3
Fjerritslev DK 38 B2
Fjordgard N 112 C6
Fjugesta S 37 C1
Flå N 32 B6
Flåbygd N 33 C5
Flaça E 91 A5
Flace F 69 B4
Fladungen D 51 C6
Flaine F 70 B1
Flaka FIN 36 B7
Flåm N 32 B4
Flamatt CH 70 B2
Flamborough UK 27 A5
Flammersfeld D 50 C3
Flassans-sur-Issole F 79 C5
Flatdal N 33 C5
Flatebø N 32 B3
Flateby N 34 C3
Flateland N 33 C4
Flateyri IS 111 A2
Flatøydegard N 32 B6
Flatråker N 32 C2
Flattach A 72 B3
Flatvarp S 37 E3
Flauenskjold DK 38 B3
Flavigny-sur-Moselle F 60 B2
Flavy-le-Martel F 59 A4
Flawil CH 71 A4
Flayosc F 79 C5
Flechtingen D 44 C3
Fleckeby D 44 A1
Fleet UK 31 C3
Fleetmark D 44 C3
Fleetwood UK 26 B2
Flehingen D 61 A4
Flekke N 32 A2
Flekkefjord N 33 D3
Flen S 37 C3
Flensburg D 39 E2
Fleringe S 37 E5
Flerohopp S 40 C5
Flers F 57 B5
Flesberg N 32 C6
Fleurance F 77 C3
Fleuré F 67 B5
Fleurier CH 69 B6
Fleurus B 49 C5
Fleury
Hérault F 78 C2
Yonne F 59 C4
Fleury-les-Aubrais F 58 C2
Fleury-sur-Andelle F 58 A2
Fleury-sur-Orne F 57 A5
Flieden D 51 C5
Flimby UK 26 A2
Flims CH 71 B4
Flines-lèz-Raches F 49 C4
Flint UK 26 B2
Flirey F 60 B1
Flirsch A 71 A5
Flisa N 34 B4
Flisby S 40 B4
Fliseryd S 40 B6
Flix E 90 B3
Flixecourt F 48 C3
Flize F 59 A5
Flobecq B 49 C4
Floby S 35 D5
Floda S 40 B2
Flodden UK 25 C5
Flogny-la-Chapelle F 59 C4
Flöha D 52 C3
Flonheim D 61 A4
Florac F 78 B2
Floreffe B 49 C5
Florence = Firenze I 81 C5
Florennes B 49 C5
Florensac F 78 C2
Florentin F 77 C5
Florenville B 59 A6
Flores de Avila E 94 B1
Floresta I 109 B3
Florești MD 11 C10
Florídia I 109 B4
Florina GR 116 B3
Florø N 114 F2
Flörsheim D 51 C4
Floss D 62 A3
Fluberg N 34 B2
Flúðir IS 111 C5
Flühli CH 70 B3
Flumet F 69 C6
Fluminimaggiore I 110 C1
Flums CH 71 A4
Flyeryd S 41 C5
Flygsfors S 40 C5
Foča BIH 84 C3
Foça TR 118 D1
Fochabers UK 23 D5
Focșani RO 11 D9
Foel UK 26 C2
Foeni RO 75 C5
Fogdö S 37 C3
Fóggia I 104 B1
Foggianise I 103 B7
Föglö FIN 36 B7
Fohnsdorf A 73 A4
Foiano della Chiana I 81 C5
Foix F 77 D4
Fojnica
BIH 84 C2
BIH 84 C3
Fokino RUS 7 E13
Fokstua N 114 E6
Földeák H 75 B5
Foldereid N 114 C9
Földes H 75 A6
Folegandros GR 117 F6
Folelli F 102 A2
Folgaria I 71 C6
Folgosinho P 92 A3
Folgoso de la Ribera E 86 B4
Folgoso do Courel E 86 B3
Foligno I 82 D1
Folkärna S 36 B3
Folkestad N 114 E3
Folkestone UK 31 C5
Follafoss N 114 D8
Folldal N 114 E6
Follebu N 34 A2
Follina I 72 C2
Föllinge S 115 D11
Follónica I 81 D4
Fölsbyn S 35 C4
Foncebadón E 86 B4
Foncine-le-Bas F 69 B6
Fondevila E 87 C2
Fondi I 103 B6
Fondo I 71 B6
Fonelas E 100 B2
Fonfría
Teruel E 90 C1
Zamora E 87 C4
Fonnes N 32 B1
Fonni I 110 B2
Fontaine F 59 B5
Fontainebleau F 58 B3
Fontaine de Vaucluse F 79 C4
Fontaine-Française F 69 A5
Fontaine-le-Dun F 58 A1
Fontan F 80 B1
Fontanarejo E 94 C2
Fontane I 80 B1
Fontanélice I 81 B5
Fontanières F 68 B2
Fontanosas E 100 A1
Fonteblanda I 102 A4
Fontenay-le-Comte F 66 B4
Fontenay-Trésigny F 59 B3
Fontevrault-l'Abbaye F 67 A5
Fontiveros E 94 B2
Fontoy F 60 A1
Fontpédrouse F 91 A5
Font-Romeu F 91 A5
Fontstown IRL 21 A5
Fonyód H 74 B2
Fonz E 90 A3
Fonzaso I 72 B1
Föppolo I 71 B4
Föra S 41 B6
Forbach
D 61 B4
F 60 A2
Forcall E 90 C2
Forcalquier F 79 C4
Forcarei E 86 B2
Forchheim D 62 A2
Forchtenau A 64 C2
Forchtenberg D 61 A5
Ford UK 24 B2
Førde
Hordaland N 33 C2
Sogn og Fjordane N 32 A2
Förderstedt D 52 B1
Førdesfjorden N 33 C2
Fordham UK 30 B4
Fordingbridge UK 29 C6
Fordon PL 47 B4
Fordongiánus I 110 C1
Forenza I 104 C1
Foresta di Búrgos I 110 B1
Forfar UK 25 B5
Forges-les-Eaux F 58 A2
Foria I 106 A2
Forio I 103 C6
Forjães P 87 C2
Førland N 33 D4
Forlì I 81 B6
Forlimpopoli I 82 B1
Formazza I 70 B3
Formby UK 26 B2
Formerie F 58 A2
Fórmia I 103 B6
Formígine I 81 B4
Formigliana I 70 C3
Formiguères F 91 A5
Fornalutx E 97 B2
Fornåsa S 37 D2
Fornelli I 110 B1
Fornells E 97 A4
Fornelos de Montes E 87 B2
Fornes E 100 C2
Forneset N 112 C8
Forni Avoltri I 72 B2
Forni di Sopra I 72 B2
Forni di Sotto I 72 B2
Forno
Piemonte I 70 C3
Piemonte I 79 A6
Forno Alpi-Gráie I 70 C2
Forno di Zoldo I 72 B2
Fornos de Algodres P 92 A3
Fornovo di Taro I 81 B4
Foros do Arrão P 92 B2
Forráskút H 75 B4
Forres UK 23 D5
Forriolo E 87 B3
Fors S 36 B3
Forsand N 33 D3
Forsbacka S 36 B3
Forserum S 40 B4
Forshaga S 35 C5
Forsheda S 40 B3
Forsinain UK 23 C5
Førslev DK 39 D5
Förslöv S 41 C2
Forsmark
Uppsala S 36 B5
Västerbotten S 115 B12
Forsmo S 115 D14
Forsnäs S 115 A15
Forsnes N 114 D5
Forssa FIN 3 F25
Forssjöbruk S 37 D3
Forst D 53 B4
Forsvik S 37 D1
Fortanete E 90 C2
Fort Augustus UK 22 D4
Forte dei Marmi I 81 C4
Fortezza I 72 B1
Forth UK 25 C4
Fort-Mahon-Plage F 48 C2
Fortrie UK 23 D6
Fortrose UK 23 D4
Fortun N 32 A4
Fortuna E 101 A4
Fortuneswell UK 29 C5
Fort William UK 24 B2
Forvik N 115 B9
Fos F 77 D3
Fosdinovo I 81 B4
Foss N 32 B6
Fossacesia I 103 A7
Fossano I 80 B1
Fossato di Vico I 82 C1
Fossbakken N 112 D7
Fosse-la-Ville B 49 C5
Fossombrone I 82 C1
Fos-sur-Mer F 78 C3
Fot H 65 C5
Fouchères F 59 B5
Fouesnant F 56 C1
Foug F 60 B1
Fougères F 57 B4
Fougerolles F 60 C2
Foulain F 59 B6
Fountainhall UK 25 C5
Fouras F 66 C3
Fourchambault F 68 A3
Fourmies F 49 C5
Fourna GR 116 C3
Fournels F 78 B2
Fourni GR 119 E1
Fournols F 68 C3
Fourques F 91 A5
Fourquevaux F 77 C4
Fours F 68 B3
Fowey UK 28 C3
Foxdale UK 26 A1
Foxford IRL 18 C2
Foyers UK 23 D4
Foynes IRL 20 B2
Foz E 86 A3
Foza I 72 C1
Foz do Arelho P 92 B1
Foz do Giraldo P 92 B3
Frabosa Soprana I 80 B1
Frades de la Sierra E 93 A5
Fraga E 90 B3
Fragagnano I 104 C3
Frailes E 100 B2
Fraire B 49 C5
Fraize F 60 B2
Framlingham UK 30 B5
Frammersbach D 51 C5
Framnes N 35 C2
França P 87 C4
Francaltroff F 60 B2
Francavilla al Mare I 103 A7
Francavilla di Sicília I 109 B4
Francavilla Fontana I 104 C3
Francavilla in Sinni I 106 A3
Francescas F 77 B3
Franco P 87 C3
Francofonte I 109 B3
Francos E 89 C3
Frändefors S 35 D4
Franeker NL 42 B2
Frangy F 69 B5
Frankenau D 51 B4
Frankenberg
Hessen D 51 B4
Sachsen D 52 C3
Frankenburg A 63 B4
Frankenfels A 63 C6
Frankenmarkt A 63 C4
Frankenthal D 61 A4
Frankfurt
Brandenburg D 45 C6
Hessen D 51 C4
Frankowo PL 47 A6
Frankrike S 115 D10
Fränsta S 115 E13
Františkovy Lázně CZ 52 C2
Franzburg D 45 A4
Frascati I 102 B5
Frasdorf D 62 C3
Fraserburgh UK 23 D6
Frashër AL 116 B2
Frasne F 69 B6
Frasnes-lez-Anvaing B 49 C4
Frasseto F 102 B2
Frastanz A 71 A4
Fratel P 92 B3
Fratta Todina I 82 D1
Frauenau D 63 B4
Frauenfeld CH 70 A3
Frauenkirchen A 64 C2
Frauenstein D 52 C3
Frauental A 73 B5
Frayssinet F 77 B4
Frayssinet-le-Gélat F 77 B4
Frechas P 87 C3
Frechen D 50 C2
Frechilla E 88 B2
Freckenhorst D 50 B3
Fredeburg D 51 B4
Fredelsloh D 51 B5
Fredeng N 34 B2
Fredensborg DK 41 D2
Fredericia DK 39 D2
Frederiks DK 39 C2
Frederikshavn DK 38 B3
Frederikssund DK 39 D5
Frederiksværk DK 39 D5
Fredrika S 115 C15
Fredriksberg S 34 B6
Fredriksdal S 40 B4
Fredrikstad N 35 C2
Fregenal de la Sierra E 99 A4
Fregene I 102 B5
Freiberg D 52 C3
Freiburg
Baden-Württemberg D 60 C3
Niedersachsen D 43 B6
Freienhagen D 51 B5
Freienhufen D 53 B3
Freienstein D 44 B4
Freihung D 62 A2
Freilassing D 62 C3
Freisen D 60 A3
Freising D 62 B2
Freistadt A 63 B5
Freital D 52 B3
Freixedas P 93 A3
Freixo de Espada à Cinta P 87 C4
Fréjus F 79 C5
Fremdingen D 61 B6
Frenštát pod Radhoštěm CZ 64 A4
Freren D 43 C4
Freshford IRL 21 B4
Freshwater UK 31 D2
Fresnay-sur-Sarthe F 57 B6
Fresneda de la Sierra E 95 B4
Fresneda de la Sierra Tiron E 89 B3
Fresnedillas E 94 B2
Fresnes-en-Woevre F 60 A1
Fresno Alhandiga E 94 B1
Fresno de la Ribera E 88 C1
Fresno de la Vega E 88 B1
Fresno de Sayago E 87 C5
Fresnoy-Folny F 58 A2
Fresnoy-le-Grand F 59 A4
Fressenville F 48 C2
Fresvik N 32 A3
Fréteval F 58 C2
Fretigney F 69 A5
Freudenberg
Baden-Württemberg D 61 A5
Nordrhein-Westfalen D 50 C3
Freudenstadt D 61 B4
Freux B 49 D6
Frévent F 48 C3
Freyburg D 52 B1
Freyenstein D 44 B4
Freyming-Merlebach F 60 A2
Freystadt D 62 A2
Freyung D 63 B4
Frías de Albarracín E 95 B5
Fribourg CH 70 B2
Frick CH 70 A3
Fridafors S 41 C4
Fridaythorpe UK 27 A5
Friedberg
A 73 A6
Bayern D 62 B1
Hessen D 51 C4
Friedeburg D 43 B4
Friedewald D 51 C5
Friedland
Brandenburg D 53 A4
Mecklenburg-Vorpommern D 45 B5
Niedersachsen D 51 B5
Friedrichroda D 51 C6
Friedrichsdorf D 51 C4
Friedrichshafen D 61 C5
Friedrichskoog D 43 A5
Friedrichstadt D 43 A6
Friedrichswalde D 45 B5
Friesach A 73 B4
Friesack D 45 C4
Friesenheim D 60 B3
Friesoythe D 43 B4
Friggesund S 115 F13
Frigiliana E 100 C2
Frihetsli N 112 D8
Frillesås S 40 B2
Frinnaryd S 40 B4
Frinton-on-Sea UK 31 C5
Friockheim UK 25 B5
Friol E 86 A3
Fristad S 40 B2
Fritsla S 40 B2
Fritzlar D 51 B5
Frizington UK 26 A2
Frödinge S 40 B6
Froges F 69 C5
Frohburg D 52 B2
Frohnhausen D 50 C4
Frohnleiten A 73 A5
Froissy F 58 A3
Frombork PL 47 A5
Frome UK 29 B5
Frómista E 88 B2
Fröndenberg D 50 B3
Fronsac F 76 B2
Front I 70 C2
Fronteira P 92 B3
Frontenay-Rohan-Rohan F 67 B4
Frontenhausen D 62 B3
Frontignan F 78 C2
Fronton F 77 C4
Fröseke S 40 C5
Frosinone I 103 B6
Frosolone I 103 B7
Frosta N 114 D7
Frøstrup DK 38 B1
Frosunda S 37 C5
Frouard F 60 B2
Frövi S 37 C2
Frøyset N 32 B2
Fruges F 48 C3
Frutigen CH 70 B2
Frýdek-Místek CZ 65 A4
Frýdlant CZ 53 C5
Frýdlant nad Ostravicí CZ 65 A4
Frygnowo PL 47 B6
Fryšták CZ 64 A3
Fucécchio I 81 C4
Fuencaliente
Ciudad Real E 94 C3
Ciudad Real E 100 A1
Fuencemillán E 95 B3
Fuendejalón E 89 C5
Fuengirola E 100 C1
Fuenlabrada E 94 B3
Fuenlabrada de los Montes E 94 C2
Fuensalida E 94 B2
Fuensanta E 101 B4
Fuensanta de Martos E 100 B2
Fuente-Alamo E 101 A4
Fuente-Álamo de Murcia E 101 B4
Fuentealbilla E 96 B1
Fuente al Olmo de Iscar E 88 C2
Fuentecén E 88 C3
Fuente Dé E 88 A2
Fuente de Cantos E 99 A4
Fuente del Arco E 99 A5
Fuente del Conde E 100 B1
Fuente del Maestre E 93 C4
Fuente de Santa Cruz E 94 A2
Fuente el Fresno E 94 C3
Fuente el Saz de Jarama E 95 B3
Fuente el Sol E 94 A2
Fuenteguinaldo E 93 A4
Fuentelapeña E 88 C1
Fuentelcésped E 89 C3
Fuentelespino de Haro E 95 C4
Fuentelespino de Moya E 95 C5
Fuentenovilla E 95 B3
Fuente Obejuna E 99 A5
Fuente Palmera E 99 B5
Fuentepelayo E 94 A2
Fuentepinilla E 89 C4
Fuenterroble de Salvatierra E 93 A5
Fuenterrobles E 96 B1
Fuentes E 95 C4
Fuentesaúco E 88 C1
Fuentesaúco E 94 A1
Fuentes de Andalucía E 99 B5
Fuentes de Ebro E 90 B2
Fuentes de Jiloca E 89 C5
Fuentes de la Alcarria E 95 B4
Fuentes de León E 99 A4
Fuentes de Nava E 88 B2
Fuentes de Oñoro E 93 A4
Fuentes de Ropel E 88 B1
Fuentespalda E 90 C3
Fuentespina E 88 C3
Fuente-Tójar E 100 B1
Fuente Vaqueros E 100 B2
Fuentidueña E 88 C3
Fuentidueña de Tajo E 95 B3
Fuerte del Rey E 100 B2
Fügen A 72 A1
Fuglebjerg DK 39 D4
Fuglevik N 35 C2
Fuhrberg D 44 C1
Fulda D 51 C5
Fulgatore I 108 B1
Fully CH 70 B2
Fulnek CZ 64 A3
Fülöpszállás H 75 B4
Fulpmes A 71 A6
Fulunäs S 34 A5
Fumay F 59 A5
Fumel F 77 B3
Funäsdalen S 115 E9
Fundão P 92 A3
Funzie UK 22 A8
Furadouro P 87 D2
Fure N 32 A2
Fürstenau D 43 C4
Furstenau D 51 B5
Fürstenberg D 45 B5
Fürstenfeldbruck D 62 B2
Fürstenstadt D 45 C6
Fürstenwalde D 45 C6
Fürstenwerder D 45 B5
Fürstenzell D 63 B4
Fürth
Bayern D 62 A1
Hessen D 61 A4
Furth im Wald D 62 A3
Furtwangen D 61 B4
Furuby S 40 C5
Furudal S 36 A2
Furuflaten N 112 C8
Furulund S 41 D3
Furusjö S 40 B3
Fusa N 32 B2
Fuscaldo I 106 B3
Fusch an der Grossglocknerstrasse A 72 A2
Fushë Arrëz AL 105 A6
Fushë-Krujë AL 105 B5
Fusina I 72 C2
Fusio CH 70 B3
Füssen D 62 C1
Fustiñana E 89 B5
Futog SRB 75 C4
Futrikelv N 112 C8
Füzesabony H 65 C6
Füzesgyarmat H 75 A6
Fužine HR 73 C4
Fyllinge S 40 C2
Fynshav DK 39 E2
Fyresdal N 33 C5

G

Gaaldorf A 73 A4
Gabaldón E 95 C5
Gabarret F 76 C2
Gabčíkovo SK 64 C3
Gąbin PL 47 C5
Gabriac F 78 B1
Gabrovo BG 11 E8
Gaby I 70 C2
Gacé F 58 B1
Gacko BIH 84 C3
Gäddede S 115 C11
Gadebusch D 44 B3
Gadmen CH 70 B3
Gádor E 101 C3
Gádoros H 75 B5
Gael F 57 B3
Găești RO 11 D8
Gaeta I 103 B6
Gafanhoeira P 92 C2
Gaflenz A 63 C5
Gagarin RUS 7 D13
Gaggenau D 61 B4
Gagliano Castelferrato I 109 B3
Gagliano del Capo I 107 B5
Gagnet S 36 B2
Gaibanella I 81 B5
Gaildorf D 61 B5
Gaillac F 77 C4
Gaillefontaine F 58 A2
Gaillon F 58 A2
Gainsborough UK 27 B5
Gairloch UK 22 D3
Gairlochy UK 24 B3
Gáiro I 110 C2
Gaj
HR 74 C2
SRB 85 B6
Gaja-la-Selve F 77 C4
Gajanejos E 95 B4
Gajary SK 64 B2
Gajdobra SRB 75 C4
Galan F 77 C3
Galanta SK 64 B3
Galapagar E 94 B2
Galápagos E 95 B3
Galaroza E 99 B4
Galashiels UK 25 C5
Galatas GR 117 E5
Galați RO 11 D10
Galatina I 107 A5
Galatista GR 116 B5
Galátone I 107 A5
Galaxidi GR 117 D4
Galdakao E 89 A4
Galeata I 81 C5
Galende E 87 B4
Galera E 101 B3
Galéria F 102 A1
Galgamácsa H 65 C5
Galgate UK 26 B3
Galgon F 76 B2
Galinduste E 93 A5
Galinoporni CY 120 A3
Galisteo E 93 B4
Galizes P 92 A3
Galków PL 55 B4
Gallarate I 70 C3
Gallardon F 58 B2
Gallegos de Argañán E 93 A4
Gallegos del Solmirón E 93 A5
Galleguillos de Campos E 88 B1
Galleno I 81 C4
Galliate I 70 C3
Gallicano I 81 B4
Gállio I 72 C1
Gallípoli I 107 A4
Gallipoli = Gelibolu TR 118 B1
Gällivare S 112 E9
Gallizien A 73 B4
Gallneukirchen A 63 B5
Gällö S 115 E12
Gallocanta E 95 B5
Gällstad S 40 B3
Gallur E 90 B1
Galmisdale UK 24 B1
Galmpton UK 29 C4
Galston UK 24 C3
Galta N 33 C2
Galtelli I 110 B2
Galten DK 39 C2
Galtür A 71 B5
Galve de Sorbe E 95 A3
Galveias P 92 B2
Gálvez E 94 C2
Galway IRL 20 A2
Gamaches F 48 D2
Gámbara I 71 C5
Gambárie I 106 C2
Gambassi Terme I 81 C4
Gambatesa I 103 B7
Gambolò I 70 C3
Gaming A 63 C6
Gamla Uppsala S 36 C4
Gamleby S 40 B6
Gamlingay UK 30 B3
Gammelgarn S 37 E5
Gammelstad S 3 D24
Gammertingen D 61 B5
Gams CH 71 A4
Gamvik
Finnmark N 113 A17
Finnmark N 113 B12
Gan F 76 C2
Gáname E 87 C4
Ganda di Martello I 71 B5
Gandarela P 87 C2
Ganddal N 33 D2
Ganderkesee D 43 B5
Gandesa E 90 B3
Gandía E 96 C2
Gandino I 71 C4
Gandrup DK 38 B3
Ganges F 78 C2
Gånghester S 40 B3
Gangi I 109 B3
Gangkofen D 62 B3
Gannat F 68 B3
Gannay-sur-Loire F 68 B3
Gänserndorf A 64 B2
Ganzlin D 44 B4
Gap F 79 B5
Gara H 75 B4
Garaballa E 96 B1
Garaguso I 104 C2
Garbayuela E 94 C1
Garbhallt UK 24 B2
Garbsen D 44 C1
Garching D 62 B3
Garciaz E 93 B5
Garcihernández E 94 B1
Garcillán E 94 B2
Garcinarro E 95 B4
Garcisobaco E 99 C5
Garda I 71 C5
Gardanne F 79 C4
Gärdås S 115 B11
Gårdby S 41 C6
Gardeja PL 47 B4
Gardelegen D 44 C3
Gardermoen N 34 B3
Gardiki GR 116 D3
Garding D 43 A5
Gardone Riviera I 71 C5
Gardone Val Trómpia I 71 C5
Gárdony H 74 A3
Gardouch F 77 C4
Gårdsjö S 37 D1
Gårdskär S 36 B4
Gards Köpinge S 41 D4
Garein F 76 B2
Gareloi ...
Garelochhead UK 24 B3
Garéoult F 79 C5
Garešnica HR 74 C1
Garéssio I 80 B2
Garforth UK 27 B4
Gargaliani GR 117 E3
Gargaligas E 93 B5
Gargallo E 90 C2
Garganta la Olla E 93 A5
Gargantiel E 100 A1
Gargellen A 71 B4
Gargilesse-Dampierre F 67 B6
Gargnano I 71 C5
Gargnäs S 115 B14
Gárgoles de Abajo E 95 B4
Gargrave UK 26 B3
Garitz D 52 B2
Garlasco I 70 C3
Garlieston UK 24 D3
Garlin F 76 C2
Garlitos E 94 D1
Garmisch-Partenkirchen D 71 A6
Garnat-sur-Engièvre F 68 B3
Garpenberg S 36 B3
Garphyttan S 37 C1
Garray E 89 C4
Garrel D 43 C5
Garriguella E 91 A6
Garrison UK 18 B3
Garrovillas E 93 B4
Garrucha E 101 B4
Gars-am-Kamp A 63 B6
Garsås S 36 B1
Garsdale Head UK 26 A3
Gärsnäs S 41 D4
Garstang UK 26 B3
Gartow D 44 B3
Gartz D 45 B6
Gærum DK 38 B3
Garvagh UK 19 B5
Garvão P 98 B2
Garve UK 22 D4
Garwolin PL 55 B6
Garz D 45 A5
Garzyn PL 54 B1
Gąsawa PL 46 C3
Gåsborn S 34 C6
Gaschurn A 71 B5
Gascueña E 95 B4
Gasny F 58 A2
Gąsocin PL 47 C6
Gastes F 76 B1
Gastouni GR 117 E3
Gastouri GR 116 C1
Gata
E 93 A4
HR 83 C5
Gata de Gorgos E 96 C3
Gatchina RUS 7 B11
Gatehouse of Fleet UK 24 D3
Gátér H 75 B4
Gateshead UK 25 D6
Gátova E 96 B2
Gattendorf A 64 B2
Gatteo a Mare I 82 B1
Gattinara I 70 C3
Gattorna I 80 B3
Gaucín E 99 C5
Gaulstad N 114 D9
Gaupne N 32 A4
Gautefall N 33 C5
Gauting D 62 B2
Gauto S 115 A13
Gava E 91 B5
Gavardo I 71 C5
Gavarnie F 76 D2
Gávavencsellő H 65 B7
Gavi I 80 B2
Gavião P 92 B3
Gavirate I 70 C3
Gävle S 36 B4
Gavoi I 110 B2
Gavorrano I 81 D4
Gavray F 57 B4
Gavrio GR 117 E6
Gävunda S 34 B6
Gaweinstal A 64 B2
Gaworzyce PL 53 B5
Gawroniec PL 46 B2
Gaydon UK 30 B2
Gayton UK 30 B4
Gazipaşa TR 119 F7
Gazoldo degli Ippoliti I 71 C5
Gazzuolo I 81 A4
Gbelce SK 65 C4
Gdańsk PL 47 A4
Gdinj HR 84 C1
Gdov RUS 7 B9
Gdów PL 65 A6
Gdynia PL 47 A4
Gea de Albarracín E 95 B5
Geary UK 22 D2
Géaudot F 59 B5
Geaune F 76 C2
Gebesee D 51 B6
Gebiz TR 119 E5
Gebze TR 118 B4
Géderlak H 75 B3
Gedern D 51 C5
Gedinne B 49 D5
Gediz TR 118 D4
Gèdre F 76 D3
Gedser DK 44 A3
Gedsted DK 38 C2
Geel B 49 B5
Geesthacht D 44 B2
Geetbets B 49 C6
Gefell D 52 C1
Gehrden D 51 A5
Gehren D 52 C1
Geilenkirchen D 50 C2
Geilo N 32 B5
Geinsheim D 61 A4
Geisa D 51 C5
Geiselhöring D 62 B3
Geiselwind D 61 A6
Geisenfeld D 62 B2
Geisenhausen D 62 B3
Geisenheim D 50 D3
Geising D 53 C3
Geisingen D 61 C4
Geislingen D 61 B5
Geistthal A 73 A5
Geiterygghytta N 32 B4
Geithain D 52 B2
Geithus N 34 C1
Gela I 109 B3
Geldermalsen NL 49 B6
Geldern D 50 B2
Geldrop NL 49 B6
Geleen NL 50 C1
Gelembe TR 118 C2
Gelendost TR 119 D6
Gelibolu = Gallipoli TR 118 B1
Gelida E 91 B4
Gelnhausen D 51 C5
Gelnica SK 65 B6
Gelsa E 90 B2
Gelse H 74 B1
Gelsenkirchen D 50 B3
Gelsted DK 39 D2
Geltendorf D 62 B2
Gelterkinden CH 70 A2
Gelting D 39 E2
Gelu RO 75 B6
Gelves E 99 B4
Gembloux B 49 C5
Gemeaux F 69 A5
Gémenos F 79 C4
Gemerská Poloma SK 65 B6
Gemerská Ves SK 65 B6
Gemert NL 50 B1
Gemla S 40 C4
Gemlik TR 118 B4
Gemmenich B 50 C1
Gemona del Friuli I 72 B3
Gémozac F 67 C4
Gemund D 50 C2
Gemünden
Bayern D 51 C5
Hessen D 51 C4
Rheinland-Pfalz D 60 A3
Genappe B 49 C5
Génave E 101 A3
Genazzano I 102 B5
Gençay F 67 B5
Gencsapáti H 74 A1
Gendringen NL 50 B2
Genelard F 69 B4
Genemuiden NL 42 C3
Generalski Stol HR 73 C5
Geneva = Genève CH 69 B6
Genevad S 40 C3
Genève = Geneva CH 69 B6
Genevriéres F 60 C1
Gengenbach D 61 B4
Genillé F 67 A6
Genk B 49 C6
Genlis F 69 A5
Gennep NL 50 B1
Genner DK 39 D2
Gennes F 67 A4
Genoa = Génova I 80 B2
Genola I 80 B1
Génova = Genoa I 80 B2
Genowefa PL 54 A3
Gensingen D 60 A3
Gent = Ghent B 49 B4
Genthin D 44 C4
Gentioux F 68 C1
Genzano di Lucánia I 104 C2
Genzano di Roma I 102 B5
Georgenthal D 51 C6
Georgsmarienhütte D 50 A4
Gera D 52 C2
Geraards-bergen B 49 C4
Gerace I 106 C3
Geraci Siculo I 109 B3
Geraki GR 117 F4
Gérardmer F 60 B2
Geras A 63 B6
Gerbéviller F 60 B2
Gerbini I 109 B3
Gerbstedt D 52 B1
Gerði IS 111 C9
Gerede TR 118 B7
Gerena E 99 B4
Geretsried D 62 C2
Gérgal E 101 B3
Gergy F 69 B4
Gerindote E 94 C2
Gerjen H 74 B3
Gerlos A 72 A2
Germay F 59 B6
Germencik TR 119 E2
Germering D 62 B2
Germersheim D 61 A4
Gërnec AL 105 C5
Gernika-Lumo E 89 A4
Gernrode D 52 B1
Gernsbach D 61 B4
Gernsheim D 61 A4
Geroda D 51 C5
Gerola Alta I 71 B4
Geroldsgrun D 52 C1
Gerolsbach D 62 B2
Gerolstein D 50 C2
Gerolzhofen D 61 A6
Gerovo HR 73 C4
Gerpinnes B 49 C5
Gerrards Cross UK 31 C3
Gerri de la Sal E 91 A4
Gersfeld D 51 C5
Gerstetten D 61 B6
Gersthofen D 62 B1
Gerstungen D 51 C6
Gerswalde D 45 B5
Gerzat F 68 C3
Gerze TR 16 A7
Gerzen D 62 B3
Gescher D 50 B3
Geseke D 51 B4
Geslau D 61 A6
Gespunsart F 59 A5
Gesté F 66 A3
Gestorf D 51 A5
Gesualda I 103 C8
Gesunda S 36 B1
Geta FIN 36 B6
Getafe E 94 B3
Getinge S 40 C2
Getxo E 89 A4
Geversdorf D 43 B6
Gevgelija NMK 116 A4
Gevora del Caudillo E 93 C4
Gevrey-Chambertin F 69 A4
Gex F 69 B6
Gey D 50 C2
Geyikli TR 118 C1
Geysir IS 111 C5
Geyve TR 118 B5
Gföhl A 63 B6
Ghedi I 71 C5
Ghent = Gent B 49 B4
Gheorgheni RO 11 C8
Ghigo I 79 B6
Ghilarza I 110 B1
Ghisonaccia F 102 A2
Ghisoni F 102 A2
Gialtra GR 116 D4
Gianitsa GR 116 B4
Giardinetto Vécchio I 103 B8
Giardini Naxos I 109 B4
Giarratana I 109 B3
Giarre I 109 B4
Giat F 68 C2
Giaveno I 80 A1
Giazza I 71 C6
Giba I 110 C1
Gibellina Nuova I 108 B1
Gibostad N 112 C7
Gibraleón E 99 B4
Gibraltar GBZ 99 C5
Gic H 74 A2
Gideå S 115 D16
Gideåkroken S 115 C14
Gidle PL 55 C4
Giebelstadt D 61 A5
Gieboldehausen D 51 B6
Gielniów PL 55 B5
Gielow D 45 B4
Gien F 58 C3
Giengen D 61 B6
Giens F 79 C5
Giera RO 75 C6
Gieselwerder D 51 B5
Giessen D 51 C4
Gieten NL 42 B3
Giethoorn NL 42 C3
Giffaumont-Champaubert F 59 B5
Gifford UK 25 C5
Gifhorn D 44 C2
Gige H 74 B2
Gignac F 78 C2
Gijón = Xixón E 88 A1
Gilching D 62 B2
Gilena E 100 B1
Gilford UK 19 B5
Gillberga S 35 C4
Gilleleje DK 41 C2
Gilley F 69 A6
Gilley-sur-Loire F 68 B3
Gillingham
Dorset UK 29 B5
Medway UK 31 C4
Gilocourt F 59 A3
Gilserberg D 51 C5
Gilsland UK 25 D5
Gilze NL 49 B5
Gimåt S 115 D15
Gimo S 36 B5
Gimont F 77 C3
Ginasservis F 79 C4
Gingelom B 49 C6
Gingst D 45 A5
Ginosa I 104 C2
Ginzling A 72 A1
Giões P 98 B3
Gióia dei Marsi I 103 B6
Gióia del Colle I 104 C2
Gióia Sannitica I 103 B7

Gióia Táuro I 106 C2
Gioiosa Iónica I 106 C3
Gioiosa Marea I 109 A3
Giosla UK 22 C2
Giovinazzo I 104 B2
Girifalco I 106 C3
Giromagny F 60 C2
Girona E 91 B5
Gironcourt-sur-Vraine F 60 B1
Gironella E 91 A4
Gironville-sous-les-Côtes F 60 B1
Girvan UK 24 C3
Gislaved S 40 B3
Gislev DK 39 D3
Gisors F 58 A2
Gissi I 103 A7
Gistad S 37 D2
Gistel B 48 B3
Gistrup DK 38 C3
Giswil CH 70 B3
Githio GR 117 F4
Giugliano in Campania I 103 C7
Giulianova I 82 D2
Giulvăz RO 75 C5
Giurgiu RO 11 E8
Give DK 39 D2
Givet F 49 C5
Givors F 69 C4
Givry
B 49 C5
F 69 B4
Givry-en-Argonne F 59 B5
Givskud DK 39 D2
Giżalki PL 54 A2
Gizeux F 67 A5
Giżycko PL 6 D6
Gizzeria I 106 C3
Gizzeria Lido I 106 C3
Gjedved DK 39 D2
Gjegjan AL 105 B6
Gjendesheim N 32 A5
Gjerde N 32 B3
Gjerlev DK 38 C3
Gjermundshamn N 32 B2
Gjerrild DK 38 C3
Gjerstad N 33 D6
Gjesås N 34 B4
Gjesvær N 113 A14
Gjirokastër AL 116 B2
Gjøfjell N 35 C2
Gjøl DK 38 B2
Gjøra N 114 E6
Gjøvik N 34 B2
Gladbeck D 50 B2
Gladenbach D 51 C4
Gladstad N 114 B8
Glamis UK 25 B5
Glamoč BIH 84 B1
Glamsbjerg DK 39 D3
Gland CH 69 B6
Glandorf D 50 A3
Glanegg A 73 B4
Glanshammar S 37 C2
Glarus CH 70 A4
Glasgow UK 24 C3
Glashütte
Bayern D 62 C2
Sachsen D 53 C3
Glastonbury UK 29 B5
Glatzau A 73 B5
Glauchau D 52 C2
Glava S 35 C4
Glavatičevo BIH 84 C3
Glavičice BIH 85 B4
Glavnik KOS 85 D6
Gledica SRB 85 C5
Glein
A 73 A4
N 115 A9
Gleinstätten A 73 B5
Gleisdorf A 73 A5
Glenamoy IRL 18 B2
Glenarm UK 19 B6
Glenavy UK 19 B5
Glenbarr UK 24 C2
Glenbeigh IRL 20 B2
Glenbrittle UK 22 D2
Glencoe UK 24 B2
Glencolumbkille IRL 18 B3
Glendalough IRL 21 A5
Glenealy IRL 21 B5
Glenelg UK 22 D3
Glenfinnan UK 24 B2
Glengarriff IRL 20 C2
Glenluce UK 24 D3
Glennamaddy IRL 18 C3
Glenrothes UK 25 B4
Glenties IRL 18 B3
Glesborg DK 38 C3
Glesien D 52 B2
Gletsch CH 70 B3
Glewitz D 45 A4
Glifada GR 117 E5
Glimåkra S 41 C4
Glin IRL 20 B2
Glina HR 73 C6
Glinde D 44 B2
Glinojeck PL 47 C6
Glinsk IRL 20 A2
Gliwice PL 54 C3
Glödnitz A 73 B4
Gloggnitz A 64 C1
Głogoczów PL 65 A5
Glogonj SRB 85 B5
Glogovac SRB 85 B6
Głogów PL 53 B6
Głogówek PL 54 C2
Glomel F 56 B2
Glomfjord N 112 F2
Glommen S 40 C2
Glommersträsk S 115 B16
Glonn D 62 C2
Glorenza I 71 B5
Gloria P 92 B2
Glosa GR 116 C5
Glossop UK 27 B4
Gloucester UK 29 B5
Głowaczów PL 55 B6
Główczyce PL 46 A3
Glöwen D 44 C4
Głowno PL 55 B4
Gložan SRB 75 C4
Głubczyce PL 54 C2
Głuchołazy PL 54 C2
Głuchów PL 55 B5
Głuchowo PL 54 A1
Glücksburg D 39 E2
Glückstadt D 43 B6
Glumina BIH 84 B4
Glumsø DK 39 D4
Glušci SRB 85 B4
Glusk BY 7 E10
Głuszyca PL 53 C6
Glyngøre DK 38 C1
Glyn Neath UK 29 B4
Gmünd
Karnten A 72 B3
Nieder Östereich A 63 B5
Gmund D 62 C2
Gmunden A 63 C4
Gnarp S 115 E14
Gnarrenburg D 43 B6
Gnesau A 72 B3
Gnesta S 37 C4
Gnięchowice PL 54 B1
Gniew PL 47 B4
Gniewkowo PL 47 C4
Gniezno PL 46 C3
Gnoien D 45 B4
Gnojnice BIH 84 C2
Gnojno PL 55 C5
Gnosall UK 26 C3
Gnosjö S 40 B3
Göbel TR 118 B3
Göçbeyli TR 118 C2
Goch D 50 B2
Gochsheim D 51 C6
Göd H 65 C5
Godalming UK 31 C3
Godby FIN 36 B6
Goðdalir IS 111 B6
Goddelsheim D 51 B4
Gódega di Sant'Urbano I 72 C2
Godegård S 37 D2
Godelheim D 51 B5
Goderville F 58 A1
Godiasco I 80 B3
Godič SLO 73 B4
Godkowo PL 47 A5
Godmanchester UK 30 B3
Gödöllö H 65 C5
Gödre H 74 B2
Godshill UK 31 D2
Godzikowice PL 54 C2
Godziszewo PL 47 A4
Goes NL 49 B4
Goetzenbrück F 60 B3
Góglio I 70 B3
Gogolin PL 54 C3
Göhren D 45 A5
Goirle NL 49 B6
Góis P 92 A2
Góito I 71 C5
Goizueta E 76 C1
Gojna Gora SRB 85 C5
Gójsk PL 47 C5
Gökçedağ TR 118 C3
Gökçen TR 119 D2
Gökçeören TR 119 D3
Gökçeyazı TR 118 C2
Göktepe TR 119 E3
Gol N 32 B5
Gola
HR 74 B2
N 34 A1
Gołańcz PL 46 C3
Gölbaşı TR 16 B6
Gölby FIN 36 B6
Gölcük
Kocaeli TR 118 B4
Niğde TR 16 B7
Golčův Jenikov CZ 63 A6
Gołczewo PL 45 B6
Goldach CH 71 A4
Goldbach D 51 C5
Goldbeck D 44 C3
Goldberg D 44 B4
Goldelund D 43 A6
Goldenstedt D 43 C5
Gołębiewo PL 47 A4
Golegã P 92 B2
Goleniów PL 45 B6
Golfo Aranci I 110 B2
Gölhisar TR 119 E4
Golina PL 54 A3
Gölle H 74 B3
Göllersdorf A 64 B2
Golling an der Salzach A 63 C4
Gölmarmara TR 118 D2
Golnice PL 53 B5
Golnik SLO 73 B4
Gölova TR 119 F5
Gölpazarı TR 118 B5
Gols A 64 C2
Golspie UK 23 D5
Golssen D 52 B3
Golubac SRB 85 B6
Golub-Dobrzyń PL 47 B5
Golubinci SRB 85 B5
Golubovci MNE 105 A5
Goluchów PL 54 B2
Golzow D 52 A2
Gomagoi I 71 B5
Gómara E 89 C4
Gomaringen D 61 B5
Gömbe TR 119 F4
Gömeç TR 118 C1
Gomel = Homyel BY 7 E11
Gomes Aires P 98 B2
Gómezserracin E 88 C2
Gommern D 52 A1
Gomulin PL 55 B4
Gonäs S 36 B2
Goncelin F 69 C5
Gończyce PL 55 B6
Gondomar
E 87 B2
P 87 C2
Gondrecourt-le-Château F 60 B1
Gondrin F 76 C3
Gönen
Balıkesir TR 118 B2
Isparta TR 119 E5
Gonfaron F 79 C5
Goñi E 76 D1
Goni
GR 116 C4
I 110 C2
Gonnesa I 110 C1
Gonnosfanádiga I 110 C1
Gönyü H 64 C3
Gonzaga I 81 B4
Goodrich UK 29 B5
Goodwick UK 28 A2
Gooik B 49 C5
Goole UK 27 B5
Goor NL 50 A2
Göpfritz an der Wild A 63 B6
Goppenstein CH 70 B2
Göppingen D 61 B5
Gor E 100 B3
Góra
Dolnośląskie PL 54 B1
Mazowieckie PL 47 C6
Gorafe E 100 B2
Góra Kalwaria PL 55 B6
Gorawino PL 46 B1
Goražde BIH 84 C3
Gordaliza del Pino E 88 B1
Gördes TR 118 D3
Gørding DK 39 D1
Górdola CH 70 B3
Gordon UK 25 C5
Gordoncillo E 88 B1
Gorebridge UK 25 C4
Gorenja Vas SLO 73 B4
Gorenje Jelenje HR 73 C4
Gorey
IRL 21 B5
UK 57 A3
Gorgonzola I 71 C4
Gorica HR 83 B4
Gorican HR 74 B1
Gorinchem NL 49 B5
Goring UK 31 C2
Goritsy RUS 7 C14
Göritz D 45 B5
Gorízia I 72 C3
Górki PL 47 C5
Gorleben D 44 B3
Gorleston-on-sea UK 30 B5
Gørlev DK 39 D4
Görlitz D 53 B4
Górliz E 89 A4
Görmin D 45 B5
Górna Grupa PL 47 B4
Gorna Oryahovitsa BG 11 E8
Gornja Gorevnica SRB 85 C5
Gornja Klina KOS 85 D5
Gornja Ploča HR 83 B4
Gornja Radgona SLO 73 B5
Gornja Sabanta SRB 85 C6
Gornja Trešnjevica SRB 85 B5
Gornja Tuzla BIH 84 B3
Gornje Polje MNE 84 D3
Gornje Ratkovo BIH 84 B1
Gornji Grad SLO 73 B4
Gornji Humac HR 83 C5
Gornji Jasenjani BIH 84 C2
Gornji Kamengrad BIH 83 B5
Gornji Kneginec HR 73 B6
Gornji Kokoti MNE 105 A5
Gornji Kosinj HR 83 B4
Gornji Milanovac SRB 85 B5
Gornji Podgradci BIH 84 A2
Gornji Ravno BIH 84 C2
Gornji Sjenicak HR 73 C5
Gornji Vakuf BIH 84 C2
Górno PL 55 C5
Görömböly H 65 B6
Górowo Iławeckie PL 47 A6
Gorran Haven UK 28 C3
Gorredijk NL 42 B3
Gorron F 57 B5
Gorseinon UK 28 B3
Gort IRL 20 A3
Gortin UK 19 B4
Görzke D 52 A2
Gorzkowice PL 55 B4
Górzno
Kujawsko-Pomorskie PL 47 B5
Zachodnio-Pomorskie PL 46 B1
Gorzów Śląski PL 54 B3
Gorzów Wielkopolski PL 45 C7
Górzyca PL 45 C6
Gorzyce PL 54 D3
Górzyn PL 53 B4
Gorzyń PL 46 C1
Gorzyno PL 46 A3
Gosaldo I 72 B1
Gosau A 63 C4
Gosberton UK 30 B3
Gościcino PL 47 A4
Gościęcin PL 54 C3
Gościm PL 46 C1
Gościno PL 46 A1
Gosdorf A 73 B5
Gosforth UK 26 A2
Goslar D 51 B6
Goslice PL 47 C5
Gospič HR 83 B4
Gosport UK 31 D2
Gössäter S 35 D5
Gossau CH 71 A4
Goss Ilsede D 51 A6
Gössnitz D 52 C2
Gössweinstein D 62 A2
Gostimë AL 105 C6
Gostkow PL 55 B4
Göstling an der Ybbs A 63 C5
Gostomia PL 46 B2
Gostycyn PL 46 B3
Gostyń PL 54 B2
Gostynin PL 47 C5
Goszczyn PL 55 B5
Göta S 35 D4
Göteborg = Gothenburg S 38 B4
Götene S 35 D5
Gotha D 51 C6
Gothem S 37 E5
Gothenburg = Göteborg S 38 B4
Gotse Delchev BG 116 A5
Gottersdorf D 62 B3
Göttingen D 51 B5
Gottne S 115 D15
Götzis A 71 A4
Gouarec F 56 B2
Gouda NL 49 A5
Goudhurst UK 31 C4
Goumenissa GR 116 B4
Goura GR 117 E4
Gourdon F 77 B4
Gourgançon F 59 B5
Gourin F 56 B2
Gournay-en-Bray F 58 A2
Gourock UK 24 C3
Gouveia P 92 A3
Gouvy B 50 C1
Gouzeacourt F 49 C4
Gouzon F 68 B2
Govedari HR 84 D2
Govérnolo I 81 A4
Gowarczów PL 55 B5
Gowerton UK 28 B3
Gowidlino PL 46 A3
Gowran IRL 21 B4
Goyatz D 53 A4
Göynük
TR 118 B5
Antalya TR 119 F5
Gozdnica PL 53 B5
Gozdowo PL 47 C5
Gozee B 49 C5
Graal-Müritz D 44 A4
Grab BIH 84 D3
Grabenstätt D 62 C3
Grabhair UK 22 C2
Gråbo S 38 B5
Grabovac
HR 84 C1
SRB 85 B5
Grabovci SRB 85 B4
Grabow D 44 B3
Grabów PL 55 A4
Grabow nad Pilicą PL 55 B6
Grabów nad Prosną PL 54 B3
Grabowno PL 46 B3
Grabs CH 71 A4
Gračac HR 83 B4
Gračanica
BIH 84 B3
KOS 85 D6
Graçay F 68 A1
Gracen AL 105 B5
Grad SLO 73 B6
Gradac
BIH 84 D3
HR 84 C2
MNE 85 C4
SRB 85 C5
Gradačac BIH 84 B3
Gradec HR 74 C1
Gradefes E 88 B1
Grades A 73 B4
Gradil P 92 C1
Gradina
HR 74 C2
MNE 85 C4
Gradisca d'Isonzo I 72 C3
Gradiška BIH 74 C2
Gradište HR 74 C3
Grado
E 86 A4
I 72 C3
Grafenau D 63 B4
Gräfenberg D 62 A2
Gräfenhainichen D 52 B2
Grafenschlag A 63 B6
Grafenstein A 73 B4
Gräfenthal D 52 C1
Grafentonna D 51 B6
Grafenwöhr D 62 A2
Grafing D 62 B2
Grafling D 62 B3
Gräfsnäs S 40 A2
Gragnano I 103 C7
Grahovo
MNE 84 D3
SLO 72 B3
Graiguenamanagh IRL 21 B5
Grain UK 31 C4
Grainau D 71 A6
Graja de Iniesta E 95 C5
Grajera E 89 C3
Gram DK 39 D2
Gramais A 71 A5
Gramat F 77 B4
Gramatneusiedl A 64 B2
Grambow D 45 B6
Grammichele I 109 B3
Gramsh AL 116 B2
Gramzow D 45 B6
Gran N 34 B2
Granada E 100 B2
Granard IRL 19 C4
Grañas E 86 A3
Granátula de Calatrava E 100 A2
Grancey-le-Château F 59 C6
Grandas de Salime E 86 A4
Grandcamp-Maisy F 57 A4
Grand-Champ F 56 C3
Grand Couronne F 58 A2
Grand-Fougeray F 57 C4
Grândola P 98 A2
Grandpré F 59 A5
Grandrieu
B 49 C5
F 78 B2
Grandson CH 70 B1
Grandvillars F 70 A1
Grandvilliers F 58 A2
Grañén E 90 B2
Grangärde S 36 B1
Grange IRL 18 B3
Grangemouth UK 25 B4
Grange-over-Sands UK 26 A3
Grängesberg S 36 B1
Granges-de Crouhens F 77 D3
Granges-sur-Vologne F 60 B2
Gräningen D 44 C4
Granitola-Torretta I 108 B1
Granja
Évora P 98 A3
Porto P 87 C2
Granja de Moreruela E 88 C1
Granja de Torrehermosa E 93 C5
Gränna S 40 A4
Grannäs
Västerbotten S 115 B13
Västerbotten S 115 B14
Granö S 115 C16
Granollers E 91 B5
Granowiec PL 54 B2
Granowo PL 54 A1
Gransee D 45 B5
Gransherad N 33 C6
Grantham UK 27 C5
Grantown-on-Spey UK 23 D5
Grantshouse UK 25 C5
Granville F 57 B4
Granvin N 32 B3
Grærup Strand DK 39 D1
Gräsås S 40 C2
Grasbakken N 113 B17
Grasberg D 43 B6
Grasmere UK 26 A2
Gräsmyr S 115 D16
Grasö S 36 B5
Grassano I 104 C2
Grassau D 62 C3
Grasse F 79 C5
Grassington UK 27 A4
Græsted DK 41 C2
Gråsten DK 39 E2
Grästorp S 35 D4
Gratkorn A 73 A5
Gråträsk S 115 B16
Gratwein A 73 A5
Graulhet F 77 C4
Graus E 90 A3
Grávalos E 89 B5
Gravberget N 34 B4
Grave NL 50 B1
Gravedona I 71 B4
Gravelines F 48 B3
Gravellona Toce I 70 C3
Gravendal S 36 B1
Gravens DK 39 D2
Gravesend UK 31 C4
Graveson F 78 C3
Gravina in Púglia I 104 C2
Gray F 69 A5
Grayrigg UK 26 A3
Grays UK 31 C4
Grayshott UK 31 C3
Grayvoron RUS 7 F13
Graz A 73 A5
Grazalema E 99 C5
Grążawy PL 47 B5
Grazzano Visconti I 80 B3
Greåker N 35 C3
Great Dunmow UK 31 C4
Great Malvern UK 29 A5
Great Torrington UK 28 C3
Great Waltham UK 31 C4
Great Yarmouth UK 30 B5
Grebbestad S 35 D3
Grebenstein D 51 B5
Grębocice PL 53 B6
Grębocin PL 47 B4
Greding D 62 A2
Gredstedbro DK 39 D1
Greencastle IRL 19 A4
Greenhead UK 25 D5
Greenisland UK 19 B6
Greenlaw UK 25 C5
Greenock UK 24 C3
Greenway UK 28 B3
Greenwich UK 31 C4
Grefrath D 50 B2
Greifenburg A 72 B3
Greiffenberg D 45 B5
Greifswald D 45 A5
Grein A 63 B5
Greipstad N 33 D4
Greiz D 52 C2
Grenaa DK 39 C3
Grenade F 77 C4
Grenade-sur-l'Adour F 76 C2
Grenchen CH 70 A2
Grendi N 33 D4
Grenivík IS 111 B7
Grenoble F 69 C5
Gréoux-les-Bains F 79 C4
Gresenhorst D 44 A4
Gressoney-la-Trinité I 70 C2
Gressoney-St-Jean I 70 C2
Gressthal D 51 C6
Gressvik N 35 C2
Gresten A 63 C6
Gretna UK 25 D4
Greussen D 51 B6
Greve in Chianti I 81 C5
Greven
Mecklenburg-Vorpommern D 44 B2
Nordrhein-Westfalen D 50 A3
Grevena GR 116 B3
Grevenbroich D 50 B2
Grevenbrück D 50 B4
Grevenmacher L 60 A2
Grevesmühlen D 44 B3
Grevestrand DK 41 D2
Grevie S 41 C2
Greystoke UK 26 A3
Greystones IRL 21 A5
Grez-Doiceau B 49 C5
Grèzec F 77 B4
Grez-en-Bouère F 57 C5
Grezzana I 71 C6
Grgar SLO 72 B3
Grgurevci SRB 85 A4
Gries A 71 A6
Griesbach D 63 B4
Griesheim D 61 A4
Gries in Sellrain A 71 A6
Grieskirchen A 63 B4
Griffen A 73 B4
Grignan F 78 B3
Grignano I 72 C3
Grigno I 72 B1
Grignols F 76 B2
Grignon F 69 C6
Grijota E 88 B2
Grijpskerk NL 42 B3
Gril AL 105 A5
Grillby S 37 C4
Grimaud F 79 C5
Grimbergen B 49 C5
Grimma D 52 B2
Grimmen D 45 A5
Grimmialp CH 70 B2
Grimsås S 40 B3
Grimsby UK 27 B5
Grimslöv S 40 C4
Grímsstaðir IS 111 B9
Grimstad N 33 D5
Grimstorp S 40 B4
Grindavík IS 111 D3
Grindelwald CH 70 B3
Grindheim N 33 D4
Grindsted DK 39 D1
Griñón E 94 B3
Gripenberg S 40 B4
Gripsholm S 37 C4
Grisolles F 77 C4
Grisslehamn S 36 B5
Gritley UK 23 C6
Grizebeck UK 26 A2
Grndina BIH 84 B1
Gröbming A 72 A3
Gröbzig D 52 B1
Grocka SRB 85 B5
Gröditz D 52 B3
Gródki PL 47 B6
Grodków PL 54 C2
Grodziec PL 54 A3
Grodzisk Mazowiecki PL 55 A5
Grodzisk Wielkopolski PL 54 A1
Groenlo NL 50 A2
Groesbeek NL 50 B1
Grohote HR 83 C5
Groitzsch D 52 B2
Groix F 56 C2
Grójec PL 55 B5
Grom PL 47 B6
Gromiljca BIH 84 C3
Grömitz D 44 A2
Gromnik PL 65 A6
Gromo I 71 C4
Gronau
Niedersachsen D 51 A5
Nordrhein-Westfalen D 50 A3
Grønbjerg DK 39 C1
Grönenbach D 61 C6
Grong N 114 C9
Grönhögen S 41 C6
Groningen
D 52 B1
NL 42 B3
Grønnestrand DK 38 B2
Grono CH 71 B4
Grönskåra S 40 B5
Grootegast NL 42 B3
Gropello Cairoli I 70 C3
Grorud N 34 C2
Grósio I 71 B5
Grošnica SRB 85 C5
Grossalmerode D 51 B5
Grossarl A 72 A3
Gross Beeren D 45 C5
Gross Berkel D 51 A5
Grossbodungen D 51 B6
Gross-botwar D 61 B5
Grossburgwedel D 44 C1
Grosschönau D 53 C4
Gross-Dölln D 45 B5
Grossenbrode D 44 A3
Grossenehrich D 51 B6
Grossengottern D 51 B6
Grossenhain D 52 B3
Grossenkneten D 43 C5
Grossenlüder D 51 C5
Grossensee D 44 B2
Grossenzersdorf A 64 B2
Grosseto I 81 D5
Gross-Gerau D 61 A4
Grossgerungs A 63 B5
Grossglobnitz A 63 B6
Grosshabersdorf D 62 A1
Grossharras A 64 B2
Grosshartmansdorf D 52 C3
Grosshöchstetten CH 70 B2
Gross Kreutz D 45 C4
Grosskrut A 64 B2
Gross Lafferde D 51 A6
Gross Leutheb D 53 A4
Grosslohra D 51 B6
Grossmehring D 62 B2
Gross Muckrow D 53 A4
Gross Oesingen D 44 C2
Grossostheim D 61 A5
Grosspertholz A 63 B5
Grosspetersdorf A 73 A6
Grosspostwitz D 53 B4
Grossraming A 63 C5
Grossräschen D 53 B4
Gross Reken D 50 B3
Grossrinderfeld D 61 A5
Grossröhrsdorf D 53 B4
Gross Sarau D 44 B2
Gross Särchen D 53 B4
Grossschirma D 52 C3
Gross Schönebeck D 45 C5
Grossschweinbarth A 64 B2
Grosssiegharts A 63 B6
Grosssölk A 72 A3
Gross Umstadt D 61 A4
Grosswarasdorf A 74 A1
Gross Warnow D 44 B3
Gross-Weikersdorf A 64 B1
Gross-Welle D 44 B4
Grosswilfersdorf A 73 A5
Gross Wokern D 44 B4
Grostenquin F 60 B2
Grosuplje SLO 73 C4
Grotli N 114 E4
Grötlingbo S 37 E5
Grottáglie I 104 C3
Grottaminarda I 103 B8
Grottammare I 82 D2
Grotte di Castro I 81 D5
Grotteria I 106 C3
Gróttole I 104 C2
Grouw NL 42 B2
Grov N 112 D6
Grova N 33 C5
Grove E 86 B2
Grua N 34 B2
Grube D 44 A3
Grubišno Polje HR 74 C2
Gruda HR 105 A4
Grude BIH 84 C2
Grudusk PL 47 B6
Grudziądz PL 47 B4
Grue N 34 B4
Gruissan F 78 C2
Grullos E 86 A4
Grumo Áppula I 104 B2
Grums S 35 C5
Grünau im Almtal A 63 C4
Grünberg D 51 C4
Grünburg A 63 C5
Grundarfjörður IS 111 C2
Gründau D 51 C5
Gründelhardt D 61 A5
Grundforsen S 34 A4
Grundlsee A 63 C4
Grundsund S 35 D3
Grunewald D 53 B3
Grungedal N 33 C4
Grunow D 53 A4
Grünstadt D 61 A4
Gruvberget S 36 A3
Gruyères CH 70 B2
Gruža SRB 85 C5
Grybów PL 65 A6
Grycksbo S 36 B2
Gryfice PL 45 B7
Gryfino PL 45 B6
Gryfów Śląski PL 53 B5
Gryllefjord N 112 C6
Grymyr N 34 B2
Gryt S 37 D3
Grytgöl S 37 D2
Grythyttan S 37 C1
Grytnäs S 37 D4
Grzmiąca PL 46 B2
Grzybno PL 45 B6
Grzywna PL 47 B4
Gschnitz A 71 A6
Gschwend D 61 B5
Gstaad CH 70 B2
Gsteig CH 70 B2
Guadahortuna E 100 B2
Guadalajara E 95 B3
Guadalaviar E 95 B5
Guadalcanal E 99 A5
Guadalcázar E 100 B1
Guadalix de la Sierra E 94 B3
Guadálmez E 100 A1
Guadalupe E 93 B5
Guadamur E 94 C2
Guadarrama E 94 B2
Guadiaro E 99 C5
Guadix E 100 B2
Guagnano I 105 C3
Guagno F 102 A1
Guajar-Faragüit E 100 C2
Gualchos E 100 C2
Gualdo Tadino I 82 C1
Gualtieri I 81 B4
Guarcino I 103 B6
Guarda P 92 A3
Guardamar del Segura E 96 C2
Guardão P 92 A2
Guardavalle I 106 C3
Guardea I 102 A5
Guárdia I 103 C8
Guardiagrele I 103 A7
Guardiarégia I 103 B7
Guárdia Sanframondi I 103 B7
Guardias Viejas E 100 C3
Guardiola de Bergueda E 91 A4
Guardo E 88 B2
Guareña E 93 C4
Guaro E 100 C1
Guarromán E 100 A2
Guasila I 110 C2
Guastalla I 81 B4
Gubbhögen S 115 C12
Gúbbio I 82 C1
Guben D 53 B4
Gubin PL 53 B4
Guča SRB 85 C5
Gudå N 114 D8
Gudavac BIH 83 B5
Guddal N 32 A2
Güderup DK 39 E2
Gudhem S 35 D5
Gudhjem DK 41 D4
Gudovac HR 74 C1
Gudow D 44 B2
Güdüı TR 118 B7
Gudvangen N 32 B3
Guebwiller F 60 C3
Guéjar-Sierra E 100 B2
Guéméné-Penfao F 57 C4
Guéméné-sur-Scorff F 56 B2
Güeñes E 89 A3
Guer F 57 C3
Guérande F 66 A2
Guéret F 68 B1
Guérigny F 68 A3
Guesa E 76 D1
Gueugnon F 68 B4
Guglionesi I 103 B7
Gühlen Glienicke D 45 B4
Guia P 92 B2
Guichen F 57 C4
Guidizzolo I 71 C5
Guidónia-Montecélio I 102 B5
Guiglia I 81 B4
Guignes F 58 B3
Guijo E 100 A1
Guijo de Coria E 93 A4
Guijo de Santa Bábera E 93 A5
Guijuelo E 93 A5
Guildford UK 31 C3
Guillaumes F 79 B5
Guillena E 99 B4
Guillestre F 79 B5
Guillos F 76 B2
Guilsfield UK 26 C2
Guilvinec F 56 C1
Guimarães P 87 C2
Guincho P 92 C1
Guînes F 48 C2
Guingamp F 56 B2
Guipavas F 56 B1
Guisborough UK 27 A4
Guiscard F 59 A4
Guiscriff F 56 B2
Guise F 59 A4
Guisona E 91 B4
Guitiriz E 86 A3
Guîtres F 76 A2
Gujan-Mestras F 76 B1
Gulbene LV 7 C9
Gulçayır TR 118 C6
Guldborg DK 39 E4
Gullabo S 40 C5
Gullane UK 25 B5
Gullbrå N 32 B3
Gullbrandstorp S 40 C2
Gulleråsen S 36 A2
Gullhaug N 35 C2
Gullringen S 40 B5
Gullspång S 35 D6
Gullstein N 114 D5
Güllük TR 119 E2
Gülnar TR 16 C6
Gülpınar TR 116 C8
Gülşehir TR 16 B7
Gulsvik N 34 B1
Gumiel de Hizán E 88 C3
Gummersbach D 50 B3
Gümüldür TR 119 D2
Gümüşhaciköy TR 16 A7
Gümüşova TR 118 B5
Gundelfingen D 61 B6
Gundel-fingen D 60 B3
Gundelsheim D 61 A5
Gunderschoffen F 60 B3
Gundertshausen A 62 B3
Gundinci HR 74 C3
Gündoğmuş TR 119 F7
Güney
Burdur TR 119 E4
Denizli TR 119 D4
Gunja HR 84 B3
Günlüce TR 119 F3
Gunnarn S 115 B14
Gunnarskog S 34 C4
Gunnebo S 40 B6
Gunnislake UK 28 C3
Günselsdorf A 64 C2
Guntersblum D 61 A4
Guntersdorf A 64 B2
Guntin E 86 B3
Günyüzü TR 118 C6
Günzburg D 61 B6
Gunzenhausen D 62 A1
Güre
Balıkesir TR 118 C1
Uşak TR 118 D4
Gurk A 73 B4
Gurrea de Gállego E 90 A2
Gürsu TR 118 B4
Gušće HR 74 C1
Gusev RUS 6 D7
Gusinje MNE 105 A5
Gusmar AL 105 C5
Gúspini I 110 C1
Gusselby S 37 C2
Güssing A 73 A6
Gusswerk A 63 C6
Gustav Adolf S 34 B5
Gustavsberg S 37 C5
Gustavsfors S 35 C4
Güstrow D 44 B4
Gusum S 37 D3
Gutcher UK 22 A7
Gutenstein A 64 C1
Gütersloh D 51 B4
Guttannen CH 70 B3
Guttaring A 73 B4
Guttau D 53 B4
Güttingen CH 61 C5
Gützkow D 45 B5
Guzów PL 55 A5
Gvardeysk RUS 6 D6
Gvarv N 33 C6
Gvozd MNE 85 D4
Gvozdansko HR 73 C6
Gwda Wielka PL 46 B2
Gwennap UK 28 C2
Gy F 69 A5
Gyál H 75 A4
Gyarmat H 74 A2
Gyékényes H 74 B2
Gyé-sur-Seine F 59 B5
Gylling DK 39 D3
Gyoma H 75 B5
Gyömöre H 74 A2
Gyömrö H 75 A4
Gyón H 75 A4
Gyöngyfa H 74 C2
Gyöngyös H 65 C5
Gyöngyöspata H 65 C5
Gyönk H 74 B3
Györ H 64 C3
Györszemere H 74 A2
Gypsera CH 70 B2
Gysinge S 36 B3
Gyttorp S 37 C1
Gyula H 75 B6
Gyulafirátót H 74 A2
Gyulaj H 74 B3

H

Haacht B 49 C5
Haag
Nieder Östereich A 63 B5
Ober Östereich A 63 B4
D 62 B3
Haaksbergen NL 50 A2
Haamstede NL 49 B4
Haan D 50 B3
Haapajärvi FIN 3 E26
Haapsalu EST 6 B7
Haarlem NL 42 C1
Habas F 76 C2
Habay B 60 A1
Habo S 40 B4
Håbol S 35 D4
Habry CZ 63 A6
Habsheim F 60 C3
Hachenburg D 50 C3
Hacıbektaş TR 16 B7
Hacılar TR 16 B7
Hacinas E 89 C3
Hackås S 115 E11
Hacketstown IRL 21 B5
Hackthorpe UK 26 A3
Hadamar D 50 C4
Hädanberg S 115 D15
Haddington UK 25 C5
Hadersdorf am Kamp A 63 B6
Haderslev DK 39 D2
Haderup DK 39 C1
Hadım TR 119 F7
Hadleigh
Essex UK 31 C4
Suffolk UK 30 B4
Hadlow UK 31 C4
Hadmersleben D 52 A1
Hadsten DK 39 C3
Hadsund DK 38 C3
Hadyach UA 7 F13
Hadžići BIH 84 C3
Hafnarfjörður IS 111 C4
Hafnir IS 111 D3
Hafslo N 32 A4
Haganj HR 74 C1
Hagby S 40 C6
Hage D 43 B4
Hægebostad N 33 D4
Hægeland N 33 D4
Hagen
Niedersachsen D 43 B5
Nordrhein-Westfalen D 50 B3
Hagenbach D 61 A4
Hagenow D 44 B3
Hagetmau F 76 C2
Hagfors S 34 B5
Häggenås S 115 D11
Hagondange F 60 A2
Hagsta S 36 B4
Haguenau F 60 B3
Hahnbach D 62 A2
Hahnslätten D 50 C4
Hahót H 74 B1
Haiger D 50 C4
Haigerloch D 61 B4
Hailsham UK 31 D4
Hainburg A 64 B2
Hainfeld A 64 B1
Hainichen D 52 C3
Hajdúböszörmény H 10 C6
Hajdučica SRB 75 C5
Hajdúszoboszló H 75 A6
Hajnáčka SK 65 B5
Hajnówka PL 6 E7
Hajós H 75 B4
Håkafot S 115 C11
Hakkas S 113 F10
Håksberg S 36 B2
Halaszi H 64 C3
Halberstadt D 52 B1
Halberton UK 29 C4
Hald Ege DK 39 C2
Haldem D 43 C5
Halden N 35 C3
Haldensleben D 52 A1
Halenbeck D 44 B4
Halesowen UK 26 C3
Halesworth UK 30 B5
Halfing D 62 C3
Halhjem N 32 B2
Håliden S 34 B5
Halifax UK 27 B4
Häljelöt S 37 D3
Halkirk UK 23 C5
Hall S 37 E5
Hälla S 115 D14
Hallabro S 41 C5
Hällabrottet S 37 C2
Halland UK 31 D4
Hällaryd S 41 C4
Hallaryd S 40 C3
Hällberga S 37 C3
Hällbybrunn S 37 C3
Halle
B 49 C5
Nordrhein-Westfalen D 51 A4
Sachsen-Anhalt D 52 B1
Hålleberga S 40 C5
Hällefors S 36 C1
Hälleforsnäs S 37 C3
Hallein A 62 C4
Hällekis S 35 D5
Hallen S 115 D11
Hållen S 36 B4
Hallenberg D 51 B4
Hällestad S 37 D2
Hällevadsholm S 35 D3
Hällevik S 41 C4
Hälleviksstrand S 35 D3
Hallingby N 34 B2
Hallingeberg S 40 B6
Hallingen N 32 B6
Hall in Tirol A 71 A6
Hällnäs S 115 A15
Hållnäs S 36 B4
Hällnäs S 115 C16
Hallormsstaður IS 111 B11
Hallsberg S 37 C2
Hållsta S 37 C3
Hallstahammar S 37 C3
Hallstatt A 72 A3
Hallstavik S 36 B5
Halltorp S 40 C6
Halluin F 49 C4
Hallviken S 115 D12
Hallworthy UK 28 C3
Halmstad S 40 C2
Hals DK 38 B3
Halsa N 114 D5
Halstead UK 31 C4
Haltdalen N 114 E8
Haltern D 50 B3
Haltwhistle UK 25 D5
Halvarsgårdarna S 36 B2
Halver D 50 B3
Halvrimmen DK 38 B2
Ham F 59 A4
Hamar N 34 B3
Hamarhaug N 32 B2
Hamarøy N 112 D4
Hambach F 60 A3
Hambergen D 43 B5
Hambergsund S 35 D3
Hambledon UK 31 D2
Hambuhren D 44 C1
Hamburg D 44 B2
Hamdibey TR 118 C2
Hamdorf D 43 A6
Hämeenlinna FIN 3 F26
Hameln = Hamlin D 51 A5
Hamersleben D 52 A1
Hamidiye TR 118 C5
Hamilton UK 24 C3
Hamina FIN 7 A9
Hamlagrø N 32 B3
Hamlin = Hameln D 51 A5
Hamm D 50 B3
Hammar S 37 D1
Hammarland FIN 36 B6
Hammarö S 35 C5
Hammarstrand S 115 D13
Hamme B 49 B5
Hammel DK 39 C2
Hammelburg D 51 C5
Hammelspring D 45 B5
Hammenhög S 41 D4
Hammerdal S 115 D12
Hammerfest N 113 B12
Hammershøj DK 38 C2
Hammerum DK 39 C2
Hamminkeln D 50 B2
Hamnavoe UK 22 A7
Hamneda S 40 C3
Hamningberg N 113 B19
Hamoir B 49 C6
Hamont B 49 B6
Hámor H 65 B6
Hamra
Gävleborg S 115 F12
Gotland S 37 F5
Hamrångefjärden S 36 B4
Hamstreet UK 31 C4
Hamsund N 112 D4
Han
MNE 84 D3
TR 118 C5
Hanaskog S 41 C4
Hanau D 51 C4
Händelöp S 40 B6
Handlová SK 65 B4
Hanerau-Hademarschen D 43 A6
Hånger S 40 B3
Hanhimaa FIN 113 E14
Han i Hotit AL 105 A5
Hanken S 37 D1
Hankensbüttel D 44 C2
Han Knežica BIH 83 A5
Hanko FIN 6 B7
Hannover D 43 C6
Hannut B 49 C6
Han Pijesak BIH 84 B3
Hansnes N 112 C8
Hanstedt D 44 B2
Hanstholm DK 38 B1
Hantsavichy BY 7 E9
Hanušovice CZ 54 C1
Haparanda S 3 D26
Haradok BY 7 D10
Harads S 3 C24
Häradsbäck S 40 C4
Häradsbygden S 36 B2
Harbo S 36 B4
Harboør DK 38 C1
Harburg
Bayern D 62 B1
Hamburg D 44 B1
Hårby DK 39 D3
Harc H 74 B3
Hardegarijp NL 42 B2
Hardegsen D 51 B5
Hardelot Plage F 48 C2
Hardenbeck D 45 B5
Hardenberg NL 42 C3
Harderwijk NL 42 C2
Hardheim D 61 A5
Hardt D 61 B4
Hareid N 114 E3
Haren
D 43 C4
NL 42 B3
Harestua N 34 B2
Harfleur F 57 A6
Harg S 36 B5
Hargicourt F 49 D4
Hargnies F 49 C5
Hargshamn S 36 B5
Härja S 40 A3
Harkány H 74 C3
Härkeberga S 37 C4
Harkebrügge D 43 B4
Harlech UK 26 C1
Harleston UK 30 B5
Hårlev DK 41 D2
Harlingen NL 42 B2
Harlösa S 41 D3
Harlow UK 31 C4
Harmancık TR 118 C4
Harmånger S 115 F14
Harmanli BG 11 F8
Härnevi S 37 C4
Härnösand S 115 E14
Haro E 89 B4
Haroldswick UK 22 A8
Háromfa H 74 B2
Haroué F 60 B2
Harpenden UK 31 C3
Harplinge S 40 C2
Harpstedt D 43 C5
Harrogate UK 27 A4
Harrow UK 31 C3
Härryda S 40 B2
Harsefeld D 43 B6
Harsewinkel D 50 B4
Hârşova RO 11 D9
Harstad N 112 D5
Harsum D 51 A5
Harsvik N 114 C7
Harta H 75 B4
Hartberg A 73 A5
Hartburn UK 25 C6
Hartennes F 59 A4
Hartest UK 30 B4
Hartha D 52 B2
Hartland UK 28 C3
Hartlepool UK 27 A4
Hartmanice CZ 63 A4
Hartmannsdorf A 73 A5
Harvassdal N 115 B11
Harwell UK 31 C2
Harwich UK 31 C5
Harzgerode D 52 B1
Häselgehr A 71 A5
Haselünne D 43 C4
Haskovo BG 11 F8
Hasköy TR 118 A1
Haslach D 61 B4
Haslach an der Mühl A 63 B5
Hasle DK 41 D4
Haslemere UK 31 C3
Haslev DK 39 D4
Hasloch D 61 A5
Hasparren F 76 C1
Hassela S 115 E13
Hasselfelde D 51 B6
Hasselfors S 37 C1
Hasselt
B 49 C6
NL 42 C3
Hassfurt D 51 C6
Hassleben D 45 B5
Hässleholm S 41 C3
Hasslö S 41 C5
Hassloch D 61 A4
Hästbo S 36 B4
Hastersboda FIN 36 B7
Hästholmen S 37 D1
Hastière-Lavaux B 49 C5
Hastigrow UK 23 C5
Hastings UK 31 D4
Hästveda S 41 C3
Hasvik N 113 B11
Hatfield
Hertfordshire UK 31 C3
South Yorkshire UK 27 B5
Hatherleigh UK 28 C3
Hathersage UK 27 B4
Hatlestrand N 32 B2
Hattem NL 42 C3
Hatten
D 43 B5
F 60 B3
Hattfjelldal N 115 B10
Hatting DK 39 D2
Hattingen D 50 B3
Hattstadt F 60 B3
Hattstedt D 43 A6
Hatvan H 65 C5
Hatvik N 32 B2
Hau D 50 B2
Haudainville F 59 A6
Hauganes IS 111 B7
Haugastøl N 32 B4
Hauge N 33 D3
Haugesund N 33 C2
Haughom N 33 D3
Haugsdal N 32 B2
Haugsdorf A 64 B2
Haukedal N 32 A3
Haukeland N 32 B2
Haukeligrend N 33 C4
Haukeliseter N 32 C4
Haukipudas FIN 3 D26
Haulerwijk NL 42 B3
Haunersdorf D 62 B3
Haus N 32 B2
Hausach D 61 B4
Hausham D 62 C2
Hausmannstätten A 73 B5
Hausvik N 33 D3
Hautajärvi FIN 113 F18
Hautefort F 67 C6
Hauterives F 69 C5
Hauteville-Lompnès F 69 C5
Haut-Fays B 49 C6
Hautmont F 49 C4
Hautrage B 49 C4
Hauzenberg D 63 B4
Havant UK 31 D3
Havdhem S 37 E5
Havdrup DK 39 D5
Havelange B 49 C6
Havelberg D 44 C4
Havelte NL 42 C3
Haverfordwest UK 28 B3
Haverhill UK 30 B4
Havering UK 31 C4
Håverud S 35 D4
Havířov CZ 65 A4
Havixbeck D 50 B3
Havlíčkův Brod CZ 63 A6
Havndal DK 38 C3
Havneby DK 39 D1
Havnebyen DK 39 D4
Havnsø DK 39 D4
Havøysund N 113 A13
Havran TR 118 C2
Havrebjerg DK 39 D4
Havsa TR 118 A1
Havstenssund S 35 D3
Havza TR 16 A7
Hawes UK 26 A3
Hawick UK 25 C5
Hawkhurst UK 31 C4
Hawkinge UK 31 C5
Haxey UK 27 B5
Hayange F 60 A2
Haydarlı TR 119 D5
Haydon Bridge UK 25 D5
Hayle UK 28 C2
Haymana TR 118 C7
Hay-on-Wye UK 29 A4
Hayrabolu TR 118 A2
Haysyn UA 11 B10
Hayvoron UA 11 B10
Haywards Heath UK 31 D3
Hazebrouck F 48 C3
Hazlov CZ 52 C2
Heacham UK 30 B4
Headcorn UK 31 C4
Headford IRL 20 A2
Heanor UK 27 B4
Héas F 76 D3
Heathfield UK 31 D4
Hebden Bridge UK 26 B3
Heberg S 40 C2
Heby S 36 C3
Hechingen D 61 B4
Hechlingen D 62 B1
Hecho E 76 D2
Hechtel B 49 B6
Hechthausen D 43 B6
Heckelberg D 45 C5
Heckington UK 27 C5
Hecklingen D 52 B1
Hed S 37 C2
Hedalen N 34 B1
Hedared S 40 B2
Heddal N 33 C6
Hédé F 57 B4
Hede S 115 E10
Hedekas S 35 D3
Hedemora S 36 B2
Hedensted DK 39 D2
Hedersleben D 52 B1
Hedesunda S 36 B4
Hedge End UK 31 D2
Hedon UK 27 B5
Heede D 43 C4
Heek D 50 A3
Heemstede NL 42 C1
Heerde NL 42 C3
Heerenveen NL 42 C2
Heerhugowaard NL 42 C1
Heerlen NL 50 C1
Heeze NL 49 B6
Heggenes N 32 A6
Hegra N 114 D8
Hegyeshalom H 64 C3
Hegyközség H 74 A1
Heia N 114 C9
Heide D 43 A6
Heidelberg D 61 A4
Heiden D 50 B2
Heidenau D 53 C3
Heidenheim D 61 B6
Heidenreichstein A 63 B6
Heikendorf D 44 A2
Heilam UK 22 C4
Heiland N 33 D5
Heilbad Heiligenstadt D 51 B6
Heilbronn D 61 A5
Heiligenblut A 72 A2
Heiligendamn D 44 A3
Heiligendorf D 44 C2
Heiligengrabe D 44 B4
Heiligenhafen D 44 A2
Heiligenhaus D 50 B2
Heiligenkreuz A 73 B6
Heiligenstadt D 62 A2
Heiloo NL 42 C1
Heilsbronn D 62 A1
Heim N 114 D6
Heimburg D 51 B6
Heimdal N 114 D7
Heinerscheid L 50 C2
Heinersdorf D 45 C6
Heining D 63 B4
Heiningen D 61 B5
Heinola FIN 3 F27
Heinsberg D 50 B2
Heist-op-den-Berg B 49 B5
Hejde S 37 E5
Hejdeby S 37 E5
Hejls DK 39 D2
Hejnice CZ 53 C5
Hel PL 47 A4
Helchteren B 49 B6
Heldburg D 51 C6
Heldrungen D 52 B1
Helechosa E 94 C2
Helensburgh UK 24 B3
Helfenberg A 63 B5
Helgen N 33 C6
Helgeroa N 35 D1
Hella
IS 111 D5
N 32 A3
Helland N 112 D5
Hellas S 35 D4
Helle N 33 D3
Helleland N 33 D3
Hellendoorn NL 42 C3
Hellenthal D 50 C2
Hellesøy N 32 B1
Hellesylt N 114 E3
Hellevoetsluis NL 49 B5
Helligskogen N 112 C9
Hellín E 101 A4
Hellissandur IS 111 C2
Hellnar IS 111 C2
Hellum DK 38 B3
Hellvi S 37 E5
Hellvik N 33 D2
Helm-brechts D 52 C1
Helmond NL 49 B6
Helmsdale UK 23 C5
Helmsley UK 27 A4
Helmstedt D 51 A6
Hel'pa SK 65 B5
Helsa D 51 B5
Helsby UK 26 B3
Helsingborg S 41 C2
Helsinge DK 41 C2
Helsingør DK 41 C2
Helsinki FIN 6 A8
Helston UK 28 C2
Hemau D 62 A2
Hemavan S 115 B12
Hemel Hempstead UK 31 C3
Hemer D 50 B3
Héming F 60 B2
Hemmet DK 39 D1
Hemmingstedt D 43 A6
Hemmoor D 43 B6
Hemnes N 35 C3
Hemnesberget N 115 A10
Hemse S 37 E5
Hemsedal N 32 B5
Hemslingen D 43 B6
Hemsworth UK 27 B4
Hen N 34 B2
Henån S 35 D3
Hendaye F 76 C1
Hendek TR 118 B5
Hendungen D 51 C6
Henfield UK 31 D3
Hengelo
Gelderland NL 50 A2
Overijssel NL 50 A2
Hengersberg D 62 B4
Hengoed UK 29 B4
Hénin-Beaumont F 48 C3
Henley-on-Thames UK 31 C3
Hennan S 115 E12
Henneberg D 51 C6
Hennebont F 56 C2
Henne Strand DK 39 D1
Hennigsdorf D 45 C5
Hennset N 114 D5
Hennstedt D 43 A6
Henrichemont F 68 A2
Henryków PL 54 C2
Henrykowo PL 47 A6
Hensås N 32 A5
Henstedt-Ulzburg D 44 B1
Heppenheim D 61 A4
Herad
Buskerud N 32 B6
Vest-Agder N 33 D3
Heradsbygd N 34 B3
Heraklion = Iraklio GR 117 G7
Herálec CZ 64 A2
Herand N 32 B3
Herbault F 58 C2
Herbern D 50 B3
Herbertstown IRL 20 B3
Herbeumont B 59 A6
Herbignac F 66 A2
Herbisse F 59 B5
Herbitzheim F 60 A3
Herbolzheim D 60 B3
Herborn D 50 C4
Herbrechtingen D 61 B6
Herby PL 54 C3
Herceg-Novi MNE 105 A4
Hercegovać HR 74 C2
Hercegovacka Goleša SRB 85 C4
Hercegszántó H 75 C3
Herchen D 50 C3
Heréd H 65 C5
Hereford UK 29 A5
Herefoss N 33 D5
Hereke TR 118 B4
Herencia E 95 C3
Herend H 74 A2
Herent B 49 C5
Herentals B 49 B5
Hérépian F 78 C2
Herfølge DK 41 D2
Herford D 51 A4
Herguijuela E 93 B5
Héric F 66 A3
Héricourt F 60 C2
Héricourt-en-Caux F 58 A1
Hérimoncourt F 70 A1
Heringsdorf D 44 A3
Herisau CH 71 A4
Hérisson F 68 B2
Herk-de-Stad B 49 C6
Herlufmagle DK 39 D4
Hermagor A 72 B3
Hermannsburg D 44 C2
Hermansverk N 32 A3
Heřmanův Městec CZ 53 D5
Herment F 68 C2
Hermeskeil D 60 A2
Hermisende E 87 C4
Hermonville F 59 A4
Hermsdorf D 52 C1
Hernani E 76 C1
Hernansancho E 94 B2
Herne D 50 B3
Herne Bay UK 31 C5
Hernes N 34 B3
Herning DK 39 C1
Herøya N 35 C1
Herramelluri E 89 B3
Herräng S 36 B5
Herre N 33 C6
Herrenberg D 61 B4
Herrera E 100 B1
Herrera de Alcántara E 92 B3
Herrera del Duque E 94 C1
Herrera de los Navarros E 90 B1
Herrera de Pisuerga E 88 B2
Herreros del Suso E 94 B1
Herrestad S 35 D3
Herrhamra S 37 D4
Herritslev DK 44 A3
Herrlisheim F 60 B3
Herrljunga S 40 A3
Herrnhut D 53 B4
Herrsching D 62 B2
Hersbruck D 62 A2
Hersby S 37 C5
Herscheid D 50 B3
Herselt B 49 B5
Herso GR 116 A4
Herstal B 49 C6
Herstmonceux UK 31 D4
Herten D 50 B3
Hertford UK 31 C3
Hervás E 93 A5
Hervik N 33 C2
Herxheim D 61 A4

Herzberg
Brandenburg D ...45 C4
Brandenburg D ...52 B3
Niedersachsen D ...51 B6
Herzbrock D ...50 B4
Herzfelde D ...45 C5
Herzlake D ...43 C4
Herzogen-aurach D ...62 A1
Herzogenbuchsee CH ...70 A2
Herzogenburg A ...63 B6
Herzsprung D ...44 B4
Hesby N ...33 C2
Hesdin F ...48 C3
Hesel D ...43 B4
Heskestad N ...33 D3
Hessdalen N ...114 E8
Hesselager DK ...39 D3
Hesseng N ...113 C18
Hessisch Lichtenau D ...51 B5
Hessisch-Oldendorf D ...51 A5
Hestra S ...40 B3
Heswall UK ...26 B2
Hetvik N ...32 B2
Hettange-Grande F ...60 A2
Hetton-le-Hole UK ...25 D6
Hettstedt D ...52 B1
Heuchin F ...48 C3
Heudicourt-sous-les-
Côtes F ...60 B1
Heunezel F ...60 B2
Heuqueville F ...57 A6
Heves H ...65 C6
Hévíz H ...74 B2
Hexham UK ...25 D5
Heysham UK ...26 A3
Heytesbury UK ...29 B5
Hidas H ...74 B3
Hieflau A ...63 C5
Hiendelaencina E ...95 A4
Hiersac F ...67 C5
High Bentham UK ...26 A3
Highclere UK ...31 C2
High Hesket UK ...25 D5
Highley UK ...26 C3
High Wycombe UK ...31 C3
Higuera de Arjona E ...100 B2
Higuera de Calatrava
E ...100 B1
Higuera de la Serena
E ...93 C5
Higuera de la Sierra E ...99 B4
Higuera de Vargas E ...93 C4
Higuera la Real E ...99 A4
Higuera de Llerena E ...93 C4
Higueruela E ...101 C5
Híjar E ...90 B2
Hilchenbach D ...50 B4
Hildburghausen D ...51 C6
Hilden D ...50 B2
Hilders D ...51 C5
Hildesheim D ...51 A5
Hilgay UK ...30 B4
Hillared S ...40 B3
Hille D ...51 A4
Hillegom NL ...49 A5
Hillerstorp S ...40 B3
Hillesheim D ...50 C2
Hillestad N ...35 C2
Hillmersdorf D ...52 B3
Hillsborough UK ...19 B5
Hillswick UK ...22 A7
Hilpoltstein D ...62 A2
Hiltpoltstein D ...62 A2
Hilvarenbeek NL ...49 B6
Hilversum NL ...49 A6
Himarë AL ...116 B1
Himbergen D ...44 B2
Himeshaza H ...74 B3
Himmelberg A ...73 B4
Himmelpforten D ...43 B6
Himód H ...51 A5
Hinckley UK ...30 B2
Hindås S ...40 B2
Hindelang D ...71 A6
Hindelbank CH ...70 A2
Hinderavåg N ...33 C2
Hindhead UK ...31 C3
Hinjosa del Valle E ...93 C4
Hinnerup DK ...39 C3
Hinneryd S ...40 C4
Hinojal E ...93 B4
Hinojales E ...99 B4
Hinojos E ...99 B4
Hinojosa del Duque E ...93 C5
Hinojosas
de Calatrava E ...100 A1
Hinterhornbach A ...71 A5
Hinterriss A ...71 A6
Hintersee
A ...63 C4
D ...45 B6
Hinterstoder A ...63 C5
Hintertux A ...72 A1
Hinterweidenthal D ...60 A3
Hinwil CH ...70 A3
Hios GR ...116 D8
Hippolytushoef NL ...42 C1
Hirschaid D ...62 A2
Hirschau D ...62 A2
Hirschfeld D ...52 B3
Hirschhorn D ...61 A4
Hirsingue F ...60 C3
Hirson F ...59 A5
Hirtshals DK ...38 B2
Hirzenhain D ...51 C5
Hisarcık TR ...118 C4
Hishult S ...41 C3
Hitchin UK ...31 C3
Hitra N ...114 D5
Hittarp S ...41 C2
Hittisau A ...71 A4
Hittun N ...32 A2
Hitzacker D ...44 B3
Hjallerup DK ...38 B3
Hjällstad S ...34 B5
Hjältevad S ...40 B5
Hjärnarp S ...41 C2
Hjartdal N ...33 C5
Hjellestad N ...32 B2
Hjelmeland N ...33 C3
Hjelset N ...114 E4
Hjerkinn N ...114 E6
Hjerm DK ...38 C1
Hjerpsted DK ...39 D1
Hjerting DK ...39 D1
Hjo S ...35 D6
Hjordkær DK ...39 D2
Hjørring DK ...38 B2
Hjørungavåg N ...114 E3
Hjortkvarn S ...37 D2
Hjortnäs S ...36 B1
Hjortsberga S ...40 C4
Hjuken S ...115 C14
Hjuksebø N ...33 C6
Hjulsjö S ...36 C1
Hliník nad Hronom SK ...65 B4
Hlinsko CZ ...64 A1
Hlío IS ...111 A10
Hlohovec CZ ...64 B3
Hluboká nad
Vltavou CZ ...63 A5
Hlučín CZ ...64 A4
Hlukhiv UA ...7 F12
Hlybokaye BY ...7 D9
Hniezdne SK ...65 A6
Hnilec SK ...65 B6
Hnúšťa SK ...65 B6
Hobol H ...74 B2
Hobro DK ...38 C2
Hobscheid L ...60 A1
Hocalar TR ...119 D4
Hochdonn D ...43 A6
Hochdorf CH ...70 A3
Hochfelden F ...60 B3
Hochspeyer D ...60 A3
Höchst im Odenwald
D ...61 A5
Höchstädt D ...61 B6
Hochstenbach D ...50 C3
Höckendorf D ...52 C3
Hockenheim D ...61 A4

Hoddesdon UK ...31 C3
Hodejov SK ...65 B5
Hodenhagen D ...43 C6
Hodkovice CZ ...53 C5
Hódmezővásárhely
H ...75 B5
Hodnet UK ...26 C3
Hodonín CZ ...64 B3
Hodslavice CZ ...64 A4
Hoedekenskerke NL ...49 B4
Hoegaarden B ...49 C5
Hoek van Holland NL ...49 B5
Hoenderlo NL ...50 A1
Hof
Bayern D ...51 C6
Hessen D ...51 C5
Hofheim
Bayern D ...51 C6
Hessen D ...51 C5
Hofkirchen im
Mühlkreis A ...63 B4
Höfn IS ...111 C10
Hofors S ...36 B3
Hofsós IS ...111 B6
Hofstad N ...114 C7
Höganäs S ...41 C2
Högbo S ...36 B3
Høgebru N ...32 A3
Högsäter S ...35 D3
Högsby S ...40 B6
Högyész H ...74 B3
Hohenau A ...64 B2
Hohenberg A ...63 C6
Hohenbucko D ...52 B3
Hohendorf D ...45 A4
Hohenems A ...71 A4
Hohenhameln D ...51 A6
Hohenhausen D ...51 A4
Hohenkirchen D ...43 B4
Hohenlinden D ...62 B2
Hohenlockstedt D ...43 B6
Hohenmölsen D ...52 B2
Hohennauen D ...44 C4
Hohen Neuendorf D ...45 C5
Hohenseeden D ...52 A2
Hohentauern A ...73 A4
Hohentengen D ...70 A3
Hohenwepel D ...51 B5
Hohenwestedt D ...43 A6
Hohenwutzen D ...45 C6
Hohenzieritz D ...45 B5
Horn
D ...51 B6
N ...34 B2
S ...40 B5
Hojer DK ...39 E1
Højslev Stby DK ...38 C2
Hok S ...40 B4
Hökerum S ...40 B3
Hökhuvud S ...36 B5
Hokksund N ...34 C1
Hörn S ...40 A6
Hola Pristan UA ...11 C12
Holbæk
Aarhus Amt. DK ...38 C3
Frederiksværk DK ...41 C2
Holberg D ...61 B4
Holbrook UK ...31 C5
Holdenstedt D ...44 C2
Holdhus N ...32 B2
Horne
Fyns Amt. DK ...39 D3
Ribe Amt. DK ...39 D1
Holeby DK ...44 A3
Hølen N ...35 C2
Hølervasseter N ...32 B6
Holešov CZ ...64 A3
Holguera E ...93 B4
Holíč
SK ...64 B3
Höljes S ...34 B4
Hollabrunn A ...64 B2
Hollandstoun UK ...23 B6
Hollen D ...33 D4
Holleben D ...52 B1
Hollfeld D ...62 A2
Hollókő H ...65 C5
Hollola FIN ...3 F26
Hollstadt D ...51 C6
Hollum NL ...42 B2
Hollviksnäs S ...41 D2
Holm N ...101 A7
Holmänik IS ...111 B4
Holmarö B ...110 B10
Holmedal S ...35 C3
Holmegil N ...35 C3
Holmen N ...39 E1
Holmestrand N ...35 C2
Holmfirth UK ...27 B4
Holmfoss N ...113 C19
Holmsbu N ...35 C2
Holmsjö S ...41 C5
Holmsund S ...115 D4
Holmsveden S ...37 E6
Holored S ...40 C4
Horsett
Norfolk UK ...30 B5
Wrexham UK ...26 B3
Holten NL ...50 A2
Holtwick D ...50 A3
Holwerd NL ...42 B2
Holycross IRL ...21 B4
Holyhead UK ...26 B1
Holýšov CZ ...62 A4
Holywell UK ...26 B2
Holzdorf D ...52 B3
Holzhausen D ...51 A4
Holzheim D ...61 B6
Holzkirchen D ...62 C2
Holzminden D ...51 B5
Holzthaleben D ...51 B6
Homberg
Hessen D ...51 B5
Hessen D ...51 C5
Homburg D ...60 A3
Homokmegy H ...75 B4
Homokszentgyörgy
H ...74 B2
Homyel = Gomel BY ...7 E11
Honaz TR ...119 E4
Hondarribia E ...76 A1
Hondón de los Frailes
E ...101 A5
Hondschoote F ...48 C3
Hønefoss N ...34 B2
Honfleur F ...57 A6
Høng DK ...39 D4
Honiton UK ...29 C4
Hönningsvåg N ...113 B14
Honrubia E ...95 C4
Hontalbilla E ...88 C2
Hontianske-Nemce SK ...65 B4

Hontoria de la Cantera
E ...88 B3
Hontoria del Pinar E ...89 C3
Hontoria de
Valdearados E ...89 C3
Hoofddorp NL ...49 A5
Hoogerheide NL ...49 B5
Hoogeveen NL ...42 C3
Hoogezand-Sappemeer
NL ...42 B3
Hoogkarspel NL ...42 C2
Hoogkerk NL ...42 B3
Hoogstede D ...42 C3
Hoogstraten B ...49 B5
Hook UK ...31 C3
Hooksiel D ...43 B5
Höör S ...41 D3
Hope UK ...26 B2
Hope under Dinmore
UK ...29 A5
Hopen N ...112 E4
Hopfgarten A ...72 A2
Hopfgarten in
Defereggen A ...72 B2
Hopseidet N ...113 B16
Hopsten D ...43 C4
Hoptrup DK ...39 D2
Hora Svatého
Sebestiána CZ ...52 C3
Horažďovice CZ ...63 A4
Horb am Neckar D ...61 B4
Horbelev DK ...39 E5
Hörby DK ...38 B3
Hörby S ...41 D3
Horcajada de la Torre
E ...95 B4
Horcajo de los Montes
E ...94 C2
Horcajo de Santiago
E ...95 C3
Horcajo-
Medianero E ...93 A5
Horche E ...95 B3
Horcajo D ...45 A4
Horda S ...40 B4
Hordabø N ...32 B1
Hordalia N ...33 D3
Hordvik N ...32 B2
Horezu RO ...11 D8
Horgen CH ...70 A3
Horgoš SRB ...75 B4
Hořice CZ ...53 C5
Horjul SLO ...73 B4
Horka D ...53 B4
Hörken S ...36 B1
Herl BY ...7 D11
Hörle S ...40 B4
Horn
Aarhus Amt. DK ...38 C3
Frederiksværk DK ...41 C2
Hornberg D ...61 B4
Hornburg D ...51 A6
Horncastle UK ...27 B5
Horndal S ...36 B3
Horndean UK ...31 D2
Horne
Fyns Amt. DK ...39 D3
Ribe Amt. DK ...39 D1
Hornes N ...33 D4
Horni Bečva CZ ...64 A4
Horni Benešov CZ ...64 A3
Horní Cerekev CZ ...63 A6
Horni Jiřetín CZ ...52 C3
Horni Lomná CZ ...65 A4
Horni Maršov CZ ...53 C5
Horný
Horni Planá CZ ...63 B5
Horni Slavkov CZ ...52 C2
Horni Vltavice CZ ...63 B5
Hornnes N ...33 D4
Horno D ...53 B4
Hornos E ...101 A3
Hornoy-le-Bourg F ...58 A2
Hornsea UK ...27 B5
Hornsjø N ...34 B2
Hornslet DK ...39 C3
Hornstein A ...64 C2
Hörnum D ...39 E1
Hornum D ...38 C2
Horný Tisovník SK ...65 B5
Horodenka UA ...11 B8
Horodnya UA ...7 F11
Horodok
Khmelnytskyy UA ...11 B7
Lviv UA ...11 B7
Horodyshche UA ...11 B11
Horokhiv UA ...11 A8
Horred S ...40 B2
Hörröd S ...41 D4
Hörsching A ...63 B5
Horsens DK ...39 D2
Horsham UK ...31 C3
Hørsholm DK ...41 D2
Horslunde DK ...39 E4
Horšovský Týn CZ ...62 A3
Horst NL ...50 B2
Horstel D ...50 A3
Horsten D ...43 B4
Horstmar D ...50 A3
Hort H ...65 C5
Horta P ...24 P2
Horten N ...35 C2
Hortezuela E ...89 C4
Hortiguela E ...89 B3
Hortobágy H ...75 A6
Horton in Ribblesdale
UK ...26 A3
Hørve DK ...39 D4
Horwich UK ...26 B3
Hosanger N ...32 B2
Hösbach D ...51 C5
Hosena D ...53 B3
Hosenfeld D ...51 C5
Hosingen L ...50 C2
Hospental CH ...70 B3
Hospital IRL ...20 B3
Hossa FIN ...3 D29
Hossegor F ...76 C1
Hosszúhetény H ...74 B3
Hostal de Ipiés E ...90 A2
Hoštálkova CZ ...64 A3
Hostalric E ...91 B5
Hostens F ...76 B2
Hostěradice CZ ...64 B2
Hostinné CZ ...53 C5
Hostomice CZ ...63 A5
Hostouň CZ ...62 A3
Hotagen S ...115 D11
Hoting S ...115 D13
Hotolisht AL ...116 A2

Hov
DK ...39 D3
N ...34 B2
Hova S ...35 D5
Høvåg N ...33 D5
Hovborg DK ...39 D2
Hovda N ...32 B6
Hovden N ...33 C4
Hove UK ...31 D3
Hovedgård DK ...39 D2
Hovelhof D ...51 B4
Hoven DK ...39 D1
Hovet N ...32 B5
Hovingham UK ...27 A5
Hovmantorp S ...40 C5
Hovsta S ...37 C2
Howden UK ...27 B5
Howe D ...44 B2
Höxter D ...51 B5
Hoya D ...43 C6
Hoya de Santa Maria
E ...99 B4
Hoya-Gonzalo E ...95 D5
Høyanger N ...32 A3
Høydalsmo N ...33 C5
Hoyerswerda D ...53 B4
Høyjord N ...35 C2
Hoylake UK ...26 B2
Høylandet N ...114 C9
Hoym D ...52 B1
Hoyocasero E ...94 B2
Hoyos E ...93 A4
Hoyos del Espino E ...93 A5
Hoyo de Manzanares
E ...94 B3
Hoyo de Pinares E ...94 B2
Hoyos E ...93 A4
Hoyos del Espino E ...93 A5
Hrabušice SK ...65 B6
Hradec Králové CZ ...53 C5
Hradec nad Moravicí
CZ ...64 A3
Hrádek CZ ...64 B2
Hrádek nad Nisou CZ ...53 C4
Hradiště CZ ...63 A4
Hrafnagil IS ...111 B7
Hrafnseyri IS ...111 B2
Hranice
Severomoravský CZ ...64 A3
Západočeský CZ ...52 C2
Hranovnica SK ...65 B6
Hrasnica BIH ...84 C3
Hrastnik SLO ...73 B5
Hrebenka UA ...11 A11
Hřensko CZ ...53 C4
Hrisova SK ...65 B5
Hrisoupoli GR ...116 B6
Hrochov CZ ...64 A2
Hrochův Tynec CZ ...53 D5
Hrodna BY ...6 E7
Hrodzyanka BY ...7 E10
Hronov CZ ...53 C5
Hrotovský Beňadik SK ...65 B4
Hrotovice CZ ...64 A2
Hrtkovci SRB ...85 B4
Hrun IS ...111 A5
Hrušov SK ...65 B5
Hrušovany nad
Jevišovkou CZ ...64 B2
Hrušín SK ...65 A5
Hrvacani BIH ...84 B2
Hrvace HR ...83 C5
Hrvatská Suča SK ...64 B3
Huben A ...72 B2
Hückel-hoven D ...50 B2
Hückeswagen D ...50 B3
Hucknall UK ...27 B4
Hucqueliers F ...48 C2
Huddersfield UK ...27 B4
Huddinge S ...37 C4
Huddunge S ...36 B3
Hude D ...43 B5
Hudiksvall S ...115 F14
Huélago E ...100 B2
Huélamo E ...95 B5
Huelgoat F ...56 B2
Huelma E ...100 B2
Huelva E ...99 B4
Huéneja E ...100 B3
Huércal de Almeria E ...101 C3
Huércal-Overa E ...101 B4
Huerta de Abajo E ...89 B3
Huerta del Rey E ...89 C3
Huerta de
Valdecarabanos E ...95 C3
Huertahernando E ...95 B4
Huesa E ...100 B2
Huesca E ...90 A2
Huéscar E ...101 B3
Huete E ...95 B4
Huétor Tájar E ...100 B1
Hüfingen D ...61 C4
Hufthamar N ...32 B2
Hugh Town UK ...28 D1
Huglfing D ...62 C2
Huissen NL ...50 B1
Huittinen FIN ...3 F25
Huizen NL ...49 A6
Hulin CZ ...64 A3
Hull D ...50 B2
Hulsig DK ...38 B3
Hulst NL ...49 B5
Hult S ...40 B5
Hulta S ...40 A6
Hulterstad S ...41 C6
Hultsfred S ...40 B5
Humanby UK ...27 A5
Humanes E ...95 B3
Humberston UK ...27 B5
Humble DK ...39 E3
Humenné SK ...10 B6
Humilladero E ...100 B1
Humlebæk DK ...41 D2
Humlum DK ...38 C1
Hummelsta S ...37 C3
Humpolec CZ ...63 A6
Humshaugh UK ...25 C5
Hundala N ...115 B9
Hundested DK ...39 D4
Hundorp N ...34 A1
Hundvåg N ...33 C2
Hundvin N ...32 B2
Hunedoara RO ...11 D7
Hünfeld D ...51 C5
Hungen D ...51 C4
Hungerford UK ...31 C2
Hunndalen N ...34 B2
Hunnebostrad S ...35 D3
Hunstanton UK ...30 B4
Huntingdon UK ...30 B3
Huntley UK ...29 B5
Huntly UK ...23 D6
Hünxe D ...50 B2
Hurbanovo SK ...64 C4
Hurdal N ...34 B3
Hurezani RO ...11 D7
Hurlford UK ...24 C3
Hurstbourne Tarrant
UK ...31 C2
Hurstpierpoint UK ...31 D3
Hurum N ...32 A5
Hurup DK ...38 C1
Húsafell IS ...111 C5
Húsavík IS ...111 A8
Husbands Bosworth
UK ...30 B2
Húsey IS ...111 B11
Husi RO ...11 C10
Husina BIH ...84 B3
Husinec CZ ...63 A4
Husinish UK ...22 D1
Huskvarna S ...40 B4
Husnes N ...33 C2
Husøy N ...112 C6
Hustad N ...114 E4
Hüsten D ...50 B4
Hustopeče CZ ...64 B2
Hustopeče nad
Bečvou CZ ...64 A3
Husum
D ...43 A6
S ...115 D16

Husvika N ...115 B9
Huta PL ...46 C2
Hutovo BIH ...84 D2
Hüttenberg A ...73 B4
Hüttlingen D ...61 B6
Hutton Cranswick UK ...27 B5
Hüttschlag A ...72 A3
Huttwil CH ...70 A2
Huy B ...49 C6
Hüyük TR ...119 E6
Hval N ...34 B2
Hvåle N ...32 B6
Hvaler N ...35 C3
Hvalpsund DK ...38 C2
Hvammstangi IS ...111 B5
Hvammur IS ...111 B6
Hvar HR ...83 C5
Hvarnes N ...35 C1
Hveragerði IS ...111 D4
Hvidbjerg DK ...38 C1
Hvide Sande DK ...39 D1
Hvittingfoss N ...35 C2
Hvolsvöllur IS ...111 D5
Hybe SK ...65 A5
Hycklinge S ...40 B5
Hydra GR ...117 E5
Hyen N ...114 F2
Hyères F ...79 C5
Hyères Plage F ...79 C5
Hylestad N ...33 C4
Hylke DK ...39 D2
Hyllestad N ...32 A2
Hyllstofta S ...41 C3
Hyltebruk S ...40 B3
Hynish UK ...24 B1
Hynnekleiv N ...33 D5
Hythe
Hampshire UK ...31 D2
Kent UK ...31 C5
Hyvinkää FIN ...3 F26

I

Iam RO ...85 A6
Iasi RO ...11 C9
Iasmos GR ...116 A7
Ibahernando E ...93 B5
Iballé AL ...105 A5
Ibarranguelua E ...89 A4
Ibbenbüren D ...50 A3
Ibeas de Juarros E ...89 B3
Ibestad N ...112 D6
Ibi E ...96 C2
Ibiza = Eivissa E ...97 C1
Ibradı TR ...119 E6
Ibriktepe TR ...118 A1
Ibros E ...100 B2
Ibstock UK ...27 C4
İçel TR ...16 C7
Ichenhausen D ...61 B6
Ichny UA ...11 A12
Ichtegem B ...49 B4
Ichtershausen D ...51 C6
Idanha-a-Novo P ...93 B3
Idar-Oberstein D ...60 A3
Idd N ...35 C3
Idiazábal E ...89 B4
Idivuoma S ...113 D10
Idkerberget S ...36 B2
Idön S ...36 B5
Idre S ...115 E9
Idritsa RUS ...7 D9
Idstein D ...50 C4
Idvor SRB ...75 C5
Iecca Mare RO ...75 C5
Ielsi I ...103 B7
Ieper = Ypres B ...48 C3
Ierapetra GR ...117 G7
Ierissos GR ...116 B5
Ifjord N ...113 B16
Igal H ...74 B3
Igea E ...89 B4
Igea Marina I ...82 B1
Igelfors S ...37 D2
Igersheim D ...61 A5
Iggesund S ...115 F14
Iglarevo KOS ...85 D5
Iglésias E ...89 B3
Iglesias I ...110 C1
Igls A ...71 A6
Igny-Comblizy F ...59 A4
Igorre E ...89 A4
Igoumenitsa GR ...116 C2
Igries E ...90 A2
Igualada E ...91 B4
Igüeña E ...86 B4
Iguerande F ...69 B4
Iharosberény H ...74 B2
Ihl'any SK ...65 A6
Ihlienworth D ...43 B5
Ihringen D ...60 B3
Ihrlerstein D ...62 B2
Ihsaniye TR ...118 C5
Iiddorp N ...42 C1
Iisalmi FIN ...3 E27
Ijevan AM ...23 B4
IJmuiden NL ...42 C1
IJsselmuiden NL ...42 C2
IJzendijke NL ...49 B4
Ikast DK ...39 C2
Ikervár H ...74 A1
Ilandža SRB ...75 C5
Ilanz CH ...71 B4
Ilava SK ...64 B4
Il Castagno I ...81 C4
Ilche E ...90 B3
Ilchester UK ...29 C5
Ilfeld D ...51 B6
Ilfracombe UK ...28 B3
Ilgaz TR ...16 A6
İlgın TR ...119 D6
Ilhavo P ...87 C2
Ilica TR ...118 C2
Ilidža BIH ...84 C3
Ilijaš BIH ...84 C3
Ilirska Bistrica SLO ...73 C4
Ilkeston UK ...27 C4
Ilkley UK ...27 B4
Illana E ...95 B4
Illano E ...86 A4
Illar E ...101 C3
Illats F ...76 B2
Illertissen D ...61 B6
Illescas E ...94 B3
Ille-sur-Têt F ...91 A5
Illfurth F ...60 C3
Illichivsk UA ...11 C11
Illiers-Combray F ...58 B2
Illkirch-
Graffenstaden F ...60 B3
Illmensee D ...61 C5
Illmitz A ...64 C2
Illora E ...100 B2
Illueca E ...89 C5
Imamoğlu TR ...16 C7
Imatra FIN ...3 F28
İmeçik TR ...119 E5
Imingen N ...32 B6
Immeln S ...41 C4
Immenhausen D ...51 B5
Immenstedt D ...43 A6
Immenstadt D ...61 C6
Ímola I ...81 B5
İmon S ...115 D16

Imotski HR ...84 C2
Impéria I ...80 C2
Imphy F ...68 B3
İmroz TR ...116 B7
İmsland N ...33 C2
Imst A ...71 A5
İnagh IRL ...20 B2
İnari FIN ...113 D15
Inca E ...97 B2
Inchnadamph UK ...22 C4
Incinillas E ...89 B3
Indal S ...115 E14
Indija SRB ...85 A5
Indre Arna N ...32 B2
Indre Billefjord N ...113 B14
Indre Brenna N ...113 B14
İğneada TR ...118 A2
İnebolu TR ...16 A6
İnecik TR ...118 A2
İnegöl TR ...118 B4
İnerthal CH ...70 A3
Infiesto E ...88 A1
Ingatorp S ...40 B5
Ingedal N ...35 C3
Ingelheim D ...50 D4
Ingelmunster B ...49 C4
Ingelstad S ...40 C4
Ingleton UK ...26 A3
Ingolfsland N ...32 C5
Ingolstadt D ...62 B2
Ingrandes
Maine-et-Loire F ...66 A4
Vienne F ...67 B5
Ingwiller F ...60 B3
İnhisar TR ...118 B5
Iniesta E ...95 C5
Inishannon IRL ...20 C3
Inishcrone IRL ...18 B2
Inke H ...74 B2
Inndyr N ...112 E3
Innellan UK ...24 C3
Innerleithen UK ...25 C4
Innermessan UK ...24 D3
Innertkirchen CH ...70 B3
İnnfjorden N ...114 E4
İnnhavet N ...112 E4
İnnsbruck A ...71 A6
Innset N ...112 D7
Innvik N ...114 F3
İnönü TR ...118 C5
İnowłódz PL ...55 B5
İnowrocław PL ...47 C4
İns CH ...70 A2
Insch UK ...23 D6
İnsjön S ...36 B2
İnstow UK ...28 B3
İntepe TR ...118 B7
İnterlaken CH ...70 B2
İntragna CH ...70 B3
İntrobio I ...71 C4
İnverallochy UK ...23 D7
İnveran
IRL ...20 A2
UK ...22 D4
İnveraray UK ...24 B2
İnverbervie UK ...25 B5
İnvergarry UK ...22 D4
İnvergordon UK ...23 D4
İnvergowrie UK ...25 B4
İnverkeilor UK ...25 B5
İnverkeithing UK ...25 B4
İnvermoriston UK ...22 D4
İnverness UK ...23 D4
İnveruno I ...70 C3
İnverurie UK ...23 D6
İoannina GR ...116 C2
İolanda di Savoia I ...81 B5
İon Corvin RO ...11 D9
İ ...106 C2
İpel I ...117 F7
İpati GR ...116 D4
İpsala TR ...118 B1
İpswich UK ...30 B5
İraklia GR ...116 A5
İrakli o = Heraklion
GR ...117 G7
İrdning A ...73 A4
İregszemcse H ...74 B3
İrgoli I ...110 B2
İrig SRB ...85 A4
İrlava LV ...6 C7
İronbridge UK ...26 C3
İrpın UA ...11 A11
İrrel D ...60 A2
İrsina I ...104 C2
İrsta S ...37 C3
İrthlingborough UK ...30 B3
İ Iruela E ...88 B1
İrun E ...76 C1
İrurita E ...76 C1
İrurzun E ...76 C1
İrvine UK ...24 C3
İrvinestown UK ...19 B4
İsaba E ...76 D2
İsabela E ...100 A2
İ Isafjörður IS ...111 A2
İsane N ...114 F2
İsaszeg H ...75 A4
İsbister UK ...22 A7
İ Iscar E ...88 C2
İ Ischgl A ...71 A5
İschia I ...103 C6
İschia di Castro I ...102 A4
İschitella I ...104 B1
İ Isdes F ...58 C3
İsen D ...62 B2
İselle I ...70 B3
İseltwald CH ...70 B2
İserlohn D ...50 B3
İsérnia I ...103 B7
İsfjorden N ...114 E4
İsigny-sur-Mer F ...57 A4
İsjum UA ...13 A5
İskenderun TR ...16 C7
İ Iskilip TR ...16 A7
İ Isla Canela E ...98 B3
İ Isla Cristina E ...98 B3
İ Islares E ...89 A3
İsleham UK ...30 B4
İsle of Whithorn UK ...24 D3
İsmaning D ...62 B2
İsna P ...92 B3
İsnestoften N ...113 B11
İsny D ...61 C6
İsokylä FIN ...3 D28
İsokyrö FIN ...3 E25
İsola F ...79 B6
İsola d'Astì I ...80 B2
İsola del Gran Sasso
d'Italia I ...103 A6
İsola della Scala I ...71 C6
İsola delle Fémmine
I ...108 A2
İsola del Liri I ...103 B6
İsola di Capo Rizzuto
I ...107 C4
İsona E ...91 A4
İspagnac F ...78 B2
İsparta TR ...119 E5
İsperih BG ...11 E9
İspica I ...109 C3
İsselburg D ...50 B2
İ Issigeac F ...77 B3
İssogne I ...70 C2
İssoire F ...68 C3
İssoncourt F ...59 B6
İssoudun F ...68 B1
İs-sur-Tille F ...69 A5
İssy-l'Évêque F ...68 B4
İstanbul TR ...118 A4
İstebna PL ...65 A4
İ İstia d'Ombrone I ...81 D5
İstok KOS ...85 D5
İstres F ...78 C3

İstvándi H ...74 B2
İtea GR ...116 D4
İthaki GR ...117 D2
İtoiz E ...76 D1
İtrabo E ...100 C2
İttireddu I ...110 B1
İttiri I ...110 B1
İtzehoe D ...43 B6
İvalo FIN ...113 D16
İvanava BY ...11 A8
İvančane Gorica SLO ...73 C4
İvančna Gorica SLO ...73 C4
İvancsa H ...74 A3
İvanec HR ...73 B6
İvanić Grad HR ...73 C6
İvanjska BIH ...84 B2
İvanka SK ...65 B4
İvankovo HR ...84 A3
İvano-Frankivsk UA ...11 B8
İvanović na Hané CZ ...64 A3
İvanska HR ...74 C1
İvarrud N ...115 B11
İvatsevichy BY ...7 E8
İvaylovgrad BG ...116 A8
İveland N ...33 D4
İvrea I ...70 C2
İvrindi TR ...118 C2
İvry-en-Montagne F ...69 A4
İvry-la-Bataille F ...58 B2
İvybridge UK ...28 C4
İwaniska PL ...55 C6
İwiny PL ...53 B5
İwuy F ...49 C4
İxworth UK ...30 B4
İ İzarra E ...89 B4
İzbica Kujawska PL ...47 C4
İzbište SRB ...85 A5
İzeda P ...87 C4
İzegem B ...49 C4
İzernore F ...69 B5
İzmayil UA ...11 D10
İzmir TR ...119 D2
İzmit = Kocaeli TR ...118 B4
İznájar E ...100 B1
İznalloz E ...100 B2
İznatoraf E ...101 A3
İznik TR ...118 B4
İ İzola SLO ...72 C3
İ Izsák H ...75 B4
İzsófalva H ...65 B6
İzyaslav UA ...11 A9

J

Jabalquinto E ...100 A2
Jablanac HR ...83 B3
Jablanica BIH ...84 C2
Jablonec nad Jizerou
CZ ...53 C5
Jablonec nad Nisou
CZ ...53 C5
Jablonica SK ...64 B3
Jablonna PL ...55 A5
Jablonné nad Orlicí CZ ...54 C1
Jablonné
Podještědi CZ ...53 C4
Jablonov nad Turňou
SK ...65 B6
Jabłonowo Pomorskie
PL ...47 B5
Jablunka CZ ...64 A3
Jablunkov CZ ...65 A4
Jabučje SRB ...85 B5
Jabuka I ...99 B4
Jabugo E ...99 B4
Jabuka
Srbija SRB ...85 B5
Vojvodina SRB ...85 B5
Jabukovac HR ...73 C6
Jaca E ...90 A2
Jáchymov CZ ...52 C2
Jaco E ...43 C5
Jagodina SRB ...85 C6
Jagodnjak HR ...74 C3
Jagodzin PL ...53 B5
Jagotin UA ...11 A11
Jagstheim D ...61 A6
Jagstzell D ...61 A6
Jajce BIH ...84 B2
Jajkowo PL ...47 B5
Ják H ...74 A1
Jakabszállás H ...75 B4
Jäkkvik S ...115 A13
Jakobsnes N ...113 C19
Jakovlje HR ...73 C5
Jakšić HR ...74 C2
Jakubany SK ...65 A6
Jalance E ...96 B1
Jalasjärvi FIN ...3 E25
Jalhay B ...50 C1
Jaligny-sur-Besbre F ...68 B3
Jallais F ...66 A4
Jalón E ...96 C2
Jâlons F ...59 B5
Jamena SRB ...84 B4
Jamilena E ...100 B2
Jämjö S ...41 C6
Jamnička Kiselica HR ...73 C5
Jamno PL ...46 A2
Jamoigne B ...59 A6
Jämsä FIN ...3 E26
Jämshög S ...41 C4
Jämjö = Ypres B ...48 C3
Janakkala FIN ...3 F26
Jandelsbrunn D ...63 B4
Jänickendorf D ...52 A3
Janikowo PL ...47 C4
Janja BIH ...85 B4
Janja BIH ...85 B4
Janjina HR ...84 D2
Janki
Łódzkie PL ...55 B4
Mazowieckie PL ...55 A5
Jankov CZ ...63 A5
Jankovo Dolne PL ...46 C3
Jánoshalma H ...75 B4
Jánoshida H ...75 A4
Jánossomorja H ...64 C3
Janovice nad Uhlavou
CZ ...63 A4
Janów PL ...55 C4
Janowiec
Wielkopolski PL ...46 C3
Janowo PL ...47 B6
Jänsmässholmen S ...115 D10
Janville F ...58 B2
Janzé F ...57 C4
Jarabá SK ...65 B5
Jaraczewo PL ...54 B2
Jaraicejo E ...93 B5
Jaráiz de la Vera E ...93 A5
Jarak SRB ...85 B4
Jarandilla de la Vera
E ...93 A5
Jarafuel E ...96 B1
Jaramillo E ...89 B3
Jarandilla de la Vera E ...93 A5
Jaraba E ...89 C5

Jaroslav CZ ...53 C6
Jaroslavice CZ ...64 B2
Jarosław PL ...11 A7
Jarosław nad Nežarkou
CZ ...63 A6
Järpås S ...35 D4
Järpen S ...115 D10
Jarrow UK ...25 D6
Järso FIN ...36 D6
Järvenpää FIN ...3 F26
Jarvornik D ...54 C2
Järvsö S ...115 F13
Jarze F ...67 A5
Jaša Tomic SRB ...75 C5
Jasenak HR ...73 C4
Jasenica BIH ...83 B5
Jasenice HR ...83 B4
Jasenova CZ ...64 C1
Jasenovac HR ...74 C1
Jasenovo
Srbija SRB ...85 C5
Vojvodina SRB ...85 B6
Jasień PL ...53 B5
Jasienica PL ...53 B5
Jasika SRB ...85 C6
Jasło PL ...10 B6
Jásová SK ...65 C4
Jastarnia PL ...47 A4
Jastrebarsko HR ...73 C5
Jastrowie PL ...46 B2
Jastrzębia-Góra PL ...47 A4
Jastrzębie Zdrój PL ...54 D3
Jászals-
Lószentgyörgy H ...75 A5
Jászapáti H ...75 A5
Jászárokszállás H ...75 A4
Jászberény H ...75 A4
Jászdózsa H ...75 A5
Jászfényszaru H ...75 A4
Jászjakóhalma H ...75 A5
Jászkarajenő H ...75 A5
Jászkisér H ...75 A5
Jászladány H ...75 A5
Jászszentlászló H ...75 B4
Jásztelek H ...75 A5
Játar E ...100 C2
Jättendal S ...115 F14
Jatznick D ...45 B5
Jaun CH ...70 B2
Jausiers F ...79 B5
Jávea E ...96 C3
Jävenitz D ...44 C3
Javerlhac F ...67 C5
Javier E ...90 A1
Javorani BIH ...84 B2
Javorina SK ...65 A6
Javron F ...57 B5
Jawor PL ...53 B6
Jaworzno PL ...55 C4
Jaworzyna Śl. PL ...54 C1
Jayena E ...100 C2
Jażow PL ...53 B4
Jebel RO ...75 C6
Jebjerg DK ...38 C2
Jedburgh UK ...25 C5
Jedlinsk PL ...55 B6
Jedlnia Letnisko PL ...55 B6
Jednorożec PL ...47 B6
Jędrychów PL ...54 C2
Jędrzejów PL ...55 C5
Jedwabno PL ...47 B6
Jeesiö FIN ...113 E15
Jeglnik PL ...47 A5
Jegun F ...77 C3
Jekabpils LV ...7 C8
Jektevik N ...33 C2
Jektvik N ...112 E7
Jelakci SRB ...85 C6
Jelcz-Laskowice PL ...54 B2
Jelenec SK ...64 B4
Jelenia Góra PL ...53 C5
Jelgava LV ...6 C7
Jelka SK ...64 B3
Jelling DK ...39 D2
Jels DK ...39 D2
Jelsa
HR ...83 C5
N ...33 C3
Jelšava SK ...65 B6
Jemgum D ...43 B4
Jemnice CZ ...63 A6
Jena D ...52 C1
Jenaz CH ...71 B4
Jenbach A ...72 A1
Jennersdorf A ...73 B6
Jenny S ...40 B6
Jerchel D ...44 C3
Jeres del
Marquesado E ...100 B2
Jerez de la Frontera E ...99 C4
Jerez de los
Caballeros E ...99 A4
Jericho D ...44 C3
Jerichow D ...44 C4
Jerka PL ...54 B2
Jermenovci SRB ...75 C6
Jerslev DK ...38 B3
Jerte E ...93 A5
Jerup DK ...38 B3
Jerxheim D ...51 A6
Jerzmanowice PL ...55 C4
Jerzu I ...110 C2
Jerzwałd PL ...47 B5
Jesberg D ...51 B5
Jeßen D ...52 B3
Jesenice
Středočeský CZ ...52 C3
Středočeský CZ ...63 A4
SLO ...73 B4
Jeseník CZ ...54 C2
Jesenké SK ...65 B6
Jesi I ...82 C2
Jesolo I ...72 C2
Jessen D ...52 B3
Jessheim N ...34 B3
Jessnitz D ...52 B2
Jesteburg D ...44 B1
Jeumont F ...49 C5
Jeven-stedt D ...43 A6
Jever D ...43 B4
Jevičko CZ ...64 A2
Jevišovice CZ ...63 B6
Jevnaker N ...34 B2
Jezerane HR ...83 A4
Jezero
BIH ...84 B2
HR ...83 A4
Jezów PL ...55 B5
Jeżewo PL ...47 B4
Jeżowe PL ...55 C6
Jičín CZ ...53 C5
Jičíněves CZ ...53 C5
Jicmeny SLO ...73 B4
Jihlava CZ ...63 A6
Jijona E ...96 C2
Jilemnice CZ ...53 C5
Jílové CZ ...53 C4
Jílové u Prahy CZ ...53 D4
Jimbolia RO ...75 C5
Jimena E ...100 B2
Jimena de la Frontera
E ...99 C5
Jimera de Libar E ...99 C5
Jimramov CZ ...64 A2
Jince CZ ...63 A5
Jindřichovice CZ ...52 C2
Jindřichúv Hradec CZ ...63 A6
Jirkov CZ ...52 C3
Jistebnice CZ ...63 A5
Joachimsthal D ...45 C5
Jochberg A ...72 A2
Jockfall S ...113 F11
Jódar E ...100 B2
Jodoigne B ...49 C5
Joensuu FIN ...3 E28
Joesjö S ...115 B11
Jõgeva EST ...7 B8
Johanngeorgenstadt
D ...52 C2
Johannishus S ...41 C5
Kale
Antalya TR ...119 F4

Johanniskirchen D ...62 B3
Johansfors S ...40 C5
John o'Groats UK ...23 C5
Johnshaven UK ...25 B5
Johnstone UK ...24 C3
Johnstown IRL ...21 B4
Jõhvi EST ...7 B9
Joigny F ...59 C4
Joinville F ...59 B6
Jokkmokk S ...112 F8
Jölenberg D ...51 A4
Jölkrad D ...44 B1
Jomala FIN ...36 D6
Jönåker S ...37 D3
Jonava LT ...6 D8
Jonchery-sur-Vesle F ...59 A4
Jondal N ...32 B3
Jondalen N ...33 C6
Joniškis LT ...6 C7
Jönköping S ...40 B4
Jonkowo PL ...47 B6
Jönnbu N ...33 C5
Jonsberg S ...37 D3
Jonsered S ...38 B5
Jonstorp S ...41 C2
Jonzac F ...67 C4
Jordanów E ...91 A5
Jordanów PL ...65 A5
Jordanów Śląski PL ...54 C1
Jordbro S ...37 C5
Jördbrua S ...115 A11
Jördenstorf D ...45 B4
Jõrdet N ...34 A4
Jordøse DK ...39 D3
Jork D ...43 B6
Jörlanda S ...38 B4
Jormlien S ...115 C10
Jormvattnet S ...115 C11
Jörn S ...115 B17
Jörpeland N ...33 C3
Jorquera E ...96 B1
Jošan HR ...83 B4
Jošanička Banja SRB ...85 C5
Jošavka BIH ...84 B2
Josipdol HR ...73 C5
Josipovac HR ...74 C3
Jössefors S ...35 C4
Josselin F ...56 C3
Jössund N ...114 C7
Jostedal N ...32 A3
Jósvafő H ...65 B6
Jou P ...87 C3
Jouarre F ...59 B4
Joué-lès-Tours F ...67 A5
Joué-sur-Erdre F ...66 A3
Joure NL ...42 C2
Joux-la-Ville F ...59 C4
Jouy F ...58 B2
Jouy-aux-Arches F ...60 A2
Jouy-en-Josas F ...58 B3
Jouy-le-Châtel F ...59 B4
Jouy-le-Potier F ...58 C2
Joyeuse F ...78 B3
Józefów
Lubelskie PL ...11 A7
Mazowieckie PL ...55 A6
Juankoski FIN ...3 E28
Juan-les-Pins F ...79 C6
Jübar D ...44 C2
Jübek D ...43 A6
Jubrique E ...99 C5
Jüchsen D ...51 C6
Judaberg N ...33 C2
Judenburg A ...73 A4
Juelsminde DK ...39 D3
Jugon-les-Lacs F ...56 B3
Juillac F ...67 C6
Juillan F ...76 C3
Juist D ...43 B4
Jukkasjärvi S ...112 E10
Jule N ...115 C10
Julianadorp NL ...42 C1
Julianstown IRL ...19 C5
Jülich D ...50 C2
Jullouville F ...57 B4
Jumeaux F ...68 C3
Jumièges F ...58 A1
Jumilhac-le-Grand F ...67 C6
Jumilla E ...101 A4
Juncosa E ...90 B3
Juneda E ...90 B3
Jung S ...35 D4
Jungingen D ...61 B5
Jungsund FIN ...3 E24
Juniville F ...59 A5
Junosuando S ...113 E11
Junqueira P ...87 C3
Junsele S ...115 D14
Juntinvaara FIN ...3 D29
Juoksenki FIN ...113 F12
Juoksgielas FIN ...113 E12
Juprelle B ...49 C6
Jurata PL ...47 A4
Jurbarkas LT ...6 D7
Jurjevo HR ...83 B3
Jurmala LV ...6 C7
Juromenha P ...93 C3
Jursla S ...37 D3
Jüssi F ...59 B5
Jussac F ...77 B5
Jussey F ...60 C1
Jussy F ...59 A4
Juta H ...74 B2
Juuka FIN ...3 E28
Juuma FIN ...3 D29
Juustad N ...34 A1
Juvigny-le-Terte F ...57 B4
Juvigny-sous-
Andaine F ...57 B5
Juzennecourt F ...59 B5
Jyderup DK ...39 D4
Jyväskylä FIN ...3 E26

K

Kaamanen FIN ...113 C16
Kaamasmukka FIN ...113 C15
Kaaresuvanto FIN ...113 D11
Kaarssen D ...44 B3
Kaatscheuvel NL ...49 B6
Kaba H ...75 A6
Kåbdalis S ...115 A17
Kačarevo SRB ...85 B5
Kačikol KOS ...85 D6
Kačkovice CZ ...53 D5
Kadaň CZ ...52 C3
Kadarkút H ...74 B2
Kadınhanı TR ...16 B6
Kaduy RUS ...7 B14
Kåfjord N ...113 C14
Kåfjordbotn N ...112 C9
Kagárol D ...44 C4
Kågeröd S ...41 D3
Kahla D ...52 C1
Kainach bei Voitsberg
A ...73 A5
Kaindorf A ...73 A5
Kainulasjärvi S ...113 F11
Kairala FIN ...113 E16
Kaisepakte S ...112 D8
Kaisersesch D ...50 C3
Kaiserslautern D ...60 A3
Kaisheim D ...62 B1
Kajaani FIN ...3 D27
Kajárpéc H ...74 A2
Kajdacs H ...74 B3
Kakanj BIH ...84 B3
Kakasd H ...74 B3
Kakerbeck D ...44 C3
Kakolewo PL ...54 B2
Kál H ...65 C6
Kålboda S ...115 D15
Kalajoki FIN ...3 D25
Kalak N ...113 B16
Kalamata GR ...117 E4
Kalambaka GR ...116 C3
Kalamos GR ...117 D5
Kalandra GR ...116 C5
Kälarne S ...115 E13
Kalasin FIN ...113 E16
Kalavrita GR ...117 D4
Kalbe D ...44 C3
Kale
Antalya TR ...119 F4
Denizli TR ...119 E3

Kalecik TR ...16 A6
Kaléem S ...51 B6
Kalefeld D ...51 B6
Kalenić SRB ...85 C5
Kalesija BIH ...84 B3
Kalety PL ...54 C3
Kalevala RUS ...3 D29
Kalhovd N ...32 B5
Kali HR ...83 B4
Kaliningrad RUS ...47 A6
Kalinkavichy BY ...7 E10
Kalinovac HR ...74 B2
Kalinovik BIH ...84 C3
Kalinovka UA ...11 B10
Kalirachi GR ...116 B6
Kaliska
Pomorskie PL ...47 A4
Pomorskie PL ...47 B4
Kalisko PL ...55 B4
Kalisz PL ...54 B3
Kalisz Pomorski PL ...46 B1
Kaljord N ...112 D4
Kalkan TR ...119 F4
Kalkar D ...50 B2
Kalkım TR ...118 C2
Kall
D ...50 C2
S ...115 D10
Källby S ...35 D5
Kållered S ...38 B5
Källerstad S ...40 B3
Kallinge S ...41 C5
Kallmeti i Madh AL ...105 B5
Kallmünz D ...62 A2
Kallo FIN ...113 E13
Källö-Knippla S ...38 B4
Kallsedet S ...115 D9
Källvik S ...37 D4
Kalmar S ...40 C6
Kalmthout B ...49 B5
Kalna SRB ...85 C4
Kalnik HR ...83 B4
Kalocsa H ...75 B3
Kalokhorio CY ...120 B2
Kalo Nero GR ...117 E3
Kaloi Limenes GR ...117 G6
Kalókastro GR ...116 B5
Kálloní GR ...116 C7
Kalló H ...65 C5
KallsKnon S ...115 D9
Kalmar S ...40 C6
Kalocsa H ...75 B3
Kalpáki GR ...116 C2
Kals A ...72 B2
Kalsdorf A ...73 B5
Kaltbrunn CH ...70 A4
Kaltenbach A ...72 A1
Kaltenkirchen D ...44 B1
Kaltennordheim D ...51 C6
Kaluga RUS ...7 D14
Kalundborg DK ...39 D4
Kalush UA ...11 B8
Kałuszyn PL ...55 A6
Kalv S ...40 B3
Kalvåg N ...114 F1
Kalvehave DK ...41 D2
Kalwang A ...73 A4
Kalwaria
Zebrzydowska PL ...65 A5
Kalyazin RUS ...7 C14
Kam H ...74 A1
Kaman TR ...16 B6
Kamares GR ...117 F6
Kambos GR ...117 E4
Kamen D ...50 B3
Kamenec-
Podil'skyy UA ...11 B9
Kamenica SK ...65 A4
Kamenicá SK ...64 C4
Kamenný Most SK ...65 C4
Kamenny Ujezd CZ ...63 B5
Kamensko HR ...84 C1
Kamenz D ...53 B4
Kameric D ...84 C1
Kamień PL ...55 B5
Kamienica PL ...65 A6
Kamieniec Zabk PL ...54 C1
Kamienka SK ...65 A6
Kamień Krajeński PL ...46 B3
Kamień Pomorski PL ...45 B6
Kaminsk PL ...55 B4
Kamiros Skala GR ...119 F2
Kamnik SLO ...73 B4
Kampen D ...39 E1
Kampinos PL ...55 A5
Kamp-Lintfort D ...50 B2
Kampor HR ...83 B3
Kamyanets-
Podil's'kyy UA ...11 B9
Kamyanka-Buz'ka UA ...11 A8
Kamýk nad Vltavou
CZ ...63 A5
Kanal SLO ...72 B3
Kanalia GR ...116 C4
Kananaskis RUS ...3 C30
Kandalaksha RUS ...3 C30
Kandanos GR ...117 G5
Kandel D ...61 A4
Kandern D ...60 C3
Kandersteg CH ...70 B2
Kandila GR ...117 E4
Kandıra TR ...118 A5
Kanfanar HR ...82 A3
Kangasala FIN ...3 F26
Kangos S ...113 E11
Kangosjärvi FIN ...113 E12
Kanjiža SRB ...75 B5
Kankaanpää FIN ...3 F25
Kannus FIN ...3 E25
Kanturk IRL ...20 B3
Kaonik SRB ...85 C6
Kapaklı TR ...118 A2
Kapellen
A ...63 C6
B ...49 B5
Kapellskär S ...37 C6
Kapfenberg A ...73 A5
Kapfenstein A ...73 B5
Kaplice CZ ...63 B5
Kápljuh BIH ...83 B5
Kápolna H ...65 C6
Kápolnásnyék H ...74 A3
Kaposfö H ...74 B2
Kaposszekcsö H ...74 B3
Kaposvár H ...74 B2
Kápolna H ...65 C6
Kappel D ...60 C3
Kappeln D ...44 A1
Kappelshamn S ...37 E5
Kappl A ...71 A5
Kaprun A ...72 A2
Kaptol HR ...74 C2
Kapuvár H ...74 A2
Karabiga TR ...118 B2
Karaburun TR ...118 D1
Karacabey TR ...118 B3
Karacaköy TR ...118 A3
Karacaören TR ...119 D5
Karacasu TR ...119 E3
Karácsond H ...65 C6
Karádasu TR ...119 E3
Karád H ...74 B2
Karahallı TR ...119 D4
Karaisali TR ...16 C7
Karaman
Balıkesir TR ...118 C3
Karaman TR ...16 C6
Karamanlı TR ...119 E4
Karamürsel TR ...118 B4
Karan SRB ...85 C4
Karancslapujtó H ...65 B5
Karaova TR ...119 E2
Karapınar TR ...16 C6
Karasjok N ...113 C15
Karasu TR ...118 A5
Karataş TR ...16 C7
Karata
Adana TR ...16 C7
Manisa TR ...119 D3

Karatoprak TR 119 E2
Karavostasi CY 120 A1
Karbenning S 36 B3
Kårberg S 37 D1
Kårböle S 115 F12
Karbunara AL 105 C5
Karby
D 44 A1
DK 38 C1
Kårby S 40 B6
Karby S 37 C5
Karcag H 75 A5
Karczew PL 55 A6
Karczów PL 54 C2
Karczowiska PL 53 B6
Kardamena GR 119 F2
Kardamila GR 116 D8
Kardamili GR 117 F4
Kardašova Rečice CZ 63 A5
Kardis S 113 F12
Karditsa GR 116 C3
Kärdla EST 6 B7
Kardoskút H 75 B5
Kardzhali BG 15 C10
Karesuando S 113 D11
Kargı TR 16 A7
Kargowa PL 53 A5
Karigasniemi FIN 113 C14
Karise DK 41 D2
Karistos GR 117 D6
Karkkila FIN 6 A8
Karlholmsbruk S 36 B4
Karlino PL 46 A1
Karl Liebknecht RUS 7 F13
Karlobag HR 83 B4
Karlovac HR 73 C5
Karlovasi GR 119 E1
Karlovčic SRB 85 B5
Karlovice CZ 54 C2
Karlovo BG 11 E8
Karlovy Vary CZ 52 C2
Karłowice PL 54 C2
Karlsborg S 37 D1
Karlshamn S 41 C4
Karlshöfen D 43 B6
Karlshus N 35 C2
Karlskoga S 37 C1
Karlskrona S 41 C5
Karlsrud N 32 B5
Karlsruhe D 61 A4
Karlstad S 35 C5
Karlstadt D 51 D5
Karlstetten A 63 B6
Karlstift A 63 B5
Karlstorp S 40 B5
Karmacs H 74 B2
Karmin PL 54 B2
Kärna S 38 B4
Karnobat BG 11 E9
Karojba HR 72 C3
Karow D 44 B4
Karpacz PL 53 C5
Karpathos GR 119 G2
Karpenisi GR 116 D3
Karpuzlu TR 119 E2
Kärrbo S 37 C3
Karrebaeksminde DK 39 D4
Karshult S 40 B3
Karsin PL 46 B3
Kårsta S 37 C5
Karstädt D 44 B3
Kartal TR 118 B4
Kartitsch A 72 B2
Kartuzy PL 47 A4
Karup DK 39 C2
Karviná CZ 65 A4
Kås DK 38 B2
Kaş TR 119 F4
Kasaba TR 119 F4
Kašava CZ 64 A3
Kåseberga S 41 D4
Kasejovice CZ 63 A4
Kasfjord N 112 D5
Kashin RUS 7 C14
Kašina HR 73 C6
Kasina-Wielka PL 65 A6
Kaskinen FIN 3 E24
Kašperské Hory CZ 63 A4
Kassandrino GR 116 B5
Kassel D 51 B5
Kassiopi GR 116 C1
Kastamonu TR 16 A6
Kastav HR 73 C4
Kasteli GR 117 G5
Kastellaun D 50 C3
Kastelli GR 117 G7
Kaštel-Stari HR 83 C5
Kaštel Zegarski HR 83 B4
Kasterlee B 49 B5
Kastl D 62 A2
Kastlösa S 41 C6
Kastorf D 44 B2
Kastoria GR 116 B3
Kastorio GR 117 E4
Kastraki GR 117 F7
Kastrosikia GR 116 C2
Kastsyukovichy BY 7 E12
Kaszaper H 75 B5
Katakolo GR 117 E3
Katapola GR 117 F7
Katastari GR 117 E2
Katerbow D 45 C4
Katerini GR 116 B4
Kathikas CY 120 B1
Kätkesuando S 113 D12
Katlenburg-Lindau D 51 B6
Kato Achaia GR 117 D3
Káto Pyrgos CY 120 A1
Katouna GR 116 D3
Katovice CZ 63 A4
Katowice PL 55 C4
Katrineberg S 36 A3
Katrineholm S 37 D3
Kattarp S 41 C2
Kattavia GR 119 G2
Katthammarsvik S 37 E5
Kattilstorp S 40 A3
Katwijk NL 49 A5
Katymár H 75 B4
Kąty Wrocławskie PL 54 B1
Katzenelnbogen D 50 C3
Katzhütte D 52 C1
Kaub D 50 C3
Kaufbeuren D 62 C1
Kauhajoki FIN 3 E25
Kauhava FIN 3 E25
Kaukonen FIN 113 E13
Kaulsdorf D 52 C1
Kaunas LT 6 D7
Kaunisvaara S 113 E12
Kaupanger N 32 A4
Kautokeino N 113 C12
Kautzen A 63 B6
Kavadarci NMK 116 A4
Kavajë AL 105 B5
Kavakköy TR 118 B1
Kavaklı TR 118 A2
Kavaklıdere TR 119 E3
Kavala GR 116 B6
Kavarna BG 11 E10
Kävlinge S 41 D3
Kawcze PL 46 A2
Kaxås S 115 D10
Kaxholmen S 40 B4
Kaymakçı TR 119 D3
Kaymaz TR 118 C6
Kaynarca TR 118 A5
Käyrämö FIN 113 F15
Kayseri TR 16 B7
Kaysersberg F 60 B3
Kazanlak BG 11 E8
Kazár H 65 B5
Kazimierza Wielka PL 55 C5
Kazincbarcika H 65 B6
Kaźmierz PL 46 C2
Kcynia PL 46 B3
Kdyně CZ 62 A4
Kea GR 117 E6
Keadew IRL 18 B3
Keady UK 19 B5
Kecel H 75 B4
Keçiborlu TR 119 E5
Kecskemét H 75 B4
Kėdainiai LT 6 D7
Kędzierzyn-Koźle PL 54 C3
Keel IRL 18 C1
Keenagh IRL 19 C4
Keerbergen B 49 B5
Kefalos GR 119 F1
Kefken TR 118 A5
Keflavík IS 111 C3
Kegworth UK 27 C4
Kehl D 60 B3
Kehrigk D 53 A3
Keighley UK 27 B4
Keila EST 6 B8
Keillmore UK 24 C2
Keiss UK 23 C5
Keith UK 23 D6
Kelberg D 50 C2
Kelbra D 51 B7
Kelč CZ 64 A3
Kelchsau A 72 A2
Këlcyrë AL 116 B2
Keld UK 26 A3
Kelebia H 75 B4
Kelekçi TR 119 E4
Kelemér H 65 B6
Keles TR 118 C4
Kelheim D 62 B2
Kell D 60 A2
Kellas UK 23 D5
Kellinghusen D 43 B6
Kelloselkä FIN 113 F17
Kells
IRL 19 C5
UK 19 B5
Kelmis B 50 C2
Kelokedhara CY 120 B1
Kelottijärvi FIN 113 D11
Kelsall UK 26 B3
Kelso UK 25 C5
Kelsterbach D 51 C4
Keltneyburn UK 24 B3
Kelujärvi FIN 113 E16
Kemaliye TR 119 D3
Kemalpaşa TR 119 D2
Kematen A 71 A6
Kemberg D 52 B2
Kemer
Antalya TR 119 F5
Burdur TR 119 E5
Muğla TR 119 F4
Kemerkaya TR 118 D6
Kemeten A 73 A6
Kemi FIN 3 D26
Kemijärvi FIN 113 F16
Kemnath D 62 A2
Kemnay UK 23 D6
Kemnitz
Brandenburg D 52 A2
Mecklenburg-Vorpommern D 45 A5
Kempen D 50 B2
Kempsey UK 29 A5
Kempten D 61 C6
Kemptthal CH 70 A3
Kendal UK 26 A3
Kenderes H 75 A5
Kengyel H 75 A5
Kenilworth UK 30 B2
Kenmare IRL 20 C2
Kenmore UK 25 B4
Kennacraig UK 24 C2
Kenyeri H 74 A2
Kenzingen D 60 B3
Kepez TR 118 B1
Kępice PL 46 A2
Kępno PL 54 B3
Kepsut TR 118 C3
Keramoti GR 116 B6
Keräntöjärvi S 113 E12
Keratea GR 117 E5
Kerava FIN 7 A8
Kerecsend H 65 C6
Kerekegyhaza H 75 B4
Kerepestarcsa H 75 A4
Keri GR 117 E2
Kérien F 56 B2
Kerkafalva H 74 B1
Kerken D 50 B2
Kerkrade NL 50 C2
Kerkyra GR 116 C1
Kerlouan F 56 B1
Kernascléden F 56 B2
Kernhof A 63 C6
Kerns CH 70 B3
Kerpen D 50 C2
Kerrysdale UK 22 D3
Kerta H 74 A2
Kerteminde DK 39 D3
Kerzers CH 70 B2
Keşan TR 118 B1
Kesgrave UK 30 B5
Kesh UK 19 B4
Keskin TR 16 B6
Kesselfall A 72 A2
Kestenga RUS 3 D29
Keswick UK 26 A2
Keszthely H 74 B2
Kétegyháza H 75 B6
Kéthely H 74 B2
Kętrzyn PL 6 D6
Kettering UK 30 B3
Kettlewell UK 26 A3
Kęty PL 65 A5
Ketzin D 45 C4
Keula D 51 B6
Keuruu FIN 3 E26
Kevelaer D 50 B2
Kevermes H 75 B6
Kevi SRB 75 C4
Keyingham UK 27 B5
Keynsham UK 29 B5
Kežmarok SK 65 A6
Kherson UA 11 C12
Khimki RUS 7 D14
Khisinev = Chişinău
MD 11 C10
Khmelnik UA 11 B9
Khmelnytskyy UA 11 B9
Khodoriv UA 11 B8
Kholm RUS 7 C11
Khorol UA 11 B12
Khotyn UA 11 B9
Khoyniki BY 7 F10
Khust UA 11 B7
Khvoynaya RUS 7 B13
Kiato GR 117 D4
Kibæk DK 39 C1
Kiberg N 113 B19
Kicasalih TR 118 A1
Kičevo NMK 116 A2
Kidderminster UK 26 C3
Kidlington UK 31 C2
Kidsgrove UK 26 B3
Kidwelly UK 28 B3
Kiefersfelden D 62 C3
Kiel D 44 A2
Kielce PL 55 C5
Kiełczygłów PL 54 B4
Kielder UK 25 C5
Kiełpino PL 47 A4
Kielpiny PL 47 B5
Kierinki FIN 113 E14
Kiernozia PL 55 A4
Kierspe D 50 B3
Kietrz PL 54 C3
Kietz D 45 C6
Kiev = Kyyiv UA 11 A11
Kiezmark PL 47 A4
Kiffisia GR 117 D5
Kifino Selo BIH 84 C3
Kihlanki
FIN 113 E12
S 113 E12
Kiistala FIN 113 E14
Kije PL 55 C5
Kijevo HR 83 C5
Kikallen N 32 B2
Kikinda SRB 75 C5
Kil
N 33 D6
Örebro S 37 C2
Värmland S 35 C5
Kila S 35 C4
Kilafors S 36 A3
Kilbaha IRL 20 B2
Kilbeggan IRL 21 A4
Kilberry UK 24 C2
Kilbirnie UK 24 C3
Kilboghamn N 112 F2
Kilbotn N 112 D5
Kilb Rabenstein A 63 B6
Kilchattan UK 24 C2
Kilchoan UK 24 B1
Kilcock IRL 21 A5
Kilconnell IRL 20 A3
Kilcormac IRL 21 A4
Kilcreggan UK 24 C3
Kilcullen IRL 21 A5
Kilcurry IRL 19 B5
Kildare IRL 21 A5
Kildinstroy RUS 3 B30
Kildonan UK 23 C5
Kildorrery IRL 20 B3
Kilegrend N 33 C5
Kilen N 33 C5
Kilgarvan IRL 20 C2
Kiliya UA 11 D10
Kilkee IRL 20 B2
Kilkeel UK 19 B5
Kilkelly IRL 18 C3
Kilkenny IRL 21 B4
Kilkieran IRL 20 A2
Kilkinlea IRL 20 B2
Kilkis GR 116 A4
Kill IRL 21 B4
Killadysert IRL 20 B2
Killala IRL 18 B2
Killaloe IRL 20 B3
Killarney IRL 20 B2
Killashandra IRL 19 B4
Killashee IRL 19 C4
Killearn UK 24 B3
Killeberg S 40 C4
Killeigh IRL 21 A4
Killenaule IRL 21 B4
Killimor IRL 20 A3
Killin UK 24 B3
Killinaboy IRL 20 B2
Killinge S 112 E9
Killinick IRL 21 B5
Killorglin IRL 20 B2
Killucan IRL 21 A4
Killybegs IRL 18 B3
Killyleagh UK 19 B6
Kilmacrenan IRL 19 A4
Kilmacthomas IRL 21 B4
Kilmaine IRL 18 C2
Kilmallock IRL 20 B3
Kilmarnock UK 24 C3
Kilmartin UK 24 B2
Kilmaurs UK 24 C3
Kilmeadan IRL 21 B4
Kilmeedy IRL 20 B3
Kilmelford UK 24 B2
Kilmore Quay IRL 21 B5
Kilmuir UK 23 D4
Kilnaleck IRL 19 C4
Kilninver UK 24 B2
Kilpisjärvi FIN 112 C9
Kilrea UK 19 B5
Kilrush IRL 20 B2
Kilsmo S 37 C2
Kilsyth UK 24 C3
Kiltoom IRL 20 A3
Kilwinning UK 24 C3
Kimasozero RUS 3 D29
Kimi GR 116 D6
Kimolos GR 117 F6
Kimovsk RUS 7 D14
Kimratshofen D 61 C6
Kimry RUS 7 C14
Kimstad S 37 D2
Kinbrace UK 23 C5
Kincardine UK 25 B4
Kincraig UK 23 D5
Kindberg A 73 A5
Kindelbruck D 52 B1
Kingarrow IRL 18 B3
Kingisepp RUS 7 B10
Kingsbridge UK 28 C4
Kingsclere UK 31 C2
Kingscourt IRL 19 C5
King's Lynn UK 30 B4
Kingsteignton UK 29 C4
Kingston
Greater London UK 31 C3
Moray UK 23 D5
Kingston Bagpuize UK 31 C2
Kingston upon Hull
UK 27 B5
Kingswear UK 29 C4
Kingswood UK 29 B5
Kington UK 29 A4
Kingussie UK 23 D4
Kınık
Antalya TR 119 F4
İzmir TR 118 C2
Kinloch
Highland UK 22 C4
Highland UK 22 D2
Kinlochbervie UK 22 C3
Kinlochewe UK 22 D3
Kinlochleven UK 24 B3
Kinlochmoidart UK 24 B2
Kinloch Rannoch UK 24 B3
Kinloss UK 23 D5
Kinlough IRL 18 B3
Kinn N 34 B2
Kinna S 40 B2
Kinnared S 40 B3
Kinnarp S 40 A3
Kinnegad IRL 21 A4
Kinne-Kleva S 35 D5
Kinnitty IRL 21 A4
Kinrooi B 50 B1
Kinross UK 25 B4
Kinsale IRL 20 C3
Kinsarvik N 32 B3
Kintarvie UK 22 C2
Kintore UK 23 D6
Kinvarra IRL 20 A3
Kioni GR 116 D2
Kiparissia GR 117 E3
Kipfenburg D 62 B2
Kippen UK 24 B3
Kiraz TR 119 D3
Kirazlı TR 118 B1
Kirberg D 50 C4
Kirchbach
in Steiermark A 73 B5
Kirchberg
CH 70 A2
Baden-Württemberg D 61 A5
Rheinland-Pfalz D 60 A3
Kirchberg am Wechsel
A 64 C1
Kirchberg an der Pielach A 63 B6
Kirchberg in Tirol A 72 A2
Kirchbichl A 72 A2
Kirchdorf
Bayern D 63 B4
Mecklenburg-Vorpommern D 44 B3
Niedersachsen D 43 C5
Kirchdorf an der Krems A 63 C5
Kirchdorf in Tirol A 72 A2
Kirchenlamitz D 52 C1
Kirchenthumbach D 62 A2
Kirchhain D 51 C4
Kirchheim
Baden-Württemberg D 61 B5
Bayern D 61 B6
Hessen D 51 C5
Kirchheimbolanden
D 61 A4
Kirchhundem D 50 B4
Kirchlintein D 43 C6
Kirchschlag A 73 A6
Kirchweidach D 62 B3
Kirchzarten D 60 C3
Kircubbin UK 19 B6
Kireç TR 118 C3
Kırıkkale TR 16 B6
Kirillov RUS 7 B15
Kirishi RUS 7 B12
Kırka TR 118 C5
Kırkağaç TR 118 C2
Kirkbean UK 25 D4
Kirkbride UK 25 D4
Kirkby UK 26 B3
Kirkby Lonsdale UK 26 A3
Kirkby Malzeard UK 27 A4
Kirkbymoorside UK 27 A5
Kirkby Stephen UK 26 A3
Kirkcaldy UK 25 B4
Kirkcolm UK 24 D2
Kirkconnel UK 24 C3
Kirkcowan UK 24 D3
Kirkcudbright UK 24 D3
Kirkehamn N 33 D3
Kirke Hyllinge DK 39 D4
Kirkenær N 34 B4
Kirkenes N 113 C19
Kirkham UK 26 B3
Kirkintilloch UK 24 C3
Kirkjubæjarklaustur
IS 111 D7
Kirkkonummi FIN 6 A8
Kırklareli TR 118 A2
Kirkmichael UK 25 B4
Kirk Michael UK 26 A1
Kirkoswald UK 24 C3
Kirkpatrick Fleming
UK 25 C4
Kirkton of Glenisla UK 25 B4
Kirkwall UK 23 C6
Kirkwhelpington UK 25 C6
Kirn D 60 A3
Kiro AL 105 A5
Kirov RUS 7 D13
Kirovohrad UA 11 B12
Kirovsk RUS 3 C30
Kirriemuir UK 25 B5
Kırşehir TR 16 B7
Kirton UK 30 B3
Kirton in Lindsey UK 27 B5
Kirtorf D 51 C5
Kiruna S 112 E9
Kisa S 40 B5
Kisač SRB 75 C4
Kisbér H 74 A3
Kiseljak BIH 84 C3
Kisielice PL 47 B5
Kisköre H 75 A5
Kiskőrös H 75 B4
Kiskunfélegyháza H 75 B4
Kiskunhalas H 75 B4
Kiskunlacháza H 75 A3
Kiskunmajsa H 75 B4
Kisláng H 74 B3
Kisslegg D 61 C5
Kissolt H 75 B4
Kissónerga CY 120 B1
Kist D 61 A5
Kistanje HR 83 C4
Kistelek H 75 B4
Kisterenye H 65 B5
Kisújszállás H 75 A5
Kisvárda H 11 B7
Kisvejke H 74 B3
Kiszkowo PL 46 C3
Kiszombor H 75 B5
Kitee FIN 3 E29
Kithnos GR 117 E6
Kiti CY 120 B2
Kitkiöjärvi S 113 E12
Kitkiöjoki S 113 E12
Kittelfjäll S 115 B12
Kittendorf D 45 B4
Kittilä FIN 113 E13
Kittlitz D 53 B4
Kittsee A 64 B3
Kitzbühel A 72 A2
Kitzingen D 61 A6
Kiuruvesi FIN 3 E27
Kivertsi UA 11 A8
Kividhes CY 120 B1
Kivik S 41 D4
Kivotos GR 116 B3
Kiwity PL 47 A6
Kıyıköy TR 118 A3
Kızılcabölük TR 119 E4
Kızılcadağ TR 119 E4
Kızılcahamam TR 16 A6
Kızılırmak TR 16 A6
Kızılkaya TR 119 E5
Kızılkuyu TR 118 D6
Kızılören
Afyon TR 119 D5
Konya TR 119 E7
Kjeldebotn N 112 D5
Kjellerup DK 39 C2
Kjellmyra N 34 B4
Kjøllefjord N 113 B16
Kjopmannskjaer N 35 C2
Kjøpsvik N 112 D5
Kl'ačno SK 65 B4
Kladanj BIH 84 B3
Kläden D 44 C3
Klädesholmen S 38 B4
Kladnica SRB 85 C5
Kladnice HR 83 C5
Kladno CZ 53 C4
Kladruby CZ 62 A3
Klagenfurt A 73 B4
Klågerup S 41 D3
Klagstorp S 41 D3
Klaipėda LT 6 D6
Klaistow D 52 A2
Klaksvík FO 2 E10
Klana HR 73 C4
Klanac HR 83 B4
Klanjec HR 73 B5
Klardorf D 62 A3
Klarup DK 38 B3
Klašnice BIH 84 B2
Klässbol S 35 C4
Klášterec nad Ohří
CZ 52 C3
Kláštor pod Znievom
SK 65 B4
Klatovy CZ 63 A4
Klaus an der Pyhrnbahn A 63 C5
Klazienaveen NL 42 C3
Kłecko PL 46 C3
Kleczew PL 47 C4
Klein Plasten D 45 B4
Klein Sankt Paul A 73 B4
Kleinsölk A 72 A3
Kleinzell A 64 C1
Klejtrup DK 38 C2
Klek SRB 75 C5
Klemensker DK 41 D4
Klenak SRB 85 B4
Klenci pod Cerchovem CZ 62 A3
Klenica PL 53 B5
Klenje SRB 85 B4
Klenoec NMK 116 A2
Klenovec SK 65 B5
Klenovica HR 83 A3
Klenovnik HR 73 B6
Kleppe N 33 D2
Kleppestø N 32 B2
Kleptow D 45 B5
Kletnya RUS 7 E12
Kleve D 50 B2
Klevshult S 40 B4
Klewki PL 47 B6
Kličevac SRB 85 B6
Kliening A 73 B4
Klietz D 44 C4
Klikuszowa PL 65 A5
Klimkovice CZ 64 A4
Klimontów PL 55 C6
Klimovichi BY 7 E11
Klimpfjäll S 115 B11
Klin RUS 7 C14
Klina KOS 85 D5
Klinča Sela HR 73 C5
Klingenbach A 64 C2
Klingenberg D 61 A5
Klingenmunster D 61 A4
Klingenthal D 52 C2
Klinken D 44 B3
Klintehamn S 37 E5
Klintsy RUS 7 E12
Kliny PL 55 B5
Kliplev DK 39 E2
Klippan S 41 C3
Klis HR 83 C5
Klitmøller DK 38 B1
Klitten S 34 A6
Klixbüll D 39 E1
Kljajićevo SRB 75 C4
Ključ BIH 83 B5
Klobouky CZ 64 B2
Kłobuck PL 54 C3
Klockestrand S 115 E14
Kłodawa
Lubuskie PL 45 C7
Wielkopolskie PL 54 A3
Kłodzko PL 54 C1
Kløfta N 34 B3
Klokkarvik N 32 B2
Klokkerholm DK 38 B3
Klokočov SK 65 A4
Kłomnice PL 55 C4
Klonowa PL 54 B3
Kloosterzande NL 49 B5
Kłopot PL 53 A4
Klos AL 116 A2
Kloštar Ivanić HR 73 C6
Kloster
D 45 A5
DK 39 C1
Klösterle A 71 A5
Klostermansfeld D 52 B1
Klosterneuburg A 64 B2
Klosters CH 71 B4
Kloten CH 70 A3
Klötze D 44 C3
Klövsjö S 115 E11
Kluczbork PL 54 C3
Kluczewo PL 46 B2
Kluisbergen B 49 C4
Klundert NL 49 B5
Klutz D 44 B3
Klwów PL 55 B5
Klyetsk BY 7 E9
Knaben N 33 D3
Knaften S 115 C15
Knapstad N 35 C3
Knäred S 40 C3
Knaresborough UK 27 A4
Knarvik N 32 B2
Knebel DK 39 C3
Knebworth UK 31 C3
Knesebeck D 44 C2
Knesselare B 49 B4
Knežak SLO 73 C4
Kneževi Vinogradi HR 74 C3
Kneževo HR 74 C3
Knić SRB 85 C5
Knighton UK 29 A4
Knin HR 83 B5
Knislinge S 41 C4
Knittelfeld A 73 A4
Knivsta S 37 C4
Knock IRL 18 C3
Knocktopher IRL 21 B4
Knokke-Heist B 49 B4
Knowle UK 30 B2
Knurów PL 54 C3
Knutby S 36 C5
Knutsford UK 26 B3
Kobarid SLO 72 B3
København = Copenhagen DK 41 D2
Kobenz A 73 A4
Kobersdorf A 64 C2
Kobiernice PL 65 A5
Kobierzyce PL 54 C1
Kobilje SLO 73 B6
Kobiór PL 54 C3
Koblenz
CH 61 C4
D 50 C3
Kobryn BY 6 E8
Kobylanka PL 45 B6
Kobylin PL 54 B2
Kobyłka PL 55 A6
Kobylniki PL 47 C6
Kocaali TR 118 A5
Kocaaliler TR 119 E5
Kocaeli = İzmit TR 118 B4
Kočani NMK 11 F7
Koçarlı TR 119 E2
Koceljevo SRB 85 B4
Kočerin BIH 84 C2
Kočevje SLO 73 C4
Kočevska Reka SLO 73 C4
Kochel am see D 62 C2
Kocs H 64 C4
Kocsér H 75 A4
Kocsola H 74 B3
Koczala PL 46 B3
Kodal N 35 C2
Kode S 38 B4
Kodersdorf D 53 B4
Kodrab PL 55 B4
Koekelare B 48 B3
Kofçaz TR 118 A2
Köflach A 73 A5
Køge DK 41 D2
Kohlberg D 62 A3
Kohtla-Järve EST 7 B9
Köinge S 40 B2
Kojetín CZ 64 A3
Kökar FIN 36 C7
Kokava SK 65 B5
Kokkinotrimithia CY 120 A2
Kokkola FIN 3 E25
Kokori BIH 84 B2
Kokoski PL 47 A4
Koksijde B 48 B3
Kola
BIH 84 B2
RUS 3 B30
Köla S 34 C4
Kołacin PL 55 B4
Kolari FIN 113 E12
Kolárovo SK 64 C3
Kolašin MNE 85 D4
Kolbäck S 37 C3
Kolbacz PL 45 B6
Kolbeinsstaðir IS 111 C3
Kolbermoor D 62 C3
Kołbiel PL 55 A6
Kolbnitz A 72 B3
Kolbotn N 34 C2
Kolbu N 34 B2
Kolby Kås DK 39 D3
Kolczewo PL 45 B6
Kolczyglowy PL 46 A3
Kolding DK 39 D2
Kölesd H 74 B3
Kolgrov N 32 A1
Kolín CZ 53 C5
Kolind DK 39 C3
Kolinec CZ 63 A4
Koljane HR 83 C5
Kølkær DK 39 C2
Kölleda D 52 B1
Kollum NL 42 B3
Köln = Cologne D 50 C2
Koło PL 54 A3
Kołobrzeg PL 46 A1
Kolochau D 52 B3
Kolomyya UA 11 B8
Kolonje AL 105 C5
Kolonowskie PL 54 C3
Koloveč CZ 62 A4
Kolpino RUS 7 B11
Kolpny RUS 7 E14
Kolrep D 44 B4
Kölsillre S 115 E12
Kolsko PL 53 B5
Kolsva S 37 C2
Kolta SK 65 B4
Kolunič BIH 83 B5
Koluszki PL 55 B4
Kolut SRB 75 C3
Kolvereid N 114 C8
Kølvrå DK 39 C2
Komagvær N 113 B19
Koman AL 105 A5
Komarica BIH 84 B2
Komárno SK 64 C4
Komárom H 64 C4
Komatou Yialou CY 120 A3
Komboti GR 116 C3
Komen SLO 72 C3
Komin HR 84 C2
Komiža HR 83 C5
Komjáti H 65 B6
Komjatice SK 64 B4
Komletinci HR 75 C3
Komló H 74 B3
Kömlo H 65 C6
Komoča SK 64 C4
Komorane KOS 85 D5
Komorniki PL 54 A1
Komorzno PL 54 B3
Komotini GR 116 A7
Konak SRB 75 C5
Konakovo RUS 7 C14
Konary PL 55 B6
Konarzyny PL 46 B3
Kondias GR 116 C7
Kondorfa H 73 B6
Kondoros H 75 B5
Kondrovo RUS 7 D13
Køng DK 39 D4
Konga S 40 C5
Köngäs FIN 113 E13
Kongerslev DK 38 C3
Kongsberg N 35 C1
Kongshamn N 33 D5
Kongsmark DK 39 D1
Kongsmoen N 115 C9
Kongsvik N 112 D5
Kongsvinger N 34 B4
Konice CZ 64 A2
Konie PL 55 B5
Koniecpol PL 55 C4
Königsberg D 51 C6
Königsbronn D 61 B6
Königsbrück D 53 B3
Königsbrunn D 62 B1
Konigsdorf D 62 C2
Königsee D 52 C1
Königshorst D 45 C4
Königslutter D 51 A6
Königssee D 62 C3
Königstein
Hessen D 51 C4
Sachsen D 53 C4
Königstetten A 64 B2
Königswartha D 53 B4
Königswiesen A 63 B5
Königswinter D 50 C3
Königs Wusterhausen D 52 A3
Konin PL 54 A3
Konispol AL 116 C2
Konitsa GR 116 B2
Köniz CH 70 B2
Konjevići BIH 85 B4
Konjevrate HR 83 C5
Konjic BIH 84 C2
Konjščina HR 73 B6
Könnern D 52 B1
Konnerud N 35 C2
Konopiska PL 54 C3
Konotop
PL 53 B5
UA 7 F12
Końskie PL 55 B5
Konsmo N 33 D4
Konstancin-Jeziorna
PL 55 A6
Konstantynów Łódzki PL 55 B4
Konstanz D 61 C5
Kontich B 49 B5
Kontiolahti FIN 3 E28
Konya TR 119 E7
Konz D 60 A2
Kópasker IS 111 A9
Kópavogur IS 111 C4
Kopčany SK 64 B3
Koper SLO 72 C3
Kopervik N 33 C2
Kópháza H 64 C2
Kopice PL 54 C2
Kopidlno CZ 53 C5
Köping S 37 C2
Köpingebro S 41 D3
Köpingsvik S 41 C6
Koplik AL 105 A5
Köpmanholmen S 115 D15
Koppang N 34 A3
Koppangen N 112 C9
Kopparberg S 36 C1
Koppelo FIN 113 D16
Koppom S 35 C4
Koprivlen BG 116 A5
Koprivna BIH 84 B3
Koprivnica HR 74 B1
Kopřivnice CZ 64 A4
Köprübaşı TR 118 D3
Koprzywnica PL 55 C6
Kopstal L 60 A2
Kopychyntsi UA 11 B8
Kopytkowo PL 47 B4
Korbach D 51 B4
Körbecke D 50 B4
Korçë AL 116 B2
Korčula HR 84 D2
Korczyców PL 53 A4
Korenevo RUS 7 F13
Korenica HR 83 B4
Korenita SRB 85 B4
Korets UA 11 A9
Korfantów PL 54 C2
Körfez TR 118 B4
Korgen N 115 A10
Korinth DK 39 D3
Korinthos = Corinth
GR 117 E4
Korita
BIH 83 B5
HR 84 D2
Korithi GR 117 E2
Korkuteli TR 119 E5
Körmend H 74 A1
Korne PL 46 A3
Korneuburg A 64 B2
Kornevo RUS 47 A6
Kórnik PL 54 A2
Kornsjø N 35 D3
Környe H 74 A3
Koromačno HR 82 B3
Koroni GR 117 F3
Koronos GR 117 E7
Koronowo PL 46 B3
Körösladány H 75 B6
Köröstarcsa H 75 B6
Korosten UA 11 A10
Korostyshev UA 11 A10
Korpilombolo S 113 F12
Korsberga
Jönköping S 40 B5
Skaraborg S 35 D6
Korshavn N 35 C2
Korskrogen S 115 F12
Korsnäs S 36 B2
Korsør DK 39 D4
Korsun Shevchenkovskiy
UA 11 B11
Kortrijk B 49 C4
Korucu TR 118 C2
Koryčany CZ 64 A3
Koryukovka UA 7 F12
Korzeńsko PL 54 B1
Korzybie PL 46 A2
Kos GR 119 F2
Kosakowo PL 47 A4
Kosanica MNE 85 C4
Kosaya Gora RUS 7 D14
Kösching D 62 B2
Kościan PL 54 A1
Kościelec PL 54 A3
Kościerzyna PL 46 A3
Koserow D 45 A5
Košetice CZ 63 A6
Košice SK 10 B6
Kosjerić SRB 85 C4
Koška HR 74 C3
Koskullskulle S 112 E9
Kosovska Mitrovica
KOS 85 D5
Kosta S 40 C5
Kostajnica
BIH 74 C1
HR 74 C1
Kostajnik SRB 85 B4
Kostanica MNE 105 A5
Kostanjevica SLO 73 C5
Kostelec nad Černými Lesy CZ 53 D4
Kostelec na Hané CZ 64 A3
Kostice CZ 53 C3
Kostkowo PL 47 A4
Kostojevići SRB 85 B4
Kostolac SRB 85 B6
Kostomłoty PL 54 B1
Kostopil UA 11 A9
Kostów PL 54 B3
Kostrzyn
Lubuskie PL 45 C6
Wielkopolskie PL 46 C3
Koszalin PL 46 A2
Koszęcin PL 54 C3
Kőszeg H 74 A1
Koszwaly PL 47 A4
Koszyce PL 55 C5
Kot SLO 73 C5
Kotala FIN 113 E17
Kotë AL 105 C5
Kötelek H 75 A5
Köthen D 52 B1
Kotka FIN 7 A9
Kotomierz PL 47 B4
Kotor MNE 105 A4
Kotoriba HR 74 B1
Kotorsko BIH 84 B3
Kotor Varoš BIH 84 B2
Kotovsk UA 11 C10
Kotraža SRB 85 C5
Kotronas GR 117 F4
Kötschach A 72 B2
Kötzting D 62 A3
Koudum NL 42 C2
Kouřim CZ 53 C4
Kout na Šumave CZ 62 A4
Kouvola FIN 3 F27
Kovačevac SRB 85 B5
Kovačica SRB 85 A5
Kovdor RUS 3 C29
Kovel' UA 11 A8
Kovilj SRB 75 C5
Kovin SRB 85 B5
Kovren MNE 85 C4
Kowal PL 47 C5
Kowalewo Pomorskie
PL 47 B4
Kowalów PL 45 C6
Kowary PL 53 C5
Köyceğiz TR 119 F3
Kozan TR 16 C7
Kozani GR 116 B3
Kozarac
BIH 84 B1
HR 73 C5
Kozárovce SK 65 B4
Kozarska Dubica BIH 74 C1
Kozelets UA 11 A11
Kozelsk RUS 7 D13
Kozica HR 84 C2
Koziegłowy PL 55 C4
Kozienice PL 55 B6
Kozina SLO 72 C3
Kozje SLO 73 B5
Kozlu TR 118 A6
Kozluk BIH 85 B4
Koźmin PL 54 B2
Koźminek PL 54 B3
Kozolupy CZ 63 A4
Kożuchów PL 53 B5
Kožuhe BIH 84 B3
Kozyatyn UA 11 B10
Kozyürük TR 118 A1
Krackow D 45 B6
Kraddsele S 115 B13
Krąg PL 46 A2
Kragenæs DK 39 E4
Kragerø N 33 D6
Krągi PL 46 B2
Kragujevac SRB 85 B5
Kraiburg D 62 B3
Krajenka PL 46 B2
Krajišnik SRB 75 C5
Krajková CZ 52 C2
Krajné SK 64 B3
Krajnik Dolny PL 45 B6
Krakača BIH 83 A4
Kräklingbo S 37 E5
Kraków = Cracow PL 55 C4
Krakow am See D 44 B4
Králíky CZ 54 C1
Kraljevica HR 73 C4
Kraljevo SRB 85 C5
Kral'ovany SK 65 A5
Král'ov Brod SK 64 B3
Kralovice CZ 52 D3
Kralupy nad Vltavou
CZ 53 C4
Králův Dvůr CZ 63 A5
Kramfors S 115 E14
Kramsach A 72 A1
Kramsk PL 54 A3
Kråmvik N 32 C5
Kranenburg D 50 B2
Krania GR 116 C3
Krania Elasonas GR 116 C4
Kranichfeld D 52 C1
Kranidi GR 117 E5
Kranj SLO 73 B4
Kranjska Gora SLO 72 B3
Krapanj HR 83 C4
Krapina HR 73 B5
Krapje HR 74 C1
Krapkowice PL 54 C2
Kraselov CZ 63 A4
Krašić HR 73 C5
Krāslava LV 7 D9
Kraslice CZ 52 C2
Krasna PL 55 B5
Krasna Lipa CZ 53 C4
Kraśnik PL 11 A7
Krašnja SLO 73 B4
Krásno SK 65 A4
Krásnohorské Podhradie SK 65 B6
Krasno Polje HR 83 B4
Krasnozavodsk RUS 7 C15
Krasnystaw PL 11 A7
Krasnyy RUS 7 D11
Krasnyy Kholm RUS 7 B14
Krasocin PL 55 C5
Kraszewice PL 54 B3
Kraszkowice PL 54 B3
Kratigos GR 118 C1
Kraubath A 73 A4
Krausnick D 53 A3
Krautheim D 61 A5
Kravaře CZ 53 C4
Kraváre CZ 64 A4
Kravarsko HR 73 C6
Kraznějov CZ 63 A4
Krčedin SRB 75 C5
Kŭrdzhali BG 116 A7
Krefeld D 50 B2
Kregme DK 39 D5
Krembz D 44 B3
Kremenchuk UA 11 B12
Kremenets UA 11 A8
Kremmen D 45 C5
Kremna SRB 85 C4
Kremnica SK 65 B4
Krempe D 43 B6
Krems A 63 B6
Kremsbrücke A 72 B3
Kremsmünster A 63 B5
Křemže CZ 63 B5
Křenov CZ 64 A2
Krepa PL 54 B3
Krępa Krajeńska PL 46 B2
Krepsko PL 46 B2
Kreševo BIH 84 C3
Kressbronn D 61 C5
Krestena GR 117 E3
Kretinga LT 6 D6
Krettsy RUS 7 B12
Kreuth D 62 C2
Kreuzau D 50 C2
Kreuzlingen CH 61 C5
Kreuztal D 50 C3
Krewelin D 45 C5
Krezluk BIH 84 B2
Krieglach A 73 A5
Kriegsfeld D 60 A3
Kriens CH 70 A3
Krimml A 72 A2
Krimpen aan de IJssel
NL 49 B5
Křinec CZ 53 C5
Kristdala S 40 B6
Kristiansand N 33 D5
Kristianstad S 41 C4
Kristiansund N 114 D4
Kristiinankaupunki
FIN 3 E24
Kristinefors S 34 B4
Kristinehamn S 35 C6
Kriváň SK 65 B5
Křivoklát CZ 53 C3
Krivoy Rog = Kryvyy Rih
UA 11 C12
Križ HR 74 C1
Křižanov CZ 64 A2
Križevci HR 74 B1
Krk HR 83 A3
Krka SLO 73 C4
Krnjača SRB 85 B5
Krnjak HR 73 C5
Krnjeuša BIH 83 B5
Krnjevo SRB 85 B6
Krnov CZ 54 C2
Krobia PL 54 B1
Kroczyce PL 55 C4
Krøderen N 34 B1
Krokees GR 117 F4
Krokek S 37 D3
Krokom S 115 D11
Krokowa PL 47 A4
Krokstad-elva N 34 C1
Kroksund N 35 C3
Krolevets UA 7 F12
Kroměříž CZ 64 A3
Krommenie NL 42 C1
Krompachy SK 65 B6
Kromy RUS 7 E13
Kronach D 52 C1
Kronshagen D 44 A2
Kronshtadt RUS 7 B10
Kröpelin D 44 A3
Kropp D 43 A6
Kroppenstedt D 52 B1
Kropstädt D 52 B2
Krościenko nad Dunajcem PL 65 A6
Kröslin D 45 A5
Krośnice PL 54 B2
Krośniewice PL 55 A4
Krosno PL 10 B6
Krosno Odrzańskie PL 53 A5
Krostitz D 52 B2
Krotoszyn PL 54 B2
Krottendorf A 73 A5
Krouna CZ 64 A2
Krowiarki PL 54 C3
Krrabë AL 105 B5
Kršan HR 73 C4
Krško SLO 73 C5
Krstac MNE 84 C3
Krstur SRB 75 B5
Křtiny CZ 64 A2
Kruft D 50 C3
Kruishoutem B 49 C4
Krujë AL 105 B5
Krulyewshchyna BY 7 D9
Krumbach
A 73 A6
D 61 B6
Krumovgrad BG 116 A7
Krün D 71 A6
Krupá CZ 53 C3
Krupa na Vrbasu BIH 84 B2
Krupanj SRB 85 B4
Krupina SK 65 B5
Krupka CZ 53 C3
Krupki BY 7 D10
Kruså DK 39 E2
Krušćica BIH 84 B2
Kruševac SRB 85 C6
Kruševo NMK 116 A3
Kruszwica PL 47 C4
Kruszyn PL 47 C5
Krute MNE 105 A5
Krychaw BY 7 E11
Krynica PL 65 A6
Krynica Morska PL 47 A5
Kryvyy Rih = Krivoy Rog UA 11 C12
Krzęcin PL 46 B1
Krzelów PL 54 B1
Krzepice PL 54 C3
Krzepielów PL 53 B6
Krzeszowice PL 55 C4
Krzeszyce PL 45 C7
Krzynowlaga Mała
PL 47 B6
Krzywiń PL 54 B1
Krzyżanowice PL 54 D3
Krzyżowa PL 65 A5
Krzyż Wielkopolski
PL 46 C2
Ksiaz Wielkopolski PL 55 C5
Książ Wielkopolski
PL 54 A2
Ktębowiec PL 46 B2
Kübekháza H 75 B5
Küblis CH 71 B4
Kuç AL 105 C5
Kuchary PL 54 B2
Kuchl A 63 C4
Kucice PL 47 C6
Kuciste HR 84 D2
Kućište KOS 85 D5
Kuçovë AL 105 C5
Küçükbahçe TR 118 D1
Küçükköy TR 118 C1
Küçükkuyu TR 118 C1
Kucura SRB 75 C4
Kuczbork-Osada PL 47 B6
Kuddby S 37 D3
Kudowa-Zdrój PL 53 C6
Kufstein A 62 C3
Kuggeboda S 41 C5
Kuggörana S 115 F14
Kühbach D 62 B2
Kuhmo FIN 3 D28
Kuhmoinen FIN 3 F26
Kuhnsdorf A 73 B4
Kuhstedt D 43 B5
Kuinre NL 42 C2
Kuivastu EST 6 B7
Kukës AL 10 E6
Kuklin PL 47 B6
Kukljica HR 83 B4
Kukujevci SRB 85 A4
Kula
Srbija SRB 85 B6
Vojvodina SRB 75 C4
TR 119 D3
Kuldīga LV 6 C6
Kulen Vakuf BIH 83 B5
Kulina BIH 84 B3
Kullstedt D 51 B6
Kulmain D 62 A2
Kulmbach D 52 C1
Kulu TR 16 B6
Kumafşarı TR 119 E4
Kumane SRB 75 C5
Kumanovo NMK 10 E6
Kumbağ TR 118 B2
Kumdanlı TR 119 D5
Kumkale TR 118 C1
Kumla S 37 C2
Kumlakyrkby S 36 C3
Kumlinge FIN 36 B7
Kumluca TR 119 F5
Kumrovec HR 73 B5
Kunadacs H 75 B4
Kunágota H 75 B6
Kunbaja H 75 B4
Kunda EST 7 B9
Kundl A 72 A1
Kunes N 113 B15
Kunfehértó H 75 B4
Kungälv S 38 B4
Kungsängen S 37 C4
Kungsäter S 40 B2
Kungsbacka S 38 B5
Kungsgården S 36 B3
Kungshamn S 35 D3
Kungs-Husby S 37 C4
Kungsör S 37 C3
Kunhegyes H 75 A5
Kunmadaras H 75 A5
Kunovice CZ 64 A3
Kunów PL 55 C6
Kunowo
Wielkopolskie PL 54 B2
Zachodnio-Pomorskie PL 45 B6
Kunštát CZ 64 A2
Kunszállás H 75 B4
Kunszentmárton H 75 B5
Kunszentmiklós H 75 A4
Kunžak CZ 63 A6
Künzelsau D 61 A5
Kuolayarvi RUS 113 F18
Kuopio FIN 3 E27
Kuosku FIN 113 E17
Kup
H 74 A2
PL 54 C2
Kupa H 65 B6
Kupari HR 84 D3
Kupci SRB 85 C6
Kupferzell D 61 A5
Kupinec HR 73 C5
Kupinečki Kraljevac
HR 73 C5
Kupinovo SRB 85 B5
Kupirovo HR 83 B5
Kupjak HR 73 C4
Kuppenheim D 61 B4
Kupres BIH 84 C2
Küps D 52 C1
Kurbnesh AL 105 B6
Kurd H 74 B3
Küre TR 16 A6
Kuressaare EST 6 B7
Kurikka FIN 3 E25
Kuřim CZ 64 A2
Kuřivody CZ 53 C4
Kurki PL 47 B6
Kurort Oberwiesenthal D 52 C2
Kurort Schmalkalden
D 51 C6
Kurort Stolberg D 51 B6
Kurort Wippra D 52 B1
Kurów PL 11 A7
Kurowice PL 55 B4
Kurravaara S 112 E9
Kursk RUS 7 F14
Kursu FIN 113 F17
Kuršumlija SRB 85 C6
Kuršumlijska Banja
SRB 85 C6
Kurşunlu
Bursa TR 118 B4
Çankırı TR 16 A6
Kurtakko FIN 113 E13
Kürten D 50 B3
Kurucaşile TR 16 A6
Kurzelów PL 55 C4
Kusadak SRB 85 B5
Kuşadası TR 119 E2
Kusel D 60 A3
Kusey D 44 C3
Küsnacht CH 70 A3
Kütahya TR 118 C4
Kutenholz D 43 B6
Kutina HR 74 C1
Kutjevo HR 74 C2
Kutná Hora CZ 53 D5
Kutno PL 55 A4
Kuttara FIN 113 D15
Küttingen CH 70 A3
Kúty SK 64 B3
Kuusamo FIN 3 D28
Kuusankoski FIN 3 F27
Kuvshinovo RUS 7 C13
Kuyucak TR 119 E3
Kuzmin SRB 85 A4
Kuźnia Raciborska PL 54 C3
Kuźnica Czarnkowska PL 46 C2
Kuźnica Żelichowska
PL 46 C2
Kvaløysletta N 112 C7
Kvalsund N 113 B12
Kvam
Nord-Trøndelag N 114 C8
Oppland N 114 F6
Kvamsøy N 32 A3
Kvænangsbotn N 113 C11
Kvanndal N 32 B3
Kvänum S 35 D5
Kværndrup DK 39 D3
Kvås N 33 D4
Kvasice CZ 64 A3
Kvelde N 35 C1
Kvenna N 114 E5
Kvernaland N 33 D2
Kvibille S 40 C2
Kvicksund S 37 C3
Kvidinge S 41 C3
Kvikkjokk S 112 F6
Kvikne N 114 E7
Kvilda CZ 63 A4
Kville S 35 D3
Kvillsfors S 40 B5
Kvinlog N 33 D3
Kvinnherad N 32 C3
Kvissel DK 38 B3
Kvissleby S 115 E14
Kviteseid N 33 C5
Kvitsøy N 33 C2
Kwakowo PL 46 A3
Kwidzyn PL 47 B4
Kwilcz PL 46 C2
Kyjov CZ 64 B3
Kyleakin UK 22 D3
Kyle of Lochalsh UK 22 D3
Kylerhea UK 22 D3
Kylestrome UK 22 C3
Kyllburg D 50 C2
Kyllini GR 117 E3
Kynšperk nad Ohří
CZ 52 C2
Kyperounda CY 120 B1
Kyrenia CY 120 A2
Kyritz D 44 C4
Kyrkesund S 38 A4
Kyrkhult S 41 C4
Kyrksæterøra N 114 D6
Kysucké Nové Mesto
SK 65 A4
Kythira GR 117 F4
Kythréa CY 120 A2
Kyustendil BG 11 E7
Kyyiv = Kiev UA 11 A11
Kyyjärvi FIN 3 E26

L

Laa an der Thaya A 64 B2
La Adrada E 94 B2
Laage D 44 B4
La Alameda E 100 A2
La Alberca E 93 A4
La Alberca de Záncara
E 95 C4
La Albergueria de Argañán E 93 A4
La Albuera E 93 C4
La Aldea del Portillo del Busto E 89 B3
La Algaba E 99 B4
La Aliseda de Tormes
E 93 A5
La Almarcha E 95 C4
La Almolda E 90 B2
La Almunia de Doña Godina E 89 C5
Laanila FIN 113 D16
La Antillas E 98 B3
La Arena E 86 A4
Laatzen D 51 A5
La Aulaga E 99 B4
La Balme-de-Sillingy
F 69 C6
La Bañeza E 88 B1
La Barca de la Florida
E 99 C5
La Barre-de-Monts F 66 B2
La Barre-en-Ouche F 58 B1
La Barrosa E 99 C4
La Barthe-de-Neste F 77 C3
La Bassée F 48 C3
La Bastide-de-Sèrou
F 77 C4
La Bastide-des-Jourdans F 79 C4
Labastide-Murat F 77 B4
La Bastide-Puylaurent F 78 B2
Labastide-Rouairoux
F 77 C5
Labastide-St Pierre F 77 C4
La Bathie F 69 C6
Lábatlan H 65 C4
La Baule-Escoublac F 66 A2
La Bazoche-Gouet F 58 B1
La Bégude-de-Mazenc F 78 B3
Labenne F 76 C1
La Bernerie-en-Retz F 66 A2
Labin HR 82 A3
La Bisbal d'Empordà
E 91 B6
Łabiszyn PL 46 C3
Lablachère F 78 B3
Lábod H 74 B2
Laboe D 44 A2
La Boissière F 57 A6
Labouheyre F 76 B2
La Bourboule F 68 C2
La Bóveda de Toro E 88 C1
Łabowa PL 65 A6
La Brède F 76 B2
La Bresse F 60 B2
La Bridoire F 69 C5
La Brillanne F 79 C4
Labrit F 76 B2
Labros E 95 A5
La Bruffière F 66 A3
Labruguière F 77 C5
Labrujo P 87 C2
L'Absie F 67 B4
La Bussière F 58 C3
Laç AL 105 B5
La Caillère F 66 B4
Lacalahorra E 100 B2
La Caletta
Cágliari I 110 C1
Núoro I 110 B2
La Calmette F 78 C3
La Calzada de Oropesa E 93 B5
La Campana E 99 B5
La Cañada E 94 B2
Lacanau F 76 B1
Lacanau-Océan F 76 A1
Lacanche F 69 A4
La Canourgue F 78 B2
La Capelle F 49 D4
Lacapelle-Marival F 77 B4
Laćarak SRB 85 A4
La Cardanchosa E 99 A5
La Caridad E 86 A4
La Carlota E 100 B1
La Carolina E 100 A2
Lacaune F 78 C1
La Cava E 90 C3
La Cavalerie F 78 B2
Laceby UK 27 B5
Lacedónia I 103 B8
La Celle-en-Moravan F 69 A4
La Celle-St Avant F 67 A5
La Cerca E 89 B3
Láces I 71 B5
La Chaise-Dieu F 68 C3
La Chaize-Giraud F 66 B3
La Chaize-le-Vicomte F 66 B3
La Chambre F 69 C6
Lachania GR 119 G2
La Chapelaude F 68 B2
La Chapelle-d'Angillon F 68 A2
La Chapelle-en-Aalgaudémar F 79 B5
La Chapelle-en-Vercors F 79 B4
La Chapelle-Glain F 57 C4
La Chapelle-la-Reine F 58 B3
La Chapelle-Laurent
F 68 C3
La Chapelle-St Luc F 59 B5
La Chapelle-sur-Erdre F 66 A3
La Chapelle-Vicomtesse F 58 C2
La Charce F 79 B4
La Charité-sur-Loire F 68 A3
La Chartre-sur-le-Loir F 58 C1
La Châtaigneraie F 67 B4
La Châtre F 68 B1
La Chaussée-sur-Marne F 59 B5
La Chaux-de-Fonds
CH 70 A1
Lachen CH 70 A3
Lachendorf D 44 C2
La Cheppe F 59 A5
La Chèze F 56 B3
Lachowice PL 65 A5
La Ciotat F 79 C4
Łąck PL 47 C5
Läckeby S 40 C6
Läckö S 35 D5
La Clayette F 69 B4
La Clusaz F 69 C6
Lacock UK 29 B5
La Codosera E 93 B3
La Concha E 88 A3
La Condamine-Châtelard F 79 B5
Láconi I 110 C2
La Contienda E 99 A4
La Coquille F 67 C5
La Coronada E 93 C5
La Côte-St André F 69 C5
La Cotinière F 66 C3
La Courtine F 68 C2
Lacq F 76 C2
La Crau F 79 C5
La Crèche F 67 B4
La Croix F 67 A5
Lacroix-Barrez F 77 B5
Lacroix-St Ouen F 58 A3
Lacroix-sur-Meuse F 60 B1
La Croix-Valmer F 79 C5
La Cumbre E 93 B5
Łącznik PL 54 C2
Lad H 74 B2
Ladbergen D 50 A3
Lądek-Zdrój PL 54 C1
Ladelund D 39 E2
Ladendorf A 64 B2
Ladignac-le-Long F 67 C6
Ladíspoli I 102 B5
Ladoeiro P 93 B3
Ladon F 58 C3
La Douze F 77 A3
Ladushkin RUS 47 A6
Ladybank UK 25 B4
Laer D 50 A3
La Espina E 86 A4
La Estrella E 94 C1
La Farga de Moles E 91 A4
La Fatarella E 90 B3
La Felipa E 95 C5

La Fère F 59 A4
La Ferrière
Indre-et-Loire F 58 C1
Vendée F 66 B3
La Ferrière-en-Parthenay F 67 B4
La-Ferté-Alais F 58 B3
La Ferté-Bernard F 58 B1
La Ferté-Frênel F 58 B1
La Ferté-Gaucher F 59 B4
La Ferté-Imbault F 68 A1
La Ferté-Macé F 57 B5
La Ferté-Milon F 59 A4
La Ferté-sous-Jouarre F 59 B4
La Ferté-St-Aubin F 58 C2
La Ferté-St-Cyr F 58 C2
La Ferté-Vidame F 58 B1
La Ferté Villeneuil F 58 C2
La Feuillie F 58 A2
Lafkos GR 116 C5
La Flèche F 57 C5
La Flotte F 66 B3
Lafnitz A 73 A6
La Font de la Figuera E 101 A5
La Fouillade F 77 B5
Lafrançaise F 77 B4
La Fregeneda E 87 D4
La Fresneda E 90 C3
La Fuencubierta E 99 B6
La Fuente de San Esteban E 87 D4
La Fulioala E 91 B4
La Gacilly F 57 C3
La Galera E 90 C3
Lagan S 40 C3
Laganadi I 109 A4
Lagarde F 77 C4
La Garde-Freinet F 79 C5
Lagares
Coimbra P 92 A3
Porto P 87 C2
La Garnache F 66 B3
Lagaro I 81 B5
La Garriga E 91 B5
La Garrovilla E 93 C4
Lagartera E 93 B5
La Gaubretière F 66 B3
Lågbol S 36 B5
Lage D 51 B4
Lägerdorf D 43 B6
Lagg UK 24 C2
Laggan UK 22 D4
Laggartorp S 35 C6
Łagiewniki PL 54 C1
La Gineta E 95 C4
Láglio I 71 C4
Lagnieu F 69 C5
Lagny-sur-Marne F 58 B3
Lago
Calabria I 106 B3
Veneto I 72 C2
Lagôa P 98 B2
Lagoaça P 87 C4
Lagonegro I 106 A2
Lagos
GR 116 A7
P 98 B2
Lagosanto I 82 B1
Łagów
Lubuskie PL 46 C1
Świętokrzyskie PL 55 C6
La Granadella
Alicante E 96 C3
Lleida E 90 B3
La Grand-Combe F 78 B3
La Grande-Croix F 69 C4
La Grande-Motte F 78 C3
La Granja d'Escarp E 90 B3
La Granjuela E 93 C5
Lagrasse F 77 C5
La Grave F 79 A5
La Gravelle F 57 B4
Laguardia E 89 B4
La Guardia E 95 C3
La Guardia de Jaén E 100 B2
Laguarres E 90 A3
Laguenne F 68 C1
Laguépie F 77 B4
La Guerche-de-Bretagne F 57 C4
La Guerche-sur-l'Aubois F 68 B2
La Guérinière F 66 B2
Laguiole F 78 B1
Laguna de Duera E 88 C2
Laguna del Marquesado E 95 B5
Laguna de Negrillos E 88 B1
Lagundo I 71 B6
Lagunilla E 93 A4
La Haba E 93 C5
Laharie F 76 B2
La Haye-du-Puits F 57 A4
La Haye-Pesnel F 57 B4
Lahden D 43 C4
La Herlière F 48 C3
La Hermida E 88 A2
La Herrera E 95 D4
Laheycourt F 59 B6
La Higuera E 101 A4
La Hiniesta E 88 C1
Lahnstein D 50 C3
Laholm S 40 C3
La Horcajada E 93 A5
La Horra E 88 C3
Lahr D 60 B3
Lahti FIN 3 F26
La Hulpe B 49 C5
La Hutte F 57 B6
Laichingen D 61 B5
L'Aigle F 58 B1
La Iglesuela E 94 B2
La Iglesuela del Cid E 90 C2
Laignes F 59 C5
Laiguéglia I 80 C2
L'Aiguillon-sur-Mer F 66 B3
Laimbach am Ostrong A 63 B6
Laina E 95 A4
Lainio S 113 E11
Lairg UK 23 C4
La Iruela E 100 B3
Laissac F 78 B1
Laisvall S 115 A14
Láives I 71 B6
La Javie F 79 B5
Lajkovac SRB 85 B5
La Jonchère-St Maurice F 67 B6
La Jonquera E 91 A5
Lajoskomárom H 74 B3
Lajosmizse H 75 A4
Lak H 65 B6
Lakenheath UK 30 B4
Laki BG 116 A6
Lakitelek H 75 B5
Lakki GR 117 G5
Lakolk DK 39 D1
Łąkorz PL 47 B5
Lakšárska Nová Ves SK 64 B3
Lakselv N 113 B13
Laksfors N 115 B10
Laktaši BIH 84 B2
La Lantejuela E 99 B5
Lalapaşa TR 118 A1
L'Albagès E 90 B3
Lalbenque F 77 B4
L'Alcudia E 96 B2
L'Aldea E 90 C3
Lalëz AL 105 B5
Lalín E 86 B2
Lalinde F 77 B3
La Línea de la Concepción E 99 C5
Lalizolle F 68 B3
La Llacuna E 91 B4
Lalley F 79 B4
Lalling D 62 B4
Lalm N 114 F6
La Londe-les-Maures F 79 C5
La Loupe F 58 B2
La Louvière B 49 C5
L'Alpe-d'Huez F 79 A5
La Luisiana E 99 B5
Laluque F 76 C1
Lam D 62 A4
La Machine F 68 B3
la Maddalena I 110 A2
Lama dei Peligni I 103 A7
Lamadrid E 88 A2
Lamagistére F 77 B3
La Mailleraye-sur-Seine F 58 A1
La Malène F 78 B2
Lama Mocogno I 81 B4
La Mamola E 100 C2
La Manresana dels Prats E 91 B4
Lamarche F 60 B1
Lamarche-sur-Saône F 69 A5
Lamargelle F 69 A4
Lamarosa P 92 B2
Lamarque F 76 A2
Lamas P 92 A2
La Masadera E 90 B2
Lamas de Moaro P 87 B2
Lamastre F 78 B3
La Mata E 94 C2
La Mata de Ledesma E 94 A1
La Mata de Monteagudo E 88 B1
Lambach A 63 B4
Lamballe F 56 B3
Lamberhurst UK 31 C4
Lambesc F 79 C4
Lambia GR 117 E3
Lambley UK 25 D5
Lambourn UK 31 C2
Lamego P 87 C3
La Meilleraye-de-Bretagne F 66 A3
La Ménitré F 67 A4
L'Ametlla de Mar E 90 C3
Lamia GR 116 D4
Lammhult S 40 B4
La Mojonera E 101 C3
La Mole F 79 C5
La Molina E 91 A4
La Monnerie-le-Montel F 68 C3
La Morera E 93 C4
La Mothe-Achard F 66 B3
Lamothe-Cassel F 77 B4
Lamothe-Montravel F 76 B3
La Mothe-St Héray F 67 B4
Lamotte-Beuvron F 58 C3
La Motte-Chalançon F 79 B4
La Motte-du-Caire F 79 B5
La Motte-Servolex F 69 C5
Lampertheim D 61 A4
Lampeter UK 28 A3
L'Ampolla E 90 C3
Lamprechtshausen A 62 C3
Lamsfeld D 53 B4
Lamspringe D 51 B6
Lamstedt D 43 B6
La Mudarra E 88 C2
La Muela E 90 B1
La Mure F 79 B4
Lamure-sur-Azergues F 69 B4
Lana I 71 B6
Lanaja E 90 B2
Lanarce F 78 B2
Lanark UK 25 C4
La Nava E 99 B4
La Nava de Ricomalillo E 94 C2
La Nava de Santiago E 93 B4
Lancaster UK 26 A3
Lanchester UK 25 D6
Lanciano I 103 A7
Lancing UK 31 D3
Lançon-Provence F 79 C4
Lancova Vas SLO 73 B5
Landau
Bayern D 62 B3
Rheinland-Pfalz D 61 A4
Landeck A 71 A5
Landen B 49 C6
Landerneau F 56 B1
Landeryd S 40 B3
Landesbergen D 43 C6
Landete E 96 B1
Landévant F 56 C2
Landévennec F 56 B1
Landeyjahöfn IS 111 D5
Landivisiau F 56 B1
Landivy F 57 B4
Landl A 62 C3
Landön S 115 D11
Landos F 78 B2
Landouzy-le-Ville F 59 A5
Landquart CH 71 B4
Landrecies F 49 C4
Landreville F 59 B5
Landriano I 71 C4
Landsberg D 62 B1
Lands-berg D 52 B2
Landsbro S 40 B4
Landscheid D 50 D2
Landshut D 62 B3
Landskrona S 41 D2
Landstuhl D 60 A3
Lanesborough IRL 19 C4
Lanester F 56 C2
Lanestosa E 89 A3
La Neuve-Lyre F 58 B1
La Neuveville CH 70 A2
Langå DK 39 C2
Langada GR 116 D8
Langadas GR 116 B5
Langa de Duero E 89 C3
Langadia GR 117 E4
Langangen N 35 C1
Långared S 40 A2
Långaröd S 41 D3
Långaryd S 40 B3
Långås S 40 C2
Långasjö S 40 C5
Langau A 63 B6
Langeac F 78 A2
Langeais F 67 A5
Langedijk NL 42 C1
Langeln D 51 B6
Langelsheim D 51 B6
Langemark-Poelkapelle B 48 C3
Langen
Hessen D 51 D4
Niedersachsen D 43 B5
Langenau D 61 B6
Langenberg D 50 B4
Langenbruck CH 70 A2
Langenburg D 61 A5
Längenfeld A 71 A5
Langenfeld D 50 B2
Langenhorn D 43 A5
Langenlois A 63 B6
Langenlonsheim D 60 A3
Langennaudorf D 52 B3
Langenneufnach D 62 B1
Langenthal CH 70 A2
Langenzenn D 62 A1
Langeoog D 43 B4
Langeskov DK 39 D3
Langesund N 35 C1
Langewiesen D 51 C6
Långflon S 34 A4
Langförden D 43 C5
Langhagen D 44 B4
Länghem S 40 B3
Langhirano I 81 B4
Langholm UK 25 C5
Langholt IS 111 D7
Långlöt S 41 C6
Langnau CH 70 B2
Langø DK 39 E4
Langogne F 78 B2
Langon F 76 B2
Langquaid D 62 B3
Långrådna S 37 D3
Langreo E 88 A1
Langres F 59 C6
Långsele S 115 D14
Långserud S 35 C4
Langset N 34 B3
Långshyttan S 36 B3
Langstrand N 113 B12
Långträsk S 115 B17
Langueux F 56 B3
Languidic F 56 C2
Längvik S 37 C5
Langwarden D 43 B5
Langwathby UK 26 A3
Langwedel D 43 C6
Langweid D 62 B1
Langwies CH 71 B4
Lanheses P 87 C2
Lanięta PL 47 C5
Lanildut F 56 B1
Lanjarón E 100 C2
Lanmeur F 56 B2
Lanna
Jönköping S 40 B3
Örebro S 37 C1
Lännaholm S 36 C4
Lannavaara S 113 D10
Lannéanou F 56 B2
Lannemezan F 77 C3
Lanneuville-sur-Meuse F 59 A6
Lannilis F 56 B1
Lannion F 56 B2
La Nocle-Maulaix F 68 B3
Lanouaille F 67 C6
Lansjärv S 113 F11
Lanškroun CZ 64 A2
Lanslebourg-Mont-Cenis F 70 C1
Lanta F 77 C4
Lantadilla E 88 B2
Lanton F 76 B1
Lantosque F 79 C6
La Nuez de Arriba E 88 B3
Lanusei I 110 C2
Lanúvio I 102 B5
Lanvollon F 56 B3
Lánycsók H 74 B3
Lanz D 44 B3
Lanza E 86 A2
Lanzada E 86 B2
Lanzahita E 94 B2
Lanžhot CZ 64 B2
Lanzo Torinese I 70 C2
Laole SRB 85 B6
Laon F 59 A4
Laons F 58 B2
La Paca E 101 B4
La Pacaudière F 68 B3
Lapalisse F 68 B3
La Palma d'Ebre E 90 B3
La Palma del Condado E 99 B4
La Palme F 78 D2
La Palmyre F 66 C3
La Parra E 93 C4
Łapczyna Wola PL 55 C4
La Pedraja de Portillo E 88 C2
La Peraleja E 95 B4
La Petit-Pierre F 60 B3
Lapeyrade F 76 B2
Lapeyrouse F 68 B2
Lapford UK 28 C4
La Pinilla E 101 B4
Lapithos CY 120 A2
La Plagne F 70 C1
La Plaza E 86 A4
Laplje Selo KOS 85 D6
Laplume F 77 B3
La Pobla de Lillet E 91 A4
La Pobla de Vallbona E 96 B2
La Pobla Llarga E 96 B2
La Pola de Gordón E 88 B1
la Porta F 102 A2
La Pouëze F 66 A4
Lapoutroie F 60 B3
La Póveda de Soria E 89 B4
Lapovo SRB 85 B6
Läppe S 37 C2
Lappeenranta FIN 3 F28
Lappoluobbal N 113 C12
La Preste F 91 A5
La Primaube F 77 B5
Lapseki TR 118 B1
Lapua FIN 3 E25
La Puebla de Almoradie E 95 C3
La Puebla de Cazalla E 99 B5
La Puebla de los Infantes E 99 B5
La Puebla del Río E 99 B4
La Puebla de Montalbán E 94 C2
La Puebla de Roda E 90 A3
La Puebla de Valdavia E 88 B2
La Puebla de Valverde E 96 A2
La Pueblanueva E 94 C2
La Puerta de Segura E 101 A3
La Punt CH 71 B4
L'Áquila I 103 A6
La Quintana E 100 B1
La Quintera E 99 B5
La Rábita
Granada E 100 C2
Jaén E 100 B1
Laracha E 86 A2
Laragh IRL 21 A5
Laragne-Montéglin F 79 B4
La Rambla E 100 B1
l'Arboç E 91 B4
L'Arbresle F 69 C4
Lärbro S 37 E5
Larceveau F 76 C1
Larche
Alpes-de-Haute-Provence F 79 B5
Corrèze F 77 A4
Lårdal N 33 C5
Lærdalsøyri N 32 A4
Lardosa P 92 B3
La Reale I 110 A1
Laredo E 89 A3
La Redondela E 98 B3
La Réole F 76 B2
Largentière F 78 B3
L'Argentière-la-Bessée F 79 B5
Largs UK 24 C3
Lari I 81 C4
La Riera E 86 A4
La Riera de Gaià E 91 B4
La Rinconada E 99 B4
Lariño E 86 B1
Larino I 103 B7
Larisa GR 116 C4
La Rivière-Thibouville F 58 A1
Larkhall UK 25 C4
Larkollen N 35 C2
Larmor-Plage F 56 C2
Larnaca CY 120 B2
Larne UK 19 B6
La Robla E 88 B1
La Roca de la Sierra E 93 B4
La Roche CH 70 B2
La Rochebeaucourtet-Argentine F 67 C5
La Roche-Bernard F 66 A2
La Roche-Canillac F 68 C1
La Roche-Chalais F 67 C5
La Roche Derrien F 56 B2
La Roche-des-Arnauds F 79 B4
La Roche-en-Ardenne B 49 C6
La Roche-en-Brénil F 69 A4
La Rochefoucauld F 67 C5
La Roche-Guyon F 58 A2
La Rochelle F 66 B3
La Roche-Posay F 67 B5
La Roche-sur-Foron F 69 B6
La Roche-sur-Yon F 66 B3
Larochette L 60 A2
La Rochette F 79 B4
La Roda
Albacete E 95 C4
Oviedo E 86 A4
La Roda de Andalucía E 100 B1
Laroquebrou F 77 B5
La Roquebrussanne F 79 C4
Laroque d'Olmes F 77 D4
La Roque-Gageac F 77 B4
La Roque-Ste Marguerite F 78 B2
Laroque-Timbaut F 77 B3
Larouco E 87 B3
Larraga E 89 B5
Larrau F 76 C2
Larrazet F 77 C4
Larsnes N 114 E2
La Rubia E 89 C4
Laruns F 76 C2
Larva E 100 B2
Larvik N 35 C2
La Sagrada E 87 D4
La Salceda E 94 A3
Lasalle F 78 B2
La Salle F 79 B5
la Salute di Livenza I 72 C2
La Salvetat-Peyralés F 77 B5
La Salvetat-sur-Agout F 78 C1
Las Arenas E 88 A2
La Sarraz CH 69 B6
Lasarte E 89 A4
Låsby DK 39 C2
Las Cabezadas E 95 A3
Las Cabezas de San Juan E 99 C5
Las Correderas E 100 A2
Las Cuevas de Cañart E 90 C2
La Seca E 88 C2
La Selva del Camp E 91 B4
La Senia E 90 C3
La Serra E 91 B4
La Seu d'Urgell E 91 A4
La Seyne-sur-Mer F 79 C4
Las Gabias E 100 B2
Las Herencias E 94 C2
Las Herrerias E 98 B3
Łasin PL 47 B5
Lask PL 55 B4
Laska PL 46 B3
Łaskarzow PL 55 B6
Laško SLO 73 B5
Laskowice PL 47 B4
Las Labores E 95 C3
Las Mesas E 95 C4
Las Minas E 101 A4
Las Navas E 100 B1
Las Navas de la Concepción E 99 B5
Las Navas del Marqués E 94 B2
Las Navillas E 94 C2
Las Negras E 101 C4
La Solana E 95 D3
La Souterraine F 67 B6
Las Pajanosas E 99 B4
Laspaules E 90 A3
Las Pedroñas E 95 C4
La Spézia I 81 B3
Las Planes d'Hostoles E 91 A5
Laspuña E 90 A3
Las Rozas
Cantabria E 88 B2
Madrid E 94 B3
Lassan D 45 B5
Lassay-les-Châteaux F 57 B5
Lasseube F 76 C2
Lassigny F 58 A3
La Storta I 102 B5
Lastovo HR 84 D1
Lastras de Cuéllar E 88 C2
Lästringe S 37 D4
Lastrup D 43 C4
Lastva BIH 84 D3
Las Uces E 87 C4
La Suze-sur-Sarthe F 57 C6
Las Veguillas E 94 B1
Las Ventas con Peña Aguilera E 94 C2
Las Ventas de San Julián E 93 A5
Las Villes E 96 A3
Latasa E 76 D1
Látera I 102 A4
Laterza I 104 C2
La Teste F 76 B1
Lathen D 43 C4
Latheron UK 23 C5
La Thuile I 70 C1
Latiano I 105 C3
Latina I 102 B5
Latisana I 72 C3
Látky SK 65 B5
La Toba E 95 B5
La Toledana E 94 C2
La Torre de Cabdella E 90 A3
La Torre de Esteban Hambrán E 94 B2
La Torre del l'Espanyol E 90 B3
La Torresaviñán E 95 B4
La Tour d'Aigues F 79 C4
La Tour de Peilz CH 70 B1
La Tour-du-Pin F 69 C5
Latowicz PL 55 A6
La Tranche-sur-Mer F 66 B3
La Tremblade F 66 C3
La Trimouille F 67 B6
La Trinité F 56 C2
La Trinité-Porhoët F 56 B3
Latrónico I 106 A3
Latronquière F 77 B5
Latterbach CH 70 B2
La Turballe F 66 A2
Laubach D 51 C4
Laubert F 78 B2
Laucha D 52 B1
Lauchhammer D 53 B3
Lauchheim D 61 B6
Lauda-Königshofen D 61 A5
Laudal N 33 D4
Lauder UK 25 C5
Lauenau D 51 A5
Lauenburg D 44 B2
Lauf D 62 A2
Laufach D 51 C5
Laufen
CH 70 A2
D 62 C3
Lauffen D 61 A5
Laugar IS 111 B8
Laugarás IS 111 C5
Laugarbakki IS 111 B5
Laugarvatn IS 111 C5
Laugharne UK 28 B3
Lauingen D 61 B6
Laujar de Andarax E 100 C3
Laukaa FIN 3 E26
Lauker S 115 B16
Laukvik N 112 E3
La Uña E 88 A1
Launceston UK 28 C3
La Unión E 101 B5
Launois-sur-Vence F 59 A5
Laupheim D 61 B5
Lauragh IRL 20 C2
Laureana di Borrello I 106 C3
Laurencekirk UK 25 B5
Laurencetown IRL 20 A3
Laurenzana I 104 C1
Lauria I 106 A2
Laurière F 67 B6
Laurieston UK 24 D3
Laurino I 103 C8
Lausanne CH 69 B6
Laussonne F 78 B3
Lauta D 53 B4
Lautenthal D 51 B6
Lauterach A 71 A4
Lauterbach D 51 C5
Lauterbrunnen CH 70 B2
Lauterecken D 60 A3
Lauterhofen D 62 A2
Lautrec F 77 C5
Lauvsnes N 114 C7
Lauvvlk N 33 D3
Lauzerte F 77 B4
Lauzès F 77 B4
Lauzun F 77 B3
Lavagna I 80 B3
Laval F 57 B5
La Vall d'Uixó E 96 B2
Lavamünd A 73 B4
Lavara GR 118 A1
Lavardac F 76 B3
Lavaris P 92 A2
Lavarone I 71 C6
Lavau F 59 C3
Lavaur F 77 C4
La Vecilla de Curueño E 88 B1
La Vega
Asturias E 88 A1
Cantabria E 88 A2
Lavelanet F 77 D4
La Velilla E 94 A3
La Velles E 94 A1
Lavello I 104 B1
Lavelsloh D 43 C5
Lavenham UK 30 B4
Laveno I 70 C3
La Ventosa E 95 B4
Lavezzola I 81 B5
Laviano I 103 C8
La Victoria E 100 B1
La Vid E 89 C3
Lavik N 32 A2
La Vilavella E 96 B2
La Vilella Baixa E 90 B3
La Villa de Don Fadrique E 95 C3
Lavilledieu F 78 B3
La Villedieu F 67 B4
La Ville Dieu-du-Temple F 77 B4
Lavinio-Lido di Enea I 102 B5
Lav ìs I 71 B6
Lavit F 77 C3
Lavoncourt F 60 C1
Lavos P 92 A2
La Voulte-sur-Rhône F 78 B3
Lavoûte-Chilhac F 68 C3
Lavradio P 92 C1
Lavre P 92 C2
Lavrio GR 117 E6
La Wantzenau F 60 B3
Lawers UK 24 B3
Ławy PL 45 C6
Laxå S 37 D1
Laxamýri IS 111 B8
Laxe E 86 A2
Laxey UK 26 A1
Laxford Bridge UK 22 C3
Laxhall S 35 D5
Laxsjö S 115 D11
Laxtjarn S 34 B6
Laxvik S 40 C2
Laxviken S 115 D11
La Yesa E 96 B2
Laza E 87 B3
Lazarevac SRB 85 B5
Lazarev Krst MNE 105 A5
Lazarevo SRB 75 C5
Lazise I 71 C5
Łaziska Grn. PL 54 C3
Lazkao E 89 A4
Lázně Bělohrad CZ 53 C5
Lázně Bohdaneč CZ 53 C5
Lázně Kynžvart CZ 52 C2
Lazonby UK 26 A3
La Zubia E 100 B2
Łazy PL 46 A2
Lazzaro I 109 B4
Lea UK 27 B5
Leadburn UK 25 C4
Leadhills UK 25 C4
Leap IRL 20 C2
Leatherhead UK 31 C3
Łeba PL 46 A3
Lebach D 60 A2
Le Barcarès F 78 D2
Le Barp F 76 B2
Le Bar-sur-Loup F 79 C5
Le Béage F 78 B3
Le Beausset F 79 C4
Lebedyn UA 7 F13
Lebekke B 49 B5
Lébény H 64 C3
Le Bessat F 69 C4
Le Blanc F 67 B6
Le Bleymard F 78 B2
Łebno PL 47 A4
Leboreiro E 87 B3
Lębork PL 46 A3
Le Boullay-Mivoye F 58 B2
Le Boulou F 91 A5
Le Bourg F 77 B4
Le Bourg-d'Oisans F 79 A5
Le Bourget-du-Lac F 69 C5
Le Bourgneuf-la-Forêt F 57 B5
Le Bousquet d'Orb F 78 C2
Le Brassus CH 69 B6
Le Breuil F 68 B3
Le Breuil-en-Auge F 57 A6
Lebrija E 99 C4
Lebring A 73 B5
Le Brusquet F 79 B5
Le Bry CH 70 B2
Le Bugue F 77 B3
Le Buisson F 77 B3
Lebus D 45 C6
Lebusa D 52 B3
Leca da Palmeira P 87 C2
Le Caloy F 76 C2
Le Cap d'Agde F 78 C2
Le Cateau Cambrésis F 49 C4
Le Caylar F 78 C2
Le Cayrol F 78 B1
Lecce I 105 C4
Lecco I 71 C4
Lécera E 90 B2
Lećevica HR 83 C5
Lech A 71 A5
Le Chambon-Feugerolles F 69 C4
Le Chambon-sur-Lignon F 78 A3
Le Château d'Oléron F 66 C3
Le Châtelard F 69 C6
Le Châtelet F 68 B2
Le Chatelet-en-Brie F 58 B3
Lechbruck D 62 C1
Lechena GR 117 E3
Le Chesne F 59 A5
Le Cheylard F 78 B3
Lechlade UK 29 B6
Lechovice CZ 64 B2
Leciñena E 90 B2
Leck D 39 E1
Le Collet-de-Deze F 78 B2
Le Conquet F 56 B1
Le Creusot F 69 B4
Le Croisic F 66 A2
Le Crotoy F 48 C2
Lectoure F 77 C3
Łęczyca
Łódzkie PL 55 A4
Zachodnio-Pomorskie PL 45 B7
Ledaña E 95 C5
Ledbury UK 29 A5
Lede B 49 C4
Ledečnad Sazavou CZ 63 A6
Ledenice CZ 63 B5
Le Deschaux F 69 B5
Ledesma E 87 C4
Lédignan F 78 C3
Lédigos E 88 B2
Ledmore UK 22 C4
Lednice CZ 64 B2
Lednicke-Rovné SK 64 A4
Le Donjon F 68 B3
Le Dorat F 67 B6
Lędyczek PL 46 B2
Lędziny PL 55 C4
Leeds UK 27 B4
Leek
NL 42 B3
UK 26 B3
Leenaun IRL 18 C2
Leens NL 42 B3
Leer D 43 B4
Leerdam NL 49 B6
Leerhafe D 43 B4
Leese D 43 C6
Leeuwarden NL 42 B2
Leezen D 44 B2
Le Faou F 56 B1
Le Faoüet F 56 B2
Lefka CY 120 A1
Lefkada GR 116 D2
Lefkimis GR 116 C2
Lefkoniko CY 120 A2
Le Folgoet F 56 B1
Le Fossat F 77 C4
Le Fousseret F 77 C4
Le Fugeret F 79 B5
Leganés E 94 B3
Legau D 61 C6
Le Gault-Soigny F 59 B4
Legbąd PL 46 B3
Legé F 66 B3
Lège-Cap-Ferret F 76 B1
Legionowo PL 55 A5
Léglise B 60 A1
Legnago I 71 C6
Legnano I 70 C3
Legnaro I 72 C1
Legnica PL 53 B6
Łęgowo PL 47 A4
Legrad HR 74 B1
Le Grand-Bornand F 69 C6
Le-Grand-Bourg F 67 B6
Le Grand-Lucé F 58 C1
Le Grand-Pressigny F 67 B5
Le Grand-Quevilly F 58 A2
Le Grau-du-Roi F 78 C3
Léguevin F 77 C4
Legutiano E 89 B4
Le Havre F 57 A6
Lehesten D 52 C1
Lehnice SK 64 B3
Lehnin D 52 A2
Le Hohwald F 60 B3
Le Houga F 76 C2
Lehrberg D 61 A6
Lehre D 51 A6
Lehrte D 44 C1
Lehsen D 44 B3
Leibnitz A 73 B5
Leicester UK 30 B2
Leiden NL 49 A5
Leidschendam NL 49 A5
Leigh UK 26 B3
Leighlinbridge IRL 21 B5
Leighton Buzzard UK 31 C3
Leignon B 49 C6
Leikanger N 114 E2
Leimen D 61 A4
Leinefelde D 51 B6
Leinesfjord N 112 E4
Leintwardine UK 29 A5
Leipojärvi S 112 E10
Leipzig D 52 B2
Leira
Nordland N 115 A10
Oppland N 32 B6
Leiråmoen N 112 F3
Leiria P 92 B2
Leirvik
Hordaland N 32 C2
Sogn og Fjordane N 32 A2
Leisach A 72 B2
Leisnig D 52 B2
Leiston UK 30 B5
Leitholm UK 25 C5
Leitrim IRL 18 C3
Leitza E 76 C1
Leitzkau D 52 A1
Lejkowo PL 46 A2
Lekani GR 116 A6
Łękawa PL 55 B4
Łekawica PL 65 A5
Lekbibaj AL 105 A5
Lekeitio E 89 A4
Lekenik HR 73 C6
Lekeryd S 40 B4
Leknes N 112 D2
Lęknica PL 53 B4
Leksand S 36 B1
Leksvik N 114 D7
Lekunberri E 76 C1
Lekvattnet S 34 B4
Le Lardin-St Lazare F 67 C6
Le Lauzet-Ubaye F 79 B5
Le Lavandou F 79 C5
Le Lion-d'Angers F 57 C5
Lelkowo PL 47 A6
Le Locle CH 70 A1
Le Loroux-Bottereau F 66 A3
Le Louroux-Béconnais F 66 A4
Lelów PL 55 C4
Le Luc F 79 C5
Le Lude F 57 C6
Lelystad NL 42 C2
Lem
Ringkøbing DK 39 C1
Viborg Amt. DK 38 C1
Le Malzieu-Ville F 78 B2
Le Mans F 57 B6
Le Mas-d'Azil F 77 C4
Le Massegros F 78 B2
Le Mayet-de-Montagne F 68 B3
Le May-sur-Evre F 66 A4
Lembach F 60 A3
Lemberg F 60 A3
Lembèye F 76 C2
Lemelerveld NL 42 C3
Le Mêle-sur-Sarthe F 58 B1
Le Ménil F 60 B2
Le Merlerault F 57 B6
Le Mesnil-sur-Oger F 59 B5
Lemförde D 43 C5
Lemgo D 51 A4
Le Miroir F 69 B5
Lemland FIN 36 B7
Lemmer NL 42 C2
Le Molay-Littry F 57 A5
Le Monastier-sur-Gazeille F 78 B2
Le Monêtier-les-Bains F 79 B5
Le Mont-Dore F 68 C2
Le Montet F 68 B3
Le Mont-St Michel F 57 B4
Lempdes F 68 C3
Le Muret F 76 B2
Le Muy F 79 C5
Lemvig DK 38 C1
Lemwerder D 43 B5
Lena N 34 B2
Lenart SLO 73 B5
Lenartovce SK 65 B6
Lenauheim RO 75 C5
Lencloître F 67 B5
Lend A 72 A3
Lendalfoot UK 24 C3
Lendava SLO 73 B6
Lendery RUS 3 E29
Lendinara I 81 A5
Lendorf A 72 B3
Lendum DK 38 B3
Le Neubourg F 58 A1
Lengefeld D 52 C3
Lengerich
Niedersachsen D 43 C4
Nordrhein-Westfalen D 50 A3
Lenggries D 62 C2
Lengyeltóti H 74 B2
Lenhovda S 40 C5
Lenk CH 70 B2
Lennartsfors S 35 C3
Lennestadt D 50 B4
Lennoxtown UK 24 C3
Leno I 71 C5
Lénola I 103 B6
Le Nouvion-en-Thiérache F 49 C4
Lens
B 49 C4
F 48 C3
Lensahn D 44 A2
Lens Lestang F 69 C5
Lensvik N 114 D6
Lentellais E 87 B3
Lentföhrden D 44 B1
Lenti H 74 B1
Lentini I 109 B3
Lenungshammar S 35 C4
Lenzburg CH 70 A3
Lenzen D 44 B3
Lenzerheide CH 71 B4
Leoben A 73 A5
Leogang A 72 A2
Leominster UK 29 A5
León E 88 B1
Léon F 76 C1
Leonberg D 61 B5
Léoncel F 79 B4
Leonding A 63 B5
Leonessa I 102 A5
Leonforte I 109 B3
Leonidio GR 117 E4
Leopoldsburg B 49 B6
Leopoldsdorf im Marchfeld A 64 B2
Leopoldshagen D 45 B5
Leova MD 11 C10
Le Palais F 66 A1
Le Parcq F 48 C3
Lepe E 98 B3
Le Péage-de-Roussillon F 69 C4
Le Pellerin F 66 A3
Lepenac
MNE 85 D4
SRB 85 C6
Lepenou GR 116 D3
Le Perthus F 91 A5
Le Pertuis F 78 A3
Le Petit-Bornand F 69 C6
Lephin UK 22 D2
L'Epine F 79 B4
Le Poët F 79 B4
Lepoglava HR 73 B6
Le Poirè-sur-Vie F 66 B3
Le Pont CH 69 B6
Le Pont-de-Montvert F 78 B2
Le Porge F 76 B1
Le Porge-Océan F 76 B1
Le Portel F 48 C2
Le Pouldu F 56 C2
Le Pouliguen F 66 A2
Leppäjärvi FIN 113 D12
Leppävirta FIN 3 E27
Leppin D 44 C3
le Prese I 71 B5
Lepsény H 74 B3
Le Puy-en-Velay F 78 A2
Le Puy-Ste Réparade F 79 C4
Le Quesnoy F 49 C4
Léquile I 105 C4
Le Rayol F 79 C5
Lercara Friddi I 108 B2
Lerdal S 35 D3
Leré F 68 A2
Lérici I 81 B3
Lerin E 89 B5
Lerma E 88 B3
Lerm-et-Musset F 76 B2
Lermoos A 71 A5
Le Roeulx B 49 C5
Le Rouget F 77 B5
Lérouville F 60 B1
Le Rozier F 78 B2
Lerum S 40 B2
Le Russey F 70 A1
Lervik N 35 C2
Lerwick UK 22 A7
Lés E 77 D3
Les Abrets F 69 C5
Les Aix-d'Angillon F 68 A2
Lešak KOS 85 C5
Lesaka E 76 C1
Les Ancizes-Comps F 68 C2
Les Andelys F 58 A2
Les Arcs
Savoie F 70 C1
Var F 79 C5
Les-Aubiers F 67 B4
Les Baux-de-Provence F 78 C3
Les Bézards F 58 C3
Les Bois CH 70 A1
Les Bordes F 58 C3
Les Borges Blanques E 90 B3
Les Borges del Camp E 91 B4
Les Brunettes F 68 B3
Lesbury UK 25 C6
Les Cabannes F 77 D4
L'Escala E 91 A6
Lescar F 76 C2
L'Escarène F 80 C1
Lesce SLO 73 B4
Lescheraines F 69 C6
Lesconil F 56 C1
Les Contamines-Montjoie F 70 C1
les Coves de Vinroma E 90 C3
Les Déserts F 69 C5
Les Deux-Alpes F 79 B5
Les Diablerets CH 70 B2
Lesdins F 59 A4
Les Echelles F 69 C5
Le Sel-de-Bretagne F 57 C4
Le Sentier CH 69 B6
Les Escaldes AND 91 A4
Les Essarts F 66 B3
Les Estables F 78 B3
Les Eyzies-de-Tayac F 77 B4
Les Gets F 70 B1
Les Grandes-Ventes F 58 A2
Les Haudères CH 70 B2
Les Herbiers F 66 B3
Les Hôpitaux-Neufs F 69 B6
Lesično SLO 73 B5
Lésina I 103 B8
Lesjaskog N 114 E5
Lesjöfors S 34 C6
Leskovac SRB 10 E6
Leskova Dolina SLO 73 C4
Leskovec
CZ 64 A3
SLO 73 C5
Leskovice CZ 63 A6
Leskovik AL 116 B2
Leslie UK 25 B4
Les Lucs-sur-Boulogne F 66 B3
Les Mages F 78 B3
Lesmahagow UK 25 C4
Les Mazures F 59 A5
Les Mées F 79 B4
Lesmont F 59 B5
Les Mureaux F 58 B2
Leśna PL 53 B5
Lesneven F 56 B1
Leśnica PL 54 C3
Lešnica SRB 85 B4
Leśniów Wielkoplski PL 53 B5
Lesnoye RUS 7 B13
Les Omergues F 79 B4
Les Ormes-sur-Voulzie F 59 B4
Les Orres F 79 B5
Le Souquet F 76 C1
Lesparre-Médoc F 66 C4
l'Espérance F 59 A4
l'Esperou F 78 B2
Les Pieux F 57 A4
Lesponne F 76 C3
Les Ponts-de-Cé F 67 A4
Les Ponts-de-Martel CH 70 B1
Les Praz F 70 C1
L'Espunyola E 91 A4
Les Riceys F 59 C5
Les Roches F 69 C4
Les Rosaires F 56 B3
Les Rosiers F 67 A4
Les Rousses F 69 B6
Les Sables-d'Olonne F 66 B3
Lessach A 72 A3
Lessay F 57 A4
Lessebo S 40 C5
Les Settons F 68 A4
Lessines B 49 C4
L'Estany E 91 B5
Les Ternes F 78 A1
Lesterps F 67 B5
Les Thilliers en-Vexin F 58 A2
Les Touches F 66 A3
Les Trois Moûtiers F 67 A5
Les Vans F 78 B3
Les Verrières CH 69 B6
Les Vignes F 78 B2
Leswalt UK 24 D2
Leszno
Mazowieckie PL 55 A5
Wielkopolskie PL 54 B1
Leszno Górne PL 53 B5
Letchworth UK 31 C3
Le Teil F 78 B3
Le Teilleul F 57 B5
Le Temple-de-Bretagne F 66 A3
Letenye H 74 B1
Le Theil F 58 B1
Le Thillot F 60 C2
Letino I 103 B7
Letohrad CZ 54 C1
Le Touquet-Paris-Plage F 48 C2
Le Touvet F 69 C5
Letovice CZ 64 A2
Le Translay F 48 D2
Le Tréport F 48 C2
Letschin D 45 C6
Letterfrack IRL 18 C2
Letterkenny IRL 19 B4
Lettermacaward IRL 18 B3
Lettoch UK 23 D5
Letur E 101 A3
Letux E 90 B2
Letzlingen D 44 C3
Leucate F 78 D2
Leuchars UK 25 B5
Leuglay F 59 C5
Leuk CH 70 B2
Leukerbad CH 70 B2
Leumrabhagh UK 22 C2
Leuna D 52 B2
Leusden NL 49 A6
Leutenberg D 52 C1
Leuterschach D 61 C6
Leutershausen D 61 A6
Leutkirch D 61 C6
Leuven B 49 C5
Leuze-en-Hainaut B 49 C4
Le Val F 79 C5
Le Val-André F 56 B3
Le Val-d'Ajol F 60 C2
Levan AL 105 C5
Levanger N 114 D8
Levanjska Varoš HR 74 C3
Lévanto I 80 B3
Levaré F 57 B5
Levata I 71 C5
Leveld N 32 B5
Leven
East Yorkshire UK 27 B5
Fife UK 25 B5
Leverano I 105 C3
Le Verdon-sur-Mer F 66 C3
Leverkusen D 50 B2
Levern D 43 C5
Le Vernet F 79 B5
Levet F 68 B2
Levice SK 65 B4
Lévico Terme I 71 B6
Levie F 102 B2
Levier F 69 B6
Le Vigan F 78 C2
Lévignen F 59 A3
le Ville I 82 C1
Levinovac HR 74 C2
Le Vivier-sur-Mer F 57 B4
Levoča SK 65 A6
Levroux F 67 B6
Lewes UK 31 D4
Lewin Brzeski PL 54 C2
Lewisham UK 31 C3
Leyburn UK 27 A4
Leyland UK 26 B3
Leysdown-on-Sea UK 31 C4
Leysin CH 70 B2
Lezajsk PL 11 A7
Lézardrieux F 56 B2
Lézat-sur-Léze F 77 C4
Lezay F 67 B4
Lezhë AL 105 B5
Lézignan-Corbières F 78 C1
Lezignan-la-Cèbe F 78 C2
Ležimir SRB 75 C4
Lézinnes F 59 C5
Lezoux F 68 C3
Lezuza E 95 D4
Lgov RUS 7 F13
Lhenice CZ 63 B5
Lherm F 77 C4
Lhommaizé F 67 B5
L'Hospitalet F 91 A4
L'Hospitalet de l'Infant E 90 C3
L'Hospitalet de Llobregat E 91 B5
L'Hospitalet-du-Larzac F 78 C2
Lhuître F 59 B5
Liancourt F 58 A3
Liart F 59 A5
Liatorp S 40 C4
Liatrie UK 22 D4
Libáň CZ 53 C5
Libceves CZ 53 C3
Liběchov CZ 53 C4
Liber E 86 B3
Liberec CZ 53 C5
Libiąż PL 55 C4
Libina CZ 64 A3
Libochovice CZ 53 C4
Libofshë AL 105 C5
Libohovë AL 116 B2
Libourne F 76 B2
Libramont B 59 A6
Librazhd AL 116 A2
Librilla E 101 B4
Libros E 96 A1
Licata I 108 B2
Licciana Nardi I 81 B4
Licenza I 102 A5
Liceros E 89 C3
Lich D 51 C4
Lichères-près-Aigremont F 59 C4
Lichfield UK 27 C4
Lichtenau
A 63 B6
D 51 B4
Lichtenberg D 52 C1
Lichtenfels D 52 C1
Lichtensteig CH 71 A4
Lichtenstein D 52 C2
Lichtenvoorde NL 50 B2
Lichtervelde B 49 B4
Lička Jesenica HR 83 A4
Lickershamn S 37 E5
Lički Osik HR 83 B4
Ličko Lešce HR 83 B4
Licodía Eubéa I 109 B3
Licques F 48 C2
Lida BY 7 E8
Lidar N 32 A6
Lidečko CZ 64 A4
Liden S 115 E13
Lidhult S 40 C3
Lidköping S 35 D5
Lido I 72 C2
Lido Azzurro I 104 C3
Lido degli Estensi I 82 B1
Lido degli Scacchi I 82 B1
Lido della Nazioni I 82 B1
Lido di Camaiore I 81 C4
Lido di Casalbordino I 103 A7
Lido di Castél Fusano I 102 B5
Lido di Cincinnato I 102 B5
Lido di Classe I 82 B1
Lido di Fermo I 82 C2
Lido di Fondi I 103 B6
Lido di Jésolo I 72 C2
Lido di Lícola I 103 C7
Lido di Metaponto I 104 C2
Lido di Óstia I 102 B5
Lido di Policoro I 106 A3
Lido di Pomposa I 82 B1
Lido di Savio I 82 B1
Lido di Scanzano I 104 C2
Lido di Siponto I 104 B1
Lido di Squillace I 106 C3
Lido di Volano I 82 B1
Lido Riccio I 103 A7
Lidoriki GR 116 D4
Lido Silvana I 104 C3
Lidsjöberg S 115 C12
Lidzbark PL 47 B5
Lidzbark Warmiński PL 47 A6
Liebenau
A 63 B5
D 43 C6
Liebenwalde D 45 C5
Lieberose D 53 B4
Liebling RO 75 C6
Lieboch A 73 B5
Liège B 49 C6
Lieksa FIN 3 E29
Lienen D 50 A3
Lienz A 72 B2
Liepāja LV 6 C6
Lier B 49 B5
Lierbyen N 34 C2
Liernais F 69 A4
Liesing A 72 B2
Liestal CH 70 A2
Liétor E 101 A4
Lieurac F 77 D4
Lieurey F 58 A1
Liévin F 48 C3
Liezen A 73 A4
Liffol-le-Grand F 60 B1
Lifford IRL 19 B4
Liffré F 57 B4
Ligardes F 77 B3
Lignano Sabbiadoro I 72 C3
Ligne F 66 A3
Lignières F 68 B2
Ligny-en-Barrois F 59 B6
Ligny-le-Châtel F 59 C4
Ligoła Polska PL 54 B2
Ligourio GR 117 E5
Ligowo PL 47 C5
Ligueil F 67 A5
Lijeva Rijeka MNE 85 D4
Likavka SK 65 A5
Likenäs S 34 B5
Likhoslavl RUS 7 C13
Liknes N 33 D3
Lild Strand DK 38 B1
L'Île-Bouchard F 67 A5
l'Île-Rousse F 102 A1
Lilienfeld A 63 B6
Lilienthal D 43 B5
Lilla Edet S 35 D4
Lilla Tjärby S 40 C3
Lille
B 49 B5
F 49 C4
Lillebonne F 58 A1
Lillehammer N 34 A2
Lillerød DK 41 D2
Lillers F 48 C3
Lillesand N 33 D5
Lillestrøm N 34 C3
Lillhärdal S 115 F11
Lillkyrka S 37 C4
Lillo E 95 C3
Lillögda S 115 C14
Lima S 34 B5
Limanowa PL 65 A6
Limassol CY 120 B2
Limavady UK 19 A5
Limbach-Oberfrohna D 52 C2
Limbaži LV 6 C8
Limbourg B 50 C1
Limburg D 50 C4
Lime DK 39 C3
Limedsforsen S 34 B5
Limenaria GR 116 B6
Limenas Chersonisou GR 117 G7
Limerick IRL 20 B3
Limes I 71 C5
Limésy F 58 A1
Limmared S 40 B3
Limni GR 116 D5
Limoges F 67 C6
Limogne-en-Quercy F 77 B4
Limoise F 68 B3
Limone Piemonte I 80 B1
Limone sul Garda I 71 C5
Limons F 68 C3
Limours F 58 B3
Limoux F 77 C5
Linares E 100 A2
Linares de Mora E 90 C2
Linares de Riofrio E 93 A5
Linaria GR 116 D6
Linas de Broto E 90 A2
Lincoln UK 27 B5
Lind DK 39 C1
Lindås N 32 B2
Lindau D 71 A4
Lindberget N 34 A3
Lindelse DK 39 E3
Lindenberg D 53 A4
Lindenberg im Allgäu D 61 C5
Lindern D 43 C4
Linderöd S 41 D3
Lindesberg S 37 C2
Lindesnäs S 36 B1
Lindesnes N 33 E4
Lindholmen S 37 C5
Lindknud DK 39 D2
Lindlar D 50 B3
Lindö S 37 D3
Lindome S 38 B5
Lindos GR 119 F3
Lindoso P 87 C2
Lindow D 45 C4
Lindsdal S 40 C6
Lindshammar S 40 B5
Lindstedt D 44 C3
Lindved DK 39 D2
Líně CZ 63 A4
Lingbo S 36 A3
Lingen D 43 C4
Linghed S 36 B2
Linghem S 37 D2
Linguaglossa I 109 B4
Linia PL 46 A3
Linie PL 45 B6
Liniewo PL 47 A4
Linkenheim D 61 A4
Linköping S 37 D2
Linksness UK 23 C5
Linlithgow UK 25 C4
Linneryd S 40 C5
Linnes Hammarby S 36 C4
Linnich D 50 C2
Linsell S 115 E10
Linslade UK 31 C3
Linthal CH 70 B4
Linyola E 90 B3
Linz
A 63 B5
D 50 C3
Liomseter N 32 A6
Lionárisso CY 120 A3
Lioni I 103 C8
Lion-sur-Mer F 57 A5
Lipany SK 65 A6
Lipar SRB 75 C4
Lípari I 106 C1
Lipcani MD 11 B9
Liperi FIN 3 E28
Liphook UK 31 C3
Lipiany PL 45 B6
Lipik HR 74 C2
Lipka PL 46 B3
Lipki Wielkie PL 46 C1
Lipnica PL 46 B3
Lipnica Murowana PL 65 A6
Lipnik PL 55 C6
Lipník nad Bečvou CZ 64 A3
Lipno
Kujawsko-Pomorskie PL 47 C5
Łódzkie PL 54 B3
Liposthey F 76 B2
Lipovac HR 84 A4
Lipovec CZ 64 A2
Lipovets UA 11 B10
Lipovljani HR 74 C1
Lipowina PL 47 A5
Lippborg D 50 B4
Lippó H 74 C3
Lippoldsberg D 51 B5
Lippstadt D 51 B4
Lipsko PL 55 B6
Liptál CZ 64 A3
Liptovská-Lúžna SK 65 B5
Liptovská Osada SK 65 B5
Liptovská-Teplička SK 65 B6
Liptovský Hrádok SK 65 A5
Liptovský Milkuláš SK 65 A5
Lipusz PL 46 A3
Lipůvka CZ 64 A2
Liré F 66 A3
Lis AL 105 B6
Lisa SRB 85 C5
Lisac BIH 84 B2
Lisbellaw UK 19 B4
Lisboa = Lisbon P 92 C1
Lisbon = Lisboa P 92 C1
Lisburn UK 19 B5
Liscannor IRL 20 B2
Lisdoonvarna IRL 20 A2
Lisewo PL 47 B4
Lisia Góra PL 55 C6
Lisięcice PL 54 C2
Lisieux F 57 A6
Lisjö S 37 C3
Liskeard UK 28 C3
L'Isle CH 69 B6
L'Isle-Adam F 58 A3
L'Isle-de-Noé F 77 C3
L'Isle-en-Dodon F 77 C3
L'Isle-Jourdain
Gers F 77 C4
Vienne F 67 B5
L'Isle-sur-la-Sorgue F 79 C4
L'Isle-sur-le Doubs F 69 A6
L'Isle-sur-Serein F 59 C5
Lisle-sur-Tarn F 77 C4
Lismore IRL 21 B4
Lisnaskea UK 19 B4
Lišov CZ 63 A5
Lisów
Lubuskie PL 45 C6
Śląskie PL 54 C3
Lisse NL 49 A5
Lissycasey IRL 20 B2
List D 39 D1
Listerby S 41 C5
Listowel IRL 20 B2
Listrac-Médoc F 76 A2
Liszki PL 55 C4
Liszkowo PL 46 B3
Lit S 115 D11
Litava SK 65 B5
Litcham UK 30 B4
Lit-et-Mixe F 76 B1
Litija SLO 73 B4
Litke H 65 B5
Litlabø N 32 C2
Litochoro GR 116 B4
Litoměřice CZ 53 C4
Litomyšl CZ 64 A2
Litovel CZ 64 A3
Litschau A 63 B6
Littlehampton UK 31 D3
Littleport UK 30 B4
Littleton IRL 21 B4
Little Walsingham UK 30 B4
Litvinov CZ 52 C3
Livadero GR 116 B3
Livadhia CY 120 B2
Livadi GR 116 B4
Livadia GR 116 D4
Livarot F 57 B6
Liveras CY 120 A1
Livernon F 77 B4
Liverovici MNE 85 D4
Liverpool UK 26 B3
Livigno I 71 B5
Livingston UK 25 C4
Livno BIH 84 C1
Livold SLO 73 C4
Livorno I 81 C4
Livorno Ferraris I 70 C3
Livron-sur-Drôme F 78 B3
Livry-Louvercy F 59 A5
Lixheim F 60 B3
Lixouri GR 117 D2
Lizard UK 28 D2
Lizy-sur-Ourcq F 59 A4
Lizzano I 104 C3
Lizzano in Belvedere I 81 B4
Lješane KOS 85 D5
Ljig SRB 85 B5
Ljørdalen N 34 A4
Ljosland N 33 D4
Ljubija BIH 83 B5
Ljubinje BIH 84 D3
Ljubljana SLO 73 B4
Ljubno ob Savinji SLO 73 B4
Ljubovija SRB 85 B4
Ljubuški BIH 84 C2
Ljugarn S 37 E5
Ljung S 40 B3
Ljunga S 37 D3
Ljungaverk S 115 E13
Ljungby S 40 C3
Ljungbyhed S 41 C3
Ljungbyholm S 40 C6
Ljungdalen S 115 E9
Ljungsarp S 40 B3
Ljungsbro S 37 D2
Ljungskile S 35 D3
Ljusdal S 115 F13
Ljusfallshammar S 37 D2